Lives & Times

Lives & Times

*Achievements of the Famous and
Remarkable, Age by Age*

Edmund Morrison

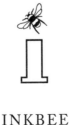

INKBEE

First published in 2013 by

Inkbee Publishing Ltd
10 York Place
Edinburgh
EH1 3EP

www.inkbeepublishing.com

2 4 6 8 10 9 7 5 3 1

British Library Cataloguing in Publication Data
A catalogue record for this book is available from the British Library

ISBN: 978–0–9572761–0–9

Set in Adobe Caslon Pro 11.5/15 pt
Typeset by Palimpsest Book Production Limited,
Falkirk, Stirlingshire

Printed and bound by CPI Group (UK) Ltd, Croydon, CRO 4YY

For Alex and Martin

Contents

Introduction

The usefulness of living lies not in duration but in what you make of it. Some have lived long and lived little. See to it while you are still here. Whether you have lived enough depends not on a count of years but on your will.

MICHEL DE MONTAIGNE

Age is that inescapable measure that we all share. As a child I was happy to attain more, to reach double figures and the teenage years – becoming a grown-up seemed a lifetime away as time dilly-dallied. Now, as I complete my fifth decade, the annual cycle feels much faster. Recurring major events highlight this illusory acceleration in the passage of time; for me, the Olympics return far quicker than their quadrennial gap would suggest.

Taking stock a few years ago, I realised that I was not only older than most professional sportspeople and pop stars, but also older than the prime minister was when he entered office. I was tempted to continue the comparisons into other spheres: which milestones had other people reached by my age, and what achievements had people gone on to accomplish?

No convenient book was available to provide the answers so, fuelled by curiosity, and hoping to gain some solace for the road ahead, I decided to write one. The initial six months I set aside evolved into more than three years before *Lives & Times* was finally finished – or at least, that's when I stopped.

My first task was to decide who to include. I wanted to try to capture a wide-ranging selection of personal achievement at a given age. Many names quickly came to mind: inventors, politicians, writers, actors, musicians, sportspeople and so on. I also sought out others associated with a notable event or discovery and added them to the list, which was soon past the thousand mark. Naturally, the number of entries dwindles at the extremes and, reflecting my own cultural background, most are from the Western world. It's been a challenge to produce the final list, to come to a halt and resist the temptation to add 'just one more'.

I also faced a further quandary: what should I do about people with more than one memorable achievement? In these instances I've usually selected the most well-known, or the most remarkable for their age; sometimes I have simply made a personal choice.

Working through the gathered names, I've found it fascinating to see the path that people have taken, especially when they have shown great determination or overcome obstacles. For example, John Moores persevered with his football pools scheme (Littlewoods) despite an unpromising start and reaped huge financial reward, while Charles Dickens triumphed over his irregular schooling and a period as a child worker to become one of the English language's foremost novelists.

With respect to age, predictable patterns emerged, such as the sporting prowess of the young or the older generation's attainment of high political office, but there was also, refreshingly, many who refused to conform to conventional expectations. For example, Sir Francis Chichester completed his solo round-the-world voyage at the age of sixty-five, whilst William Pitt became prime minister at the tender age of twenty-four.

Whether you simply dip in to check the entries at your own age, or take a more systematic approach, I hope my selection gives you the sense that age should never be something to hold us back, whatever our ambitions.

Note on the Text

The headline for each entry typically lists one person (occasionally more), indicated in bold, and the selected event which is used to define their age at that moment in time. These ages, grouped into chapters for each decade, are used to place the entries in ascending order. Within a particular age, the entries are ordered chronologically from the earliest event to the most recent.

Please note that the biographical entries are not intended to be a definitive listing of all of a person's awards and achievements. For more information on a particular individual, please consult the Further Reading section. Although great care has been taken to ensure accuracy, I warmly welcome any corrections or clarifications.

Edmund Morrison
February 2013

Lives & Times

CHAPTER ONE

Predenarians

The childhood shows the man,
As morning shows the day.

JOHN MILTON

5

FIVE

Wolfgang Mozart completed his first recorded compositions in 1761.

Mozart's baptismal certificate records his name, in Latin, as Joannes Chrysostomus Wolfgangus Theophilus Mozart, but as an adult he would usually adopt the form Wolfgang Amadè Mozart (Amadeus, a Latin form for Theophilus, only gained ground posthumously as his quoted middle name). The seventh, and last, child of the family, only Mozart and his sister Maria Anna (also musically gifted and known as Nannerl) would survive infancy. His first recorded musical composition, aged five, is believed to be 'Andante in C'. Transcribed by his father, it was only ten bars in length. More compositions followed and one year later Mozart's musical gifts were displayed on a European grand tour accompanied by his father Leopold (a court musician), his mother Anna Maria and his sister. Mozart's talent continued to blossom and by the age of thirteen the range of his compositions included operas, concertos and symphonies. His later operas included *The Marriage of Figaro*, first performed in 1786 when Mozart was thirty, and *Don Giovanni* – which premiered the following year. Mozart's final opera, *The Magic Flute*, received its first performance shortly before his death in Vienna, in 1791, at the age of thirty-five.

6

SIX

In 1935 Shirley Temple received a special Academy Award for her 'outstanding contribution to screen entertainment' in the previous year.

Temple, who started her career with a series of short films at the age of three, appeared in several films that were released in 1934, including *Stand Up and Cheer!* and *Baby Take a Bow*. The year closed with top billing for the six-year-old in *Bright Eyes*, which featured her signature tune, 'On the Good Ship Lollipop'. Further leading roles followed in films such as *Our Little Girl* (1935), *Curly Top* (1935) and *Dimples* (1936), but in the next decade Temple's popularity waned. Her last film, *A Kiss for Corliss*, was released in 1949 when she was twenty-one, and one year later Temple announced her official retirement from film-making. Her attachment to Republican politics brought her back to a prominent public role twenty years later when she was appointed as a United States representative to the UN General Assembly by President Nixon. She also served as ambassador to Ghana (1974–76) and Czechoslovakia (1989–92). Temple remains the youngest person ever to be honoured with an Academy Award.

7

SEVEN

Ludwig van Beethoven *made his first known public performance in 1778.*

Seven-year-old Beethoven made his public debut in Cologne, billed by his father as being a year younger. Beethoven published his first three piano sonatas at the age of twelve, and four years later he travelled to Vienna to meet Mozart, but his visit was cut short due to his mother's illness. He returned to Vienna in 1792 (Mozart had died the previous year), shortly before his twenty-second birthday, and lived there for the rest of his life. It was in Vienna that the first of his nine symphonies received its debut performance eight years later. Beethoven's oeuvre also encompassed concertos, overtures, sonatas and one opera, *Fidelio*. He started to suffer from diminished hearing in his late twenties and by his mid-forties was profoundly deaf, although he continued to compose. His ninth and final symphony (the 'choral') was premiered in 1824, three years before his death at the age of fifty-six.

Drew Barrymore *appeared as Gertie in 'E.T.: The Extra-Terrestrial', released in 1982.*

Barrymore made her cinematic debut two years earlier with a role in *Altered States*, but it was her performance in *E.T.* that made the seven-year-old a star. Her next film was *Firestarter* (1984), based on the book by Stephen King, and she was kept busy throughout her childhood with subsequent features for cinema and television. The 1990s saw Barrymore make a successful progression to adult roles with appearances in films such as *Scream* (1996), *The Wedding Singer* (1998) and *Never Been Kissed* (1999), the latter also marking her first credit as an executive producer. Her other films include *Charlie's Angels* (2000) and *Donnie Darko* (2001). Barrymore made her debut as a feature-film director with *Whip It* in 2009.

8

EIGHT

Television test card 'F', which featured **Carole Hersee** *and her puppet clown 'Bubbles', was introduced in 1967.*

Test cards are static images which are broadcast to enable a television receiver's settings to be adjusted to achieve the best picture quality. Once a familiar feature to viewers, the prevalence of round-the-clock programming means that they are now rarely transmitted. Test card 'F' was the first to feature an image of a person and to use colour. It was developed by Hersee's father, BBC engineer George Hersee. The X in the game of noughts and crosses played by the eight-year-old Hersee and Bubbles marked the centre of the screen. Test card 'F' was used for test-card broadcasts for over thirty years, but has been replaced by updated variants (for example, to accommodate widescreen and high-definition transmissions) which continue to use Carole Hersee's image. As an adult, Hersee maintained her connection with the entertainment industry in her career as a theatrical costumier.

In 1980 **Justin Henry** *was nominated for an Academy Award, for best supporting actor, for his portrayal of Billy Kramer in 'Kramer vs. Kramer'.*

The youngest Academy Awards nominee to date, eight-year-old Henry took on the role, in what became the year's best picture Oscar winner, with no prior acting experience. By contrast, the best supporting actor Oscar went to the 79-year-old Melvyn Douglas for his performance in

Being There (1979). Henry's next feature film was *Sixteen Candles* (1984), and after some further appearances, he took a break of several years to further his college education. He subsequently returned to acting, playing parts in various television and cinema productions. His most recent big-screen appearance was in *Lost* (2004).

9

NINE

*In 1931 **Jackie Cooper** was nominated for an Academy Award for his role as Skippy in 'Skippy Skinner'.*

Cooper lost out to Lionel Barrymore for the top male acting award, but the film won his uncle, Norman Taurog, the Oscar for best director at the age of thirty-two, and Taurog remains the youngest to receive this accolade from the Academy. During one scene in which he needed Cooper to cry, Taurog ordered for Cooper's dog to be shot. The deception worked and Cooper's weepy state continued even when the scene was over and he was told his dog was safe. The incident made a lasting impression on the young star who would later call his autobiography *Please Don't Shoot My Dog*. Cooper followed his Oscar nomination for best actor with numerous starring film roles in the 1930s and 1940s. As an adult, he increasingly appeared in television roles. He only made one film appearance in the 1960s, but several more in the next two decades including the role of Perry White in the Superman series (1978–1987). Cooper also moved into directing, and won Emmy Awards in this field for the comedy series *M*A*S*H* in 1974 and for *The White Shadow* in 1979. Cooper continues to hold the record as the youngest Oscar nominee, aged nine, for a lead acting role. He died in 2011 at the age of eighty-eight.

*In 1972 **Jimmy Osmond** reached number one in the UK singles chart with 'Long Haired Lover From Liverpool'.*

Osmond, the junior member of the musical family, is the youngest person to reach the top spot in the UK singles chart. The song was the 1972 Christmas number one and spent five weeks at the top of the chart.

Osmond had two more singles in the UK top twenty as a solo artist – his next, with the Mike Curb Congregation, entitled 'Tweedlee Dee' reached number four in 1973, and the subsequent 'I'm Gonna Knock On Your Door' made it to number eleven the following year. Osmond also enjoyed success two years before his British number one, at the age of seven, when he received a gold disc for his Japanese recording of 'My Little Darling'. As well as collecting several more such awards, Osmond has also had success with his own advertising agency, and in the entertainment production business.

*In 2013 **Quvenzhané Wallis** was nominated for an Academy Award for best actress for her debut role, as Hushpuppy, in 'Beasts of the Southern Wild'.*

Wallis is the youngest ever Oscar nominee for best actress. She was only five when she won the audition, beating approximately 4,000 other candidates in the process, and completed filming when she was seven. *Beasts of the Southern Wild* received its premiere at the 2012 Sundance Film Festival. Prior to her Oscar nomination, Wallis had already picked up a number of awards for her debut performance.

CHAPTER TWO

Denarians

Sweet childish days, that were as long
As twenty days are now.

WILLIAM WORDSWORTH

10

TEN

*In 1974 **Tatum O'Neal** won the Academy Award for best supporting actress, for the role of Addie Loggins in 'Paper Moon'.*

Paper Moon, which also starred her father Ryan O'Neal, was adapted from the novel *Addie Pray* by Joe David Brown. Tatum O'Neal, then only ten, is the youngest person to date to have won a competitive Academy Award. Her next films included *Nickelodeon* (1976), in which she again starred with her father, and *International Velvet* (1978). As an adult she has starred in films that include *Certain Fury* (1985), *Basquiat* (1996), *The Scoundrel's Wife* (2002) and, more recently, *The Runaways* (2010).

__Macaulay Culkin__ starred as Kevin McCallister in 'Home Alone', released in 1990.

Culkin made his stage debut aged four and his film debut as Cy Blue Black in *Rocket Gilbraltar* (1988), aged eight. Two years later his breakthrough role in *Home Alone* (1990), which took over $285 million at the US box office, gained him a Golden Globe nomination. Culkin's other work for the cinema includes the sequel, *Home Alone 2: Lost in New York* (1992), *My Girl* (1991) and *Saved!* (2004).

11

ELEVEN

*In 1840 **John Everett Millais** became the youngest person ever to be admitted to the Royal Academy Schools in London.*

Millais first participated in the Royal Academy exhibition in 1846 with his canvas entitled *Pizarro Seizing the Inca of Peru*. Millais met William Holman Hunt at the Academy and their shared view on the state and direction of British art led them to found, along with Dante Gabriel Rossetti, the Pre-Raphaelite Brotherhood in 1848, when Millais was nineteen. Soon joined by others, their aim was to break away from the conventions of the Royal Academy and to return to a more truthful, realistic form of representation that they associated with the period before the Italian High Renaissance painter Raphael, who was born in the late 15th century. Their artwork and their cause attracted attention, especially after Millais's *Christ in the House of His Parents* (1850) was critically reviled for what was seen as a non-reverential treatment of its subject matter. His popular Pre-Raphaelite work *Ophelia* was completed in 1852 and required his model, Elizabeth Siddal, to pose fully dressed in a bath full of water. After the temperature of the water dropped one day, Siddal (who was also muse to Rossetti) became seriously ill. Millais was elected as a Royal Academician in 1863. His later work shows a departure from Pre-Raphaelite principles and reflects his admiration for old masters such as Rembrandt and Velázquez. His historical canvas *The Boyhood of Raleigh* (1870) proved very popular and his painting of his young grandson, *Bubbles* (1886), was used to advertise Pears soap. Millais was given a baronetcy in 1885 – the first native British artist to be accorded a hereditary title. He became president of the Royal Academy in 1896 shortly before his death, that same year, at the age of sixty-seven.

Cecilia Colledge *competed for Great Britain at the 1932 Winter Olympic Games held at Lake Placid, New York State.*

Colledge, who holds the record as Britain's youngest Olympic competitor, finished eighth in the women's individual figure skating competition. Her path to the Games began four years earlier when the seven-year-old and her mother attended the 1928 World Figure Skating Championships, held in London, where they watched Sonja Henie clinch the world title. The visit proved to be inspirational. Colledge's mother subsequently arranged the coaching for Cecilia that took her to her first Olympics, in 1932, when she competed against Henie who was still on winning form. Colledge fared better at the next Winter Olympics in 1936, held in Garmisch-Partenkirchen. Aged fifteen, she was narrowly beaten by the reigning world champion Henie into second place. The following year Colledge won the British, European and world titles. She was also a pioneer in skating technique, developing her own manoeuvres, and was the first woman to successfully accomplish a double jump in competition. Colledge died in 2008 at the age of eighty-seven.

12

TWELVE

'National Velvet' starring **Elizabeth Taylor** *was released in 1944.*

The success of *National Velvet* in which Taylor played young horsewoman Velvet Brown, propelled her to stardom. Born in London to American parents, the family moved to Los Angeles when she was seven. Taylor made an early entry into the world of film with her debut appearance in the 1942 release of *There's One Born Every Minute*. Following *National Velvet* her career continued on an upwards trajectory as she successfully took on adult roles. Taylor's first Academy Award nomination was, in 1958, for *Raintree County* (1957). After two further nominations, for *Cat on a Hot Tin Roof* (1958) and *Suddenly, Last Summer* (1959), she won the best actress category for *Butterfield 8* (1960), and again for *Who's Afraid of Virginia Woolf?* (1966). *Cleopatra* (1963) was the first of eleven films in which she co-starred with her future husband, Richard Burton. She was made a Dame, for services to acting and charity, in 2000. Taylor died in 2011 at the age of seventy-nine.

Lester Piggott *had his first win as a jockey, riding The Chase at Haydock Park, in 1948.*

The first of Piggott's nine Derby victories came six years later at the age of eighteen, riding Never Say Die (his last was in 1983 with Teenoso). His father Keith was a successful jockey and trainer whilst his grandfather, Ernie, secured a total of three Grand National victories as a rider. Piggott achieved thirty Classic wins in his riding career, adding to his Derby successes with eight victories in the St. Leger, five in the 2,000 Guineas and two in the 1,000 Guineas. His last Classic win, in 1992 at the age of fifty-six, was in the 2,000 Guineas. He rode his final winner at Haydock Park, the course of his debut triumph, two years later. Piggott was also champion jockey eleven times between 1960 and 1982. The Lesters, the annual jockey awards that were founded in 1990, are named in his honour.

'*The Jazz Soul of Little Stevie*', the debut album of **Stevie Wonder**, was released in 1962.

The opening track of the album is the studio version of 'Fingertips', the live recording of which gave Wonder his first US number one hit the following year. The disc from which it was culled, *Recorded Live: The 12 Year Old Genius*, also made the top spot in the US chart. Wonder is the youngest person to have reached the number one position in the US music chart and the first to have a simultaneous single and album chart topper. Born blind, Wonder displayed his talent for music at an early age and attracted the attention of Tamla Motown chief Berry Gordy who signed him to his fledgling label. Wonder continued to develop his career, and by the early seventies had negotiated full creative control over his work, though he continued to record for Motown. Despite a string of hits in the UK singles chart it wasn't until 1984 that Wonder made the number one position with 'I Just Called To Say I Love You'. Winner of many Grammy Awards, he has received three for 'album of the year', the last in 1976 for *Songs in the Key of Life*.

Neil Reid, with his self-titled debut, reached number one in the UK album chart in 1972.

The twelve-year-old Reid remains the youngest person to top the UK album chart. The Scottish-born singer came to prominence at the end of the previous year by winning the television talent show *Opportunity Knocks* singing 'Mother of Mine', and subsequently took the song to number two in the UK singles chart. A follow-up single 'That's What I Want To Be' and album, *Smile*, both reached the top fifty in 1972 and became his last chart entries.

Fu Mingxia won a gold medal for the 10m platform dive at the 1991 World Championships.

Mingxia switched from gymnastics to diving as a young child and, at the age of nine, attended a diving school in Beijing. She followed her success at the World Championships with a gold medal at the Barcelona Olympics in 1992, aged thirteen. Mingxia retained her world title in 1994 and, two years later, at the Atlanta Olympics she took home gold in both the 10m platform and 3m springboard events while still only seventeen. She retired from diving and studied economics at Qinghua University, Beijing. However, she decided to return to competing and won gold in Sydney at the 2000 Olympics, for the 3m springboard, before finally retiring from the sport.

In 1998 **Charlotte Church** *released her debut album 'Voice of an Angel'.*

Church's album reached number four in the UK chart and she became the youngest person ever to take the top spot in the classical listings as her album went on to sell over half a million copies in the UK alone. Her big break came the previous year when she sang 'Pie Jesu' on the TV game show *Talking Telephone Numbers*, which led to a record deal with Sony. Her fifth album, *Tissues and Issues*, was released in 2005. It was her first pop collection and gave her a number two UK single for the track 'Crazy Chick'. *Tissues and Issues* spawned three further top twenty entries for the Welsh songstress, who also co-wrote eight of the album's twelve songs. The follow-up, *Back to Scratch*, was released in 2010.

Daniel Radcliffe *starred as the title character in 'Harry Potter and the Philosopher's Stone', released in 2001.*

Radcliffe's feature-film debut, as Mark Pendel in *The Tailor of Panama* (2001), was followed by his starring role in the first instalment in the Harry Potter cinema series. His maiden screen appearance was on television as a young David Copperfield, which premiered on Christmas Day 1999. Radcliffe played Harry Potter in all eight of the film adaptations based on J.K. Rowling's books, concluding with *Harry Potter and the Deathly Hallows: Part II*, released in 2011.

13
THIRTEEN

In 1812 the 'Western Flying Post' reported the extraction of the first fossilised skeleton, discovered by **Mary Anning**, *of what would later be called an 'Icthyosaurus'.*

The fossil find was made on the Dorset coast at Lyme. The skull had initially been spotted by Anning's older brother Joseph a year earlier.

Anning's interest in fossil hunting had been inspired by her late father's efforts to provide specimens for sale to visitors to the region. Anning's skill and expertise led her to make further significant discoveries in the 1820s, including skeletons of a plesiosaurus and a pterodactyl. Largely self-educated, Anning's growing reputation drew her into communication with the scientific community, who often visited her to benefit from her insights. In Anning's later years, before her death in 1847 at the age of forty-seven, her work was recognised with the award of an annuity, principally raised from the members of the British Association for the Advancement of Science.

Marjorie Gestring *won a gold medal at the 1936 Berlin Olympics for the 3m springboard diving event.*

Thirteen-year-old Gestring, who represented the US, is the youngest individual gold medallist in Olympic history, and the youngest ever at the summer Games. It was to be her last appearance at the competition since World War Two brought the cancellation of the next two scheduled Olympics and she then narrowly missed out in qualifying for the 1948 Games in London. Gestring died at the age of sixty-nine in 1992.

'Got To Be There,' the first solo single by **Michael Jackson**, *was released in 1971.*

Jackson had already been a US chart topper as part of the Jackson Five two years earlier, and would reach the number four position in the US Billboard Hot 100 with his solo debut release, aged thirteen. He would go on to become a popular music phenomenon. Jackson's 1979 album, *Off the Wall*, marked his first collaboration with producer Quincy Jones, with whom he would work again on his next album, *Thriller*. Released in 1982, with a title track written by former Heatwave member Rod Temperton, *Thriller* went on to become the biggest-selling album of all time. Jackson recorded four more studio collections, beginning with *Bad* (1987) and closing with *Invincible* (2001). His seven solo UK number one singles include 'Billie Jean' (1983), 'Black or White' (1991) and his last 'Blood on the Dancefloor' (1997). Jackson was in the midst of rehearsing for a series of London concerts when he died, at the age of fifty, in 2009.

In 1985 **Ruth Lawrence** *was awarded a first-class degree in mathematics from the University of Oxford.*

Lawrence, at the age of thirteen, became the youngest Briton to earn a first-class degree, completed in two years rather than the standard three. She gained her doctorate four years later. Lawrence had already made headlines when she achieved an A grade in the pure mathematics A-level, which she sat at the age of nine. She was home schooled, with her father giving up his job to concentrate on the task full-time. Lawrence later accepted various academic positions, most recently to become an associate professor of mathematics at the Hebrew University of Jerusalem.

In 2004 **Keisha Castle-Hughes** *was nominated for the best actress Academy Award for her role as Paikea Apirana in the film 'Whale Rider'.*

At the time, Castle-Hughes was the youngest person to have been nominated for best actress at the Oscars. Her next cinematic appearances were as the Queen of Naboo in *Star Wars: Episode III – Revenge of the Sith* (2005), followed by Mary in *The Nativity Story* (2006). Castle-Hughes has recently starred in the films *Vampire* (2011) and *Red Dog* (2011).

Ellie Simmonds *won two gold medals at the 2008 Paralympic Games in Beijing, China.*

Simmonds came first in the S6 100m and 400m freestyle swimming events. Weeks later she turned fourteen and rounded off the year with the BBC Young Sports Personality of the Year award, as well as the announcement in the 2009 New Year Honours list that she was to become the youngest ever MBE. In 2009, Simmonds won six World Championship and five European Championship gold medals; the following year, she claimed a further four world titles. At the 2012 London Paralympics, she defended her 400m freestyle title and also won the 200m SM6 individual medley, setting world-record times in both finals. She took her Games medal tally to four with silver for the S6 100m freestyle and bronze for the S6 50m freestyle. She was awarded an OBE in the 2013 New Year Honours.

Jordan Romero *reached the summit of Mount Everest in 2010.*

Romero, aged thirteen, was accompanied on the expedition by his father and stepmother as he became the youngest person to climb the world's tallest mountain. They had to make the ascent from the Tibetan side of the peak since Nepal does not issue Everest climbing licences to those under sixteen. (A similar restriction on young mountaineers was introduced by the Chinese authorities after Romero's achievement.) Everest was the sixth summit conquered by Romero as he chased the goal of ascending the highest peaks on all seven continents. He scaled the first of these, Mount Kilimanjaro in Africa, at the age of ten, and reached the top of the Vinson Massif, Antarctica's highest peak, in 2011 to become, aged fifteen, the youngest climber to complete the ascent of the 'seven summits'.

14

FOURTEEN

*In 1961 **Helen Shapiro** reached number one in the UK chart with her second hit single, 'You Don't Know'.*

'You Don't Know' spent three weeks at number one and the fourteen-year-old Shapiro remains the youngest female solo artist to top the UK singles chart. Her next single, 'Walkin' Back to Happiness' did likewise, and Shapiro achieved a number two position for its follow-up, 'Tell Me What He Said'. These records, combined with the performance of her debut release, 'Don't Treat Me Like a Child' – which made the number three position – gave Shapiro four top-three chart placings before her sixteenth birthday. She topped the bill on a nationwide tour of Britain that began in early 1963, which also provided one of her supporting acts, the Beatles, with their first national outing; though their gathering success saw them leave the line-up before its conclusion. Shapiro's last UK singles chart entry was in 1964, with 'Fever'.

***Nadia Comăneci** won three gold medals (individual all-round, asymmetric bars and beam), and one bronze medal (floor), for gymnastics at the 1976 Montreal Olympics.*

Comăneci also won a silver medal with Romania in the team competition in what was the fourteen-year-old's debut Olympics. As well as her medal success, Comăneci became famous as the first gymnast to be awarded a perfect score of ten out of ten at the Olympics, a feat she repeated a further six times at the Montreal Games. Comăneci defended her Olympic beam title in Moscow four years later and also took gold for the floor exercises, as well as two silver medals for the individual all-round and team competitions.

Declan Donnelly and Anthony McPartlin first appeared in the kids' BBC drama series 'Byker Grove' in 1989 and 1990 respectively.

Donnelly and McPartlin became friends as well as colleagues and went on to launch a pop career, initially under their characters' names (PJ & Duncan), which notched up twelve top-twenty UK hits in the 1990s. Billed as 'Ant and Dec' they went on to a successful career as television presenters with their own shows, and also as hosts for the popular ITV programmes *I'm a Celebrity Get Me Out of Here!*, first screened in 2002; and *Britain's Got Talent* which debuted in 2007.

In 2001 Jamie Bell won the Bafta Award for best actor for the title role in 'Billy Elliot'.

Fourteen-year-old Bell, who won the part from his audition performance, is the youngest ever winner of the best actor category at the Baftas. Similar to his on-screen character in the film, who pursues his balletic ambitions, Bell also took up dancing at an early age. Since *Billy Elliot* he has appeared in over a dozen feature films including the Peter Jackson remake of *King Kong* (2005), *Flags of Our Fathers* (2006), *Hallam Foe* (2007) and *Defiance* (2008).

15
FIFTEEN

In 1790 Joseph Turner participated in his first Royal Academy summer exhibition.

Turner, who made his summer exhibition debut with a watercolour of the Archbishop's Palace at Lambeth, had been admitted as a student at the Royal Academy late in the previous year. For the 1796 exhibition, in addition to several watercolours, Turner also exhibited his first oil painting: *Fishermen at Sea*. He is renowned for his landscape painting, while his style and use of colour are regarded as prefiguring that of the impressionists. Turner died in 1851 at the age of seventy-six, and bequeathed around three hundred oil paintings and approximately twenty thousand watercolours to the nation. In a 2005 BBC Radio 4 poll, Turner's *The Fighting Temeraire, tugged to her last berth to be broken up, 1838*, which he painted when he was in his sixties, was voted the greatest painting in Britain.

Louis Braille *completed his six-dot system, which enabled blind people to read and write more easily, in 1824.*

Braille's method was developed from a code of twelve raised dots that Charles Barbier had invented to allow soldiers to communicate silently in darkness, and which he demonstrated to Braille and others at the National Institute for the Blind in Paris. Braille simplified the code to one of six raised dots, arranged in a 2 x 3 pattern, thus allowing a single fingertip touch to read one encoded letter or symbol. Braille's blindness was the result of an accident at the age of three when he stabbed himself in one eye with a stitching awl. The other eye then became infected (a condition known as sympathetic ophthalmia), leaving Braille completely blind. It wasn't until after his death in 1852, at the age of forty-three, that Braille's system would start to become widely adopted.

In 1825 'Rondo in C minor' by **Frédéric Chopin** *became his first commercially published composition.*

The fifteen-year-old Chopin, who was born in the Duchy of Warsaw to a French father and Polish mother, had already been composing for several years before his first commercial publication. Also a celebrated pianist, Chopin completed well over two hundred compositions before his death in Paris at the age of thirty-nine. His remains are buried at Père Lachaise cemetery, but his heart (by his own request) was removed and returned to his native Poland where it was interred inside a pillar of the Holy Cross Church in Warsaw.

Lottie Dod won the Wimbledon Ladies' Singles Championship in 1887.

Dod is the youngest Wimbledon singles winner, and captured the title on another four occasions. She faced Blanche Hillyard (who became a six-time champion) in all five finals, the last of which took place in 1893. A formidable all-rounder, her sporting prowess was not confined to tennis. Dod played for England at hockey, won the Ladies' Open Golf Championship in 1904, and took a silver medal at the 1908 London Olympics for archery. Her interests also included winter sports such as skating and tobogganing, as well as mountaineering. Dod died in 1960 at the age of eighty-eight, reportedly while listening to radio commentary from Wimbledon.

Billy Wright made his first team debut for Wolverhampton Wanderers, against Notts County, in a friendly match in 1939.

The league programme was suspended during the war years, but when it resumed Wright became a key member of the Wolves team, and was club captain by the time they won their first post-war silverware – the FA Cup – after defeating Leicester City by three goals to one in 1949. He had been made England captain a year earlier, and his international career would see him become the first player in the world to receive 100 caps, his final total increasing to 105. He also captained England ninety times and played in seventy consecutive internationals. Wright was the England captain at the three World Cup finals held in the 1950s. Domestically, in addition to the FA Cup win, he led Wolves to three League Championship titles. They were his only senior side and Wright signed for them despite some misgivings about his potential from their then manager, Major Frank Buckley. Wright was never booked or sent off in his professional career, and retired from the game in 1959, receiving a CBE in the same year. He died at the age of seventy in 1994.

Lulu and the Luvvers reached number seven with their debut single, 'Shout', in 1964.

Lulu, real name Marie Lawrie, left the group to embark on a solo career which gave her a US number one three years later at the age of eighteen, singing the title track from *To Sir With Love* (1967) – in which she also made her feature film debut. A Eurovision Song Contest win came in 1969 with 'Boom Bang-a-Bang' (the year there was a four-way tie for the top spot), as well as hit singles over the next four decades. At the age of forty-four, in 1993, Lulu made it to number one in the UK for the first time, singing 'Relight my Fire' with Take That.

Jenny Agutter starred as Bobbie in the BBC television production of 'The Railway Children', first shown in 1968.

Agutter, who had already made her movie debut four years earlier in *East of Sudan* (1964), went on to reprise her role of Bobbie in the 1970 cinema production of *The Railway Children*. Her other film credits include *Walkabout* (1971); *Logan's Run* (1976); *An American Werewolf in London* (1981); and *Equus* (1977), which won her a Bafta Award for best supporting actress. Prior to this Agutter picked up an Emmy for her role in *The Snow Goose*, first broadcast by the BBC in 1971. She returned to *The Railway Children* in a new television adaptation in 2000, this time playing the role of Bobbie's mother. Agutter was awarded an OBE in the 2012 Queen's Birthday Honours.

Frankie Dettori won his first race as a jockey in Turin, Italy, in 1986.

Just over six months later Dettori (who had turned sixteen), recorded his first victory in Britain riding Lizzy Hare at Goodwood. In addition to winning all the British horse racing Classics, Dettori's other notable achievements include being the first teenager since Lester Piggott to have 100 wins in a season, and the first rider to win all seven races in one day, which he did at Ascot in September 1996. Dettori had to wait until he was thirty-six for his first Derby win, in 2007, on Authorized. Flat racing champion jockey three times, he was awarded an MBE in 2000.

Judit Polgár became a chess Grandmaster in 1991, setting a record as the youngest ever at that time.

Polgár has been the world's number one female chess player since 1989, and was ranked eighth overall in 2005 – becoming the first woman to break into the top ten. She was home schooled by her parents who decided, even before she was born, that she should become a chess player, and therefore placed special emphasis on the study of the game from an early age. Both of Polgár's older sisters are also accomplished chess champions: Sofia is a Woman Grandmaster, and Susan a Grandmaster.

*In 1998 **Ian Thorpe** became the youngest ever male swimmer to win gold at the World Championships when he triumphed in the 400m freestyle event in Perth, Australia.*

Thorpe also collected a gold medal as part of the 4x200m freestyle relay team. Thorpe began swimming at the age of five, and first represented Australia at the age of fourteen, one year before taking his first world title. At the Sydney Olympics in 2000, Thorpe won three gold and two silver medals. He added to his total, in Athens in 2004, with two gold, one silver and one bronze medal – making him Australia's most successful Olympian.

*In 1998 'Because We Want To', the first release by **Billie Piper**, went straight to number one in the UK singles chart.*

Piper's follow-up, 'Girlfriend,' did likewise, and she went on to become the first female artist to have three number one hits before her eighteenth birthday ('Day and Night' was the third in 2000). She moved into acting and, as Rose Tyler, became the first assistant to the eponymous *Doctor Who* when the programme was relaunched by the BBC in 2005. Piper left the role, which brought her a clutch of acting awards, at the end of the second series, but has since returned to make occasional appearances.

***Tom Daley** won a gold medal for the 10m platform dive at the 2009 World Championships.*

Daley's success at the Rome meeting made him not only Britain's first world diving champion, but also the youngest British world champion in any sport. It was Daley's debut appearance at the World Championships, held biannually, and followed on from his seventh position in the same event, achieved at the age of fourteen, at the Beijing Olympics in the previous year. Daley won his first Olympic medal, bronze for the 10m platform dive, at the 2012 London Games.

***Rūta Meilutytė** won a gold medal for the 100m breaststroke at the 2012 London Olympics.*

Meilutytė beat the 100m and 200m breaststroke world champion, Rebecca Soni, to clinch the gold medal after setting a new European record in the semi-final. Meilutytė, the first swimmer to win a medal for

Lithuania, moved to Plymouth aged twelve and took advantage of the coaching offered at the Plymouth Leander swimming club. Meilutytė is the youngest person to win a gold medal at the 2012 London Games and the youngest ever winner of the women's 100m breaststroke at the Olympics.

16

SIXTEEN

Gordon Richards won his first race riding Gay Lord for the Apprentices' Plate at Leicester, in 1921.

Four years later, Richards became champion jockey for the first time; a title he would retain for all but three seasons until 1953 when he secured his last crown. Richards, who rode 4,870 winners during his career, was knighted in the Queen's Coronation Honours in 1953 for services to horse racing. Less than a week later, at the age of forty-nine, he won the Derby for the first time riding Pinza, beating the Queen's horse Aureole into second place. Richards was the first, and so far only, jockey to receive a knighthood. His retirement from racing in 1954 was brought forwards after he was thrown by his mount Abergeldie and injured. Richards died in 1986 at the age of eighty-two.

*In 1966 **Twiggy** was declared to be the 'Face of '66' by the 'Daily Express' newspaper.*

The centre-page *Daily Express* spread, published in March 1966, effectively launched Twiggy's career as she became one of the most successful models of the decade. In the following years Twiggy (born Leslie Hornby) moved into acting. Her debut feature-film appearance, as Polly Browne in *The Boy Friend* (1971), won her Golden Globe awards for best actress in a musical/comedy and most promising female newcomer. She has since worked widely on stage, on television and in the cinema, including a cameo role in *The Blues Brothers* (1980). Twiggy also had a UK top twenty hit in 1976 with 'Here I Go Again'.

William Hague thrilled delegates with his speech at the 1977 Conservative Party Conference.

Hague went on to graduate from Magdalen College, Oxford, where he read philosophy, politics and economics. He entered Parliament in a by-election at the age of twenty-seven, and was given his first government post the following year. Hague became a cabinet member as secretary of state for Wales in 1995; a post he maintained until the Conservative defeat in the 1997 general election. When John Major stepped down as party leader, Hague, at the age of thirty-six, was elected to succeed him. The Conservatives lost the next general election in 2001, and Hague resigned the leadership. He returned to front-bench politics with his appointment as shadow foreign secretary in 2005, and took up the same role on the government benches following the general election of 2010.

*In 1997 **Martina Hingis** became the youngest tennis player to reach number one in the world rankings.*

Hingis spent eighty consecutive weeks at the top of the rankings and notched up over 200 weeks in total. Her first Grand Slam success, at the age of sixteen, came in the ladies' doubles at Wimbledon in 1996. Hingis began the following year with victory in her first Grand Slam singles final at the Australian Open where she became the youngest winner of the event in its history. Hingis proceeded to reach the other three Grand Slam singles finals that year and recorded victories in two of these: Wimbledon and the US Open. She later added two more Australian singles titles, and brought her total of Grand Slam doubles successes to nine, before retiring from the game at the age of twenty-two. Hingis made a comeback two years later before announcing her final retirement from professional tennis in 2007, at the age of twenty-seven.

*The debut album from Destiny's Child, featuring **Beyoncé Knowles**, was released in 1998.*

Beyoncé was one of the founding members of the group Girl's Tyme in 1990, from which, with fellow members LeToya Luckett and LaTavia Robertson (later joined by Kelly Rowland), Destiny's Child would emerge five years later. They released their first US single entitled 'No No No' in 1997 which reached number three in the Billboard Hot 100, and made it to the number five position in the UK in 1998. Their first British number one single came in late 2000 with 'Independent Women Part 1'. The subsequent release, 'Survivor', also topped the UK chart as did the album of the same name. Beyoncé's solo career started with a number seven position for 'Work It Out', and she has so far clocked up four number ones in the UK, the last of which was 'If I Were a Boy' in 2008. Her mother's maiden name was the source of Beyoncé's first name.

In 2002 **Wayne Rooney** *made his professional football debut.*

Rooney was part of the Everton side that drew 2–2 with Tottenham Hotspur in an August Premier League game. Rooney's first goals for the club came weeks later when he scored two against Wrexham in the League Cup and shortly after netted the winner against Arsenal in a league match. His ninetieth minute strike ended Arsenal's thirty game unbeaten run and, still days short of his seventeenth birthday, made him the youngest player to score in the Premier League at that time. Rooney played his first game for England in a friendly match against Australia at the age of seventeen. He spent two seasons at Everton before moving to Manchester United for a fee of approximately £25 million. Rooney netted a hat-trick in his debut game for the club as they recorded a 6–2 victory over Fenerbahçe in the Champions League. His honours, during his time so far with United, include four League Championships, two League Cups and one UEFA Champions League medal.

17
SEVENTEEN

Henry VIII *became King of England in 1509 after succeeding his father, Henry VII.*

Henry thus fulfilled the role that would have been accorded to his older brother, Arthur, who had died seven years previously. Another major consequence of his brother's early death was that Henry married Arthur's widow, Catherine of Aragon, thus setting in motion a train of events that would lead to a break from Rome and Henry's instalment as head of the church in England. The marriage, which received a special papal dispensation, took place only weeks after his accession to the throne when Henry was still seventeen. After many years of matrimony there was only one surviving female child, Mary, and thus no male heir. Henry, smitten by Anne Boleyn and the desire to ensure the succession with a son, pursued an end to his marriage to Catherine. After several years, papal agreement was still not forthcoming, so in 1533 Henry wed Anne on his own terms. In the following year he was declared the Supreme Head of the Church of England. His union with Anne also produced a surviving daughter only, the future Queen Elizabeth, and their marriage ended with Anne's execution in 1536. Henry went through four further marriages, with his last wife, Catherine Parr, surviving him upon his death in 1547 at the age of fifty-five. His successor was Edward VI, his son by his third wife, Jane Seymour.

In 1810 the gothic novel 'Zastrozzi', by **Percy Shelley**, *became his first published work.*

Shelley's next novel, *St Irvyne; or, The Rosicrucian*, appeared later that year. A major figure in English literature's Romantic movement, Shelley refused to live a conventional life. He was expelled from Oxford University for his contribution to the pamphlet *The Necessity of Atheism*. Later, Shelley eloped to Scotland with the sixteen-year-old Harriet Westbrook. The marriage did not endure, and Shelley later formed a relationship with Mary Godwin whom he would marry after Harriet's suicide. The Shelleys left for Italy in 1818. His later works would include *Prometheus Unbound* and *The Defence of Poetry*, while his wife Mary would write *Frankenstein*. In 1822 Shelley died, shortly before his thirtieth birthday, when he drowned with two others after their boat was caught in a storm off Livorno on the Tuscan coast.

'Young' **Tom Morris** *won golf's Open Championship in 1868.*

Morris's victory was the first of four consecutive Open titles (a unique golfing achievement), and the seventeen-year-old remains the youngest player to have won the championship, and indeed any golf major. All his victories were obtained at the Prestwick Golf Club, where his father, Tom, also a four-time Open champion, was greenkeeper for a period. Tragically,

Morris's life ended prematurely at the age of twenty-four on Christmas Day 1875, less than four months after the death of his wife and baby during childbirth.

In 1919 'Any Old Place with You' was the first **Richard Rodgers** *composition to be featured in a Broadway production ('A Lonely Romeo').*

'Any Old Place with You' was written by Rodgers in partnership with lyricist Lorenz Hart. The duo's first hit shows came in the following decade, and their success continued until Hart's death in November 1943. Their famous songs include 'Falling in Love with Love' and 'The Lady is a Tramp'. Rodgers formed a new partnership with Oscar Hammerstein II, and their first musical, *Oklahoma!*, was premiered in 1943. Further success was to follow with, amongst others, *Carousel* (1945), *South Pacific* (1949), *The King and I* (1951) and *The Sound of Music* (1959). Rodgers died in 1979 at the age of seventy-seven.

Bruce Hobbs *won the 1938 Grand National, riding Battleship.*

Hobbs, aged seventeen, remains the youngest jockey to have won the race, when he defeated Dan Moore riding Royal Danieli by a head. (Moore went on to win the 1975 Grand National as a trainer with L'Escargot.) Battleship, trained by his father Reg, was a 40–1 outsider. Born on Long Island, New York, the Hobbs family returned to England when Bruce was one-year-old. Boyhood riding tuition led to his first winner at the age of fifteen. A serious fall in the same year as his National win hospitalised him for three months, but he recovered and rode again before the outbreak of the Second World War. He was awarded the Military Cross in 1943. He switched to horse training after the end of the war, and died in 2005 at the age of eighty-four.

'The Wizard of Oz', which starred **Judy Garland** *as Dorothy Gale, was released in 1939.*

Garland's breakthrough performance in *The Wizard of Oz* helped to secure her a special juvenile Oscar in the following year. Garland was born Frances Ethel Gumm in Grand Rapids, Minnesota, to parents who were both vaudeville performers (her father also worked in theatre management). The youngest of three sisters, she joined her older siblings' singing act in which they were accompanied by their mother on the piano. Originally billed as the Gumm Sisters, they were later renamed the Garland Sisters. Before she reached the age of five, the family relocated to California, known for its expanding film industry, and at the age of thirteen Judy was awarded a contract at Metro-Goldwyn-Mayer (MGM). She made her debut in *Every Sunday* (1936), a short musical feature, and completed several other films before her starring role in *The Wizard of Oz* (1939). Garland's success thrust her into a flurry of work in the next decade, which included the films *Meet Me in St. Louis* (1944) and *Easter Parade* (1948). Her performance in *A Star is Born* (1954) led to her only Academy Award nomination for best actress, but she also picked up a best supporting actress Oscar nomination for *Judgement at Nuremberg* (1961). In later life she returned to her singing roots, and received accolades for both her recordings and her concert performances. The album of a 1961 appearance at Carnegie Hall won multiple Grammy Awards and sold over two million copies. Garland's last film, *I Could Go On Singing*, was released in 1963. She died six years later in London at the age of forty-seven.

Ingvar Kamprad *founded Ikea in 1943.*

The Ikea company name was formed from Kamprad's initials and the first letters of the farm and village where he grew up (Elmtaryd and Agunnaryd respectively). Prior to establishing his company, Kamprad had already been involved in commerce: buying and selling items such as Christmas cards, pens and seeds. He moved into furniture sales after the war. In 1952, Ikea announced that it would concentrate on furniture and domestic items. The company opened a showroom the following year, where customers could view items and then place an order. Five years later in 1958 the first Ikea store opened in Älmhult, Sweden. Ikea continued to grow, expanding from its Swedish base into international markets, in the process making Kamprad a multibillionaire.

Gary Sobers *made his test cricket debut for the West Indies, against England, in 1954.*

Born in Bridgetown, Barbados, Sobers played ninety-three test matches in his twenty-year test career. Just four years after his test debut he set a record of 365 not out against England, which would stand for over thirty-five years as a world test record. Playing at county level for Nottinghamshire, he hit six sixes in a single six ball over in 1968 – the first player to do so in first-class competition. Sobers was knighted in 1975 for services to cricket.

Judy Grinham won a gold medal at the 1956 Melbourne Olympic Games for the 100m backstroke.

The 100m backstroke final ended as a close finish between Grinham and Carin Cone from the US, with both being given the same world-record time, but the judges awarded the gold medal to Grinham and she became the first British swimmer to win at the Olympics since 1924. Grinham won gold again for the backstroke at the subsequent European and Commonwealth Games in 1958 and retired from the sport the following year. She was awarded an MBE for services to swimming in the 2006 Queen's Birthday Honours.

*The debut single by **Cliff Richard** and the Drifters, 'Move it!', was released in 1958.*

'Move it!' went on to reach number two in the UK singles chart. The Drifters would later change their name to the Shadows, and Richard, primarily as a solo artist from the late sixties onwards, would go on to have hits in each of the next five decades. Among over ninety top-twenty entries he has achieved the number one position in the UK fourteen times, beginning with 'Living Doll' in 1959. Other hits include 'The Young Ones', 'Summer Holiday', 'We Don't Talk Anymore' and his most recent 'The Millennium Prayer' at the end of 1999. Richard was knighted in 1995 for services to charity.

Margaret Court won her first tennis Grand Slam, the Australian Championship, in 1960.

Competing under her maiden name of Smith, it was the first of her eleven victories in the event over the next thirteen years. Her inaugural French and US titles came in 1962 and, in the following year, she became the first Australian woman to triumph in the singles at Wimbledon when she defeated Billie Jean Moffitt (the future Mrs King) in straight sets.

Court won Wimbledon on two more occasions, in 1965 and 1970, and in addition to further wins in the US and French tournaments, amassed a total of twenty-four Grand Slam singles championships – a record which still stands. In 1970 she became the second person to win all four Grand Slams in one calendar year, and the first to do so in the open era of tennis. She also won thirty-eight doubles titles, half of those for the mixed event, to give her an unsurpassed total of sixty-two Grand Slams before her retirement from the game in 1975.

In 1967 the Bee Gees, brothers Barry, **Robin** *and* **Maurice Gibb***, scored their first UK number one hit single with 'Massachusetts'.*

The brothers, Barry (the oldest by three years) and twins Robin and Maurice, were born on the Isle of Man, but the family moved to Australia in the late fifties where their musical pursuits eventually led to a record deal. In 1966, they had their first number one in Australia: 'Spicks and Specks'. Arriving back in Britain soon after, they entered the chart with their first UK hit, 'New York Mining Disaster 1941', which reached number twelve in 1967. The Bee Gees' career was given fresh impetus in the seventies with their disco-based compositions for the film *Saturday Night Fever* (1977). Their most recent number one hit came twenty years after their first, with 'You Win Again', in 1987. The Bee Gees have also written hit songs for many other artists including Diana Ross, Barbra Streisand and Dionne Warwick. Their last studio album, prior to Maurice's sudden death in 2003, at the age of fifty-three, *This is Where I Came In*, was released in 2001. Robin died in 2012 at the age of sixty-two. The Bee Gees were awarded CBEs in 2002 New Year Honours.

Gymnast **Olga Korbut** *won individual gold medals for the beam and the floor exercise, as well as a team gold medal, representing the USSR, at the 1972 Munich Olympic Games.*

Korbut, from Grodno, which was then part of the Byelorussian Soviet Socialist Republic (now independent Belarus), also took silver in the asymmetric bars with a routine that included a memorable back flip. She was the first gymnast to accomplish this difficult manoeuvre, which is no longer allowed in competition. At the next Olympics she won gold again in the team competition and an individual silver for the beam. She moved to the USA in 1991, and now lives in Arizona where she teaches gymnastics.

In 1982 **Norman Whiteside** *became the youngest footballer ever to play in the World Cup finals.*

Whiteside, wearing the number sixteen shirt, made his international debut in Northern Ireland's opening game against Yugoslavia and started all four of their remaining matches as the team made it through to the second round in Spain. Weeks before his appearance, he became one of the youngest footballers to play for Manchester United when he made his debut against Brighton & Hove Albion in a league game less than a fortnight before his seventeenth birthday. In the 1983 FA Cup final, Whiteside scored in the replay, helping United to a 4–0 victory over Brighton & Hove Albion. Having also scored Manchester United's only goal against Liverpool in a 2–1 defeat in the League Cup final, he became the youngest player to score in English football's two major cup competitions. In 1989 he transferred to Everton; however, a knee injury cut short his career, aged twenty-six. He had already won thirty-eight international caps.

In 1985 **Boris Becker** *won his first Wimbledon singles final to become the youngest men's champion in the tournament's history.*

The unseeded Becker defeated Kevin Curren in four sets to take the title. He repeated his triumph the following year, this time defeating the then world number one, Ivan Lendl, in the final. Becker appeared in five more Wimbledon singles finals, three of them against Stefan Edberg who he defeated in 1989 to win his third All England title. Becker also added one US and two Australian Open wins to reach a total of six Grand Slam singles titles during his tennis career.

In 1989 **Michael Chang** *won the French Open to become the youngest ever male winner of a tennis Grand Slam singles tournament.*

Chang defeated Stefan Edberg in five sets to take what would be his only Grand Slam title. On his way to the final, he had to come back from two sets down against world number one Ivan Lendl, a three-time winner of the French Open, in the fourth round. Chang achieved his highest world rating, number two, in 1996, the year in which he was runner-up in both the Australian and US Opens – his only other Grand Slam final appearances. Chang retired from competition in 2003.

Michael Adams *won the British Chess Championship in 1989.*

Adams also became a chess Grandmaster in the same year at the age of seventeen, making him, at the time, the youngest Briton ever to reach this level. His highest world-ranking position to date, number four, was first achieved in 2000. Adams was one of the eight players to take part in the 2005 FIDE World Chess Championships and finished in joint sixth position.

In 1991 ***Robbie Williams*** *had his first UK chart hit, as a member of Take That, with 'Promises'.*

Take That's first number one single didn't come until their eighth release, 'Pray', two years later, with the band going on to notch up another seven chart toppers before splitting up in 1996. Williams had left the previous year and went on to solo success with six top twenty singles, one of which was 'Angels' (his biggest seller to date), before 'Millennium' gave him his first UK number one in 1998. He has enjoyed a further five number one singles in the UK, and his first seven studio albums, beginning with *Life Thru a Lens* in 1997, have all reached the top of the UK album chart. Williams rejoined Take That in 2010, and their first album release as the original line-up since 1995, *Progress*, debuted in the November of that year and went straight to the top of the UK chart.

David Beckham *made his professional football debut, playing for Manchester United, in 1992.*

Beckham came on as a substitute in a League Cup match against Brighton & Hove Albion. This was his only appearance that season for the club and he didn't feature in the next campaign. In the following season he made his league debut, and scored his first goal for the team against Galatasaray in the Champions League. By the end of the 2003 season, after which he left the club for Real Madrid, Beckham had collected six Premier League and two FA Cup medals. His Champions League medal came in 1999 when Manchester United completed 'the treble' by also winning the Premier League and the FA Cup. In 2007 he won the Spanish Championship in his last season with Real Madrid, before joining Los Angeles Galaxy. Beckham's international career started in 1996 at the age of twenty-one, and has included appearances at three World Cup finals. His injury-time goal against Greece, at Old Trafford in 2001, secured England's qualification for the 2002 finals in spectacular fashion. Beckham's total of 115 international caps is an England record for an outfield player. He is also famous for his marriage, in 1999, to Victoria Adams of the Spice Girls. Beckham was awarded an OBE in 2003.

Ronnie O'Sullivan won snooker's UK Championship in 1993.

O'Sullivan, who had turned professional the previous year, holds the record as the youngest winner of a snooker ranking event after his defeat of reigning world champion Stephen Hendry in the final. In the first round of the 1997 World Championship, O'Sullivan made the fastest recorded maximum break in a time of five minutes and twenty seconds; one of eleven maximum breaks in his professional career. In 2001 he won the world title for the first time. O'Sullivan has won three more, most recently in 2012 at the age of thirty-six.

*'. . . Baby One More Time', the debut single by **Britney Spears**, reached number one in the UK chart in 1999.*

'. . . Baby One More Time', the title track from Spears's debut album, was the biggest-selling single of the year in the UK and the first of five British number ones for the Mississippi-born singer. Though she is yet to reach the top of the UK album chart, six of Spears's seven studio albums, including *In The Zone* (2003) and *Femme Fatale* (2011), have made it to the US number one spot, with combined worldwide sales of over seventy million.

*In 2006 **Theo Walcott** became the youngest person to play for the England football team.*

Walcott made his international debut in a friendly match against Hungary that England won by three goals to one. In the previous year he made his inaugural first team professional appearance as a Southampton player and months later transferred to Arsenal where he made his Premier League debut nearly three months after his first game for England. In 2008, at the age of nineteen, Walcott became the youngest person to score a hat-trick for England, against Croatia in a World Cup qualifier in Zagreb.

18

EIGHTEEN

Victoria became Queen of the United Kingdom of Great Britain and Ireland in 1837, succeeding her uncle William IV.

Victoria, the granddaughter of George III, was the last Hanoverian monarch. Her reign lasted for nearly sixty-four years, the longest to date of any British ruler. At the age of twenty she married her cousin, Prince Albert of Saxe-Coburg and Gotha. They had four sons and five daughters; most of whom would connect to Europe's other royal families through marriage. Their eldest son, Prince Albert Edward, would reign after Victoria as Edward VII. She was widowed at the age of forty-two and the loss of her husband was a profound blow to the Queen, who began a prolonged period of mourning. Her reign saw a flourishing of the British Empire, and the further evolution of Britain into a modern constitutional monarchy. Victoria died in 1901 at Osborne House on the Isle of Wight, aged eighty-one.

William Perkin filed his patent for 'Dyeing Fabrics' in 1856.

Perkin's document described the technique for producing the first synthetic dye. It was while Perkin, then a student, was on his Easter holiday from the Royal College of Chemistry that he decided to try to artificially produce quinine in his home laboratory. Though he didn't succeed in this task, he stumbled upon a purple-coloured liquid which proved to have excellent properties as a dye. With the help of his father and brother, Perkin set up a factory to produce the dye, later known as mauveine, in 1858. He became a wealthy man, selling his business in 1874, but continuing with his chemical research. Perkin was knighted in 1906 and died the following year at the age of sixty-nine.

Johnny Weissmuller broke swimming's 100m freestyle record in 1922 with a time of 58.6 seconds, and became the first man to officially swim the distance in under one minute.

Two years later at the Paris Olympics Weissmuller won gold for the same event, as well as for the 400m freestyle and the 4x200m freestyle relay. At the next Olympics, in Amsterdam, he again took home gold medals for the 100m and 4x200m freestyle events. During his career, Weissmuller set a total of sixty-seven world records. He is also famous for his portrayal of Tarzan in many films, the first of which, *Tarzan the Ape Man*, was released in 1932. Weissmuller died in 1984 at the age of seventy-nine.

*'And Death Shall Have No Dominion', by **Dylan Thomas**, was published in 1933.*

The poem, which appeared in *New English Weekly*, was Thomas's first to be published outside his native Wales. His debut collection, *18 Poems*, appeared in the subsequent year. Thomas also produced short stories as well as scripts for radio and film. A large proportion of his published poems were created in his late teenage years. A celebrated later work, 'Do not go gentle into that good night', was written for his dying father. Thomas is also remembered for his 'play for voices', *Under Milk Wood*, completed only months before his death, in 1953, at the age of thirty-nine.

***Freddie Trueman** made his first-class cricket debut, for Yorkshire, in 1949.*

Trueman's test debut came three years later against India at Leeds where he made a sparkling start by taking three wickets for no runs. A renowned fast bowler, in his thirteen year career as an England player he became the first cricketer to take three hundred test wickets (his final tally was 307). Trueman, who was awarded an OBE in 1989, died in 2006 at the age of seventy-five.

*McFly, featuring **Tom Fletcher** and **Danny Jones**, both on lead vocals and guitar; **Harry Judd** on drums; and Dougie Poynter on bass, reached number one in the UK with their debut album, 'Room on the 3rd Floor', in 2004.*

With an average age of eighteen, McFly took over from the Beatles as the youngest group to top the UK album chart. Fletcher and Jones, the founding members of the band, have the most songwriting credits on the album, with Jones also contributing the only solo effort, 'Not Alone'. Judd and bass player Dougie Poynter, the youngest band member who was sixteen when they first reached number one, also share four co-writing citations. The group's other studio albums include the UK number one *Wonderland* (2005) and more recently *Above the Noise* (2010). They have had seven number one singles in the UK.

In 2007 **Samantha Larson** *reached the summit of Mount Everest.*

Larson's conquest of Everest made her the youngest woman to climb the 'seven summits' – the highest peaks on the seven continents – based on the list created by Richard Bass. Larson also climbed (while still eighteen) Carstensz Pyramid which is regarded by some as the qualifying highest peak for the Australian continent. (Mount Kosciuszko, on the Bass list, is located in Australia, whereas the higher Carstensz Pyramid is situated in Papua New Guinea.) Larson, who reached the summit of South America's highest peak, Aconcagua, when just thirteen, and success-fully scaled Africa's Mount Kilimanjaro aged twelve, was accompanied on her climbs of the 'seven summits' by her father, David.

19

NINETEEN

In 1862 the suite of incidental music composed by **Arthur Sullivan** *for Shakespeare's 'The Tempest' was performed in London.*

The performance, as part of the Saturday Crystal Palace concerts, garnered critical praise and helped establish Sullivan's reputation. The composition was a revised version of Sullivan's graduation piece, which had been performed the previous year in Leipzig. In order to better generate an income, Sullivan also created more popular compositions, such as ballads and hymns (for example, his 'St Gertrude' became the standard accompaniment to 'Onward Christian Soldiers'). He is best remembered though for his 'comic operas', most famously produced in a partnership with librettist William Gilbert; titles include *The Pirates of Penzance, The*

Mikado and *The Gondoliers.* Sullivan was knighted by Queen Victoria in 1883. He died in 1900 at the age of fifty-eight.

Don Bradman *made his first-class cricket debut in 1927, when he played for New South Wales against South Australia.*

Bradman made an impressive opening with 118 runs in the first innings, but South Australia won the match by one wicket. He made his test debut a year later in Brisbane against England, who won the match by a record margin of 675 runs, with Bradman making 18 runs in the first innings and a meagre one in the second. Bradman performed better in the third test against England when he hit 79 and 112. In 1930 his run-making ability saw him amass a score of 974 in a test series against England for the Ashes, which still remains a record. By the end of his test career, in 1948, Bradman had recorded an exceptional batting average (total number of runs divided by the number of times out) of 99.94 – an achievement which remains well clear of the next highest figure. Bradman was only four runs away from making it 100, but was bowled for nought in his last innings against England at the Oval. He was knighted in the 1949 New Year Honours list for services to cricket. Bradman died in 2001 at the age of ninety-two.

Edwin Land *filed his first US patent, entitled 'Polarizing Refracting Bodies', in 1929.*

In the patent, Land detailed his invention of a commercially viable film which could be used to produce polarised light. He had been a student of chemistry at Harvard, but took a leave of absence after his first year and moved to New York City where he would carry out his work on light polarisation. In 1932 the Land–Wheelwright Laboratories were established, in conjunction with George Wheelwright, who at the time was a physics professor at Harvard, to commercially exploit Land's invention. In 1937 they formed the Polaroid Corporation. This would become famous for another of Land's inventions – instant photography – which was first demonstrated in 1947. Near the end of the following year the first Polaroid instant camera went on sale (initially, it only produced sepia-tinted pictures). A colour version appeared in 1963, and 1972 saw the launch of the SX-70 camera which now had dry film which could be developed in daylight. Land never returned to complete his studies and graduate from Harvard, though he subsequently received many honorary degrees. He filed over five hundred patents before his death at the age of eighty-one in 1991.

In 1942 **Richard Attenborough** *made his film debut in 'In Which We Serve'.*

Attenborough's breakthrough role, as the small-time gangster Pinkie Brown, came five years later in the film adaptation of Graham Greene's *Brighton Rock* (1947). Attenborough worked prolifically as an actor for the next thirty years, which included an appearance in the prisoner-of-war epic *The Great Escape* (1963). He also moved into roles behind the camera; *Oh! What a Lovely War* (1969) marked his directorial debut. Academy Award success came in 1984 when he won the category of best director for *Gandhi* (1983) which also scooped the best picture prize. Attenborough returned to acting after a gap of many years to play Dr John Hammond in *Jurassic Park* (1993). He was knighted in 1976 and became a life peer in 1993.

Elvis Presley *released his first single, 'That's All Right', in 1954.*

Written by Arthur Crudup, 'That's All Right' was teamed with the flipside of 'Blue Moon of Kentucky'. Presley was the younger of twins born in Tupelo, Mississippi, but his brother, Jesse Garon, was stillborn. Presley had no other siblings. The family moved to Memphis, the location of Sun Records, when he was a teenager. Presley paid for his first demo recordings; however, he attracted the attention of Sun Records boss Sam Philips who partnered Presley with musicians Scotty Moore on guitar and Bill Black on bass. The trio gelled in rehearsals and created a memorable sound with their rendition of 'That's All Right'. Four more singles followed before RCA Victor bought out Presley's Sun contract in late 1955. Presley's initial single for his new label, 'Heartbreak Hotel', gave him his first US number one in 1956 and Presley's debut album achieved similar status. In the UK singles chart, Presley would achieve sixteen number ones in his lifetime (his first, in 1957, was 'All Shook Up'), and, when added to his posthumous career total, gives him the record for the most UK chart-toppers. He made over thirty films, primarily light entertainment vehicles to showcase his singing talent – his most successful include

Jailhouse Rock (1957), *Blue Hawaii* (1961) and *Viva Las Vegas* (1964). *G.I. Blues* (1960) was inspired by Presley's posting to Germany as part of his two-year National Service. Dubbed the 'King of Rock and Roll', Presley died in 1977 at the age of forty-two, in Memphis, Tennessee.

Anita Lonsbrough *won a gold medal for the 200m breaststroke at the 1960 Rome Olympics in a new world-record time.*

Lonsbrough's accomplishment would not be equalled by a British female swimmer for another forty-eight years, when Rebecca Adlington won gold twice and also broke the 800m freestyle world record at the Beijing Olympics. At the half-way stage, Lonsbrough was two seconds behind Wiltrud Urselmann of Germany who had gone off fast, but came back to take the lead and claim victory. She went on to win the same event at the 1962 European Championships and, in the same year, became the first woman to win the BBC Sports Personality of the Year award. In 1964 Lonsbrough was awarded an MBE, and at the Tokyo Olympics became the first woman to carry the flag for the British team at the opening ceremony.

In 1962 the Beatles, featuring **George Harrison** *on lead guitar, released their debut single.*

'Love Me Do' would make it to no higher than number seventeen in the chart on its first release, but the group went on to dominate popular music in the sixties, with eleven consecutive number one songs. Harrison, the youngest member of the band, also influenced their exploration of eastern culture and music, incorporating the sitar into several recordings. His first composition to feature on a Beatles' release was 'Don't Bother Me', which appeared on their second album, *With the Beatles*. Harrison continued to make regular songwriting contributions and his first Beatles' single 'A' side, 'Something', was released in 1969. It would become one of the group's most covered songs. After the band's break-up, Harrison was, in 1971, the first to record a solo UK number one with 'My Sweet Lord', taken from his acclaimed debut triple album, *All Things Must Pass*, which also topped the UK chart. In the same year he organised a concert for Bangladesh, the first major charity fundraiser of its type. Harrison also became involved in film production, setting up Handmade Films to finance

Monty Python's *Life of Brian* (1979). He died in 2001 at the age of fifty-eight.

*The Rolling Stones, with lead singer **Mick Jagger** and guitarist **Keith Richards**, first entered the UK singles chart in 1963 with 'Come On'.*

A cover version of a Chuck Berry song, 'Come On' lodged just one place outside the top twenty. The Stones' early reliance on covers continued until 1965 when 'The Last Time' became the first Jagger/Richards composition to reach number one. It was the third of five consecutive chart toppers for the band, and they would enjoy three more UK number ones before the end of the decade. Jagger and Richards had first met at primary school in Kent and, after attending different secondary schools, met again and discovered a shared interest in blues and R&B music that would eventually lead to the founding of the Rolling Stones, with Jagger abandoning his studies at the London School of Economics. The band signed to Decca, who had previously rejected the Beatles, and their impressive recording career commenced. Now into their fifth decade, the Rolling Stones continue to record and perform. Both Jagger and Richards have also released solo albums. Jagger was knighted in 2003 for services to music.

*The debut performance of 'Joseph and the Amazing Technicolour Dreamcoat', with music by **Andrew Lloyd Webber** and lyrics by Tim Rice, took place in 1968.*

This, the first Webber and Rice collaboration to be performed, was part of a school end-of-term concert, and the original fifteen-minute work was subsequently augmented to become a two-hour stage show. Lloyd Webber came from a musical family (there has been renewed interest in his late father's work as a composer), and displayed his own talent in this sphere at an early age. The first work that he created in conjunction with Tim Rice, *The Likes of Us*, was completed in 1965 but, due to a lack of backing at the time, did not receive its first performance until forty years later. They were more fortunate with their third musical: *Jesus Christ Superstar* (1970), which was a hit. Six years later they teamed up again for *Evita* (1976). The film treatment released in 1996 brought Lloyd Webber and Rice their first Oscar for the song 'You Must Love Me'. Lloyd Webber, as a composer, has also scored major successes with *Cats* (1981) and *The*

Phantom of the Opera (1986), the latter of which has become the longest-running musical on Broadway. Lloyd Webber has collected numerous awards including seven Tonys and seven Oliviers. He was knighted in 1992 and ennobled as a life peer, Baron Lloyd-Webber, in 1997.

In 1975 **Bill Gates** *and Paul Allen developed the first Microsoft product – a version of the programming language BASIC for the Altair 8800 microcomputer.*

Gates, then a second-year student at Harvard, and Allen were inspired by seeing the Altair 8800 microcomputer on the cover of *Popular Electronics* magazine. Their creation was subsequently demonstrated to the Altair's manufacturer, MITS, who became Gates and Allen's first customer. Gates took a leave of absence from Harvard (never to return to his studies) and the name Microsoft (originally hyphenated) was registered in 1976. In its early years, the company focused on programming languages for different computing platforms. IBM's entry into the personal computer (PC) market at the start of the eighties provided Microsoft with an outstanding opportunity. Initially contracted by IBM to provide a BASIC interpreter, Microsoft also supplied the operating system. It was purchased from Seattle Computer Products and adapted to run on the IBM PC. Crucially, Microsoft retained the copyright on the operating system which was dubbed PC-DOS, and with the proliferation of IBM PC clones in the following years the company found itself in a dominant and lucrative position in the software market, further enhanced by its Windows operating system, and the broadening of its product range into applications such as word processing, spreadsheets and presentations. In 2008 Gates stepped down from his role at Microsoft to concentrate on his and his wife's philanthropic work through the Bill and Melinda Gates Foundation. The Gates themselves have donated more than $26 billion to the foundation.

In 1978 **Kate Bush** *made it to number one in the UK chart with her debut offering, 'Wuthering Heights'.*

Bush became the first woman to have composed and performed a British chart topping single. 'Wuthering Heights' was also featured on her debut album, *The Kick Inside*, which reached number three in the same year. Bush was signed to EMI Records after she was championed by Pink Floyd's David Gilmour, who was made aware of her talent through a friend of the family. Her original demos had been turned down by various record companies, but eventually a Gilmour-financed professional production of three tracks secured a contract. Her second single, 'The Man With The Child In His Eyes' which reached number six in 1978, was actually written several years earlier and featured on the Gilmour demo completed in 1975. It was one of the large number of songs that she composed in her teenage years. Bush has completed eight studio albums with the latest, *50 Words For Snow*, debuting in 2011. In the same year she also released *Director's Cut*, a selection of reworked tracks from *The Sensual World* and *The Red Shoes*. Bush shares her birthday with Emily Brontë, author of the novel *Wuthering Heights*. She was awarded a CBE in 2013.

*'For You', the debut album by **Prince**, was released in 1978.*

The Minneapolis-born songwriter and multi-instrumentalist, full name Prince Roger Nelson, was credited with the album's production, arrangement, composition and performance. It sold moderately, but it was with his 1982 offering *1999* that he achieved a breakthrough both in the US and internationally. Prince's next album, *Purple Rain*, the soundtrack to the 1984 film in which he starred as 'The Kid', further boosted his reputation and garnered him an Oscar for 'best music, original song score'. Further albums released in the eighties such as *Parade* and *Sign 'O' The Times* cemented his position in the musical firmament. Prince's first UK number one single was as a songwriter with Sinéad O'Connor's version of 'Nothing Compares 2 U' in 1990. He made the top spot in his own right with 'The Most Beautiful Girl In The World' in 1994 (by this time Prince had accumulated five US number one singles). In the previous year, he had changed his name to an unpronounceable symbol, which led to him generally being referred to as 'The Artist Formerly Known as Prince', but he returned to his original moniker in 2000. A prodigious songwriter, Prince released his twenty-sixth studio album, *20Ten*, in 2010.

*In 1987 **Kylie Minogue** began her pop career with a number one hit in Australia, singing 'The Locomotion'.*

Minogue's version of 'The Locomotion' topped the chart for seven weeks and became the biggest-selling Australian single of the decade. Her UK chart career got off to a similar start with the Stock, Aitken and Waterman production of 'I Should Be So Lucky'. It topped the UK singles chart for five weeks in early 1988 and was the first of thirteen consecutive top-ten hits that included three more number ones. Minogue had already made her name in Britain as a television actress playing Charlene Robinson in the series *Neighbours*, which made its UK debut on BBC1 in 1986. However, she remains best known for her music career and after a gap of ten years returned to the top of the UK singles chart with 'Spinning Around' in 2000. Minogue has had two more number ones since then, 'Can't Get You Out of My Head' in 2001, which became her best-selling single, and 'Slow' in 2003. Her eleventh studio collection, *Aphrodite*, was released in 2010 and became her fifth number one album in the UK. She was awarded an OBE in the 2008 New Year Honours.

In 1988 **Steffi Graf** *won a gold medal at the Seoul Olympics for the women's singles.*

Tennis returned to the Olympic Games after a gap of sixty-four years, with Graf capturing a gold medal by defeating Gabriela Sabatini in straight sets. Graf had already won the four Grand Slam tournaments in 1988, so her Olympic victory gave her a 'Golden Slam', an achievement which no other player has yet emulated. (Andre Agassi, Rafael Nadal and Serena Williams have all achieved career 'Golden Slams' – i.e. they have won the four major titles and the Olympic gold, but not in the same year). Graf won her first Grand Slam title, the 1987 French Open, at the age of seventeen. Her clean sweep of the tennis majors the following year added to her career total of twenty-two Grand Slam singles, making her second only to Margaret Court with twenty-four. Graf had begun playing tennis before she was five and turned professional when she was thirteen. She retired from tennis in 1999, the year of her last Grand Slam victory, at the French Open.

Westlife, featuring **Shane Filan**, **Brian McFadden**, **Kian Egan**, *Mark Feehily and Nicky Byrne, reached number one with their debut single 'Swear It Again' in 1999.*

'Swear It Again' was the first of fourteen UK number one singles for Westlife, a total only surpassed by Elvis Presley and the Beatles. McFadden left the group in 2004 to pursue a solo career, which began with a number one for his co-written debut release 'Real to Me' later in the year. Westlife went on to have two more number one singles in the UK, 'You Raise Me Up' (2004) and 'The Rose' (2006). The band split up in June 2012 after their farewell tour, which ended with a concert held in Croke Park, Dublin.

Mark Zuckerberg launched the social networking website Facebook from his dormitory room at Harvard in 2004.

Initially membership of Facebook, co-founded with Dustin Moskovitz, Chris Hughes and Eduardo Saverin, was exclusively for Harvard students, but it was soon expanded to include other educational establishments such as Stanford, Cornell and Yale. Facebook embraced more universities, colleges and high schools, and eventually by the autumn of 2006 it would be open to everyone older than thirteen. Zuckerberg, a second-year student at the time of the site's launch, left his studies to concentrate on Facebook, relocating the company to Palo Alto, California. Membership of the site has increased dramatically. In July 2012, Facebook stated that it had 955 million monthly active users. Zuckerberg was named as *Time* magazine's Person of the Year for 2010.

In 2004 Scarlett Johansson won the Bafta Award for best actress for her performance as Charlotte in 'Lost In Translation'.

Johansson, who is the youngest to be awarded the Bafta accolade of best actress, also scored a Golden Globe nomination for *Lost In Translation*. Her film debut came ten years earlier with a minor part in *North* (1994), directed by Rob Reiner, and further roles followed with Johansson earning plaudits for her portrayal of Grace MacLean in *The Horse Whisperer* (1998). In the same year as her Bafta success, Johansson was also Bafta and Golden Globe nominated for *Girl with a Pearl Earring* (2003). She has completed a trio of Woody Allen films: *Match Point* (2005), *Scoop* (2006) and *Vicky Cristina Barcelona* (2008) – the first of which brought Johansson her fourth Golden Globe nomination.

In 2006 Rob Gauntlett and his climbing partner James Hooper became the youngest Britons to climb Mount Everest.

Gauntlett, the younger of the duo, and Hooper both reached their 19th birthday at base camp prior to the ascent. It was only three years before their Everest achievement that the two friends had decided that they wanted to scale the world's highest peak. In 2008 they successfully completed a journey, using only human or natural power, between the north and south magnetic poles. Tragedy struck in 2009 when the 21-year-old Gauntlett and his fellow climber, James Atkinson, were killed whilst ice climbing in the Alps.

*In 2008 '19', the debut album by **Adele**, went straight to number one in the UK album chart.*

Singer-songwriter Adele Adkins came to the notice of her label, XL Recordings, with a three-song demo on her Myspace page; she was signed in 2006. The album featured her first four singles, with 'Chasing Pavements' reaching number two in the UK chart in 2008. Adele released her second album, *21*, at the start of 2011, which also entered the chart at number one and spent eleven consecutive weeks at the top – a record for a female solo artist. It has since become the biggest-selling album of the twenty-first century in the UK. The second single culled from *21*, 'Someone Like You', gave Adele her first UK number one single at the end of February 2011. In 2012 Adele won six Grammy Awards including Album of the Year for *21*, and Record and Song of the Year for the opening track 'Rolling in the Deep', which was also her first US number one single.

*****Rebecca Adlington** won two gold medals, for the 400m and 800m freestyle swimming events, at the 2008 Beijing Olympic Games.*

Adlington also broke the world record in the final of the 800m that had stood for nineteen years and remains the current record holder. Her victories were the first for a British female swimmer at the Olympics since Anita Lonsbrough in 1960. She also became the first Briton since Henry Taylor at the 1908 Olympic Games to win two individual swimming golds. At the 2011 World Championships, Adlington won gold for the 800m freestyle and silver for the 400m freestyle. The following year, she won bronze for both these events at the London Olympics. She was awarded an OBE in the 2009 New Year Honours list.

*****Jade Jones** won a gold medal for taekwondo at the 2012 London Olympics.*

Jones, who was victorious in the 57kg category, was Britain's youngest gold medallist at the London Games. She is also the first Briton to win a gold medal for taekwondo. Twice a European Championship bronze medallist, she also won a gold medal at the Youth Olympic Games in 2010. Jones defeated China's Yuzhuo Hou in the final at the London Games, thereby reversing the result when the pair met in the 2011 World Championship final when Jones had to settle for silver. Jones was awarded an MBE in the 2013 New Year Honours.

Jonnie Peacock won a gold medal for the 100m at the 2012 London Paralympics.
Competing in the T44 class, Peacock won the 100m in a time of 10.9 seconds, setting a new Paralympic record. The Cambridge-born sprinter, who lost his right leg below the knee to meningitis aged five, attended a Paralympic talent-spotting event in 2008 that identified his potential. Three months before the London Paralympics, Peacock set a new world record of 10.85 seconds at the US Paralympic track-and-field trials. He was awarded an MBE in the 2013 New Year Honours.

CHAPTER THREE

Vicenarians

Oh, talk not to me of a name great in story;
The days of our youth are the days of our glory;
And the myrtle and ivy of sweet two-and—twenty
Are worth all your laurels, though ever so plenty.

LORD BYRON

20

TWENTY

*The first published poem of **John Keats**, 'O Solitude!', appeared in 'The Examiner' in 1816.*

Keats's first volume of poetry was published in the following year and his celebrated work *Lamia, Isabella, The Eve of St Agnes, and other Poems* in 1820. It contained his odes (which include 'To a Nightingale'), and was to be the last work he would see in print. Keats died in Rome in 1821 at the age of twenty-five. His gravestone does not contain his name, as he requested, but describes him as a young English poet ending with his chosen words: 'Here lies One Whose Name was Writ in Water'.

*'Frankenstein: or, The Modern Prometheus', the first novel by **Mary Shelley**, was published in 1818.*

Mary (née Godwin) eloped with Percy Shelley in 1814, and they married two years later following the death of Shelley's first wife, Harriet. The story of Frankenstein was conceived while they were staying close to Lake Geneva, Switzerland, with company that included Lord Byron. After Percy Shelley died in 1822, Mary and their son returned to England where she continued to write novels, short stories, biographies and travelogues. She also promoted the publication and appreciation of her late husband's work. Mary Shelley died in 1851 at the age of fifty-three.

*In 1848 **Dante Gabriel Rossetti** was one of the founders of the Pre-Raphaelite Brotherhood.*

Rossetti formed the group, which sought to take a different direction in British art from the conventional Royal Academy approach, in conjunction with John Millais and William Holman Hunt; others were to join the trio later in the year. Rossetti's first significant oil paintings, *The Girlhood of Mary Virgin* and *Ecce Ancilla Domini*, were exhibited in 1849 and 1850 respectively. His first volume of poetry was published in 1870 and drew upon many of the poems that he had buried with his wife Elizabeth Siddal, but was later persuaded to have exhumed from her grave. Siddal was an important model for the Pre-Raphaelites and Rossetti in particular, and they married after an engagement that lasted a decade. However, less than two years after their union, Siddal died of an overdose of laudanum. Rossetti published a further volume of poems in 1881, the year before his death at the age of fifty-three.

In 1919 **Jack Cohen** *decided to start selling groceries from a market stall in London – the beginning of what would become the supermarket Tesco.*

Instead of returning to tailoring after service in the Royal Flying Corps, Cohen used some of his £30 demobilisation gratuity to buy surplus grocery stock and sell it on a Hackney stall. The name Tesco, initially deployed on his own brand of tea, would come a few years later, formed from the initials of T. E. Stockwell (a partner in the firm of his tea suppliers), and the first two letters of Cohen's surname. Cohen concentrated on market trading for several years before deciding to obtain premises. A decade after first starting out, he opened the first Tesco store in the Greater London suburb of Burnt Oak. The business continued to expand in and around London in the 1930s, with up to one hundred stores in place before the end of the decade. After the war, Tesco was among the first to introduce self-service supermarkets based on the American format. The sixties saw further growth, aided by acquisitions, and by the end of the seventies sales had reached £1 billion. Cohen was knighted in 1969. He died ten years later, at the age of eighty.

The first West End production by **Noël Coward**, *'I'll Leave It to You', was given its London premiere at the New Theatre in 1920.*

Coward, who also starred in the play, had been a child actor – making his professional stage debut at the age of eleven as Prince Mussel in *The Goldfish*. However, he is best-known as a playwright, and it was his play of 1924, *The Vortex*, that gave him his first major success. Other hits followed – including *Hay Fever*, *Private Lives* and *Blithe Spirit*. Coward was also a composer of numerous songs (including 'Mad Dogs and Englishmen' and 'Mad About the Boy'). In the cinematic arena he wrote, produced, co-directed and starred in the patriotic war film *In Which We Serve* (1942).

His plays were also adapted for the screen, including *Still Life* which formed the basis for *Brief Encounter* (1945). Coward received a knighthood in 1969, four years before his death at his home in Jamaica at the age of seventy-three. The New Theatre was renamed the Noël Coward Theatre in 2006.

In 1926 **Gertrude Ederle** *became the first woman to swim across the English Channel.*

Nearly fifty-one years after the Channel was first swum by Matthew Webb, Ederle completed the route in a record fourteen hours and thirty-nine minutes, swimming from France to England. She was already a successful record-breaking competitive swimmer. Representing the United States at the 1924 Olympics in Paris, Ederle won gold as part of the 4x100m freestyle relay team, and bronze in both the 100m and 400m freestyle. She first attempted to swim the Channel in 1925, but after twenty-three miles she was disqualified when one of her supporting crew grabbed her in the belief that she was in trouble. During her successful crossing the following year, Ederle had to contend with stormy weather which lengthened her route from a possible twenty-one to thirty-five miles. Despite this, her time remained unbeaten by anyone until 1950. Ederle's triumph was recognised with a ticker-tape parade in New York and a role, as herself, in the film *Swim Girl, Swim* (1927). Childhood measles had impaired her hearing which was worsened by her swimming exploits, resulting in complete deafness for nearly the latter two thirds of her life. Ederle died in 2003 at the age of ninety-eight.

Clive Sinclair *founded Sinclair Radionics in 1961.*

Sinclair chose not to go to university and instead set his sights on starting an electronics business. As a teenager he wrote articles for *Practical Wireless*, and soon ended up running the magazine. He next joined Bernard Babini's publishing company, for whom he wrote successful books on electronics such as *Modern Transistor Circuits for Beginners*, first published in 1962. In November of that year, Sinclair Radionics advertised its first product, a Micro-amplifier. The company went on to develop a number of miniature products, including small transistor radios which were offered in kit form. In the seventies they brought out their first pocket calculator, and launched a miniature television towards the end of the decade, although it wasn't a commercial success. Sinclair Radionics was wound up shortly after when the government's National Enterprise Board, who had a controlling stake, sought a buyer for the calculator and TV side of the business. Clive Sinclair carried on with further companies that bore his name, producing home computers such as the ZX81 and the Spectrum, and the ill-fated battery-assisted vehicle known as the Sinclair C5. He was knighted in 1983 and served for seventeen years as the chairman of Mensa.

The self-titled debut album from **Bob Dylan** *was released in 1962.*

Only two of the album's thirteen tracks were Dylan compositions: 'Talkin' New York' and 'Song for Woody'. This situation was reversed for his second album, *The Freewheelin' Bob Dylan* (1963), which contained eleven self-penned tracks including 'Blowin' in the Wind' and 'A Hard Rain's a-Gonna Fall'. It was a critical and commercial success for the socially conscious songwriter and gave him his first UK number one album in 1965 (it was not until 1974's *Planet Waves*, his thirteenth studio album, that he would reach number one in the US billboard chart). Dylan's fifth album, *Bringing it all Back Home*, was significant for being the first of his releases to include recordings using electric instruments. His 2009 studio album *Together Through Life* brought him his first UK number one for nearly forty years. Dylan has received numerous accolades throughout his career, including an Academy Award in 2001 for best original song – 'Things Have Changed' from *Wonder Boys* (2000).

The Beatles, with **Paul McCartney** *on bass guitar, first entered the UK singles chart in 1962 with the Lennon/McCartney composition 'Love Me Do'.*

On its initial release, 'Love Me Do' reached number seventeen. The next Beatles' single, 'Please Please Me', peaked at number two on the *Record Retailer* chart, the forerunner of today's official chart. The band's third offering, 'From Me To You', became the first of eleven consecutive number ones for the band that culminated with the double 'A' side 'Yellow Submarine/Eleanor Rigby' in 1966. The Beatles achieved a further six number one singles before they split up in 1970. McCartney went on to form Wings, whose 1977 Christmas number one, 'Mull of Kintyre' (co-written with Denny Laine), became one of the biggest-selling singles of all time, beating the Beatles' top seller, 'She Loves You'. McCartney's songwriting prowess has made him one of the most successful composers in popular music – his song 'Yesterday' is the most covered in the world, with hundreds of versions by other artists in existence. McCartney was knighted in 1997.

*Led Zeppelin, with lead singer **Robert Plant**, played their first concert in 1968.*

Led Zeppelin originally came together as an offshoot of the Yardbirds, which in its last incarnation featured future Zeppelin guitarist Jimmy Page. When the Yardbirds split up in 1968, Page and fellow member Chris Dreja decided to assemble a new line-up that would be able to fulfil tour dates already booked for The Yardbirds. Terry Reid was the first choice for lead vocals, however he declined and recommended Robert Plant – who introduced drummer John Bonham to the line-up. Dreja left and was replaced on bass by John Paul Jones, to complete the formation of Led Zeppelin. The band's debut album was released the following year, launching a highly successful recording career. Led Zeppelin was disbanded following the death of drummer John Bonham in 1980, although the remaining three members have played together since then, reuniting in 2007 for a benefit concert.

*In 1976 **Björn Borg** won the first of his five consecutive Wimbledon singles titles when he defeated Ilie Nastase in straight sets.*

Borg never lost a set during his first successful Wimbledon campaign and would not lose another match in the championships until he was defeated by John McEnroe in the 1981 final. Borg never won the US or Australian Opens, however he won the French Open on six occasions, and is the only male player to have won both this title and Wimbledon in three consecutive years (1978–1980). Like many other young tennis champions, Borg's interest began in childhood. His first success at the All England club came at the age of sixteen when he won the junior Wimbledon crown. He announced his retirement from world tennis at the age of twenty-six, though in the early 1990s he made an undistinguished return to the professional game before finally quitting in 1993, aged thirty-seven.

Edwin Moses won a gold medal at the 1976 Montreal Olympics for the 400m hurdles in a new world-record time of 47.64 seconds.

Moses, using his thirteen-stride pattern between the hurdles, dominated this event for the next decade, winning 122 consecutive races (107 of these were finals), and setting world-record times on four occasions. He missed the 1980 Moscow Olympics due to the USA boycott, but took gold again in Los Angeles in 1984. His last Olympic final came four years later in Seoul, where he was beaten into third place in what was his last competitive race.

In 1976 John Lydon first entered the UK singles chart as the vocalist with the Sex Pistols.

The Sex Pistols' debut release 'Anarchy in the UK', co-written by Lydon (also known as Johnny Rotten at the time), reached number thirty-eight. Its entry into the UK chart came after the band's notorious teatime appearance on Thames Television's *Today* programme where the group, interviewed by Bill Grundy, were a last-minute substitute for EMI stablemates Queen. The resulting media backlash against their on-air swearing resulted in the cancellation of tour gigs and thrust the Sex Pistols, and punk rock, into the public consciousness. The band released three further singles and an album, *Never Mind the Bollocks, Here's the Sex Pistols*, before Lydon left the group in early 1978. He then formed Public Image Limited, whose debut album appeared later that year. The band charted frequently in the 1980s with Lydon remaining the only constant member. In the mid 1990s, the original line-up of the Sex Pistols reformed for a series of live dates and have performed occasionally since then. A reconstituted Public Image Limited also took to the stage after a gap approaching two decades in 2009 and the band released their ninth studio album, *This is PIL*, in 2012.

Carrie Fisher played Princess Leia in 'Star Wars', released in 1977.

Star Wars was Fisher's second film, following her debut two years earlier in *Shampoo* (1975). She also appeared in the latter two instalments of the original Star Wars trilogy: *The Empire Strikes Back* (1980) and *Return of the Jedi* (1983). Her cinematic career has also included roles in films such as *The Blues Brothers* (1980), *Hannah and Her Sisters* (1986) and *Wonderland* (2003). Fisher is also a writer and her first, semi-autobiographical novel,

Postcards from the Edge, achieved both critical and commercial success following its publication in 1987. She also wrote the screenplay for its film adaptation, released in 1990.

Rory Underwood *made his England rugby union debut in 1984.*

England defeated Ireland in the Five Nations game that gave Underwood the first of his eighty-five caps. He holds the record for the most tries by an England player, with a total of forty-nine, and also scored one playing for the Lions against New Zealand. Underwood played for England at the first three Rugby World Cups in 1987, 1991 and 1995, and ended his international career where he began, in a Five Nations match against Ireland at Twickenham, in 1996. Underwood played most of his club rugby for Leicester Tigers, winning two English Premierships, before joining Bedford Blues for his final professional season which ended in 1998. He was awarded an MBE in 1992.

In 1991 Take That secured their first UK chart hit with 'Promises', co-written by band member **Gary Barlow**.

'Promises' reached number thirty-eight, but Take That's next release, a cover of 'It Only Takes A Minute', broke into the top ten. The group, which also included Robbie Williams, Mark Owen, Jason Orange and Howard Donald, hit their stride and in their first period together, before the split in 1996, scored eight number one singles. The first of these was 'Pray' in 1993, penned by Gary Barlow. As the band's main songwriter, he also wrote another three of their number ones in this period, and co-wrote another pair: 'Everything Changes' and 'Sure'. During Take That's hiatus between 1996 and their reunion tour in 2006, Barlow had two solo number one hits, the first of which was the self-penned 'Forever Love'. His debut album, *Open Road*, also reached the top of the chart. The band's later career has seen them notch up another three number one singles, all with songwriting contributions by Barlow. He has also written for many other artists and has been the recipient of five Ivor Novello awards.

In 1996 **Kate Winslet** *won her first Bafta Award, for best supporting actress, for her role as Marianne Dashwood in 'Sense and Sensibility' (1995).*

Winslet made her film debut in the Peter Jackson directed *Heavenly*

Creatures (1994), for which she won both the London Critics' Circle Award and the *Empire* magazine British Actress of the Year Award. She earned her first Academy Award nomination, as well as a Bafta, for her third film, *Sense and Sensibility* (1995). Her next Oscar nomination, this time for best actress, was for her part as Rose in the hugely successful *Titanic* (1997). Her performance as the young Iris Murdoch in *Iris* (2001) brought her Oscar, Bafta and Golden Globe nominations for best supporting actress. After two further nominations for best actress for each of these awards, Winslet finally won all three, aged thirty-three, for her performance as Hanna Schmitz in *The Reader* (2008). She was awarded a CBE in the 2012 Queen's Birthday Honours.

Andrew Flintoff made his test cricket debut for England against South Africa in 1998.

England, the home side, won the match by eight wickets, with Flintoff making seventeen runs and taking one wicket. 'Freddie' Flintoff made his maiden test century against New Zealand in 2002, when he chalked up 137 as England won the first test on their way to victory in the three test series. The Ashes series in 2005 is seen by many to be the high point of Flintoff's career, where his batting totals of 68 and 73 runs in each of the innings (including nine sixes) and his capture of seven Australian wickets helped propel England to victory in the second test by two runs. England won the series by two tests to one; their first Ashes victory since 1987. Flintoff was captain of the side for the next series, 'Down Under', in 2007, but the visitors lost all five tests as the Australians regained the Ashes. Flintoff made his last test appearance in the concluding test of the next Ashes encounter, which England won to clinch the series 2–1. Recurring injury problems forced Flintoff to retire from the game, at the age of thirty-two, in 2010. He received an MBE in 2006.

In 2006 Keira Knightley was nominated for an Academy Award for best actress for her portrayal of Elizabeth Bennet in 'Pride and Prejudice'.

Knightley is the youngest British actress to be nominated in the Academy's best actress category (the third youngest overall). The daughter of an actor and a playwright (father and mother respectively), Knightley was destined for a stage career. She completed her first feature, the television film *A Village Affair* (1995), at the age of nine, and continued to add to her portfolio throughout her childhood. Her role as Jules Paxton in *Bend it Like Beckham* (2002) brought her to prominence, and she has had further success with productions that include the first three Pirates of the Caribbean films (2003–2007) and *Atonement* (2007).

21

TWENTY-ONE

Gustav Kirchoff *announced his two laws for electrical circuits in 1845, while still a student at the University of Königsberg.*

Kirchoff stated that the sum of electrical current into a circuit node must equal the sum of the electrical current out of the node, and that the sum of all the voltages around a loop of an electrical circuit must equal zero. These laws are still widely used in electrical engineering, and form the basis of many computer programs that simulate the behaviour of electrical circuits. Later a professor at both Heidelberg and Berlin universities, Kirchoff also made important contributions to spectroscopy and thermal radiation. He died in 1887 at the age of sixty-three.

Thomas Edison *obtained his first patent, for an 'Electrographic Vote Recorder and Register', in 1869.*

Designed to speed up the process of vote taking by legislative bodies, Edison's machine did not find favour. However, he proved to have a prodigious talent for invention, and would go on to register over one thousand US patents during his lifetime. These included the phonograph (1877), the carbon microphone (1878) – used in the telephone – and his commercially-viable incandescent light bulb (1880). Edison, the seventh and last child of the family, received little formal education, but he had a great capacity for reading and self-improvement. Edison became an operator for the telegraph, improvements to which would form the basis of many of his first patent submissions. An early success was his stock ticker, the funds from which helped to establish his Menlo Park research lab, where Edison and his staff came up with many more inventions. He patented and set up the first electricity distribution system, based on direct current, which began operating in 1882. However, the direct current system would be gradually replaced, for sound technical reasons, by one based on alternating current. Edison died in 1931, aged eighty-four.

In 1896 **Launceston Elliot** *became the first Olympic champion to represent Great Britain and Ireland when he won the one-handed lift competition at the inaugural modern Olympic Games in Athens.*

Elliot, of Scottish lineage, was born in India, and named after the place of his conception, Launceston, Tasmania. In his early teens the family moved to England, where Elliot's prowess as a weightlifter became apparent when he took the British title in 1894. Two years later, Elliot travelled to Athens for the first modern Olympics. He first came close to success in the two-handed lift. Although Elliot lifted the same weight as the winner, he lost out on style and had to make do with the runner-up spot. He made amends in the one-handed event, taking the winner's silver medal (retrospectively classified as gold). Elliot also competed in the 100m, wrestling and the rope-climbing competition. His post-Olympic career saw him tour the music halls as a professional strongman before moving to Australia in his late forties, where he died at the age of fifty-six in 1930.

In 1922 on his twenty-first birthday, **William Lyons**, *in partnership with William Walmsley, formed the Swallow Sidecar Company, the forerunner of Jaguar Cars.*

Initially Lyons and Walmsley's business focused on the making of motorcycle sidecars but after a few years they moved into coachbuilding by creating special bodies for cars such as the Austin Seven. In the early 1930s, the SS 1 coupé, with the chassis and engine supplied by the Standard Motor Company, proved to be a success. SS Cars Ltd was established in late 1933 and shortly after, Walmsley left the company. It was also in the thirties that the name Jaguar would be used for the first time on one of Lyons's cars, and it became the company's identity after the war. The unveiling of the XK120, with its Jaguar-designed engine, at the 1948 Earl's Court Motor Show caused a sensation and, along with the company's racing success in the next decade, firmly established Jaguar's reputation.

Further accolades came with the launch of the E-type sports car in 1961. Lyons was knighted in 1956, and although Jaguar was subsequently absorbed into the British Leyland empire in the sixties, it re-emerged as an independent company in 1984 following privatisation. The Ford Motor Company took control in the late eighties, relinquishing it to Tata Motors in 2008. Lyons died in 1985 at the age of eighty-three.

Jeanette Altwegg won a gold medal for figure skating at the 1952 Winter Olympic Games in Oslo, Norway.

Altwegg's success made her the first British woman to win an individual gold at the Winter Olympics. She was also a promising tennis player and competed in the Junior Championships at Wimbledon before opting to focus on skating. In 1948, in the Olympics held at St. Moritz, Switzerland, Altwegg took home a bronze medal despite, due to a technical problem, having to skate the last thirty seconds of her routine without any music. Prior to her gold in Oslo she became the World and European champion in 1951. She retired from the sport after her Olympic victory and was awarded a CBE in the 1953 Coronation Honours list.

*In 1954 **Colin Cowdrey** made his test cricket debut playing for England against Australia.*

The initials of his full name, Michael Colin Cowdrey, were selected to coincide with those of the famous Marylebone Cricket Club. He first played at Lord's as a thirteen-year-old in a school fixture between Tonbridge and Clifton, making him arguably the youngest ever player to appear at the ground. His long test career continued until 1975 when, at the age of forty-two, he was called into service against the Australians. Cowdrey was the first cricketer to play 100 tests, ultimately notching up 114 and achieving 7624 runs in the process. He was knighted in 1992 and became Lord Cowdrey of Tonbridge in 1997, three years before his death at the age of sixty-seven.

*The Crickets, featuring **Buddy Holly** on guitar and vocals, reached number one in the UK chart in 1957 with a song co-written by Holly – 'That'll Be The Day'.*

Holly's follow-up hits with the Crickets included 'Oh Boy' and 'Maybe Baby'. He achieved further chart success in his solo career with, amongst others, 'Peggy Sue' and 'Heartbeat'. Holly, aged twenty-two, and three others – pilot Roger Peterson, Ritchie Valens and J. P. 'The Big Bopper' Richardson – were killed when their light aircraft crashed in early 1959. Weeks later 'It Doesn't Matter Anymore' gave Holly a posthumous UK number one. Holly was a major figure in the development of rock 'n' roll, and the first to use what became the standard configuration of guitar, bass and drums. He influenced many of the major artists of the sixties including the Beatles (whose chosen name resounded with that of The Crickets). 'That'll Be The Day', co-written by Holly, was the first song ever recorded by John Lennon, Paul McCartney and George Harrison, when as members of the Quarrymen they paid to make a one-off recording in 1958.

In 1962, four days before the twenty-second birthday of rhythm guitarist and co-founder **John Lennon**, *the Beatles' first single, 'Love Me Do', was released.*

The first Lennon/McCartney composition to chart, 'Love Me Do' went on to reach number seventeen on its first release. The Beatles' third single, 'From Me To You', was the first of seventeen to reach the number one spot in the UK in the sixties, which along with their album chart performance (eleven number ones by the end of 1970) and continuing popularity has made them one of the most successful bands in the history of popular music. Their later career was devoted to studio work and produced, in 1967, the landmark album *Sergeant Pepper's Lonely Hearts Club Band*. The break-up of the Beatles was announced in 1970 – although by this time Lennon's solo career was underway in collaboration with his second wife Yoko Ono, whom he had married in 1969. They produced three avant-garde experimental albums before *John Lennon and the Plastic Ono Band* appeared in 1971, joined later in the year by *Imagine*. Following a self-imposed period of creative abstinence, Lennon returned with the album *Double Fantasy*, co-credited to Yoko Ono, in 1980. However, weeks after its release, he was shot and killed near his home in New York, aged forty.

The Rolling Stones, with guitarist and founding member **Brian Jones**, *first entered the UK singles chart in 1963 with their single 'Come On'.*

Jones left his native Cheltenham for London where, in the early 1960s, he became involved with the blues scene and decided to form his own rhythm and blues band. The first familiar line-up of the Rolling Stones:

Mick Jagger, Keith Richards, Charlie Watts, Bill Wyman and Jones, then emerged. Their name, provided by Jones, was culled from a Muddy Waters song. Jones did much to drive the band forwards musically – contributing many divergent instrumental performances on, for example, the sitar, organ, marimba and saxophone. However, Jones became increasingly detached from the others and, with personal issues marring his ability to contribute to the group, a parting of the ways took place in the summer of 1969. Jones was found dead weeks later, at the age of twenty-seven, in his swimming pool. The coroner recorded a verdict of misadventure.

In 1966 **Alan Ball** *played in the England team that won the football World Cup at Wembley, when they defeated West Germany 4–2 after extra time.*

A Blackpool player, Ball was the youngest member of the squad, and his sparkling performance led many to declare him 'man of the match'. Shortly after the final, he transferred to Everton for a then record fee between English clubs of £110,000. He would win his only domestic honour in the game when Everton won the League Championship in 1970. Ball, who also had lengthy spells as a player at Arsenal and Southampton, made seventy-two appearances for England (the last six as captain), and scored eight goals in an international career which ended at the age of thirty. He later moved into management and took Portsmouth into the top division in 1987. Ball was awarded an MBE in 2000. He died in 2007 at the age of sixty-one.

Pink Floyd's debut release, 'Arnold Layne', written by **Syd Barrett**, *reached number twenty in the UK singles chart in 1967.*

Roger Barrett, nicknamed Syd, was the driving force behind the band in its formative years as vocalist, guitarist and principal songwriter. He was also responsible for their identity, a juxtaposition of the first names of two US blues artists – Pink Anderson and Floyd Council. The band's second single 'See Emily Play' (also written by Barrett) reached number six, as did their debut album *The Piper at the Gates of Dawn*. However, the pressures of success and drug misuse took their toll and Barrett's health declined. His erratic behaviour was difficult to accommodate within the band and led to his departure in early 1968. He recorded two solo albums, before leaving the limelight to live quietly in Cambridge. Barrett remains an iconic figure and was celebrated by his former bandmates in their 1975 album *Wish You Were Here*. He died at the age of sixty in 2006.

*In 1968 **Alan Sugar** founded Amstrad.*

The Amstrad company name was a contraction of Alan Michael Sugar Trading. His business initially traded in electrical goods, but began manufacturing audio equipment two years later. In the 1980s Amstrad became a major player in the home computer arena, with its word processor products proving particularly popular. Its IBM-compatible personal computer, launched in 1986, secured a large portion of the European market although Amstrad's success diminished in this area in the following decade. The company further diversified into satellite-television equipment which resulted in its ultimate acquisition by BSkyB, the satellite broadcaster, in 2007. He was the chairman of Tottenham Hotspur for nearly a decade between 1991 and 2001, during which they won the League Cup in 1999. In 2005, he starred in the first television series of *The Apprentice*; the prize for the first six series was employment in one of Sugar's companies. He was knighted in 2000 and received a peerage in 2009.

***Steve Jobs**, Steve Wozniak and Ron Wayne founded Apple Computer on 1 April 1976.*

The first Apple product, a computer designed and built by Wozniak, was sold in kit form (it came without a case and a keyboard), and was initially priced at $666.66. It was superseded in the following year by the Apple II which did come with a case, keyboard and the ability to display colour graphics. The Macintosh with its graphical user interface appeared in 1984. Jobs resigned from Apple the following year and set up a new venture called NeXT, but returned to the fold when NeXT was bought out by Apple in 1997 and subsequently became CEO of the company. He joined the Disney board of directors in 2006 after Disney's purchase of Pixar Animation (makers of *Toy Story*), where Jobs was the CEO and majority shareholder. Ron Wayne, who held 10% of the company, sold his share within a fortnight of the company's founding over concerns about his potential liability for any Apple debts, while Wozniak retired from Apple in 1985. Jobs stepped down as Apple's CEO in 2011 and died weeks later at the age of fifty-six.

Ian Botham *made his test cricket debut for England, against Australia, at Trent Bridge in 1977.*

England went on to win what was the third test in the series against the Australians. Botham took five wickets in his first innings against the visitors, and went on to amass a test career total of 383 – which remains a record for an English bowler. His performance against the Australians in the 1981 Ashes, a total of 399 runs and 34 wickets, played a huge part in England's victory. Botham made his last test appearance in 1992 against Pakistan, the same year that he was awarded an OBE. Since then he has also become well known for his long-distance charity fundraising walks, which have raised millions of pounds. He was knighted in 2007.

Daley Thompson *won a gold medal for the decathlon at the 1980 Moscow Olympic Games.*

During the next few years, Thompson broke the world record four times and took the World Championship crown in 1983 before winning gold again at the Los Angeles Olympic Games in 1984. His hopes for a third consecutive Olympic gold medal were dashed in Seoul, where he finished fourth, and injury forced his retirement in 1992. Thompson has been honoured with an MBE, OBE and, in 2000, a CBE. He remains the British record-holder in the decathlon, courtesy of his performance at the 1984 Olympics.

In 1982 *Carol Vorderman* *appeared in the first edition of 'Countdown'.*

Countdown, the letters and numbers game show, was the first programme to be broadcast on Britain's fourth terrestrial television station, Channel 4. Vorderman gained the job after responding to a newspaper advert that her mother had noticed. Credited as the 'vital statistician' in the opening programme, the 21-year-old's initial screen task was to demonstrate the solution of the numbers game and she became famed for her quick on-screen calculations. As the long-running show developed she also took over the letter and number selection duties, effectively becoming the co-presenter with original host Richard Whiteley. Following his death in 2005, she continued with the show for three more years. Vorderman has also had a number of other presenting roles on television and has written several books. She was awarded an MBE in 2000 for services to broadcasting.

*'Risky Business', the breakthrough film for **Tom Cruise**, was released in 1983.*

Cruise made his screen debut with a minor part in *Endless Love* (1981), but it was his portrayal of the teenage Joel Goodson in *Risky Business* (1983) that heralded his arrival as a star. Cruise went on to become one of the most recognised actors of his generation with box office successes that include *Top Gun* (1986), *Rain Man* (1988), *Mission: Impossible* (1996) and *War of the Worlds* (2005). Together with his then wife Nicole Kidman, he worked with Stanley Kubrick on the director's last picture: *Eyes Wide Shut* (1999). His two best actor nominations at the Academy Awards have been for *Born on the Fourth of July* (1989) and *Jerry Maguire* (1996).

*In 1987 **Marlee Matlin** won the Academy Award for best actress for her debut film appearance as Sarah Norman in 'Children of a Lesser God'.*

Despite the disadvantage of being deaf from a very early age, Matlin made her stage debut at the age of seven. She had previously played the role of Sarah Norman on stage before it became her first film part, one which also brought her a Golden Globe award for best actress. Her work in television has garnered further Golden Globe, as well as Emmy, nominations. Matlin is currently the youngest recipient of the best actress Oscar.

***Stephen Hendry** won his first World Snooker Championship, in 1990, when he defeated Jimmy White by eighteen frames to twelve.*

Hendry also faced White in his next three world finals, winning all of them, and later added a further two wins to take his total to six by the end of the nineties. Hendry first took up the game at the age of twelve, made his first century break at thirteen and turned professional at sixteen. He remains the youngest winner of the World Snooker Championship. At the age of forty-three, he announced his retirement from the game after reaching the quarter-finals of the 2012 World Championship.

***Brian Lara** made his test cricket debut for the West Indies, against Pakistan, in 1990.*

A formidable batsman, Lara holds the record for the highest individual run total in first-class cricket when he posted 501 not out for Warwickshire against Durham in 1994. His 375 runs against England in 1994 set a new innings test record which he would eclipse with a total of 400 not out, again against England, in 2004, when he reclaimed the record from Australia's Matthew Hayden.

In 1991 **Linus Torvalds** *made public his creation of a unix-based operating system for the personal computer – later to be called linux.*

Torvalds, at the time a second-year computer science student at the University of Helsinki, announced in a newsgroup posting in 1991 that he'd developed an operating system for the personal computer, similar to the established unix operating system. One month later he uploaded the first version of linux. From the start, Torvalds wanted linux to be open source and freely available – linux's development was therefore boosted by the contributions of many other programmers. Linux is now used widely for servers, supercomputers and desktop PCs. The Android operating system for mobile devices, which currently has the largest market share, is linux based. Torvalds continues to oversee linux in his work with the Linux Foundation.

In 1997 **Tiger Woods** *won his first golf major, the Masters.*

Only eight months after he turned professional, the 21-year-old Woods beat Tom Kite into second place by a record margin of twelve strokes, to become the youngest winner in the tournament's history. Woods's golfing skills were first seen on television at the age of two when he featured in a putting competition with comedian Bob Hope. He went on to demonstrate his precocity with, amongst other tournament successes, multiple wins at the Junior World Golf Championships. Woods also became the youngest US junior amateur champion at the age of fifteen. Since his 1997 Masters win, he has added another thirteen major golf titles including three wins at the Open – the first coming in 2000, at the age of twenty-four, at St Andrews. In 2001 he became the first golfer to simultaneously hold the four major titles (Open, US Open, Masters and PGA Championship). Woods's actual first name is Eldrick, with Tiger originating from the nickname of a South Vietnamese soldier his father had fought alongside in South-East Asia.

*In 2003 **Roger Federer** won the first of five consecutive Wimbledon singles titles when he defeated Mark Philippoussis in straight sets.*

Federer's 2003 Wimbledon campaign was also the first time that he had made it past the quarter-final stage in a Grand Slam tournament. His reign as Wimbledon champion ended in 2008 with defeat by Rafael Nadal in the longest final in the tournament's history, but Federer returned the following year to reclaim the title. In 2012 he won his seventeenth Grand Slam, a record for a male tennis player, after defeating Andy Murray at Wimbledon. His seventh victory at the tournament also returned Federer, at the age of thirty, to the number one ranking position. Four weeks later, Federer won a silver medal at the London Olympics, after Murray defeated him in the singles final.

***Beth Tweddle** won a gold medal for the uneven bars at the World Gymnastics Championships in 2006.*

Tweddle became Britain's first ever winner at the World Gymnastics Championships, adding the title to her European Championship victory for the same apparatus earlier in the year, which was also a first for a British gymnast at that level. In 2009 Tweddle won gold again at the European Championships for both the uneven bars and the floor exercises. She also won the World Championship in the latter discipline in the same year, when it was held in London. Tweddle retained her European titles in 2010 and also reclaimed the uneven bars world title that she had first won four years earlier. In 2011 she won her fourth European gold for the uneven bars. At the London Games the following year, Tweddle won her first Olympic medal, at the age of twenty-seven, when she finished third in the individual uneven bars competition. Tweddle was awarded an MBE in the 2010 New Year Honours list.

*In 2006 **Leona Lewis** reached number one in the UK chart with her debut single 'A Moment Like This'.*

Lewis's chart triumph followed her success in winning the television talent show *The X Factor*, and 'A Moment Like This' holds the record as the fastest-selling single in the UK. Her debut album *Spirit* went straight to number one in the UK. Upon its release in America, she chalked up another achievement when it became the first debut album by a UK solo artist to go straight to number one in the Billboard 200.

Usain Bolt won the 100m at the 2008 Beijing Olympic Games, breaking his own world record as he claimed victory in 9.69 seconds.

Bolt became the first Jamaican athlete to win the event and also took home a further two gold medals, for the 200m and the 4x100m relay – both of these also run in world-record times. Apart from the relay record, he repeated these feats at the 2009 World Championships in Berlin, setting a new 100m world-record time of 9.58 seconds. Disqualification following a false start ended his hopes of retaining his 100m title at the 2011 World Championships, but Bolt recovered to take gold for the 200m and as part of the 4x100m relay team. At the 2012 London Olympics, Bolt became the first athlete to defend both the 100m and 200m titles. Bolt also anchored the Jamaican 4x100m relay team to a second consecutive Olympic victory, in a new world-record time, to win his sixth Olympic gold medal.

22

TWENTY-TWO

George III ascended to the throne in 1760 to reign as King of Great Britain and Ireland.

George III's monarchy, which lasted for nearly sixty years, was witness to several significant events such as the American Revolutionary War, which led to the independence of the USA; the union of Great Britain and Ireland, which took effect on New Year's Day 1801; and the wars against France, which would end with Napoleon's final defeat at Waterloo in 1815. The King suffered from ill health later in life with the oldest of his fifteen children, George (subsequently George IV), acting as regent for nearly the last decade of his reign, which ended with his death in 1820 at the age of eighty-one. His third son, William, was also crowned as king, to become William IV (succeeding George IV). He in turn was followed by the daughter of George III's fifth child, Edward, who reigned as Queen Victoria – the last monarch of the House of Hanover.

John Cadbury *began business as a tea and coffee dealer in 1824.*

Seven years later, in 1831, Cadbury obtained premises in order to begin the manufacture of chocolate and cocoa products on a larger scale. The chocolate was mostly for drinking, but an 1842 price list, the earliest surviving one from Cadbury, showed that he also supplied one line of 'French Eating Chocolate'. He received a royal warrant from Queen Victoria in 1854 for his products. Seven years later he retired from the business, which had gone into decline, passing it on to two of his sons – Richard and George – who were both in their twenties. They turned it around and, in 1879, were in a position to open a new factory on the outskirts of Birmingham on an estate they renamed 'Bournville'. The brothers were able to improve working conditions for their staff and also provided some housing (later expanded further) and other benefits. Their father lived to see their success, but died ten years after the opening of Bournville, at the age of eighty-seven.

Guglielmo Marconi *submitted his patent application entitled 'Improvements in Transmitting Electrical Impulses and Signals, and in Apparatus therefor' in 1896.*

Marconi's patent was the first to document a practical system for the wireless transmission and reception of signals: in other words, radio. He was born in Bologna, Italy, to Giuseppe and Annie (née Jameson – from the family of famous Irish Whiskey distillers). Bilingual in Italian and English, he was educated privately and although he was never to enrol as a university student he attended lectures on physics at the Leghorn Lyceum and received private tutoring. Access to a laboratory at the University of Bologna gave Marconi further insight into the type of apparatus Heinrich Hertz had used to discover radio waves. Improving on this equipment and now working in his own laboratory at his father's country estate, in 1895 he was able to transmit and receive over increasing distances, establishing a range of approximately 2.5 km. Marconi approached the Italian government with his invention, but there was no interest. He travelled to England, filed his patent application and was able to demonstrate a transmission and reception range of more than 14km on Salisbury Plain to an audience that included the British military. Further improvements followed and in 1901 Marconi was able to demonstrate successful transmission across the Atlantic when the morse code for S (three dots) was received in Newfoundland from Cornwall. Marconi shared the 1909 Nobel Prize in Physics for his work with Karl Braun and continued to work in his chosen field until his death, in 1937, at the age of sixty-three.

Working as an assistant to Frederick Banting, **Charles Best** *co-discovered the hormone insulin, essential for the control of blood sugar levels, in 1921.*

In early 1922 the first human subject, a fourteen-year-old diabetic boy, was successfully treated with insulin injections. Banting and John Macleod, Professor of Physiology at the University of Toronto where the work on insulin was carried out, shared the 1923 Nobel Prize in Physiology or Medicine for the discovery. The omission of Best from the honour prompted Banting to offer him half of his prize money. Best's involvement in the breakthrough hinged on the toss of a coin, since the two students (Clark Noble was the other) assigned to Banting by Macleod used this method to decide who should work for him first in 1921. Due to the proficiency he had acquired in the necessary lab techniques, Banting opted to keep Best involved and so Noble did not share in the discovery (he did however become involved later in the study of insulin). Best died at the age of seventy-nine in 1978.

Eric Liddell won a gold medal for the 400m at the 1924 Olympic Games, held in Paris.

Liddell also took home the bronze medal for the 200m at the Paris Games. He declined to participate in the 100m event since the heats were to take place on a Sunday, and Liddell, a committed Christian, did not want to break the Sabbath (the race was won instead by Harold Abrahams, representing Great Britain). Liddell was born the son of a Scottish missionary, in Tianjin, China, in 1902, but came to Britain when he was five. His talent for athletics came to the fore at school, and continued at the University of Edinburgh – from where he graduated only days after his gold medal performance in Paris. Liddell, like his father, became a

Christian missionary and returned to China where he was ultimately interned in 1943, by the Japanese. He died two years later from a brain tumour at the age of forty-three. Liddell (and Abraham's) story was told in the Oscar-winning film *Chariots of Fire* (1981).

In 1930 **Frank Whittle** *filed his patent which described a practical turbojet engine.*

Whittle had first recorded his interest in jet propulsion in 1928, when he included it in his thesis entitled 'Future Developments in Aircraft Design', written when he was a flight cadet at the RAF College Cranwell. Following his 1930 patent application, Whittle failed to interest the Air Ministry or the business world in his invention. His patent elapsed in 1935, but soon after he was contacted by two ex-RAF officers (Rolf Dudley-Williams and James Tinling) who believed they could succeed in realising Whittle's ideas. They secured the backing of an investment bank and, in 1936, formed Power Jets Ltd. One year later the first test run of Whittle's engine took place. Development continued and the Air Ministry began to show an interest. Whittle was placed on the RAF's special duty list, allowing him to continue his work on the engine. The first flight trial of a British jet powered plane (the Gloster E28/39) took place in May 1941 and the first similarly propelled Gloster Meteor aircraft arrived for service at the RAF three years later. Whittle left the RAF in 1948 at the rank of Air Commodore. He was knighted the same year and appointed to the Order of Merit in 1986. He accepted various positions as a technical adviser, and in his late sixties moved to the United States where he died, aged eighty-nine, in 1996.

Jesse Owens won four gold medals at the 1936 Berlin Olympic Games.

Born James Cleveland Owens ('J. C.' became 'Jesse' after being misheard by a schoolteacher) in Danville, Alabama, he was victorious in the 100m, 200m, the long jump and as a member of the 4x100m relay team at the Berlin Games. Despite Owens's athletic achievements, there was little fanfare and no well-paid contracts awaiting him on his return to the United States. He took a variety of jobs to earn a living, though later in life he would find success as a motivational speaker. Official recognition came with the award of the Presidential Medal of Freedom, bestowed by Gerald Ford in 1976, four years before Owens's death at the age of sixty-six.

John Surtees won the 500cc World Motorcycle Championship in 1956.

Riding for MV Agusta, Surtees won all three of the 500cc races he entered to take the title by a margin of eight points. He achieved a third-place finish in the following season, but then won both the 350cc and 500cc World Championships for three years in succession beginning in 1958. For the first two of these he won every race he entered, and in the third he became the first rider to win the Isle of Man TT senior race three times in succession. Surtees switched to four wheels and made his Formula One debut driving for Lotus in the 1960 Monaco Grand Prix. He finished second in his next race that season, the British Grand Prix at Silverstone. Now with Ferrari, Surtees's first Formula One win came at the 1963 German Grand Prix. The following season, at the age of thirty, Surtees won the Formula One World Championship to become the first, and so far only, person to have won world titles on both two and four wheels. Surtees, who retired from competitive driving in 1972, also managed his own racing team in the sixties and seventies. He was awarded an OBE in the 2008 Queen's Birthday Honours.

John Haynes founded the publishing company which bears his name in 1960.

While still at school in the mid-fifties, Haynes had produced his first booklet in which he documented the procedure to create an Austin 7 special (the transformation of a saloon into an open two-seater sports car) – something that Haynes had done for himself as a sixteen-year-old. The first edition sold out within ten days, and Haynes went on to produce more publications in this vein. In 1960, following the completion of his National Service in the RAF, J. H. Haynes & Co. Ltd was formed. The first Haynes title to feature the words 'owners workshop manual' was written by Stanley Page for the Ford Anglia, but the first to appear in the recognisable step-by-step illustrated format came in 1966 – a combined volume for the Austin-Healey Sprite and MG Midget – written by John Haynes himself. Since then, over 150 million Haynes manuals have been sold and in recent years the format has also been applied to subjects outside the automotive sphere. Haynes, who was awarded an OBE in the 1995 Queen's Birthday Honours, stepped down as chairman in 2010 at the age of seventy-two.

*In 1960 **Peter Cook** along with Dudley Moore, Alan Bennett and Jonathan Miller performed the revue 'Beyond the Fringe' as part of the Edinburgh festival.*

Cook wrote much of the material and its irreverent and satirical tone struck a chord in post-1950s Britain. After a successful stay in London, the show transferred to New York in 1962. Cook, who also helped to establish the satirical magazine *Private Eye* in the early 1960s, continued his comedy partnership with Dudley Moore in the television series *Not only . . . But Also*, first aired in 1965, as well as in films such as *The Wrong Box* (1966) and *Bedazzled* (1967). The 1970s saw them make recordings as a foul-mouthed double-act called 'Derek and Clive', which featured material too outrageous for broadcast. Cook died in 1995, aged fifty-seven.

*In 1962 **Ringo Starr** replaced drummer Pete Best in the Beatles.*

Two months after Starr had joined the Beatles, their debut single 'Love Me Do' entered the chart, going on to reach number seventeen. Starr was the lead singer on a number of Beatles' songs, including 'With a Little Help From My Friends' and 'Yellow Submarine', as well as the self-penned 'Octopus's Garden' which featured on the album *Abbey Road*. Starr had first met the Beatles in Hamburg when he was with Rory Storm and the Hurricanes, and had occasionally stood in as their drummer before officially joining the group. His post-Beatles solo career included four top-ten hits in the seventies with 'Back of Boogaloo' just missing the number one spot. Since 1989, he has toured and recorded with his All-Starr Band. Along with the other members of the Beatles he was awarded an MBE in 1965.

*Cassius Clay, soon after to become **Muhammad Ali**, won the World Heavyweight Boxing Championship when he defeated Sonny Liston in 1964.*

The fight ended after six rounds, with Liston unable to reappear for the seventh. Ali became one of the youngest boxers to take the title by defeating the reigning champion, but his refusal to serve in the US Army led to him being stripped of it three years later. Ali's appeal against his conviction would eventually be upheld by the Supreme Court in 1971, the same year that he fought heavyweight champion Joe Frazier for the title. Frazier won with a unanimous decision, but Ali would regain the championship in 1974 when he defeated George Foreman in Zaire in what was dubbed the 'rumble in the jungle'. He held the heavyweight crown until his defeat by Leon Spinks in 1978, though Ali would reclaim it for a record second time months later. He retired shortly after, in 1979, though he made a brief unsuccessful comeback at the start of the eighties.

Lynn Davies won a gold medal for the long jump at the 1964 Tokyo Olympic Games.

Davies's victory, on his Games debut, was Britain's first triumph in an Olympic athletics field event for fifty-six years. Davies also won gold for the long jump at the 1966 European Championships in Budapest and competed at the next two Olympic Games, in Mexico City and Munich. He was awarded a CBE in 2006.

Elton John released his first solo album, 'Empty Sky', in 1969.

Empty Sky featured nine songs, all written by John, with lyrics provided by Bernie Taupin whom John was teamed up with after they answered the same advert placed by Ray Williams at Liberty Records. It was Elton John's eponymous second album which would first bring success, featuring his debut chart single 'Your Song', which reached number seven in the UK in 1971. 'Rocket Man' made it to number two in the following year and John became one of the biggest-selling artists both in the UK and the US, although he would have to wait until 1990 for his first UK number one single: 'Sacrifice/Healing Hands'. He played the reworded 'Candle in the Wind' at the funeral service of Diana, Princess of Wales, in 1997. This became the world's biggest-selling single, with sales of over thirty-five million copies; the proceeds going to the Diana, Princess of Wales Memorial Fund. John has also worked with other lyricists – his collaboration with Tim Rice for the soundtrack of *The Lion King* (1994), brought them an Oscar for best original song, and he teamed up with Lee Hall for *Billy Elliot The Musical*, which premiered in 2005. John, who has released thirty studio albums in his career, was knighted in 1998.

David Bowie had his first chart hit in the UK with 'Space Oddity', which reached number five in 1969.

Bowie had released his first single five years earlier when he was seventeen, but 'Liza Jane', credited to Davie Jones and the King Bees, failed to make the charts. A similar fate befell further singles and an album, during which time he changed his surname to Bowie. His next hit after 'Space Oddity' came in 1972 with 'Starman', which reached the top ten and was taken from his first chart album: *The Rise and Fall of Ziggy Stardust and the Spiders from Mars*. Bowie became a leading figure in the glam rock era, but decided to retire the character of Ziggy and embrace a new musical direction with a soul and funk orientated sound, manifested in the album *Young Americans* in 1975. In the same year, a re-released 'Space Oddity' gave Bowie his first solo UK number one single. (He reached the top again with 'Ashes to Ashes' in 1980 and 'Let's Dance' in 1983.) Changes in musical style would continue to define his career, such as when he explored an electronic, European sound in Berlin for the albums *Low* and *Heroes*, released in the late 1970s. Bowie has also made an impact as an actor with starring roles in films that include *The Man Who Fell to Earth* (1976) and *Merry Christmas, Mr. Lawrence* (1983). His twenty-fourth solo studio album, *Reality*, was released in 2003, his last until *The Next Day* in 2013.

Alex Higgins beat John Spencer to win his first World Snooker Championship in 1972.

Higgins was the youngest player to win the tournament at that time, a record which remained intact until Stephen Hendry's victory eighteen years later. Nicknamed the 'Hurricane', his flamboyant play and skill at the table became a major draw for the watching public. He was the losing finalist on two occasions before he reclaimed the title for a second time in 1982. Higgins died in 2010 at the age of sixty-one.

Mark Spitz won seven gold medals for swimming at the 1972 Munich Olympic Games.

Spitz achieved a world-record time in each of the four individual races (freestyle and butterfly at 100m and 200m), and with his team-mates did likewise in the three relay events (4x100m freestyle, 4x200m freestyle and 4x100m medley). His gold medal haul at a single Olympics would not be surpassed until swimmer Michael Phelps went one better at the Beijing Games in 2008. Spitz also picked up two team golds at the Mexico City Games in 1968. In 1999, the International Olympic Committee declared Spitz to be one of its five 'athletes of the century'.

In 1973 Virgin Records, co-founded by **Richard Branson**, *released their first albums, including Mike Oldfield's 'Tubular Bells'.*

Branson's debut business venture was a magazine called *Student*, the first edition of which was published when he was seventeen. He then moved into record sales and with his business partners Simon Draper and Nik Powell subsequently launched Virgin Records. Oldfield, who had been turned down by many other record companies, was the first artist signed to the label. The four inaugural Virgin albums were released on the same day, but *Tubular Bells* was accorded the first catalogue number, V2001, and is recognised as the label's debut disc. An instrumental recording, composed and mostly performed by Oldfield, it proved to be a major success for Virgin Records and helped to establish the company. Branson turned to the business of air travel in the next decade and decided to invest in an airline that planned to operate between London Gatwick and the US. The 33-year-old Branson was aboard the maiden Virgin Atlantic flight in 1984, which also featured performances by a juggler, illusionist and a pop group. Branson has also made several transportation-based world-record attempts and has recorded achievements for sailing and ballooning. His business interests have continued to expand and, in addition to further terrestrial enterprises, his Virgin Group created Virgin Galactic in 2004, aimed at providing paying passengers with the chance to experience sub-orbital spaceflight. Branson received his knighthood in 2000.

David Wilkie won a gold medal at the 1976 Montreal Olympic Games for swimming in the 200m breaststroke.

Wilkie won the race in a new world-record time and became the first British male swimmer to win gold since the London Olympics in 1908. His victory was the culmination of four years of training when he was based in Miami, Florida. Wilkie also collected a silver medal at the same Games for the 100m breaststroke. His first major podium finish was at the Edinburgh Commonwealth Games in 1970, aged sixteen, when he took bronze in his Olympic-winning event.

Eric Bristow won the World Professional Darts Championship in 1980.

Bristow, nicknamed the 'Crafty Cockney', dominated professional darts in the 1980s, and won another four world titles, the last of these in 1986.

In addition he was runner-up on five occasions between 1983 and 1991. Bristow's successes came prior to the split in darts in the 1990s which saw a rival grouping to the BDO (British Darts Organisation) emerge, ultimately called the Professional Darts Corporation (PDC), and the existence of two competing World Championships since 1994. Bristow reached the semi-finals of the PDC tournament in 1997, but lost out to the eventual winner, Phil Taylor. He was awarded an MBE in 1989.

John McEnroe brought Björn Borg's winning run at Wimbledon to an end when he defeated the Swede in four sets in 1981, to claim his first All England title.

Borg's attempt to win six consecutive singles titles was ended by McEnroe, who took home prize money of £21,600 (ten years later it would climb to £240,000). The left-hander had already made an impact at Wimbledon in earlier years. As an amateur in 1977, he reached the semi-finals, where he lost to Jimmy Connors. Three years later he competed in his first Wimbledon final but lost to Borg. McEnroe won Wimbledon on two more occasions – in 1983 and 1984, the latter in the same year as the last of his four victories at the US Open. His vehement disputes with the umpires and line judges at Wimbledon often added further colour to his appearances. McEnroe retired from professional tennis in 1992, but made a return in 2006 when he played two doubles tournaments, winning the SAP Open with Jonas Björkman. McEnroe commentates on the sport for media organisations on both sides of the Atlantic.

*In 1983 U2, with lead singer **Bono**, first reached number one in the UK album chart with 'War'.*

The album, which was their third, also provided their first top-twenty hit, 'New Year's Day', which reached number ten in the singles chart in 1983. The band had come together in Bono's (born Paul Hewson) home city of Dublin in response to an advert placed by drummer Larry Mullen in 1976. Two years later their name, U2, and the four man line-up with The Edge on guitar, Adam Clayton on bass and Mullen on drums, were established. The band achieved international success in the 1980s; their 1987 album, *The Joshua Tree*, gave them their first US number one. Their seventh studio album, *Achtung Baby*, released in 1991, also reached the top in the US and spawned five UK hit singles including their second number one, 'The Fly'. Of their twelve studio albums, nine in the UK and seven in the US have reached the number one spot. Bono has also been widely recognised for his humanitarian work, including his campaigns to reduce poverty in Africa. Among other awards, he was presented with an honorary knighthood in 2007 and received France's Légion d'honneur in 2003.

Victoria Beckham and *Melanie Chisholm*, *as members of the Spice Girls, reached number one in the UK chart with their debut single 'Wannabe' in 1996.*

In addition to Beckham (née Adams) and Chisholm, the group, which became the first to have their six singles reach number one, also featured 20-year-old Emma Bunton, 21-year-old Melanie Brown and 23-year-old Geri Halliwell. The Spice Girls formed in 1994 in response to an advertisement in *The Stage*, with Bunton later replacing original member Michelle Stephenson. 'Wannabe' spent seven weeks at number one and was featured on their debut album *Spice* (1996), which also reached the top spot in the UK, US and other countries. Geri Halliwell left the band in 1998 and returned to the chart the following year with a number two position for her solo debut 'Look At Me', the first of nine top-thirty singles, four of which reached number one. The remaining members decided to take a break in 2001 and concentrate on their own solo careers. Beckham began hers with a number two for her single 'Out of Your Mind' in 2000, the year after her marriage to footballer David Beckham. Chisholm, also known as Melanie C, has co-written eleven UK number ones, the latter two as part of her post-Spice Girls career, and established her own record company in 2004. Bunton's debut solo single, 'What Took You So Long', reached number one in 2001. Brown was the first to reach the singles top spot outside of the Spice Girls with her first solo single (also featuring Missy Elliott) 'I Want you back' in 1998. The group, including Geri Halliwell, completed a reunion tour in 2007.

The debut single of **Lady Gaga** *(featuring Colby O'Donis), 'Just Dance', reached number one in the UK chart in 2009.*

Co-written by Lady Gaga, real name Stefani Germanotta, the song spent three weeks at the top of the chart, and was also a number one in the United States. The stage name of the New York-born singer/songwriter was inspired by the Queen song 'Radio Ga Ga'. She learned piano as a child and started to write her own material as a teenager. She gained admission to the Tisch School of the Arts, New York University, when she was seventeen, but left during her second year to concentrate on her musical career. Gaga first signed to Island Def Jam, but was dropped by the label weeks later, which meant that they missed out on the success of her debut album, *The Fame*, a global sensation which reached number one in the UK in 2009. Her second studio collection, *Born This Way*, was released in 2011 and went straight to number one in several countries, including the US and the UK.

Rory McIlroy won golf's US Open in 2011.

McIlroy tasted his first triumph in a golf major at the Congressional Country Club in Maryland where he won by eight strokes to become the youngest US Open champion for nearly ninety years. McIlroy, born in County Down, enjoyed a distinguished career as an amateur and earned first place in the world rankings in 2007; the year that he turned professional. In 2010, 21-year-old McIlroy was the youngest member of the European Ryder Cup team that defeated the US by a single point. In 2012, aged twenty-two, McIlroy became the world's number one ranked golfer. Months later, after turning twenty-three, he won his second major tournament, the PGA Championship, by a record margin of eight strokes.

23
TWENTY-THREE

Robert William Thomson applied for a patent for his invention of the pneumatic tyre in 1845.

Although Thomson's invention, which he called the 'aerial wheel', was demonstrated to improve the quality of ride when applied to horse-drawn carriages, there was little interest or demand, for the potentially large market offered by bicycles and cars was still to appear. The pneumatic tyre would be re-invented by John Boyd Dunlop, who is usually credited as the originator, over forty years later. Thomson was a prolific inventor and his other creations included a portable steam crane, electrically detonated explosive charges and a fountain pen. He died in Edinburgh, at the age of fifty, in 1873.

In 1887 **William Randolph Hearst** *took control, from his father, of his first newspaper, 'The Examiner' in San Francisco.*

The Californian daily was the start of Hearst's publishing empire which grew with the introduction of new titles and also by acquisition. Hearst boosted circulation with the introduction of banner headlines and sensationalist stories – tagged 'yellow journalism'. In the opinion of many, coverage of the Cuban struggle for independence by his newspapers stoked the clamour for military action, which led to the Spanish–American War in 1898. Hearst also became involved in politics. At the start of the twentieth century, he spent four years as a Democratic Representative for New York in the US Congress and also made unsuccessful bids to become governor of New York and US president. By the end of the 1920s, the Hearst organisation owned twenty-eight newspapers as well as magazines and radio stations. However, during the subsequent Depression, newspaper circulation fell, corporate debt accumulated and in 1937 he was forced to cede financial control of his empire. A large portion of his vast, extravagantly funded art collection was put up for sale and building work on his Californian castle, San Simeon, and other properties halted. Soon afterwards, *Citizen Kane* (1941), directed by and starring Orson Welles, was released. The central character, Charles Foster Kane, was inspired by Hearst, who tried – mainly unsuccessfully – to suppress the film, which is today regarded as one of cinema's finest productions. In 1945, at the age of eighty-one, Hearst regained control of a slimmed-down organisation; however, it was still the largest news corporation in the US at the time of his death in 1951 at the age of eighty-eight.

The first paper by **Werner Heisenberg**, *in which he described his groundbreaking theory of quantum mechanics, was published in 1925.*

Heisenberg based his theory only on the observable properties of the atomic system, and therefore abandoned the idea of the planetary visualisation of the atom in which electrons were deemed to circle the nucleus in defined orbits. Max Born, who reviewed Heisenberg's paper before publication, saw the potential of using mathematical matrices to describe Heisenberg's theory and, along with Pascual Jordan, published a paper on this development not long after Heisenberg. The three men then co-authored a third paper on the subject, also submitted before the end of 1925. Heisenberg is also remembered for the 'uncertainty principle', which he published two years later. It stated that certain pairs of variables, such as position and momentum, cannot be measured simultaneously with the same degree of precision; a consequence of the act of measurement influencing the quantities to be determined. Though the errors are not significant in the day-to-day world they become an important factor at the atomic level when, for example, describing the behaviour of an electron. For his work in quantum mechanics and its applications, Heisenberg was awarded the 1932 Nobel Prize in Physics (presented in 1933), and as a result became one of the youngest Nobel laureates. He died in 1976 at the age of seventy-four.

W. H. Auden (Wystan Hugh) commercially published his first book, entitled 'Poems', in 1930.

A small number of copies of a similarly-titled volume by Auden had been printed privately two years previously. Its namesake was accepted for commercial publication by T. S. Eliot, then working at the publishers Faber and Faber. The 1930s were eventful for Auden: he married Erika Mann in order to give her a route out of pre-war Germany, he went to Spain to support the Republican cause in the civil war and, in 1939, he moved to America, later becoming a US citizen. Also in the same decade, Auden worked for a spell in the General Post Office film unit, writing commentaries for, amongst others, *Coal Face* (1935) and *Night Mail* (1936). His collaboration with Christopher Isherwood produced three plays, the first of which was *The Dog Beneath the Skin*. In 1956, Auden became professor of poetry at the University of Oxford for a five-year term, though he remained based in America during the winter months until 1972, the year before his death at the age of sixty-six. Auden's later volumes of poetry include *About the House* (1965), *City Without Walls* (1969) and *Thank You, Fog* which was published posthumously in 1974. His poem 'Funeral Blues' found a wide audience when it featured in the hit film *Four Weddings and a Funeral* (1994).

Richard Dimbleby, the BBC's first radio news reporter, performed his debut assignment for the BBC in 1936.

Dimbleby covered the annual Conference for the Preservation of Rural England, held in Torquay, the month after his appointment by the BBC. Prior to this he had briefly worked on the Dimbleby family paper, the *Richmond and Twickenham Times*, and then at the *Bournemouth Echo* and the *Advertisers Weekly*. Dimbleby became the first BBC war correspondent in 1939, when he reported on the Spanish Civil War. He later became a freelance broadcaster, commentating on major events such as the coronation of Queen Elizabeth II and the funeral of President Kennedy. Beginning in 1955, he also presented the BBC current-affairs programme *Panorama* for a decade, participating in its famous 'spaghetti tree' April fool in 1957. Already an OBE, Dimbleby was awarded a CBE in 1959. His last major outside broadcast was the funeral of Winston Churchill in 1965 – Dimbleby died later that year at the age of fifty-two. The BBC established an annual lecture in his honour in 1972. Two of his sons, David and Jonathan, have also become successful broadcasters.

Joe Louis won the World Heavyweight Boxing Championship when he defeated James Braddock in an eighth-round knockout in 1937.

Louis retained the title until his retirement in 1949; a duration of eleven years and 252 days which still stands as a record. He defended his heavyweight crown twenty-five times, with only four of those contests going the distance. Despite his enforced return to the boxing ring over two years after his retirement to meet his tax demands, which brought two defeats out of ten bouts, Louis's legacy as one of the greatest heavyweight champions remains intact. He died in 1981 at the age of sixty-six and was, at the behest of President Reagan, who waived the qualifying conditions, interred in Arlington National Cemetery. He was accorded a funeral with full military honours.

*The first record to feature vocals by **Frank Sinatra**, 'From the Bottom of My Heart', was released in 1939.*

Harry James and his Orchestra provided the music for Sinatra's debut, and with sales of less than ten thousand, the 78 rpm disc has become a much sought-after collector's item. Soon afterwards, he moved to the

Tommy Dorsey band with whom he would have his first best-selling record. Sinatra left Dorsey's band in the early 1940s to become a solo performer and in 1946 released his debut album, *The Voice of Frank Sinatra*, which reached the number one spot in the US. The 1940s also saw the start of his acting career; his portrayal of Private Angelo Maggio in *From Here to Eternity* (1953) won him an Academy Award for best supporting actor. The win also rejuvenated his singing career and over the next few years he produced such albums as *Songs for Swingin' Lovers* and *Come Fly with Me*. The iconic 'My Way' was released in 1969 and although it would only reach number five in the UK chart, combined with various re-entries it has spent more weeks in the UK top forty than any other single. Sinatra returned to touring in the 1990s. He died in 1998, aged eighty-two.

Ivor Broadis became player/manager of Carlisle United in 1946.

Broadis's actual first name is Ivan, but was misread as Ivor when he played as an amateur for Tottenham Hotspur during the Second World War. Broadis stuck with his new moniker for his subsequent football career. As well as being the youngest player/manager in Football League history, Broadis also became the first manager to transfer himself to another club when he joined Sunderland in 1949 for a fee of £18,000. He also spent time at Manchester City and Newcastle United before returning to Carlisle. Broadis ended his playing career at Scottish club Queen of the South. He played for England fourteen times, scored eight goals and made his last international appearances at the 1954 World Cup finals in Switzerland.

Colin Chapman co-founded the Lotus Engineering Company in 1952.

Four years previously, Chapman had created his first Lotus car – the mark 1 – a modified Austin 7, which he raced successfully. Further designs followed and, shortly after the establishment of Lotus Engineering, Chapman was able to leave his job at the British Aluminium Company and devote himself fully to the development of his racing creations. The Lotus 7 appeared in 1957, and would be manufactured in-house for the next fifteen years before the rights were sold to Caterham, who still produce the car today. Although Lotus became a successful manufacturer of sports cars, Chapman also had a profound impact on Formula One, where his innovation and design philosophy introduced advances in automotive engineering and aerodynamics that frequently set the pace in motor sport. His cars' competitive edge would lead to seven constructors' titles between 1963 and 1978. On all but one of these occasions, a Lotus driver also won the Formula One World Championship. Chapman, who received a CBE in 1970, died in 1982 at the age fifty-four. The badge of Lotus Cars bears his initials – C.A.B.C.

David Frost *presented the first edition of 'That Was The Week That Was' in 1962.*

The groundbreaking satirical show was the brainchild of Ned Sherrin, and Frost hosted it for two series before it finished at the end of 1963. He maintained his presence on television with, among others, *The Frost Report*, first broadcast in 1966, and also the *Frost Programme*. He duplicated his success across the Atlantic with a parallel career on US television. Frost is particularly well-known for his interviews with significant political figures that include every British prime minister since Harold Wilson and all US presidents from Richard Nixon to George W. Bush. Many of these were aired in his programme, *Breakfast with Frost*, which ran for over twelve years in a BBC Sunday morning slot until 2005. Frost, an OBE since 1970, was knighted in 1993. He received the Bafta fellowship in 2005.

John Travolta *starred as Tony Manero in 'Saturday Night Fever', which premiered in New York in 1977.*

Travolta, born and raised in New Jersey, first gained national prominence in the USA with his role as Vinnie Barbarino in the TV series *Welcome Back, Kotter*, which made its network debut in 1975. Travolta appeared in his first feature film, *The Devil's Rain*, in the same year, and then took a role in another horror movie, *Carrie* (1976), prior to landing the lead in *Saturday Night Fever* (1977). His performance as Tony Manero brought him an Academy Award nomination for best actor as well as a Golden Globe nomination for best actor in a musical/comedy. He swiftly followed this with another hit film, the musical *Grease* (1978), where he played Danny Zuko opposite Olivia Newton-John's Sandy. His career dipped in the next decade but then enjoyed a resurgence as a result of his role as Vincent Vega in Quentin Tarantino's *Pulp Fiction* (1994), which also garnered him a second Academy Award nomination for best actor. Since then, he has won a best actor Golden Globe for *Get Shorty* (1995), and was nominated again for *Primary Colors* (1998) and his supporting role in *Hairspray* (2007). Travolta is a keen pilot and owns several planes, including a Boeing 707.

Mel Gibson starred as the eponymous 'Mad Max', released in 1979.

Gibson was born in New York, but spent his later childhood in Australia, where he trained as an actor. He returned to the character of Max Rockatansky, his breakthrough role, in two sequels (1981 and 1985), before embarking on another trilogy, beginning in 1987, which was to be even more successful at the box office: Lethal Weapon. He has also enjoyed success behind the camera. *Braveheart* (1995), in which he also starred as the Scottish hero William Wallace, won Gibson an Oscar for best director as well as taking the best picture prize. His next directorial project, *The Passion of the Christ* (2004), proved to be an even bigger commercial success, and also picked up three Academy Award nominations. He then directed *Apocalypto* (2006) which, similar to *The Passion of the Christ*, featured non-English dialogue and garnered an identical number of Oscar nominations. His other well-known films as an actor include *Ransom* (1996), *The Patriot* (2000) and *Signs* (2002).

Sebastian Coe won a gold medal at the 1980 Moscow Olympics for the 1,500m.

Coe also took silver in the 800m in Moscow. Four years later he won the same medals for the same events at the Los Angeles Olympic Games. Coe captured the attention of the athletics world in 1979 when he set three different world records (for the 800m, 1,500m and mile) in a six-week period. He added the 1,000m world record the following year and briefly became the first, and so far only, person to hold all four world records simultaneously. After retiring from athletics, he served as a Conservative MP for five years until 1997. Three years later he received a peerage, becoming Baron Coe of Ranmore in the County of Surrey. Coe led the successful London bid for the 2012 Olympics and became the chairman of the organising committee for the Games.

Steve Davis won his first World Professional Snooker Championship when he defeated Doug Mountjoy by eighteen frames to twelve in 1981.

Davis won five more World Championships, the last in 1989. He also took part in the famous final in 1985, against Dennis Taylor, where the match was decided on the last black ball of the final frame. Taylor potted the ball to become champion, watched by over eighteen million television viewers. Davis turned professional at the age of twenty-one in 1978 and played his first televised game against his veteran namesake Fred in the BBC series *Pot Black*. In 1982 Davis became the first player to record a maximum 147 break in front of the TV cameras.

Charles Kennedy was elected as the MP for Ross, Cromarty and Skye at the 1983 general election.

Kennedy became the youngest member of the Commons and was one of only six Social Democratic Party (SDP) MPs returned who, along with the seventeen Liberal MPs, formed the SDP–Liberal Alliance in Parliament. He'd spent a short period as a BBC journalist and broadcaster in between graduating from Glasgow University and his election victory. Kennedy became the UK party president of the Liberal Democrats in 1990, and nine years later was elected as the leader to replace Paddy Ashdown. In the 2005 general election the Liberal Democrats won sixty-two seats: the best third-party performance for decades. Kennedy resigned as leader in 2006 and was succeeded by Sir Menzies Campbell.

Carl Lewis won his first Olympic gold medal, for the 100m, at the 1984 Los Angeles Games.

The reigning 100m world champion, Lewis also took gold for the 200m, the long jump and as a member of the US 4x100m relay team, to emulate the achievement of Jesse Owens at the Berlin Olympics in 1936. At the next Games in Seoul, South Korea, Lewis defended his 100m title (following the disqualification of Ben Johnson) and again won gold for the long jump. Lewis, at the age of thirty, produced his best 100m performance in the 1991 World Championships when he won his third consecutive title in a world-record time of 9.86s. That competition also saw him record his best ever distance in the long jump, although it was not enough to win gold as Mike Powell achieved a distance of 8.95m to take Bob

Beamon's 23-year-old world record. Lewis won another three Olympic golds before his retirement, two at the 1992 Barcelona Games for the 4x100m relay and the long jump, and one at the 1996 Atlanta Olympics for the long jump, which was his fourth successive gold in this event.

Chris Boardman won a gold medal for cycling's individual pursuit at the 1992 Barcelona Olympics.

Boardman, riding a streamlined carbon-fibre Lotus-made bicycle, set a new world record for the 4,000m individual pursuit and registered Britain's opening gold medal at the Barcelona Games; the first British cycling medal since 1920. He was awarded an MBE in the 1993 New Year Honours list. Boardman became a professional later in the year and set several world records including the 'UCI hour', in 2000, when he completed a distance of 49.441 km, a measure which stood for nearly five years. Boardman, who also won bronze for the individual time trial at the 1996 Olympics, retired from competitive cycling in 2000. He led British cycling's research and development team in their preparations for the 2008 Beijing Olympics, where UK competitors returned with fourteen medals from the fourteen road and track cycling events, eight of them gold.

Jamie Oliver presented the first edition of 'The Naked Chef' in 1999.

Oliver left school at sixteen to attend Westminster Catering College. After various jobs, his position at the River Café restaurant in London gave him his big break: it was featured in a television documentary and, as a result, Oliver landed his own show. He completed three series of *The Naked Chef*, the first of many television vehicles that have included *Jamie's Kitchen* and also *Jamie's School Dinners* (2005), which campaigned to improve the nutritional quality of school meals and attracted considerable media and political interest. Oliver is also a successful culinary author, with nearly twenty publications to his credit. He was awarded an MBE in the 2003 Queen's Birthday Honours.

Ben Ainslie won a gold medal at the 2000 Sidney Olympics for sailing (Laser class).

Ainslie had already won silver at the same event at the 1996 Atlanta Olympics and went on to win gold at the 2004 and 2008 Games (both for the Finn class), making him Britain's most successful sailing Olympian. Ainslie began his nautical career, aged eight, when he lived in Cornwall. Already an MBE and OBE, he was appointed CBE in 2009. In the following year he became the International Sailing Federation (ISAF) world match racing champion. At the 2012 London Games, 35-year-old Ainslie won his fourth gold medal to become the most successful Olympic sailor of all time. He was knighted in the 2013 New Year Honours.

In 2002 **Will Young** *became the first winner of the talent show 'Pop Idol'.*

Young emerged from thousands of hopefuls as the winner of ITV's *Pop Idol* and then spent three weeks at the top of the UK chart with his debut release 'Anything Is Possible/Evergreen', which became the best-selling single of the decade. Solo follow-ups 'Light My Fire' and 'Leave Right Now' also made it to number one as did his debut album *From Now On* (2002). Young's other albums include *Friday's Child* (2003) and *Echoes* (2011), both of which also reached the top of the UK chart. He made his acting debut in the feature *Mrs Henderson Presents* (2005).

In only his second season in the sport, **Lewis Hamilton** *won the Formula One World Championship in 2008, driving for the Vodafone McLaren Mercedes team.*

Hamilton's racing career began at the age of eight with kart racing, and he was signed to the McLaren Driver Development Support Programme in 1998, aged thirteen. (Hamilton first spoke to McLaren team boss Ron Dennis when he was only ten, telling him that he wanted to race his cars one day.) Two years later he won the European karting title and also became the world number one. He made his racing car debut in 2001 in the British Formula Renault class and then stepped up to Formula Three and GP2. His first Formula One season, in 2007, began with a third place in his debut grand prix and almost ended in a championship success as he lost out by only one point, after the final race of the year, to Kimi Räikkönen.

Sebastian Vettel *won the Formula One World Championship in 2010.*

Vettel is the youngest driver to take the title, beating the previous record holder, Lewis Hamilton, by a matter of months. Amongst many age-related records, he is also the youngest driver to win a grand prix after triumphing in the 2008 Italian Grand Prix at the age of twenty-one. Vettel took his first Formula One point at the age of nineteen, when he finished eighth in the 2007 US Grand Prix. He began driving for the Red Bull team in 2009 and finished the season as the championship runner-up to Jensen Button. In the 2011 season, Vettel won nine of the first fifteen grand prix meetings as he clinched his second World Championship with four races to go. Aged twenty-five, he won the Formula One title again in 2012, making him the youngest to win three consecutive titles.

24

TWENTY-FOUR

William Pitt *became prime minister and chancellor of the exchequer in 1783.*

Pitt is believed to be the youngest person (at age fourteen) to have become an undergraduate at Cambridge. He left three years later with a master of arts degree, gained without examination as per his entitlement as the son of a nobleman. He was the fourth child and second son of William Pitt, who had been prime minister for over two years in the 1760s. Although Pitt the younger was called to the bar and a legal career beckoned for him, his political destiny started to take shape when he became an MP at the age of twenty-one in 1781. He impressed his fellow parliamentarians with his maiden speech in the chamber, given unprepared on an economic reform bill. In 1782 Pitt became the youngest chancellor of the exchequer on record, under the Earl of Shelburne. He would remain in this office for less than a year, but in December 1783 Pitt returned both as chancellor and first lord of the treasury (prime minister), becoming at the age of twenty-four the youngest to hold this position in Britain. His tenure was also to be one of the longest, enduring for over seventeen years, until 1801, during which time his ministry tackled the national debt, reformed the relationship with the British East India Company, and also created the union between Great Britain and Ireland which came into effect on New Year's Day 1801. War with post-revolutionary France began in 1793 and continued, apart from one interruption, throughout the remainder of Pitt's government. The reduction in trade and thus in associated revenue contributed to the introduction of Britain's first income tax in 1799. Following union with Ireland, Pitt wanted to introduce Catholic emancipation. However, King George III wouldn't give his agreement so Pitt resigned in 1801. He returned to office in 1804 and agreed an alliance with Austria, Russia and Sweden (the Third Coalition) to try to counter the increasing power of Napoleon in Europe. In 1805 Britain's naval supremacy was confirmed with Nelson's victory at Trafalgar, which removed the threat of a French invasion. However, the Third Coalition broke down following the defeat of the Austrians by the French at Ulm and then at Austerlitz, where the Austrians were fighting alongside the Russians. Pitt died early in 1806 at the age of forty-six. He never married and left debts totalling around £40,000, which were settled by Parliament.

The debut novel by **Charles Dickens**, *'The Pickwick Papers', was first serialised in 1836.*

Dickens was born in the Portsmouth suburb of Landport where his father worked as a clerk in the Navy Pay Office, an occupation that took the family to London and then Chatham, where Dickens spent the early years of his boyhood and began school. His first period of formal education stopped when the family returned to London in 1822. Two years later, when Dickens was twelve, his father was sent to a debtor's prison and Dickens was put to work labelling bottles in a blacking warehouse, a harsh experience which left a lasting impression. His father's release and an improvement in their finances allowed Dickens to return to school. He left at the age of fifteen and first worked as a solicitor's clerk, but in the next year gave this up to become a newspaper reporter. His first published literary work was the story 'A Dinner at Poplar Walk' which appeared in *The Monthly Magazine* at the end of 1833. More followed, and his fifty-six 'Sketches of London' were collected and published together in a two-volume set as *Sketches by Boz* in February 1836. Shortly after, the first instalment of Dickens's debut novel was published. Originally titled *The Posthumous Papers of the Pickwick Club*, but commonly referred to as *The Pickwick Papers*, the novel extended to twenty parts and proved to be a tremendous success, which he followed up with *Oliver Twist* in the next year. Dickens became one of the most popular authors of the Victorian age and his appeal has endured with many adaptations of his work being made for the stage and screen, including *David Copperfield*, *A Christmas Carol*, *A Tale of Two Cities*, *Great Expectations* and *Bleak House*. Dickens, noted for his vivid characterisation, social compassion and vibrant story-telling, remains one of the most widely-read novelists in English literature. He died in 1870 at the age of fifty-eight, leaving the last manuscript that he was working on, *The Mystery of Edwin Drood*, unfinished.

John Sainsbury and his wife Mary Ann founded their grocery business in 1869.

The first Sainsbury store was located in Drury Lane, London and sold dairy products. An early slogan was 'Quality perfect, prices lower', and by 1882 Sainsbury had several shops operating in the capital. He continued to grow the company and gave his six sons senior positions within it (the couple also had five daughters). Sainsbury became governing director and life chairman of J. Sainsbury Ltd, which was incorporated in 1922. Shareholding was restricted to the Sainsbury family and their descendants until 1973. John Sainsbury died in 1928 at the age of eighty-three.

Herman Hollerith applied for his first patent, entitled 'Art of Compiling Statistics', in 1884.

The patent detailed Hollerith's machine for the tabulation of data, which used punched cards to automate the process. Hollerith trained as a mining engineer, but it was his work at the US Census Office which highlighted a growing need to mechanise the collection of data. The Census Office tested two other schemes in conjunction with Hollerith's in order to choose one for the upcoming 1890 census. His system triumphed and was duly implemented, making the census results available sooner and at less cost than before. Hollerith founded the Tabulating Machine Company in 1896, and this business would later merge with three others in 1911 to form the Computing Tabulating Recording Corporation. It was renamed the International Business Machines Corporation (IBM) in 1924. Hollerith died five years later at the age of sixty-nine.

In 1905 Alf Common became the first footballer to be transferred for a fee of £1,000 when he moved from Sunderland to nearby rivals Middlesbrough.

Common, an England international and FA Cup winner with Sheffield United, scored from a penalty in his first game for his new club as they won away at Sheffield United by one goal to nil. Middlesbrough's signing of Common had been prompted by the threat of relegation, and the move was to pay dividends as the club avoided the drop into division two. He spent five years with them before moving on to Woolwich Arsenal and then Preston North End prior to his retirement from the game in 1914, after which he became a pub landlord. Common died in 1946 at the age of sixty-five.

Thomas Sopwith set up the Sopwith Aviation Company Ltd in 1912.

Sopwith's business supplied more than 18,000 aircraft during World War One, including nearly 6,000 Sopwith Camel single-seat fighters. Sopwith first took to the air in 1910 and went on to win several aviation prizes, using the funds to help him set up his own company. He had also inherited money due to the death of his father on a family holiday, who was tragically killed when a gun, lying across ten-year-old Thomas's knee, accidentally fired. Following the end of World War One, production levels at Sopwith's company plummeted. The business went bankrupt and was wound up in 1920. Shortly afterwards, Sopwith started the H. G. Hawker Engineering Company Ltd with Fred Sigrist and Harry Hawker. With Sopwith as chairman, the company would also produce a fighter plane, used to great effect in the Second World War – the Hawker Hurricane. Sopwith also presided over the creation of Hawker Siddeley Aircraft in 1935, which combined the companies of Avro, Gloster and Armstrong–Whitworth among others. De Havilland was added to the group in the late fifties. Sopwith, who was knighted in 1953, remained as chairman until the age of seventy-five. He died nine days after his 101st birthday in 1989.

Charlie Chaplin made his first appearance as his famous character 'the tramp' in the film 'Kid Auto Races at Venice', released in 1914.

Kid Auto Races at Venice was Chaplin's second film and his comic creation of 'the tramp' would become one of the most recognisable and popular of the silent-film era. Chaplin was born in England to parents who were both music-hall entertainers. He first took to the stage as a child, and as a teenager joined Fred Karno's vaudeville troupe. While touring America with the company, Chaplin was spotted and signed to Max Sennett's Keystone Film Company, with whom he would make his cinema debut in 1914. He appeared in over thirty, mostly short, comedy films in that year alone. The advent of sound for motion pictures challenged Chaplin as to how his tramp character, heavily reliant on mime, could adapt. He responded with another 'silent' film, *City Lights* (1931), and with the dialogue-free *Modern Times* (1936). The latter is regarded as the final film of the silent era, though for the first time at the end of the picture Chaplin's voice is heard as he sings a song in a fictitious language. His first 'talking feature' came in 1940 with *The Great Dictator*, for which he received two Academy Award nominations: for best actor and best writing/original screenplay. His only 'competitive' academy win came in 1973 when *Limelight* (1952) won him a share of the best music/original dramatic score category (the film was released in Los Angeles in 1972, which made it eligible for an award in the following year's ceremony). Chaplin lived in Switzerland for the last two decades of his life. He was knighted in 1975, at the age of eighty-five, and died two years later, on Christmas day, at the age of eighty-eight.

'See America First', with music and lyrics by **Cole Porter**, had its New York debut in 1916.

Porter came from a prosperous Indiana family and, encouraged by his mother, took up the violin and piano at an early age. He later studied at Yale, where he composed prolifically, and then attended Harvard Law School, although he changed to a music course after a year. Following *See America First*, which only ran for fifteen performances, Porter's next Broadway piece, *Hitchy-Koo of 1919*, fared better, but again was not a resounding success. Porter settled in Europe, but his return to Broadway with the musical *Paris* in 1928 was well received. It was followed by the popular success of *Fifty Million Frenchmen* in 1929. A golden period then ensued, with shows such as *Anything Goes* in 1934. However, a riding accident in 1937 left his lower limbs badly injured and would result in the eventual amputation of his right leg twenty-one years later. Porter continued to write during this period, and *Kiss me Kate*, in 1948, gave him a Tony Award for best composer and lyricist. He died in 1964 at the age of seventy-three. Many of his songs such as 'Let's Do It (Let's Fall in Love)' and 'Night and Day' have become standards of the American popular music repertoire.

'Always You', the first musical by **Oscar Hammerstein II**, *opened in New York in 1920, with music composed by Herbert Stothart.*

Seven years later, Hammerstein's collaboration with Jerome Kern resulted in *Showboat*, a major success at the time, and a work which has remained a favourite through the decades. His writing partnership with Richard Rodgers, which began in the 1940s, was particularly successful and long lasting. Together they produced *Oklahoma!* (1943), which was followed by other musicals including *Carousel* (1945), *South Pacific* (1949), *The King and I* (1951) and *The Sound of Music* (1959). Each of these was successfully adapted for the cinema. Hammerstein won two Academy Awards in the 1940s for 'best music, original song', the first shared with Jerome Kern and the second with Richard Rodgers. (Hammerstein is so far the only person named Oscar to actually win an 'Oscar'.) Also the recipient of eight Tony Awards, he died in 1960 at the age of sixty-five.

In 1922 a collection of poems, 'Child Whispers', was the first book to be published by **Enid Blyton**.

Blyton's output was prodigious and amounted to hundreds of books, mainly aimed at children. These included series such as the Famous Five (beginning with *Five on a Treasure Island* published in 1942), the Secret Seven (fifteen titles published between 1949 and 1963) and *Noddy* (who first appeared in 1949). Blyton is also one of the world's most translated authors. She died in 1968 at the age of seventy-one.

At the Paris Games in 1924, **Harold Abrahams** *became the first Briton to win an Olympic gold medal for the 100m.*

In what was Abrahams's second time at the Games, he also took home a silver medal for his part in the 4x100m relay. Four years previously at the Antwerp Games, he did not manage to make it beyond the second round of the 100m, but with the subsequent guidance of his coach Sam Mussabini, he would secure victory in Paris – beating the reigning Olympic champion in the process. An injury sustained during a long-jump competition in 1925 prematurely ended Abrahams's athletic career. He practised as a barrister and subsequently became a journalist and commentator. He was awarded a CBE in 1957. Abrahams died in 1978, at the age of seventy-eight, and so did not live to see the portrayal of his Olympic triumph in the Oscar-winning film *Chariots of Fire* (1981).

'The Man Within', the first novel by **Graham Greene**, *also became his first published book in 1929.*

Greene studied history at Oxford and after graduating began a career in journalism, later becoming a sub-editor at *The Times*. Encouraged by the success of his first book, Greene left *The Times* to pursue a career as a novelist. However, his next two books were not particularly well received. Greene, though, bounced back with the extremely successful *Stamboul Train* in 1932, which gave his literary ambitions a much-needed boost. The novel was adapted for the cinema as *Orient Express* in 1934. With Greene's career as an author assured, he produced further acclaimed novels including *Brighton Rock* (1938), *The Power and the Glory* (1940) and *The Heart of the Matter* (1948). He also wrote screenplays including *The Fallen Idol* (1948) and *The Third Man* (1949). As a playwright he made his debut with *The Living Room* in 1953. During the Second World War, Greene was employed for a time as an agent for MI6. He was appointed to the Order of Merit in 1986 and died, five years later, at the age of eighty-six.

Hedy Lamarr *starred in her first Hollywood film, 'Algiers', in 1938.*

Born Hedwig Kiesler in Vienna, Lamarr began her career appearing in German and Czech films in the early 1930s, culminating with an appearance in *Ekstase* (1933). Her nude scenes in the movie created a sensation and also opposition to its release in the US. Although the ban on its importation was lifted in 1935, its screenings continued to be limited. In 1933 she married Fritz Mandl, a wealthy Austrian munitions manufacturer. However, his controlling nature and constant surveillance proved unbearable, and she disguised herself as a maid and escaped to Paris. From there she went to London where an introduction to movie mogul Louis B. Mayer secured her a contract with MGM in the US. Lamarr worked consistently for MGM throughout the 1940s, starring in such films as *Come Live with Me* (1941) and *Tortilla Flat* (1942), and registered a major commercial success when she played the female title character in *Samson and Delilah* (1949). She was also an inventor. In 1941, along with George Antheil, she lodged a patent application for a 'Secret Communication

System', the basis of which was a 'frequency hopping' technique which would preserve the integrity of a message by altering in a defined way the frequency used to transmit it. Though difficult to implement successfully at the time, the concept has been applied to forms of today's radio communication systems such as mobile telephony. Her last film appearance was a starring role in *The Female Animal* (1958). Lamarr died in 2000, aged eighty-six.

In 1947 **Chuck Yeager** *became the first person to officially fly faster than the speed of sound.*

Yeager had served with the United States Army Air Force in World War Two. Although he was shot down in France, he had managed, with the help of the resistance, to eventually return to his base in England and resume his combat duties. He remained in the air force after the end of the war and became a test pilot. The speed of sound varies with temperature and atmospheric pressure. Piloting the Bell X-1 at over eight miles high, Yeager broke through the sound barrier at 662mph and reached a final speed of 700mph. Although not the first to reach twice the speed of sound, in 1953 he flew a Bell X-1A to Mach 2.44 (1650mph). He was awarded a special congressional silver medal in 1976 for his sound-barrier-breaking flight.

'Fear and Desire', the first feature film to be directed by **Stanley Kubrick**, *was released in 1953.*

Kubrick spent four years working as a staff photographer for *Look* magazine, before making his directorial debut with a short documentary called *Day of the Fight* (1951). His first Hollywood film, *Paths of Glory* (1957), was followed by *Spartacus* (1960). In the early sixties Kubrick, a native of New York, moved permanently to England where his first production was *Lolita* (1962). Further films such as *2001: A Space Odyssey* (1968) and *A Clockwork Orange* (1971) strengthened his reputation. Kubrick, known for his meticulous preparation and perfectionism, made thirteen feature films, with his last, *Eyes Wide Shut*, appearing in 1999, the year of his death at the age of seventy. Despite his status as a director Kubrick would only receive one personal Academy Award – for the special effects used in *2001: A Space Odyssey* (1968).

*In 1954 **Audrey Hepburn** won the Academy Award for best actress for her role as Princess Ann in the film 'Roman Holiday'.*

Born in Brussels, Hepburn spent her later childhood in Holland where after the war she made her film debut with a minor part as an air stewardess in *Nederlands in 7 Lessen* (1948). She moved to London where she continued to study ballet and also worked as a model. Her British film career began with a role as a hotel receptionist in *One Wild Oat* (1951), but her career breakthrough came with her Broadway appearance in the title role of *Gigi* which opened at the end of 1951. A starring part in her first major US film, *Roman Holiday* (1953), came next and won her the Academy Award for best actress. In 1954 she also won a Tony Award for best actress as the title character in *Ondine*. Hepburn, whose on-screen style also made her a cultural icon, was nominated a further four times for the best actress Oscar, including for her portrayal of Holly Golightly in *Breakfast at Tiffany's* (1961), and lastly for her role as Susy Hendrix in *Wait Until Dark* (1967). She won best British actress three times at the Baftas for *Roman Holiday* (1953), *The Nun's Story* (1959) and *Charade* (1963). Hepburn took a break from acting in the late sixties, but returned to complete a brace of films in the next decade. Her last appearance was in the Steven Spielberg film *Always* (1989). Hepburn was also made a UNICEF Goodwill Ambassador in 1988 and she was awarded the Presidential Medal of Freedom in 1992 for her charitable work. She also won a Bafta lifetime achievement award in the same year, one year before her death at the age of sixty-three.

James Dean starred in his first major film, 'East of Eden', released in 1955.

Dean was born in Marion, Indiana. The family moved to California when he was five, but he moved back to Indiana four years later, following the death of his mother. After completing high school he returned to California, where he attended drama classes. He moved to New York in 1951 and became a member of the Actor's Studio, then under the leadership of Lee Strasberg. Dean's screen career began in the same year with minor parts in television and uncredited film appearances. He made his Broadway debut as Wally Wilkins in *See the Jaguar*, which opened in 1952, but it was his next theatrical production, *The Immortalist* (1954), which won him the attention of film director Elia Kazan who cast him as Cal

Trask in *East of Eden* (1955). In his second feature, *Rebel Without a Cause* (1955), Dean's embodiment of disaffected youth and rebellion in his performance as teenage misfit Jim Stark made him a cultural icon. He completed work on one more film, *Giant* (1956), before dying at the age of twenty-four in a car accident. Neither of his last two films were released in his lifetime. In 1956 he received the first posthumous Academy Award nomination for best actor for *East of Eden* (1955) and a second one the following year for *Giant* (1956).

Just Fontaine scored thirteen goals in the 1958 football World Cup finals hosted by Sweden.

Fontaine's World Cup total, accumulated over six matches, remains a record for a single tournament. He scored four goals against the reigning champions West Germany in the third place play-off match, a hat-trick against Paraguay and netted, at least once, in every other game. Born in Marrakesh to a French father and Spanish mother, Fontaine began his club career with USM Casablanca. He moved to France in 1953, where he won the French Cup and Championship with Nice. After transferring to Stade de Reims, he enjoyed a Championship and Cup double in 1958, followed by two further league titles and an appearance in the 1960 European Cup final, where Reims were defeated by Real Madrid. Injury forced his early retirement at the age of twenty-eight. Fontaine later had spells in management, including one with the French national side.

In 1959 Henry Cooper outpointed Brian London to win the British and Empire (Commonwealth) heavyweight boxing titles at Earl's Court, London.

Cooper held the titles almost continuously for the next twelve years, and also became the European heavyweight champion in 1968. He first fought Muhammed Ali (then Cassius Clay) in a non-title fight in 1963, in what was Ali's first overseas contest, and famously knocked down his opponent close to the end of the fourth round. Many believe that the bell saved Ali from a defeat by giving him extra time to recover and win the bout, stopped due to Cooper's cuts in the fifth round. They boxed for a second time in 1966, this time for the world title, but again the bout would be stopped in Ali's favour after Cooper suffered a bad cut over his left eye. In 1971 Cooper retired from boxing, at the age of thirty-six, after his defeat by Joe Bugner who claimed his titles by the margin of one quarter of a point. Cooper was knighted in 2000. He died in 2011 at the age of seventy-six.

The first episode of the series 'Coronation Street', created by **Tony Warren**, *was broadcast in December 1960.*

Warren overcame some reluctance at Granada television to launch what would become one of British television's most watched programmes and a doyen of the ITV network. *Coronation Street*, which celebrated its fiftieth anniversary in 2010, has also become the world's longest-running TV soap opera. Originally to be called *Florizel Street*, Warren single-handedly wrote all of the thirteen initial episodes of the twice-weekly drama, which was soon top of the ratings. In the 1990s Warren published four novels, including *The Lights of Manchester* (1992) and *Full Steam Ahead* (1998). He was awarded an MBE in 1976.

Mary Rand *won a gold medal for the long jump at the 1964 Tokyo Olympics.*

Rand became the first British female athlete to win a track-and-field gold medal at the Olympics, breaking the world record in the process. She completed her set of medals at the Tokyo Games with a silver in the pentathlon and bronze for the 4x100m relay. Rand's triumph in the long jump laid to rest her disappointment four years earlier at the Rome Games when, despite performing well in the qualifying round, she finished in ninth place. Injury prevented her defending her title at the next Olympics, and also prompted her sporting retirement. Rand was awarded an MBE in the 1965 New Year Honours list.

In 1964 **Tom Jones** *reached number one in the UK chart for the first time with 'It's Not Unusual'.*

'It's Not Unusual' was written by Jones's manager, Gordon Mills, and Les Reed. It was Mills who recognised Jones's potential as a singer on a visit to South Wales when he spotted him fronting the group 'Tommy Scott and the Senators'. At Mills's suggestion Tom Jones Woodward became simply Tom Jones. His first single for Decca didn't chart, but although the BBC declined to play 'It's Not Unusual', the pirate station Radio Caroline gave it airtime and the song went to number one. Mills continued to guide Jones's career, which saw him record a James Bond theme (*Thunderball*) in 1965 and also become an established entertainer in the US. Following Mills's death in 1986, his son Mark took over, and Jones returned to the UK singles chart the following year, after a ten-year gap, with the number two hit 'A Boy from Nowhere'. His 1999 album, *Reload*, became his biggest selling and gave him the top spot for the second time. Jones was awarded an OBE in 1999 and was knighted in 2006.

Geoff Hurst scored a hat-trick as England beat West Germany, 4–2 after extra time, to win the football World Cup in 1966.

Hurst remains the only player to have scored three goals in a World Cup final. He made his international debut against West Germany at Wembley, five months before the historic World Cup final game, when England triumphed by one goal to nil. Coincidentally, he also made his last appearance for England against West Germany, again at Wembley. The World Cup final was Hurst's eighth game for his country, and he had scored on two previous occasions, once against Scotland and also against Argentina in the World Cup quarter-final. Hurst scored 24 times for England in his 49 appearances. His club honours were achieved with West Ham United, his longest-serving senior side – the FA cup in 1964 and, in the following year, the European Cup Winners' Cup, won in another Wembley final against German opposition in the form of 1860 Munich. Hurst was awarded an MBE in 1975 and knighted in 1998.

Tony Blackburn became the first disc jockey to broadcast on BBC Radio 1 when it was launched in September 1967.

Blackburn had first worked as a disc jockey for the pirate broadcasters Radio Caroline and Radio London, whose broadcasting style the new Radio 1 largely imitated. Blackburn presented the Radio 1 breakfast show for six years, before he moved on to the mid-morning and afternoon slots. He left the BBC in 1988 and moved to commercial radio, but returned to the BBC to work in local radio in 2004. Six years later, he was back on a BBC national network as the host of Radio 2's *Pick of the Pops*. In 2002, he became the first winner of the ITV series *I'm a Celebrity . . . Get Me Out of Here!*

*In 1974 Abba, with vocalists **Agnetha Fältskog** and Anna-Frid Lyngstad, won the Eurovision Song Contest in Brighton with 'Waterloo'.*

'Waterloo' gave Abba their first number one in the UK. The group would dominate the chart in the following years, with another eight number ones and ten further singles that reached the top ten. Success in her native Sweden had come earlier for Fältskog. Her first single release, the self-penned 'Jag Var så Kär' (I Was So in Love), made it to number one in the Swedish chart when she was seventeen. Her self-titled debut album was released in 1968, and three more albums were to follow before Abba's Eurovision success.

*

Philippe Petit *performed a high-wire walk between the twin towers of the World Trade Center in 1974.*

Petit had spent several months covertly planning the New York spectacle with his assistants. On the day, he spent around forty-five minutes on the cable, suspended approximately 1,350 feet in the air. Petit crossed back and forth, even lying down and sitting, as onlookers gazed from below. Although arrested when he finally left the wire, all charges were dropped in return for a free show for the children of New York City in Central Park. Prior to his World Trade Center achievement, Petit, who taught himself wire-walking as a teenager, had also crossed between the towers of Notre Dame Cathedral in Paris, and between those of Sydney Harbour Bridge. The film *Man on Wire* (2008), which recounted the story of his World Trade Center achievement, won an Academy Award for best documentary.

*

*In 1979 **Trevor Francis** became the first footballer to be transferred between English clubs for a fee of £1 million.*

Francis was signed by Nottingham Forest, then managed by Brian Clough, from Birmingham City with the final fee (including taxes and other costs) in excess of £1 million. He went on to score the only goal in the 1979 European Cup final as Forest defeated Malmö to become the third English side to lift the trophy, but he missed Forest's victory in the subsequent final due to injury. Francis was transferred to Manchester City in 1981 for a fee of approximately £1.2 million. He made twenty-six appearances for the club before moving to Italian side Sampdoria where he won a Coppa Italia medal. Francis played for another Italian side, Atalanta, before returning to Britain, this time signing for Rangers in 1987 with whom he picked up another honour – the Scottish League Cup. Francis won the corresponding English trophy at Sheffield Wednesday, his last senior club as a player, before he moved into management.

The Cambridge Footlights, which included **Stephen Fry** *as a member, won the first Perrier Comedy Award at the 1981 Edinburgh Fringe Festival.*

Fry, a graduate of Queens' College, Cambridge, had made his television debut in the previous year as a contestant on *University Challenge* – the team finished as runners-up. The success of the Edinburgh Fringe show led to his participation in the ITV sketch series, *There's Nothing to Worry About!* and its second season, re-billed as *Alfresco.* He had prominent roles in the second and fourth series of *Blackadder* playing members of the Melchett dynasty, latterly as a World War One general. Fry and Hugh Lawrie, a recurring collaborator from the Footlights days, maintained their comedy partnership with their own BBC series, *A Bit of Fry and Laurie,* first aired in 1989. They also teamed up, at the start of the 1990s, as the title characters in *Jeeves and Wooster,* with Fry in the former role. That decade also saw the publication of Fry's first novel, *The Liar,* in 1993, in addition to film appearances which included *Peter's Friends* (1992) and the Golden Globe nominated lead role in the Oscar Wilde biopic *Wilde* (1997). Fry has also been active in the theatre (his first play, *Latin!,* won an award at the Edinburgh Fringe in 1980) and on radio. In 2003 he began hosting the television quiz show *QI* – now in its tenth series. A self-confessed technophile, Fry has amassed over five million followers on the messaging service Twitter. He has also published two volumes of autobiography, *Moab is My Washpot* (1997) and *The Fry Chronicles* (2010).

In 1982 **Madonna** *released her debut single, 'Everybody'.*

Born Madonna Louise Ciccone in Bay City, Michigan, she moved to New York in the late 1970s to pursue her interest in dance. She also became involved in the city's music scene and played in various bands before signing a solo deal with Sire Records. Madonna's debut, the self-penned 'Everybody', was a dance chart hit in the US, but her breakthrough came with her third single, 'Holiday', which reached number sixteen in the US Hot 100. It also provided her UK chart debut with a placing of number six in 1984, and heralded the start of a remarkable career which has seen her become one of the best-selling artists in the world. Madonna's first UK number one single was 'Into the Groove' in 1985, and she has had a further twelve chart toppers, including 'True Blue', 'Like a Prayer' and 'Frozen'. 'Into the Groove' also featured in her first critical and commercial film success, *Desperately Seeking Susan* (1985), in which she played the title character. Her other films include *Dick Tracy* (1990); *A League of Their Own* (1992); and *Evita* (1996), which won her a Golden Globe award for best actress. In 2012, at the age of fifty-three, she released her twelfth studio album, *MDNA*. Her first for four years, similar to most of its predecessors *MDNA* reached number one in several countries including the UK and US.

*In 1982 **Jools Holland** co-presented the first edition of Channel 4's music show 'The Tube'.*

The popular Friday evening series continued for over four years. Prior to that, Holland was a founding member of the group Squeeze, who first enjoyed chart success in the late seventies. His musical career away from the group saw him form the Jools Holland Big Band in 1987, which later became Jools Holland and His Rhythm & Blues Orchestra. Since 1992 he has been the presenter of *Later . . . with Jools Holland*, the BBC's flagship popular music programme. He was awarded an OBE in 2003.

***Michael J. Fox** starred as Marty McFly in 'Back to the Future', released in 1985.*

Fox played the seventeen-year-old who, accidentally transported back to 1955, must ensure his future parents get together in order for him to return to his own time in 1985. Fox, who made his feature-film debut in *Midnight Madness* (1980), starred again as McFly in two sequels. The television-comedy series *Family Ties*, first broadcast in 1982, brought him Emmy and Golden Globe recognition, and a seven-year stretch as the character Alex P. Keaton. His other films include *Teen Wolf* (1985), *The Secret of My Success* (1987) and *Casualties of War* (1989). Fox voiced the eponymous animated mouse in the Stuart Little trilogy (1999–2005), while the television series *Spin City*, first aired in 1996, brought him further Emmy and Golden Globe success. He was diagnosed with Parkinson's disease in 1991 and launched the Michael J. Fox Foundation for Parkinson's Research in 2000, which has raised more than $230 million.

Jonny Wilkinson scored the winning drop goal in the last minute of extra time in the 2003 Rugby World Cup final, as England beat the hosts Australia to win the trophy for the first time.

Wilkinson was also the leading points scorer in the tournament, with a total of 113. He rounded off the year by winning the BBC Sports Personality of the Year award, and was also named the International Rugby Board (IRB) player of the year. Injury hampered the fly-half's career following the World Cup, but he competed in the next World Cup final in 2007; England this time losing out to South Africa, despite his two penalties. Wilkinson is the only player to have scored in two Rugby World Cup finals. In his club career he spent a dozen years with Newcastle Falcons, winning the Premiership with them in 1998, before transferring to French side Toulon in 2009. Wilkinson, who made his England debut aged eighteen, announced in 2011 that he was retiring from international rugby after ninety-one appearances. He is England's record points scorer, with 1,179 to his credit, and played his last game for the team at the 2011 Rugby World Cup. In what was his fourth consecutive appearance at the tournament, Wilkinson increased his overall Rugby World Cup points total to a record 277. He was awarded an OBE in the 2004 New Year Honours list.

Amy Winehouse won five Grammy Awards in 2008.

Winehouse became the first British artist to scoop five Grammys – her song 'Rehab' won record of the year, song of the year and best female pop vocal performance, while *Back to Black* was named as best pop vocal album. Winehouse also triumphed in the best new artist category. She released her debut album, *Frank*, at the age of twenty in 2003. *Back to Black*, predominantly written by Winehouse, emerged three years later and first reached the UK number one position in January 2007. The opening track of the album 'Rehab' gave her a first top-ten position in the UK singles chart. Following her death in 2011 at the age of twenty-seven, *Back to Black* returned to the top of the chart and has since become one of the UK's biggest-selling albums of the twenty-first century.

Christine Ohuruogu won a gold medal at the 2008 Beijing Olympic Games for the 400m.

Ohuruogu was the only British track-and-field gold medallist at the Games, and she is also the first British female winner of the event in Olympic history. Ohuruogu also won the world title over the same distance in 2007 and Commonwealth gold in 2006. Despite a late surge, Ohuruogu narrowly failed to defend her Olympic title at the 2012 London Games and had to settle for a silver medal. She received an MBE in the 2009 New Year Honours.

In 2010 Rafael Nadal won his first US Open tennis tournament, thereby completing a career Grand Slam.

Nadal's victory in the US Open against Novak Djokovic, made him the youngest male player to win a career Grand Slam in the open era of tennis. Encouraged by his uncle, Nadal began playing tennis aged four and won a regional tennis tournament for the under-12s when he was only eight. Two days after his nineteenth birthday he scored his first Grand Slam title at the 2005 French Open. Nadal's first win at Wimbledon came three years later, in 2008, after an epic final encounter with defending champion Roger Federer, in which Nadal took victory by nine games to seven in the fifth set. At nearly five hours long it was the longest final in the history of the Wimbledon Championships. Nadal has recorded eleven Grand Slam tournament wins and, with seven of them coming on the clay surface of the French Open, more than any other player, he has been dubbed the 'king of clay'. In the same year as his debut Wimbledon triumph, he also won a gold medal at the Beijing Olympic Games for the men's singles, which together with his acquisition of the four major titles has made him one of only four tennis players, alongside Steffi Graf, Andre Agassi and Serena Williams, to achieve a career 'Golden Slam'.

Alistair Brownlee won a gold medal for the men's triathlon at the 2012 London Olympics.

Brownlee is the first British winner of the Olympic triathlon, which made its debut at the Sydney Games in 2000. The event consists of a 1,500m swim, 40km cycle and a 10km road run. Brownlee had already achieved success at international level. He won the European Championship in 2010 and 2011, and won the World Championship in 2009 and 2011. Brownlee was joined on the Olympic podium by his younger brother Jonathan, who took the bronze medal. Alistair was awarded an MBE in the 2013 New Year Honours.

25
TWENTY-FIVE

Elizabeth I *became Queen of England in 1558.*

Elizabeth, the daughter of Henry VIII and his second wife, Anne Boleyn, was the last Tudor monarch. She ascended to the throne after the death of her half sister, Queen Mary I, Henry VIII's daughter by Catherine of Aragon. Elizabeth's monarchy saw the full establishment of the Church of England, the defeat of the Spanish Armada in 1588 and the encouragement of seafaring and exploration by Francis Drake and others. She did not marry and was succeeded, after her death in 1603 at the age of sixty-nine, by James VI of Scotland, who ruled England as James I, and became the first joint monarch of the two realms.

Edmond Halley *observed the comet that would later bear his name in 1682.*

Halley compared its orbital path with that of previous comet appearances in 1531 and 1607, and concluded that these were in fact the same object. In 1705 he predicted its return in 1758, and was proved correct when it was spotted in the sky close to Christmas Day. (Halley though had died sixteen years prior to this event.) Although best remembered for the comet, Halley also made other notable contributions to science. He established the link between barometric pressure and height above sea level, urged Newton to publish his great work *Principia* (which Halley funded at his own expense) and was the first to propose that the moon was speeding up in its orbit around the earth. He also made a significant contribution to the field of actuarial science with his study of the mortality rates of the city of Breslau which allowed him to show how to calculate, based on an analysis of the population statistics, how much individuals should pay in order to receive an annuity. In 1720 Halley was appointed as the second astronomer royal, an office that he was to hold until his death in 1742 at the age of eighty-five.

Henry Petty-Fitzmaurice became chancellor of the exchequer, in 1806, in the administration of Lord Grenville.

Petty-Fitzmaurice was only able to present two budgets, as he was out of office in the following year. Following the death of his father and his older half-brother he became the third Marquess of Lansdowne and took his seat in the House of Lords in 1810. In 1827 he returned to high office as home secretary, although again he would only hold the position for a matter of months. He died in 1863 at the age of eighty-two.

Isabella Beeton published in a single volume her 'Book of Household Management' in 1861.

The contents first appeared between 1859 and 1861 as monthly supplements of the *Englishwoman's Domestic Magazine*, a title published by Beeton's husband, Samuel. The book version ran to over one thousand pages and contained hundreds of recipes, as well as wide-ranging advice on the running of a household with topics that included domestic servants and the rearing of children. Beeton died shortly after the birth of her fourth child, at the age of twenty-eight, in 1865. Her best-selling book lived on and was purchased along with the rest of Samuel Beeton's publishing interests by the company Ward, Lock and Tyler, who in the early 1880s stated that it had sold in excess of 300,000 copies. The book continued to be revised and up-dated, and many more titles were published under her name, such as *Mrs Beeton's Family Cookery*.

*La femme à la robe verte (The Woman in the Green Dress), was one of the first paintings by **Claude Monet** to attract attention, when it was exhibited in the Paris Salon in 1866.*

Monet's painting is also referred to by the first name of its subject, Camille Doncieux, who would appear in many of his works and later become his wife. The title of Monet's 1872 painting *Impression, soleil levant* (*Impression, Sunrise*) gave rise to the name of the art movement, Impressionism, of which he would become a major exponent. His move to Giverny in 1883 marked the start of a period that would see the creation of what are now seen as his most famous works. It was there, inspired by his flower garden, that he produced the 'Water Lilies' series. Monet painted and resided in Giverny until his death in 1926 at the age of eighty-six.

George Eastman filed his patent for a method to coat photographic plates in 1879.

Eastman, the youngest of three siblings, was born in Waterville, New York State, and started work as an office boy at the age of thirteen. Six years later he took a job as a bank clerk and within twelve months Eastman had become an assistant bookkeeper. He bought his first camera at the age of twenty-three. The wet plates which it used to capture an image were not convenient. They had to be prepared immediately before use and, following exposure, developed within minutes before the chemicals dried. Outside photography also required the use of a tent as a darkroom. Eastman was inspired to find a way to simplify the process and drawing on magazine articles which described dry plate formulations, and experiments at home, he developed and patented his own machine for making dry plates. Shortly after, he began their commercial manufacture and founded the Eastman Dry Plate Company with Henry Strong in 1881. Eastman left his bank job and in 1884 lodged two patents for photographic roll film, the second for an improved version developed with William Walker. Four years later, in 1888, Eastman also patented the camera which could use the film and registered the trademark 'Kodak'. The camera was sold with enough film to take 100 pictures and then had to be returned to Kodak for processing and reloading. The famous 'Brownie' model was launched in 1900, priced at $1. The company's success made Eastman wealthy and he became a leading philanthropist. He donated millions to the Massachusetts Institute of Technology, the University of Rochester and others. Faced with deteriorating health as a result of a spinal condition, Eastman committed suicide in 1932 at the age of seventy-seven, leaving a note which said 'My work is done. Why wait?'

William Lawrence Bragg shared the 1915 Nobel Prize in Physics with his father, William Henry Bragg, for their work in the field of X-ray crystallography.

The 25-year-old William Lawrence Bragg is the youngest recipient of a Nobel Prize. Born in Adelaide, Australia, he went to the University of Adelaide, where his father was a professor of mathematics and physics, when he was only fifteen. He graduated in 1908 with first-class honours in mathematics; the subsidiary course in physics gave him his first academic introduction to the subject. The family relocated to England in 1909, and Bragg read mathematics and physics at Trinity College, Cambridge. He again graduated with first-class honours. In 1912 he first described how the structure of materials can be elucidated from their interaction with X-rays. Bragg and his father developed this concept further and detailed it in *X-rays and Crystal Structure*, which led to their joint Nobel Prize award. Bragg later became head of the Cavendish Laboratory at Cambridge, and during his tenure X-ray crystallography was to play a key part in the discovery of the structure of DNA. Bragg was knighted in 1941. He died in 1971, aged eighty-one.

*In 1927 **Charles Lindbergh** completed the first solo non-stop transatlantic flight.*
Lindbergh flew from Roosevelt Field on New York's Long Island to Le Bourget Field near Paris, piloting his single engine Ryan monoplane named *Spirit of St. Louis*. The flight took approximately thirty-three-and-a-half hours, and won the $25,000 Orteig Prize which had been offered since 1919 by a New York hotel businessman for the first non-stop New York to Paris flight. Lindbergh returned home with his plane, on board the USS *Memphis*, to a hero's welcome. He received the Congressional Medal of Honor and the first ever Distinguished Flying Cross from the US government. Lindbergh, who also helped to design his aircraft and planned the flight to Paris, had secured the necessary financial backing in St. Louis. He had no radio equipment or parachute (both sacrificed for more fuel), and no front facing view from his cockpit: all reasons to further admire his achievement, which came only four years after his first solo aeroplane flight. Lindbergh died in 1974 at the age of seventy-two.

*The first London gallery exhibition to feature work by **Barbara Hepworth** took place at the Beaux Arts Gallery in 1928.*
Yorkshire-born Hepworth studied at the Leeds School of Art, and then at the Royal College of Art in London where, at the age of twenty, she gained her diploma. The award of a scholarship for one year's travel took her to Italy for further study, where she learnt to carve marble, after which she returned to London in 1926. Her early work included figurative pieces such as *Mother and Child* (1927), but by the mid-1930s, Hepworth's focus was the abstract and would remain so for the rest of her career, with works

such as *Three Forms* (1935), *Wood and Strings* (1944) and *The Family of Man* (1970). She moved to St Ives, Cornwall, in 1939, where she would live and work until her death, in 1975, at the age of seventy-two. Hepworth's commissions include *Single Form*, located at the United Nations building in New York and created in memory of her friend Dag Hammarskjöld, the UN secretary-general, who was killed in a plane crash. Hepworth was awarded a damehood in 1965.

Fred Perry won his first Wimbledon Men's Singles Championship in 1934.
Perry's victory, in straight sets against the defending champion Jack Crawford, was also the first British win after a gap of twenty-five years. He repeated his success at the next two Wimbledon Championships, and he remains the last British male tennis player to win a Wimbledon singles final. Perry won the US Open three times and the Australian Open once. His victory at the French Open in 1935 made him the first man to win all four major titles and complete a career Grand Slam. Perry did not take up tennis until he was fifteen – his first sporting success came in table tennis, in which he became the world champion at the age of nineteen. Perry died in 1995 at the age of eighty-five.

Stanford University graduates **William Hewlett** *and David Packard founded the Hewlett-Packard Company in 1939, from a garage in Palo Alto, California.*
Hewlett and Packard (who was one year older) met when they were both engineering students at Stanford University. They tossed a coin to decide on the order of their names for the company's identity. Their first product was the 200A audio oscillator – an instrument used to test sound equipment – and an early customer was the Walt Disney Company. World War Two provided a boost to the fledgling business as US government orders increased. In 1947 the Hewlett-Packard (HP) catalogue featured thirty-nine products and HP had annual revenue in excess of $850,000. Over the subsequent decades the business continued to expand and diversify; in 1972 HP launched the world's first handheld scientific calculator, the HP-35. The company decided to change tack slightly in the 1990s, and in 1999 spun off several interests such as its original core offering, measurement equipment, into a new business in order to concentrate on computing, printing and imaging. Packard, a recipient of the Presidential

Medal of Freedom, died in 1996 at the age of eighty-three. Hewlett died five years later, at the age of eighty-seven. Neither lived to see the completed restoration in 2005 of the garage in California where it all began for the company, which many consider to be the founder of 'Silicon Valley'.

Orson Welles *directed, produced, co-wrote and starred in the film 'Citizen Kane', released in 1941.*

Welles's cinematic tour de force, in which he plays Charles Foster Kane, was his first feature film and frequently tops lists of the greatest films ever made. *Citizen Kane* received nine Oscar nominations including best picture, best actor and best director (the latter two categories for Welles), but ultimately only picked up one Academy Award, shared between Herman Mankiewicz and Welles for best original screenplay. The film's central figure, and narrative, draws parallels with the life of the newspaper magnate William Randolph Hearst, who sought to suppress the unflattering depiction using all the media resources at his disposal. Welles had already hit the headlines as a result of his direction and narration of a radio adaptation of *The War of the Worlds*, in 1938. Newspapers reported that the broadcast had made many listeners panic because they believed that an alien invasion was actually taking place. Welles followed *Citizen Kane* with *The Magnificent Ambersons* (1942), and although his original vision for the movie was overridden by the studio, RKO, it is still regarded as one of his masterpieces. Welles's other films include *The Lady from Shanghai* (1948), *Othello* (1952), *Touch of Evil* (1958) and *Chimes at Midnight* (1967). As an actor he memorably played Harry Lime in *The Third Man* (1949), and contributed the famous 'cuckoo clock' speech to the script. Welles, who received an honorary Oscar in 1971, died in 1985 at the age of seventy.

In 1942, 'Shot Down over Libya: An RAF Pilot's Factual Account' became the first published work of **Roald Dahl** *when it appeared in the 'Saturday Evening Post'.*

Dahl had volunteered for the Royal Air Force at the outbreak of the Second World War and was badly injured when his Gloster Gladiator, low on fuel, crashed on landing in the Libyan desert. After recuperating he returned to the war effort, piloting a Hawker Hurricane in the Battle of Athens before being invalided home to England. He then became an assistant air attaché in Washington. There, the author C.S. Forester prompted Dahl to write about his experience of war and this resulted in Dahl's first piece in the *Saturday Evening Post*. His first book for children was *The Gremlins*, published in 1943, but Dahl's initial literary efforts were focused on adult fiction. His short stories, published in collections such as *Lamb to the Slaughter*, blended macabre and comic elements and featured in the television series *Roald Dahl's Tales of the Unexpected*, which first aired in 1979. He is perhaps most famous for his children's books, which include *James and the Giant Peach*, *Charlie and the Chocolate Factory*, *The Twits*, *Matilda* and *The Witches*. Dahl fashioned two Ian Fleming books into screenplays. The first to appear was the James Bond tale *You Only Live Twice* (1967), followed by the children's automotive fantasy *Chitty Chitty Bang Bang* (1968). Dahl died in 1990, aged seventy-four.

Leonard Bernstein made his conducting debut with the New York Philharmonic Orchestra in 1943.

The concert, in which Bernstein replaced the ill Bruno Walter at short notice, was also broadcast on the radio, and – with a review on the front page of the next day's *New York Times* – Bernstein was catapulted into the public eye. Fourteen years later, he was appointed as the first American-born music director of the New York Philharmonic. Bernstein was also a talented pianist and composer, probably best remembered for his work on *West Side Story* and *On the Town*. His compositional canon also includes orchestral scores, choral music and ballet. Bernstein died at the age of seventy-two in 1990.

Akio Morita and Masaru Ibuka co-founded the Tokyo Telecommunications Engineering Corporation (Tokyo-Tsushin-Kogyo), later renamed Sony, in 1946.

Morita was born into a family of sake brewers, but he was more inter-ested in technical subjects and studied for a degree in physics at Osaka Imperial University. After the Second World War, he read an article in a newspaper about Masaru Ibuka, nearly thirteen years his senior, who had founded a research institute. They arranged to meet and subsequently formed a partnership to create a new company, Tokyo-Tsushin-Kogyo. It produced the first Japanese tape recorder and Ibuka's visit to the United

States in 1952 led to the business becoming the first Asian company to be granted a licence by Western Electric for the transistor. They produced Japan's first radio to use the new devices, which went on sale in 1955 and was branded as Sony. This was adopted as the corporate name three years later, its derivation coming from a combination of the Latin word *sonus* (sound) and sonny. Sony went on to produce other innovative products such as the Trinitron TV tube and Walkman personal stereo, and developed commercial audio CD technology with Philips – the first CD players were launched in 1982. Morita died in 1999, aged seventy-eight, two years after Ibuka's death at eighty-nine.

Elizabeth II *succeeded to the British throne following the death of her father, George VI, in 1952.*

The abdication of Elizabeth's uncle, Edward VIII, in 1936 made her father king and set Elizabeth, as his older daughter, on her path to the throne. She married Prince Philip of Greece and Denmark in 1947, and in the following year their first child, Charles, was born, to be followed by Anne, Andrew and Edward. Her coronation in 1953 was the first to be shown on television – a medium that has expanded considerably from the one BBC channel available at the time. When Elizabeth inherited the throne, Winston Churchill was prime minister and Harry Truman was the US president; there have since been eleven further holders of each office. The monarch of sixteen independent states including Canada, Australia and Papua New Guinea as well as the UK, Elizabeth celebrated her golden jubilee in 2002 and her diamond jubilee in 2012. Second only to Queen Victoria in British history for the duration of her reign, Elizabeth is set to surpass her great-great-grandmother's record in September 2015.

James Watson *was one of the co-discoverers of the structure of deoxyribose nucleic acid (DNA) in 1953.*

The paper that announced their finding, 'A Structure for Deoxyribose Nucleic Acid', which Watson co-authored with his colleague, Francis Crick, was published in the journal *Nature* in 1953. The same issue also contained two further papers by researchers at King's College London, who were also investigating DNA using a technique called X-ray crystallography. The data that they produced, in particular that obtained by

Rosalind Franklin, helped Watson and Crick to formulate the double helix model of DNA. Maurice Wilkins of King's College, lead author on one of the papers, shared the 1962 Nobel Prize with Watson and Crick. (Rosalind Franklin, co-author of the other paper with Raymond Gosling, died in 1958. Since the Nobel Prize is not awarded posthumously, she could not receive any consideration as a joint winner.) Watson was born in Chicago and entered Indiana University at the age of fifteen. He graduated with a degree in zoology, and seven years later was awarded his doctorate at the same institution. His first post-doctoral position was in Copenhagen, but in early October 1952 his interest in the determination of the structure of DNA took him to the Cavendish Laboratory in Cambridge where he would collaborate with Francis Crick. It was only months later that history would be made when their model of the molecule's structure was published.

In 1954 **Roger Bannister** *ran the first official sub-four-minute mile when he recorded a time of 3 minutes 59.4 seconds at the Iffley Road track in Oxford.*

Bannister's achievement took place during the annual match between the Amateur Athletic Association and Oxford University. He was helped by pace setting from his fellow team members, Chris Chataway and Chris Brasher. Bannister won gold at the British Empire and Commonwealth Games for the mile, and was also victorious at the European Championships in 1954. He retired from athletics later in that year to concentrate on his medical career and he later became a specialist in neurology. Bannister was knighted in 1975.

Stirling Moss *achieved his first Formula One win at the British Grand Prix in 1955.*

Driving a Mercedes W196, Moss took the first ever victory for a British driver in the event, and returned to the Aintree track two years later to repeat his success. Moss's Formula One career began in 1951 and spanned more than ten years, with his last seven seasons producing four consecutive second-place finishes in the championship followed by three third places. Driving for the Vanwall team, he narrowly missed out on the 1958 title by a single point. Three years previously, London-born Moss, along with navigator Denis Jenkinson, became the only British winners of the

Mille Miglia Italian road race, recording a near 100mph average speed in the process. A bad crash at Goodwood in 1962 brought forwards his retirement from motor sport. Already an OBE since 1959, Moss received a knighthood in 2000.

Luciano Pavarotti *made his operatic debut as Rodolfo in Puccini's La Bohème at the Teatro Reggio Emilia in 1961.*

Four years later, Pavarotti made his debut appearance at La Scala (again in *La Bohème*) and also performed in the US for the first time as Edgardo in *Lucia di Lammermoor*. He reached a wider audience with his recording of 'Nessun Dorma' from Puccini's *Turandot*, which was used to great effect as the BBC theme for the 1990 World Cup in Italy and subsequently rose to number two in the UK singles chart. Pavarotti played many outdoor concerts in the 1990s, with approximately half a million people gathering to listen to his free performance in New York's Central Park in 1993. He died in 2007, aged seventy-one.

In 1961 **Gherman Titov** *flew into space aboard Vostok 2 to become the second man to orbit the earth.*

Titov's mission came just under four months after Yuri Gagarin became the first man in space. Titov made seventeen complete orbits of the earth in a mission that lasted for over a day and therefore included the first period of extra-terrestrial sleep. He remains the youngest person to travel into space. Titov died in 2000 at the age of sixty-five.

Valerie Singleton *joined 'Blue Peter' as a presenter in 1962.*

Singleton regularly co-hosted the long-running children's television programme until 1972, and is the second longest-serving female presenter in the show's history, after Konnie Huq. Singleton studied at Rada, but was diverted from a theatrical career when she took a job as a BBC continuity announcer and subsequently as a presenter on *Blue Peter*. After leaving her full-time position on the show, she continued her association with the programme in the spin-off series *Blue Peter Special Assignment* which saw her report back from various locations around the globe. Singleton's other presenting duties include *The Money Programme* and Radio 4's *PM*. She received an OBE in 1994 for services to broadcasting.

Bobby Moore *captained England to victory in the 1966 World Cup final.*

The World Cup win against West Germany, 4–2 after extra-time, was the pinnacle of Moore's professional footballing career, which began at West Ham United in 1958 with a debut against Manchester United. Moore spent nearly sixteen years at the club where he picked up his only domestic silverware, the FA Cup, in 1964. In the following year, Moore lifted the UEFA Cup Winners' Cup at Wembley, after his team beat 1860 Munich. Moore's playing career ended with a spell at Fulham which brought him one last Wembley appearance, on the losing side in the 1975 FA Cup final, against his former club West Ham. In his international career, Moore won a record 108 caps for an outfield player (only eclipsed by David Beckham in 2009), played in three World Cup finals and captained the England side on ninety occasions. He received an OBE in the 1967 New Year Honours. Moore died in 1993 at the age of fifty-one.

In 1969 **Tony Jacklin** *won golf's Open Championship at Royal Lytham & St Annes.*

Jacklin won by two strokes to take the first prize of £4,250. He was the first British winner since Max Faulkner's victory in 1951 at the Royal Portrush course in Northern Ireland (the only time that the tournament has not been played in either Scotland or England). Jacklin went on to win the US Open in 1970, the first triumph in the tournament by a British player for forty-five years. He became a successful Ryder Cup captain and presided over victories in 1985, the first for twenty-eight years, and a famous first ever win on US soil in 1987. He has been awarded both an OBE and a CBE.

Mark Hamil *starred as Luke Skywalker in 'Star Wars', released in 1977.*

Hamil had worked in television for several years, before taking his first major film role in *Star Wars*. Leading parts in productions such as *Corvette Summer* (1978) and *The Night the Lights Went Out in Georgia* (1981) followed, but he remains best known for the character of Skywalker, reprised in the sequels *The Empire Strikes Back* (1980) and *Return of the Jedi* (1983). Since the 1990s, he has worked extensively as a voice artist both in film and video games.

Barry McGuigan *won the WBA World Featherweight Boxing Championship when he defeated Eusebio Pedroza on points in 1985.*

McGuigan, nicknamed the 'Clones Cyclone' after his hometown in County Monaghan, Ireland, made two successful defences and held the title for just over a year before being outpointed by Steve Cruz over fifteen rounds. He retired from boxing after the bout, though he returned to the ring two years later for four more fights, finally hanging up his gloves in 1989. McGuigan was awarded an MBE in 1994.

Gary Lineker *was the top scorer at the 1986 Mexico World Cup finals with a total of six goals.*

Lineker is the only England player to be top scorer at the World Cup finals. He headed the goal-scoring list despite England only reaching the quarter-finals, where they were defeated by Argentina in the controversial 'Hand of God' match. Lineker added a further four goals to his tally at the 1990 tournament held in Italy, and with a total of ten goals remains England's highest overall scorer at the World Cup finals. His international tally of forty-eight goals is only one behind England's leading scorer Bobby Charlton. Lineker's club career began at his home-town club, Leicester City and continued at Everton, Barcelona and Tottenham Hotspur before ending at Japanese club Nagoya Grampus Eight. Lineker has never won a league championship title with any of his clubs, although he did win cup competitions with Everton, Barcelona and Tottenham. He is one of the few players never to have received a yellow or red card in the professional game. Following his retirement from football, Lineker, who was awarded the OBE in 1992, embarked on a successful media career.

Matthew Perry *and* ***Jennifer Aniston*** *starred in the first episode of 'Friends', broadcast in 1994.*

Perry played Chandler Bing in the hit TV comedy, set in New York, which ran for ten series until 2004. The youngest of the six cast members, Perry made his feature-film debut in *A Night in the Life of Jimmy Reardon* (1988). His most recent films include *Birds of America* (2008) and *17 Again* (2009). Although originally considered for the role of Monica Geller, Aniston instead took the part of Rachel Green. Aniston had some television appearances and one feature film, *Leprechaun* (1993), to her credit before her breakthrough with *Friends*. Her other films include *She's the One* (1996), *Office Space* (1999), *Bruce Almighty* (2003) and *Marley and Me* (2008).

Michael Schumacher *won his first Formula One World Championship in 1994 after the final race of the season – the Australian Grand Prix.*

Schumacher took the title by one point from Damon Hill, with both drivers' cars being retired after they collided as Hill tried to pass his rival on an inside bend. Schumacher's slender lead in the championship going into the final race was therefore preserved. The following season Schumacher, still driving for Benetton, celebrated another championship victory. He joined Ferrari in 1996, and won five consecutive titles between 2000 and 2004. Schumacher retired at the end of the 2006 season, but made a comeback, driving for the Mercedes GP Petronas team, in 2010, to finish ninth in the championship. Schumacher holds various Formula One records including most championships and most race victories.

Joe Calzaghe *won the WBO super middleweight boxing title in 1997.*

Calzaghe's defeat of Chris Eubank on points marked the start of a ten-year reign for Calzaghe as the WBO champion in this weight division. He added the IBF title in 2006, though he relinquished this after his first defence due to contractual issues. In the following year, Calzaghe defeated Mikkel Kessler as he collected the WBA and WBC titles after a unanimous decision, to become the undisputed super middleweight champion. He moved up to the light heavyweight division for his last two professional fights, in 2008, which ended, as did the previous forty-four, in victory. Calzaghe retired undefeated in 2009. He received an MBE in 2003 and a CBE in 2008.

Google, founded by **Larry Page** *and* **Sergey Brin**, *was incorporated in 1998.*

Page and Brin met when they were both computer science PhD students at Stanford. Their collaboration on a research project known as *BackRub* would lead to the creation of Google. Together they devised a system which would rank web pages on a given topic by significance, with the significance being determined by the number of links to that page, weighted to take account of importance. In essence, their technique would return a list of pages ranked by relevance, and not just keywords, as the result of a search enquiry. *BackRub* was renamed Google – an adaptation of the word googol, which is the mathematical term for the number one followed by one hundred zeros. Ten years after it was founded, Google posted revenue of nearly $22 billion and a net income of over $4 billion.

Nicole Cooke won Britain's first gold medal of the 2008 Beijing Olympic Games, for the women's cycling road race.

Cooke's achievement was also notable for being the 200th gold medal that Britain had won since the inauguration of the modern Olympics, and was also the first by a Welsh competitor for thirty-six years. She also made history by becoming the first woman in cycling to win both the Olympics and World Championships in the same year when she achieved victory at the latter event held in Varese, Italy. Swansea-born Cooke began her racing career at the age of eleven. In 1999 aged sixteen, she won the British national Road Race Championship; the youngest ever to do so. Cooke went on to win the event a further nine times between 2001 and 2009. She won her first world title in 2000 with victory in the Junior World Road Race. Her other cycling successes include becoming the first Briton to win the Grande Boucle Féminine, unofficially known as the women's Tour de France, in 2006. She won again the following year. In 2013, at the age of twenty-nine, Cooke announced her retirement from cycling. She was awarded an MBE in the 2009 New Year Honours.

Andy Murray won his first tennis Grand Slam title, the US Open, in 2012.

Murray defeated the defending champion, Novak Djokovic, to become the first British man to win a tennis Grand Slam tournament since Fred Perry's victory in the US Open in 1936. Murray made his tournament debut at the age of five in his home town of Dunblane in an event for the under-10s. He won the US Open junior title aged seventeen in 2004 and the following year turned professional. In 2006, he won his first ATP tour title and became the British number one. Murray made his first Grand Slam final appearance in the 2008 US Open, but lost out to Roger Federer. Next, he was the runner-up at the Australian Open in 2010 and 2011. His fourth Grand Slam final appearance was at Wimbledon in 2012 against Federer, when he became the first male British player to reach the final for seventy-four years. Four weeks later the pair met again in the 2012 Olympic singles final. Murray won in straight sets to become the first Briton to win the men's singles at the Olympics since Josiah Ritchie in 1908 (Murray also won a silver medal for the mixed doubles with Laura Robson). Murray reached his third consecutive Grand Slam final (and sixth overall) at the start of 2013, when he was runner-up in the Australian Open to Djokovic. He was awarded an OBE in the 2013 New Year Honours.

26

TWENTY-SIX

Samuel Pepys began to write his diary on New Year's Day 1660.

Pepys was born in London in 1633. The son of a tailor and the fifth of eleven children, he was the oldest to reach adulthood. After schooling in Huntingdon and London, Pepys graduated from Magdalene College, Cambridge, in 1654. Soon after, Pepys began work back in London for his father's cousin, Edward Montagu, a member of the Cromwellian protectorate's council of state. In 1658 Pepys survived a potentially life-threatening operation to remove a kidney stone – a recovery he vowed to celebrate on each anniversary. Later in the year, Pepys secured an appointment in the office of George Downing, a teller of the exchequer. It was while in this post that he began his diary. It recounts both Pepys's personal life and contemporary political and national events including the plague of 1665, the Great Fire of London in 1666 and the arrival of the Dutch fleet in the Thames during the second Anglo-Dutch war in 1667. The diary was written in a form of shorthand and was first transcribed in the early nineteenth century. Concerned for his eyesight, Pepys stopped writing his diary at the end of May 1669 and never resumed it. Montagu was made the Earl of Sandwich in 1660, and in the same year his patronage provided Pepys with a post as the clerk of the acts at the Navy Board. Pepys's career flourished and he became the secretary to the Admiralty in 1673, introducing many reforms. He was also elected as an MP and spent two years in the 1680s as the president of the Royal Society. He died in 1703, aged seventy. Pepys's diary and the rest of his extensive library of some 3,000 volumes are in the care of Magdalene College.

In 1831 HMS Beagle set out from Plymouth Sound under the command of **Robert Fitzroy**.

HMS *Beagle* circumnavigated the globe in a voyage which lasted almost five years. Its primary task was to undertake a hydrographic survey along the coast of South America. The voyage also gave the 22-year-old Charles Darwin, chosen as the ship's naturalist and companion for Fitzroy, the opportunity to study the geology and natural history of many far-flung locations first hand, which laid the groundwork for his theory of evolution. Fitzroy was appointed as the second governor of New Zealand in 1843, but he was recalled in 1845. Three years later he became the superintendent of the Woolwich dockyard. His last naval command before retiring from active service in 1850 was HMS *Arrogant*. Four years later, Fitzroy became the head of what would develop into the UK meteorological office. He gathered weather data using a network of telegraphic stations and pioneered weather charts and forecasting. In 1863 Fitzroy published his *Weather Book* and was also promoted to vice admiral, but ill health led him to take his own life in 1865 at the age of fifty-nine. In 2002 the shipping-forecast area Finisterre was renamed Fitzroy in his honour.

Isambard Kingdom Brunel *was appointed chief engineer for the Great Western Railway (GWR) in 1833.*

The GWR, under Brunel's technical guidance, constructed the first line between London and Bristol. The project showcased his engineering talent, and was also novel with its adoption of a wider gauge (7 feet, 0 ¼ inch) than that previously used. Brunel believed that this would offer better high-speed performance, although after his death the GWR network was converted to standard gauge. Brunel also designed large steamships: *Great Western* (which made its first transatlantic crossing in 1838), *Great Britain* (the first large iron screw-propelled ship, launched in 1843) and the *Great Eastern* (launched in 1858, then the largest ship ever built). Brunel is also remembered for his design of the Clifton suspension bridge. The foundation stone was laid when he was only twenty-four, but due to financing issues it was not completed during his lifetime, with the bridge towers on either side of the river Avon standing alone for close to twenty years. Construction restarted after his death (in 1859 at the age of fifty-three), and the bridge was opened in 1864.

Jesse Boot began an advertising campaign in the 'Nottingham Daily Express' for his herbalist shop in 1877.

In 1877 Boot also took full control of the business that had been started by his late father, John. Under Jesse's stewardship it flourished and by the outbreak of World War One there were over 550 shops throughout Britain. Boot remained at the helm until he was seventy when he sold the business to the United Drug Company of America and retired to Jersey (Boots returned to British ownership in 1933). Boot, who gave generously to his home city of Nottingham, was honoured with a knighthood in 1909, made a baronet in 1916 and became Baron Trent of Nottingham in 1928, three years before his death, in 1931, at the age of eighty-one.

Harry Vardon won golf's Open Championship in 1896.

This was the first of six Open victories for Vardon, a record which still stands. As the nineteenth century gave way to the twentieth, Vardon was at the top of his form with a triumph in the 1900 US Open, in addition to his Open wins in this period (1898, 1899 and 1903). Vardon popularised the grip – the one most commonly used by professionals – which bears his name. Ill health due to tuberculosis and trouble with his putting saw his fortunes wane after his 1903 Open victory, but he was able to recapture the title again in 1911 and for the last time in 1914. A late career highlight was a second place at the US Open at the age of fifty in 1920. Vardon also designed courses and wrote successfully on how to play the game. He died in 1937 at the age of sixty-six. The Vardon trophy was instituted by the US PGA in his honour.

*In 1905 a paper by **Albert Einstein** entitled 'Zur Elektrodynamik Bewegter Körper' (On the electrodynamics of moving bodies) was published in the journal 'Annalen der Physik'.*

Einstein's paper contained what would later be referred to as his special theory of relativity. It considered 'non-accelerating frames of reference' and stated that the speed of light was fixed for everyone and was not influenced by, or relative to, the speed of motion of an observer, or the speed of a light-emitting source. Using this postulate, Einstein was able to adjust the laws of mechanics to accommodate James Clerk Maxwell's electromagnetic theory, formulated forty years previously. Produced while he worked as a patent officer in Berne, his publication revolutionised physics as it challenged the accepted Newtonian view of the relationship between space and time. In the same year (referred to as his *annus mirabilis*), Einstein published three other papers. One of these on the photo-electric effect would be cited for his award of the 1921 Nobel Prize in Physics. He also published a paper on Brownian motion and his fourth contribution in that year introduced the famous equation which states the relationship between energy [E] and mass [m]: $E=mc^2$ (*c* refers to the speed of light). Einstein's general theory of relativity was published in 1916. This dealt with gravitation and introduced the concept of the curved nature of 'space-time'. A key prediction of the theory was validated by Arthur Eddington's expedition in 1919, which observed a solar eclipse and showed that the path of light near to the sun was being bent as expected on its way to the earth by the sun's gravitational field. Einstein moved to the US in 1933, where he died in 1955 at the age of seventy-six.

*In 1919 **John Alcock** and Arthur Brown became the first people to fly non-stop across the Atlantic Ocean.*

Alcock, who was the pilot, and Brown, the navigator, flew the modified Vickers Vimy bomber from Newfoundland, Canada, to Galway, Ireland, in nearly sixteen-and-a-half hours. Alcock had gained his Royal Aero Club aviator's certificate shortly after his twentieth birthday. He served with the Royal Naval Air Service during the First World War and was awarded the Distinguished Service Cross for an attack on three German seaplanes in the Eastern Mediterranean. Later, he was held as a prisoner of war by Turkey after engine problems had forced his plane down. Following his release and return to England, Alcock put himself forwards and was accepted by Vickers as the pilot for their transatlantic attempt. The successful flight won the prize of £10,000 offered by the *Daily Mail* – which was presented to them by Winston Churchill (then the minister for war) at the Savoy hotel. Knighthoods were also bestowed on both men by George V. Alcock continued his flying career with Vickers, although it ended tragically when he crashed in fog en route to Paris in a new Vickers aircraft later that year. Alcock survived the accident but died hours later from his injuries. He was twenty-seven.

'The Pleasure Garden', the debut feature of director **Alfred Hitchcock**, *was released in Germany in 1925.*

Hitchcock had started directing a film called *Number 13* three years previously, but it was not completed due to a lack of finance and all traces of the footage have been lost. His early films include *The 39 Steps* (1935), *Sabotage* (1936) and *The Lady Vanishes* (1938) prior to his move to Hollywood in 1939. Hitchcock's first US-based production, *Rebecca* (1940), brought him an Academy Award nomination for best director, but despite receiving four more nominations, the last being for *Psycho* (1960), Hitchcock was to remain unsuccessful in this category both at the Oscars and the Baftas. Renowned for his suspense-laden thrillers, he also made cameo appearances in each of his films from *Rebecca* onwards. Hitchcock was knighted months before his death, in 1980, at the age of eighty.

The first Mickey Mouse cartoon entitled 'Plane Crazy', produced by **Walt Disney**, *was released in 1928.*

Plane Crazy made little impact, but a few months later a third Mickey Mouse animation, *Steamboat Willie* (1928), became the first Disney feature to use synchronised sound. It was an immediate success following its release on 18 November 1928, the date that would later be assigned as Mickey's 'birthday'. Walt Disney was the original voice of Mickey up until the mid 1940s and had initially intended for him to be called Mortimer, before his wife Lillian intervened. Disney capitalised on the popularity of the character and, bolstered by his success, went on to produce the first animated feature film in 1937: *Snow White and the Seven Dwarfs*. Though many in the industry doubted the wisdom of this move, Disney was proved right and, as well as commercial success, it also gained him an honorary Academy Award in 1939. Further feature-length cartoons such as *Pinocchio* (1940) and *Bambi* (1942) followed. In addition to his film interests, Disney also established the first Disneyland theme park in 1955. He won a record breaking twenty-six Academy Awards (including four special awards) over the course of his career. Walt Disney died in 1966, at the age of sixty-five, less than a year before the last animated film he worked on, *The Jungle Book* (1967), was released.

*In 1930 **Amy Johnson**, piloting her Gipsy Moth aircraft named 'Jason', became the first woman to fly solo from Britain to Australia.*

The journey, from Croydon to Darwin, took nearly three weeks and earned Johnson a prize of £10,000 from the *Daily Mail*, and also a CBE. She took part in further long-distance flights and in her last, in 1936, she regained the record she had previously set for a flight between London and Cape Town. During the Second World War she joined the Air Transport Auxiliary as a pilot, but during a flight in early 1941 to deliver a plane she went off course and ditched in the Thames estuary. Johnson baled out and was seen alive, but attempts to rescue her failed. Her body was never recovered. She was thirty-seven.

***Vivien Leigh** won an Academy Award for best actress for her portrayal of Scarlett O'Hara in 'Gone with the Wind'.*

Born Vivien Hartley in Darjeeling, India, Leigh arrived in England as a six-year-old in 1920 to attend boarding school in Roehampton. An ambition to become an actress took her to Rada and she made her film debut with one line in *Things are Looking Up* (1935). Her performance on stage in the play *The Mask of Virtue* brought her critical acclaim and a five-year contract with producer Alexander Korda. The first film of this agreement, *Fire Over England* (1937), also starred Laurence Olivier, whom she married in 1940; their union lasted for two decades. Her casting as Scarlett O'Hara surprised many who had been expecting an American actress to land the part, and the performance brought her international recognition. Leigh's other film roles included the title role in *Anna Karenina* (1948) and as Blanche DuBois in *A Streetcar Named Desire* (1951), which brought her a second Academy Award for best actress in 1952. Her last film was *Ship of Fools* (1965). She died in 1967 at the age of fifty-three.

*'Look Back in Anger' by **John Osborne** premiered at the Royal Court Theatre in London in 1956.*

Written in a matter of weeks, the success of *Look Back in Anger* and its departure in tone and style from the established British theatrical offerings would prove to be highly influential, and spawned the term 'angry young man', represented by the play's main protagonist, Jimmy Porter. It transferred to Broadway and was nominated for a Tony Award for best play in 1958. *Look Back in Anger* and his next play, *The Entertainer*, established Osborne as a leading British dramatist. He also wrote for television and won an Academy Award for his adapted screenplay of *Tom Jones* (1963). Osborne died thirty years later at the age of sixty-five.

In 1957 **Ted Hughes** *won a competition for a first book of poems.*

The prize was publication of Hughes's first volume, *The Hawk in the Rain*, several months later, which was greeted with critical acclaim. His wife at the time, fellow poet Sylvia Plath, had typed out nearly all the poems in the collection and entered them into the competition. His second book of poetry, *Lupercal*, appeared in 1960. Hughes and Plath separated in 1962, and Plath and their two children moved from the family home in Devon to London. Months later Plath committed suicide. This had a profound effect on Hughes, with some blaming her death on his actions, and curtailed his poetic writing. He published Plath's posthumous volume, *Ariel*, in 1965. Hughes's next collection, *Wodwo*, appeared in 1967 and was followed by *Crow* three years later. Hughes also wrote books for children including *Nessie the Mannerless Monster* (1964) and later *The Iron Man* (1968). He succeeded John Betjeman as Poet Laureate in 1984. His last poetry collection, *Birthday Letters* (1998), addressed his relationship with Plath and won multiple awards. Hughes was appointed to the Order of Merit in 1998, months before his death at the age of sixty-eight.

Alan Bennett *first came to prominence with his appearance in the satirical revue 'Beyond the Fringe', staged as part of the Edinburgh Festival in 1960.*

The performance also featured Jonathan Miller, Peter Cook and Dudley Moore. Bennett won a scholarship to Exeter College, Oxford, where he read history. The success of *Beyond the Fringe* diverted him from academia and he turned to writing full-time. His initial contributions to the BBC blossomed into a six part comedy sketch series, *On the Margin* (1966), which he wrote and also starred in. Bennett's first stage play, *Forty Years*

On, debuted two years later. Numerous works for television, radio and stage followed, alongside acting appearances and volumes of prose. His most famous works include the plays *The Madness of King George III* (1991), and *The History Boys* (2004), both of which transferred to the cinema with a screenplay by Bennett (the former also gained him an Oscar nomination), and two series of his television monologues *Talking Heads* (1988 and 1998).

Valentina Tereshkova became the first woman in space when she spent nearly three days in orbit as the pilot of Vostok 6 in 1963.

Tereshkova's flight, during which she had the call sign 'chayka' (seagull), was the last launch of the Vostok spacecraft, and it would be over nineteen years before another woman, Svetlana Savitskaya, would journey into space. A key requirement for potential female cosmonauts was that they were parachutists, since it was necessary to leave the spacecraft in this manner as it neared the ground following re-entry. Tereshkova met this constraint since she had already demonstrated an interest in skydiving and parachuting, making her first jump at the age of twenty-two. Vostok 6 was her only spaceflight and she remains the youngest woman to travel into space.

*'The Andromeda Strain' by **Michael Crichton** was published in 1969.*

Crichton's first bestseller, *The Andromeda Strain* was made into a film in 1971 – many of his later novels also reached the big screen including *Jurassic Park*, *Congo*, *Rising Sun* and *Disclosure*. He published his first book, *Odds On*, under the pseudonym of John Lange while a student at Harvard Medical School in 1966. His cinematic directorial debut came with the self-penned film *Westworld* (1973). Crichton was also the creator of the highly successful medical drama TV series *ER*. In 1994, he had the unique distinction of simultaneously holding the number one US ranking in film (*Jurassic Park*), books (*Disclosure*) and television (*ER*). Crichton died in 2008, aged sixty-six.

*The first episode of 'Monty Python's Flying Circus', featuring **Michael Palin** and **Eric Idle**, was broadcast in 1969.*

Palin and Idle, along with the four other members of the team, Terry Jones, Graham Chapman, Terry Gilliam and John Cleese, devised, wrote and acted in this innovative comedy that would extend to four series and several films including *Monty Python and the Holy Grail* (1975) and *Life of Brian* (1979). Palin also co-wrote, with Terry Jones, and starred in the comedy series *Ripping Yarns* in the 1970s. The end of the next decade saw Palin pick up a Bafta best supporting actor award for *A Fish Called Wanda* (1988). He also became famous as a presenter of travel documentaries with his attempt in *Around the World in 80 Days* to complete the circumnavigation goal set in the similarly named Jules Verne novel. He followed this with a pole-to-pole journey, first broadcast in 1992, and further travel exploits. Palin received a CBE in 2000. Eric Idle, in addition to his comic offerings, also furnished the Python team with musical contributions that included 'Always Look on the Bright Side of Life', which made it to number three in the UK singles chart in 1991. Idle's first post-Python TV series, *Rutland Weekend Television*, aired in the mid-seventies and also gave birth to another musical creation (with Neil Innes) – the Rutles, a Beatles parody. More recently, Idle converted *Monty Python and the Holy Grail* (1975) into the musical *Spamalot*, which opened in 2005. He provided the lyrics and co-wrote the music of the production which won three Tony Awards in 2005, including best musical.

In 1971 **Rod Stewart** *reached number one in the UK singles chart for the first time with 'Maggie May'.*

'Maggie May', written by Stewart and Martin Quittenton, was originally the 'B' side of the single 'Reason to Believe', but radio DJs preferred it to the 'A' side and it was reclassified, going on to become Stewart's first US number one single. The album from which it was taken, *Every Picture Tells a Story*, also reached the top on both sides of the Atlantic, which resulted in Stewart becoming the first artist to simultaneously hold the number one spot in the singles and album charts both in the UK and the US. Stewart's next four studio albums all topped the British chart and he has notched up another five UK number one singles, the best-selling of which was 'Sailing' in 1975. Stewart was awarded a CBE in 2007. His 2010 album *Fly Me to the Moon . . . The Great American Songbook Volume V* reached the top five in the UK and US. It was followed by *Merry Christmas, Baby* in 2012.

In 1974 'Carrie' was the first novel by **Stephen King** *to be published.*

The success of *Carrie* allowed King to leave his job as an English teacher and take up writing full-time. He followed *Carrie* with *Salem's Lot* and his further novels include *The Shining, The Stand, Christine* and *Misery*. Many of his books have been adapted for the screen, with *Carrie* the first to be released in 1976. Other notable film treatments of his work include *Stand by Me* (1986) and *The Shawshank Redemption* (1994). King has published over fifty novels, as well as non-fiction and short story collections.

At the 1976 Winter Games in Innsbruck, Austria, **John Curry** *became Britain's first male Olympic figure skating champion.*

Curry also triumphed at the world and European Championships in the same year and afterwards turned professional, forming his own company of ice dancers. Dancing was his original interest, but parental disapproval provoked his switch to skating. Curry's distinctive style incorporated balletic dance elements into his artistic routines. His first competitive win came at the age of eight and in 1970 Curry became the British champion for the first time at the age of twenty-one. He was awarded an OBE in the 1976 Queen's Birthday Honours. Curry died in 1994 at the age of forty-four.

The 'Gossamer Albatross', piloted and powered by **Bryan Allen**, *crossed the English Channel in 1979.*

Allen, an amateur cyclist, took nearly three hours to complete the first human-powered flight from England to France, as he pedalled the *Gossamer Albatross* to an average altitude of five feet. The plane had a special lightweight construction, with an empty weight of only 32kg. Its designer, Paul MacCready, won the second Kremer Prize (£100,000) as a result of the successful crossing. MacCready also won the inaugural Kremer Prize for the first human-powered flight around a specified figure-of-eight course – achieved in 1977 with Bryan Allen piloting the *Gossamer Condor*.

On Valentine's Day 1984, **Jayne Torvill** *and Christopher Dean won a gold medal for ice dancing at the Winter Olympics in Sarajevo, Yugoslavia.*

Torvill and Dean's memorable free dance to the music of Ravel's *Bolero* received a perfect score for artistic impression, with all nine judges awarding the maximum six marks available, and a further three sixes for technical merit. Already European champions, the duo also won the world title for the fourth successive time before turning professional. They were awarded the BBC Sports Personality of the Year award in 1984, and ten years later they made a surprise return to Olympic competition in Lillehammer, Norway, when they took home the bronze medal. The pair announced the retirement of their skating partnership in 1998. Torvill had begun skating at the age of eight and first paired with Dean in 1975. Together they have won seven British, four European and four World Ice Dancing Championships. They were each awarded an MBE in 1981 and an OBE in 2000.

Ian Hislop became the editor of the magazine 'Private Eye' in 1986.

Four years later Hislop, who graduated from Magdalen College, Oxford, with a degree in English literature, took his place as one of the regular panellists on the BBC panel show *Have I Got News for You*, and has taken part in every edition to date. He has also written for radio and television (including such comedies as *Gush* and *My Dad's the Prime Minister*), and was a contributor to the satirical ITV puppet show *Spitting Image*.

'The Last Resort with Jonathan Ross' made its television debut on Channel 4 in 1987.

The show, with a format devised by Ross in partnership with Alan Marke, was his first presenting role on TV. After completing four series, Ross went on to feature in various radio and television shows over the next decade. He took over the helm of the BBC's film review programme in 1999 as well as starting his Saturday morning Radio 2 programme in the same year. His television chat show *Friday Night with Jonathan Ross* aired between 2001 and 2010. He was awarded an OBE in 2005 for services to broadcasting. In 2010 Ross announced his departure from the BBC and launched his new ITV show in the following year.

Chris Evans co-hosted with Gaby Roslin the launch of Channel 4's 'The Big Breakfast' in 1992.

The Big Breakfast was the first of a number of media triumphs for Evans – who went on to form his own company, Ginger Productions, which produced Evans-fronted shows such as *Don't Forget Your Toothbrush* and *TFI Friday*. He became the presenter of the BBC Radio 1 breakfast show in 1995 but left in 1997 and subsequently moved to Virgin Radio. The station was later acquired by his Ginger Media Group, which he then sold in a multimillion-pound deal. Evans returned to the BBC in 2006 as the presenter of the Radio 2 drive-time slot. At the start of 2010, he took over the Radio 2 breakfast show previously presented by Terry Wogan.

Matthew Dent was announced as the winner of the competition to redesign seven of the UK's coins (from the 1p to the £1) in 2008.

Dent's entry split the image of the Royal Arms across six of the pieces, with the pound coin showing the complete shield. Dent studied art at Coleg Menai in Bangor, Wales, and completed a degree in graphic design at the University of Brighton. He received a total prize of £35,000 for his winning submission, which heralded the first change in the design of Britain's coinage for approximately forty years.

Alastair Cook became the youngest Englishman to reach 5,000 runs in test cricket, during England's victorious 2010–11 Ashes series in Australia.

Cook amassed 766 runs during seven innings as England won the Ashes in Australia for the first time in twenty-four years. Already assured of victory after the fourth test, England won the fifth to take the series by three to one, with Cook's 189 runs taking him past the 5,000 mark. Only Sachin Tendulkar, at twenty-five, has reached this milestone at an earlier age. Cook faced India in his 2006 test debut, when he recorded a maiden test century with 104 in the second innings to add to his 60 runs in the first. Since his first appearance in 2003, Cook has played all his county cricket for Essex. He was awarded an MBE in 2011. Cook succeeded Andrew Strauss as the captain of the England cricket team in 2012.

Jessica Ennis won a gold medal for the heptathlon at the 2012 London Olympics.

Ennis had been unable to compete at the previous Games in Beijing due to injury, but her debut Olympic appearance in London saw her take gold as she set a new British record of 6,955 points. Ennis began the event with a personal best performance in the 100m hurdles; her time of 12.54 seconds was the best ever in the heptathlon and also set a new British record. Her parents sparked her interest in athletics at the age of ten when they took her to summer holiday sessions aimed at giving children experience of the sport. The following year she joined the City of Sheffield

Athletic Club and five years later won the high jump competition at the English Schools Championship. Ennis's first senior podium finish was in the 2006 Commonwealth Games where she won bronze for the heptathlon. She became Britain's first world champion in the event in 2009 and one year later added the European title. She was awarded an MBE in 2011 and a CBE in the 2013 New Year Honours.

27
TWENTY-SEVEN

*The first volume of poetry by **Robert Burns** to appear in print, entitled 'Poems, Chiefly in the Scottish Dialect', was published in 1786.*

Burns was born in Alloway, Ayrshire, the son of a tenant farmer and the eldest of seven children. His father's hard work on the farm was beset by misfortune and he died when Robert was twenty-five. Burns and his brother Gilbert then leased another farm, which again proved difficult to work. Two years later in 1786, Robert transferred his interest in the venture to Gilbert and made plans to immigrate to Jamaica, before the success of his debut volume helped to prompt a rethink. *Poems, Chiefly in the Scottish Dialect*, which includes 'To a Mouse', 'Address to the Deil' and 'The Cotter's Saturday Night', sold out within a month. Burns remained in Scotland and an expanded second edition was published in Edinburgh in 1787. He also worked on the *The Scots Musical Museum*, a project by James Johnson to gather together the lyrics and music of all Scottish songs. It was published as six volumes between 1787 and 1803. Burns was the de facto editor and major contributor, providing approximately two hundred songs – some collected and reworked by Burns such as 'A Red, Red Rose' and 'Auld Lang Syne', but the majority of which were original, including 'Ae Fond Kiss' and 'Sweet Afton'. Burns married Jean Armour in 1788, but only three of their nine children would survive infancy. He began work as an excise officer in 1789, although he also made a brief return to farming near Dumfries. His narrative poem 'Tam O'Shanter' appeared two years later. Burns died at the age of thirty-seven in 1796 on the same day that his last son, Maxwell, was born. Regarded as the national poet of Scotland, his life and work are celebrated on 25 January (his birthday) with the social occasion known as a 'Burns supper'.

In 1875 **Matthew Webb** *became the first person to swim the English Channel.*
   This was Webb's second attempt in less than two weeks and, covered in porpoise oil, he made the crossing in 21 hours and 45 minutes. Formerly a merchant navy captain, Webb took up a career as a professional swimmer, but his 1883 attempt to swim through the treacherous whirlpool rapids below Niagara Falls ended in his tragic death. Webb, who was thirty-five, was buried in a cemetery near the Falls.

Frank Woolworth *opened his first successful store in Lancaster, Pennsylvania, in 1879.*
   Woolworth had started his career in retail six years earlier with a job as a sales assistant in a dry-goods store in New York where he worked for free for the first three months. During his time there, Woolworth got the idea for his 'five and dime' stores when he saw surplus stock being sold off at a fixed price of five cents. He saw the potential in having a whole store organised on this basis and with the backing of his former employer, William Moore, opened his first shop in 1879 with all goods priced at five cents. It didn't succeed but Woolworth tried again shortly afterwards in a better location, this time broadening the range to include ten-cent items. The store was a success and by the time of his death in 1919, at the age of sixty-six, Woolworth's retail empire encompassed over one thousand outlets. The first Woolworth store in the UK was opened in Liverpool in 1909, and the name would be a fixture in numerous British towns until early 2009. Woolworth's legacy includes the Woolworth building in New York which was the tallest in the world when it was completed in 1913, and was paid for in cash.

Willis Carrier *filed his patent for an 'Apparatus for Treating Air' in 1904.*
   Carrier's patent was the first of many that he would lodge related to air conditioning. He had initially solved the problem of humidity control for a New York printer in 1902, and after further development he submitted his patent application, which was granted in 1906. Carrier was still working for the Buffalo Forge Company at this time, where he would remain until

1915 when he and several other engineers founded the Carrier Engineering Corporation. He died in 1950 at the age of seventy-three.

*The new British Medical Association building, which featured the first London sculptural commission of **Jacob Epstein**, opened in 1908.*

The eighteen nude sculptures that Epstein created, collectively called *Ages of Man*, proved to be controversial for the Edwardian public. (The building is now Zimbabwe House, and functions as the Embassy of Zimbabwe.) It would not be the last time that Epstein's work attracted such a reaction; his sculptures of 1929 entitled *Day and Night* (located at the present-day head office of London Underground) also aroused controversy. Epstein also became noted for his bronze portrait studies, which included subjects such as Albert Einstein and T.S. Eliot. His sculpture *St Michael's Victory over the Devil* adorns the rebuilt Coventry Cathedral and was completed one year before his death, in 1959, at the age of seventy-eight. He was knighted in 1954.

*'The Sun Also Rises', the first full-length novel by **Ernest Hemingway**, was published in 1926.*

Hemingway's semi-autobiographical work, centred on a group of expatriate Americans in Paris and Spain, gave him his first major success. *The Sun Also Rises* was renamed *Fiesta* when released in Britain, and included scenes of the 'running of the bulls' in Pamplona. As well as short-story collections and non-fiction, Hemingway had another five novels published in his lifetime. The last of these, *The Old Man and the Sea*, was published in 1952. Two years later, Hemingway was awarded the Nobel Prize in Literature. He committed suicide in 1961, at the age of sixty-one, using a shotgun.

*In 1931 **Salvador Dalí** completed the painting of 'The Persistence of Memory'.*

The striking image of melted, limp watch faces has arguably become Dalí's most famous work and was first exhibited in Paris shortly after its completion. Dalí, who was born in Figueres in the Catalonia region of north-east Spain, began painting in boyhood and studied at the École des Beaux-Arts in Madrid. The subconscious was a major theme of his work (the dream theories of Sigmund Freud were a key influence) and

Dalí became a leading member of the Surrealists in the late 1920s. He also contributed to the movement with two films, *Un Chien Andalou* (*An Andalusian Dog*) and *L'Age d'Or* (*Age of Gold*), released in 1929 and 1930 respectively. These were co-written with Luis Buñuel whom he had met as a student in Madrid. Differences with the Surrealists led to his expulsion from the group in the 1930s. To the wider public Dalí became not just known for his artwork but also for his eccentric, flamboyant persona – he once dressed in a deep-sea diving suit to give a lecture and filled a borrowed Rolls Royce with cauliflower before driving it to Paris. Around the time of his split from the Surrealists, Dalí's paintings became more classical in style and frequently reflected scientific and religious themes. Famous works in this period include *Exploding Raphaelesque Head* (1951), *Christ of St. John of the Cross* (1951) and *The Disintegration of the Persistence of Memory* (1952-54) in which the limp watch faces returned as he disassembled the earlier painting on which it was based. Dalí spent his last years back in Figueres where he died in 1989, aged eighty-four.

Roy Plunkett *discovered polytetrafluoroethylene, which would later be trademarked as Teflon, in 1938.*
   While working at DuPont's Jackson Laboratory in New Jersey, Plunkett noticed during an experiment related to refrigerants that one sample had turned into a waxy solid overnight. The substance aroused his curiosity and he found that it exhibited some remarkable properties such as being unaffected by corrosive acids, had a low coefficient of friction and was a good electrical insulator. Teflon has since found many uses including as a coating for 'non-stick' cookware. Plunkett remained at DuPont until his retirement in 1975. He died in 1994, aged eighty-three.

The flight of the first jet-powered aircraft, a Heinkel He 178, with an engine designed by **Hans von Ohain**, *took place in August 1939.*
   The first jet-powered flight took place three years after Ohain had received a patent for his jet-engine design. (Frank Whittle, working independently, had registered his first jet patent in 1930.) Ohain continued with the development of his engine during the war. He left Germany for the United States in 1947, and began work at the Wright-Patterson Air Force Base as a research scientist. By the mid-1970s he was chief scientist

of the Aero Propulsion Laboratory, and retired in 1979. Ohain died in 1998 at the age of eighty-six.

In 1939, shortly after the outbreak of World War Two, **Alan Turing** *reported to the government's code-breaking centre at Bletchley Park.*

Turing's contribution was key to the breaking of the German enigma code used for encrypted transmissions. He was also a pioneer in the theory of computing, and gave his name to the test he proposed to determine whether or not a machine can be said to have intelligence. He described this test in his 1950 paper entitled 'Computing Machinery and Intelligence'. Turing died in 1954 at the age of forty-one, with the inquest concluding that he had committed suicide.

Sam Walton *opened his first retail store in Newport, Arkansas, in 1945.*

A graduate from the University of Missouri, Walton's first retail experience was as a management trainee for J. C. Penney. After serving in the army, Walton returned to retailing with his own store in Newport, aided by a loan from his father-in-law. The store was successfully operated under the Ben Franklin franchise, but Walton had to give it up when the lease expired nearly five years later. His next venture, a store called Walton's Five and Dime, opened in Bentonville, Arkansas, in 1951 (it is now the Wal-Mart visitor's centre). Walton opened more stores in partnership with family members and others, many under the Ben Franklin franchise, until in 1962, at the age of forty-four, he opened the first Wal-Mart in Rogers, Arkansas. Walton and his wife provided 95% of the funds needed, borrowing heavily to create the beginning of a chain that would make Walton a multibillionaire. He died in 1992, aged seventy-four. Seven years later Wal-Mart established a presence in Britain with the purchase of the Asda supermarket chain.

In 1953 **Richard Burton** *received the first of his seven Academy Award nominations, for best supporting actor, for his role as Philip Ashley in 'My Cousin Rachel'.*

Burton made his Hollywood debut in *My Cousin Rachel* (1952) and his performance won him a Golden Globe in 1953 for most promising newcomer. The following year, he was Oscar nominated for his appearance in *The Robe* (1953) – the first of six best actor nominations that concluded with *Equus* (1977). Burton (originally Jenkins) took his surname from a teacher at Port Talbot secondary school who took him under his wing, became his legal guardian and encouraged him to be an actor. He made his London theatre debut at the age of eighteen in 1944. Following service with the RAF during the war, Burton returned to acting and made his film debut in *The Last Days of Dolwyn* (1949). In the theatre his Shakespearean performances drew critical acclaim. Burton's relationship with actress Elizabeth Taylor generated much media interest: they made eleven films together, beginning with *Cleopatra* (1963), and were married to each other twice. His last film performance was as O'Brien in *Nineteen Eighty-Four* (1984), also the year of his death at the age of fifty-eight.

Hugh Hefner *launched 'Playboy' magazine in 1953.*

A few years after leaving university, Hefner found work as a copywriter for *Esquire* magazine. When his request for a $5 rise was rejected, Hefner decided to start his own publication, but failed to gather enough investment. Undeterred, and after a short period during which he figured that there was a gap in the market for a men's magazine, Hefner raised money from family and friends. This, along with $600 he had borrowed (giving his furniture as the loan guarantee), was used to publish the first issue of *Playboy* with its nude centrefold of Marilyn Monroe. It sold over 50,000 copies, a figure that would rise to seven million a month for editions of the magazine in the 1970s. Hefner, now in his eighties, is editor-in-chief and chief creative officer of Playboy Enterprises, Inc.

Yuri Gagarin *became the first man in space, and the first to orbit the earth, in 1961.*

Gagarin, born in Klushino, Russia, qualified as a pilot with the Soviet Air Force before being selected for cosmonaut training. His mission into space aboard Vostok 1 had an official duration of one hour and forty-eight minutes, with Gagarin, after re-entry, completing the final part of the descent by parachute as planned. It was to be his only spaceflight. Just under seven years after his historic journey Gagarin was killed, at the age of thirty-four, when a MiG-15UTI he was piloting crashed while on a training mission. The accident, the definitive cause of which has never been established, also killed his instructor Vladimir Seryogin.

Brian Epstein *became the manager of the Beatles in 1961.*

The Beatles came to Epstein's attention when he was working in the family-retail business in Liverpool, managing a large record shop. The band would become his first management appointment in the music business. Epstein created a new image for the group – matching suits and haircuts – and encouraged them to cultivate a more professional tone on stage. The Beatles attended an audition at Decca Records on New Year's Day 1962, but failed to secure a record contract; a fate that befell them on several other occasions. Eventually they were signed to the Parlophone label by George Martin later in 1962, and had their first chart success with 'Love Me Do'. Epstein took on the management of many more artists, including Gerry and the Pacemakers and Cilla Black. He died in 1967 at the age of thirty-two.

Jim Clark *won his first Formula One World Championship in 1963.*

Driving a Lotus, Clark won seven out of the ten races to take the drivers' title in 1963. He won the championship again two years later, and was also victorious in the Indianapolis 500 – the first win by a non-American for over forty years. The son of a farmer, Clark's motorsport career began at the age of twenty and after various local and national events he made his Formula One debut at the 1960 Dutch Grand Prix behind the wheel of a Lotus. He achieved his first grand prix win in 1962 and went on to become the championship runner-up. He was awarded an OBE two years later. Regarded as one of the finest drivers of all time, Clark's last victory, in 1968, took his total number of wins to twenty-five and surpassed the record held by Juan Fangio. Three months later at the age of thirty-two, Clark was killed when his car left the track, possibly due to a puncture, during a Formula Two race at Hockenheim.

Abba, with **Benny Andersson** *on keyboards, won the 1974 Eurovision Song Contest held in Brighton.*

In 1974 the contest was decided by the votes of the ten-strong 'Eurovision jury' in each country, who each assigned one point to their favourite song. Five countries, including the UK, awarded zero points to Abba. However, their song 'Waterloo', co-written by Andersson along with Björn Ulvaeus and Stig Anderson, still won the contest. It went on to reach number one in the UK and was a major hit in many other countries. Andersson had already tasted musical success in his homeland with the Hep Stars: at one point they had three songs in the Swedish top ten. By the end of the sixties the four members of Abba had met and had started collaborating musically; the two couples would later marry. 'People Need Love' gave them a first hit in Sweden in 1972. In the next year they came third in the contest to select Sweden's entry for the Eurovision Song Contest, before winning the following year and going on to become one of the biggest-selling groups of all time.

The Police, with lead singer and bassist **Sting**, *reached number one in the UK singles chart with 'Message in a Bottle'.*

Written by Sting, 'Message in a Bottle' was the first of five number one UK singles for the band, which came together in 1977. Born Gordon Sumner in Wallsend in the north-east of England, Sting qualified as a teacher in the mid-seventies, while also continuing to play bass with various local bands. His nickname came from a black and yellow striped sweater he wore on stage. In 1977 Sting moved to London and soon after helped form the Police. Sting was the main songwriter for the trio and penned their UK number ones, including their last 'Every Breath You Take' in 1983. The Police released five studio albums, with the final four all making the top spot in the UK. The last to be released, *Synchronicity*, also gave them a US number one. Although the band split in 1984, Sting went on to have a successful solo career. So far, he has released ten studio albums, won numerous awards, including a Golden Globe, and was awarded a CBE in 2002.

Sandy Lyle *won golf's Open Championship in 1985.*

Lyle's victory at Sandwich, by one stroke over American Payne Stewart, was the first by a British golfer for sixteen years. Lyle also played in the winning Ryder Cup team that year, the first time the US had been defeated for nearly thirty years, and helped to defend the trophy two years later. Further success came in 1988 with his victory in the US Masters, which made him, at the age of thirty, the first British golfer to don the winner's celebrated green jacket. Similar to his other major win at the Open, Lyle took the US Masters' title by a one stroke margin.

Helen Sharman became the first Briton in space when she was a crew member of Soyuz TM–12 in 1991.

Sharman returned to earth nearly eight days later on board Soyuz TM–11 after visiting the Soviet space station *Mir*, where she carried out various experiments while in orbit. Sharman was selected after she had answered an advertisement looking for someone to become the first British astronaut, with the funding for the project, named Juno, provided by a private consortium. There were approximately 13,000 applications and Sharman was the only woman to make it to the final four. Two candidates were selected for months of training in the Soviet Union before Sharman was finally chosen for the flight. She was awarded an OBE in 1992.

Lennox Lewis was declared to be the WBC heavyweight boxing champion in 1993.

Lewis had been the number one challenger to the WBC incumbent, Riddick Bowe, but his refusal to fight Lewis saw him stripped of his title. It was transferred to Lewis, making him the first British-born fighter to hold a heavyweight world title in the twentieth century. The last of his three successful defences of the WBC crown was an all-British clash against Frank Bruno. A technical knockout ended his reign in the next fight, but Lewis exacted revenge on his opponent, Oliver McCall, by reclaiming the title in 1997. Two years later Lewis faced Evander Holyfield in two bouts – at which the WBC, IBF and WBA heavyweight crowns were at stake. Following a draw in the first fight, Lewis won the second on points to become the undisputed world heavyweight champion (he later forfeited his WBA title over a disagreement about his next opponent). He won his next three fights, but lost his IBF, WBC and IBO (awarded after his win over Holyfield) titles to Hasim Rahman in 2001. In the rematch less than seven months later, Lewis again reclaimed his titles. He boxed successfully on two more occasions, the next of these a round eight knockout of Mike Tyson, before retiring, at the age of thirty-eight, in 2004. Lewis was awarded a CBE in 2002.

Colin McRae won the World Rally Championship in 1995.

Driving a Subaru Impreza, McRae became the youngest driver and the first Briton to win the world rally title, as he took victory in the last round of the season, in Britain, to clinch the championship. He was runner-up in the two successive championships and, after switching to the Ford team, was again second in 2001. McRae made his World Rally Championship debut in 1987 behind the wheel of a Vauxhall Nova. He became Scottish rally champion the following year and notched up two British rally titles in 1991 and 1992. McRae was killed in 2007, at the age of thirty-nine, when the helicopter he was piloting crashed. The accident also claimed the life of his son, aged five, and two friends. McRae was awarded an MBE in 1996.

Paula Radcliffe won the long course gold medal at the World Cross-Country Championships in 2001.

Radcliffe defended her title in the following year and also won her debut London Marathon as she set the second fastest time in marathon history and established a new European record. She improved on this performance later in the season when she set a new world record at the Chicago Marathon and subsequently broke it at the next London event in 2003 with a time that remains the current world best for a woman. Radcliffe showed her early promise with victory in the junior race at the 1992 World Cross-Country Championships when she was eighteen, but surprisingly, despite her many successes, she has yet to win an Olympic medal. She finished just outside a podium placing for the 10,000m at the 2000 Games in Sydney, and in the next two Olympics her chances of a medal were hampered by injury; in 2004 she had to retire from the marathon and in 2008 she could only manage a finish in 23rd place. Injury also forced her to withdraw from the 2012 London Olympics only one week before the marathon. Radcliffe was awarded an MBE in 2002.

Victoria Pendleton won a gold medal at the 2008 Beijing Olympic Games for the women's individual sprint cycling event.

Pendleton was aged nine when she entered her first cycling race. Her interest in the sport had been sparked by her father, himself an avid cyclist and former cycling champion. Pendleton won her first world individual sprint champion title at the 2005 World Championships – a feat that she has repeated on five further occasions between 2007 and 2012. Along with team-mate Jessica Varnish, Pendleton broke the world record in a qualifying round for the team sprint at the 2012 London Olympics, but the British pair was disqualified in the semi-final for a changeover infringement. Pendleton recovered from this disappointment to win her second Olympic gold medal, for the keirin, and also silver for the individual sprint at the London Games. She was awarded a CBE in 2013.

Matt Smith *made his television debut as Doctor Who in 2010.*

The eleventh actor to play Doctor Who on television, Smith is also the youngest. He had originally wanted to be a professional footballer and Smith played for the youth sides of Nottingham Forest and Leicester City before a serious back injury terminated his ambitions. He was guided to a future in drama by a teacher at his school in Northampton and subsequently studied the subject, as well as creative writing, at the University of East Anglia. Smith (a one-time member of the National Youth Theatre) first made an impression on the stage, with his performance in *That Face* earning him a London Evening Standard best newcomer award in 2008. His first major television role was in *Political Animals* (2007), in which he played a political researcher.

Amy Williams *won a gold medal for the bob skeleton at the 2010 Winter Olympics in Vancouver, Canada.*

Williams became Britain's first individual gold medallist at the Games since Robin Cousins in 1980, and the first solo female winner since Jeanette Altwegg in 1952. She also broke the track record twice during her four runs down the Vancouver course. The women's skeleton event made its first appearance at the Salt Lake City Olympics in 2002. It involves travelling along an ice track, face down and head first, on a sled which can reach speeds of over 80mph.

Michael Phelps *won four gold and two silver medals at the 2012 London Olympics.*

Phelps's six medals at the Games took his overall Olympic total to twenty-two, and beat the previous record holder, the gymnast Larisa Latynina, who won eighteen medals between 1956 and 1964. Phelps also holds the record for the most gold medals won at a single Olympics, when he won eight at the 2008 Beijing Games. When his London and

Beijing gold medal wins are added to the six he won at the 2004 Athens Games, his gold medal total is double that of his nearest challenger, Latynina. At the London Games, Phelps's victory in the 200m individual medley made him the first swimmer to win the same event at three consecutive Olympics, a feat which he repeated twenty-four hours later when he took gold in the 100m butterfly. Phelps has also won twenty-six gold medals at the World Championships and is the current world-record holder for the 100m butterfly, 200m butterfly and the 400m individual medley.

28

TWENTY-EIGHT

John Flamsteed became the first astronomer royal in 1675.

The post, inaugurated in the reign of Charles II, was described as 'astronomical observator' in the warrant of appointment, with the more familiar term coming into currency later. Flamsteed became the director of the new Royal Observatory at Greenwich, completed in 1676. The publication of his star catalogue, *Historia Coelestis,* in 1712 caused controversy since it was done without his permission and under the editorship of Edmond Halley, whom Flamsteed disliked and distrusted. Flamsteed strongly believed that the release of his data, which Isaac Newton and Halley had both been pressing for, was premature since he hadn't completed his mapping of the stars and also wanted to be sure of the data's accuracy before publication. He later secured 300 of the 400 copies printed, retained the pages that he was satisfied with and burnt the rest on a bonfire in Greenwich Park. With his death in 1719 at the age of seventy-three, he did not live to see the publication of his own version, which appeared in 1725.

In 1876 Alexander Graham Bell lodged his patent application for the telephone.

Bell's patent was granted less than a month later and despite challenges (for example by Antonio Meucci and Elisha Gray, with Gray lodging his patent caveat on the same day as Bell), he was able to defend it successfully. Bell was born in Edinburgh, but left for Canada at the age of twenty-three, and then moved to America where he took US citizenship in 1874. He continued his work with the deaf, which he had started in Britain, and became professor of vocal physiology and elocution at Boston University in 1873. The success of the telephone gave Bell the means to continue his inventive pursuits. He developed the photophone (which used light beams to transmit speech) with Charles Tainter, first patented in 1880. Other areas of interest for Bell included hydrofoils and aviation. Bell died in Canada in 1922 at the age of seventy-five. Although usually referred to by his full name, he only adopted his middle name at the age of eleven.

In 1887 'A Study in Scarlet' by **Arthur Conan Doyle** *became the first Sherlock Holmes story to be published when it appeared in 'Beeton's Christmas Annual'.*
Conan Doyle drew inspiration from Professor Joseph Bell when creating his most famous character, Sherlock Holmes. He met Bell, famed for his observant manner and deductive powers, while studying medicine at the University of Edinburgh. Holmes features in four novels and fifty-six short stories, and such was the popularity of the character that Conan Doyle was even forced to bring him back after Holmes's apparent death in *The Final Problem*. Conan Doyle also wrote many other works including *Rodney Stone* and *The White Company*. He served as a doctor during the Boer War and his book *The War in South Africa: its Cause and Conduct*, published in 1902, set out his defence of British policy and was instrumental in his award of a knighthood in the same year. He died in 1930 at the age of seventy-one.

Harold Harmsworth, *in partnership with his brother Alfred, launched the 'Daily Mail' in 1896.*
Within a few years of its launch, the circulation of the *Daily Mail* was over a million a day; the first newspaper to achieve this level of sales. The paper offered many prizes for aviation 'firsts' at the start of the twentieth century such as £1,000 for the first cross-channel flight. In 1910 Harold Harmsworth, the younger of the brothers, became a baronet, and, in 1914, Baron Rothermere. By the 1920s, he controlled a large press empire of both national and local titles. Rothermere died in 1940, aged seventy-two.

*Rolls–Royce was founded in 1906, sealing a partnership between Henry Royce and **Charles Rolls** that began with a lunchtime meeting in a Manchester hotel.*

Rolls, who owned a car dealership, agreed an exclusive contract with Royce to sell his motor cars which would be badged as Rolls-Royce. While Royce did the engineering, Rolls helped to publicise the cars with endeavours such as setting a new record for the London to Monte Carlo run in 1906. He also took a great interest in aviation and tried, with little support, to introduce aircraft manufacture to Rolls-Royce. He had already crossed the English Channel by balloon, and, in 1910, he became the first person to cross it both ways non-stop by aeroplane. However, tragedy struck just over one month later when, at the age of thirty-two, he crashed while making a landing in Bournemouth. Rolls became the first British person to be killed in an aeroplane accident.

*In 1909 **Ettore Bugatti** left his job at Deutz and set about establishing his own car factory, based in Molsheim near Strasbourg.*

The first Bugatti model to be produced, in 1910, was the Type 13. It had a four-cylinder, 1.3 litre engine that gave the car a top speed of 60mph. The First World War not only interrupted Bugatti production, but also resulted in the transfer of the Molsheim factory from German to French territory, when the region of Alsace-Lorraine was transferred to French jurisdiction by the 1919 Treaty of Versailles. After the war, Bugatti cars won races at Le Mans and the inaugural Monaco Grand Prix in 1929, where they were victorious on three further occasions in the next four years. The company's racing success added to its reputation for engineering finesse and beautiful design. World War Two brought more trouble for Bugatti as the occupation of France in 1940 forced the sale of his factory. He died in 1947 at the age of sixty-five. Attempts to revive the brand after the war were to fail and manufacturing ended in the 1950s. In 1998 Volkswagen purchased the Bugatti marque and built a new factory at Molsheim for the manufacture of the Bugatti Veyron. First produced in 2005, the Veyron claimed the record for the world's fastest production car with a top speed of 253mph. The Super Sport version reclaimed the record in 2010 when it achieved a speed of nearly 268mph.

*In 1924 **John Moores** co-founded Littlewoods football pools.*

The first four thousand football coupons were distributed outside Manchester United's Old Trafford ground; however, only thirty-five were returned. The continuing poor performance of the enterprise prompted Moores's two partners to leave the business before the end of the year. Moores bought them out, although one did give his original birth name, Littlewood, to the business. However, the perseverance of Moores was rewarded – the pools took off and less than ten years after starting out he became a millionaire. He also started the Littlewoods mail-order business in 1932 and later added a chain of department stores. Moores received a knighthood in 1980. He is also remembered for his charitable work, and in 1992, the year before his death at the age of ninety-seven, Liverpool John Moores University was named in his honour.

***Alan Blumlein** lodged his patent application for two channel sound reproduction in 1931.*

Blumlein referred to it as 'binaural' sound, better known today as stereo, and his patent covered both records and film soundtracks. It was granted in 1933, but his employer, EMI, did not commercially exploit the technology at the time. Blumlein's focus switched to the emerging technology of electronic television – many of the over one hundred patents that Blumlein filed were in this area. Blumlein also headed the EMI team whose all-electronic television system was chosen by the BBC in 1937 over John Logie Baird's mechanical-based one. During the Second World War he was involved in the development of radar systems and it was during a radar test flight that the 38-year-old Blumlein was killed when the Halifax bomber that he was aboard crashed in Wales.

***Roy Plomley** presented the first edition of 'Desert Island Discs', the radio show whose format he created, in 1942.*

The comedian Vic Oliver was Plomley's first guest, or 'castaway'. He was asked to choose his eight favourite records to take with him to the fictional island. In subsequent years the choice was extended to include one luxury item and one book. Plomley presented nearly eighteen hundred editions of the show until his death in 1985 at the age of seventy-one, making *Desert Island Discs* one of the longest-running radio shows (it continues to be broadcast today on Radio 4 with host Kirsty Young). In addition to other presenting duties on radio and television, Plomley was also a participant in panel games, wrote more than a dozen plays (*Cold Turkey* was his most successful) and was awarded an OBE in 1975.

Bill Haley and his Comets released 'Rock Around the Clock' in 1954.

'Rock Around the Clock' reached number seventeen in the UK singles chart in 1955, and was later a hit in the US, where its use in the film *Blackboard Jungle* (1955) propelled it to the number one spot. It would reach a similar position in the UK after it re-entered the chart in October 1955 following the film's release in Britain. 'Rock Around the Clock' became the UK's biggest-selling single of the 1950s and returned to the chart in the sixties and in 1974 when it registered a number twelve hit for the then 48-year-old Haley. The band's other chart entries include 'See You Later, Alligator' and 'Rockin' Through The Rye'. Haley died in 1981, aged fifty-five.

*In 1954 **David Attenborough** began presenting the television series 'Zoo Quest'.*

Attenborough graduated from Clare College, Cambridge, with a degree in natural sciences and spent two years in the Royal Navy for his National Service. He then went to work for a publisher and applied for a BBC radio job after seeing a newspaper advert. Although not selected for the position, he later accepted the offer of a place on a three-month training course and so began his long association with the BBC. *Zoo Quest*, which gave Attenborough the opportunity to go on location and report on wildlife in its natural habitat, was aired from 1954 until 1963. In 1965, Attenborough became the controller of the fledgling channel BBC2. Two years later, the station began transmitting the first colour broadcasts in the UK. He then became Director of Programmes at the BBC in 1969, but resigned three years later in order to return to making documentaries. His landmark natural history series *Life on Earth* made its debut in 1979, and it has been followed by other acclaimed series that explore the natural world – including *The Living Planet* (1984), *The Trials of Life* (1990), *The Life of Mammals* (2002) and more recently

Frozen Planet (2011). Attenborough was knighted in 1985 and appointed to the Order of Merit in 2005.

Chris Brasher *won a gold medal at the 1956 Melbourne Olympics for the 3,000m steeplechase.*

Brasher's victory was Britain's first athletics win at the Olympics for twenty years. Two years earlier he had helped set the pace, along with Chris Chataway, for Roger Bannister's record-breaking sub-four-minute mile. Brasher would be the only one of the trio to win an Olympic gold. Following his athletics achievements, Brasher enjoyed a career as a sports journalist and broadcaster. He was also the driving force behind the creation of the London Marathon in 1981, and completed the inaugural course himself in just under three hours, aged fifty-two. He was awarded a CBE in 1996. Brasher died in 2003, aged seventy-four.

William Roache *appeared as Ken Barlow in the first episode of 'Coronation Street', broadcast in December 1960.*

Roache is the only member of the original cast to have still been part of the series when it celebrated its fiftieth anniversary in 2010. A native of Derbyshire, Roache was largely educated in Wales and then spent five years in the Royal Welch Fusiliers, rising to the rank of captain. His portrayal of Ken Barlow won him a lifetime achievement award at the inaugural British Soap Awards in 1999. He received an MBE in 2001.

Julie Andrews *starred as the title character in the feature film 'Mary Poppins', released in 1964.*

Andrew's debut film appearance as the magical nanny won her both the Academy Award and Golden Globe for best actress. *Mary Poppins*, which mixed animation and live action, was the first Disney production to be nominated for a best picture Academy Award. Andrews had made her first professional solo stage appearance in 1947 at the age of twelve, and one year later appeared in the Royal Variety Performance. Famed for both the quality of her voice and its exceptional range, she was already a Broadway and television star by the time she was cast as the eponymous Mary Poppins. *The Sound of Music* (1965) and *Victor Victoria* (1982) brought Andrews further best actress Oscar nominations. She was made a Dame in 2000.

Bobby Charlton *was a member of the England football team that beat West Germany 4–2 to win the World Cup in 1966.*

Charlton scored England's first goal in the tournament and netted both of the team's goals in the semi-final match against Portugal to take England through to their Wembley encounter with West Germany. Charlton, a survivor of the Munich air disaster in 1958 which killed eight of his Manchester United team-mates and fifteen others, played virtually all his senior football for the Old Trafford side. His total of 758 appearances for the club, during which he won three league titles and one FA Cup medal, as well as captaining the side when they became the first English team (in 1968) to win the European cup, has only recently been surpassed by Ryan Giggs. Charlton still remains Manchester United's, and England's, top scorer with a total of 249 and 49 goals respectively. He ended his England career in 1970, at the age of 32, having amassed a record 106 caps. Charlton's last international game was a World Cup quarter-final appearance against West Germany; although on that occasion the Germans won after extra time. Charlton received a CBE in 1974 and was knighted twenty years later.

John Peel *joined the newly launched BBC Radio 1 in 1967.*

Peel initially co-hosted radio programmes on the BBC's new station, but early in 1968 he became a solo presenter. His path to a broadcasting career began in 1960 when (still under his original name of Ravenscroft) he was offered a ticket to the US by his father, the aim being to learn more about the cotton industry. Later he switched to the insurance business, but more significantly he obtained his first experience in radio as an unpaid presenter for a Dallas station. His Liverpudlian connections provided a boost to his career as the Beatles grew in popularity and further radio work followed in Dallas as well as Oklahoma and California. On his return to Britain in 1967, he became a disc jockey on the pirate station Radio London, which along with the others operating in the North Sea would soon be outlawed. This clampdown led to the re-organisation of the BBC's radio service and the emergence of Radio 1 in 1967. Peel, famed for his championing of fresh musical styles and new bands, became the longest-serving disc jockey on the station, continuing to broadcast until his sudden death, at the age of sixty-five, in 2004. His gravestone bears a line from his favourite song, The Undertones' 'Teenage Kicks', as he had requested.

Björn Ulvaeus and **Anni-Frid Lyngstad** *were members of Abba when they won the 1974 Eurovision Song Contest.*

Abba's winning song, 'Waterloo', was co-written by Ulvaeus, Benny Andersson and Stig Anderson. Ulvaeus, then a member of the hit Swedish folk group The Hootenanny Singers, first met Andersson in 1966. The pair began working together, culminating, with the addition of their respective female partners, Agnetha Fältskog and Anni-Frid Lyngstad, in the forma-tion of Abba. 'Waterloo' was the group's first UK number one though they would have to wait nearly two years before returning to the top with 'Mamma Mia' in 1976. Seven further Abba songs made it to the UK number spot, the last of which was 'Super Trouper' in 1980. After Abba's demise in 1982, Ulvaeus and Andersson collaborated with Tim Rice on the musical *Chess*. Lyngstad was born in Norway, but grew up in Sweden where she won a national talent contest in 1967. Lyngstad reached number one in Sweden for the first time with 'Min Egen Stad' in 1971 and her debut solo album, entitled *Frida*, was released in the same year. She has released four more studio albums, the latest of these being *Djupa Andetag* in 1996.

'Jaws', directed by **Steven Spielberg**, *was released in 1975.*

Often cited as the first summer 'blockbuster', *Jaws* was only the second major film release to be directed by Spielberg, following on from *The Sugarland Express* in 1974. A huge commercial success, *Jaws* won three Oscars (editing, original music score and sound), was nominated for best picture, and gave Spielberg his first Bafta nomination for best director. A keen teenage amateur film maker, Spielberg, at the age of seventeen, attended the premiere of his first full-length feature, *Firelight* (1964), at a local Arizona cinema. Five years later his short film *Amblin'* (1969) brought his creative skills to the attention of Universal Studios (and also provided the name for the production company he would form in the mid-1980s). During the early seventies, Spielberg worked in television on various series and also directed three TV movies including the Golden Globe nominated *Duel* (1971). After *Jaws*, Spielberg's career continued on an upward trajectory with *Close Encounters of the Third Kind* (1977) providing the first of his Academy Award nominations for best director. He has also been nominated for *Raiders of the Lost Ark* (1981), *E.T.: The Extra-Terrestrial* (1982), *Munich* (2005) and *Lincoln* (2012). Spielberg won his first best director Oscar for *Schindler's List* (1993) and won again for *Saving Private Ryan* (1998). Other major successes include *The Color Purple* (1985), *Jurassic Park* (1993), *Minority Report* (2002) and *War of the Worlds* (2005). Spielberg has also produced or executive produced other box-office hits such as the Back to the Future trilogy (1985–1990), the Men in Black trilogy (1997–2012) and the three latest Transformers films (2005–2011).

Allan Wells won a gold medal at the 1980 Moscow Olympics for the 100m, to become the second British winner of the event in Olympic history.

Edinburgh-born Wells also took the silver medal in the 200m, beaten by only two hundredths of a second by Pietro Mennea of Italy. Wells had originally competed as a long jumper and triple jumper before deciding to focus on sprinting. After the Moscow Olympics, he had further major sprint victories at the Commonwealth Games and in the European Cup. More than thirty years later, the times he set at the 1980 Olympics for the 100m (10.11 seconds) and 200m (20.21 seconds) remain Scottish records.

Florence Griffith-Joyner set a new world record for the 100m in 1988.

Griffith-Joyner's time of 10.49 seconds, set in the US Olympic trial, beat the previous time of 10.76 seconds achieved by Evelyn Ashford, and remains the current world record. Griffith-Joyner won three gold medals at the 1988 Seoul Olympics for the 100m, 200m and 4x100m relay events and set a world-record time, which still stands today, in the 200m final of 21.34 seconds. She also won silver for the 4x400m relay in Seoul. Griffith-Joyner retired from athletics after the Games and died only ten years later at the age of thirty-eight as a result of an epileptic seizure.

Jeremy Clarkson first appeared as a presenter on the BBC motoring show 'Top Gear' in 1988.

Clarkson, who worked as a journalist for various regional newspapers, formed the Motoring Press Agency in 1984 to road test cars and provide reports for local papers and automotive magazines. His reviews started to attract attention and four years later Clarkson made his debut on *Top Gear*. The show was re-launched with a new format in 2002, with Clarkson joined in the presenting duties by Richard Hammond and, since 2003, by James May. Clarkson has also written many books including *The World According to Clarkson* and *Don't Stop Me Now!*

In 1992 'Reservoir Dogs', written and directed by **Quentin Tarantino**, *received its premiere at the Sundance Film Festival.*

Tarantino also played one of the colour-coded criminals, Mr Brown, in the heist movie, which was his debut feature release. Tarantino's first experience of directing was with an amateur project called *My Best Friend's Birthday*, completed in 1987, although a fire destroyed the final reel of the finished film. *Reservoir Dogs* was critically acclaimed and Tarantino's next film, *Pulp Fiction* (1994), brought him an Academy Award best director nomination and an Oscar win for the screenplay, shared with Roger Avary. His other films include *Jackie Brown* (1997) and *Inglourious Basterds* (2009), which gained him a second Oscar nomination for best director. He won a second screenplay Oscar for *Django Unchained* (2012).

Stelios Haji-Ioannou *founded the airline easyJet in 1995.*

Haji-Ioannou began working for his father's shipping company in 1988 and, with a cash injection from his father, set up his own version called Stelmar Shipping in 1992. It was successfully floated on the New York Stock Exchange in 2001. The establishment of easyJet, with its low-cost model, helped to fuel the growth of budget air travel in Europe. Haji-Ioannou has also applied the 'easy' business philosophy to other areas such as car rental and hotels. His easyGroup, founded in 1998, manages the brand. Haji-Ioannou received a knighthood in 2006 and is the founder of the Stelios Philanthropic Foundation.

Pierre Omidyar *launched Auction Web, later to be renamed eBay, in 1995.*

Omidyar, a graduate of computer science from Tufts University, was working as a software developer when he started Auction Web and wrote the code for the site's launch over a weekend. A broken laser pointer was the first item to be sold for the sum of $14.83. The company was renamed eBay in 1997 – Omidyar's first choice of domain name, echobay (the name of his consultancy), was already registered so he opted for an alternative. The company went public in 1998 with the shares closing at the end of the first day at over $47, nearly $30 above the offer price. By the middle of 2010, eBay had over 94 million active accounts around the world and in the same year recorded $9.2 billion in revenue. Omidyar is currently a director of the company and chairman of the board.

Michael Johnson won a gold medal for the 200m at the 1996 Olympic Games in Atlanta to complete a unique double triumph.

Johnson's victory in the 200m, in a new world-record time of 19.32s, came only three days after he won the 400m, making him the first athlete to take gold at both events. Four years later in Sydney, the US athlete also became the first to successfully defend a 400m Olympic title. In the previous year Johnson had set a new world record, which still stands, of 43.18s. He also achieved six individual wins at the World Championships including, in 1995, a 200m and 400m double that prefigured his Olympic triumph.

Denise Lewis won a gold medal for the heptathlon at the 2000 Sydney Olympics.

Lewis was already the European champion in the heptathlon, a discipline which she first competed in as a teenager. The nineties saw her succeed on the international stage with golds in two Commonwealth Games and the runner-up spot in two World Championships. At the 1996 Atlantic Olympics, Lewis was Britain's only female track-and-field medallist when she won bronze. Her winning performance in Sydney was achieved despite crossing the line of the final 800m event with her lower left leg bandaged to ameliorate an Achilles problem. Injury, however, forced her to withdraw from the defence of her Olympic title in Athens, and she retired from the sport in 2005. Already an MBE, she was awarded an OBE in the 2001 New Year Honours list.

Ellen MacArthur broke the world record for a solo round-the-world voyage in 2005, completing the approximately 27,000 mile route in 71 days, 14 hours, 18 minutes and 33 seconds.

MacArthur, sailing in her boat named *B&Q*, beat the previous record by over a day in what was her first world-record attempt. Her success was many years in the making – MacArthur's first major sailing achievement was to sail solo around Britain when she was aged eighteen. On her return to England after her record-breaking success, MacArthur was awarded a damehood. In 2008 Francis Joyon reclaimed the world record he had lost to MacArthur.

Rebecca Romero won a gold medal for cycling's individual pursuit at the 2008 Olympic Games in Beijing.

Romero won a silver medal for rowing at the previous Games in Athens and thus her victory in cycling at the 2008 Olympics made her the first British woman, and only the second woman ever, to win Olympic medals at two different disciplines. Romero, who also took gold at the 2008 World Championships for the 3km individual pursuit and the women's team pursuit, was awarded an MBE in 2009.

29
TWENTY-NINE

*'Wuthering Heights' by **Emily Brontë** was first published under the pen name of Ellis Bell in 1847.*

Brontë was the fifth of six children. The elder two, Maria and Elizabeth, both died in childhood leaving Emily with two sisters, Charlotte and Anne, and one brother, Branwell. Emily received little formal schooling and was mainly educated at home by her father and aunt. In 1846, Brontë and her sisters, Charlotte and Anne, made their publication debut with a self-financed collection of their poems. Next, Brontë wrote *Wuthering Heights*, a tale of destructive passion set against the backdrop of the Yorkshire moors, which was to be her only novel. She had difficulty finding a publisher, and when she did find one agreeable she had to contribute financially to the undertaking. The book was not well received on publication, but is now regarded as one of the classic English novels. Brontë lost her brother to tuberculosis in 1848 and she herself was to die of the same illness nearly three months later at the age of thirty.

*In 1865 **Elizabeth Garrett Anderson** became the first woman to qualify as a medical practitioner in Britain when she obtained her licence from the Society of Apothecaries of London.*

The reluctance of the medical schools of the day to admit women was a barrier to Anderson's ambitions. She resorted to private tuition and, since women weren't explicitly barred from sitting the exams of the Society of Apothecaries, Anderson was able to take them and qualify as a doctor (the society then changed the rules to prevent other women following this path). In 1870 she added to her qualifications with an MD from the University of Paris. Anderson founded the New Hospital for Women in London in 1871 and it became the first hospital in Britain staffed wholly by women (she employed those with overseas degrees as house officers). Five years later, an Act of Parliament was passed which permitted women to become medical practitioners. Anderson retired in 1902 and six years later became the first female mayor in England at Aldeburgh. She died in 1917, aged eighty-one.

*William **Wrigley Jr.** founded the Wrigley Company in 1891.*

The son of a soap manufacturer, Wrigley's new business began by selling soap to the wholesale trade. As an incentive to his customers, Wrigley offered free baking powder, which proved so popular that he made it his main offering instead of soap. In 1892 he decided to offer chewing gum with the baking powder. The additional product again proved to be more popular, and Wrigley switched to the chewing-gum business. The familiar Juicy Fruit brand appeared in 1893, followed by Wrigley's Spearmint later that year. The Wrigley Company grew to be the biggest chewing-gum manufacturer in the world and was headed by a member of the Wrigley family until 2006. William Wrigley died in 1932, aged seventy.

***Frederick Banting**, under the aegis of John Macleod, and with his assistant Charles Best, discovered the hormone insulin in 1921.*

In 1922, fourteen-year-old diabetic Leonard Thompson became the first person to receive insulin injections. The initial dose was not pure enough to effect an improvement in his condition, but a second purer form, prepared by James Collip, successfully alleviated his diabetic symptoms. Banting and Macleod shared the 1923 Nobel Prize in Physiology or

Medicine, with Banting splitting his portion with Best – Macleod did likewise with James Collip. Banting was knighted in 1934 and died seven years later in a plane crash. He remains the youngest recipient of a Nobel Prize in Physiology or Medicine.

The first solo exhibition by **Henry Moore** *opened at the Warren Gallery in London in 1928.*

Moore's debut solo exhibition comprised fifty-one drawings and forty-two sculptures, including *Mother and Child* whose theme would be a recurring element in his life's work. Later in 1928, Moore was also awarded his first public commission and created the Portland stone relief *West Wind* to adorn the façade of the new headquarters of London Underground. Moore was born in Castleford, Yorkshire, and as a schoolboy decided to become a sculptor. After active service in the First World War, during which he took part in the Battle of Cambrai and was gassed, Moore studied first at the Leeds School of Art and then at the Royal College of Art in London where he took up a part-time appointment as an instructor in sculpture after graduating in 1924. In 1931 he joined the Chelsea School of Art, and established its first department of sculpture during his eight-year tenure. Moore's major commissions include *Madonna and Child* for St Matthew's Church, Northampton, and *Reclining Figure*, for the UNESCO headquarters in Paris. The latter, a large travertine marble piece unveiled in 1958, is an example of another of Moore's central themes that he frequently returned to during his career: reclining abstractions of the human figure. In addition to sculpture, Moore also won praise for his shelter drawings of Londoners taking refuge from the blitz. Moore declined a knighthood but was made a Companion of Honour in 1955 and appointed to the Order of Merit in 1963. He died in 1986 at the age of eighty-eight.

In 1945 **Joseph Cyril Bamford** *made his first product, a farm trailer, which marked the start of the business that would become better known as 'JCB'.*

Bamford had eschewed a career in the family firm, a farm-machinery business, in order to start up on his own. Three years later, he marketed Europe's first hydraulic tipping trailer. His classic product, the backhoe loader, usually simply referred to as a 'JCB' (the term has entered the

Oxford English Dictionary) appeared in 1953 and helped his business become a world leader in its sector. Bamford was awarded a CBE in 1969 and retired in 1975, passing the business on to his two sons. He died in 2001, aged eighty-four.

Emil Zátopek *won a unique trio of gold medals, for the 5,000m, 10,000m and the marathon, at the 1952 Olympic Games in Helsinki.*

At the previous Games, in London, Zátopek went home with two medals, gold for the 10,000m and silver for the 5,000m. His triple triumph in Helsinki was all the more remarkable given that he only entered the marathon at the last minute, and it was the Czech runner's first race over the 26 mile 385 yard distance. Not only that, but he won the event in a new Olympic-record time of 2 hours 23 minutes and 3.2 seconds (he had also set new Olympic-record times in the 5,000m and 10,000m at the same Games). Zátopek was posthumously awarded the Pierre de Coubertin medal shortly after his death in 2000, at the age of seventy-eight.

Mike Hawthorn *won the Formula One World Championship in 1958.*

Hawthorn, driving for Ferrari, became the first British driver to be crowned Formula One champion as he took the title by the slender margin of one point from his compatriot, Stirling Moss. The final placings were not decided until the last grand prix of the season, in Morocco. Moss won the race and also recorded the fastest lap (to gain an extra point), but Hawthorn's second place was enough to secure the championship. Hawthorn's other major motor sport triumph, driving a Jaguar D-Type, was in the Le Mans 24-hour race of 1955, partnered with fellow driver Ivor Bueb. Despite a horrendous accident which killed over eighty spectators and the Mercedes-Benz driver Pierre Levegh, the race continued and the pair took first place. In late 1958, shortly after his victorious, seventh season in Formula One, Hawthorn announced his retirement. In the January of the following year he was killed, aged twenty-nine, when he crashed his Jaguar on the Guildford bypass.

'What's New Pussycat?', the debut film of **Woody Allen**, *was released in 1965.*

As well as appearing in *What's New Pussycat?*, Allen also wrote the screenplay. He became a joke writer in his teens and before he turned twenty was providing material for television shows such as *Caesar's Hour*. In the early 1960s, he became a stand-up comedian. Allen's film directorial debut was *Take the Money and Run* (1969), while *Annie Hall* (1977) brought his first Academy Award wins for best director and best screenplay (shared with Marshall Brickman). Allen has been nominated twenty-three times by the Academy, but rarely attends the awards ceremony – his last appearance was in 2002, when he introduced a tribute to New York. He remains a prolific film-maker and continues to produce, on average, one feature per year. His most recent Oscar nominations for best screenplay have been for *Mighty Aphrodite* (1995), *Deconstructing Harry* (1997), *Match Point* (2005) and *Midnight in Paris* (2011), the latter of which brought him his fourth Oscar win.

In 1970 **Spencer Silver** *filed his patent for 'Acrylate Copolymer Microspheres', the adhesive that would be used on Post-it notes several years later.*

Silver, who worked for the manufacturing company 3M, whose products include Scotch tape, had first discovered the adhesive in 1968. It was his colleague, Art Fry, who came up with the perfect application for the not-so-sticky glue after realising that it would be ideal for making a bookmark which didn't keep falling out of his church choir hymnal. Following product development and customer trials, Post-it notes were launched across the United States in 1980 and in Europe the following year. Silver retired from 3M in 1996 after thirty years of service.

Bobby Fischer *won the World Chess Championship in 1972.*

In early 1958 Fischer became the US chess champion at the age of fourteen, a title that he subsequently retained for the following seven tournaments. He took the world title following his defeat of Boris Spassky in their 1972 meeting held in Reykjavik, Iceland. The match received unprecedented media interest, and was billed as a 'Cold War battle' between the US and the USSR as much as a contest between Fischer and the champion. Fischer never defended his title, since the chess ruling body, FIDE, would not agree to his demand that if the next championship was drawn at nine games all he should retain the title. Fischer played no official competitive chess after his World Championship victory, but re-appeared in 1992 to take on Spassky and beat him again. The contest took place in Belgrade, Yugoslavia, then subject to UN sanctions which extended to sporting events, and thus earned Fischer an arrest warrant from the United States. He became an outspoken critic of his home country and lived the remainder of his life in exile, eventually moving to Iceland where he died, in 2008, at the age of sixty-four.

Pink Floyd, co-founded by **Roger Waters**, *released the album 'The Dark Side of the Moon' in 1973.*

The Dark Side of the Moon is one of the biggest-selling albums in rock history despite only reaching number two in the UK chart. Waters, the group's bass player, was a school-friend of Syd Barrett, who along with Richard Wright and Nick Mason formed the group in 1964. Waters wrote the lyrics to all the songs on the album and co-wrote the music for four tracks. 'Money' was one of three songs with words and music by Waters and it gave the group their first US top-twenty hit single in 1973. Pink Floyd's follow-up to *The Dark Side of the Moon, Wish You Were Here,* was partly a homage to Barrett, who left the group in 1968 (the band then returned to a four-piece line-up that included guitarist David Gilmour who had joined earlier that year). By the time of their next album, *Animals,* released in 1977, Waters had become the group's main songwriter. *The Wall* followed two years later, which contained the track 'Another Brick in the Wall (Part 2)'. The band's biggest hit single, it gave them a Christmas number one in the UK in 1979, and also reached the top in the US and many other countries. *The Final Cut,* released in 1983, was the last Pink Floyd album to feature Waters, who left the group in 1985. He continued with a solo career, but reunited with his former bandmates to perform at the 'Live 8' concert in 2005. In the same year his opera, *Ça Ira,* received its official premiere and topped the UK classical album chart.

In 1975 **Freddie Mercury** *reached number one in the UK singles chart for the first time, with the group Queen.*

Queen's approximately six-minute-long 'Bohemian Rhapsody', penned by Mercury, would remain at the top for nine weeks before it was replaced by Abba's 'Mamma Mia' in January 1976. Mercury was born Farrokh Bulsara, in Zanzibar, but spent part of his childhood in India before coming to England with his family when he was seventeen. Mercury studied at Ealing Art College, and became a member of various bands until he met future members of Queen, Brian May (guitar) and Roger Taylor (drums). Bass player John Deacon joined the band in 1971 and the group's first hit, 'Seven Seas of Rhye', reached the top ten in the UK singles chart in 1974. *A Night at the Opera*, which featured 'Bohemian Rhapsody', gave them their first number one album in the UK. A further six of Queen's studio albums made it to the top of the UK chart, including their final offering, *Made in Heaven*, in 1995. This was the last album to feature Mercury who had recorded as much material as possible for the band to work with prior to his death from Aids, in 1991, at the age of forty-five. The group's compilation album *Greatest Hits (Volume One)* is the biggest-selling album in the UK.

*In 1976 **James Hunt** won the Formula One World Championship.*

Driving for McLaren, Hunt came third in the final race of the season, the Japanese Grand Prix, and took the four points which were enough to overhaul Niki Lauda's lead in the championship by a single point. Lauda, almost fatally injured earlier in the campaign, retired from the final race after one lap due to the heavy rain. It was to be Hunt's only championship success. He finished fifth and thirteenth in the next two seasons and retired from the sport in 1979. Hunt moved into commentating for the BBC. He died of a heart attack in 1993 at the age of forty-five.

*In 1978 **Naomi James** became the first woman to sail solo around the world via Cape Horn.*

The voyage, which beat Sir Francis Chichester's record for a solo circumnavigation, took 272 days to complete. James, originally from New Zealand, survived a near disaster when her boat, *Express Crusader*, capsized in rough seas but self-righted itself with the mast intact. Repairs to the boat necessitated stops in Cape Town and the Falkland Islands, before her safe arrival back in Dartmouth, Devon. James was made a DBE in 1979.

***Sigourney Weaver** starred as Ellen Ripley in the film 'Alien' released in 1979.*

Weaver's character in *Alien* is one of her most famous roles and one which she reprised in three sequels, picking up her first Academy Award nomination for the second film in the series, *Aliens* (1986). Two years later she was simultaneously nominated for best supporting actress for *Working Girl* (1988) and best actress for *Gorillas in the Mist: The Story of Dian Fossey* (1988). Her original first name is Susan – Sigourney was adopted in 1963 after the character Sigourney Howard in the F. Scott Fitzgerald novel *The Great Gatsby*. Since the last Aliens instalment Weaver, who made her debut in *Annie Hall* (1977), has appeared in films such as *Heartbreakers* (2001) and *Avatar* (2009), and was the voice of the ship's computer in the Pixar animation *Wall-E* (2008).

Phil Taylor *won his first World Professional Darts Championship in 1990.*

Taylor defeated Eric Bristow in the final and also took the title again in 1992. The following year saw the game's last unified championship as a rival organisation, ultimately called the Professional Darts Corporation (PDC), was formed in competition to the BDO. Taylor won the second PDC world crown in 1995, and went on to dominate the tournament, only losing three times – in 2003, 2007 and 2008 – between 1995 and 2010. He holds the record (nine) in televised matches for the most nine dart finishes (the minimum number needed to finish from the starting point of 501).

Kenneth Branagh *won the Bafta Award for best director in 1990 for 'Henry V'.*

Branagh, who also starred as the king in what was his directorial debut, is the youngest recipient of this award category at the Baftas. *Henry V* also brought him Academy Award nominations for acting and directing. Branagh returned to Shakespeare for other celluloid adaptations such as *Much Ado About Nothing* (1993) and *Hamlet* (1996), the latter of which gained him another Oscar nomination, this time for the screenplay. Branagh was born in Belfast, but moved with his family to England when he was still at primary school. He studied at Rada and joined the Royal Shakespeare Company when he was twenty-three. Branagh co-founded the Renaissance Theatre Company in 1987. In 2010 he won a Bafta best actor TV award for his role as the title character in the detective series *Wallander*. Branagh was knighted in the 2012 Queen's Birthday Honours.

Adrien Brody won the Academy Award for best actor in 2003 for his portrayal of Władysław Szpilman in 'The Pianist'.

Brody, who made his film debut in *New York Stories* (1989), is the youngest person to win best actor at the Academy Awards. He was up against four former Oscar winners: Jack Nicholson, Daniel Day-Lewis, Nicolas Cage and Michael Caine. Since *The Pianist*, Brody has taken on roles such as Jack Driscoll in Peter Jackson's remake of *King Kong* (2005), Louis Simo in *Hollywoodland* (2006), Peter Whitman in *The Darjeeling Limited* (2007) and Clive Nicoli in *Splice* (2009).

Jason Robinson was a member of the England squad that won the 2003 Rugby World Cup.

Robinson played in all seven of England's matches that culminated in a win against the host nation, Australia, by 20 points to 17 in the final, with Robinson scoring England's only try in the game. He began his playing career in rugby league and, after many years with Wigan, with whom his honours included four challenge cups and five premiership titles, Robinson transferred to rugby union to play for Sale Sharks in 2000. His international debut in rugby union came the following year against Italy and his England career continued until 2007 when he made his last appearance against South Africa in the World Cup final. Robinson was awarded an MBE in 2004 and an OBE four years later.

Jenson Button won the Formula One World Championship in 2009.

Button, driving for the Brawn GP team, won six of the first seven races on his way to winning the championship by a margin of eleven points over Sebastian Vettel. Button began his motorsport career in karting, and made his Formula One debut in 2000. His first win at this level came in 2006 at the Hungarian Grand Prix and was to be his last until his championship-winning 2009 season. Button was awarded an MBE in the 2010 New Year Honours list.

Nicola Adams won a gold medal at the 2012 London Olympics in boxing's flyweight division.

Adams's victory made her the first woman to become an Olympic boxing champion. The bout was a rematch of the 2012 and 2010 world amateur flyweight finals when Adams took silver medals after being defeated by the Chinese boxer Ren Cancan. Adams also won silver, this time in the bantamweight division, at the 2008 World Amateur Championships. In 2011 Adams won her first major international title when she defeated Karolina Michalczuk in the flyweight final of the Women's European Union Amateur Boxing Championships. Adams was awarded an MBE in the 2013 New Year Honours.

Mo Farah won gold medals for the 5,000m and 10,000m at the 2012 London Olympics.

Farah is the first British athlete to win the Olympic 10,000m title and only the sixth runner ever to complete the Olympic double at these distances. Farah had failed to make the 5,000m final at the previous 2008 Games in Beijing, but two years later he became the European champion at 5,000m and 10,000m. In 2011 he successfully defended the 3,000m title at the European Indoor Championships that he had won in 2009, and later in 2011 he won gold for the 5,000m and silver for the 10,000m at the World Championships held in Daegu, South Korea. The Somalia-born athlete came to the UK when he was eight and is the current European-record holder for the 10,000m. Farah was awarded a CBE in the 2013 New Year Honours.

CHAPTER FOUR

Tricenarians

*Life is not long, and too much of it must not pass
in idle deliberation how it shall be spent.*

SAMUEL JOHNSON

30

THIRTY

Napoleon Bonaparte became first consul of France, following a coup d'état, in 1799.

Napoleon became first consul for life in 1802 and two years later was installed as emperor; each time the appointment was approved by a large majority in a plebiscite. Born in Corsica in 1769, he was educated at military schools, commissioned as an artillery officer and rose rapidly to command the French Army in Italy in his mid to late twenties, where his success established his reputation as a military leader. As ruler of France, Napoleon reorganised government, created a central bank, introduced the metric system and established the civil code that remains the basis of the French legal system today. His influence in Europe was extended by victory over Austria and Russia at Austerlitz in 1805, but his troops eventually suffered a reversal in the Peninsular War, which began in 1808, as the British helped to drive the French from Portugal and Spain. In 1812, Napoleon was victorious against the Russians in the Battle of Borodino and went on to occupy Moscow. However, he was forced to retreat and lost thousands of men to the bitter winter conditions and dwindling provisions. In 1813, Napoleon was outnumbered and defeated at the Battle of Leipzig, and in the following year the capture of Paris by the coalition ranged against him precipitated his abdication and exile to the island of Elba. He escaped in 1815 and regained power, but his army was decisively defeated at Waterloo three months later. This time Napoleon was banished to the island of St Helena in the Atlantic where he died, at the age of fifty-one, in 1821.

The first collection of 'Fairy Tales' by **Hans Christian Andersen** *was published in 1835.*

Andersen's first book to be published, *Ungdoms-Forsøg (Youthful attempts)*, in 1822, was unsuccessful, but his 1829 work proved more popular and is regarded as his proper debut: *Fodreise fra Holmens Kanal til Østpynten af Amager I Aarene 1828 og 1829* (*A walking tour from Holmen's canal to the eastern point of Amager in the years 1828 to 1829*). The first edition quickly sold out. Andersen's debut collection of fairy tales appeared six years later and more followed, including works such as *The Emperor's New Clothes*, *The Little Mermaid* and *The Ugly Duckling*, which sealed his reputation as a great storyteller. Andersen died in 1875, aged seventy.

John D. Rockefeller was the principal founder of the Standard Oil Company in 1870.

Standard Oil's success was to make Rockefeller, the company's largest shareholder, one of the world's richest men. Within ten years of its founding, Standard controlled approximately 90% of the United States' oil refining capacity and was a major player in its transportation and storage. Standard's monopolistic position led to the order for its break-up in 1911 under the Sherman Antitrust Act. Rockefeller, who died in 1937 at the age of ninety-seven, is also remembered for his extensive philanthropic work. He established the Rockefeller Foundation in 1913 and his donations also led to the founding of the University of Chicago and Rockefeller University.

'Treasure Island' by **Robert Louis Stevenson** *was published as a novel in 1883.*

Stevenson had started writing *Treasure Island*, originally called *The Sea Cook*, in 1881. It first appeared in serial format in the boys' magazine *Young Folks* in the same year, under the pen name of Captain George North. *Treasure Island* was Stevenson's first success as an author, and has been adapted numerous times for film and television. The Stevenson family background was in engineering, particularly the building of lighthouses (Robert, his grandfather, and Thomas, his father, were both chief engineers to the Northern Lighthouse Board), and he was expected to enter the profession. Stevenson's interest though was in literature and, giving up his engineering studies at the University of Edinburgh, he read law instead. Once qualified, he devoted himself to writing. Stevenson's travels, initially to Europe, inspired his early work. His first book, a travelogue called *An Inland Voyage* (1878), recounts a canoe trip he made through France and

Belgium. He also journeyed to America where he married Fanny Osborne in San Francisco in 1880. The couple returned to Scotland, but soon left for Switzerland where they sought a better climate to alleviate Stevenson's lung condition. Further travels took them to the south of France, Bournemouth and America again, from where they embarked on their South Sea voyages, eventually settling in Samoa in 1890. Stevenson died there four years later at the age of forty-four. His other famous works include *Kidnapped* (1886), *The Master of Ballantrae* (1889) and *Strange Case of Dr Jekyll and Mr Hyde* (1886). Stevenson's last novel, *Weir of Hermiston*, was unfinished at the time of his death.

*The experimental work of **Heinrich Hertz**, which resulted in the first transmission and reception of radio waves, was published in the journal 'Annalen der Physik' in 1887.*

Hertz was able to demonstrate that the velocity of radio waves was equivalent to that of light, with which they shared other properties, thereby discovering part of the electromagnetic spectrum predicted theoretically by James Clerk Maxwell over twenty years earlier. Hertz's work also confirmed the electromagnetic nature of light itself. In 1887 he was the first person to report the photoelectric effect, the phenomenon whereby electrons are emitted from a material by the action of light; this effect was later explained in a paper by Albert Einstein in 1905. Hertz did not live to see this, or indeed the development of radio communication, as he died in 1894 at the age of thirty-six, and was buried in his native city of Hamburg. The unit for frequency measurement was named in his honour.

*The first novel written by **Agatha Christie** to be published in the UK was 'The Mysterious Affair at Styles' in 1921.*

Christie's debut also introduced the fictional Belgian detective, Hercule Poirot, who would go on to feature in over thirty of her novels, including *The Murder of Roger Ackroyd*, *Murder on the Orient Express* and *Death on the Nile*. Her other famous investigator, Miss Marple, made her first appearance in a full-length novel in *The Murder at the Vicarage*, published in 1930. Christie was born Agatha Miller in Devon to affluent parents. She had little formal education and was mostly schooled at home by a series of governesses. She married Archibald Christie in 1914, months after the outbreak of the First World War that saw her take work in a hospital and a dispensary. Their marriage ended in divorce in 1928 and she married an archaeologist, Max Mallowan, two years later. Christie's travels with Mallowan to the Middle East provided material that she incorporated into her writing. By the time of her death in 1976 at the age of eighty-five, Christie had penned over seventy novels, numerous short stories and, in addition to other works, close to twenty stage plays – one of which, *The Mousetrap*, has been performed continuously in London's West End since 1952 and holds the record for the longest-running show in the world. Christie is the world's best-selling fiction author, with sales of over two billion. She received a damehood in the 1971 New Year Honours.

The first posters of the London Underground map, designed by **Harry Beck**, *were printed in 1933.*

Pocket-sized copies of Beck's London Underground map were made available to the general public at the beginning of the year. Its radical new approach was to simplify the depiction of the network by removing the link to geographical reality, thus concentrating on the stations' relative position on each line and any interconnections to other lines. The map, updated regularly to reflect changes in the Underground network, is now considered to be a design classic, and has influenced the style of other transport network maps across the world. Beck, who worked as a draughtsman with London Underground, created the map in his own time as a personal project. When he first presented it to the management in 1931, they showed no enthusiasm for its design, but Beck persevered and resubmitted the map in the following year, this time winning approval. He continued to be involved with updating the map until the end of the 1950s. Beck died in 1974, aged seventy-two.

Dustin Hoffman *starred as Benjamin Braddock in the 1967 film of 'The Graduate', based on the novel by Charles Webb.*

Although their characters are separated by a generation, Hoffman's co-star in the film, Anne Bancroft (Mrs Robinson), was actually only six years older than Hoffman. His performance, in what was his second feature film, won him both Bafta and Golden Globe most promising newcomer awards, and also brought him an Academy Award nomination for best actor. Hoffman has been Oscar nominated a further six times for best actor for films that include *Midnight Cowboy* (1969), *Lenny* (1974) and *Tootsie* (1982), and has won the accolade on two occasions: for *Kramer vs. Kramer* (1979) and *Rain Man* (1988).

*In 1969 **Robin Knox-Johnston** became the first person to circumnavigate the globe single-handed and non-stop by boat.*

Knox-Johnston was the only finisher out of nine competitors in the first round-the-world yacht race: the Sunday Times Golden Globe Race. He departed from Falmouth, Devon, aboard his yacht *Suhaili* and returned over ten months later, after rounding both capes, to claim the trophy and a prize of £5,000 for the fastest voyage (which he donated to the family of a fellow competitor who had committed suicide during the race). Knox-Johnson was awarded a CBE in 1969 and was knighted in 1995.

*In 1969 **Ann Jones** won the Wimbledon Ladies' Singles Championship.*

Jones faced Billie Jean King in the Wimbledon final for the second time, having lost their first encounter in 1967. However, on this occasion she was victorious against King, the defending champion, despite losing the first set. Jones was a frequent presence in major singles finals during the sixties. She was twice runner-up in the US Championships (1961 and 1967) and chalked up appearances in six French finals with wins in 1961 and 1966. The Birmingham-born left-hander also won five Grand Slam doubles titles. Jones's sporting career began with table tennis – she played in several World Championships during the 1950s.

***Jackie Stewart**, with his win in the Italian Grand Prix, was assured of the 1969 Formula One World Championship.*

The title came four years after Stewart's first grand prix victory in his debut season, when he finished third overall. By the time he retired in 1973, Stewart had won another two championships (1971 and 1973), and had accumulated twenty-seven grand prix wins to set a new record which would endure for fourteen years until surpassed by Alain Prost. Stewart was knighted in 2001.

Ernő Rubik applied for a Hungarian patent in 1975, for what he referred to as the 'Magic Cube'.

Following the puzzle's initial release in Budapest in the late 1970s, a deal was struck with Ideal Toys, and the renamed Rubik's Cube was displayed at major toy fairs in Europe at the start of 1980. It went on to become one of the most popular puzzle games of all time, with global sales of over three hundred million.

Sylvester Stallone starred in 'Rocky', which premiered in New York in 1976.

Stallone also wrote the script for *Rocky* and in his studio pitches he was steadfast in demanding the lead role for himself. The film received ten Academy Award nominations including two for Stallone – best actor and best writing (directly for the screen) – and won in three categories: best picture, best director and film editing. *Rocky* spawned five sequels, the most recent, *Rocky Balboa*, was released thirty years after the original. Stallone also starred in another successful series, *Rambo*, which has so far extended to four movies. His other films include *Cliffhanger* (1993), *Get Carter* (2000) and more recently *The Expendables* (2010).

In 1980 Meryl Streep won the Academy Award for best supporting actress for her role as Joanna Kramer in 'Kramer vs. Kramer'.

Streep is the most nominated actress or actor by the Academy, being cited on seventeen occasions (fourteen for best actress). She made her feature-film debut in *Julia* (1977), and was Oscar nominated for her next film, *The Deer Hunter* (1978). Her performance in *Sophie's Choice* (1982) gave the star her first best actress Academy Award. Streep's other nominated films include: *Silkwood* (1983), *Ironweed* (1987), *The Bridges of Madison County* (1995) and *Adaptation* (2002). After a gap of nearly thirty years, she won her second Oscar for best actress for her portrayal of Margaret Thatcher in *The Iron Lady* (2011). The role also won her a second Bafta Award for best actress to add to her first for *The French Lieutenant's Woman* (1981) and gave her an eighth Golden Globe.

'The Terminator', co-written and directed by James Cameron, was released in 1984.

A sci-fi thriller, *The Terminator* was Cameron's proper directorial debut following a two-and-a-half week stint in the chair for *Piranha II: The Spawning* (1981). *The Terminator* was made on a low budget of approximately $6.5 million and went on to gross more than ten times that figure. Cameron's subsequent films have all proved to be lucrative at the box office and include *Aliens* (1986), *The Abyss* (1989) and *Terminator 2: Judgment Day* (1991). *Titanic* (1997), directed and written by Cameron, became the highest-grossing film of all time and scooped a record-equalling eleven Oscars, including best director and best picture. His next major feature film, *Avatar* (2009), picked up three Academy Awards and overtook *Titanic* in box office receipts.

Nick Faldo won golf's Open Championship at Muirfield in 1987.
As a fourteen-year-old, Faldo's interest in golf was sparked when he watched the 1971 Masters tournament at Augusta, Georgia, on television. Six years later, at the age of twenty, Faldo took part in the Ryder Cup – he went on to become one of the competition's most successful players. Faldo has won the Open on three occasions – in 1987, 1990 and 1992. He is also a three-time winner at the Masters (1989, 1990 and 1996), and has finished as the runner-up in golf's other two majors: the US Open (1988) and the PGA Championship (1992). He became an MBE in 1998 and was knighted in 2009 for services to golf.

Lynne Cox became the first person to swim from the United States to the Soviet Union, by crossing the Bering Strait between Alaska and Siberia, in 1987.
The water temperature for the 2.7 mile route across the Bering Strait was approximately 5°C. Cox's swim, which took two hours and six minutes, made more impact in the Soviet Union (she was lauded by Soviet President Mikhail Gorbachev) than at home in the US. The Bering Strait crossing was the latest in a succession of global long-distance achievements by Cox that began when she swam the twenty-seven-mile Catalina Channel off the Californian coast in 1971 at the age of fourteen. In 1972, Cox broke the men's and women's records for a crossing of the English Channel with a time under ten hours – a feat she repeated the following year. Her other exploits include swimming between New Zealand's North and South Islands, traversing the Strait of Magellan and, in 2007, a quartet of Northwest Passage swims.

In 1993 **Rachel Whiteread** *became the first woman to win the Turner Prize.*

Whiteread studied at Brighton Polytechnic and the Slade School of Art, London. She is famous for her casts of the space in and around objects, exemplified by her piece for the Turner Prize exhibition: *Untitled (Room)*. Her large-scale work *House*, completed less than a month before the award ceremony, consisted of a concrete cast of the inside of a Victorian terraced house that had been scheduled for demolition. Despite pleas by many admirers to have it preserved, *House* was demolished by the local council in the following year. Whiteread's other works include *Ghost* (1990), *Untitled (One Hundred Spaces)* (1997) and *Untitled Monument* (2001). She was awarded a CBE in the 2006 New Year Honours list.

Damien Hirst *won the 1995 Turner Prize.*

Bristol-born Hirst attended Goldsmiths College in London, where in his second year he was the major force behind the conception and staging of the student art show 'Freeze' in London's docklands in 1988. Hirst became a leading figure in the group referred to as the 'Young British Artists' and in 1992 he received his first nomination for the Turner Prize. In the same year, his *Physical Impossibility of Death in the Mind of Someone Living* (a shark in a glass tank of formaldehyde) was exhibited at the Saatchi Gallery. *Mother and Child, Divided*, which consists of a cow and a calf, both sliced in half and preserved in formaldehyde, was exhibited at the 1993 Venice Biennale and subsequently at Hirst's 1995 Turner Prize show. This also included a 'spot' painting, one of hundreds which Hirst or his assistants have produced since 1986. In financial terms, Hirst is one of the most successful living artists of all time; in 2008 he sold a complete exhibition by auction which raised over £100 million.

Steve McQueen *won the 1999 Turner Prize.*

McQueen's silent film *Deadpan* (1997) was featured in his Turner Prize exhibition. Four and a half minutes long, *Deadpan* recreates a famous Buster Keaton stunt, with McQueen as the participant, in which the gable end of a house falls on him, but doesn't hit him because he is standing where there is a missing window. McQueen made his debut as a feature-film director with *Hunger* (2008), which picked up many awards, including a Bafta for most promising newcomer for McQueen himself. He was elevated from OBE to CBE in the 2011 New Year Honours.

Richard Burns *won the World Rally Championship in 2001.*

Driving a Subaru Impreza, Burns, and his co-driver Richard Reid, took the title with a third-place finish in the season's last rally, held in Great Britain. His success followed runner-up spots in the previous two World Rally Championships (WRC). Burns made his debut in 1988 and claimed the British Rally Championship twice in the following decade (1992 and 1993). The first of his ten WRC race victories came in 1998 in the Kenyan safari rally, driving a Mitsubishi Lancer Evo IV. He joined the Subaru team in the following season for the first of four WRC campaigns that culminated in his 2001 victory, the first for an English driver, before switching to Peugeot for his final two seasons. He died four years to the day after winning his world title, at the age of thirty-four, as a result of a brain tumour.

Graeme McDowell *won golf's US Open Championship in 2010.*

The US Open was the first major win for McDowell, from Portrush, Northern Ireland, and the first by a European player for forty years. He turned professional in 2002 and made his Ryder Cup debut in 2008, winning his singles match, but Europe lost to the US for the first time in nine years. In the next Ryder Cup in 2010, McDowell defeated Hunter Mahan in the last singles match to clinch victory for Europe.

31
THIRTY-ONE

Jean-François Champollion *reported his success in understanding the system of Egyptian hieroglyphs to the Academie des Inscriptions in 1822.*

Shortly afterwards, Champollion sent a more detailed report to the secretary of the Academy, now referred to as the 'Letter to Monsieur Dacier', and this was followed two years later by a comprehensive analysis. The Rosetta Stone contains the same text in Greek, demotic and hieroglyphic and provided the key with which scholars who understood Greek and demotic could begin to decipher hieroglyphics. Champollion's achievement was aided by his linguistic abilities – he had learned six ancient oriental languages by the age of sixteen. Regarded as the father of Egyptology, Champollion died at the age of forty-one in 1832.

In 1847 'The Macdermots of Ballycloran' became the first published novel by **Anthony Trollope**.

Trollope's publishing debut was set in Ireland, where he was employed at the time by the Post Office. He wrote three further Irish novels, but none of these were particularly successful. Trollope returned to England, and, still working for the Post Office, wrote *The Warden*, the first of six novels that would become known collectively as the *Chronicles of Barsetshire*. He produced another major series – the *Palliser* novels – and became one of the best-selling authors in the Victorian era. He is also credited with the introduction of the pillar box (originally rectangular in shape and painted green) to the UK, which were first placed in the Channel Islands in 1854. Trollope died in 1882 at the age of sixty-seven.

In 1847 'Jane Eyre' by **Charlotte Brontë** *was published*.

The first edition of *Jane Eyre*, one of the most famous English novels, credited Brontë's pseudonym, Currer Bell, as editor. In the previous year, Charlotte and her sisters, Emily and Anne (who adopted the pen names Ellis and Acton Bell respectively), had financed their first publication: a joint volume of verse entitled *Poems*. Jane Eyre's experiences often echoed events in Charlotte's life such as the death of her two older sisters, Maria and Elizabeth, from tuberculosis, which left Charlotte the senior member of the four surviving Brontë siblings. She would see only two more of her novels published in her lifetime: *Shirley* in 1849 and *Villette* in 1853. Charlotte married in 1854, by which time she had lost her sisters and brother. In the following year Charlotte also died, at the age of thirty-eight, while carrying her unborn child. Her first book, *The Professor*, originally rejected by publishers, was released posthumously.

Nikola Tesla *filed his patent application for an electro-magnetic motor in 1887.*

The document described Tesla's alternating current (AC) motor and showed how AC sources could be used to form the necessary rotating magnetic field. It was one of numerous patents issued to Tesla. Many of these concerned AC electricity and included its application to generators, transformers and distribution systems. Tesla was born in Smiljan (now in modern-day Croatia), to parents who were both Serbian. He studied at what is now the Graz University of Technology and the University of Prague, but did not graduate from either institution. Tesla was employed in Budapest (in the Central Telegraph office) and Paris (in Edison's Continental Company), before he left for the US in 1884 at the age of twenty-seven. He worked for Edison for one year before a dispute prompted him to form his own company. Edison advocated direct current (DC) electricity distribution and came to oppose the idea of AC championed by Tesla. George Westinghouse, engineer and businessman, purchased Tesla's patents in this domain and the stage was set for the 'battle of the currents'. The Westinghouse power station at Niagara Falls was based in part on Tesla's AC work and became operational in 1895. Despite Edison's attempts, such as grimly executing animals to demonstrate its dangers, AC, with its advantages for high voltage transmission, was to be the winner. Tesla was also a pioneer of radio transmission and registered many patents in the subject. In 1943 the US Supreme Court upheld Tesla's claim of priority over Marconi with regard to the invention of radio. Tesla had died months earlier, impoverished despite his inventions, at the age of eighty-six at the Hotel New Yorker where he had lived for the last few years of his life. The SI unit for magnetic flux density was posthumously named in his honour.

*In 1894 **Pierre de Coubertin** advocated a revival of the ancient Olympic Games during an international congress in Paris.*

Coubertin's proposal resulted in the foundation of the International Olympic Committee (IOC) and the first modern Games took place two years later in Athens, Greece, in 1896. Coubertin had been inspired by his visit to England in 1890, where he met William Penny Brookes who had inaugurated the Olympian Games in Much Wenlock, Shropshire, in 1850, which featured a mixture of athletics and country sports. Brookes was a long-standing advocate for an international Olympic version to be staged in Greece. Coubertin pressed on with his desire to see a modern Olympics staged and served as the first president of the IOC until 1925. He died twelve years later at the age of seventy-four.

*The sheet music for 'Original Rag', by **Scott Joplin**, was published in 1899.*

'Original Rag' was Joplin's first ragtime piece to be published and was followed later that year by the more successful 'Maple Leaf Rag'. Ragtime's popularity waned but a strong revival of interest in Joplin's music was sparked by its use in the Oscar-winning film *The Sting* (1973). Marvin Hamlisch, who adapted Joplin's work for the production, won an Academy Award for his efforts and also scored a hit with its theme, 'The Entertainer'. Joplin died in 1917 at the age of forty-nine.

*In 1899 the first session began at the new Glasgow School of Art building designed by **Charles Rennie Mackintosh**.*

Regarded as Mackintosh's architectural masterpiece, the opening marked the completion of the first phase of the Glasgow School of Art building. Due to a lack of funds the western portion was constructed later, between 1907 and 1909. Mackintosh was born in Glasgow and his native city has the greatest number of Mackintosh-designed buildings. These include, in addition to the School of Art, the Scotland Street School, the Glasgow Herald building (now called The Lighthouse) and his only ecclesiastical commission, Queen's Cross Church. Mackintosh not only designed the exterior of buildings, but also the interior, including furniture and decorations, as exemplified by the Willow Tearooms in Glasgow's Sauchiehall Street, which also boast a façade by Mackintosh. Though his work was influential in a European context, Mackintosh failed in his lifetime to enjoy the recognition that, in recent years, he has been afforded in his homeland. He moved to England and spent his last years in the south of France, where he focused on painting watercolours. Ill health brought him back to London for treatment, where he died in 1928 at the age of sixty. The *House for an Art Lover*, based on a 1901 competition design by Mackintosh, was built in Glasgow's Bellahouston Park, and opened in 1996.

Paul Dirac *received the Nobel Prize in Physics in 1933 for 'the discovery of new productive forms of atomic theory'.*

Dirac graduated in electrical engineering and then mathematics from Bristol University before attending St John's College, Cambridge, where he obtained his doctorate in 1926. It was at Cambridge that Dirac became interested in the recently announced theory of quantum mechanics, to which he would make important contributions including, in 1928, the 'relativistic wave equation' that could be used to explain properties of the electron and the characteristics of the hydrogen spectrum. Dirac's theoretical work predicted the existence of the positron (a positively charged sub-atomic particle which is the antimatter counterpart of the electron), subsequently discovered soon after by Carl Anderson. Dirac held the post of Lucasian Professor of Mathematics at Cambridge from 1932 to 1969, and was admitted to the Order of Merit in 1973. Dirac died at the age of eighty-two in 1984. He shared the 1933 Nobel Prize with Erwin Schrödinger.

Benjamin Britten's opera 'Peter Grimes' premiered at Sadler's Wells Theatre in 1945.

Peter Grimes, inspired by a poem by George Crabbe and with a libretto provided by Montagu Slater, was an early success for Britten. He showed exceptional musical talent as a child, passing piano at grade eight when he was twelve, and becoming a prodigious composer in his teenage years. Later, in the 1930s, he worked with W.H. Auden on the documentary films *Coal Face* and *Night Mail* produced by the GPO film unit. After *Peter Grimes*, Britten composed several more operas including *Gloriana* (1953), *A Midsummer Night's Dream* (1960) and his last, *Death in Venice* (1973). His other work was wide ranging and included orchestral, choral and vocal compositions. Britten was admitted to the Order of Merit in 1965. He was the first British composer to be honoured with a life peerage and became Baron Britten in 1976, the year of his death at the age of sixty-three.

*The characters of 'Steptoe and Son', created by **Ray Galton** and Alan Simpson, made their first appearance on BBC television in 1962.*

Galton and Simpson (one year older at thirty-two), had previously worked together as writers for *Hancock's Half Hour* which began as a radio show in the 1950s and subsequently transferred to television. They met in 1948 at a sanatorium in Surrey where they were both being treated for tuberculosis. It was there that their comedy writing partnership was formed and within a few years they were writing for the BBC. The first half-hour show to feature the Steptoe characters, called 'The Offer', was one of six in the *Comedy Playhouse* slot and led to the spin-off series *Steptoe and Son*.

Galton and Simpson wrote eight series featuring the rag-and-bone men, the last of which was broadcast in 1974. They were each awarded an OBE in 2000.

John Noakes became a presenter on 'Blue Peter' in 1965.

Noakes is the programme's longest-serving presenter, with a twelve-and-a-half-year stint that lasted until 1978. After initially training to be an aircraft engine fitter he turned to acting and took on some minor roles on television, until he landed the job at *Blue Peter*. Noakes became the most intrepid of the show's presenters at the time, and one of his most famous exploits was when he became the first civilian to make a five-mile free-fall parachute jump in 1973. He also presented the spin-off series *Go With Noakes* which continued until 1980 and also featured his collie Shep. His second attempt to sail around the world with his wife, in 1984, ended prematurely in Majorca after they decided to stay and make their home on the island.

In 1971 Chay Blyth became the first person to sail non-stop around the world the 'wrong way', by travelling from east to west.

Blyth completed his 292-day journey aboard *British Steel* in August 1971. Prior to that he spent nearly a decade in the Parachute Regiment, towards the end of which, in 1966, he rowed across the Atlantic with John Ridgway in an open boat, in a 92-day voyage. Blyth circumnavigated the globe again in the 1970s, this time in the conventional direction, with a crew of paratroopers, in the first Whitbread Round the World Yacht Race. Awarded a CBE in 1972, Blyth has continued to be involved in maritime challenges, both as a competitor and organiser. He was knighted in 1997 for his services to sailing.

Arthur Ashe won the Wimbledon men's singles final in 1975, beating Jimmy Connors in four sets.

The victory was to be Ashe's third and last Grand Slam title win as he became the oldest men's singles winner at Wimbledon in the open era of tennis (from 1968 onwards). Ashe also won the inaugural US Open in 1968 and the Australian Open in 1970. He died in 1993 at the age of forty-nine.

Virginia Wade won the Wimbledon Ladies Singles Championship in 1977.

Wade lost the first set against Betty Stove, before claiming the next two 6–3, 6–1, to win the 1977 Wimbledon title. The Queen, in her silver jubilee year, was there to spectate and award the trophy, in what was also the centenary year of the Wimbledon Championships. Wade won the first US Open tournament in 1968, when she scored a straight sets victory over Billie Jean King. Four years later, she added the Australian Open title. Wade also won four Grand Slam doubles championships. Her last Wimbledon singles appearance was in 1985, but she returned in the following year (during which she also received an OBE to add to her MBE) to compete in the doubles for the last time. Wade is the last female British tennis player to win a Grand Slam singles title.

The first Wallace and Gromit feature, 'A Grand Day Out', directed and co-written by **Nick Park**, *made its television debut on Christmas Day 1989.*

'A Grand Day Out' had been seven years in the making and started life as Park's graduation project for the National Film and Television School. The animation received an Oscar nomination in 1991, but lost out to another Nick Park work: *Creature Comforts*. Three further short *Wallace and Gromit* films have been made as well as a full-length feature, *Wallace & Gromit: The Curse of The Were-Rabbit* (2005). These have garnered three Oscar wins between them. Park was awarded a CBE in 1997.

'Friends', starring **Lisa Kudrow** *as Phoebe Buffay, made its debut on US television in 1994.*

Kudrow was the oldest of the six main cast members, and came to the role after playing Phoebe's twin sister, Ursula, in the TV series *Mad About You* – a character who would also feature in a later episode of *Friends*. Kudrow made her television and film debuts in the late 1980s, and achieved her first cinematic top billing in *Romy and Michele's High School Reunion* (1997) alongside Mira Sorvino. *Friends* gained her a handful of Emmy nominations as supporting actress and one win in 1998. Her film credits include *The Opposite of Sex* (1998), *Analyze This* (1999) and *Kabluey* (2007).

Amazon.com, founded by **Jeff Bezos**, *was launched online in 1995.*

Named after the world's longest river, Amazon has grown from its bookseller roots to become one of the major online retailers of a wide variety of goods. Bezos graduated from Princeton with a degree in computer science and electrical engineering, and went to work in the financial sector, where technical skills were becoming increasingly sought after to conduct market analysis. Bezos spotted the potential offered by the growing use of the internet and decided to capitalise on this by setting up an online bookshop. He abandoned his financial career and set off for Seattle where he would start Amazon in 1994, the year before its online debut. Bezos was selected as *Time* magazine's Person of the Year in 1999.

'Harry Potter and the Philosopher's Stone', written by **J. K. Rowling** *(Joanne Kathleen) was published in 1997.*

Initially turned down by several publishers, Rowling's first Harry Potter book, and the six others which followed in the series, became a publishing phenomenon. In 2011 the worldwide sales of the Harry Potter books, which have been translated into seventy languages, had reached approximately 450 million copies. It was whilst on a crowded train journey from Manchester to London that Rowling first came up with the story of the boy wizard Harry Potter. Her publisher asked Rowling to use initials rather than her first name, Joanne, so as not to potentially alienate young male readers. Having no middle name, Rowling selected K for Kathleen, the name of her paternal grandmother. The series concluded with *Harry Potter and the Deathly Hallows* in 2007. Rowling was presented with an OBE in 2001 for services to children's literature. The Harry Potter books have also been made into a highly successful film series, released between 2001 and 2011. *The Casual Vacancy*, Rowling's first book since *The Tales of Beedle the Bard* in 2008, and her first novel for adult readers, was published in 2012.

In 2003 **Lawrence Dallaglio** *was a member of the England team which won the Rugby World Cup in Australia.*

Dallaglio, who amassed a total of 85 international caps, holds the distinction of being the only member of the squad to have played in every minute of the tournament. He also played in the 2007 final, when England finished runners-up to South Africa. Dallaglio's only domestic senior club was (London) Wasps who he helped to five Premiership titles, the last of these in 2008, in his final game before retirement. His other medals include two for Wasps' Heineken Cup victories in 2004 and 2007. Dallaglio was awarded an OBE to add to his MBE in 2008. Less well known is that he was part of the school choir who sang backing vocals for Tina Turner's 1985 hit 'We Don't Need Another Hero'.

32
THIRTY-TWO

James Watt *obtained his first steam engine patent in 1769.*

Watt's patent contained his breakthrough improvement to the existing Newcomen engine – a separate condensing chamber – which resulted in much greater efficiency and a consequent reduction in the amount of coal consumed. Watt was working as an instrument maker at the University of Glasgow where his experience of repairing a Newcomen engine led him to consider how it might be improved. Watt went into partnership with John Roebuck, whose interest in the patent was later taken over by Matthew Boulton, a Midlands factory owner, who secured an extension to Watt's patent in 1775. The engine formed the basis of a successful business as it supplanted the inferior Newcomen version. Watt patented further improvements and, in 1785, both he and Boulton were elected as fellows of the Royal Society. Watt died in 1819 at the age of eighty-three. The SI unit of power, the Watt, is named in his honour.

The first railway locomotive, constructed by **Richard Trevithick***, transported its first passengers in a demonstration run in 1804.*

The journey took place at the Penydarren ironworks, near Merthyr Tydfil in south Wales, where Trevithick's engine hauled five wagons, ten tons of iron and seventy men over nine miles before the track failed due to the higher than normal loading. Trevithick's father was a tin-mine manager, and the employment of steam power by the industry was to provide Trevithick with the opportunity to develop his engineering talents. He advanced the principle of using high-pressure steam and patented his ideas in 1802. Trevithick died in 1833, at the age of sixty-two.

Thomas Cook organised the first package tour in 1841.

The trip, for a group of over five hundred temperance campaigners, consisted of a rail journey from Leicester to Loughborough (Cook himself was a keen promoter of temperance). Further tours followed and the business expanded with Cook's son John becoming a partner. The company were soon offering trips to Europe, and in the early 1870s Thomas Cook took the first organised tourist party around the world. John Cook did much to further the enterprise, eventually taking charge in 1879. Thomas Cook died in 1892 at the age of eighty-three.

Vincent Van Gogh completed his painting of the 'Potato Eaters' in 1885.

A multi-figure composition depicting impoverished peasants, it is regarded by many as his first major work and was created only a few years after he had started painting. In an artistic career which was to last only another five years and ended with his death in 1890 at the age of thirty-seven, Van Gogh, produced over eight hundred and fifty paintings. His other famous works include *Starry Night* and *Sunflowers*, but Van Gogh only sold one painting during his lifetime and was supported financially in his artistic endeavours by his brother, Theo. Appreciation and demand for his work grew in the twentieth century. The highest price paid at auction for one of his paintings is $82.5 million for his *Portrait of Dr Gachet* in 1990.

Orville Wright made the first controlled, powered flight in a 'heavier than air machine', the Wright Flyer, in 1903.

The *Wright Flyer* had been constructed with his older brother Wilbur. The toss of a coin decided who flew first. Wilbur won, but *Flyer* stalled on his attempt and was damaged when it came to a halt. Three days later, after repairs had been made, Orville travelled a distance of 120 feet in about twelve seconds to make the first flight. After Wilbur had taken the next shot in *Flyer*, Orville made his second attempt and increased the distance travelled to just over 200 feet. Orville died in 1948 at the age of seventy-six.

Louis Chevrolet co-founded the Chevrolet Motor Car Company with William Durant in 1911.

Chevrolet, the son of a watchmaker, was born on Christmas Day 1878, in Switzerland. He moved to Canada where he worked as a chauffeur and mechanic, before heading to the US. Chevrolet also became a racing driver for Fiat, and later joined the Buick racing team (Buick became part of General Motors (GM), which was controlled by Durant). When Durant was forced out of GM, he partnered with Chevrolet who designed their first car – the Chevrolet Classic Six. However, the pair did not agree on the direction of the company and Chevrolet left and sold his stock. Though he continued to work in the automobile industry, Chevrolet's commercial ventures eventually failed. In the early 1930s, he found employment as a mechanic in the Chevrolet division of General Motors. He died in 1941 at the age of sixty-two.

*In 1919 **Arthur Brown** completed the first non-stop transatlantic flight with John Alcock.*

Brown was the navigator on the historic flight from Newfoundland to Galway, which took 16 hours and 27 minutes. He was born in Glasgow, to American parents, but took British citizenship in 1914 and served in the First World War, initially with the army and then the Royal Flying Corps. Brown was unemployed in 1919 when he sought a position at Vickers of Weybridge. Shortly afterwards, the company decided to attempt the non-stop flight, which carried a prize of £10,000 offered by the *Daily Mail*. Brown was chosen to accompany Alcock in the modified Vickers Vimy bomber and both were knighted one week after their successful flight by King George V at Windsor Castle. Brown died in 1948 at the age of sixty-two.

***Chester Carlson** filed his first patent for 'Electron Photography' in 1938.*

Carlson's work led, in 1959, to the production of the first photocopier which could use plain paper: the Xerox 914. Carlson came from an impoverished background and, inspired by inventors such as Edison, hoped one day to invent something significant. He studied physics at university but found it difficult to obtain a job in Depression-era America. Carlson went to work at Bell Labs, but was laid off shortly afterwards; he then worked in the patent department of an electronic manufacturer, where it occurred to him that a machine that could easily copy documents would be of great benefit. Carlson's researches drew him to the photoconductivity work of

Hungarian physicist Paul Selenyi and this inspired the experiments he began in his kitchen to develop 'electrophotography'. Carlson moved to a small self-funded lab, engaged an assistant, and in 1938 they produced the world's first photocopy. Despite no interest from large corporations at the time, Carlson persevered and eventually in 1944 received backing from the Battelle Memorial Institute, a non-profit research organisation. This led to an agreement with the Haloid Company (later to be renamed Xerox). The company – and their products – went on to become hugely successful. Carlson died in 1968 at the age of sixty-two.

'Catcher in the Rye' by J. D. Salinger (Jerome David) was published in 1951.

Salinger's first novel, *Catcher in the Rye* charts several days in the life of the book's narrator and main protagonist, the teenage Holden Caulfield. Despite huge interest and acclaim for the work, Salinger refused to allow any film adaptations of the novel. He shunned interviews, preferring to live privately at his home in New Hampshire until his death in 2010, at the age of ninety-one. He is also the author of *Franny and Zooey* (1961) and *Raise High the Roof Beam, Carpenters and Seymour: An Introduction* (1963).

In 1953 the journal 'Nature' published an X-ray diffraction image of DNA, produced by Rosalind Franklin.

Franklin completed her undergraduate studies at Newnham College, Cambridge, in 1941, and then worked towards her doctorate. She spent four years in Paris where she developed her expertise in the technique of X-ray crystallography before accepting a research position at King's College London, in 1951, where she investigated the structure of DNA. Franklin's experimental skills helped her to elucidate many of the important features of the molecule. One X-ray diffraction picture of DNA, produced at King's, was shared, unbeknown to her, with James Watson. This image assisted Watson and his colleague, Francis Crick, in the formulation of their famous double helix model for DNA, published in *Nature* in 1953. Franklin and her assistant, Raymond Gosling, reported on their work in the same edition. Franklin died of cancer five years later, at the age of thirty-seven; four years before Crick, Watson and Maurice Wilkins received the Nobel Prize for their work on DNA (Franklin's contribution could not be considered for the Nobel Prize as it is not awarded posthumously).

Marilyn Monroe starred as Sugar Kane Kowalczyk in Billy Wilder's 'Some Like it Hot', released in 1959.

Monroe won her only US acting award – a Golden Globe for best actress in a musical or comedy – for her performance in *Some Like it Hot.* She was born Norma Jeane Mortenson in 1926, though baptised as Norma Jeane Baker. Monroe's film debut came with an uncredited part in *The Shocking Miss Pilgrim* (1947). The next decade saw her move from a minor role in *The Asphalt Jungle* (1950), to starring performances in films such as *Gentlemen Prefer Blondes* (1953), *The Seven Year Itch* (1955) and *Bus Stop* (1956), the latter of which earned her a Golden Globe nomination. The last film she completed, before her death in 1962 at the age of thirty-six, was *The Misfits* (1961).

Theodore Maiman demonstrated the world's first working laser in 1960.

The theoretical groundwork for the laser (its name derived from Light Amplification by Stimulated Emission of Radiation) stretched back several decades to Albert Einstein, with subsequent contributions by many others. A similar device, the maser, was produced in 1953, which used microwaves rather than visible light. Maiman's ruby laser, which could produce short bursts of light, was first demonstrated at the Hughes Research Laboratories in Malibu, California. He beat several other groups to achieve the first practical demonstration. Maiman continued to work in this field, both for his own companies and as a consultant. He died in 2007 at the age of seventy-nine.

Written by clarinettist Acker Bilk, 'Stranger on the Shore', was released in 1961.

Performed by Bilk and the Leon Young String Chorale, it reached number two the following year during a fifty-five week stay in the UK chart. The biggest seller of 1962, with over a million copies purchased, it also made it to the top of the US Billboard chart. A doyen of the trad jazz scene, Bilk and his Paramount Jazz Band first entered the British singles chart in 1960 with a number five placing for 'Summer Set', their first of several hits. After a gap of thirteen years, Bilk made his next UK chart appearance, at the age of forty-seven, with a number five-spot for his solo single 'Aria'. He was awarded an MBE in 2001.

Sean Connery *made his first appearance as James Bond in the 1962 film 'Dr. No'.*

Connery's portrayal of the British secret agent transformed him into an international star and he played the role in a further five 'official' (EON produced) Bond films, the last of which was *Diamonds Are Forever* (1971). Connery's next films included *Murder on the Orient Express* (1974) and *The Man Who Would be King* (1975), before he returned to the role of James Bond in a Warner Bros. adaptation of *Thunderball*, *Never Say Never Again* (1983), released when Connery was fifty-three. Born in Edinburgh, Thomas Sean Connery found his way into acting after three years of service in the navy, and a number of different occupations including lifeguard and coffin polisher. His first credited film appearance was in *No Road Back* (1957) and the following year he had a more prominent role in *Another Time, Another Place* (1958). Connery won the best supporting actor Academy Award in 1988 for his role as Jim Malone in *The Untouchables*. His performance in *The Name of the Rose* (1986) brought him a Bafta best actor award and he was nominated again for *The Hunt for Red October* (1990). Connery received the Bafta fellowship in 1998 and was knighted in 2000.

In 1974 **John Thaw** *first played Jack Regan in the TV drama, 'Regan'.*

Thaw returned to the part of Detective Inspector Regan in the following year for the first of four series of *The Sweeney*, the London police drama which, with its gritty realism, reshaped the depiction of law enforcement on British television. Thaw attended Rada and made his film debut in *The Loneliness of the Long Distance Runner* (1962). His other most identifiable role was as the eponymous Oxford detective *Inspector Morse*, first shown in 1987, which earned him two Bafta Awards. He was nominated, in the Bafta film section, for best supporting actor for *Cry Freedom* (1987), and in 2001 received the Bafta fellowship. Thaw died in 2002, aged sixty.

The **Oprah Winfrey** *Show was first broadcast nationally in the US in 1986.*

Winfrey's programme would go on to become the leading US talk show and win her consecutive Emmy Awards, as well as the International Radio and Television Society's 'Broadcaster of the Year' award. Winfrey had a troubled childhood, but got a break aged seventeen, when she was offered work by a local radio station in Nashville following her win in the Nashville Miss Fire Prevention contest. From there she progressed to local television, attended university and, after a move to Baltimore, hosted her first talk show for WJZ-TV. Winfrey is also an Oscar-nominated actress for her supporting role in *The Color Purple* (1985). The last edition of her talk show, which ran for twenty-five years, aired in 2011.

In 1990 **Daniel Day-Lewis** *won both the Academy Award and Bafta for best actor, for his performance in 'My Left Foot: The Story of Christy Brown'.*

Day-Lewis studied at the Bristol Old Vic Theatre School, and after some stage and television work landed his first major film role in *The Bounty* (1984). His next features included *My Beautiful Laundrette* (1985), *Room with a View* (1985) and *The Unbearable Lightness of Being* (1988). Known for his thorough preparation and versatility, Day-Lewis has been a regular best actor nominee at both the Academy and Bafta Awards, winning a second Oscar, and third Bafta, for *There Will Be Blood* (2007). *Gangs of New York* (2002) also provided him with a Bafta win and another Oscar nomination. He has also been Bafta nominated for *The Last of the Mohicans* (1992) and *In the Name of the Father* (1993). The title role in *Lincoln* (2012) won him a fourth Bafta, and a record third Oscar, for best actor.

Ben Okri *won the 1991 Booker Prize for his novel 'The Famished Road'.*

The Famished Road was the third novel by the Nigerian-born author, the youngest ever winner of the prize, who made his publishing debut with *Flowers and Shadows* in 1980. *The Famished Road* charts the story of its narrator Azaro, a 'spirit child' who can transfer between the real world and a place inhabited by the spirits. His subsequent novels include *Songs of Enchantment* (1993), as well as *Astonishing the Gods* (1995), *Infinite Riches* (1998) and *In Arcadia* (2002). Okri was awarded an OBE in 2001.

Linford Christie *won a gold medal at the 1992 Olympic Games in Barcelona for the 100m.*

Christie's victory made him the oldest 100m Olympic sprint champion, and the third Briton to win the race (after Harold Abrahams in 1924 and

Allan Wells in 1980). The following year he claimed the 100m title at the World Championships, and became the first man to simultaneously hold the Olympic, European, World and Commonwealth crowns. His British record for the 100m, set in 1993, still stands. Christie was awarded an MBE in 1990 and an OBE in 1998.

Chris Hoy won three gold medals at the 2008 Olympic Games in Beijing.

Hoy was the first British man for a hundred years to win three gold medals at a single Olympic Games. His cycling wins were achieved in the keirin, men's team sprint and the men's individual sprint. Hoy, who was knighted in 2009, also won gold at the 2004 Olympics in Athens for the 1km track time trial. At the 2012 London Olympics, Hoy won gold for both the keirin and the team sprint, helping to set a new world record for the latter. With a total of six gold medals and one silver, Edinburgh-born Hoy is Britain's most successful Olympian.

Andrew Strauss captained England to an Ashes series victory at the Oval in 2009.

England's opening batsman, Strauss was also the most prolific run maker of the series with a total of 474, as England regained the Ashes by the margin of two tests to one. His 161 first innings total in the second test at Lord's helped England to a 115 run victory against Australia – the first at the London venue since 1934. Strauss, who made his test debut against New Zealand in 2004, had already tasted Ashes success in 2005 when he made two centuries as England triumphed for the first time since 1987. The team were unable to retain the urn in the next series, but England achieved a successful defence in the 2010–11 Ashes, as Strauss captained England for a consecutive triumph against the Australians. Strauss, who was awarded an OBE in 2011, gave up the England captaincy in 2012 and also announced his retirement from professional cricket, bringing an end to his fourteen-year career with Middlesex.

Bradley Wiggins won the 2012 Tour de France.

Wiggins is the first British rider to win the prestigious cycling event since its inception in 1903. The 2012 Tour de France began in Liège, Belgium, and covered nearly 2,200 miles in just over three weeks before ending in Paris. Wiggins finished 3 minutes and 21 seconds ahead of team-mate, Chris Froome. Only ten days after his victory, Wiggins won the men's cycling time trial at the London Olympics to complete a unique sporting double. It was his fourth Olympic gold medal following success in the individual pursuit at the 2004 Games, and in both the individual pursuit and team pursuit at the 2008 Games. Wiggins, who also has one silver and two bronze medals, shares the record for the most Olympic medals won by a British athlete with Sir Chris Hoy. Wiggins has also recorded six wins at the UCI Track Cycling World Championships. Already a CBE, he was knighted in the 2013 New Year Honours.

33
THIRTY-THREE

Augustus Fitzroy (third Duke of Grafton) became prime minister in 1768 under the monarchy of George III.

Fitzroy is the second youngest British prime minister. He entered Parliament in 1756 aged twenty-one and months later, following the death of his grandfather, he moved to the House of Lords as the third Duke of Grafton (he had lost his father at the age of five). After a brief period as secretary of state for the northern department under the Marquess of Rockingham, Fitzroy became first lord of the Treasury in Pitt the elder's government in 1766. Pitt's ill health and absence from London meant that Fitzroy increasingly took the lead in Parliament and he formally replaced Pitt when he resigned in 1768. Fitzroy's term as prime minister lasted less than sixteenth months before he too resigned. His position had been weakened by attacks in the press, some in open letters by an anonymous writer who used the pen name 'Junius', and by Pitt's opposition following his return to Parliament in 1769. Later, Fitzroy had two spells as lord privy seal, the second of which ended in 1783. He died in 1811 at the age of seventy-five.

Charles Fox became the first foreign secretary of Great Britain in 1782.

Fox's tenure ended with the death of the prime minister, Lord Rockingham, just over three months later, although he returned to the post briefly on two further occasions. Fox was an outspoken and prominent critic of the 'American War' that was to end in 1783 with the Treaty of Paris, which recognised the independence of the American colonies. Though Fox would spend the vast majority of his political career in opposition, his third spell as foreign secretary, in 1806, was marked by his patronage of the bill to abolish the slave trade, duly passed in 1807, months after his death at the age of fifty-seven.

James Clerk Maxwell presented his 'Dynamic Theory of the Electro-Magnetic Field' to the Royal Society of London in 1864.

Maxwell's presentation included his groundbreaking deduction that light is an electromagnetic wave. He said that radiant heat and 'other radiation, if any' was also similarly constructed and thereby foresaw the electromagnetic spectrum yet to be fully discovered (for example, the existence of X-rays and radio waves were not demonstrated until later in the nineteenth century). His mathematical treatment of the relationship between electric and magnetic fields, already evidenced by the experimental work of Michael Faraday and others, was summarised in a celebrated set of equations, known as Maxwell's equations. Born in Edinburgh in 1831, Maxwell's early promise was manifested at the age of fourteen when his first scientific paper (on the geometry of ellipses and curves) was presented to the Royal Society of Edinburgh. His university education began in Edinburgh and was completed at Trinity College, Cambridge, where Maxwell graduated second in his year in mathematics. At the age of twenty-five he took up a post as professor of natural philosophy at Marischal College, Aberdeen, but following the merger with King's College to create the University of Aberdeen, he was made redundant. In 1860 Maxwell joined King's College London. Over a decade later he became the first Cavendish professor of physics at Cambridge University and oversaw the establishment of the Cavendish Laboratory. In addition to his work on electromagnetism, Maxwell also made significant contributions in other areas such as optics, colour theory, kinetic theory and thermodynamics. He also provided a physical explanation for the rings of Saturn. Maxwell's scientific contribution is regarded as comparable to that of Newton and Einstein, although he was never officially recognised during his lifetime. He died in 1879 at the age of forty-eight.

Lewis Carroll *(the pen name of Charles Dodgson) had his novel 'Alice's Adventures in Wonderland' published in 1865.*

Alice's Adventures in Wonderland has its origins in a boat trip on the Thames, taken by Dodgson in 1862. He was accompanied by the Reverend Robinson Duckworth and the three daughters (Lorina, Alice and Edith) of Henry George Liddell, the dean of Christ Church College, Oxford, where Dodgson lectured in mathematics. He created the tale to entertain the boating party and it was Alice who requested that he write it down. A sequel, *Through the Looking-Glass and What Alice Found There*, was published six years later. He died in 1898 at the age of sixty-five.

Alfred Nobel *was granted his British patent for dynamite in 1867.*

Nobel had been successful in producing a safer, more easily handled form of nitroglycerine (an explosive liquid invented by Ascanio Sobrero) by blending it with an inert substance, thus opening up commercial opportunities. He also invented gelignite, but he is perhaps best known for the awards which were established in his name – he bequeathed money for the purpose in his will. The first prizes were presented in 1901, five years after his death at the age of sixty-three.

Rudolf Diesel *lodged his first patent application for what would become known as the diesel engine, in 1892.*

The first working prototype of Diesel's engine was produced in 1897. No separate spark was needed to ignite the fuel, which was instead carried out by sufficient compression to raise the air temperature in the cylinder, leading to greater engine efficiency. Diesel disappeared at sea en route from Antwerp to Harwich in 1913. His body was found some days later, but the circumstances which led to his death, at the age of fifty-five, remain a mystery.

John Reith *became the first managing director of the British Broadcasting Company in 1922.*

Reith, the youngest of seven children, was born in Stonehaven, Aberdeenshire, the son of a church minister. He did not attend university but instead became an engineering apprentice. Reith served in the First World War, and came close to death when he was hit on the left cheek by a bullet. After the war he gave up his job in Glasgow, moved to London and, after seeing an advert in *The Morning Post*, applied for the job of general manager at the BBC. He was knighted shortly before it became a corporation five years later, when he became the first director-general. Reith set the tone for public service broadcasting and remained at the BBC until 1938. Two years later, he was made Baron Reith and served in government during the Second World War. The annual BBC Reith lectures, started in 1948, are held in his honour. Reith died in 1971 at the age of eighty-one.

'The Three Railway Engines', written by **Wilbert Awdry**, *was published in 1945.*

This was the first book in the Railway Series and was joined by *Thomas the Tank Engine* the following year, in which the title character made his debut. Awdry, a Church of England minister and a keen railway enthusiast, was inspired to create the characters to entertain his son, Christopher, who was ill with measles. Awdry wrote twenty-six books in the Railway Series, while Christopher went on to write a further sixteen – the latest of which was published in 2011. Thomas the Tank Engine first appeared on television in 1984, and has become an enduring children's favourite. Awdry received an OBE in 1996 and died the following year at the age of eighty-five.

The radio show 'Crazy People', co-created by **Spike Milligan** *and later known as 'The Goon Show', was first broadcast in 1951 on the BBC Home Service.*

Milligan was the principal writer of *The Goon Show*, which also starred Michael Bentine, Harry Secombe and Peter Sellers. Bentine left after the second series, but the popular show continued until 1960 and became an influential force in the development of British comedy. Milligan went on to have further success both in television (including *Q5* and its successors) and writing (for example, the *Puckoon* war memoirs). He received an honorary knighthood (Milligan was an Irish national) in 2000, two years before his death at the age of eighty-three. Milligan's humorous sugges-tion for his epitaph, 'I told you I was ill', was deemed to be inappropriate by the diocese in East Sussex where he is buried, but they did allow the words to be inscribed in Irish instead.

Edmund Hillary and Tenzing Norgay reached the summit of Mount Everest in 1953 – the first men known to have done so.

Hillary was born in New Zealand where his first major climb was to reach the summit of its highest peak, Aoraki/Mount Cook, in 1947. He was invited to join the 1953 Everest expedition led by John Hunt, which comprised over 400 people and in excess of 8,000kg of equipment. The team's first attempt on the summit, by Tom Bourdillon and Charles Evans, came within 300ft when they had to retreat due to oxygen failure. Three days later, and nearly three months after the start of the expedition, Hillary and Norgay were successful. Hillary famously snapped Norgay on the summit, but there was to be no corresponding picture of Hillary. Shortly after their success, Hillary was knighted by the newly crowned Queen Elizabeth II. Over forty years later, he was also made a Knight of the Order of the Garter. He died in 2008 at the age of eighty-eight.

*Paintings of soup cans by **Andy Warhol** made their exhibition debut at the Ferus Gallery, Los Angeles, in 1962.*

Warhol created thirty-two canvasses, each of which consists of a painting of a Campbell's soup can (one for each flavour available). A leading figure in the pop art movement, he was born Andrew Warhola in Pittsburgh, PA, to parents who had emigrated from Ruthenia (now part of Slovakia). He studied commercial art and worked successfully in this field following graduation. Warhol, whose studio was known as 'The Factory', also made arthouse films such as *Sleep* (1963), which consisted of over five hours of footage of someone sleeping, and *Empire* (1964), which featured several hours of the same shot of the Empire State Building. Warhol died in 1987, at the age of fifty-eight, following a routine operation. His bequest established the 'Andy Warhol Foundation for the Visual Arts'.

Graham Hill won the Formula One World Championship in 1962, driving for BRM (British Racing Motors), who also took the constructors' title.

Hill's victory was clinched in the last grand prix of the season in South Africa, when the race leader and fellow championship contender, Jim Clark, had to retire after mechanical failure. Hill, who was twenty-four when he obtained his ordinary driver's licence, became only the second British driver to win the title, and he won again, this time driving for

Lotus, six years later. He received the OBE in 1968 and is the only driver to have won the Formula One World Championship, the Indianapolis 500 (1966) and the Le Mans 24-Hour race (1972). Hill was killed in 1975, at the age of forty-six, along with five members of his racing team, when the plane he was piloting crashed in fog. His son Damon became world champion in 1996.

Steve McQueen *starred as Virgil Hilts in the 1963 film 'The Great Escape'.*

McQueen rose from a troubled background (he had a spell in a reform school) to become a highly successful actor. He also had a passion for motor sport and famously performed many of his own automotive stunts, although the adventurous motorcycle leap in *The Great Escape* was carried out by stuntman and personal friend Bud Ekins. His other notable films include *Bullitt* (1968), *The Thomas Crown Affair* (1968), *Papillion* (1973) and *The Sand Pebbles* (1966) for which he received an Academy Award best actor nomination. McQueen's last film, before his death in 1980 at the age of fifty, was *The Hunter* (1980).

Terry Wogan *hosted his first BBC Radio 2 Breakfast Show in 1972.*

Born in Limerick, Ireland, Wogan worked in banking until he got a part-time post at the Irish broadcaster Raidió Éireann. He became a full-time employee in 1961 and a few years later also began freelancing for the BBC; in 1967, Wogan presented *Late Night Extra* on the newly created Radio 1. Five years later he took over the breakfast time slot on Radio 2. He left in 1984 to devote himself to his eponymous BBC1 chat show, which was aired three times a week in the eighties, but returned to the Radio 2 breakfast show in 1993. Wogan is also famous for presenting BBC's annual Children in Need appeal and for his Eurovision Song Contest commentaries, the last of which he gave in 2008. He was knighted in 2005 (the year that he also took British citizenship). Wogan presented his final Radio 2 breakfast show in December 2009, but began presenting a new Sunday show on the same network in the following year.

Brian Josephson *was awarded the Nobel Prize in Physics in 1973 for his work on 'Josephson Junctions'.*

A native of Cardiff, Josephson completed his undergraduate and postgraduate studies at the University of Cambridge. Josephson junctions are made from two layers of superconducting material separated by a thin insulating layer (in a superconductor, the electrical resistance can be reduced to essentially zero at a certain temperature). In 1962, Josephson predicted that a current could flow across the junction between the superconductors and also described its behaviour. His theory was later proved to be correct. Josephson junctions have found important applications in sensitive measuring equipment used to study magnetic fields. Josephson shared the 1973 Nobel Prize in Physics with Leo Esaki and Ivar Giaver for their work on tunnelling phenomena.

'Star Wars', written and directed by **George Lucas***, was released in the USA in 1977.*

The teenage Lucas survived a serious car crash to go on and study at the University of Southern California's School of Cinema-Television. His first box office success was as the writer and director of *American Graffiti* (1973), for which he also received two Academy Award nominations. The film helped Lucas to secure a deal with 20th Century Fox for *Star Wars* after it had been turned down by rival studios United Artists and Universal. *Star Wars*, written and directed by Lucas, became one of the highest-grossing films of all time after its release in 1977. The film won a total of seven Academy Awards, with Lucas garnering a nomination for best director. He has also worked as a writer, producer and story contributor for the *Indiana Jones* films. After the completion of the original Star Wars trilogy with *The Empire Strikes Back* (1980) and *The Return of the Jedi* (1983), Lucas revisited his creation to write and direct three 'prequels', released between 1999 and 2005.

The Live Aid concert, co-organised by **Bob Geldof** *and Midge Ure, took place at Wembley Stadium in 1985.*

A parallel concert was also staged at the John F. Kennedy Stadium in Philadelphia. These events followed on from the success, in 1984, of the Band Aid single 'Do They Know It's Christmas' (co-written by Geldof and Ure) which was inspired by news reports on the humanitarian crisis in drought-stricken Ethiopia. The record raised millions for famine relief in Africa. Geldof first came to prominence as the lead singer of the

Boomtown Rats who scored the first new wave number one in the UK singles chart with 'Rat Trap' in 1978. He has also recorded five solo albums, the latest of which, *How To Compose Popular Songs That Will Sell*, was released in 2011.

*The Simpsons, created by **Matt Groening**, made their television debut on 'The Tracey Ullman Show' in 1987.*

Groening came up with the idea of the dysfunctional family after being contacted by James L. Brooks, producer of US television's *The Tracey Ullman Show*, about an animation project he was considering for the programme. Brooks had seen Groening's *Life in Hell* cartoon strip, which was first published in 1977, and had thought its characters could be adapted for the project. However, Groening did not want to lose the rights to these characters and so the Simpsons were born as a makeshift replacement. Lisa, Maggie, Marge and Homer are all named after members of Groening's family. The animation developed into thirty-minute episodes and made its debut in this format in 1989. The winner of numerous awards, a big-screen version of Groening's creation, *The Simpsons Movie*, was released in 2007.

*In 1989 **Tim Berners-Lee** described his idea for what became known as the World Wide Web in a paper called 'Information Management: A Proposal'.*

Berners-Lee was working for CERN (the European organisation for nuclear research) at the time and was trying to find a solution to their information distribution and management requirements. His 1989 paper discussed combining hypertext with the internet to create a global information sharing platform. Referred to as 'Mesh' in this document, the following year Berners-Lee renamed it the World Wide Web. The first website was launched at CERN in August 1991 (http://info.cern.ch). Berners-Lee, who was knighted in the 2004 New Year Honours list and admitted to the Order of Merit three years later, also created the first web browser and editor.

*In 1993 **Emma Thompson** won the Academy Award for best actress, for her role as Margaret Schlegel in 'Howards End'.*

Thompson read English at Newnham College, Cambridge, where she was a member of the Footlights theatrical club. She later joined fellow members Stephen Fry and Hugh Laurie in the TV comedy sketch show *Alfresco*, first broadcast in 1983. Four years later, her roles as Suzi Kettles in cult TV drama *Tutti Frutti*, and as Harriet Pringle in *Fortunes of War*, won her a Bafta best actress award. She made her film debut the following year in *The Tall Guy* (1989). The year after her first Oscar win, Thompson returned to the nomination list in the best actress and best supporting actress categories for *Remains of the Day* (1993) and *In the Name of the Father* (1993) respectively. The role of Elinor Dashwood in *Sense and Sensibility* (1995) brought her a third best actress nomination and also an Academy Award for best adapted screenplay. Since then, Thompson has appeared in films that include *Primary Colors* (1998), *Stranger than Fiction* (2006) and *Brideshead Revisited* (2008).

Frank Bruno won the WBC heavyweight boxing title in 1995.

In what was his fourth world championship bout, Bruno outpointed Oliver McCall at Wembley Stadium to take the title. His first defence was against Mike Tyson six months later, whom Bruno had previously faced in a world title contest in 1989. A stoppage in round three brought an end to Bruno's reign in what became his last professional fight. Bruno became the Amateur Boxing Association heavyweight champion aged eighteen, and began his professional career in 1982. At its close almost exactly sixteen years later, his record showed forty wins out of forty-five fights, thirty-eight of these inside the distance. He was awarded an MBE in 1990.

*In 2002 the Turner Prize was awarded to **Keith Tyson**.*

Tyson had his first solo exhibition, *From the Artmachine*, in the mid 1990s. This featured works created in response to the output from his 'Artmachine' – a system the Cumbrian-born artist produced to create random proposals for pieces of work for him to execute. One such example is *AMCHII – the KFC Notebooks and the UCT*, which consists of the offerings from the entire Kentucky Fried Chicken menu cast in lead. Tyson was nominated for his exhibitions in Venice, London and Zurich, and his Turner Prize show included paintings using mixed media on two aluminium panels entitled *Bubble Chambers: 2 Discrete Molecules of Simultaneity*.

Martin Johnson *captained the England side which won the Rugby World Cup in 2003.*

Johnson retired from international rugby soon after the Rugby World Cup final, ending an England career which began in 1993. He won honours at club level at Leicester, with five Premiership titles between 1995 and 2002, and two consecutive Heineken Cup wins (2001 and 2002). England were victorious in all but one of his last thirty games and Johnson, who was awarded a CBE in 2004, returned to the side as manager in 2008. He led them to a Six Nations victory in 2011, adding to the five he had won as a player, two of which were Grand Slams. Johnson resigned as manager weeks after England's return from the 2011 Rugby World Cup where they reached the quarter-finals in the tournament hosted by New Zealand.

Matthew Pinsent *won his fourth Olympic gold medal at the 2004 Games in Athens as a member of the coxless four rowing team.*

Pinsent retired from rowing later that year and was knighted in the following New Year Honours list. He first won Olympic gold when he partnered Steve Redgrave in the coxless pairs in the 1992 Barcelona Olympics. They repeated this success four years later and then changed to the coxless four category, with Pinsent winning his third and Redgrave his fifth gold, in the Sydney Games in 2000. Pinsent, who has also clocked up ten victories at the World Rowing Championships, is also the recipient of both an MBE and CBE.

Aravind Adiga *won the 2008 Man Booker Prize for his debut novel 'The White Tiger'.*

Adiga, born in Madras (now Chennai, India), was educated at Columbia University and Magdalen College, Oxford, before he embarked on a career in journalism. *The White Tiger* recounts the story of Balram, who dreams of escape from the poverty of his native Indian village. Adiga has also published a collection of short stories, *Between the Assassinations*, in 2008. His second novel, *Last Man in Tower*, was published in 2011.

David Weir *won four gold medals at the 2012 Paralympic Games in London.*

On the track, Weir was victorious in the 800m, 1,500m and 5,000m T54 wheelchair races and then won Britain's last gold medal of the Games in the marathon. Weir first competed at the Paralympics in 1996 as a seventeen-year-old. He missed the next Games in Sydney, but returned in 2004 to win silver and bronze in Athens. The Beijing Paralympics brought more success as he won two gold medals (for the T54 800m and 1,500m), one silver and one bronze. Weir is also a six-time winner of the London wheelchair marathon and the winner of six world titles from 100m to 5,000m. He was awarded an MBE in 2009 and a CBE in the 2013 New Year Honours.

34
THIRTY-FOUR

Arthur Guinness *took out a 9,000-year lease on a former brewery at St. James's Gate, Dublin, in 1759.*

The annual fee for Guinness's Dublin premises was set at £45 and by the late nineteenth century it had become the largest brewery in the world. Guinness had first entered the brewing business three years previously when he started out in nearby Leixlip. At the Dublin brewery, the popularity of his dark beer 'porter', the forerunner of today's modern Guinness, resulted in the site being turned over to its exclusive production by the end of the eighteenth century. Guinness was succeeded after his death, in 1803 at the age of seventy-seven, by one of his sons, also called Arthur, who would oversee the continued development of the business. It became, in the mid-nineteenth century, one of the largest in Ireland and is a globally recognised brand today.

Henry Cavendish *presented his first paper on 'Experiments on Factitious Air' to the Royal Society in 1766.*

Cavendish's paper was the first to recognise the elemental nature of hydrogen gas (referred to as 'inflammable air'). Cavendish, a reclusive and solitary man, attended Peterhouse College, Cambridge, but left three years later without a degree. Nonetheless, coming from a wealthy family, he was able to pursue his scientific interests further, including experiments to determine the density of the earth. Many of his other findings did not emerge until after his death (in 1810 at the age of seventy-eight), and often after others had been credited instead.

In 1846 **Johann Galle** *became the first person to knowingly observe the planet Neptune.*

Guided by the predictions he had received from Urbain Le Verrier, Galle observed the planet from the Berlin Observatory where he worked as an assistant to Johann Encke. Initially referred to as Le Verrier's planet, it was ultimately named after the Roman god of the sea and is the eighth, and outermost, planet in the solar system (Pluto was reclassified as a dwarf planet in 2006). Neptune is also the only one which cannot be seen without the use of a telescope. Galle, who later became professor of astronomy at Breslau, now has a crater on the moon and also one on Mars named after him. He took a special interest in comets and would discover three of these celestial bodies himself. Galle was ninety-eight when he died in 1910.

In 1854 **Florence Nightingale** *led a party of thirty-eight nurses to tend to the wounded of the Crimean War.*

Named Florence after her birthplace in Italy, Nightingale improved the organisation of the nursing effort in the Barrack Hospital, Scutari (present-day Üsküdar, Turkey), and her visible presence in the wards at night as she tended to the patients gave rise to her image as 'the Lady with the Lamp'. Nightingale returned to England in 1856. Her experiences in the Crimea led her to press for healthcare reform and a Royal Commission was subsequently set up. In 1860 she established the Nightingale School of Nursing at St. Thomas's Hospital in London and published *Notes on Nursing: What It Is and What It Is Not* which conveyed her ideas to a wider audience. In 1907, Nightingale became the first woman to receive the Order of Merit. She died three years later at the age of ninety.

The first novel by **Jules Verne***, 'Cinq Semaines en Ballon' (Five Weeks in a Balloon), was published in 1863.*

Born in Nantes, France, Verne studied Law in Paris, but then turned to writing. This career choice blossomed when he met the publisher Pierre-Jules Hetzel, with whom he would launch his literary debut. An early protagonist of the science-fiction genre, Verne's later works included *A Journey to the Centre of the Earth*, *From the Earth to the Moon* and *Around the World in Eighty Days*. His books have been widely translated and many film treatments have been made of his work. Verne died in 1905 at the age of seventy-seven.

'Far from the Madding Crowd' by **Thomas Hardy** *was published in 1874.*

Hardy's fourth published novel, *Far from the Madding Crowd* was the first of his books set in the fictional region of Wessex, and his first major success. Prior to its appearance in book form, it had been serialised in monthly instalments throughout 1874 in the *Cornhill Magazine*. His debut novel, *The Poor Man and the Lady*, completed some seven years earlier, remained unpublished, but in 1871 his second attempt, *Desperate Remedies*, found a publisher. Hardy's later works include *The Mayor of Casterbridge*, *Tess of the D'Urbervilles* and *Jude the Obscure*. He concentrated on poetry in his later years, with his *Wessex Poems and Other Verses* appearing in 1898. Hardy continued to publish poetry collections up until his death, in 1928, at the age of eighty-seven.

William Boeing *founded the Pacific Aero Products Company in July 1916.*

In the year after its founding, Pacific Aero Products was renamed as the Boeing Airplane Company. Boeing's father was a German immigrant to the US who, with his purchase of timberland and its associated mineral rights, was to leave a significant inheritance. He died when William was eight. Boeing studied at Yale, but left to enter the timber business himself. His fascination for flying developed into an interest in aeroplane manufacture – the first fruits of which were the B&W Model 1 seaplane/ biplane, designed with George Westervelt, which made its maiden flight a month before the founding of Pacific Aero Products in 1916. The company struggled after World War One, turning to the manufacture of furniture amongst other things, in order to remain solvent. However, success in the airmail business that started in the late 1920s proved lucrative. In 1934, Boeing resigned as chairman as anti-trust laws forced the division of the company into United Air Lines, United Aircraft Corporation and the Boeing Airplane Company. Boeing died in 1956 at the age of seventy-four.

John Cockcroft and Ernest Walton designed and developed the particle accelerator, which was first used in 1932 to successfully disintegrate lithium nuclei.

Cockcroft and Walton's apparatus directed a proton beam of sufficient energy at lithium atoms to split them and form helium nuclei (alpha particles). The experiment also vindicated Einstein's famous assertion concerning the equivalence of mass and energy ($E=mc^2$). Cockcroft and Walton shared the 1951 Nobel Prize in Physics for their work. Cockcroft became the first director of the Atomic Energy Research Establishment at Harwell in 1946 and was knighted two years later. He was made a KCB in 1953 and appointed to the Order of Merit ten years before his death, at the age of seventy, in 1967.

In 1932 Amelia Earhart became the first woman to fly solo, non-stop, across the Atlantic.

Earhart's flight, which lasted nearly fifteen hours, took her from Newfoundland to Northern Ireland. Earhart experienced her first air trip at the age of twenty-three; a ten-minute flight which inspired her to become a pilot. Shortly after, she took her first flying lesson and then saved for six months in order to buy a plane. In 1922, at the age of twenty-five, she set an altitude record for a woman pilot. Six years later, alongside pilot Bill Stultz and co-pilot Louis Gordon, she became the first woman to fly across the Atlantic. In 1937 Earhart's plane went missing over the Pacific during an attempt, with navigator Fred Noonan, to fly around the world. She was thirty-nine at the time and neither the plane nor their bodies have ever been found.

Fred Astaire starred in his first film, 'Dancing Lady', released in 1933.

Astaire (born Frederick Austerlitz) first danced as a child performer in partnership with his older sister, Adele. They appeared on Broadway, but Adele left the duo when she married in 1932. Astaire made the move into films and an audition report for RKO pictures is reputed to have said: 'Can't act. Can't sing. Balding. Can dance a little'. His first on-screen dance partner, in *Dancing Lady* (1933), was Joan Crawford. It was in his second film, *Flying Down to Rio* (1933), that he first paired with Ginger Rogers with whom he made nine more features, concluding with *The Barkleys of Broadway* (1949). Astaire's contribution to films was recognised with an honorary Oscar in 1950. Later in his career, he concentrated on straight acting. His role as Harlee Claiborne in *The Towering Inferno* (1974) brought him a Bafta win for best supporting actor and an Oscar nomination, at the age of seventy-six. He made his last feature-film appearance in *Ghost Story* (1981). Astaire died in 1987 at the age of eighty-eight.

The Richter scale, used for measuring the intensity of earthquakes, was created by **Charles Richter** *and Beno Gutenberg and first published in 1935.*

Originally developed to quantify earth tremors in southern California, the Richter scale, which is expressed in whole numbers and decimal fractions, was adapted to have global application. It is also logarithmic – therefore each whole number increase represents a tenfold rise in earthquake amplitude. Richter died in 1985 at the age of eighty-five.

In 1955 **Donald Campbell** *set his first water-speed world record at Ullswater.*

Campbell's Bluebird K7 craft achieved an average speed over its two timed runs of 202.32mph, and in 1964 he further increased the record, reaching 276.33mph. Campbell also took the official land-speed world record that year, driving another Bluebird, to become the first (and to date only) person to break both the official land and water-speed records in the same year. He died in 1967, at the age of forty-five, during an attempt to increase the water-speed world record to over 300mph. His body was recovered in 2001. Campbell's father (Sir Malcolm) was also a speed-record holder on both land and water.

In 1957 **Patrick Moore** *presented the first edition of the BBC astronomy series 'The Sky at Night'.*

Moore, who presented the 700th edition in 2011 and celebrated the fifty-fifth anniversary in 2012, continued to host the programme until his death in 2012, at the age of eighty-nine. *The Sky at Night* is the longest-running television programme with the same presenter (Moore only missed one show, in 2004, as a consequence of suspected food poisoning). Due to ill health, Moore was mostly schooled at home, and his interest in astronomy was kindled at the age of six when he saw his mother's copy of *The Story of the Solar System* by G. F. Chambers. Moore, who had a particular interest in the study of the moon, authored over sixty books on astronomy, all written on his 1908 typewriter. Knighted in 2001, he was also a self-taught musician and composer, and served in the RAF as a navigator during World War Two.

In 1963 **Martin Luther King, Jr.** *made his 'I have a dream' speech from the steps of the Lincoln Memorial, Washington D.C.*

King spoke of his longing for the peaceful co-existence of all people and an end to prejudice and racial injustice. King's father was a Baptist minister, and he would follow in his footsteps by becoming a pastor in Montgomery, Alabama. He became a prominent civil rights leader urging non-violent confrontation as the means to advance the African-American civil rights movement. King was awarded the Nobel Peace Prize in 1964 and he contributed to the passing of the Civil Rights Act in 1964 and the Voting Rights Act in 1965. He was assassinated in March 1968 at the age of thirty-nine. First observed in the US in 1986, Martin Luther King Day is held on the third Monday of January to commemorate his achievements.

In 1971 **Glenda Jackson** *won her first Academy Award for best actress for her portrayal of Gudrun Brangwen in 'Women in Love'.*

Jackson studied at Rada, and made her theatrical debut in 1957. Predominantly a stage actress, she made her first appearance on screen, uncredited, in the rugby league drama *This Sporting Life* (1963). In the Peter Brook directed *Marat/Sade* (1967) Jackson, then a member of the Royal Shakespeare Company, reprised her stage portrayal of Charlotte Corday. She won her second best actress Oscar for *A Touch of Class* (1973) and received two other Academy best actress nominations for *Sunday Bloody Sunday* (1971) and *Hedda* (1976), the former of which provided her only Bafta win. Jackson left acting in 1992 to pursue a career in politics. She became the MP for Hampstead and Highgate at the general election that year, and continues to represent the constituency in Parliament. Jackson was awarded a CBE in 1978.

In 1975 **Doug Scott** *and Dougal Haston became the first Britons to reach the summit of Mount Everest.*

In an expedition led by Chris Bonnington, Scott and Haston (who was one year older) were also the first to scale Mount Everest by taking the difficult route up the south-west face. Haston, who was born in Currie, near Edinburgh, was killed two years later in an avalanche, at the age of thirty-six, while skiing alone in the Bernese Alps. Scott, a native of Nottingham, began his climbing career at the age of twelve. He has achieved many first ascents as well as reaching the highest peaks on all seven continents – 'the seven summits'. Scott was awarded a CBE in 1994.

Harrison Ford starred as Han Solo in 'Star Wars', released in 1977.

Ford's early acting career was dominated by minor roles and he turned to carpentry to provide a more stable income. The catalyst for the change in his fortunes was his acquaintance with George Lucas who cast him as Bob Falfa in *American Graffiti* (1973), and then subsequently directed him in *Star Wars* (1977). Ford returned to the role of Han Solo in the subsequent sequels, and also starred in the successful Indiana Jones film series, beginning with *Raiders of the Lost Art* (1981). Other memorable Harrison Ford roles include that of Rick Deckard in the sci-fi classic *Blade Runner* (1982) and as John Book in *Witness* (1985), which earned him an Academy Award nomination for best actor. Many of his other films have also been popular at the box office including *The Fugitive* (1993), *Clear and Present Danger* (1994) and *Air Force One* (1997).

Salman Rushdie won the 1981 Booker Prize for his novel 'Midnight's Children'.

Midnight's Children was published six years after his debut novel, *Grimus*. Rushdie was born in Bombay (now Mumbai), India, and was educated there and later in England, at Rugby. He went on to read history at King's College, Cambridge. Rushdie worked as an advertising copywriter in Britain before his literary success allowed him to become a full-time writer. His fourth novel, *The Satanic Verses*, published in 1988, was declared blasphemous by Ayatollah Khomeini, the supreme leader of Iran at the time. A *fatwa* was issued that called for the death of Rushdie, who was forced into hiding. His next book, the children's volume *Haroun and the Sea of Stories*, appeared in 1990. Rushdie's other works include *The Moor's Last Sigh* (1995), *Shalimar the Clown* (2005) and *The Enchantress of Florence* (2008). Rushdie was knighted in 2007.

Alec Jeffreys observed the world's first 'genetic fingerprint' in 1984.

Jeffreys, working at the University of Leicester, described it as a 'eureka' moment when he saw the highly variable DNA patterns taken from his lab technician and her parents. Human DNA sequences are approximately 99.9% similar; however, by examining the distinctive areas it is possible to discern one individual from another. The first application of DNA finger-printing was in an immigration case in 1985. Jeffreys' fascination with science began as a boy and he read biochemistry at Oxford, followed by a DPhil in Genetics. Jeffreys has received many awards for his work, including a knighthood in 1994.

Kazuo Ishiguro won the 1989 Booker Prize for his third novel, 'The Remains of the Day'.

The Remains of the Day, adapted for the screen in 1993, is about an English butler, Stevens, as he looks back on his life of service in the employ of Lord Darlington. Ishiguro was born in Nagasaki, Japan, but moved with his family to England at the age of five. He was first nominated for the Booker Prize in 1986 for *An Artist of the Floating World*, and received two more nominations for *When We Were Orphans* (2000) and *Never Let Me Go* (2005). Ishiguro was awarded an OBE for services to literature in 1995.

In 2000 Sam Mendes won the Academy Award for best director for 'American Beauty'.

Mendes had previously worked in the theatre including with the Royal Shakespeare Company. *American Beauty* (1999), his debut as a film director, collected a total of five Academy Awards including best picture and best actor for Kevin Spacey. His other films include *Road to Perdition* (2002) and *Revolutionary Road* (2008). Mendes is the youngest British recipient, and third youngest overall, to receive the Academy Award for best director. He was awarded a CBE in the 2000 Queen's Birthday Honours.

Jonathan Edwards won a gold medal at the Sydney Olympic Games in 2000 for the triple jump.

Edwards had secured the bronze medal in the triple jump at the previous Olympics. At the 1995 World Championships in Gothenburg, on his way to the gold medal, Edwards twice broke the world record setting an ulti-mate distance of 18.29 metres that still stands today. He was awarded a CBE in 2001.

Kelly Holmes won two gold medals at the 2004 Olympic Games in Athens for the 800m and 1,500m.

Holmes took up running at the age of twelve and two years later was inspired to become an Olympic champion after watching Sebastian Coe's gold-winning performance over 1500m at the 1984 Los Angeles Olympics. She joined the Women's Royal Army Corps (WRAC), and continued her sporting development by becoming a physical training instructor. Holmes left the army to concentrate full-time on athletics in 1997, the same year that she was regarded as the favourite for the 1500m at the World Championships in Athens. However, she had to withdraw during the first heat due to injury. Seven years later, Holmes returned to Athens to savour double Olympic success at the 800m and 1500m. Already an MBE, she was made a Dame in the 2005 New Year Honours list. Holmes is still the UK-record holder over 600m, 800m 1,000m and 1,500m.

Sarah Storey won four gold medals at the 2012 Paralympic Games in London.

Storey won Britain's first gold medal of the Games, in the cycling C5 individual pursuit, on the opening day of competition. She then won gold for the C4-5 500m time trial, the C5 individual road time trial and finally the C4-5 individual road race, taking her London Games gold-medal total to four and her overall Paralympic tally to eleven. Aged fourteen, Storey first competed at the Paralympics as a swimmer at the Barcelona Games in 1992, where she won two golds, three silvers and a bronze. At the next three Paralympics she amassed a further three gold, five silver and two bronze medals in the pool, before switching sports to cycling in 2005. Three years later, she won two cycling gold medals at the Beijing Paralympics and also beat an able-bodied field to win the 3,000m indi-vidual pursuit at the British Track Cycling Championships. Storey success-fully defended her title the following year. In 2010, she became the first Paralympic cyclist to compete for England at the Commonwealth Games. Storey was awarded an MBE in 1998, an OBE in 2009 and a damehood in the 2013 New Year Honours.

35
THIRTY-FIVE

In 1599 'Julius Caesar' was one of the first plays by **William Shakespeare** *to be performed at the newly opened Globe Theatre in London.*

Shakespeare was baptised in Stratford-upon-Avon in 1564. Firm details on his boyhood are scant, but it is recorded that he was married, at the age of eighteen, to Anne Hathaway, eight years his senior. Their first child, Susanna, was born six months later. Information is again scarce on the next few years of Shakespeare's life, but by his late twenties he was known to be an actor and playwright in London (his earliest works for the stage include *Henry VI* and *Richard III*). He also became a prominent member of the Lord Chamberlain's Men (later renamed the King's Men after the accession of James I to the English throne in 1603) – a company of actors that from 1594 onwards was the sole performer of his plays. Shakespeare also had a share in the partnership of company members that built the Globe Theatre, which was opened in 1599, on London's south bank. By this time, Shakespeare was midway through his career as a playwright, and had completed works such as *Romeo and Juliet*, *A Midsummer Night's Dream*, *The Merchant of Venice* and *Henry V*. After adding to his literary canon with plays that included *Hamlet*, *Othello*, *King Lear*, *Macbeth* and, one of his last, *The Tempest*, he retired to Stratford for the last few years of his life. Shakespeare's 154 sonnets were published in a single volume in 1609. He died in 1616 at the age of fifty-two. The first collection of his plays (known as the *First Folio*) was published seven years later.

In 1721 Christian Ludwig, Margrave of Brandenburg-Schwedt, received the manuscript for the Brandenburg Concertos by **Johann Sebastian Bach**.

Bach's collection of instrumentals, the Brandenburg Concertos, was originally known as *Six Concerts avec plusieurs instruments*, and was assembled by him from works dating back to his early twenties to showcase his talent with a view to gaining the Margrave of Brandenburg-Schwedt's patronage. There is no record of Ludwig acknowledging their receipt or of any performances. Ludwig died in 1734 and Bach's autographed manuscript remained in the family archives until its rediscovery in 1849; one year later, the concertos were published for the first time. Bach was born in Eisenach, in present day Germany, in 1685. He was initially taught the violin and harpsichord by his father, but his tutelage and care was transferred to an elder brother, an organist, after the death of their father when Bach was ten. Their mother had died only eight months previously. Bach became a celebrated master of the keyboard and a court musician, first in Weimar and then in Köthen, during which time he composed cantatas, organ music, concertos and orchestral suites. Bach's last and longest position, as the Cantor of Thomasschule in Leipzig, began in 1723. He was also the director of music at two of the city's principal churches, and it was during this period that Bach composed the *St. Matthew Passion*, *St John Passion*, the *Christmas Oratorio* and his *Mass in B Minor*. Bach's *The Art of Fuge* was unfinished at his death, at the age of sixty-five, in 1750.

*The third Eddystone Lighthouse, designed by **John Smeaton**, was completed in 1759.*

Smeaton's Eddystone Lighthouse had two innovations that contributed to its success and which were influential in future lighthouse design: its interlocking stone blocks and a quick-drying, water-resistant mortar. The structure, which stood for approximately 120 years, was replaced when the rock on which it stood started to erode. It was reassembled on Plymouth Hoe where it remains as a tourist attraction. Smeaton's other work included bridges and canals, and he is looked upon as a founder of the civil engineering profession. He died in 1792 at the age of sixty-eight.

*The first published novel by **Jane Austen** was 'Sense and Sensibility' in 1811.*

Sense and Sensibility, with its authorship attributed to 'A Lady', was published on a commission basis, with Austen responsible for any losses. However, this did not prove to be a problem as the first edition sold out and Austen took a share of the profits. Austen was born in Steventon, Hampshire, to the Reverend George Austen and his wife Cassandra. The second youngest of six brothers and two sisters, Austen spent her first twenty-five years living in the Steventon rectory. By around the age of eleven she was already writing plays, novellas and other prose. She completed her first novel, *First Impressions*, at the age of twenty-one, but this was turned down by a publisher. Later renamed *Pride and Prejudice*, it became her second published novel in 1813 when she was in her late thirties. She saw only two more novels published in her lifetime, *Mansfield Park* in 1814 and *Emma* in 1816, before her death in 1817 at the age of forty-one. *Northanger Abbey* and *Persuasion* were published posthumously later that year with a note by her brother Henry, which for the first time identified her as the author of her six novels. Although courtship and marriage figured prominently in her writing, Austen never married, although she did accept a proposal when she was twenty-six, but quickly changed her mind. She remains one of the most popular English novelists and her work has featured in many film and television adaptations.

***Charles Blondin** (born Jean-Francois Gravelet) crossed the Niagara River on a tightrope in 1859.*

Blondin, watched by a crowd of thousands, first crossed from the American side, stopping half way to take a drink of water raised from a boat below, before making the return journey. He repeated the tightrope crossing several times over the coming weeks and added further excitement for the watching crowd since he would, amongst other variations, perform it in a sack, stop and stand on his head and even carry his manager (Harry Colcord) over on his back. As interest grew, special trains and steamers were laid on to convey spectators to the area. Blondin made his final tightrope performance in Belfast in 1896. He died the following year at the age of seventy-two.

***Dmitri Mendeleev** presented his work 'On the Relationship of the Properties of the Elements to their Atomic Weights' to the Russian Chemical Society in 1869.*

Mendeleev showed the society his arrangement of the known chemical elements into a table which importantly left gaps for undiscovered elements, some of which had their properties predicted by Mendeleev based on their position in the table. His work would be developed further into the modern, complete periodic table of the elements. Mendeleev died in 1907 at the age of seventy-two.

The first joint work by **William Gilbert** *and Arthur Sullivan, 'Thespis, or, The Gods Grown Old' was first performed in 1871.*

Known by his middle name of 'Schwenk' within the family (from the surname of his great aunt), Gilbert was called to the Bar in 1863 and practised for a short time before becoming a magazine contributor and playwright. Following *Thespis*, Gilbert and Sullivan did not collaborate for another three years until *Trial by Jury*, which proved to be a great success. They went on to complete a further twelve comic operas – which include *The Pirates of Penzance*, *The Mikado* and their last, *The Grand Duke*, first performed in 1896. Gilbert was knighted in 1907 and died in 1911 at the age of seventy-four.

Emile Berliner filed his patent for the gramophone in 1887.

Berliner's gramophone patent was granted six months later, and in the following year his invention was demonstrated at the Franklin Institute in Philadelphia. Unlike Edison's phonograph, which used cylinders, Berliner's invention used a disc to record sound. Recorded discs were easier to mass manufacture than cylinders and also easier to store. The two systems remained in competition, but Berliner's discs, or records, had won out by the end of the First World War. The format was developed further (the microgroove long-playing disc was introduced in 1948) and became the dominant means of domestic sound-reproduction until the advent of compact discs in the early 1980s. Berliner, who had little formal education, also patented many improvements to the newly invented telephone. He died in 1929 at the age of seventy-eight.

Production of the first Morris car (the Oxford) was started in 1913 by W.R.M. Motors Ltd, founded the previous year by **William Morris**.

The Oxford, designed by Morris, was a two-seater car with an 8.9 horsepower engine that was dubbed the 'bullnose' on account of its distinctive radiator shape. Morris's first business venture was as a cycle repairer at the age of sixteen. He soon moved into bicycle manufacturing, followed by motorcycle work – then car sales, repair and hire. Following World War One, Morris's company increased car production and by the late 1920s it was supplying a third of British-made cars. Faced with greater competition, Morris merged his business with Austin to create the British

Motor Corporation (BMC) in 1952. Morris, who was honoured with an OBE, was also made a Baronet, a Baron and finally became Viscount Nuffield in 1938. He died in 1963 at the age of eighty-five. He is also remembered for his philanthropic work; he founded Nuffield College at the University of Oxford and also the Nuffield Foundation. The Morris name was last used on cars in the early 1980s, though the MG (Morris Garages) marque has continued to feature since then. Both are now owned by the Shanghai Automotive Industry Corporation.

Oliver Hardy starred in the first 'Stan and Ollie' film, 'The Second Hundred Years', released in 1927.

Hardy and Stan Laurel had appeared together in earlier films, though not as the comedy pairing that would make them famous. As a duo, they went on to make over one hundred pictures, most of them short features. Their last movie, *Atoll K* (also known as *Utopia*), was released in 1951. Hardy used his father's first name rather than his own (Norvell), and made his film debut in 1914 (billed as O.N. Hardy). He died in 1957 at the age of sixty-five.

The Morecambe and Wise Show, starring **Eric Morecambe** *and* **Ernie Wise**, *began on ATV and other regional independent stations in 1961.*

Morecambe (originally John Eric Bartholomew) first met Wise (a contraction of Wiseman), when they were both juvenile performers. Morecambe's mother Sadie was the inspiration behind the formation of the comedy duo and they made their stage debut, billed as Bartholomew and Wise, in 1941. Wartime service in the merchant navy for Wise, and for Morecambe in the mines as a 'Bevin boy', broke up their partnership, but it was resumed in 1947. They plied their trade on the variety circuit and also began to feature on radio and television. This led to their first TV series, *Running Wild* (1954); however, it was not a success and only ran for six episodes. Following more variety work and appearances on television, the pair began their next series, this time on ITV, in 1961. The show gave them their first television award two years later and established their popularity. The duo also made three feature films before transferring to the BBC in 1968, after which they enjoyed even greater success, particularly with the Christmas specials; the 1977 edition drew an estimated audience of over 28 million. They returned to ITV in the following year, but Morecambe, previously afflicted by heart problems, collapsed shortly after appearing on stage in 1984 and died a few hours later. He was fifty-eight. Wise, who ceremonially made Britain's first mobile phone call on New Year's Day 1985, died in 1999 at the age of seventy-three. Morecambe and Wise both received an OBE in 1976.

In 1964 **Tony Richardson** *won the Academy Award for best director for 'Tom Jones'.*

Richardson was a leading figure in the British New Wave of film directors who explored working-class themes in their films in the late 1950s and early 1960s. *Tom Jones* (1963), for which he also picked up the best picture prize, was Richardson's sixth feature film as a director in a career that began with *Look Back in Anger* (1959), and continued with films such as *The Entertainer* (1960) and *A Taste of Honey* (1961). His flamboyant costume drama *The Charge of the Light Brigade* (1968) scored six Bafta nominations. Richardson directed Mick Jagger in *Ned Kelly* (1970), but he had to leave his next project, *Mahogany* (1975), starring singer Diana Ross, after a disagreement with Berry Gordy Jr., the producer. Richardson's last film, *Blue Sky*, was released three years after his death, in 1991, at the age of sixty-three. He was survived by two daughters from his marriage to Vanessa Redgrave – Joely and Natasha (who died as a result of a skiing accident in 2009) both became successful actresses.

Leonard Nimoy *and* **William Shatner** *starred in the series 'Star Trek', first shown on US television in 1966.*

Shatner took the role of Captain James T. Kirk in the second pilot episode 'Where No Man Has Gone Before', replacing Jeffrey Hunter who played Captain Christopher Pike, the previous commander of the starship *Enterprise*. Shatner notched up numerous television appearances in the fifties and sixties, and also landed roles in films such as *The Brothers Karamazov* (1958) and *Judgement at Nuremberg* (1961). *Star Trek*'s original television run ended in 1969, but ten years later *Star Trek: The Motion Picture* revived the space series for cinema audiences and for Shatner himself, who went on to play Captain Kirk in five more films. Nimoy played the half human/half Vulcan science officer Mr Spock in the television series and films. He also directed two of the Star Trek cinema releases. Nimoy has written two autobiographies: *I Am Not Spock* (1977) and *I Am Spock* (1995).

In 1970 **Maggie Smith** *won both the Academy Award and Bafta for best actress for her portrayal of the titular character in 'The Prime of Miss Jean Brodie'.*

Smith first trod the boards at the age of seventeen with the Oxford University Dramatic Society, and made her Broadway debut in 1956. Her first major film role in *Nowhere to Go* (1958) earned her a Bafta nomination for most promising newcomer. Smith has since been Bafta nominated another fifteen times, both for her work in television and in cinema. In addition to her win for *The Prime of Miss Jean Brodie* (1969), Smith has won a further three best actress Bafta film awards for *A Private Function* (1984), *A Room with a View* (1985) and *The Lonely Passion of Judith Hearne* (1987). She picked up a second Oscar, for best supporting actress, for *California Suite* (1978). Smith has also won Emmys, Golden Globes and *Evening Standard* Theatre Awards, and received the Bafta fellowship in 1996. In the past decade, she has also starred in the Harry Potter film series as Minerva McGonagall. Smith was awarded a CBE in 1970 and a damehood twenty years later.

In 1975 **John Cleese** *starred as Basil Fawlty in the first episode of the BBC comedy series 'Fawlty Towers', co-written with Connie Booth.*

Cleese and Booth (his wife at the time) produced two six-episode series of the hotel-based comedy, first broadcast on BBC2. Cleese read law at Cambridge, where he became a member of the 'Footlights Revue', playing at the Edinburgh Fringe, the West End in London, and abroad. In the sixties, he was involved in many successful projects including *The Frost Report*, and *Monty Python's Flying Circus* (1969). Following *Fawlty Towers*, Cleese tasted big-screen success with *Life of Brian* (1979) and *A Fish Called Wanda* (1988), the latter of which gained him a best original screenplay Oscar nomination, shared with Charles Crichton.

John Hurt *won a Bafta Award for best actor for his portrayal of Quentin Crisp in 'The Naked Civil Servant', first broadcast on television in 1975.*

Hurt made his film debut in *The Wild and The Willing* (1962), and received his first Bafta nomination (best supporting actor) for *10 Rillington Place*

(1971). He won a Bafta in the same category for his role in *Midnight Express* (1978), which also gave him his first Oscar nomination and Golden Globe win. *Alien* (1979), in which his character meets a famously gruesome end, earned him another Bafta nomination. His next film, *The Elephant Man* (1980), brought him a Bafta best actor win as well as an Academy Award nomination. His other notable film credits include *Scandal* (1989) and *The Field* (1990), the latter of which resulted in a Bafta nomination for best supporting actor. Hurt returned to the role of Quentin Crisp for the 2009 film *An Englishman in New York*. He was awarded a CBE in 2004.

In 1980 **Reinhold Messner** *became the first man to reach the summit of Mount Everest solo.*

Messner also completed the ascent without using additional oxygen. Two years previously, he and Peter Habeler had been the first climbers to reach the summit of Everest in this manner. In 1986 Messner conquered Lhotse in the Himalayas, making him the first person to have climbed all fourteen peaks above 8,000m.

In 1985 Dire Straits, led by **Mark Knopfler**, *reached number one in the UK album chart with 'Brothers in Arms'.*

Dire Straits' fifth and penultimate studio collection, *Brothers in Arms*, became not only their greatest commercial success, but also one of the biggest-selling albums ever in the UK. It was also one of the first releases in which the compact disc version (then a relatively new medium) was longer than the traditional vinyl long-playing format. Knopfler wrote all nine tracks, with one ('Money for Nothing') co-credited to Sting. Knopfler released his first solo album, *Golden Heart*, in 1996. His film-score work for *Local Hero* (1983) and *The Princess Bride* (1987) received Bafta and Grammy nominations respectively. He was awarded an OBE in the 2000 New Year Honours list.

Kenny Dalglish *was player–manager of Liverpool when they beat Everton in the FA Cup final to complete the double of League Championship and FA Cup in 1986.*

Liverpool's success in 1986 was only the fifth time that 'the double' had been achieved in English football history. One week previously, they had also beaten Everton by two points to take the league title. It had been Dalglish's first season in charge, following eight years as a player at Anfield after he had joined from Celtic, in 1977, for a then record British transfer fee of £440,000. Dalglish won the League Championship and the FA Cup on two further occasions, each with Liverpool, and in 1995 steered Blackburn to the FA Premier League title. As a player he has won every major domestic honour in both Scotland and England, as well as three European cup medals. Dalglish is the most capped Scottish player with 102 appearances, and joint top Scotland goal scorer (thirty) with Denis Law. Dalglish, who last played for Liverpool at the age of thirty-nine, returned to the Anfield side in 2011 as caretaker manager. Near the end of the season, he was given a three-year managerial contract. Despite his team winning the League Cup and also reaching the final of the FA Cup in 2012, Dalglish's contract was terminated. Liverpool had finished eighth in the Premier League in his first full season back in charge. He was awarded an MBE in 1984.

*In 1992 **Michael Foale** became the first British man in space.*

A crew member of the STS-45 space shuttle flight, Foale's dual UK-US nationality (his mother is from the US) allowed him to pursue more easily his boyhood dream of becoming an astronaut. Foale, who has a PhD from the University of Cambridge, is now a veteran of six missions and has clocked up nearly 374 days in space. On his third shuttle flight, he became the first person born in the UK to perform a space walk. He received a CBE in the 2005 New Year Honours list.

Roddy Doyle *won the 1993 Booker Prize for his novel 'Paddy Clarke Ha Ha Ha'.*

Paddy Clarke Ha Ha Ha, the fourth novel by Doyle, shows the world through the eyes of its ten-year-old central character who lives in Doyle's hometown, Dublin, in the 1960s. He wrote the novel after his Barrytown trilogy which consisted of *The Commitments* (1987), *The Snapper* (1990) and *The Van* (1991), the latter of which was shortlisted for the Booker Prize. All three novels were subsequently turned into films. Doyle's other books include *The Woman Who Walked into Doors* (1996) and The Last Roundup trilogy that concluded with *The Dead Republic* in 2010.

Tanni Grey-Thompson won two gold medals at the 2004 Athens Paralympic Games.

Grey-Thompson's victories in the 100m and 400m wheelchair races took the Cardiff-born athlete's overall tally of gold medals at the Paralympics to eleven. Her first appearance at the Games was in 1988, at the age of nineteen, when she won bronze in Seoul. At the next Paralympics in Barcelona she won four gold medals (100m, 200m, 400m and 800m) – a feat which she repeated again in Sydney in 2000. Her other Paralympic medals include one gold at Atlanta in 1996 and a total of four silver medals. She has also won the London wheelchair marathon six times. Grey-Thompson was made a Dame in 2005 and five years later was elevated to the peerage as a Baroness. She has also been honoured with an MBE in 1992 and an OBE in 2000.

Pádraig Harrington won golf's Open Championship in 2007.

Harrington defeated Sergio García in a four-hole play-off, by one stroke, to clinch victory at Carnoustie. He defended the title in the following year, and also won another golf major, the PGA Championship, becoming the first European-born winner in nearly eighty years. Harrington took up golf as a boy and his amateur career culminated with a Walker Cup win in 1995. He joined the professional ranks later that year, at the age of twenty-four, and picked up his first European tour title, the Spanish Open, in 1996. Since 1999, he has also played in six consecutive Ryder Cup teams and has been on the winning side on four occasions.

In 2010 A. P. McCoy (Anthony Peter) won his first Grand National.

McCoy rode Don't Push It to victory in what was his fifteenth attempt to win the famous Aintree race, in which his previous best placing had been third. McCoy, from County Antrim, Northern Ireland, rode his first winner at the age of seventeen. He crossed the Irish Sea less than three years later and recorded his first win in England in 1994. At the age of twenty-one, in 1996, McCoy became the National Hunt champion jockey (awarded to the rider with the most wins in the season) for the first time. He has won the title every year since. McCoy's total of 289 winners in the 2001/02 season set a new British record. In 2010, McCoy became the first jockey to win the BBC Sports Personality of the Year award in its fifty-six year history. He was awarded an MBE in 2003 and an OBE in 2010.

36
THIRTY-SIX

Humphry Davy invented his miner's safety lamp in 1815.

Davy proved that it was the gas methane which, when mixed with air at a high temperature, resulted in an explosion in the mine. His lamp, which he declined to patent, enclosed the flame inside a mesh fine enough to allow gas in, but also able to prevent the flame coming out. Davy, who was knighted in 1812 and awarded a baronetcy in 1818, also discovered the anaesthetic property of nitrous oxide (laughing gas), and isolated several elements including sodium and potassium. Davy was also responsible for getting Michael Faraday's scientific career underway; he offered him a position at the Royal Institution as his assistant in 1813. Davy died in Geneva at the age of fifty in 1829.

Democrat John Breckinridge was inaugurated as US vice-president in 1857, under the presidency of James Buchanan.

Breckinridge, the fourteenth US vice-president, is the youngest to hold the office. He contested the 1860 election as a presidential candidate and came third in the popular vote, which was won by Abraham Lincoln. Breckinridge joined the Confederate States Army in the American Civil War, and ultimately served as a Major General. Following their defeat, he fled to Europe, but returned after an amnesty was granted. Breckinridge died in 1875 at the age of fifty-four.

The first part of 'War and Peace', by Count Leo Tolstoy, was published in the periodical 'Russkiy Vestnik' in 1865.

Further portions of *War and Peace* would be published in the following years, but Tolstoy, unhappy with his work, rewrote the novel before it was published in book form in 1869. The epic tale is set against the backdrop of historical events that affected Russia in the early nineteenth century, including Napoleon's invasion of Moscow. Born into the Russian nobility, Tolstoy had lost both his parents before the age of ten. He was tutored at home before attending the University of Kazan where he first studied oriental languages and then law. However, he left, without a degree, in 1847 and returned to the management of his estate at Yasnaya Polyana. A few years later, Tolstoy joined the army and served in the Crimean War, his military experiences inspiring early literary works such as *The Raid* (1852) and the *Sevastopol Sketches* (1855–56). He married Sophia Behrs in 1862 and, back on his estate, began writing *War and Peace*. Tolstoy's other major novel, *Anna Karenina*, was published in the following decade. His later writing reflected his move from traditional Christianity to his own radical version that emphasised non-resistance to evil (his ideas in this sphere would later influence Gandhi among others). As part of his new belief system, Tolstoy, already forward-thinking in his treatment of the serfs on his estate, also adopted a simpler lifestyle. His beliefs resulted in domestic discord, particularly with his wife, and in 1910 at the age of eighty-two he abandoned the family home. A few days later at Astapovo railway station, Tolstoy contracted pneumonia and died.

The ballet 'Swan Lake', with a musical score by **Pyotr Tchaikovsky**, *was premiered at the Bolshoi Theatre in Moscow in 1877.*

Swan Lake was Tchaikovsky's first ballet and he composed two more: *The Sleeping Beauty* and *The Nutcracker*. Tchaikovsky, who began learning the piano at the age of five, spent a few years working as a civil servant before deciding to devote his life to music. His first symphony was premiered shortly afterwards, when he was twenty-five. Approximately ten years later, the financial support of a wealthy widow, Nadezhda von Meck, enabled Tchaikovsky to concentrate on his compositions. They agreed never to meet and instead communicated copiously by letter for many years until the latter half of 1890 when she wrote to tell him that she was unable to continue with his allowance and also their correspondence. Tchaikovsky died three years later at the age of fifty-three.

Torakusu Yamaha *established his musical instrument business in 1887.*

Yamaha's first product was a reed organ, an instrument which he first came into contact with when a local school needed one repaired. Fascinated by it, Yamaha subsequently built his own. He founded the Nippon Gakki Company in 1897, and went on to produce pianos and other instruments. Yamaha died in 1916 at the age of sixty-five, but the business continued to grow and diversify – the first Yamaha motorcycle was produced in 1954. The company symbol of three crossed tuning forks refers to its musical heritage, and on its hundredth anniversary in 1987, it was officially renamed as the Yamaha Corporation.

The only novel by **Oscar Wilde**, *'The Picture of Dorian Gray', was published in book form in 1891.*

Born in Dublin, Wilde studied Classics at Trinity College, then at Magdalen College, Oxford. At his own expense, his first book of poetry, *Poems*, was published at the age of twenty-six. Wilde was a prominent and flamboyant figure of the aesthetic movement, which espoused a philosophy of 'art for art's sake'. *The Picture of Dorian Gray* was first published in *Lippincott's Monthly Magazine* in 1890. Wilde revised the text and added six chapters for its publication in book form the following year. He also included a preface to address criticism of the novel, in which the title character's appearance remains youthful while his portrait ages instead, following its magazine publication. His reputation as a dramatist was secured with plays including *Lady Windermere's Fan* (1892), *An Ideal Husband* (1895) and *The Importance of Being Earnest* (1895). In 1895 Wilde brought a libel action against John Douglas, the Marquess of Queensberry, but the evidence presented by Queensberry's counsel drew attention to Wilde's homosexuality. Wilde stopped the prosecution, but was then arrested and stood trial. Part of the evidence presented against him was excerpts from the Lippincott version of *Dorian Gray*. Wilde was sentenced to two years imprisonment with hard labour for 'gross indecency'. Once released, he moved to France and for a time used the pseudonym Sebastian Melmoth. His last complete published work, *The Ballad of Reading Gaol*, appeared in 1898. Wilde died two years later at the age of forty-six.

Marie Curie *became the first woman to win a Nobel Prize when she received the 1903 Nobel Prize in Physics for her work in studying radioactivity.*

The term 'radioactivity' was coined by Marie Curie to describe the phenomenon first discovered by Henri Becquerel – who shared the Nobel

Prize along with Curie and her husband Pierre. She also won the 1911 Nobel Prize in Chemistry for the discovery of the elements radium and polonium, and the study of the former, making her the only person to have won the Nobel Prize for two separate scientific disciplines. Marie Curie was born Maria Skłodowska in Warsaw in the Kingdom of Poland. She completed her high-school education at the age of fifteen, and moved to Paris at the age of twenty-four to study mathematics and physics at the Sorbonne. There she met Pierre Curie and began both a working and personal relationship that would last until her death. Her daughter Irene and son-in-law Frederic Joliot-Curie would also go on to share a Nobel Prize in 1935 for their discovery of artificial radioactivity, although Curie would not live to see this achievement. She died in 1934, aged sixty-six.

In 1903 **Wilbur Wright** *made the second controlled, powered flight in a 'heavier than air machine' – the 'Wright Flyer'.*

Wright took to the air immediately after his younger brother Orville (the toss of a coin had decided who flew first). Wilbur travelled a distance of approximately 175 feet at Kitty Hawk, North Carolina. For his second flight that day (and the brothers' fourth overall), he covered 852 feet in 59 seconds. The brothers had started their first business, a printing company, when Wilbur was twenty-two. Later, they became involved in bicycle repair and manufacture before developing an interest in aviation. They built their own engine for *Flyer*, constructed in sections in the back room of their cycle shop. Wilbur could have been the first to achieve powered flight (he had actually won the coin toss), but a stall on take-off resulted in a crash and some minor damage. Once repaired, it was then Orville's turn to try and achieve the first flight three days later. Wilbur died in 1912 at the age of forty-five.

David Niven *starred in the film 'A Matter of Life and Death', which was selected for the first ever Royal Film Performance.*

In November 1946, the King, Queen and Princesses Elizabeth and Margaret all attended the showing at the Empire Cinema, Leicester Square, in aid of the Cinematograph Trade Benevolent Fund. *A Matter of Life and Death*, in which Niven played squadron leader Peter Carter who is shot down but escapes death due to an 'error' in the bureaucracy of the afterlife, was his first film after the war. Niven went on to win the 1958 Academy Award and also a Golden Globe for best actor for his role as Major Angus Pollock in *Separate Tables* (1957). His other films include *Carrington V.C.* (1955), which gave him a Bafta best British actor award, *The Pink Panther* (1963) and a turn as James Bond in *Casino Royale* (1967). Niven died in 1983, aged seventy-three.

Francis Crick and James Watson co-authored the paper 'A Structure for Deoxyribose Nucleic Acid', which was published in the journal 'Nature' in 1953.

In their paper, one of the landmark moments in twentieth-century science, Crick and Watson outlined their double helix structure for DNA. Crick's first degree was in physics and during the World War Two he worked for the British Admiralty, primarily designing mines. Afterwards he was given a permanent position with the Admiralty, but he decided to become a researcher in the field of biophysics, initially at the Strangeways Laboratory, Cambridge. In 1949 he moved to the Cavendish Laboratory, Cambridge, where he met the post-doctoral student James Watson who became his ally in the search for the structure of DNA. An important contribution to their success in determining the correct model was the X-ray diffraction work on DNA carried out by Maurice Wilkins and Rosalind Franklin at King's College London. (Wilkins and Franklin both co-authored papers on their studies in the same edition of the journal *Nature*.) Crick, Watson and Wilkins received the 1962 Nobel Prize for the discovery of the structure of DNA. Crick died in 2004 at the age of eighty-eight.

George Martin produced the first Beatles' single, 'Love Me Do', which entered the UK singles chart in 1962.

Martin also signed the Beatles (who had been turned down by many others) to EMI label Parlophone after an audition at Abbey Road studios in 1962. He continued to produce the Beatles' records until their break-up in 1970. Martin studied at the Guildhall School of Music in London and joined EMI in 1950 as the assistant to the head of Parlophone Records, Oscar Preuss. When Preuss retired five years later, Martin replaced him.

In 1961, he scored his first number one as a producer with The Temperance Seven's 'You're Driving Me Crazy'. In addition to the Beatles, Martin also produced chart toppers for Gerry and the Pacemakers, Billy J Kramer and The Dakotas, Cilla Black and Paul McCartney. His most recent number one single was Elton John's 1997 version of 'Candle in the Wind', recorded as a tribute to the late Princess Diana. Martin has also many credits as a composer, including the soundtrack for the James Bond adventure *Live and Let Die* (1973). Martin was awarded a CBE in 1988 and received a knighthood in 1996.

In 1965 'Trapped in the Sky', produced by **Gerry Anderson**, *was the first Thunderbirds adventure to be broadcast on television.*

Thunderbirds follows the adventures of a futuristic rescue organisation run by the Tracy family. A total of thirty-two episodes and two feature films were eventually made. The programme, devised by Gerry and his then wife Sylvia, became a massive success. *Thunderbirds* gained popularity with a new generation when it began a repeat showing on BBC television in 1991, in what was its debut national network airing. Anderson's first TV puppet show, *The Adventures of Twizzle*, (1957) was followed by others such as *Supercar*, *Fireball XL5*, *Stingray* and of course *Thunderbirds*. He moved into live action productions with series that included *UFO* and *Space 1999*. Anderson received an MBE in 2001. He died in 2012 at the age of eighty-three.

Michael Parkinson hosted the first edition of his eponymous chat show in 1971.

Parkinson's debut featured the unofficial royal photographer, Ray Bellisario; the tennis player, Arthur Ashe; and the actor, Terry-Thomas. Parkinson began his career as a journalist at *The Barnsley Chronicle*. National Service in the army intervened and, promoted to the rank of captain, Parkinson was part of the military operation which tried to regain control of the Suez Canal in 1956. His first work in television was for Granada in the 1960s and included hosting the *Cinema* film review slot. The original run of his Saturday night BBC chat show ended in 1982, but the format was revived in 1998. It crossed over to ITV for the final three years, before ending in 2007 when he retired. Parkinson received a CBE in 2000 and was knighted in 2008.

The first six 'Mr. Men' books, written by **Roger Hargreaves**, *were published in 1971.*

Mr. Greedy, Mr. Happy, Mr. Nosey, Mr. Sneeze, Mr. Bump and Hargreaves's original character, *Mr. Tickle*, became the first of a highly successful children's book series. Hargreaves had settled into a career as an advertising copywriter following his National Service, but gave this up in 1977 to concentrate full-time on the *Mr. Men* series. He is estimated to have sold 85 million books by the time of his death, at the age of fifty-three, in 1988.

In 1972 **Charles Duke** *became the tenth man to walk on the moon.*

Duke was the youngest of the Apollo astronauts to set foot on the moon. He was the lunar module pilot for Apollo 16 and landed on the surface of the moon with mission commander John Young. Their stay was to be the longest of the Apollo era at nearly three days. Duke was also 'capsule communicator' (capcom) during the Apollo 11 mission, the first to land men on the moon, and as such was the first person to speak to Neil Armstrong and Buzz Aldrin after they had touched down on the lunar surface. A former fighter pilot, Apollo 16 was Duke's only space flight.

In 1975 **Francis Ford Coppola** *won both the Academy Award for best director and best adapted screenplay (shared with Mario Puzo) for 'The Godfather Part II' (1974).*

The Godfather Part II, which gave Coppola his first Oscar for directing, won another four awards including best picture – the only sequel to ever do so. Two years earlier, *The Godfather* (1972) also won a best 'adapted screenplay' Oscar for Coppola and Puzo. After obtaining a degree in drama, Coppola undertook graduate film studies at UCLA. He won his first Academy Award, shared with Edmund North, in 1971 for his screenwriting contribution to *Patton* (1970). Coppola's other films include *Apocalypse Now* (1979) and *The Godfather Part III* (1990), both of which received Academy Award best picture and best director nominations (for Coppola), with the former winning him a Bafta in 1980.

*The first **Jeffrey Archer** novel, 'Not a Penny More, Not a Penny Less', was published in 1976.*

Near to bankruptcy after being the victim of an investment fraud, Archer resigned as an MP in 1974 and began what would become a commercially successful literary career. He returned to politics in the 1980s as the deputy Conservative Party chairman and in 1992 he was elevated to the peerage. Although selected as a candidate for the first London mayoral election in 2000, he withdrew when faced with a charge of perjury. Convicted at the subsequent trial, he was sentenced to four years in prison but released after twenty-four months. This experience was the inspiration for his Prison Diaries trilogy (2002–2004). Archer published his fifteenth novel, *The Sins of the Father*, in 2012.

__Ian Dury__ and the Blockheads reached number one in the UK with 'Hit Me With Your Rhythm Stick' in 1979.

Dury studied at the Royal College of Art in the sixties and worked as an art teacher while developing his music career. In 1970 he formed his first band, Kilburn and the High Roads. They split up in 1975, but Dury struck up a songwriting partnership with Chas Jankel, which led to the formation of the Blockheads – who became part of the new wave of British music in the late seventies. With no major label interest forthcoming, the band signed with the independent Stiff Records and scored a hit with their debut album *New Boots and Panties*. The band took the follow-up, *Do It Yourself*, to number two in the chart in 1979. In the 1980s, Dury also began to work as an actor. He died in 2000 at the age of fifty-seven.

*Corbiere, trained by **Jenny Pitman** and ridden by Ben de Haan, won the 1983 Grand National.*

The victory made Pitman the first female trainer of a Grand National winner. She repeated her success in 1995, this time with Royal Athlete. It was also Pitman's horse, Esha Ness, which was first past the post in the 1993 Grand National which was declared void due to a false start. Amongst other notable wins, Pitman has also recorded two Cheltenham Gold Cup victories. She was awarded an OBE in 1998.

Dennis Taylor *won the World Snooker Championship in 1985 when he defeated Steve Davis in the final.*

The match between Taylor and Davis was decided by the potting of the last black ball in the final frame. Taylor had recovered from being eight frames to zero down after the first session of play. The live television audience was estimated to be over 18 million for the conclusion of the final, a sixty-eight-minute-long last frame, which finished after midnight. Taylor was runner-up in his first World Championship final in 1979. He retired from the professional game in 2000.

Marina Stepanova *broke the woman's world record for the 400m hurdles at Tashkent, USSR, in 1986, in a time of 52.94 seconds.*

Stepanova is the oldest woman to set a world record on the athletics track. Her record stood for nearly seven years before being beaten by Sally Gunnell by two tenths of a second. Stepanova won a gold medal at the 1986 European Championships for the women's 400m hurdles; however, she was never to compete in this event at the Olympics. It was introduced to the Olympics for the 1984 Games, and, owing to the boycott by the Soviet Union whom she represented, she did not attend. By the time of the next Games, she had retired from athletics.

Konstantin Novoselov *and Andre Geim were awarded the 2010 Nobel Prize in Physics for their 'groundbreaking' work on the material graphene.*

Graphene is a two-dimensional form of carbon, only one atom thick, which possesses a number of unique properties. The thinnest and strongest material to be isolated, graphene also conducts electricity as well as copper and is the most effective conductor of heat. A range of applications are anticipated for graphene, including the creation of faster electronic devices. Novoselov, Geim and their co-workers published their first paper on graphene in 2004. Novoselov, a native of Russia, took his doctorate at the University of Nijmegen in the Netherlands (where he was supervised by Geim), and joined the University of Manchester, along with Geim, in 2001. The Manchester University researchers first used adhesive tape to produce graphene from a piece of graphite, the material commonly used in lead pencils.

Katherine Grainger *and Anna Watkins won the gold medal for the double sculls at the 2012 London Olympics.*

Although a six-time gold medallist at the World Championships, Glasgow-born Grainger, who began rowing in 1993 at the University of Edinburgh where she was studying for a law degree, had only won silver at the three previous Olympics. She began her rowing partnership with Anna Watkins, who won bronze in the double sculls at the 2008 Beijing Games, in 2010. The pair remains undefeated, winning the World Championship in 2010 and 2011, and set a new Olympic record in qualifying for the 2012 final. Grainger, who was awarded an MBE in 2006 and a CBE in 2013, is Britain's most successful female rower. She is also the first British woman to win medals at four consecutive Olympics.

37
THIRTY-SEVEN

In 1512 **Michelangelo di Lodovico Buonarroti Simoni** *completed the painting of the Vatican's Sistine Chapel ceiling.*

Michelangelo was born in the Tuscan village of Caprese, but his family returned months later to Florence where he was brought up. He was apprenticed to the Florentine painter Domenico Ghirlandaio at the age of thirteen and then after a year, on Ghirlandaio's recommendation, joined the household of Lorenzo de'Medici, the ruler of Florence and a patron of the arts. Lorenzo died in 1492 and was succeeded by his son Piero, but he lost power two years later. Michelangelo had already moved to Bologna, but later returned to Florence before going to Rome. There he sculpted his first masterpiece, the *Pietà*, a commission for Saint Peter's Basilica depicting the dead Jesus on the lap of his mother Mary. Completed in his mid-twenties, the two figures were carved out of a single block of marble; it is also the only work which Michelangelo ever signed. He returned to Florence where he produced another masterpiece, his statue of *David*, completed in 1504. The following year Michelangelo was back in Rome at the behest of Pope Julius II who wanted him to work on his tomb, but this project was never completed as originally envisaged, partly due to other demands on Michelangelo such as the painting of the Sistine Chapel ceiling, also commissioned by Julius. Michelangelo was reluctant to undertake the work, but after labouring for four years he produced an artistic triumph of the Italian Renaissance, which includes scenes from the Book of Genesis (from the Creation to Noah's Ark), prophets, sybils and other figures from the Old Testament. Once completed, he resumed work on Julius's tomb, but the project was scaled back following Julius's death in 1513. His statue of Moses for the tomb was completed two years later. Julius's successor, Pope Leo X, of the Medici family, engaged Michelangelo to create a façade for the church of San Lorenzo in Florence. Although this project was never realised, his architectural and sculptural work for the Medici Chapel again demonstrated his supreme talent. In 1534, Michelangelo left Florence and returned to Rome. His next papal commission was to paint the fresco of the *Last Judgement* in the Sistine Chapel which he completed in 1541 at the age of sixty-six. Five years later, he was appointed architect of Saint Peter's Basilica and designed its dome, which was completed after his death in 1564, at the age of eighty-eight.

In 1609 'Astronomia Nova' by **Johannes Kepler** *was published, in which he stated his first two laws of planetary motion.*

Kepler wrote that all planets move in elliptical orbits around the sun and that a line from the planet to the sun sweeps out equal areas in equal periods of time during its orbit. Kepler's move away from the idea of circular orbits was based on his desire to find a solution to the trajectory of Mars. Detailed observations had recently been provided by the Danish astronomer Tyco Brahe, which failed to conform to the circular orbit model. Kepler's third law followed ten years later. It states the relationship between a planet's mean distance from the sun and the time it takes to complete one orbit, known as the planet's period. (More specifically, Kepler's third law states that the period squared is directly proportional to the mean distance cubed.) Kepler died in 1630 at the age of fifty-eight.

Anne, *the last monarch of the House of Stuart, became Queen of England, Scotland and Ireland in 1702.*

Anne was the younger sister of Queen Mary II, who had ruled with her husband, William III, until her death. Anne succeeded William in

1702. Following the Act of Union in 1707, Anne became, on 1 May that year, the first monarch of the newly formed Kingdom of Great Britain. Her reign, which lasted for over twelve years, saw party politics gain greater significance whilst the War of the Spanish Succession became the dominant foreign policy issue. None of Anne's children survived into adulthood and she was succeeded by her second cousin, George I, Elector of Hanover, after her death at the age of forty-nine in 1714.

John Dalton announced the first table of atomic weights in 1803.

Five years later the first part of Dalton's book *A New System of Chemical Philosophy* was published, containing his atomic theory. Dalton described how atoms were the smallest unit of any chemical element, and could be distinguished from each other by their relative atomic weight. He created a nomenclature which showed how different atoms could combine to form other chemical compounds. Dalton died in 1844, aged seventy-seven.

*In 1859 **Elizabeth Blackwell** became the first woman to have her name recorded in the General Medical Council's register as a doctor.*

Blackwell qualified in the United States and was admitted to the register under a clause in the Medical Act of 1858 which recognised doctors with foreign degrees practising in Britain before 1 October 1858. She was born in Bristol and spent her early life in the city before the Blackwell family, including eleven-year-old Elizabeth, moved to New York. In her late teenage years her father died and Blackwell helped to support the family by teaching. She decided to become a physician, studied privately and eventually, after many rejections, was admitted to the Geneva Medical School in New York state in 1847. She graduated two years later, becoming the first qualified woman doctor. She spent the latter half of her life back in England, where she also became involved in social reform. Blackwell died in 1910 at the age of eighty-nine.

*The Savoy Theatre, built for **Richard D'Oyly Carte**, opened in London in 1881.*

The Savoy was one of the world's first public buildings to be illuminated throughout by electric light (using Joseph Swan's incandescent lamps). Carte worked at his father's business, which made woodwind instruments, before embarking on a career as an impresario. He was responsible for bringing together Gilbert and Sullivan, and later the 'Mr R. D'Oyly Carte Opera Company' produced the bulk of their operettas. As well as providing the money to build the Savoy Theatre, Carte also built the Savoy hotel, which opened in 1889. Carte died two years later at the age of fifty-six.

In 1901 **Frank Hornby** *lodged his patent application entitled 'Improvements in Toy or Educational Devices for Children and Young People', which described his invention of what would become known as 'Meccano'.*

Hornby's first Meccano sets went on sale in the following year under the name *Mechanics Made Easy*. A few years later he changed the name to Meccano. After World War One, Hornby also started making model trains and accessories, as well as miniature vehicles in the Dinky toys range. He entered Parliament at the age of sixty-eight as the member for Liverpool Everton, but resigned before the 1935 general election due to business demands and poor health. Hornby died the following year at the age of seventy-three.

Ernest Rutherford *won the Nobel Prize in Chemistry in 1908 for 'his investigations into the disintegration of the elements, and the chemistry of radioactive substances'.*

Born in New Zealand, Rutherford was the fourth child in a family of twelve. Following his graduation from the University of New Zealand, Rutherford won a scholarship which enabled him to join the Cavendish Laboratory at Cambridge in 1895 where he worked under J.J. Thomson, and began to study the newly discovered X-rays. He was offered a professorship at McGill University in Canada and there, with Frederick Soddy, he put forward the theory of atomic disintegration. Four years after his return to England in 1907, Rutherford proposed his model of the atom. A conclusion of his alpha particle scattering experiments, Rutherford stated that the atom was mostly free space with a small charged nucleus. This was a major contribution to atomic physics, as were his experiments following World War One which, for the first time, resulted in the transmutation of one element into another. Amongst many honours he was knighted in 1914, appointed to the Order of Merit in 1925 and made a baron in 1931. Rutherford died in 1937 at the age of sixty-six.

Louis Blériot became the first person to cross the English Channel by the means of powered flight when his monoplane, the Blériot XI, touched down near Dover in 1909.

Blériot's forty-six-minute flight won him the £1,000 prize offered by the *Daily Mail* newspaper for a successful crossing. British customs officials had not encountered anyone arriving by aeroplane, so recorded Blériot as a ship's master and his plane as a yacht. He returned to France on board the destroyer *Escopette*, the ship assigned to escort his historic voyage, but which Blériot had soon outpaced. Blériot died in 1936 at the age of sixty-four.

*The first perfume from **Gabrielle 'Coco' Chanel**, Chanel No. 5, was launched in 1921.*

The classic fragrance, chosen by Chanel, was reputedly the fifth in a range of ten scents created and presented to her by perfumer Ernest Beaux. Chanel No. 5, which became the world's best-selling perfume, blends aldehydes (organic compounds synthesised in the laboratory) with floral essences to create its distinctive aroma. Chanel spent the latter years of her childhood in an orphanage, where she learned to be a seamstress. Moving to Paris she was able to open her first establishment, a millinery shop, in 1910. Chanel is credited with revolutionising women's fashion with her modernist, elegant style. She died in 1971 at the age of eighty-seven.

*In 1926 **John Logie Baird** gave a public demonstration of his thirty-line television system.*

In the previous year Baird had demonstrated at Selfridge's in London the transmission of simple shapes, but these images lacked resolution and only had two tones, dark or light. In the following months Baird made further improvements to his electro-mechanical apparatus, which used a disc with a spiral of apertures, invented by Paul Nipkow, to scan the subject. These developments increased the resolution by using a scan of thirty lines and also allowed differences in tone to be rendered. In 1926 in an attic room in Soho, he gave his first public demonstration of this system. Baird showed both a person speaking and the movement of a ventriloquist's doll to an audience that included approximately forty members of the Royal

Institution. It was the first ever demonstration of what could be regarded as 'true television'. In 1929 the Baird Television Company began experimental broadcasts using a BBC transmitter in London. The BBC took over programme making in 1932 and continued the thirty-line broadcasts for another three years. In 1936 a contest was held to select a system for a high-definition service. Baird's electro-mechanical system (now improved to 240 lines) was pitted against the all-electronic 405-line system of Marconi-EMI, each transmitting on alternate weeks. The benefits of the Marconi-EMI option were apparent and the Baird system was finally abandoned months later in 1937. Undaunted, Baird continued to work on other aspects of television such as colour and stereoscopic reproduction, both of which he first demonstrated in 1928. In 1942, he applied for a patent for his multi-gun colour television tube, dubbed the Telechrome. He died four years later at the age of fifty-seven, and is buried in his birthplace of Helensburgh, Dunbartonshire.

Stan Laurel starred in the first 'Stan and Ollie' film, 'The Second Hundred Years', released in 1927.

Laurel, originally Arthur Stanley Jefferson, was born in Ulverston, Lancashire. His father was a theatre manager and his mother an actress. Laurel's first stage appearance was in a music hall in Glasgow in 1906, although he did not adopt his stage name until after he had moved to the US some years later. Laurel made his film debut in 1917 in the short feature *Nuts in May*, billed as Stan Jefferson. He first appeared with Oliver Hardy in *The Lucky Dog* (1921), and the duo went on to form a comedy partnership that would last for more than one hundred films. Laurel received an honorary Academy Award in 1961, four years before his death at the age of seventy-four.

'Brave New World', by **Aldous Huxley**, was published in 1932.

Huxley's fifth and most famous novel described a future where human cloning is commonplace. He read English language and literature at Balliol College, Oxford, where he graduated with first-class honours. His life as a student was made harder by his near blindness – a result of contracting an infection some years earlier – which also prevented him from pursuing his first choice of a career in medicine. Huxley published his debut novel,

Chrome Yellow, in 1921, and his other novels include *Eyeless in Gaza* (1936) and *The Doors of Perception* (1954). He died in 1963 at the age of sixty-nine.

Spencer Tracy *won the Academy Award for best actor in 1938.*

Tracy won the award for his role as Manuel Fidello in *Captains Courageous* (1937), and picked up another best actor Oscar twelve months later for *Boys Town* (1938). He collected a further seven best actor nominations, including one for his last film, *Guess Who's Coming to Dinner* (1967), which he finished shooting shortly before his death at the age of sixty-seven. (Tom Hanks is the only other actor, coincidentally at the same age as Tracy, to win two consecutive Oscars for best actor.)

Enrico Fermi *received the 1938 Nobel Prize in Physics for his work on neutron irradiation and nuclear reactions instigated by slow neutrons.*

Fermi used neutrons (elementary particles with no electric charge) to bombard the chemical elements. The result was new radioactive substances and, with uranium as the target material, he succeeded in creating new elements outside the existing periodic table. He also found that slow or low-speed neutrons were more easily absorbed by the atomic nucleus during this process. Immediately following the award of his Nobel Prize, Fermi, who had become a professor at the University of Rome in his mid-twenties, headed for the US due to the political climate in pre-war Italy. There Fermi directed the construction of the first nuclear reactor (built on a squash court underneath the University of Chicago football stadium) which produced the first controlled nuclear chain reaction in December 1942. Fermi died in 1954 at the age of fifty-three. The element fermium, with atomic number 100, was named in his honour.

The first edition of 'American Letter' by **Alistair Cooke** *was broadcast in 1946.*

American Letter later became *Letter from America* and the series would run until shortly before Cooke's death in 2004 at the age of ninety-five. He chalked up nearly 3,000 programmes to make it the longest-running speech radio show to be hosted by one person. He was born Alfred Cooke in Salford and moved with his family to Blackpool when he was eight. He won a scholarship to Jesus College, Cambridge, where he read English and won a two-year fellowship to study in the US. His first job for the

BBC was as a film critic in 1934, and later he attracted the attention of the American network NBC who hired him to broadcast a weekly *London Letter* to New York. Cooke immigrated to the USA in 1937 and became a US citizen four years later. He received an honorary KBE in 1973.

*In 1951 **Jersey Joe Walcott** won the World Heavyweight Boxing Championship when he knocked out Ezzard Charles during his fifth title attempt.*

Walcott, whose real name was Arnold Cream, remains the oldest first-time winner of the world heavyweight boxing title – a victory that came after over twenty years as a professional boxer. Walcott successfully defended his title in a rematch against Charles, but in his next fight lost out to Rocky Marciano by a knockout. Walcott died in 1994 at the age of eighty.

***Godtfred Kirk Christiansen** filed the patent for the modern Lego brick in 1958.*

Christiansen became head of the Lego Group in 1958, weeks after the Lego brick patent was lodged. He took over from his father, Ole, a master carpenter, who founded the business in the 1930s and named it from the first two letters of the Danish words *leg godt* which means 'play well'. The company's initial toys were made of wood, and their other products included stepladders and ironing boards. The purchase of a plastic-injection-moulding machine in 1947 allowed the company to start making 'Automatic Binding Bricks' two years later. These had studs, but lacked the inner tubes which gave added stability and which were described in Christiansen's patent. Lego bricks manufactured from 1958 onwards are still compatible with today's version. Godtfred died in 1995 at the age of seventy-five. His son Kjeld took over as president and chief executive officer of the Lego Group in 1979.

*The first television series with a theme by **Ron Grainer**, 'The Men from Room Thriteen', was first broadcast in 1959.*

The Australian-born Grainer composed many of the famous television theme tunes of the next two decades including *Maigret, Doctor Who, Steptoe and Son, The Prisoner, Tales of the Unexpected* and *Man in a Suitcase* (later re-used on *TFI Friday*). His film scores include *The Mouse on the Moon* (1963), *Hoffman* (1971) and *Mutiny on the Buses* (1972). Grainer died in 1981 at the age of fifty-eight.

Dana Zátopková won the silver medal at the 1960 Rome Olympics for the women's javelin.

Zátopková holds the record as the oldest woman to win a medal in athletics at the Games. The Czech athlete won a gold medal at the same event eight years earlier – which was also the Olympics where her husband, the long-distance runner Emil Zátopek, won a trio of gold medals. Zátopková was also European champion twice and set a world record for the javelin at the age of thirty-five.

Rupert Murdoch gained ownership of his first British newspaper, 'News of the World', in 1969.

Murdoch won control after defeating a rival bid from publisher Robert Maxwell. Later in the year Murdoch took over another Fleet Street title, *The Sun*, which had first been published five years earlier by International Press Corporation, but had been suffering from poor sales. Murdoch inherited control of the Adelaide paper *The News* on the death of his father, when he was twenty-two. He expanded the Murdoch newspaper stable, beginning in his native Australia and then abroad. He entered the US newspaper market in 1973, and widened his American media interests with the purchase of the film studio Twentieth Century Fox and the creation of the Fox Broadcasting Company in 1986. Murdoch added to his British newspaper titles with the acquisition of *The Times* and *The Sunday Times* in 1981. Twenty years after acquiring *The Sun*, Murdoch launched Sky satellite television in 1989, which merged the following year with the rival British Satellite Broadcasting to create BSkyB. Now in his eighties, Murdoch continues to serve as the chairman and chief executive officer of News Corporation. In 2011 the company decided to close the *News of the World*, nearly 168 years after it first appeared, as a result of a phone-hacking scandal. Several months later in 2012, the company launched a Sunday edition of *The Sun*.

Ken Rosewall won tennis's 1972 Australian Open.

Rosewall won in straight sets against Malcolm Anderson to claim his eighth and last singles Grand Slam title, nineteen years after his first win – also at the Australian Open. He is the oldest tennis player to win a Grand Slam in the 'open era' (post 1968). In 1974, at the age of thirty-nine, Rosewall competed in two more Grand Slam finals – Wimbledon and the US Open – losing out on each occasion to Jimmy Connors. This was Rosewall's fourth appearance in a Wimbledon final, two decades after he first contested one, and it would remain the only Grand Slam title that eluded him.

Derby County, managed by **Brian Clough**, *won their first Football League Championship in 1972.*

Clough's playing career in senior football as a striker, first for Middlesbrough and then for local rivals Sunderland, was ended by injury at the age of twenty-nine. He had scored an impressive 251 goals in 275 appearances, and played for the full England side twice. Clough turned to management, and, at the age of thirty, secured his first job in the Football League at fourth division Hartlepools United (now Hartlepool United). He was joined by Peter Taylor, who would become his assistant for most of the next twenty years. They moved on, in 1967, to Derby County, then in the second division. In their second season at the club, Derby recorded a twenty-two game unbeaten run and won promotion as champions. The 1972 League Championship win came in their third season in division one, but in the following year Clough and Taylor resigned. Clough then had spells at Brighton and Leeds United, the latter ending after a brief forty-four days, before joining Nottingham Forest in 1975. Taylor rejoined him at the second division club, which under their guidance won promotion, and then in the following season took the division one title. European success was also achieved with back-to-back European Cup wins in 1979 and 1980. His partnership with Taylor ended in 1982, and Clough retired from management in 1993, during which time he had added two more League Cup wins (1989 and 1990) to his total of four at Forest. His team also reached the FA Cup final in 1991 (the year he received an OBE), but lost out to Tottenham Hotspur by two goals to one. Clough died in 2004 at the age of sixty-nine.

'The Terminator', starring **Arnold Schwarzenegger**, *was released in 1984.*

Born in Thal, Austria, Schwarzenegger first achieved success as a bodybuilding champion, winning the amateur Mr. Universe contest when he was twenty and the professional Mr. Universe title three years running. He had already moved to the US when he made his film debut in *Hercules in New York* (1970). Despite this he was still able to win a Golden Globe for 'best male acting debut in a motion picture' for *Stay Hungry* (1976) several years later. The title role in *Conan the Barbarian* (1982) gave him his first big box-office success. He followed it with a sequel prior to his first outing as a cyborg from the future in *The Terminator* (1984). Perhaps his most famous role, its international success boosted his reputation as an action-movie star. In addition to further Terminator films, he has appeared in box-office hits such as *Predator* (1987), *Total Recall* (1990) and *True Lies* (1993). Schwarzenegger, a Republican, was elected as the governor of California in October 2003, re-elected in 2006, and completed his tenure in January 2011.

The sculptor **Anish Kapoor** *won the 1991 Turner Prize.*

Born in Mumbai (formerly Bombay), Kapoor studied in London, initially at the Hornsey College of Art and then at the Chelsea College of Art. His early sculptural work was characterised by its vibrant colours, which often extended onto the gallery floor in the form of powdered pigment, such as in *White Sand, Red Millet, Many Flowers* (1982). At the Venice Biennale in 1990, Kapoor won the *Premio Duemila* for the 'Best Young Artist'. For his Turner Prize exhibition in the following year Kapoor chose one untitled piece, completed in sandstone. He has also produced much bigger works – for example *Marsyas* (2002) which fills the Turbine Hall of the Tate Modern in London. Kapoor's public works include large pieces such as *Cloud Gate* (2004), located in the Millennium Park, Chicago. Kapoor collaborated with structural engineer Cecil Balmond on the design of the *ArcelorMittal Orbit* tower for the new Olympic Park in London. At a height of nearly 115 metres, it is the tallest item of public art in Britain. Kapoor was awarded a CBE in 2003.

In 1994 **Tom Hanks** *won his first Academy Award for best actor.*

Hanks was honoured for his role as lawyer Andrew Beckett in *Philadelphia* (1993), and scooped the same award again, this time as the eponymous *Forrest Gump* (1994), in the following year, to become only the second man, after Spencer Tracy, to win consecutive best actor Oscars. Hanks made his movie debut in *He Knows You're Alone* (1980), and scored an early box-office hit with the mermaid fantasy *Splash* (1984). He received the first of his five Academy Award best actor nominations for *Big* (1988), and he has also been nominated for *Saving Private Ryan* (1998) and *Cast Away* (2000). His other films include *Apollo 13* (1995), *The Green Mile* (1999), *The Polar Express* (2004) and *The Da Vinci Code* (2006). Hanks also voiced the character of Woody in the Toy Story trilogy (1995-2010). He made his feature-film debut as a director with *That Thing You Do!* (1996), which he also wrote and starred in, and has also co-produced several movies including *Cast Away* (2000) and *Charlie Wilson's War* (2007).

38

THIRTY-EIGHT

Robert Stevenson was the resident engineer for the construction of the Bell Rock Lighthouse, which was first lit in 1811.

A masterpiece of civil engineering, the Bell Rock Lighthouse was constructed on a dangerous reef, usually fully submerged, approximately twelve miles east of Dundee. The reef had been responsible for numerous shipwrecks. Stevenson proposed the building of a lighthouse and the Northern Lighthouse Board agreed – on the basis that the more experienced John Rennie would be the chief engineer for the project. There has been debate ever since as to the relative contributions of both men. Rennie did visit the rock on occasion, but Stevenson was in day-to-day charge and he has received the lion's share of the acclaim for the actual building of the structure. The design was modelled on that of John Smeaton's for the Eddystone Lighthouse, but modified to take into account the harsh weather of its location. Rennie has been credited as specifying the curvature required at the base to ensure stability. Construction began in 1807 and included temporary barracks to house the workers, and even a rail system. The lighthouse, automated since 1988, is still in use today and survived a helicopter accident in 1955, which killed both pilots. Stevenson went on to become a major builder of lighthouses in Scottish waters as well as a consultant for other civil engineering projects. His grandson was the writer Robert Louis Stevenson. Robert Stevenson died in 1850 at the age of seventy-eight.

Georg Ohm *published his book 'Die galvanische Kette, mathematisch bearbeitet' (The galvanic circuit investigated mathematically) in 1827.*

Ohm's volume contained the results of his experiments on electricity and stated the relationship between voltage (V), current (I) and resistance (R), which became known as 'Ohm's law' (namely, $V/I = R$). The unit of electrical resistance bears his name. He died in 1854 at the age of sixty-five.

In 1839 ***Charles Goodyear*** *invented his treatment of rubber which became known as vulcanisation.*

Goodyear's technique transformed rubber, which was temperature sensitive and of limited use, into a stable material fit for many applications. Goodyear had struggled for many years to determine the required process and his financial devotion to his rubber obsession resulted in imprisonment for debt on more than one occasion. Goodyear did not patent his invention until 1844, and was also slow to take out foreign patents. Specimens of his 'cured' rubber were shown in England in 1842 and the following year Thomas Hancock applied for a British patent which Goodyear challenged unsuccessfully. Goodyear died in 1860 at the age of fifty-nine, heavily in debt due to poor business deals and an inability to properly protect his invention. The Goodyear Tire & Rubber Company, which had no family connection, was founded in Ohio in 1898 and named in his honour.

Alfred Harmsworth *founded the 'Daily Mirror' in November 1903.*

Initially designed as a newspaper for women, the *Daily Mirror* also had an all-female staff. However, a lack of instant success prompted a relaunch approximately two months later as the *Illustrated Daily Mirror* with a male editor and a tag line of 'a paper for men and women'. The paper reverted to its original name soon after. Harmsworth, who also co-founded the *Daily Mail*, became a baronet in 1904 and in the following year was ennobled as Baron Northcliffe. He died in 1922 at the age of fifty-seven.

'The Man of Property', by ***John Galsworthy***, *was published in 1906.*

The opening volume of Galsworthy's *Forsyte Saga*, *The Man of Property* was published at the time as a stand-alone work which examined the lifestyle of the upper middle class. The second instalment, *In Chancery*, did not appear until fourteen years later and the final volume, *To Let* was published in 1921, though he did continue the saga with further volumes. Galsworthy, whose first published work was a collection of short stories, *From the Four Winds*, in 1897, under the pseudonym John Sinjohn, also wrote many plays including *Strife* (1909) and *The Skin Game* (1920). He was awarded the 1932 Nobel Prize in Literature. Galsworthy died in the following year at the age of sixty-five.

Geoffrey de Havilland *founded the De Havilland Aircraft Company in 1920.*
De Havilland, the son of a clergyman, was educated at the Crystal Palace School of Engineering. After a short spell in the fledgling car and bus industry, he left to pursue his interest in aviation. De Havilland designed and built his first aeroplane, which he first flew in 1910, and in a later model set a new British altitude record in 1912. The De Havilland Aircraft Company produced aeroplanes such as the Tiger Moth Trainer, the Mosquito (which had plywood construction) and the post-war Comet airliner – the first commercial jet-powered aircraft. De Havilland was knighted in 1944. He died in 1965 at the age of eighty-two.

Ethel Muckelt *won a bronze medal at the 1924 Winter Olympics held in Chamonix, France, in the ladies' singles figure skating competition.*
The Games were originally billed as a 'Winter Sports Week' and were retrospectively accredited as the first Winter Olympics by the IOC in 1926. Muckelt's bronze medal was the first for Britain at a Winter Games. She also came fourth in the pairs competition with Jack Page, the partner with whom she would win nine consecutive national pairs titles between 1923 and 1931, the last at the age of forty-five. Muckelt died in 1953 at the age of sixty-eight.

'The Cocoanuts', the first feature-length film to be released which featured ***Groucho Marx*** *and his brothers, was premiered in 1929.*
The Cocoanuts was adapted from the Broadway play of the same name which debuted four years earlier. The Marx Brothers first came to prominence on stage, although they soon progressed from Vaudeville to Broadway. Their first film, *Humor Risk* (1921), was a silent short, previewed once and believed to be destroyed. The wise-cracking Groucho (Julius Henry) appeared in fifteen films with his brothers, including *Monkey*

Business, *Duck Soup* and *A Night at the Opera*. He also appeared solo in many features, and was the long-running host of the television and radio game show *You Bet Your Life*. Marx died in 1977 at the age of eighty-six.

*In 1935 the DuPont Company research group led by **Wallace Carothers** succeeded in producing the first sample of a material that would later be called 'nylon'.*

Charles Stine, vice-president and director of the DuPont Company, announced the invention of nylon, patented in Carothers's name, in 1938. Stine had been instrumental in establishing the company's pure research programme that had lured Carothers from his academic post at Harvard in the late 1920s. Nylon, the original synthetic fibre, was first used to create toothbrush bristles; commercial manufacture began in 1939. Prior to its invention, Carothers's lab also produced the first synthetic rubber: neoprene. He did not live to see the full success of these inventions – Carothers took his own life in 1938 at the age of forty-one.

László Bíró first applied for a patent for his ballpoint pen in 1938.

A Hungarian native, Bíró immigrated to Argentina in 1940, where the invention was re-patented three years later. Bíró worked as a journalist in Hungary and was inspired to create a pen that could use quick-drying ink similar to that employed in newspaper printing. He enlisted the assistance of his brother György, a chemist, and the modern ballpoint pen was born. The pens were made under licence in Britain and found favour with RAF aircrews in World War Two as they didn't leak at high altitudes like fountain pens. Initially an expensive item (in 1945 the first pens sold in Britain cost 55 shillings), the price fell with increased competition and improved manufacturing techniques. Marcel Bich purchased Bíró's patents in 1950 and produced the pens under the name Bic. Lászlo Bíró was responsible for many other inventions including a pick-proof lock. Argentina celebrates its inventor's day on his birthday, 29 September. Bíró died at the age of eighty-six in 1985.

*In 1948 **William Shockley** filed his patent application for a 'Circuit Element Utilizing Semiconductive Material', which was subsequently granted in 1951.*

Shockley's patent described his invention of the junction transistor which essentially superseded the point contact transistor first demonstrated by John Bardeen and Walter Brattain in 1947. At the time all three worked for Bell Labs, with Shockley heading up their research group. Bardeen and Brattain made the first crucial transistor breakthrough, which drove Shockley to develop the theory and construction of his alternative format. The junction transistor was easier to fabricate than the point contact device. Its invention marked the start of the modern electronics era and gave birth to the multibillion-dollar silicon chip industry. Shockley, Bardeen and Brattain received the 1956 Nobel Prize in Physics for their work. In 1956 Shockley became director of a semiconductor enterprise financed by Beckman Instruments. However, rather than allowing Shockley to capitalise on the new technology he had developed, his difficult management style led to eight of the employees breaking away to form their own company, Fairchild Semiconductor, which in turn led to the creation of others, including Intel, which was the largest semiconductor maker by the end of the century. Shockley returned to academia, at Stanford University, in 1963. He died in 1989 at the age of seventy-nine.

*The novel 'Catch-22' by **Joseph Heller** was published in 1961.*

Approximately seven years in the writing, *Catch-22*, Heller's debut, recounts the story of Captain Joseph Yossarian, a member of a US bomber crew in World War Two, as he attempts to avoid flying further missions. The title has passed into the English language to describe a no-win situation. Heller himself flew with the US air force and completed sixty bombing missions over Europe during World War Two. He wrote a sequel, *Closing Time*, published in 1994. Heller died five years later at the age of seventy-six. His other novels include *Something Happened* (1974), *Picture This* (1988) and his last, *Portrait of an Artist, as an Old Man* (2000).

*In 1964 **Jean Alexander** played the role of Hilda Ogden for the first time in the television series 'Coronation Street'.*

The Ogden family moved into number thirteen and the character of Hilda remained in the series until Christmas 1987. Alexander had appeared in the show before – she played landlady Mrs Webb in 1962, two years before her debut as Mrs Ogden. She was voted 'Greatest Soap Opera Star of All Time' in a *TV Times* magazine poll in 2005. Alexander joined the cast of another long-running programme, *Last of the Summer Wine*, in 1988, and continued to play the character of Auntie Wainwright until the final series in 2010.

In 1969 **Neil Armstrong** *became the first man to walk on the moon.*

Armstrong had seen active service in the Korean War as a naval pilot, and later became a test pilot, clocking up several flights in the experimental high-speed plane, the X-15. Selected for astronaut training, his first venture into space was as the commander of *Gemini 8* in 1965 which performed the first docking between two spacecraft – a vital technique for the future Apollo programme. It was during the fifth manned Apollo spaceflight (Apollo 11) that Armstrong, the mission commander, and Buzz Aldrin left Michael Collins in the command module *Columbia* and made the first ever attempt at a moon landing. As they descended close to the surface in the lunar module, named *Eagle*, Armstrong took manual control of the craft, landing it safely in the Sea of Tranquillity. His first words when he stepped onto the moon were 'That's one small step for [a] man, one giant leap for mankind'. Armstrong and Aldrin spent approximately two and a half hours outside the lunar module on their only 'extra vehicular activity', the shortest time of all the Apollo landings. The mission was Armstrong's last spaceflight. He left NASA in 1971 and took up a professorship at the University of Cincinnati where he remained until 1979. In 1969, Armstrong, Aldrin and Collins were all awarded the Presidential Medal of Freedom, the highest civilian honour in the US. Armstrong died in 2012 at the age of eighty-two.

In December 1972 **Eugene Cernan** *became the 'last man on the moon' as commander of the final Apollo mission.*

Apollo 17 was Cernan's third and last spaceflight. He had previously travelled into space on board Gemini 9A, when he became the second American to walk in space. Aboard Apollo 10's lunar module, he descended close to the lunar surface in the mission that preceded the historic landing, by Neil Armstrong and Buzz Aldrin, two months later. Cernan is the last man, out of the twelve that landed, to have walked on the moon.

J. G. Farrell *(James Gordon) won the 1973 Booker Prize for his novel 'The Siege of Krishnapur'.*

Set during the Indian rebellion against the British in 1857, *The Siege of*

Krishnapur was the second book in Farrell's Empire trilogy that began with *Troubles* in 1970 and concluded with *The Singapore Grip* in 1978. His debut novel, *A Man From Elsewhere*, was published in 1963. Farrell was found drowned off the Irish coast at the age of forty-four. In 2010, *Troubles* was selected as the winner of the 'lost' Booker Prize of 1970. (The rules of the competition changed in 1971 and moved from being retrospective to include only novels published in the year of the award. As a result there were many books published in 1970 which missed out on being considered for the award.)

In 1976 **Jack Nicholson** *won his first Academy Award for best actor for his role as Randle P. McMurphy in 'One Flew Over the Cuckoo's Nest'.*

Nicholson made his film debut in *The Cry Baby Killer* (1958) and worked steadily through the sixties until his big break came with the part of George Hanson in *Easy Rider* (1969). The performance earned Nicholson his first Academy Award nomination (for best supporting actor). He won this category in 1984 for *Terms of Endearment* (1983) and picked up a second best actor award, at the age of sixty, in 1998, for *As Good as it Gets* (1997). This was his eleventh Academy Award acting nomination, seven of which were for best actor, making him the most nominated male actor in Oscar history. A further best actor Academy Award nomination five years later for *About Schmidt* (2002) took his overall total to twelve.

David Steel *was elected as the leader of the Liberal Party in 1976.*

Steel entered the House of Commons in 1965 at the age of twenty-six. His period as Liberal leader was marked first by the 'Lib–Lab' pact with the Callaghan government, and then by the alliance with the newly formed Social Democratic Party in the 1980s. Steel called for the merger of the two parties following the 1987 general election, and less than nine months later the Liberal Democrats were formed. He was knighted in 1990, and in 1997 became Baron Steel of Aikwood. Steel became the first presiding officer of the newly created Scottish Parliament in 1999, and went on to serve a four-year term. In 2004, he was made a Knight of the Order of the Thistle.

David Owen became foreign secretary in the Labour government of James Callaghan, in 1977.

Owen, who was the youngest foreign secretary since Anthony Eden in 1935, read medicine at Cambridge and was first elected to Parliament in 1966, at the age of twenty-seven. Out of office following the victory of Margaret Thatcher in 1979, Owen then became one of 'the gang of four' that broke away from the Labour Party to form the Social Democratic Party (SDP) in 1981. An alliance with the Liberal Party failed to erode the dominance of the Conservative and Labour parties in the 1983 general election, although it was close to Labour in terms of the percentage of the vote. The SDP and Liberals merged after the 1987 election, but the union did not gain unanimous support and Owen resigned as leader prior to their amalgamation. He returned to lead the remnants of the SDP until the party's final demise in 1990. Two years later, he became Lord Owen and also the EU co-chairman of the Conference for the Former Yugoslavia alongside US representative Cyrus Vance.

*In 1978 **Melvyn Bragg** presented the first edition of 'The South Bank Show'.*

Bragg presented and produced *The South Bank Show*, ITV's flagship arts programme, for over thirty years. It was notable for its broad subject range and inclusion of popular culture; the opening edition featured Paul McCartney, Germaine Greer and Gerald Scarfe. Following the conclusion of *The South Bank Show* on ITV, BSkyB relaunched the programme in 2012 with Bragg returning as its presenter. Bragg, who started in television at the BBC in 1961, has also had an extensive radio career and has presented the BBC Radio 4 series *In Our Time* since 1998. He has also written numerous works. These include the novels *The Hired Man* (1969) and *A Time to Dance* (1990), as well as non-fiction books that include a biography of Richard Burton and *Twelve Books That Changed the World* (2006). He was made a life peer in 1998.

***Richard Whiteley** presented the debut edition of Countdown in 1982.*

Countdown was the first programme to be broadcast on the UK's fourth terrestrial television station, Channel 4, after its launch in November 1982. Whitely read English at Cambridge University and after working at ITN joined Yorkshire television in the 1960s. The game show *Calendar Countdown* appeared on Yorkshire television in the summer of 1982, with Whiteley as host. He continued in this role when it transferred to Channel 4 and presented the programme until his death, in 2005, at the age of sixty-one. Whiteley was awarded an OBE in the 2004 Queen's Birthday Honours.

*'Toy Story', the first computer-animated feature film, directed and co-written by **John Lasseter**, premiered in 1995.*

Lasseter, whose boyhood ambition was to work in animation, took a new course at the California Institute of the Arts, taught by veteran Disney artists. After graduation, Lasseter went to work for Disney as an animator; however, his employers didn't share his vision for computer animation and he found himself out of a job when the project he was working on was cancelled. He joined Lucasfilm Computer Graphics, which was bought by Apple co-founder Steve Jobs in 1986 and renamed Pixar. Lasseter shared with William Reeves an Academy Award nomination for best animated short film for *Luxo Jr.* (1986) and the pair won the Oscar two years later with *Tin Toy* (1988). Pixar signed a deal with Disney to produce *Toy Story* (1995), for which Lasseter won a special achievement Academy Award. He has been nominated by the Academy on three more occasions, for *Monsters, Inc.*, *Cars* and *Toy Story 3* (2010). He returned to Disney in 2006 as chief creative officer of both studios, after their purchase of Pixar Animation.

***Steve Redgrave** won his fifth Olympic gold medal, at the 2000 Sydney Games, as a member of the men's coxless four rowing team.*

In a thrilling race, the British crew's winning margin was 0.38 seconds as they beat the Italian four into second place. Redgrave retired from the sport following the Games and was knighted in 2001. He is the only British athlete to have won gold medals at five consecutive Games. Redgrave also won nine World Championship rowing titles between 1986 and 1999. His Olympic medal tally is actually six, since he also won a bronze at the 1988 Games for the coxed pairs. Redgrave received an MBE in 1987, a CBE ten years later and was knighted in 2001.

*The fourth novel by **Dan Brown**, 'The Da Vinci Code', was published in 2003.*

The Da Vinci Code went on to sell over eighty million copies worldwide and was made into a film in 2006. Brown had tried to make a living as a songwriter, writing and producing four albums of original music, but his career failed to take off. He was inspired to become an author by reading a book called *The Doomsday Conspiracy* in 1993. Brown's first literary success was *187 Men to Avoid*, a self-help book credited to the female pseudonym of Danielle Brown and published in 1995. His first novel, *Digital Fortress*, appeared three years later.

Daniel Craig *made his debut as James Bond in 'Casino Royale', released in 2006.*

Craig's performance earned him a Bafta nomination for best actor, the first for an actor playing Bond. The screenplay was based on the first novel by Ian Fleming to feature the secret agent. After school, Craig joined the National Youth Theatre and later studied at the Guildhall School of Music and Drama, graduating in 1991. He made his film debut the following year in *The Power of One*. Craig also notched up several television appearances and had a starring role in the series *Our Friends in the North* (1996). His other films include *Layer Cake* (2004), *Munich* (2005) and his second Bond film, *Quantum of Solace* (2008). Craig made his third appearance as the British secret agent in *Skyfall* (2012).

*Abstract painter **Tomma Abts** won the 2006 Turner Prize.*

Abts, the first female painter to win the prize, was born in Kiel, Germany, but had been living and working in England prior to the award. She was nominated for her solo exhibitions in London and Basel. Abts uses a canvas with dimensions of 48cm by 38cm for her work, which is made using both acrylic and oil paint. Each finished picture is given a German first name as its title. She begins each project with no plan as to its form, but instead lets the abstract images develop during the painting process.

George Osborne *became chancellor of the exchequer in 2010.*

Osborne is the youngest person to hold the office of chancellor since Lord Randolph Churchill in 1886. A graduate in modern history from Magdalen College, Oxford, he has served as the MP for Tatton since 2001. After a short spell in journalism Osborne accepted a post at the Conservative Research Department in 1994. This marked the commencement of his active political career. Osborne spent five years as shadow chancellor before transferring to the government benches as part of the Conservative/Liberal Democrat coalition following the 2010 general election.

39
THIRTY-NINE

Michael Faraday discovered the phenomenon of electromagnetic induction in 1831.

Faraday made his discovery with apparatus that consisted of two coils of wire in close proximity. He found that when an electric current is introduced into one coil, a current is momentarily induced in the second coil. Similarly, when the current in the first coil is stopped, another transient current is observed in the second coil. This is the principle under which the electrical transformer operates. Faraday also showed that electricity could be generated by moving a magnet within a coil of wire, thus demonstrating the first dynamo. Faraday only received a basic education as a child, but an apprenticeship to a bookbinder gave him access to a wide range of reading material. His scientific career began at the age of twenty-one when he worked as an assistant to Sir Humphry Davy. Faraday had attended his lectures in London and came to Davy's attention when he sent him a bound copy of his lecture notes, hoping to gain entry to a scientific career. Following an accident that affected Davy's eyesight, he took on Faraday as a secretary for a brief period, after which Faraday returned to bookbinding. However, in early 1813, Davy asked him to fill a vacancy for a laboratory assistant at the Royal Institution. Faraday is now regarded by many as the greatest experimentalist in his field. He also established the Royal Institution Christmas Lectures for children, which continue to this day. The SI unit of capacitance, the Farad, is named in his honour. (Capacitance measures a body's ability to store electric charge.) Faraday died in 1867 at the age of seventy-five.

In 1851 Isaac Singer was issued with a US patent for his improvements to the sewing machine.

Singer did not invent the sewing machine, which by that time had been developed and patented by several others. However, his contribution, which was to make him very wealthy, was to make it a practical item. Singer's previous success as an inventor – he patented a rock-drilling machine in 1839 – enabled him to pursue his acting ambitions and he toured for several years with his own troupe until the money ran out. Singer next came up with a metal and wood carving machine, but it was his encounter with the Lerow and Blodgett sewing machine at the Boston machine shop of Orson Phelps in 1850 that kick-started his biggest success. In less than two weeks, Singer had redesigned the mechanism and built a working prototype. His first sewing-machine patent, granted in 1851, led to the creation of the I.M. Singer & Company with Phelps and George Zieber. New York lawyer Edward Clark also became a partner in 1852. Patent disputes followed with other manufacturers and inventor Elias Howe, though a settlement was reached in 1856 to pool their patents. By 1860 Singer was the world's largest sewing machine company. The first Singer facility to be built outside of the United States was in Glasgow, which opened in 1867. The nearby Clydebank premises, opened in 1884, became the world's largest sewing-machine factory. Back in the US, the Singer building in New York, built in 1908, was one of the world's first skyscrapers. Singer's personal life was complicated. He had twenty-four children by five different women, two of whom he married. Near the end of his life Singer settled in Devon, where he was to die, in 1875, at the age of sixty-three. His estate was valued at approximately $14 million and his mansion, Oldway, in Paignton, still stands and is now owned by the local council.

The first novel by **George Eliot**, *'Adam Bede', was published in 1859.*

Adam Bede was a major critical and commercial success which Eliot followed up with her next novel, *The Mill on the Floss*. Born Mary Ann Evans, she adopted the pseudonym George Eliot because she was concerned that she wouldn't be taken as seriously as a female author, and also because she wanted to protect her identity. Her domestic arrangements were unconventional for the time – she remained unmarried to her partner George Lewes although they lived together as man and wife. Eighteen months after his death she married John Cross, who was twenty years her junior. She died seven months later at their Chelsea home, in 1880, at the age of sixty-one.

Henry Ford founded the motor company which bears his name in 1903.

Ford came from a farming family, but opted instead to work in industry, first as an apprentice machinist and then later with the Edison Illuminating Company, becoming its chief engineer in 1893. He finished building his first car, called the quadricycle, in a shed behind his home at the age of thirty-two. Ford left his job to begin manufacturing cars and, after two false starts, founded the Ford Motor Company in 1903. The Model T appeared five years later. The car's appeal, Ford's introduction of the assembly-line process, and his generous pay deals for the workers, all contributed to his company's dominance in the marketplace. By the end of the First World War half of all cars in America were Ford Model Ts, although Ford had slipped to third place in the early 1930s due to increased competition. Ford died at the age of eighty-three in 1947.

In 1903 Austen Chamberlain became chancellor of the exchequer in the government led by Arthur Balfour.

Chamberlain's father had also been active in politics and encouraged his son to follow in his footsteps. Austen Chamberlain spent two periods at the Exchequer, but his longest cabinet position was as foreign secretary where he arguably made his greatest contribution, playing a key role in the negotiations that resulted in the Locarno Pact in 1925. This attempted to stabilise Europe by, amongst other things, settling the Franco–German frontier. Chamberlain won the 1925 Nobel Peace Prize for his efforts, and in the same year was appointed a Knight of the Garter. His half-brother was Neville Chamberlain, prime minister at the outbreak of the Second World War. Austen died in 1937 at the age of seventy-three.

Herbert Austin formed the Austin Motor Company in 1905.

Educated in England, Austin then served his apprenticeship in Australia, and later became the chief engineer for the Wolseley Sheep Shearing Machine Company. The business relocated to England where Austin promoted the expansion of its product range into machine tool manufacture and other areas. Increasingly interested in the emerging automobile industry, Austin produced his own three-wheeled vehicle in his spare time. He created the first four-wheeled Wolseley car in 1899 and by the early twentieth century Wolseley was the largest car manufacturer in Britain.

Austin left to set up on his own and his company produced its first vehicle, the Austin Endcliffe Phaeton, in 1906. During the First World War the company's product range diversified to include armoured cars, aeroplanes and artillery shells, among other items. Austin was subsequently knighted for helping the war effort. The business struggled to adapt to peacetime, but the launch of the Austin Seven (known as 'the baby Austin') in 1922 revived the company's fortunes. Designed by Austin himself, the car was manufactured until 1939. (Production of this vehicle under licence in Japan would also help to establish the Datsun – later to be called Nissan – Car Company.) He was made Baron Austin of Longbridge in 1936. He is also remembered for his philanthropy, with hospitals in Birmingham and Cambridge University's Cavendish Laboratory receiving donations. Austin died in 1941 at the age of eighty-two. The Austin Motor Company merged with the Nuffield Organisation (makers of Morris cars) to create the British Motor Corporation (BMC) in 1952.

In 1911 **Roald Amundsen** *led the Norwegian expedition which was the first to reach the South Pole.*

Amundsen, and four members of his team, beat Scott's attempt to reach the Pole by two months. Amundsen came from a family of sea captains and shipowners, and gave up his medical studies in order to pursue a maritime career. A previous achievement of Amundsen was the navigation of the entire length of the Northwest Passage, completed in 1906. In 1928, Amundsen and five others disappeared whilst flying on a mission in the Arctic to rescue the crew of a missing airship. Neither the plane nor his body has ever been recovered. He was fifty-five.

Malcolm Campbell *broke the land-speed world record for the first time, in 1924, when he reached 146.16mph in his V12 Sunbeam.*

Campbell continued to set more records over the next decade, and was the first to drive at over 150mph and 300mph (the latter reached in 1935 during his last record-winning attempt). Campbell also held the water-speed world record on four occasions. His son Donald went on to emulate his father by also achieving speed records on land and water. Malcolm Campbell was knighted in 1931. He died in 1948 at the age of sixty-three.

Carl Erhardt captained the British ice hockey team that won a gold medal at the 1936 Winter Olympics at Garmisch-Partenkirchen.

Erhardt is the oldest ice hockey player to have achieved Olympic gold. The British team, including Erhardt, also won the European Championships in the same year. He died in 1988 at the age of ninety-one.

*'White Christmas', sung by **Bing Crosby**, reached number one in the US for the first time in 1942.*

'White Christmas' became one of the biggest-selling singles ever, with estimated total worldwide sales of over forty million. Crosby also performed the song in the musical *Holiday Inn* (1942), for which it won the Academy Award for best original song. Crosby's film career began at the start of the 1930s. A decade later he made the first in a series of seven 'road' movies, *Road to Singapore* (1940), in which he played opposite Bob Hope. Crosby won a best actor Oscar for his portrayal of Father Chuck O'Malley in *Going My Way* (1944), although the movie *White Christmas* (1954), in which he sang the title song, would prove to be his most popular. His signature tune, 'White Christmas' was three times a US number one and made its highest ever chart appearance in the UK at number five in 1977, weeks after his death at the age of seventy-four.

***Ernst Chain** and Howard Florey received the 1945 Nobel Prize in Physiology or Medicine (shared with Alexander Fleming) for their work on penicillin, the first antibiotic drug.*

Following on from Fleming's discovery of penicillin approximately ten years earlier, Chain (a biochemist) and Florey (professor of pathology at Oxford) were able to isolate and manufacture the active ingredient, and demonstrate its efficacy in treating bacterial infections. Chain was born in Berlin, but came to England in 1933 following the rise to power of the Nazis. Knighted in 1969, he died ten years later at the age of seventy-three.

*In 1947 **Earl Tupper** filed the patent for his plastic container with a sealing lid.*

Tupper was a keen inventor, recording innovations such as a 'fish powered boat' and a 'no-drip cone' amongst his creations. He also trained as a tree surgeon and ran a landscaping business that went bankrupt in the mid 1930s, forcing him to get a job with the DuPont Company. He spent one year in the plastics division where he obtained some polyethylene slag, a waste product, and succeeded in transforming it into a much more user-friendly material. Tupper then founded his own company to design and engineer industrial plastics in 1938. Military contracts during the Second World War ensured the business prospered. After the War, he focused on the emerging consumer market. Tupper began producing plastic containers for food, with the important patented sealing lid and 'Tupperware' was born. The product was a major success, largely because of the 'Tupperware Party' sales model, instigated by saleswoman Brownie Wise. In 1958 Tupper sold his company for $16 million, purchased an island, and relocated to Costa Rica. He continued to invent, producing unusual devices such as a portable plastic cylinder for manually washing clothes, in which the required agitation was provided by the user carrying out a set of specified exercises. Tupper died in 1983 at the age of seventy-six.

The transistor was first demonstrated by **John Bardeen** *and Walter Brattain in December 1947.*

Developed at Bell Labs in the United States, the transistor was referred to as a 'three electrode circuit element' (the name transistor was later coined by John Pierce). Bardeen and Brattain had created a 'point contact' device, which was superseded by the 'junction' transistor conceived by William Shockley, their research group leader. The trio of Bardeen, Brattain and Shockley shared the 1956 Nobel Prize in Physics for their work on the transistor. Bardeen left Bell Labs in 1951 and went to work at the University of Illinois at Urbana-Champaign where he remained for the rest of his academic career. In 1957, in collaboration with Leon Cooper and Bob Schrieffer, Bardeen proposed the first satisfactory explanation of superconductivity (the ability of extremely cold metals to have zero electrical resistance). For what became known as the BCS theory, the trio were awarded the 1972 Nobel Prize in Physics. John Bardeen is one of only four individuals who have received two Nobel Prizes, and is the only person who has been a physics laureate twice. He died in 1991 at the age of eighty-two.

In 1953 **Tenzing Norgay** *and Edmund Hillary became the first men officially recognised to have reached the summit of Mount Everest.*

In the previous year Tenzing had made an ascent of Everest with a Swiss team to within a thousand feet of the summit. When Tenzing and Hillary reached the peak in 1953, Hillary famously captured Tenzing's image as he held an ice axe with the flags of the UN, Britain, Nepal and India attached. Later, his nephew, son and grandson would also conquer Everest. Tenzing died in 1986 at the age of seventy-one.

'Time for a Tiger', the first published novel by **Anthony Burgess**, *appeared in 1956.*

The first in Burgess's Malayan trilogy, *Time for a Tiger* was inspired by a period he spent working in Malaya and Borneo as an education officer for the British Colonial Service. In 1958 he was diagnosed with a brain tumour, which prompted him to write several novels within the space of a year in order to make provision for his wife, Lynne. However, the prognosis proved to be incorrect and Burgess outlived her by twenty-five years. His most famous work, *A Clockwork Orange* (1962), follows the savage exploits of the teenage Alex and society's attempt to rehabilitate him. The book's fame is also due in part to Stanley Kubrick's 1971 film adaptation. Its violent tone aroused much controversy and Kubrick withdrew the film from circulation, a situation that was only relaxed after his death in 1999. Burgess's other novels include *Napoleon Symphony* (1974), *Earthly Powers* (1980) and *Any Old Iron* (1988). Burgess died in 1993 at the age of seventy-six.

Richard Tompkins *founded the Green Shield Trading Stamp Company in 1957.*

Tompkins's first jobs after leaving school at fourteen included delivering laundry and working as a filling-station attendant. He later became an engineering draughtsman, an occupation he continued during the Second World War. The purchase of an old printing machine in 1945 was the beginning of a new career for Tompkins as a printer. Inspired by trading stamp schemes he had seen when on holiday in the US in the fifties, Tompkins decided to introduce the concept to the UK; the venture also fitted well with his printing business. His Green Shield stamps were a success, with consumers receiving them for certain purchases. Once they had saved the required amount, they could be exchanged for gifts. The business declined in the seventies but the use of catalogues, and shops where the stamps could be exchanged for goods, were elements that Tompkins retained when he launched the Argos chain in 1973. He sold this business for £35 million in 1979. Tompkins was awarded a CBE in 1992 and died later that year, at the age of seventy-four.

*In 1967 the television series 'The Prisoner' made its UK television debut starring **Patrick McGoohan** as Number Six.*

McGoohan, who was born in New York to Irish parents, was also involved in the creation of *The Prisoner*. He directed and wrote several episodes, and penned the climax of the series. *The Prisoner* features a secret agent who is incarcerated in a mysterious village where the authorities try to find out why he resigned from his job. He is referred to as Number Six (no names, only numbers are used in the village), and constantly tries to escape. Prior to *The Prisoner*, McGoohan had himself resigned from the series *Danger Man* in which he played secret agent John Drake. The supremo of Associated Television (ATV), Lew Grade, was keen for another McGoohan vehicle and gave him the go ahead to make *The Prisoner*. McGoohan is also remembered for his roles in many films such as *Ice Station Zebra* (1968), *Escape from Alcatraz* (1979) and *Braveheart* (1995). McGoohan died in 2009 at the age of eighty.

***Gordon Moore** and Robert Noyce founded Intel Corporation in 1968.*

Both Moore, who received his PhD from the California Institute of Technology, and Noyce had left Fairchild Semiconductor to start Intel. The company was briefly called NM Electronics before the change was made to Intel, derived from the first letters of the words 'integrated electronics'. In 1965 Moore stated in an article that the number of transistors per chip would double every year (revised ten years later to every two years) and this became known as Moore's law – a prediction for the growth in complexity of integrated circuits that has held true for more than forty years. Intel was floated on the stock market in 1971, the same year that the company introduced the first single-chip microprocessor, the four-bit 4004. Ten years later the company was selected to provide the microprocessor, the 8088, for the first IBM personal computer (PC) and this is a market sector which Intel has dominated ever since. Intel has been the world's largest semiconductor manufacturer since the early 1990s.

Rolf Harris reached number one in the UK singles chart with 'Two Little Boys' in 1969.

'Two Little Boys' was the 1969 Christmas number one and remained at the top for six weeks to become the first chart topper of the 1970s. Harris first made the UK top ten in 1960 with his self-penned 'Tie Me Kangaroo Down, Sport'. His other chart entries include a version of Led Zeppelin's 'Stairway to Heaven' in 1993, when he was aged sixty-two. Harris was born and grew up in Perth, Australia, and left for England at the age of twenty-one to study art. Soon afterwards he began his career on British television, and by 1967 he was hosting his own show. Latterly he presented the long-running series *Animal Hospital*, first broadcast in 1994, and returned to his creative roots with *Rolf on Art*. He was commissioned to paint a portrait of the Queen, unveiled in 2006, to celebrate her eightieth birthday. Harris, who already held an MBE and OBE, was awarded a CBE in 2006. He was appointed as a member of the Order of Australia in 1989.

In 1983 Ben Kingsley won both the Academy Award and Bafta for best actor for his portrayal of the title character in 'Gandhi'.

Kingsley joined the Royal Shakespeare Company in 1967, and his early television credits include *Coronation Street* (as Ron Jenkins), the legal drama series *Crown Court* and playing Dante Gabriel Rossetti in *The Love School*. His first film appearance was a supporting role in *Fear is the Key* (1972), but it was his portrayal of Gandhi in 1982 that brought him critical and commercial success. Kingsley, who received a CBE in 2000 and was knighted in 2002, has notched up three further Academy Award nominations since *Gandhi*: *Bugsy* (1991) and *Sexy Beast* (2000) for best supporting actor and *House of Sand and Fog* (2003) for best actor.

Jeremy Paxman presented his first edition of 'Newsnight' in 1989.

Born in Leeds, Paxman read English at St Catharine's College, Cambridge, and soon after graduating joined the BBC where his early years included a stint in Northern Ireland as a reporter. After returning to London he took on assignments for the *Tonight* programme and *Panorama*, before landing his role as anchor on *Newsnight*. He has chaired the revived quiz show *University Challenge* since 1994. Paxman has also presented *Start the Week* on Radio 4, and has written several books including *The English: A Portrait of a People* and *Empire: What Ruling the World Did to the British*. He has won many accolades for his broadcasting, twice receiving the Bafta Richard Dimbleby Award.

Nigel Mansell won the Formula One World Championship in 1992.

Mansell's career in motor sport began with karting, and he won his first race at the age of fourteen. He then worked his way through Formula Ford (1977 champion) and Formula Three to become a Formula One driver with the Lotus team in 1980. His first grand prix victory was at Brands Hatch, in the 1985 European Grand Prix, driving for the Williams Honda team. Mansell left Formula One after his championship victory, and the following year became the CART IndyCar champion, and the first driver to hold both titles simultaneously. He returned to Formula One for a handful of races in the mid-nineties finally bowing out from the sport at the 1995 Spanish Grand Prix.

Yann Martel won the 2002 Man Booker Prize for 'Life of Pi'.

Life of Pi was the second novel by the Spanish-born writer, who has Canadian parentage. Martel studied philosophy at university and embarked on a career in writing in his late twenties. His short-story collection *The Facts Behind the Helsinki Roccamatios* was published in 1993, and his debut novel, *Self*, followed three years later. More recently, Martel has published the novel *Beatrice and Virgil* in 2010 and *101 Letters to a Prime Minister* in 2012. The latter book is based on a project by Martel in which he sent the Canadian prime minister, Stephen Harper, one book every two weeks for a period of four years.

CHAPTER FIVE

Quadragenarians

I'm not young enough to know everything.

J. M. BARRIE

40
FORTY

*In 1580 **Francis Drake** sailed into Plymouth after commanding the first circumnavigation of the world by an English ship.*

Drake had set out from Plymouth in 1577 in his vessel The Pelican, which was renamed the *Golden Hind* during the voyage. It was the sole member of a five-ship fleet that was able to complete the round-the-world trip (only one other vessel, *The Elizabeth*, managed to return home). Drake was born near Tavistock, Devon in 1540. He was related to the seafaring Hawkins family and gained maritime experience on their slave-trading voyages. By his late twenties, Drake had command of a ship on a trading mission, but they were attacked by the Spanish. He escaped with his ship, but bore the Spanish a lasting enmity. Drake later exacted his revenge with marauding raids on the Spanish Main that netted him considerable wealth. His round-the-world trip, undertaken with the backing of several investors, including Queen Elizabeth I who awarded Drake a knighthood the year after its completion, also proved profitable, mainly because of raids on the Spanish interests along the Pacific coast. As vice admiral, Drake helped inflict further misery on the Spanish with the defeat of the Armada in 1588. Seven years later he began his final voyage to the West Indies with his cousin, Sir John Hawkins. Their attack on the Canary Islands was repulsed and they encountered further Spanish resistance during an unsuccessful attack on Puerto Rico. Drake continued to try to capture the Spanish possessions in the region, but in early 1596 he contracted dysentery and died at the age of fifty-five. Drake was buried at sea in a lead coffin off the coast of Panama.

*In 1841 **William Henry Fox Talbot** filed his patent for 'Improvements in Obtaining Pictures or Representations of Objects'.*

The patent detailed Talbot's 'calotype' process, the first photographic method to use a negative to make positive prints, which is still the basis of most modern film photography. Talbot's technique was superior to the rival daguerreotype process since it was possible to make multiple copies of the image – Louis Daguerre's method could only produce one unique picture per exposure. Talbot was inspired to invent a new photographic process some eight years earlier when he failed to satisfactorily capture the scenery near Lake Como, Italy, in a sketch. Soon after his return, Talbot began working to develop his process. A major step forward occurred in 1840, when he realised that a short exposure time, although it left no visible image on the paper, could, through the use of a developer, produce a satisfactory negative. Talbot was also active in other areas including representing Chippenham in Parliament for a brief period and producing translations of the Assyrian cuneiform script. He died in 1877 at the age of seventy-seven.

J. J. Thomson (Joseph John) announced at the Royal Institution in 1897 his identification of particles called 'corpuscles', later termed 'electrons'.

Thomson had been studying what were known as 'cathode rays' at the Cavendish Laboratory in Cambridge and his experiments showed that they were composed of negatively charged particles. He went on to demonstrate that they had a constant charge-to-mass ratio and that they had the same characteristics regardless of their source material. The electron was thus the first sub-atomic particle to be identified. Thomson was awarded the 1906 Nobel Prize in Physics for his work and was knighted two years later. He graduated with a degree in mathematics from Trinity College, Cambridge, in 1880 and subsequently worked at the Cavendish Laboratory. It was there, aged twenty-eight, that he succeeded Lord Rayleigh as the professor of experimental physics. The lab's eminence in its field saw several of his students also gain Nobel Prizes, including his son George, in 1937, for his work on the electron. Thomson died in 1940 at the age of eighty-three. His ashes were interred in the nave of Westminster Abbey.

Ernest Shackleton set out as the leader of the Imperial Trans-Antarctic Expedition in 1914, which aimed to cross Antarctica overland via the South Pole.

Shackleton, who was born in Kilkea, Ireland, had taken part in two previous expeditions to the Antarctic. He was a member of Robert Falcon

Scott's *Discovery* expedition (1901–1904) and led the British Antarctic (*Nimrod*) expedition (1907–1909), after which he was knighted. Five years later his third voyage to the continent ran into difficulties when his ship, *Endurance*, became trapped in ice in the Weddell Sea and eventually sank. Using lifeboats, the crew made it to the remote Elephant Island located off the coast of Antarctica. From there, Shackleton led five of his men on an eight-hundred-mile voyage to South Georgia in a twenty-two-foot open boat, the *James Caird*. They then had to cross the island's rugged interior to reach the whaling stations on the other side, arriving just under a month after setting out from Elephant Island. Shackleton was able to organise the rescue of his remaining men, found to be safe and well when they were reached, in August 1916, four months after the *James Caird* had departed for the voyage across the Southern Ocean. Shackleton organised another Antarctic expedition which departed from Britain in 1921; however, he died of a heart attack in South Georgia, aged forty-seven, before reaching the southernmost continent. He was buried in South Georgia in accordance with what his relatives believed would have been his wish for his final resting place.

Nancy Astor *became the first woman to sit as an MP in Britain* when she took her seat in the House of Commons in 1919.*

A native of the American state of Virginia, Astor succeeded her husband Waldorf Astor as the Unionist (Conservative) member for Plymouth Sutton. He had been required to leave the Commons when he was elevated to the peerage as the second Viscount Astor following his father's death. Lady Astor was elected with a majority of over five thousand and served in Parliament until she stood down before the 1945 general election. She died nineteen years later at the age of eighty-four.

The first edition of 'Ulysses' by **James Joyce** *was published in Paris in 1922.*

Ulysses was first serialised in an American journal called *The Little Review*, making its debut in 1918. The book was then published in its entirety in 1922 by the American-born Sylvia Beach, who owned the

---

* In 1918 Constance Markiewicz became the first woman to be elected as an MP, but as per the policy of her party, Sinn Féin, she did not attend Parliament.

Shakespeare and Company bookshop in Paris. *Ulysses* recounts the journey of Leopold Bloom through Dublin on one particular day: 16 June 1904. The book proved controversial and was banned in the United States until 1933. A British edition did not appear until 1936. *Ulysses* took several years to complete and Joyce, who had published only one novel previously – *Portrait of the Artist as a Young Man* in 1914 – would only publish one more after it, *Finnegan's Wake*, in 1939. He also wrote poetry (his first collection, *Chamber Music*, was published in 1907) and a short story collection, *The Dubliners*, published in 1914. Joyce largely lived abroad from his mid-twenties onwards and died in Switzerland, in 1941, at the age of fifty-eight.

In 1927 **Clarence Birdseye** *filed his patent application for a 'Method of Preparing Food Products' which contained his invention for the quick freezing of fish and meat.*

The roots of Birdseye's technique lay in his time spent living and working in Alaska between 1912 and 1915. Here, he observed how fish caught by Eskimos and frozen instantly by the climate tasted fresh once thawed. This observation inspired Birdseye to discover a way to replicate the process, a task that would take many years and culminate in the method documented in his 1927 patent application. In 1929 he sold a controlling interest in his company, as well as the associated patents, to Postum Inc. for nearly $11 million, and the remaining 49% of the business to Goldman Sachs Trading Corporation for close to $13 million. (Postum was subsequently renamed as the General Foods Corporation and also acquired the Goldman Sachs interest in the concern.) In 1930 the first food products under the 'Birds Eye' brand appeared in the shops. Birdseye died in 1956 at the age of sixty-nine.

The journal 'Nature' published a paper by **James Chadwick** *entitled 'Possible Existence of a Neutron' in 1932.*

Chadwick stated in his paper that the radiation released when the element beryllium was bombarded by alpha particles could be best described by an entity with a mass of one atomic unit and an electric charge of zero: the 'neutron'. The existence of such a particle had been suggested twelve years earlier by Sir Ernest Rutherford, while in charge of the Cavendish Laboratory in Cambridge where Chadwick worked. Chadwick followed up his paper with another shortly after, in which he proved the existence of neutrons. He was awarded the 1935 Nobel Prize in Physics for his discovery which, as well as adding to our understanding of the composition of the atom, also paved the way for further studies of nuclear disintegration that included the splitting of heavy elements such as uranium. Chadwick studied physics at the University of Manchester and graduated in 1911. He was in Berlin doing post-graduate work when the First World War broke out and as a result he was interned for four years as an enemy alien. Upon release, Chadwick returned to England and resumed his working relationship with Rutherford. Chadwick, who was knighted in 1945, died in 1974 at the age of eighty-two.

The Supermarine Spitfire, designed by **Reginald Mitchell**, *took to the sky for the first time in 1936.*

Following his apprenticeship with a locomotive engineering company, Mitchell secured a post as an assistant at the Supermarine Aviation Works. He rose rapidly through the company: by his mid-twenties he was chief designer and shortly afterwards he was made chief engineer. The Spitfire effectively combined many of the technical developments at the time, but Mitchell did not live to see the plane in action during World War Two as he succumbed to cancer in 1937, at the age of forty-two.

George VI ascended to the throne in 1936 following the abdication of his brother, Edward VIII.

Edward gave up his position as king in order to marry the twice-divorced Wallis Simpson, whose marital status was unacceptable to the establishment. George VI's reign encompassed the Second World War, and his presence alongside that of his Queen, Elizabeth Bowes-Lyon, in wartime London became a symbol of the country's determination in the struggle for victory (they continued to live either at Buckingham Palace or at nearby Windsor Castle). The royal couple also undertook morale-boosting visits to bomb-damaged areas across the country. George VI was the last Emperor of India before it was granted independence in 1947. He died five years later, in 1952, at the age of fifty-six. The throne passed to his elder daughter, Elizabeth.

*In 1954 **Malcolm McLean** filed a patent for a containerised system for trans-porting goods.*

McLean's patent, 'Apparatus for Shipping Freight', detailed his scheme for using standardised containers to transport goods on both sea and land. These units could be loaded and unloaded easily, with the contents secure inside. Two years after McLean had filed his patent, the first container ship (*SS Ideal-X*) left Newark, New Jersey, bound for the Port of Houston. McLean had built a successful trucking business in the United States from scratch, but sold up in 1955 in order to develop his idea for container-based transportation. He bought the Pan Atlantic Steamship Company and purchased two tankers for conversion, one of which was the *Ideal-X*. A special flat spar deck was added to carry the containers. A revised loading arrangement was introduced in 1957 for the ship *Gateway City*, which had been adapted to carry containers stacked on top of each other both above and below deck. His shipping company was renamed Sea-Land Service Inc. in 1960 and quickly grew to be the largest cargo-shipping enterprise in the world. He sold a controlling interest in his business in 1969 and left in 1977, but re-entered the container market the following year with a new venture. (Sea-Land's container business became part of the A.P. Moller-Maersk Group in 1999.) Containerisation revolutionised world commerce and is seen by many as the engine of globalisation. McLean died in 2001, aged eighty-seven.

*The success of the trial of the first safe vaccine for poliomyelitis, developed by a team led by **Jonas Salk**, was declared publicly in 1955.*

The announcement was greeted with tremendous joy as polio was one of the most feared diseases of the post-war era. Salk was feted as a hero, received many awards and went on to establish the Salk Institute for Biological Studies in La Jolla, California, which opened in 1963. He continued to work on vaccine development, notably for HIV, before his death in 1995 at the age of eighty.

*In 1968 **Frank Borman, Jim Lovell** and Bill Anders flew to the moon as the crew of Apollo 8 – the first manned spacecraft to leave earth orbit.*

Borman was the commander of the mission, which was the first manned flight to use the powerful Saturn V rocket system employed for all subsequent Apollo launches. Borman was accompanied by Lovell, the command module pilot, and 35-year-old Bill Anders, the designated lunar module pilot. The crew completed ten lunar orbits during the mission, conducted over the Christmas period in 1968. It was Borman and Anders' final journey into space, but Lovell would make the trip again, this time as the commander of Apollo 13 in 1970, which came perilously close to disaster after an explosion in the craft's service module. The planned moon landing was abandoned, although Lovell again came close to the lunar surface as a result of the crippled spacecraft's 'slingshot' trajectory around the moon that was required to return it to earth. This was Lovell's fourth (and last) spaceflight, and he wrote a book about his experiences that was later turned into the film *Apollo 13* (1995).

Tom Baker succeeded Jon Pertwee in 1974 to become the fourth actor to play Doctor Who on television.

Baker, who clocked up seven series in as many years, holds the record as the longest-serving Doctor. After leaving school, he decided to become a monk and spent over five years in a monastery before abandoning his religious vocation. Baker then did two years National Service, where his interest in acting was sparked by his participation in the Medical Corps' amateur dramatic productions. His first major film role was his portrayal of Rastputin in *Nicholas and Alexandra* (1971), which brought him two Golden Globe nominations. More recently, Baker was the narrator for the BBC comedy series *Little Britain*, first broadcast in 2003.

Goalkeeper Dino Zoff became the oldest winner of the football World Cup when Italy beat West Germany in 1982.

Italy, captained by Zoff, triumphed 3–1 in the final, played at the Bernabéu Stadium in Madrid. Zoff played 112 times for his national side before his retirement in 1983. He spent eleven years as a player at his last senior club, Juventus, where he won six 'Seria A' titles, two 'Coppa Italia' trophies and, in 1977, the UEFA Cup.

Goalkeeper Peter Shilton made his last appearance for England, in the third place play-off game against hosts Italy, at the 1990 World Cup.

The game, which ended 2–1 to Italy, was his 125th international match, which still stands as a record number of caps for an England player. Shilton, who made his league debut for Leicester City against Everton as a sixteen-year-old, notched up 1,005 senior-level appearances in a playing career that began in 1966 and lasted for over thirty years. His most successful period was with Nottingham Forest, when they won a League Championship, a League Cup and two consecutive European Cups in 1979 and 1980. Shilton received an MBE in the 1986 New Year Honours and an OBE five years later, both for services to football.

Merlene Ottey won a silver medal as part of the Jamaican 4x100m relay squad at the 2000 Sydney Olympics.

Ottey ran the anchor leg in the race and crossed the finishing line to become the oldest Olympic track-and-field medallist to date. At the same event, following the disqualification of winner Marion Jones, Ottey's fourth place in the 100m was upgraded to the bronze position. Ottey also competed in the 2004 Athens Games, her seventh consecutive Olympics, where she made it to the semi-final of the 100m at the age of forty-four. She narrowly missed qualifying for the 2008 Games. Over her Olympic career Ottey has won three silver medals and six bronze. She came agonisingly close at the 1996 Olympics to the coveted first prize, but lost out in a photo finish to Gail Devers in the 100m final (both athletes were given the same time of 10.94 seconds). Ottey has won gold at the World Championships on two occasions for the 200m (the latter in 1995 at the age of thirty-five), as well as for the 4x100m relay in 1991. Her total of fourteen World Championship medals is the highest for a woman. Ottey moved to Slovenia in 1998 and became a Slovenian citizen. She represented her new country at the European Championships in 2006, when she reached the semi-final of the 100m. At the age of fifty-two, Ottey became the oldest athlete to participate in the European Championships when she anchored the Slovenian team in the semi-final of the 4x100m relay in 2012.

*The first episode of 'The Office', starring **Ricky Gervais** as David Brent, was shown in 2001.*

Gervais, who also co-wrote *The Office* with Stephen Merchant, played the inept office manager for two series and also in a two-part finale that aired during Christmas 2003. After its BBC2 debut, *The Office* grew in popularity, earned critical acclaim and won 'best situation comedy' at the 2002 Bafta Awards. Gervais also won an award for best comedy performance (a feat he repeated in 2003 and 2004). The role brought him a Golden Globe Award in 2004. Before *The Office*, Gervais had a spot on Channel 4's *The 11 O'Clock Show* and hosted the series *Meet Ricky Gervais* in 2000. Gervais and Merchant followed up *The Office* with *Extras* (2005-2007), which also gained a clutch of awards. The duo's first collaboration for the big screen (as writers and directors), *Cemetery Junction*, was released in 2010.

Nick Clegg was elected as the leader of the Liberal Democrats in 2007.

Clegg studied social anthropology at Robinson College, Cambridge, and subsequently undertook post-graduate studies at the University of Minnesota and the College of Europe in Bruges. He worked as a trainee journalist and later for the European Commission (EC) in Brussels. Clegg's career as an elected politician began with his success in the 1999 European Parliament elections when he was returned as a representative for the East Midlands. Clegg served a five-year term and in 2005 was elected to the House of Commons as the member for Sheffield Hallam. He fought his first general election as the leader of the Liberal Democrats in 2010 and helped make history when he took part in the first ever British prime ministerial debates on television alongside his rivals for number ten – David Cameron and Gordon Brown. The first debate resulted in a surge in the opinion polls for the Liberal Democrats, but the enhanced level of support was not sustained on polling day. The Party only slightly increased their share of the vote, losing five seats in the process. However, the lack of an overall majority for any party resulted in the formation of the first coalition government for seventy years, formed by the Conservatives and Liberal Democrats. At the age of forty-three, Clegg was appointed deputy prime minister in the newly formed cabinet, the first to feature members of the Liberal Democrats (or the parties it evolved from) since the Second World War.

Ed Miliband was elected as the leader of the Labour Party in 2010.

Miliband won the race to become the new leader of the opposition, beating his brother David into second place. Miliband, who has a degree in politics, philosophy and economics from Oxford University, worked for the Labour Party in various roles before becoming the MP for Doncaster North in 2005. He joined the cabinet two years later at the start of Gordon Brown's premiership. In 2008 he was promoted to secretary of state for energy and climate change, a position he held until Labour's 2010 election defeat.

41

FORTY-ONE

Joseph Priestley isolated oxygen, which he called 'dephlogisticated air', in 1774.
Oxygen had first been discovered by Carl Scheele earlier in the decade, but his findings were not published until 1777. It is therefore usually Priestley who is credited with its discovery. Priestley did not fully appreciate the significance of the 'new air', but described his experiment to Antoine Lavoisier whom he visited in 1774. It was Lavoisier who realised that oxygen was a chemical element, gave the gas its modern name and demonstrated its role in combustion. Priestley rejected Lavoisier's interpretation and doggedly stuck to the 'phlogiston theory', which stated that phlogiston was a substance contained by all flammable materials released in the act of burning. A dissenting clergyman and polymath, Priestley made his first major scientific contribution with his book *The History and Present State of Electricity*, published in 1767, which reported his discovery that charcoal, as well as metals and water, could conduct electricity. Priestley also discovered many other gases including nitrous oxide – also known as 'laughing gas' and later used as an anaesthetic. In 1772 his *Directions for Impregnating Water with Fixed Air* was published; it was the first written work to describe the preparation of carbonated drinks (carbon dioxide was referred to as 'fixed air'). Priestley died in 1804, aged seventy.

*Composed by **Johann Strauss II**, 'An der Schönen Blauen Donau' (the Blue Danube) was first performed in 1867.*
Despite strong discouragement from his father, also a composer and also named Johann, the younger Strauss was determined to embrace a

musical career and made his concert debut in 1844. He forged a reputation that led him to be dubbed 'The Waltz King', although Strauss also composed other musical forms such as polkas, quadrilles, operettas (including *Die Fledermaus*) and one ballet (*Aschenbrödel*). He died at the age of seventy-three in 1899.

In 1886 **Karl Benz** *filed the patent for his internal combustion engine-powered vehicle.*

Benz described in his patent what is generally regarded as the first car: the Benz Patent-Motorwagen. His vehicle had three wheels and was powered by a 958cc single cylinder engine mounted at the rear. Two years later, Benz's 'Model 3' became the first automobile to be offered for commercial sale. In 1926 the company he founded, Benz & Cie., merged with Daimler Motoren Gesellschaft to become Daimler-Benz, which thereafter branded all of its cars Mercedes-Benz. Benz died three years later at the age of eighty-four.

The novella 'Heart of Darkness' by **Joseph Conrad** *was first published, as a three-part serial, in 'Blackwood's Magazine' in 1899.*

Conrad was born Józef Korzeniowski to Polish parents in Ukraine. He left for Marseille and embarked on a seafaring career which would influence his later work as a writer. It also took him to England, where he gained his master's certificate in sailing. By 1894 Conrad's maritime career was over and he turned to writing. His first novel, *Almayer's Folly*, was published in 1895. The narrative of *Heart of Darkness*, which recounts Charles Marlow's African quest for the mysterious Mr Kurtz, formed the basis for the 1979 film *Apocalypse Now*, directed by Francis Ford Coppola. Conrad's other books include *Lord Jim* (1900); *Nostromo* (1904); and *Suspense: A Napoleonic Novel*, unfinished upon his death in 1924 at the age of sixty-six.

Rudyard Kipling *won the Nobel Prize in Literature in 1907, becoming the first English-language writer to receive the award since its inception in 1901.*

Born in India, Joseph Rudyard Kipling was always referred to by his middle name, which was inspired by the place where his parents had first met: Lake Rudyard in Staffordshire. He arrived in England at the age of five. His parents returned to India soon after, leaving the care of

Kipling and his younger sister to a couple who provided a fostering service (a common practice at the time). He was schooled in England until his return to India at the age of sixteen, where he took up a position as a sub-editor on the *Civil and Military Gazette*. Kipling also wrote for the paper and many of his contributions would re-emerge in his first book, *Departmental Ditties*, published at the age of twenty. He returned to England in 1889, where his literary career gathered pace. Kipling's first full-length novel, *The Light that Failed*, was published in 1891 and over the years he added prolifically to his canon with works such as *Barrack-Room Ballads*, the two *Jungle Books*, *Kim* and *Puck of Pook's Hill*. Kipling lost his only son in the First World War. His output declined in the following years, but did include a history of the Irish Guards (his son's regiment) and his autobiography, *Something of Myself*, before his death in 1936 at the age of seventy. He remains the youngest Nobel laureate in literature.

In 1908 **Samuel Cody** *made the first powered aeroplane flight in Britain.*

Originally from Iowa, USA, Cody (formerly Cowdery) worked as a showman and 'wild west' entertainer before he became interested in aviation. He toured Europe with his cowboy act and settled in England in the late 1890s. At the turn of the century Cody's first aerial pastime was kite flying and in 1901 he filed his patent for a 'man-carrying kite', which was granted the following year. There was some interest from the military and Cody was enlisted to brief a group of Royal Engineers on the subject. He was appointed chief instructor in kite-flying by the war office in 1906 for a period of three years. Cody became a British subject in 1909 and, in subsequent years, built a number of aeroplanes, winning many aviation prizes. He died in 1913 at the age of forty-six when his latest aircraft crashed near Farnborough, also killing his passenger, the cricketer William Evans. Cody, who was accorded full military honours for his funeral and subsequent burial in Aldershot military cemetery, had been planning a flight across the Atlantic in the following year.

Arthur Gore *won the Wimbledon Men's Singles Championship in 1909.*

Gore, who was the defending champion, is the oldest winner of the men's singles at Wimbledon. It was his third victory in the tournament (his first was in 1901). Gore was also triumphant in the men's doubles, partnered with Herbert Barrett. In the previous year, the pair had won Olympic gold at the first London Olympics for the indoor doubles event. In addition, Gore took home a second gold medal for the indoor singles. His appearances at Wimbledon spanned the years 1888 to 1922, with Gore making his last appearance in the singles competition at the age of fifty-four. He died six years later. Gore's 1909 victory in the men's singles was the last by a British player until Fred Perry won the first of his three consecutive championships in 1934.

Charles Barkla *was awarded the 1917 Nobel Prize in Physics (in 1918*) for his discovery of the characteristic X-rays of the elements.*

Barkla was the first to discover that the X-rays emitted from a chemical element when it was irradiated with X-rays contained two components: one formed from the primary beam and the other a characteristic emission of the element itself. Barkla also demonstrated that X-rays, like light, can be polarised. He studied at the universities of Liverpool and Cambridge, and at the time of the Nobel award was a professor of natural philosophy at the University of Edinburgh, a position that he held until his death in 1944 at the age of sixty-seven.

Edward VIII *ascended to the throne of the United Kingdom in 1936.*

Known as David by his family, his middle names included those of the patron saints of England, Scotland, Ireland and Wales. He became the heir to the throne at the age of fifteen in 1910. Edward was keen to see action in the First World War, but although such direct participation was ruled out, he was able to visit the front line and lend royal support to the troops. He first met Wallis Simpson in 1931, and as their relationship developed, his desire to marry the twice-divorced American provoked a constitutional crisis. He abdicated in December 1936, less than a year after becoming king, and the crown then passed to his brother Prince Albert, Duke of York. Edward was given the title 'Duke of Windsor' and married Mrs Simpson in June 1937. They spent most of their later life living in

* The 1917 Nobel Prize in Physics was conferred one year later. None of the nominations in 1917 were deemed to meet the required criteria and the prize was reserved until 1918. Barkla was forty-one at the time of the prize ceremony.

France and their marriage lasted until his death in 1972, at the age of seventy-seven.

The Preston bypass, Britain's first length of motorway, with a range of new signs designed by **Jock Kinneir** *and Margaret Calvert, was officially opened in 1958.*

Kinneir and Calvert's signage system, developed specifically for motorways, was evaluated on the new road and subsequently approved for future motorway routes. Kinneir's first major design commission was for Gatwick Airport, opened in 1958. He engaged as his assistant Margaret Calvert, a student at Chelsea School of Art where he taught part-time. In 1964 Calvert became a partner in Kinneir's design practice, which was renamed Kinneir Calvert Associates. They went on to design new signage for Britain's roads, creating a system that was consistent and easily understood. In fact, Calvert often drew inspiration from her own life (the silhouette of the girl on the 'school-children crossing' sign was based on a photograph of her as a child). Their other design work included the Rail Alphabet typeface which was adopted for all British Rail signage in the sixties. Kinneir died in 1994 at the age of seventy-seven.

Mel Brooks *made his directorial debut with 'The Producers', which was released in 1968.*

The Producers won Brooks an Academy Award for 'best writing, story and screenplay – written directly for the screen'. Over thirty years later he adapted it as a Broadway production, which collected a record-breaking twelve Tony Awards in 2001, including best musical. Brooks started out in the entertainment business as a stand-up comic, and he later became a comedy writer for television. His other films include *Blazing Saddles* (1974), *Young Frankenstein* (1974) and *High Anxiety* (1977). Brooks is one of the few people to have won an Oscar, Emmy, Grammy and Tony Award.

Richard Briers *starred as Tom Good in the first episode of 'The Good Life' in 1975.*

The Good Life charts the attempts at full-time suburban self-sufficiency by Tom and his wife Barbara, played by Felicity Kendal. The show ran for four series and culminated in a special Royal Command Performance in the presence of the Queen in 1978. Briers had already starred in a long-running sitcom in the 1960s – *Marriage Lines* – as George Starling. His role as Martin Bryce in *Ever Decreasing Circles*, two decades later, gave him a third comedy series hit. Rada trained, Briers has also worked extensively on stage and joined Kenneth Branagh's Renaissance Theatre Company in 1987. He made his film debut in *Bottoms Up* (1960) and more recently has featured in many Kenneth Branagh productions including *Henry V* (1989) and *Frankenstein* (1994). He was awarded an OBE in 1989 and a CBE in 2004. Briers died in 2013 at the age of seventy-nine.

'Alien', directed by **Ridley Scott**, *was released in 1979.*

Alien, Scott's second feature film and first major commercial success, spawned three sequels (although none of these were directed by Scott). He followed *Alien* with another influential science fiction offering, *Blade Runner*, in 1982. He has also received three best director Academy Award nominations for *Thelma and Louise* (1991), *Gladiator* (2000) and *Black Hawk Down* (2001), with *Gladiator* winning for best picture, among other categories. Scott was knighted in 2003.

David Jason *first starred as Derek 'Del-Boy' Trotter, in the BBC comedy series 'Only Fools and Horses' in 1981.*

Only Fools and Horses ran for seven seasons with several Christmas specials and was a critical and popular success. It won six Bafta Awards for Jason, who also received the Bafta Academy Fellowship in 2003. His first television role was in the ATV serial *Crossroads* in 1964. He went on to become one of Britain's most popular actors, playing characters such as Granville in *Open All Hours*, Pop Larkin in *The Darling Buds of May* and DI Jack Frost in *A Touch of Frost*. He was knighted in 2005.

Neil Kinnock *was elected as the leader of the Labour Party in 1983.*

Kinnock, first elected to Parliament in 1970, did not serve as a minister in the Labour government of the 1970s, but joined the shadow cabinet as education spokesman after the Conservative general election victory in 1979. Kinnock's early years as leader were marked by his struggle to moderate the more extreme elements within the party. Although he was largely successful, Labour was still defeated at the next two general elections and Kinnock resigned in 1992. He left the Commons three years later, subsequently becoming a member of the European Commission and then a vice-president in 1999. He stood down from his European post in 2004 and became a life peer with the title Baron Kinnock of Bedwellty in 2005.

Wendy Richard made her debut as Pauline Fowler in the opening episode of 'EastEnders' in 1985.

Richard was born as Wendy Emerton in Middlesbrough, but the family moved south when she was a baby, eventually settling in London. She studied at the Italia Conti Academy of Theatre Arts and first began appearing on television in the early 1960s in minor roles. She made her uncredited film debut in *Doctor in Clover* (1966) and, in 1962, spent two weeks at the top of the pop chart as a result of her spoken vocal contribution to the Mike Sarne song 'Come Outside'. Richard's television profile was boosted by landing the part of Joyce Harker in the BBC soap opera *The Newcomers* which ran for four years until 1969. The seventies brought fame as Miss Shirley Brahms in the popular BBC comedy series *Are you Being Served?* The show continued for ten series until 1985, the same year that Richard made her debut in *EastEnders*. She was a regular cast member of the London-based soap until Christmas 2006. Richard was awarded an MBE in 2000. She died in 2009 at the age of sixty-five.

Goalkeeper *Pat Jennings* played the last of his 119 matches for Northern Ireland, against Brazil, in the 1986 World Cup in Mexico.

The day of the game, which Brazil won, was also his 41st birthday and Jennings holds the record as the oldest goalkeeper to play in the World Cup. He began his professional career in England at the age of seventeen with Watford, before moving after one season to Tottenham Hotspur where he notched up 472 appearances. He won the FA Cup and the UEFA Cup with the club and also enjoyed two League Cup triumphs. Unusually for a goalkeeper, Jennings also scored a goal when a long-range kick from his own box in the 1967 Charity Shield match defeated the Manchester United goalkeeper Alex Stepney. The game ended in a three-all draw. Jennings transferred from Spurs to London rivals Arsenal in 1977, where he spent eight seasons and collected another FA Cup medal. He was awarded an MBE in 1976.

The musical 'Mamma Mia!', based on a concept by **Judy Craymer**, *opened in London in 1999.*

The first night of *Mamma Mia!* coincided with the twenty-fifth anniversary of Abba's Eurovision Song Contest win with 'Waterloo' (Craymer was sixteen at the time). Craymer had worked for several years to make her idea of a musical, based on the songs of Abba, a reality. A graduate of the Guildhall School of Music, she began her theatrical career as an assistant stage manager at the Haymarket Theatre in Leicester. Craymer later worked at the Old Vic and on the original London production of the musical *Cats*. She became an assistant to Tim Rice in 1982, an appointment that led to her meeting Björn Ulvaeus and Benny Andersson from Abba. She developed her idea to use the group's songs over a ten-year period, finally settling on a storyline for a musical that involved a mother and her daughter. Craymer secured the permission of Ulvaeus and Andersson to use their songs, enlisted a scriptwriter, Catherine Johnson, and added Phyllida Lloyd as director. Her devotion to the project saw her amass a substantial overdraft and forced the sale of her flat, but the show's instant success dramatically reversed her financial fortunes. The musical has since become an outstanding hit and has sold over forty million tickets worldwide. A film adaptation starring Meryl Streep was released in 2008.

The debut series of 'Pop Idol', which featured **Simon Cowell** *as a judge, was first broadcast in 2001.*

Pop Idol, a television talent show for aspiring singers, also set Cowell on the path to celebrity status. He completed a second series of the show in the UK before launching his own format, *The X Factor*, in 2004. Cowell also scored another TV hit with *Britain's Got Talent*, first aired in 2007. Cowell left school at the age of sixteen and his father Eric, an EMI executive, tried to get him a start in a suitable career. Potential openings included the building trade and the civil service before Cowell took a job as a post boy with EMI music publishing. Cowell left after a year, but later returned to EMI, this time with the task of finding artists for EMI-owned songs. He left the company again and started E & S Music with Ellis Rich, his former EMI boss, but it was with Fanfare Records that he first achieved significant success in the 1980s. Cowell's first signing, Sinitta, gave the label its debut UK hit when she reached number two in 1986 with 'So

Macho'. A string of chart hits followed, before Cowell moved to BMG Records in 1989. The first number one single under his auspices came in 1995 with Robson & Jerome's version of 'Unchained Melody', and his artists have sold over 150 million records to date. In 2002 Cowell established Syco Records through which he signs the winners of *The X Factor*.

*Astronaut **Sunita Williams** returned to earth on board the space shuttle 'Atlantis' in 2007 after 195 days in space, the longest duration achieved by a woman.*

Williams was based at the International Space Station (ISS), and became the first person to run a marathon in earth orbit. Using a treadmill, she ran the distance at the same time as the Boston Marathon in a time of four hours and twenty-four minutes. A naval officer, Williams joined NASA in 1998. She performed four spacewalks during her ISS residency.

***Dara Torres** won silver medals at the 2008 Beijing Olympic Games for the 50m freestyle, 4x100m freestyle and the 4x100m medley swimming events.*

Torres's trio of medals at the Beijing Games took her Olympic tally to twelve. She'd won her first Olympic medal, a gold, twenty-four years earlier for the 4x100m freestyle at the 1984 Los Angeles Games. She also won Olympic medals in 1988 in Seoul (one silver, one bronze); four years later in Barcelona (one gold); and, at the age of thirty-three, at the Sydney Games in 2000 (two gold, three bronze). Torres set a new US record for the 50m freestyle at the Beijing Olympics and only missed out on the gold medal by 1/100th of a second; she had first set the US record for this event at the age of fifteen. At the age of forty-two, she set a new US record for the 50m butterfly which, like her 50m freestyle record, still stands. Torres is the oldest swimmer both to compete at the Olympics and also to win a medal.

42

FORTY-TWO

***William Herschel** discovered the planet Uranus in 1781.*

Born in Hanover, Herschel moved to England as a young man and worked as a musician and composer. By his mid-twenties he had completed six symphonies, and went on to build a successful career as a performer and teacher. Through music he became interested in the mathematical theory of harmony, which led him to study other topics in mathematics and also optics. He developed a passion for astronomy and spent long hours building his own telescopes and observing the night sky. It was while using one of his own telescopes that Herschel discovered Uranus, which he thought at first might be a comet (previous observers of Uranus had assumed it was a star). He originally named the newly discovered planet, *Georgium Sidus*, in honour of King George III, and in 1782 he was appointed as the King's personal astronomer. Herschel continued to build telescopes and made further discoveries, including two moons of Uranus (Titania and Oberon) and two moons of Saturn (Mimas and Enceladus). He created the first catalogue of 'double stars' and went on to discover that each was in orbit around the other. In 1816 he was made a Knight of the Royal Guelphic Order. Herschel died six years later at the age of eighty-three.

Joseph-Michel Montgolfier and his brother Jacques-Étienne first demonstrated their hot air balloon to a public audience in June 1783.

The sons of a successful paper manufacturer, Joseph-Michel and Jacques-Étienne, his younger brother by four years, continued their balloon experiments. In September 1783 a sheep, a duck and a rooster became the first living creatures to be sent up in a balloon. The first untethered manned flight took place two months later, in Paris, when Jean François Pilâtre de Rozier and François Laurent, Marquis d'Arlandes, took to the sky for a flight that lasted approximately twenty-five minutes. Joseph-Michel died in 1810 at the age of sixty-nine, eleven years after his brother Étienne who died at the age of fifty-four.

Robert Banks Jenkinson (second Earl of Liverpool) became prime minister in 1812 when he replaced the assassinated Spencer Percival.

Aged thirty, Jenkinson (also known as Lord Hawkesbury) first joined the Cabinet as foreign secretary in 1801 to serve in Henry Addington's government. He headed the British team of negotiators during the talks with France that led to the Treaty of Amiens in 1802 and resulted in peace between the two nations for approximately one year during the

French revolutionary wars. Jenkinson moved to the position of home secretary in 1804 and three years later accepted the post of secretary for war and the colonies. In 1808, on the death of his father, he became Lord Liverpool. He was appointed as prime minister the day after his forty-second birthday and remains the youngest incumbent of the post since William Pitt (who first came to power in 1783). Lord Liverpool's first years in power saw the climax of the Napoleonic Wars with victory at Waterloo in 1815. Domestic unrest after the wars, mainly due to economic conditions, spilled over in the 'Peterloo' massacre that took place in 1819, in which a mass gathering in Manchester to campaign for parliamentary reform was charged by the cavalry, causing an estimated eighteen deaths. Lord Liverpool's government brought in the 'Six Acts' in response to the incident which limited freedom of assembly and freedom of speech. These measures in part inspired the 'Cato Street' conspiracy which aimed to assassinate Liverpool and his cabinet in 1820. It was under Liverpool's governance that the Corn Laws, which restricted grain imports unless the price rose above a certain amount, were introduced in 1815. After nearly fifteen years as prime minister, he retired in 1827 following a stroke. Liverpool died the following year at the age of fifty-eight.

Elisha Otis sold his first lift in 1853.

Otis's lift incorporated his invention of an automatic safety device to stop it from free-falling if the chain or rope-lifting mechanism broke. Otis had come up with his invention while working as a master mechanic in a bedstead factory; he resigned to set up his own lift business. The first lift was for freight only. In 1854 Otis dramatically demonstrated his safety mechanism at the Crystal Palace Exposition in New York, by ascending in a lift and having the cable hoisting it cut with an axe. Otis's safety device worked and the lift car only dropped a few inches. The visible success of his invention overcame people's reluctance to use elevators and as a result brought Otis orders. Three years later, the first lift for customers was installed in a department store in New York City. Otis died in 1861 at the age of forty-nine, leaving his two sons to expand the business. The company is now part of the United Technologies Corporation, and continues to be one of the world's leading lift suppliers. Otis lifts have been installed in the Eiffel Tower, Balmoral Castle, the Kremlin, the Blackpool Tower and the Empire State Building.

Gregor Mendel presented his paper entitled 'Experiments with Plant Hybrids' to the Brünn Natural History Society in 1865.

The paper summarised Mendel's work and findings from several years of research, conducted using thousands of pea plants he had grown in the garden at St Thomas's Abbey in Brno (now in the Czech Republic; the German name is *Brünn*). There, Mendel was a member of the Augustinian order, an ordained priest and a teacher of physics and natural history at the Brünn *Realschule*. Mendel studied the inheritance of seven of the pea plant's basic traits such as height, colour of the pods etc., through successive generations. He showed how characteristics are inherited intact from both parents and are not the result of combination, and that some were more dominant than others. His work, subsequently published in 1866, was largely ignored and forgotten over the next thirty years, but became the basis of modern genetics in the twentieth century and led to the formulation of what became known as Mendel's laws of inheritance. Mendel became abbot of the monastery in 1868 and lived there until his death in 1884, at the age of sixty-one.

'Variations on an Original Theme for Orchestra, Op. 36 ('Enigma')', composed by Edward Elgar, premiered in 1899.

Elgar's first major composition for the orchestra, the fourteen variations are musical portraits of his wife, friends and himself. He was largely self-taught as a musician and availed himself of the opportunities afforded by his father's music shop. He found work as an organist, violinist, conductor and teacher, but it wasn't until the 1890s that his reputation as a composer started to build. Elgar followed the successful *Enigma Variations* with another major work, *The Dream of Gerontius*, premiered in 1900. The first *Pomp and Circumstance* march, written in 1901, contained the melody to which the words for 'Land of Hope and Glory' were added by Arthur Benson. It has become a familiar fixture at the last night of the Proms, as well as an unofficial national anthem for England. Elgar was knighted in 1904 and made 'Master of the King's Musick' in 1924. He died at the age of seventy-six in 1934.

*In 1900 **Max Planck** introduced into physics the concept of 'energy quanta' in order to arrive at a complete explanation of the light spectrum emitted by a 'black body' (a perfect emitter and absorber of radiation).*

Planck's paper, *On the Distribution of Energy in a Normal Spectrum*, was presented to the German Physical Society. For his explanation of the black body spectrum, Planck needed to assert that electromagnetic energy was not emitted continuously from such an object, but only in discrete packets as a multiple of a fundamental unit, given by the relationship $E = hv$ (where E is energy, h is Planck's constant and v is the frequency of the radiation). His breakthrough signified the beginning of quantum theory, and provided a means to explain phenomena which had defeated Newtonian classical physics. Planck received the 1918 Nobel Prize in Physics for his work relating to energy quanta (awarded in 1920). In addition to his talent for physics, Planck was also an accomplished musician, but he chose science as his profession and received his doctorate at the age of twenty-one. Planck was sixty-two at the time of his Nobel presentation and by then had endured the loss of his first wife, their two daughters (both in childbirth), and one of their sons in the First World War. Their remaining son was executed in World War Two for participating in the failed assassination of Hitler. Planck died in 1947 at the age of eighty-nine, and was survived by his second wife and their son.

*In 1901, following the assassination of William McKinley, Vice-President **Theodore Roosevelt** became the twenty-sixth president of the United States.*

Roosevelt remains the youngest incumbent of the White House, and was re-elected to serve a second term (John F. Kennedy, at the age of forty-three, became the youngest elected president). During his presidency Roosevelt promoted the construction of the Panama Canal, and also put forward his domestic 'square deal' policy aimed at delivering fairness to both workers and employers. Roosevelt became the first United States president to win the Nobel Peace Prize, which was awarded in 1906 for his role in the negotiations which ended the Russo–Japanese War (he is also the first US citizen to become a Nobel laureate). Choosing not to stand in the 1908 election, Roosevelt went on an African safari, but returned to try to win the Republican nomination against the sitting president, William Taft, for the 1912 election. When this attempt failed, he chose to stand as a presidential candidate for the Progressive Party (known popularly as the Bull Moose Party). Although he defeated Taft in the presidential election poll, Roosevelt lost to the Democratic candidate Woodrow Wilson. Roosevelt was fond of outdoor pursuits, although he refused to shoot a bear that had been specially cornered for him during a hunting trip because he considered it unsporting. The resulting publicity inspired the creation of the 'teddy bear' toy. Roosevelt is also one of the four presidents to be featured on Mount Rushmore in South Dakota. He died in 1919 at the age of sixty.

Henry Royce and Charles Rolls founded the car company that bears their names in 1906.

Royce and Rolls's business association started with a lunchtime meeting in the Midland Hotel, Manchester, in 1904. They later agreed that they would sell Royce's cars, badged as Rolls Royce, exclusively through Rolls's dealership. Royce provided the engineering expertise that complemented Rolls's flair for business. Royce's skills as an engineer were first forged as an apprentice for the Great Northern Railway locomotive works, but when funds to support him (provided by an aunt) ran out after three years, he was forced to abandon his apprenticeship. Royce briefly found work with a machine tool maker before he got a job with the Electric Light and Power Company. He continued his studies at evening classes, and impressed his employers enough to become chief electrical engineer for a subsidiary outfit, tasked with introducing electric lighting to Liverpool. This company failed, but, at the age of twenty-one, Royce launched his own business – producing products such as electric dynamos and later electric cranes. The pressures of competition prompted Royce to search for a new product, and he decided on the motor car. He completed his first vehicle in 1904, applying high standards to its engineering and manufacture. Two more Royce cars were built before a member of the company board arranged a meeting between his friend Charles Rolls and Royce, which led to the formation of Rolls-Royce Ltd. Rolls died in 1910, and soon after Royce moved away from the factory for health reasons, but continued to oversee the design of the company's products, including its move into aero engines. He was made a baronet in 1930 and died three years later at the age of seventy.

*In 1913 **Harry Brearley** produced what would become known as 'stainless steel', while working as the head of the Brown-Firth research laboratory in Sheffield.*

Brearley, who had started working in the steel industry as a cellar lad at the age of twelve, was trying to produce a steel which had better resistance to the heat produced in a gun barrel when he discovered that steel containing large amounts of the element chromium (approximately 13%) was much more resistant to corrosion. Brearley was working independently, but others in the United States (such as Elwood Haynes) and Europe (for example, Eduard Maurer and Benno Strauss), had also investigated and patented formulations of steel with chromium that showed resistance to corrosion. (The relevant patents of Haynes and Brearley were subsequently combined in the American Stainless Steel Company, formed in 1917.) Brearley quickly spotted the potential for the new steel (initially termed 'rustless steel') in applications such as cutlery. He left Brown-Firth in 1915 and joined the Sheffield steelworks of Brown Bayley where he became a director ten years later. Brearley died in 1948 at the age of seventy-seven.

*In 1913 **Arthur Wynne** created what is recognised as the first English language crossword puzzle to be published.*

Wynne came up with a diamond-shaped array of squares (with no black spaces) for the word game that he called 'word-cross' and which first appeared in the newspaper *New York World*. Wynne was born in Liverpool, but moved to the United States in his mid-twenties, and soon found a job on a newspaper. It was while working for the *New York World* that he introduced the crossword in order to fill some space to meet the print deadline. In the 1920s a craze for the game developed, and it became a feature in nearly every newspaper in the United States. *The Times* newspaper started to publish its own daily crossword puzzles in 1930. Wynne never tried to patent the crossword. He died in 1945 at the age of seventy-three.

*In 1935 **Robert Watson-Watt** and Arnold Wilkins demonstrated the first use of radio waves in Britain to detect aircraft (later known as radar, from radio detection and ranging).*

Watson-Watt and Wilkins used the BBC's short-wave transmitter at Daventry for the successful trial. Under Watson-Watts's leadership, this led to the establishment of a chain of radar stations along the British coastline that were a vital asset in the Battle of Britain in 1940. Watson-Watt was knighted in 1942, and ten years later he received over half of the money (approximately £50,000) gifted to the radar team by the Royal Commission on Awards to Inventors. Watson-Watt died in 1973, aged eighty-one.

'Casablanca', starring **Humphrey Bogart** *as Rick Blaine, premiered in New York City in 1942.*

Bogart's performance in *Casablanca* earned him his first Academy Award nomination, although he lost out to Paul Lukas at the ceremony in March 1944. His first major film success was as Duke Mantee in *The Petrified Forest* (1936), which led to a long-term contract with Warner Brothers. Bogart's performances in the films *High Sierra* and *The Maltese Falcon*, both released in 1941, won him further acclaim. His portrayal of Charlie Allnut in *The African Queen* (1951) gave him his only best actor Oscar, while his performance as Philip Queeg in *The Caine Mutiny* (1954), earned him his third and final Academy Award nomination in this category. Bogart's other notable films include *The Big Sleep* (1946) and *The Treasure of the Sierra Madre* (1948). He died in 1957 at the age of fifty-seven.

In 1953 **John Hunt** *led the first successful expedition to climb Mount Everest.*

Hunt was born in Simla, India, and was educated at Marlborough College before beginning officer training at Sandhurst. He received his first commission in 1930 and was posted to India the following year. Hunt took advantage of his proximity to the Himalayas, where he was able to indulge his interest in mountaineering. He led a battalion in the Italian campaign during the Second World War and was awarded a Distinguished Service Order (DSO). His military and climbing background meant he was admirably suited to the task of expedition leader for what would be Britain's last attempt on Everest for at least three years (the French and the Swiss had permission to climb in 1954 and 1955 respectively). Hunt, the oldest of the party, reached over 27,000 feet during the expedition that saw Edmund Hillary and Tenzing Norgay reach the summit. Hunt was knighted in 1953 and retired from the army three years later. He was made Baron Hunt, of Llanvair Waterdine, in 1966, and became the first chairman of the parole board the following year. He died in 1998 at the age of eighty-eight.

Margot Fonteyn first performed with Rudolf Nureyev in 1962.
Fonteyn and Nureyev danced together in the Royal Ballet's production of *Giselle* at Covent Garden and their partnership instantly won acclaim. Nureyev's presence did much to extend and enhance Fonteyn's career, which some had believed was drawing to a close. The pair forged a dance partnership that transcended the nineteen years between them. Fonteyn was born Margaret Hookham in Surrey, with a mix of English, Irish and Brazilian ancestry. Her stage name was an adaptation of her maternal grandfather's surname, Fontes. She began dance classes at the age of four, and these continued throughout her childhood in various locations abroad, as the family moved on account of her father's employment. She joined the Vic-Wells Ballet School in 1933, and later became a member of the Vic-Wells Ballet, the forerunner of the Royal Ballet with whom she would spend the rest of her career. Fonteyn first took on the part of Odette in *Swan Lake* at the age of sixteen and, just over thirteen months later, the title role in *Giselle*. She was nineteen when she made her debut as Aurora in *The Sleeping Beauty* in 1939. Fonteyn was made a DBE in 1956 and in 1979 her eminence as a ballet dancer was recognised with the title *prima ballerina assoluta*. In later life, she retired along with her husband, the Panamanian politician Dr Robert Arias, to his home country where she died, in 1991, at the age of seventy-one.

Magnus Magnusson was the quizmaster for the first edition of 'Mastermind' in 1972.
Magnusson was born in Iceland and moved to Scotland with his family as a baby. They settled in Edinburgh, where his father served as Iceland's consul-general. He attended Edinburgh Academy, then Jesus College, Oxford, where he read English. Magnusson worked as a journalist and broadcaster before the launch of *Mastermind*, which he hosted for twenty-five years until 1997. He died ten years later at the age of seventy-seven.

*The 1973 Grand National was won by Red Rum, trained by **Ginger McCain**.*
Ridden by Brian Fletcher, Red Rum beat Crisp, the race leader from

early on, to win by three quarters of a length in a dramatic finish. Red Rum and McCain repeated their Grand National success in 1974 and 1977, as well as finishing second in the intervening years. McCain's fourth victory in the Aintree race came in 2004, at the age of seventy-three, with Amberleigh House, and he holds the record with Fred Rimell for the most Grand National wins as a trainer. McCain began training horses in 1952, but it wasn't until 1965 that he had his first winner, *San Lorenzo*. He retired after the 2006 Grand National. Red Rum died in 1995 at the age of thirty and is buried at the Aintree finishing line. McCain passed away in 2011, two days before what would have been his eighty-first birthday.

Cilla Black hosted the first edition of the dating show 'Blind Date' in 1985.
Born Priscilla White in Liverpool, Black became the first female artist to be signed by the Beatles' manager Brian Epstein. A recording contract with the group's label, Parlophone, quickly followed, as did her debut single, the Lennon/McCartney composition 'Love of the Loved', which gave her a first top-forty hit at the age of twenty. Black's next two releases both hit number one: 'Anyone Who Had a Heart' and 'You're My World'. She had another nine top-ten chart entries during the sixties and early seventies. Black also became a major television personality. She began hosting her own show on the BBC in 1968, the last series of which was broadcast in 1976. Black moved to ITV to present *Surprise Surprise!*, which first aired in 1984, and in the following year hosted the first episode of *Blind Date*. After eighteen years, she announced her departure from *Blind Date* in the first live edition of the show in 2003. She was awarded an OBE in 1997.

In 1991 Jeremy Irons won the Academy Award for best actor for his role as Claus von Bülow in 'Reversal of Fortune'.
Irons first achieved fame ten years earlier with his portrayal of Charles Ryder in the celebrated 1981 TV production of *Brideshead Revisited*, and for his starring role alongside Meryl Streep in *The French Lieutenant's Woman* (1981). He had made his film debut in the previous year as Mikhail Fokine in *Nijinsky* (1980). Irons's work in the theatre won him a Tony Award for *The Real Thing* (1984). His other films include *The Mission* (1986),

Dead Ringers (1988), *Damage* (1993), *The Man in the Iron Mask* (1998) and *Being Julia* (2004).

Roger Milla *played for Cameroon at the 1994 football World Cup.*

Milla's participation made him the oldest player to appear in the finals. He netted the only Cameroon goal in a 6-1 defeat by Russia in their final group game, which extended his existing record as the oldest person to score in the World Cup finals (four years earlier in Italy, 38-year-old Milla had made headlines by scoring four times to help Cameroon reach the World Cup quarter-finals – the first time that an African nation had made it to that stage of the competition). They eventually bowed out as a result of a 3–2 extra time defeat by England. In 2007, Milla was voted as the best African player of the previous fifty years in a poll organised by the Confederation of African Football (CAF).

Pierce Brosnan *first played James Bond in 'Goldeneye', released in 1995.*

Goldeneye was the first Bond film since Timothy Dalton's second outing as the British secret agent in *Licence to Kill* (1989). Brosnan starred as Bond in three more films: *Tomorrow Never Dies* (1997), *The World Is Not Enough* (1999) and *Die Another Day* (2002). Born in Drogheda, Ireland, he came to London at the age of eleven and became involved in acting in the early 1970s. He had broken into television by the end of the decade and soon after he was cast, in a US-produced series, as the popular detective Remington Steele. In the eighties he landed his first starring film role in *Nomads* (1984). Brosnan formed a production company, Irish DreamTime, with Beau St. Clair in 1996. Its first film, which also starred Brosnan, was the remake of *The Thomas Crown Affair* (1999).

DBC Pierre *won the 2003 Booker Prize for his debut novel 'Vernon God Little'.*

Born Peter Finlay to English parents in Australia, his pseudonym is an augmented form of his childhood nickname, Pierre, which itself came from a cartoon character called *Dirty Pierre* (DBC stands for Dirty but Clean). He had a prosperous and privileged upbringing in Mexico, but in his later teenage years his father became seriously ill and died. The family's financial assets were then depleted by the economic crisis in

Mexico in the early 1980s. Pierre spent the next few years living a colourful existence, working as a cartoonist and treasure hunter among other things. Along the way he amassed considerable debt, which he pledged his prize money (£50,000) to help repay. His second novel, *Ludmilla's Broken English*, was published in 2006, and his third, *Lights Out in Wonderland*, in 2010.

In 2004 **Peter Jackson** *won the Academy Award for best director for the film 'The Lord of the Rings: The Return of the King'.*

Jackson also shared the prizes for best picture and 'best writing, adapted screenplay'. The film won all eleven of its nominated categories to equal the record set by *Ben-Hur* (1959) and *Titanic* (1997). Born in New Zealand, Jackson began making his own movies at the age of eight using a Super 8 cine camera, and from early on he pioneered his own special effects. In his twenties he worked on his biggest project to date, the low-budget alien drama *Bad Taste* (1987), which took around four years to complete and flagged up Jackson's film-making potential. He directed Kate Winslet in her film debut in *Heavenly Creatures* (1994), which also brought Jackson a shared Academy Award nomination for 'best writing, screenplay written directly for the screen'. The first instalment in his Lord of the Rings trilogy was released in 2001 and won Jackson best director at the Baftas, as well as best picture. His other films include *King Kong* (2005) and *The Lovely Bones* (2009). Jackson was knighted in 2010 for services to film.

Darren Clarke *won golf's Open Championship in 2011.*

Clarke's victory at Royal St George's by three strokes was his first major tournament win and came twenty years after his debut appearance at the Open. The Northern Ireland-born golfer's previous best finishes in the Open were in 1997 when he took joint-second place and four years later when he shared third position. Clarke won his first European tour title, the Belgian Open, in 1993, and was the first person to win the English Open on three occasions, between 1999 and 2002. He has made five appearances as a player in the Ryder Cup, with four of these ending in success for the European team. In 2010 Clarke was a non-playing vice-captain when the Europeans beat the US by one point.

43

FORTY-THREE

Henry Addington became prime minister in 1801 following the resignation of William Pitt (the younger).

Addington resigned just over three years later, after a decline in parliamentary support, and Pitt assumed the premiership once more. During Addington's tenure, the Treaty of Amiens was concluded with France in 1802, which brought a fourteen-month respite in the war between Britain and France. Addington also simultaneously fulfilled the role of chancellor of the exchequer, and one of his last duties before his resignation was to present the budget to the House. Made Viscount Sidmouth in 1805, Addington returned to high office in 1812, when he became home secretary under Lord Liverpool. He served for more than nine years until 1822, during which time he presided over the 'Six Acts', which limited rights of assembly and free speech. Addington died in 1844 at the age of eighty-six.

In 1856 Henry Bessemer presented his process for making mild steel from pig iron to a meeting of the British Association for the Advancement of Science.

Bessemer's process involved blowing air through molten pig iron contained in a vessel, which became known as a converter. The oxygen in the air reacted with the carbon in the pig iron to reduce the carbon content of the metal sufficiently to produce mild steel. However, early commercial attempts were unsatisfactory because the carbon content was too low. Metallurgist Robert Mushet found a solution for the problem and this, along with process improvements by others, ensured the success of Bessemer's technique. Mushet's ideas entered the public domain due to a lapsed patent, and after some dispute with Bessemer over priority, Mushet was eventually awarded an annual pension by him. Bessemer also had to fight claims from the American William Kelly who patented a similar steel-making method in the United States in 1857. Bessemer, although best remembered for his converter, was a prolific inventor and filed over one hundred patents. He made his first fortune from automating the production of bronze powder used to simulate decorative gold paint (although this was one invention Bessemer did not patent, instead relying on secrecy for protection). Prone to sea-sickness he also, later in life, invented and built a boat, *The Bessemer*, which featured his solution: one saloon had a floor which used a hydraulic mechanism, under the control of a crew member, to counteract any roll in the ship and keep the floor level. The boat made a return journey to Calais from Dover, but was not effective in practice and the idea was abandoned. Bessemer was knighted in 1879. He died at the age of eighty-five in 1898.

Nikolaus Otto built the first practical four-stroke internal combustion engine in 1876.

Inspired by news of Étienne Lenoir's invention of the first combustion engine, Otto, a travelling salesman, became interested in engine building and, with the financial assistance of Eugen Langen, formed a manufacturing company in 1864 to exploit Otto's ideas. Further investors became involved, and the company was eventually renamed Gasmotoren-Fabrik Deutz AG in 1872. Five years later, Otto's four-stroke engines went into mass production. He patented his engine, but years after he had built his first four-stroke model, a prior patent registered by Alphonse Beau de Rochas was discovered. It too described the four-stroke engine so Otto's patent was revoked (Beau de Rochas never built his engine). Otto died in 1891 at the age of fifty-eight. Deutz AG still manufactures engines today.

*'Symphony No.1 in C minor, Op. 68', by **Johannes Brahms**, received its premiere in 1876.*

Brahms was born in Hamburg in 1833. His first musical education came from his father, a double bassist, and while still a boy, Brahms played the piano in local theatres, restaurants and other venues in order to boost the family's income. The patronage of the composer Robert Schumann did much to raise awareness of Brahms's compositional ability and establish his career. Brahms's first published work, at the age of twenty, was *Piano Sonata No. 1, Op. 1*, and five years later the first of his two piano concertos was completed. His choral work, *A German Requiem, Op. 45*, was premiered in Bremen in 1868 and was a major success. Brahms completed his first symphony eight years later. Sometimes nicknamed 'Beethoven's tenth', it had a gestation period of approximately twenty years. His second symphony, however, swiftly followed in 1877, while his third and fourth symphonies premiered in 1883 and 1885. Brahms died in 1897 at the age of sixty-three.

In 1896 **Henri Becquerel** *reported to the French Academy of Science his observation of 'invisible rays emitted by phosphorescent bodies'.*

The phenomenon observed by Becquerel was subsequently termed radiation by Marie Curie. His investigations were inspired by the findings of Wilhelm Röntgen in 1895 regarding X-rays. Becquerel first observed that uranium salts, after exposure to sunlight, would leave an image on a photographic plate. He then confirmed that light was not required for the effect to manifest itself and deduced that it was not related to the phosphorescent properties of the material. Becquerel continued to study the unusual rays, which for a time were named after him. In 1903 the significance of his discovery was recognised by the award of the Nobel Prize in Physics, shared that year with Marie and Pierre Curie. Becquerel was following in the footsteps of his grandfather and father, both of whom had been eminent physicists, and the SI unit for radioactivity, symbol Bq, is named in his honour. He died in 1908 at the age of fifty-five.

In 1897 **Marcus Samuel** *and his brother Sam founded the Shell Transport and Trading Company.*

The Samuel brothers inherited a business from their father who had dealt in antiques and in oriental shells, the latter of which were so popular that he started importing them from the Far East. Marcus and Sam added further items to the range and established a successful import/export enterprise. On a business trip to Japan, Marcus became interested in the petroleum industry and, realising its potential, decided to begin shipping oil. The brothers commissioned a fleet of bulk tankers, approved for use in the newly opened Suez Canal, and struck a deal to export oil from the Russian oilfields owned by the Rothschilds to Asia. They also found an oil source in Borneo, which was closer to their Far East markets. The brothers formed the Shell Trading and Transport Company in 1897, the name inspired by their family's earlier business interest. Rivalry with the Royal Dutch Petroleum Company resulted in a merger of the two concerns in 1907 to become the Royal Dutch Shell Group. Marcus Samuel was knighted in 1898 for Shell's assistance in salvaging HMS *Victorious* after she ran aground. He had a spell as the Lord Mayor of London, was made a baron in 1921 and a viscount four years later. Marcus Samuel died in 1927 at the age of seventy-three.

Leo Baekeland filed his patent for the invention of the first synthetic plastic, Bakelite, in 1907.

Baekeland's thermosetting material, made from phenol and formaldehyde, found many applications, some of which took advantage of its property as an electrical insulator. It was used in telephone manufacture and in the growing automobile industry as well as to make domestic items such as clock cases, radios, lamps and bowls. Baekeland completed his doctorate in chemistry in his native Belgium and travelled to the United States in his mid-twenties. Bakelite was not his first success as an inventor. In the late 1890s, he sold the rights to his Velox photographic paper, which could be used in lower light conditions than existing versions, to George Eastman of the Kodak Company for a considerable sum. The money, as well as giving Baekeland financial security, allowed him to set up his own laboratory. He chose to work on synthetic resins and started looking for a replacement for shellac (a resin secreted by the lac beetle). Bakelite was his solution, and he founded the General Bakelite Company in 1910 to commercialise his invention. Baekeland died at the age of eighty in 1944.

Robert Falcon Scott led the sledge party consisting of Edward Wilson, Lawrence Oates, Henry Bowers and Edgar Evans that reached the South Pole in January 1912.

Scott and the rest of the party arrived to find that Roald Amundsen and his team had already reached the Pole in the previous month. Dejected, Scott's party began the trek home, but, hampered by adverse weather and a shortage of rations, all perished. Scott first ventured to the southern polar region in 1901, as the commander of the British National Antarctic Expedition, aboard the ship *Discovery*. The expedition explored the Ross

Sea area and a team of three men (Scott, Edward Wilson and Ernest Shackleton) reached the farthest southerly point then recorded. On his return to Britain, Scott was hailed as a hero and promoted to the rank of captain by the Royal Navy. In 1906 he resumed his full-time naval career, only leaving to make his last, fateful expedition to the South Pole on the *Terra Nova*, which departed from Cardiff in 1910.

In 1926 **Robert Goddard** *launched the world's first liquid-fuelled rocket in Auburn, Massachusetts.*

From its launch pad at Goddard's Aunt Effie's farm, his rocket (named Nell) ascended approximately twelve metres, fuelled by petrol and liquid oxygen. Goddard became interested in science as a child, and received his PhD in physics in 1911. Two years later, he filed his first patent for a 'Rocket Apparatus', which was accepted in 1914. The following year he successfully demonstrated that a rocket could work in a vacuum, and therefore in space. His seminal text, *A Method of Reaching Extreme Altitudes*, was published in 1919 by the Smithsonian Institute. Goddard envisaged space probes and flights to the moon, but his vision for the future was ridiculed on more than one occasion by the press. Goddard continued to work on rocket development until his death, at the age of sixty-two, in 1945. Liquid-fuelled rockets powered all manned launches into space, until the introduction of the Space Shuttle in 1981. It used two solid rocket boosters (SRBs), in addition to the orbiter's liquid-fuelled engines, to provide the thrust needed for lift off. (A fault in one of these SRBs led to the *Challenger* disaster in 1986.)

The film 'Frankenstein', which starred **Boris Karloff** *as the monster, was released in 1931.*

Karloff was born William Henry Pratt in London, the youngest of nine children, and moved to Canada in his early twenties. He took a variety of acting jobs, but major success eluded him until he was cast as Frankenstein's monster. Following his breakthrough role, horror films featured regularly in Karloff's oeuvre, and he revisited the role of the famous monster in the sequels *Bride of Frankenstein* (1935) and *Son of Frankenstein* (1939). Karloff returned to England later in life where he died, aged eighty-one, in 1969.

Percy Shaw lodged his patent application for 'Improvements Relating to Blocks for Road Surface Marking', better known as 'cat's eyes', in 1934.

Shaw stated in a television interview in the 1960s that he was inspired to create his invention when he was travelling home on a foggy night and realised that the reflective studs on a road sign would be beneficial on the road surface as well. He filed another patent for cat's eyes in 1935, which added the important self-cleaning mechanism. In the same year, Shaw also established a company, Reflecting Roadstuds, to manufacture the product. Sales were sluggish initially, but were boosted by the government's endorsement of their deployment on Britain's roads and the enforced blackout during the Second World War. Despite his success, Shaw lived an unostentatious lifestyle. His few luxuries included Two Rolls Royces and four television sets, three of which were tuned to one of the existing stations at the time, while the fourth served as a backup. Shaw also remained in the house that he had moved to at the age of two until his death in 1976, at the age of eighty-six. He was awarded an OBE in 1965.

*In 1958 **Alec Guinness** won the Academy Award for best actor for his role as Colonel Nicholson in 'Bridge on the River Kwai'.*

Guinness's stage career began in his early twenties and, following the Second World War, he made his accredited film debut in *Great Expectations* (1946). Guinness demonstrated his versatility when he played eight different characters in the first of his several Ealing comedies, *Kind Hearts and Coronets* (1949). His first Oscar nomination was for another Ealing comedy, *The Lavendar Hill Mob* (1951). Four years later, Guinness received his first Bafta nomination for *The Prisoner* (1955). His portrayal of Lieutenant Colonel Nicholson in *Bridge on the River Kwai* (1957) brought him a slew of awards, including a Bafta for best British actor and a Golden Globe, in addition to his Oscar. Guinness was knighted in 1959. In the latter part of his career, he attracted a new audience with his role as Ben (Obi-Wan) Kenobi in *Star Wars* (1977), which also brought him his penultimate Academy Award nomination, for best supporting actor, in 1978. He received an honorary Oscar in 1980, and the Bafta Fellowship in 1989. His final Oscar nomination, for best supporting actor, came at the age of seventy-four for *Little Dorrit* (1988). He died in 2000 at the age of eighty-six.

In 1961 **John F. Kennedy** *was sworn in as the thirty-fifth president of the United States, following a close election victory over his Republican rival, Richard Nixon.*

During the campaign Kennedy and Nixon had both taken part in the first televised presidential candidate debates, which contrasted the youthful, relaxed image of Kennedy with that of a more nervous-looking Nixon. Kennedy is still the youngest person to be elected president (Theodore Roosevelt was forty-two, but assumed office as vice-president). Kennedy was a decorated World War Two hero who was elected to the House of Representatives after the war, and became a senator in 1952. His three years as president saw events such as the first manned spaceflights, the construction of the Berlin Wall and the Cuban Missile Crisis, the latter of which brought the world closer than at any other time to the spectre of nuclear war. However, the situation was peacefully defused, and in 1963 a partial Test Ban Treaty covering nuclear weapons was agreed between the US, the USSR and the UK. In 1961, Kennedy announced the goal of putting a man on the moon before the end of the decade, which was duly accomplished by Apollo 11 in July 1969. His domestic policies included the extension of civil rights, and his administration supported moves to end racial discrimination. Kennedy was assassinated in 1963 while travelling in his Dallas motorcade. He was forty-six and was succeeded by his vice-president, Lyndon Johnson.

In 1973 **Ronnie Barker** *first appeared as Norman Stanley Fletcher in an episode of the series 'Seven of One' called 'Prisoner and Escort'.*

The *Seven of One* spin-off series *Porridge* ran for three seasons, and the character of Fletcher became one of Barker's most popular comedy roles. His stage career began in 1948 when he joined the Manchester Repertory Theatre, then based in Aylesbury. About eight years later he moved into radio work, becoming a regular cast member of *The Navy Lark*, which first aired in 1959. His television career also got underway, with its turning point being *The Frost Report* in 1966, which also brought him into contact with Ronnie Corbett; he would later front *The Two Ronnies* (1971–1987) with Corbett. As well as performing, Barker also wrote material for many of his shows, using pseudonyms such as Gerald Wiley to be sure that his contributions were being accepted on merit alone. Another long-running

Barker comedy series was *Open All Hours*, in which he starred as Arkwright the grocer. He retired from broadcasting in 1988, but returned to the screen for occasional appearances after 1999. Awarded an OBE in 1978, Barker died in 2005 at the age of seventy-six.

*In 1981 **Joyce Smith** was the first woman to cross the line of the inaugural London Marathon.*

Smith also won the race the following year at the age of forty-four, becoming the oldest female winner to date. In 1984, at the age of forty-six, Smith competed in the first women's Olympic Marathon at the Los Angeles Games where she finished in eleventh position, just under eight minutes behind the winner Joan Benoit of the US. Smith holds the record as the oldest female athletic competitor at the Olympics. During her running career, which began in the 1950s, Smith also won three English Cross Country Championships between 1959 and 1973, won gold at the 1972 World Cross Country Championships and won the Tokyo International Women's Marathon in 1979 and 1980. Smith retired from the sport in 1986, two years after she was awarded an MBE.

***J. M. Coetzee** (John Maxwell) won the Booker Prize in 1983 for his novel 'The Life and Times of Michael K'.*

The Life and Times of Michael K is set in Coetzee's native South Africa, and recounts the journey of the title character back to his mother's birthplace in the Western Cape. Coetzee's first book, *Dusklands*, was published in 1974. An English and mathematics graduate, Coetzee also worked for a time as a computer programmer during the 1960s. He subsequently attended the University of Texas at Austin where he completed his PhD in 1968. Coetzee then held various academic positions while simultaneously pursuing a career as a writer. He won the Booker Prize for a second time in 1999 with *Disgrace*, and was awarded the 2003 Nobel Prize in Literature.

*In 1997 **Anthony Minghella** won the Academy Award for best director for 'The English Patient'.*

The English Patient received twelve nominations, including best picture, and lost out in only three categories, one of which was best adapted screenplay for Minghella, although he did secure the equivalent Bafta. Three years later his writing skills brought Minghella a further Oscar nomination, this time for *The Talented Mr. Ripley* (1999). A graduate of the University of Hull, where he subsequently also taught drama, Minghella's first job in entertainment was as a general assistant, or 'runner', on the children's magazine programme *Magpie*. He moved on to writing and script editing for *Grange Hill*, *EastEnders* and *Boon*, and penned a trio of *Inspector Morse* episodes. As a playwright he picked up awards in the 1980s for both stage and radio productions, including *Made in Bangkok* and *Cigarettes and Chocolate*. His first major cinema release, *Truly, Madly, Deeply* (1990), which he wrote and directed, won him a Bafta Award for best original screenplay. Minghella's other films include *Cold Mountain* (2003), and *Breaking and Entering* (2006). He was awarded a CBE in 2001 and died in 2008, aged fifty-four.

Following Labour's general election victory in May 1997, **Tony Blair** *became prime minister.*

Blair was the youngest British prime minister since Lord Liverpool in 1812 (an achievement since eclipsed by David Cameron). The second son of a barrister and lecturer, Blair was born in Edinburgh, but spent most of his early childhood in Durham. He returned to his birthplace to board at Fettes College between 1966 and 1971. After a year out, Blair studied law at Oxford, becoming a barrister in due course, and first stood for Parliament in 1982 in a by-election for the safe Conservative seat of Beaconsfield. He gained 10% of the vote and lost his deposit. The following year he was successful in the general election, winning the constituency of Sedgefield and entering Westminster at the age of thirty. Blair was elected leader of the Labour Party eleven years later following the sudden death of John Smith. He is the only Labour leader to have won three consecutive general elections. An early success in his premiership was the signing of the Good Friday (or Belfast) Agreement in 1998, which advanced the Northern Ireland peace process and paved the way for a power sharing assembly. His second and third terms were overshadowed by the 11 September terrorist attacks in the United States in 2001. This led to British and US military intervention in Afghanistan and, more controversially, in Iraq. After ten years in office, he stepped down in June 2007 to be succeeded by Gordon Brown.

Grayson Perry won the Turner Prize in 2003.

Perry made it on to the Turner shortlist for his exhibitions at the Barbican Art Gallery in London and the Stedelijk Museum in Amsterdam, and is the first artist working in ceramics to win the award. Perry, a fine art graduate of Portsmouth Polytechnic, collected the Turner Prize dressed as his female alter ego Claire, and also included one of her garments entitled *Coming Out Dress* in his prize show. His Turner show also featured a selection of his vases, traditional in shape, but decorated with images and words that tackle difficult social issues.

David Cameron became prime minister in May 2010, the youngest holder of the office in nearly two hundred years.

Cameron gained a first in philosophy, politics and economics at Brasenose College, Oxford, before joining the Conservative Party research department. He later worked for Carlton Communications for several years as director of corporate affairs. Cameron first stood as a candidate for Parliament at the age of thirty in the 1997 general election, but came second in the constituency of Stafford. He was, however, successful with his next attempt when he was returned as the member for Whitney in the 2001 general election. Four years later, he was elected as the leader of the Conservative Party. In the 2010 general election, Cameron saw his party gain nearly one hundred seats to become the largest group in the new House of Commons, but fall short of an overall majority. After several days of negotiation a coalition deal with the Liberal Democrats was agreed, and Cameron became the first Conservative successor to a Labour prime minister since Margaret Thatcher in 1979.

In 2012 Felix Baumgartner set the world record for the highest ever skydive and also became the first skydiver to travel faster than the speed of sound.

Baumgartner jumped from his balloon at an altitude of 127,852.4ft (nearly 39km) and took nine minutes and three seconds to reach the ground. He achieved a maximum velocity of 843.6mph during his four minutes and twenty seconds of freefall, and beat the previous altitude record of 31km set by Joe Kittinger in 1960. Kittinger was part of Baumgartner's team for the record-breaking jump, which took place sixty-five years to the day after Chuck Yeager first officially flew faster than the speed of sound in the Bell X-1. Austrian-born Baumgartner's other exploits include numerous base jumps (a leap from a fixed object with only a parachute) from structures such as the 1,667ft tall Taipei 101 Tower in 2007 – the world's tallest building at the time. In 2003 he also skydived across the English Channel using a carbon wing.

44

FORTY-FOUR

*The magnum opus of **Isaac Newton**, 'Philosophiae Naturalis Principia Mathematica' (Mathematical Principles of Natural Philosophy), was published in 1687.*

In *Principia*, Newton stated his three laws of motion and fully explained his law of gravitation. He was slow to publish his major work – it took nearly twenty years for *Principia* to emerge and only after some prompting from Edmond Halley (famous for predicting the return of the comet which bears his name), who also financed its publication. Newton was born on Christmas Day 1642 (as per the Julian calendar then in use in England), less than three months after the death of his father whom he was named after. When Newton was three his mother remarried, left him in Woolsthorpe with his grandmother and moved away to nearby North Witham. Following the death of her husband seven years later, Newton's mother returned to Woolsthorpe, enlarging the family by bringing with her his half-brother and two half-sisters. Newton began attending Grantham grammar school when he was ten and started at Trinity College, Cambridge, aged eighteen, graduating four years later in 1665. Due to the threat of the Great Plague, the university closed for a period and Newton returned home. It was his mathematical and scientific advances during 1665 and 1666 that Newton later claimed were the foundation for all his major achievements. This included his early work on optics and 'fluxions' or calculus. A dispute later arose between Newton and Gottfried Leibniz as to who had invented calculus first, but it is generally accepted that they arrived at their discovery independently. Shortly after his return to Cambridge, Newton was appointed as the Lucasian professor of mathematics at the age of twenty-six. The first lecture course he gave, in 1669, was on optics and this formed the first chapter of his treatise on light, *Opticks*, published twenty-five years later in 1704. Newton became master of the Mint in 1699 and president of the Royal Society in 1703, positions which he would hold until his death in 1727 at the age of eighty-four. He was knighted by Queen Anne in 1705. Newton's *Principia* remains a landmark work in the annals of science.

***Robert Walpole**, generally regarded as the first prime minister, was reappointed as the first lord of the Treasury* in 1721.*

The office of prime minister was not officially recognised until the start of the twentieth century, but Walpole is considered to be the first true occupant of the role. He was the fifth of seventeen children and, with the death of his two elder brothers, became heir to his father's estate. Walpole also followed his father into Parliament, becoming a Whig member in 1701, secretary at war in 1708 and treasurer of the navy, in addition, two years later. The Tories won power in 1710, but worse was to come for Walpole. He was accused of corruption and, convicted by the Tory-dominated House of Lords, spent nearly six months incarcerated in the Tower of London during 1712. Walpole returned to Parliament the following year. George I took the throne in 1714 and this marked the start of a period of political ascendancy for the Whigs. Soon after, Walpole was made first lord of the Treasury and held the position for eighteen months until his resignation in 1717. He returned to the role in 1721 and also became chancellor of the exchequer and leader of the Commons. Walpole was knighted in 1725, but his power at this point was restricted because he had to accommodate Charles Townshend, his brother-in-law and the secretary for the Northern Department. Townshend resigned in 1730, leaving Walpole as the undisputed leader of the administration and it is from this date that his 'prime ministership' is often recorded. George II, who came to the throne in 1727, presented Walpole with 10 Downing Street as a gift, and he moved there in 1735. Walpole's term as first lord of the Treasury ended after nearly twenty-one years with his resignation

---

* A title held by virtually all prime ministers since Walpole. It adorns the letterbox of 10 Downing Street.

in 1742. Walpole, who was made the Earl of Orford after leaving office, died three years later at the age of sixty-eight.

*'The Hay Wain' by **John Constable** was first publicly displayed at the 1821 Royal Academy exhibition in London.*

Constable's *The Hay Wain* was originally called *Landscape: Noon*, and failed to attract a buyer during its exhibition debut. However, it was awarded a gold medal at the Paris Salon in 1824. The Suffolk-born son of a mill owner, Constable preferred a career as an artist to one in the family business and entered the Royal Academy Schools in London at the age of twenty-two. His oil sketch of *Dedham Vale* (1802) is an early example of Constable's passion for capturing the English countryside, particularly that around his native Suffolk. Although he is best remembered as a landscape artist, Constable also painted portraits, but these were usually embarked upon to provide an income and were a diversion from his preferred rural theme. *The White Horse* (1819) is the first of his large canvases, the 'six footers', and was exhibited at the Royal Academy in 1819. *The Hay Wain* was of a similar magnitude and others include *A View On The Stour Near Dedham* (1822) and *The Leaping Horse* (1925). Constable never travelled abroad despite the success of his work in Paris. Recognition and commercial demand for his paintings were slow to appear in his homeland; he had to wait until he was fifty-two to be elected a member of the Royal Academy. Constable died eight years later at the age of sixty.

***George Stephenson** was the engineer for the Stockton to Darlington railway which opened in September 1825 and was the first to carry passengers.*

Horses were originally envisaged as the means of traction for the line, but Stephenson persuaded the main promoter of the project, Edward Pease, to use steam-powered locomotives instead. The engine *Locomotion*, built by the Stephenson works in Newcastle-upon-Tyne, hauled the train on the opening day, driven by George Stephenson himself. He subsequently worked on the Liverpool to Manchester railway, and together with his son Robert won the competition, held at Rainhill, to provide the locomotives. However, their winning entry, *Rocket*, struck down the MP William Huskisson on the line's opening day in 1830, making him the first fatality of the railway era. As well as Stephenson's contribution to rail travel (including the setting of the standard gauge at 4 feet 8½ inches), he also invented a miner's safety lamp in 1818, around the same time as Sir Humphry Davy. Stephenson died in 1848 at the age of sixty-seven.

*The uniform penny post, as advocated by **Rowland Hill**, was established in 1840.*

Three years previously, Hill had published his proposals for the reform of the postage system. He sought to move away from a complicated structure (in which the cost of sending a letter, usually paid for by the recipient, generally depended on the number of sheets it contained and the distance conveyed) to one with a common price for delivery, based on weight, to anywhere in the British Isles. The introduction of Hill's system allowed all letters to be pre-paid, with the first postage stamps (Penny Black and Two Penny Blue) becoming available a few months after the start of the service. These featured the young Queen Victoria, who had come to the throne only three years earlier. For the cost of one penny, a letter of no more than half an ounce in weight would be delivered anywhere within the United Kingdom. Although the system proved popular, and despite the increased volume of mail, it took around twenty years for the post office's net income to reach a comparable level to that attained prior to the changes. Hill was knighted in 1860 and died in 1879, aged eighty-three.

*The play 'Peter Pan, or The Boy Who Would Not Grow Up' by **J. M. Barrie** (James Matthew) was first performed at the Duke of York's Theatre, London, in 1904.*

Peter Pan proved to be a great success, and it was subsequently published as a novel, *Peter and Wendy*, in 1911. Barrie hailed from Kirriemuir, Scotland, and after graduating from the University of Edinburgh worked as a journalist in Nottingham for two years, before moving south to London to become a freelance writer in 1885. His early novels include *Auld Licht Idylls* (1888) and *A Window in Thrums* (1890). Barrie turned his attention to the stage, and had considerable success with *Quality Street* and *The Admirable Crichton* at the start of the twentieth century. He was made a baronet in 1913, awarded the Order of Merit in 1922 and died in 1937 at the age of seventy-seven. Barrie had previously gifted the copyright of *Peter Pan* to the Great Ormond Street Hospital in London in 1929. It expired fifty years after his death in 1987, but an exception was made in law to extend its protection. The hospital is therefore still entitled to any royalties from UK performances.

George V ascended to the throne as King of the United Kingdom and its Dominions as well as Emperor of India in 1910.

George V's twenty-five-year reign was witness to many significant events including the First World War, the establishment of the Irish Free State, the first Labour government and the 1926 general strike. Formerly a member of the House of Saxe-Coburg and Gotha, George V changed the name of the royal house to Windsor in 1917, and at the same time all German titles held by the family were relinquished. He succeeded his father, King Edward VII, although as the second son it was not expected that he would inherit the throne. However, the death of his elder brother, Albert Victor, at the age of twenty-eight meant that George became heir apparent. He also married Albert's fiancée, Mary of Teck, the following year. They had five sons (including the future Edward VIII and George VI) and one daughter. George was a keen philatelist and also instituted the Christmas broadcasts in 1932. He died in 1936 at the age of seventy, the year after celebrating his silver jubilee.

*In 1918 the orchestral suite 'The Planets', by **Gustav Holst**, received its premiere in front of an invited audience.*

The first full public performance of *The Planets* took place two years later. Each of the seven movements is named after a planet in the solar system, excluding Earth. Holst was born into a musical family in Cheltenham, and in 1895 he won a scholarship to the Royal College of Music in London (he had initially attended in 1893 with money borrowed by his father). Holst held various teaching posts for the last thirty years of his life while continuing to compose. His other major works include *The Perfect Fool* and *Egdon Heath*. Holst died in 1934 at the age of fifty-nine.

*In 1925 it was announced that **Giles Gilbert Scott** had won the competition to design a new telephone kiosk.*

Scott's winning design, later dubbed the 'K2', was first sited in London.

He updated it at the request of the Post Office for King George V's silver jubilee in 1936 and this version, referred to as the 'K6', was deployed in much greater numbers in its familiar shade of red throughout Britain. Scott was already an established architect. At the age of twenty-two, he won the competition to design the new Anglican cathedral in Liverpool. He was asked to work with the more experienced architect George Bodley, but they had a difficult relationship and Scott continued alone following Bodley's death in 1907. His original design for the cathedral envisaged two towers, but the committee agreed to his proposal for a new design in 1910, which only had a single tower. The cathedral was consecrated in 1924, the year of his knighthood, but not completed until 1978, eighteen years after his death at the age of seventy-nine. Scott designed many other churches, and also secular buildings such as the Cambridge University Library and the Bankside Power Station (later converted into the Tate Modern art gallery). He was also a design consultant to Battersea Power Station and was appointed to reconstruct the bomb-damaged House of Commons in the mid 1940s.

George de Mestral first applied for a patent for his hook and loop fastening invention in 1951.

De Mestral's patent was granted four years later. His system would become better known by the trademark Velcro, a word formed from the French words for velvet (*velours*) and hook (*crochet*). De Mestral, an electrical engineer by profession, first had the idea for his alternative to the zip in the 1940s, after noticing seed burrs attached to his clothing (and his dog) after a walk in the woods. It took him several years to develop his innovation. De Mestral started his own company to manufacture the product, but later sold the business and his patent rights. His inventive streak was demonstrated at an early age when he patented a toy aeroplane at the age of twelve. De Mestral died at the age of eighty-two in 1990.

*'Casino Royale', the debut novel of **Ian Fleming**, was published in 1953.*

Born in London, Fleming was one of four brothers. His father, an army major, was killed in action during the First World War when Fleming was eight. After leaving Eton, Fleming was unsuccessful in the Foreign

Office entrance examinations and took a job at the news agency Reuters. During the Second World War he worked in naval intelligence with the rank of lieutenant commander, an experience that would prove helpful for his future literary career. Fleming reputedly wrote *Casino Royale*, the first book to feature his character of James Bond, within the space of a few weeks during 1952. The next to be published was *Live and Let Die* in 1954 and by the time of his death in 1964 at the age of fifty-six, Fleming had completed twelve novels and two short-story collections featuring the British Secret Service agent. He also penned the children's story *Chitty Chitty Bang Bang*, which was made into a successful film in 1968. Fleming lived to see only the first two Bond films, *Dr. No* (1962) and *From Russia with Love* (1963), released.

*'Carry on Sergeant', produced by **Peter Rogers**, was released in 1958.*

Carry on Sergeant was the first in one of the longest-running film series ever made, comprising thirty original films. The last, *Carry on Columbus*, was released in 1992 after a fourteen-year gap. Rogers first worked as a journalist and an appointment to interview Sydney Box, then the head of Gainsborough Studios, resulted in him becoming a full-time scriptwriter and later a film producer. His career-defining moment came when he received an unsolicited script entitled *The Bull Boys*. Reworked and renamed, it would launch the 'Carry On' franchise. The series would also make Rogers wealthy; he fastidiously kept production costs down – by, among other things, shooting quickly and making do with local alternatives to exotic locations (for example, Snowdonia doubled up as India in *Carry on up the Khyber*). Rogers died in 2009 at the age of ninety-five.

*Tottenham Hotspur, managed by **Bill Nicholson**, won the 1963 European Cup Winners' Cup to become the first British side to claim a major European football trophy.*

Spurs was Nicholson's only professional club, both as a player and a manager. He joined the north London side as a teenager and made his first team debut before the start of the Second World War. He returned to the club after military service and in 1951 was part of the side that won the League Championship, the first in Tottenham's history. Shortly afterwards, Nicholson scored for England in what was his one and only international appearance. The championship was Nicholson's only major honour in the game as a player, but he would pick up another eight as manager following his appointment to the post, at the age of thirty-nine, in 1958. His first game in charge saw Tottenham defeat Everton at home by the remarkable score of 10–4. Nicholson's trophy haul as a manager began with a league and cup 'double' in 1961 – the first since Aston Villa's success at the end of the nineteenth century. Spurs retained the FA Cup for a further season, and then in 1963 defeated Atlético Madrid by five goals to one, in Rotterdam, to lift the European Cup Winners' Cup – the first victory at that level by a British side. Nicholson presided over another FA Cup victory (1967), two football League Cups (1971, 1973) and a second European trophy, the UEFA Cup, in 1972. He took Spurs to a third European final two years later and announced his retirement as manager a few months later. Nicholson received an OBE in 1975. He had a brief period as a West Ham scout before returning to Spurs where he became club president in 1991. Nicholson died in 2004 at the age of eighty-five.

In 1967 Celtic, managed by **Jock Stein***, became the first British team to win the European Cup when they beat Inter Milan by two goals to one.*

Stein's team would again reach the final of Europe's top club tournament in 1970, the year in which he received a CBE, but they lost out 2–1 in extra time to Dutch champions Feyenoord. Stein began his senior football career with Albion Rovers, although he continued to work as a miner in the Lanarkshire coalfield. Playing as a centre-half, he left after eight years for a short spell at Llanelli Town before joining Celtic in 1951. He scored two goals for the Glasgow club in nearly 150 appearances. His managerial career started at Dunfermline Athletic with whom he won his first silverware, the Scottish FA Cup, in 1961, when they beat Celtic. Stein then moved to Hibernian in 1964 and the following year rejoined Celtic, this time as manager. In addition to European success, Stein won ten Scottish League Championships (nine of them consecutively), nine Scottish FA Cups and six Scottish League Cups. He was the first Celtic manager to win the 'treble' of major domestic trophies. Stein left Celtic in 1978 and, after a brief period at Leeds United, became the Scotland manager. He took the side to the 1982 World Cup, but during a qualification game against Wales in 1985 for the next tournament, Stein suffered a fatal heart attack at the age of sixty-two.

*'Dad's Army', written by **Jimmy Perry** and David Croft, made its debut on British television in 1968 with the episode 'The Man and the Hour'.*

Perry based the show on his own wartime experiences as a teenage member of the home guard prior to his enlistment in the regular forces. After the war, Perry studied at Rada and worked in repertory theatre for several years, before minor roles in BBC television comedy brought him into contact with Croft. *Dad's Army* ran for nine series, until 1977, but the Perry–Croft writing partnership continued with the situation comedies *It Ain't Half Hot Mum* (1974–81) and *Hi-de-Hi!* (1980–88). Both series drew again on the personal experiences of Perry, who had attended army concert parties in the Second World War and had also worked in Butlin's holiday camps. Their last collaboration was *You Rang, M'Lord* (1988–93). Perry was awarded an OBE in 1978.

*In 1970 **John Schlesinger** won both the Academy Award and Bafta for best director for 'Midnight Cowboy'.*

A graduate of Balliol College, Oxford, Schlesinger worked as an actor in the 1950s. His interest in film-making (he had already produced several amateur reels) was nurtured by his stint in the BBC documentary unit. The success of *Terminus* (1960), a thirty minute drama-documentary set in London's Waterloo station, which won a Bafta Award for best short film, led to Schlesinger's feature-film debut as a director with *A Kind of Loving* (1960). His next film, *Billy Liar* (1963), picked up six Bafta nominations and his third, *Darling* (1965), starring Julie Christie, earned him his first Academy Award nomination. As well as an Oscar and Bafta Award for Schlesinger, *Midnight Cowboy* (1969) also won the Academy Award for best picture. He won his second best director Bafta Award for *Sunday Bloody Sunday* (1971). Schlesinger's later films included *Marathon Man* (1976), *Pacific Heights* (1990) and his last, in which he directed Madonna, *The Next Best Thing* (2000). Arguably his best work in the latter part of his career was for television, with Bafta wins for *An Englishman Abroad* (1983) and *A Question of Attribution* (1991).

Schlesinger was awarded a CBE in 1970. He died in 2003 at the age of seventy-seven.

*In 1973 **Martin Cooper** made the first public telephone call using a handheld mobile phone.*

Cooper saw the need to create a more portable means of communication than the car-based system that was available at the time. He led the Motorola team that designed the first personal handset and was one of eight inventors cited on the US patent in October 1973 for a 'radio telephone system'. Cooper phoned Joel Engel, then head of research at Bell Laboratories, from a New York street to mark the first public demonstration of the mobile phone in 1973. The handset weighed approximately one kilogramme, but continued development resulted in the weight being halved for the Motorola DynaTAC 8000X, the first mobile phone to receive official US approval. It went into commercial service in 1983. Cooper left Motorola in the same year and went on to start Cellular Business Systems (which was later sold to Cincinnati Bell) and ArrayComm in 1992.

*The first Inspector Morse book, written by **Colin Dexter**, was published in 1975.*

Dexter's debut novel, *Last Train to Woodstock*, was the first of thirteen in the Inspector Morse series, with the final book *The Remorseful Day* appearing in 1999. Dexter read classics at Christ's College, Cambridge, and later taught the subject at school. The character of Morse reflected many of his own interests such as a love of cryptic crosswords. The detective first appeared on television in 1987, played by John Thaw, and Dexter usually made a cameo appearance in the productions. He was awarded an OBE in 2000.

*In 1981 **Robert Redford** won the Academy Award for best director for 'Ordinary People'.*

Redford's directorial debut, *Ordinary People* gave him his only competitive Oscar win to date. His acting career began with minor roles on television and in the theatre before he made his film debut in *War Hunt* (1962). Redford's first major success came with *Barefoot in the Park* (1967) in which he reprised his stage role of Paul Bratter. Two years later he teamed up with Paul Newman for the first time in *Butch Cassidy and the Sundance Kid* (1969). Their second and final pairing, *The Sting* (1973), brought him his only Academy Award nomination as an actor. Redford's other films include *All the President's Men* (1976), *Indecent Proposal* (1993) and *The Horse Whisperer* (1998). He received a best director Oscar nomination for *Quiz Show* (1994). Redford founded the Sundance Institute in 1981, which has managed the Sundance Film Festival since the mid eighties. The Sundance Institute is dedicated to the promotion of independent film-makers and Redford's honorary Oscar in 2002 cited his role in its success.

Alex Ferguson was appointed as the manager of Manchester United in 1986.

In 1974 Ferguson started his first managerial job at Falkirk-based Scottish second-division side East Stirlingshire, at the age of thirty-two. Four months later, he left to take up the manager's job at St. Mirren. Ferguson had already agreed a move to Aberdeen when he was dismissed four years later by the Paisley club. At Aberdeen he achieved both domestic and European success, including three Scottish League titles and the UEFA Cup Winners' Cup, but he left in 1986 to replace Ron Atkinson at Manchester United. It took Ferguson some years to restore United's fortunes. In January 1990, after seven league defeats in a row, his position looked vulnerable. However, a 1–0 away win at Nottingham Forest in the FA Cup proved to be a turning point, with United going on to win the trophy that year, setting Ferguson on course to become Britain's most successful football manager of all time. By the end of the 2011–12 season he had secured four more FA Cup wins, twelve Premier League titles, four League Cup wins, two UEFA Champions League trophies and his first European honour with Manchester United: the UEFA Cup Winners' Cup. Ferguson was knighted in 1999, at the end of a season in which United won the unique treble of Premier League, FA Cup and UEFA Champions League. Ferguson is the only manager to have won every major domestic competition (league, cup and league cup) in both Scotland and England as well as European trophies with clubs on either side of the border.

*The sculptor **Antony Gormley** won the Turner Prize in 1994.*

Gormley's Turner Prize exhibition featured two works, *Testing a World View* and *Sense*, and the prize citation made special mention of his work *Field* – of which several versions exist. Each contains thousands of small terracotta figures arranged on the gallery floor to face the viewer. The 40,000 figures of *Field for the British Isles* were handmade by a group of one hundred people in St Helens, Lancashire, under Gormley's guidance. The human form features prominently in Gormley's work, with the artist himself usually acting as the model for the statues. Examples include the *Angel of the North*, completed in 1998 and situated close to the A1 trunk road at Gateshead, and *Another Place*, consisting of one hundred cast-iron figures placed looking out to sea on Crosby beach, installed in 2005. Gormley was awarded an OBE in 1997. He is also a Royal Academician and a trustee of the British Museum.

45
FORTY-FIVE

*'A Dictionary of the English Language' by **Samuel Johnson** was published in 1755.*

Johnson took almost nine years to produce what became the definitive work of its type and one that remained unrivalled for over a century. The son of a bookseller, Johnson was able to indulge his passion for reading, and he was admitted to Oxford University in 1728. However, he was forced to leave without a degree after a year for financial reasons. He married the widower Elizabeth Porter, senior to him by twenty-one years, in 1735. Two years later Johnson, aged twenty-eight, set off for London to try to establish himself as a writer. He started to contribute to the *Gentleman's Magazine* and his first major original work *London: a Poem in Imitation of the Third Satire of Juvenal* was published in 1738. In 1746 Johnson agreed the contract for the production of his dictionary, an undertaking promoted and financed by a group of booksellers. He then enlisted the help of half a dozen assistants, who were tasked with transcribing material in an attic room. When the dictionary was finally published in 1755, its significance was quickly recognised. In it Johnson also displayed his wit with definitions such as that for lexicographer: 'a writer of dictionaries, a harmless drudge'. Johnson's literary reputation rests not only on his dictionary, but also on his poems, essays for *The Rambler*, 'The Idler' essays and other work which spanned subjects such as literary criticism, travel writing and biography. He received a pension from George III in 1762 which finally gave him financial security. Johnson died in 1784, aged seventy-five.

In 1820 **André-Marie Ampère** *demonstrated that two parallel wires carrying electric currents interact magnetically.*

Ampère showed that if the currents flow in the same direction the wires attract each other, but if they flow in different directions they repulse each other. Ampère was inspired to investigate this effect by Hans Christian Ørsted's discovery earlier in 1820 that a magnetic needle was deflected when placed close to a current-carrying wire. The findings of Ørsted and Ampère laid the groundwork for the study of electromagnetism. Ampère came from a prosperous family who would suffer during the French Revolution; his father, a justice of the peace in Lyon, was executed in 1793. Ampère married in 1799, but had to endure more tragedy when his wife died only four years later when he was twenty-eight. Soon after, he moved to Paris and took up a post at the École Polytechnique, where he became a professor of mathematics in 1809. Ampère died in 1836, aged sixty-one. The SI unit of electric current, the amp, is named in his honour.

In 1902 **Ronald Ross** *was awarded the Nobel Prize in Physiology or Medicine for his work on malaria.*

Ross first showed that malaria could be transmitted to a mosquito after it had bitten an infected human. Then, in experiments using birds, he was able to demonstrate the complete life cycle of the parasite that causes malaria and prove that it was the bite of an insect that induced transmission. Ross was born in India, but was educated largely in England where he later studied medicine. He returned to India to join the medical service but on a later visit to England contacted Patrick Manson, a leading expert on tropical diseases. Manson shared with Ross his own ideas about the cause of malaria; he suspected that the mosquito played a part in the disease's transmission, but the mechanism was not known.

Ross and Manson corresponded frequently while Ross made his break-through discoveries. In 1898, Ross's findings on the transmission of malaria were published in Britain and he returned to England the following year. His Nobel award was contested by Giovanni Grassi, who was working in the same area, but Ross prevailed. He was awarded a KCB in 1911 and a KCMG seven years later. Ross died in 1932 at the age of seventy-five.

Emmeline Pankhurst was one of the founding members of the Women's Social and Political Union (WSPU) in 1903.

Pankhurst and her daughter Christabel were the leaders of the group, which was commonly referred to as the Suffragettes. Their campaign for votes for women became increasingly militant as they took direct action in support of their aims. WSPU members smashed windows, committed arson and arranged violent demonstrations, while one member, Emily Davison, was killed when she threw herself under the King's horse at the Derby. Imprisoned suffragettes also later used hunger strikes as a way to increase the pressure on the government. It responded with force-feeding and the 'Cat and Mouse Act', which allowed the hunger strikers to be released and then re-arrested once their health had improved. Pankhurst was incarcerated on numerous occasions and also took part in the hunger strikes. The militant policy of the WSPU was suspended during the First World War. In 1918, before the end of the war, women over the age of thirty (subject to certain qualifications) were granted the right to vote. Shortly before Pankhurst's death, in 1928 at the age of sixty-nine, women were given the same voting rights as men in the UK.

Will Keith Kellogg founded the Battle Creek Toasted Corn Flake Company in 1906.

Cornflakes were invented in the Battle Creek Sanitarium where Will Kellogg's brother John was the superintendent. They wanted to find an alternative, healthier, breakfast food for the residents. Experimenting in the kitchen, the brothers discovered that flaked wheat grains might be the answer. They proved popular with the patients and later Will, a former broom salesman, found that corn was the ideal cereal to use for the product. Will and John started the Sanitas Food Company in the late 1890s, but a disagreement led to Will launching his own business in 1906. It would become known simply as Kellogg's and develop into a multibillion-dollar concern. Will Kellogg died in 1951, aged ninety-one.

'Nineteen Eighty-Four', by **George Orwell**, *was published in 1949.*

Completed in the previous year, *Nineteen Eighty-Four* presents a bleak vision of a future totalitarian society where the surveillance of individuals is the norm. Born Eric Blair in India, Orwell was schooled in England and won a scholarship to Eton. Rather than go to university he joined the Burma police, but he resigned after less than five years of service with the ambition of becoming a writer. His first book to be published, *Down and Out in Paris and London*, appeared in 1933 and was based on his own experiences of poverty; he set out to immerse himself in poorer parts of the two cities so he could write about them successfully. *Burmese Days*, his first novel, was published the following year. He wrote three further novels including *Animal Farm*, published in 1945, which became one of his most celebrated works. *Nineteen Eighty-Four* was his last novel. Suffering from tuberculosis, Orwell died in 1950 at the age of forty-six.

Christopher Cockerell *applied for a patent for his invention of the hovercraft in 1955.*

Initially there was little interest from industry or the military for Cockerell's creation, referred to in his patent title as a vehicle 'for travelling over land and/or water'. However, with the backing of the government's National Research Development Council, the Saunders Roe Company produced the first full-sized machine in 1959. Dubbed the SR-N1, it made the first crossing of the English Channel by hovercraft later that year, on the fiftieth anniversary of the first cross-channel flight. Three years later the first scheduled commercial hovercraft (or hovercoach as it was called) service commenced between Rhyl and Wallasey. A cross-channel service was established in 1968 which ran for over thirty years. Prior to the hovercraft, Cockerell had already demonstrated his inventiveness in his work at Marconi, which he joined not long after graduating from Peterhouse College, Cambridge. He filed over thirty patents during his time at Marconi and worked on radar during the war years. Cockerell was awarded a CBE in 1966 and was knighted in 1969. He died in 1999 at the age of eighty-eight.

Peter Medawar was awarded the 1960 Nobel Prize in Physiology or Medicine for the 'discovery of acquired immunological tolerance'.

In experiments with mice, Medawar showed that embryos exposed to mouse tissue from a different strain did not reject that tissue when re-exposed to it after birth. In other words, the immune response of the host had been modified to accept the foreign cells. Medawar's work also demonstrated that immunity is only fully developed some time after birth, and can therefore be altered while still in the womb. Medawar was knighted in 1965 and admitted to the Order of Merit in 1981. He died six years later, aged seventy-two. The Nobel Prize award was shared with Sir Frank Burnet.

In 1962 Maurice Wilkins was awarded the Nobel Prize in Physiology or Medicine, with Francis Crick and James Watson, for their work in determining the molecular structure of DNA.

Wilkins was born in New Zealand, but moved to England at the age of six with his family. He studied physics at Cambridge University, later obtaining his PhD at the University of Birmingham in 1940. Wilkins became involved in the Manhattan Project to build the atomic bomb, but his ethical anxieties prompted him to move into the field of biophysics. He joined a new research unit established in this area at King's College London. It was there that Wilkins and a graduate student, Raymond Gosling, produced the first X-ray diffraction patterns of DNA. Wilkins showed the image at a conference the following year, which inspired a member of the audience, James Watson, to take up the search for the structure of DNA. Wilkins also welcomed a new arrival at the lab, Rosalind Franklin, who became involved with the work on DNA. However, rather than collaborating they ended up working independently. Franklin, using a better DNA sample, produced an excellent diffraction image in 1952 and this was shared with James Watson by Wilkins in early 1953 after Franklin had left King's College (it had been passed to Wilkins under no restrictions by Raymond Gosling, Franklin's research student). Crick and Watson were also given access to a report containing more of Franklin's data by

Max Perutz of the MRC committee. The Crick and Watson 'double helix' paper was published several weeks later in the journal *Nature*. Wilkins declined to be a co-author, but published a separate paper in the same edition (along with Alec Stokes and Herbert Wilson) covering the King's College X-ray diffraction work. Franklin and Gosling also contributed a paper. Wilkins continued to work on the subject in order to refine and validate the proposed DNA model. He was awarded a CBE in 1963. Wilkins lived to celebrate the fiftieth anniversary of the discovery of the structure of DNA in 2003, but died the following year at the age of eighty-seven.

In 1967 **Paul Scofield** *won both the Academy Award and Bafta for best actor for his portrayal of Sir Thomas More in 'A Man for all Seasons'.*

Scofield, who also won a Golden Globe for his performance, first played the role of Sir Thomas More on stage in London, and subsequently took it to Broadway, winning a Tony Award in the process. Scofield began his initial training at the Croydon Repertory Theatre School at the age of seventeen. Primarily a stage actor, he made relatively rare forays into film work during his career. These include appearances as King Charles VI of France in Kenneth Branagh's production of *Henry V* (1989) and as Mark Van Doren in *Quiz Show* (1994), which brought him an Academy Award nomination for best supporting actor at the age of seventy-three. Scofield's last film appearance was as Judge Danforth in *The Crucible* (1996) for which he won a Bafta Award for best supporting actor. He was awarded a CBE in 1956. Scofield died in 2008 at the age of eighty-six.

Christiaan Barnard *performed the first successful human heart transplant in 1967.*

Barnard led the team of surgeons who performed the operation at the Groote Schuur Hospital in Cape Town, South Africa. The recipient, Louis Washkansky, died eighteen days later due to pneumonia, his immune system weakened by the drugs administered to prevent rejection of his new heart. Barnard performed his second transplant operation a few weeks later and this time the patient, Philip Blaiberg, lived for nearly six hundred days. Currently in the UK, around half of the people who have received a heart transplant live for at least ten years. Barnard died in 2001, aged seventy-eight.

Brian Trubshaw piloted the first British flight of Concorde in 1969.

The debut flight of Concorde 002 at Filton, near Bristol, lasted for twenty-two minutes and followed the maiden flight of the French aircraft, Concorde 001, weeks earlier (Trubshaw had already piloted the French plane). Sixteen airlines had placed seventy-four options to purchase production models of the supersonic passenger jet, but this level of demand was not sustained and they only went into service with British Airways (BA) and Air France, who acquired seven Concordes each. BA and Air France began scheduled Concorde flights in 1976, with BA operating a London–Bahrain service. Washington was added as a destination later in the year. The entire fleet was grounded after the crash in 2000 of an Air France Concorde shortly after take-off from Paris, which killed all those on board and four people on the ground. The planes returned to service after safety modifications in 2001, but lower passenger numbers and increasing maintenance costs led to the decision to retire the Concorde fleet. The last commercial flights took place in 2003. Trubshaw, Concorde's first British pilot, became interested in aviation as a boy and joined the RAF at the age of eighteen. Following the Second World War he was a pilot for the King's Flight, the monarch's official air transport, but then left the RAF to become a test pilot. Trubshaw received an OBE in 1964 and a CBE in 1970. He died in 2001 at the age of seventy-seven.

Roger Moore made his debut as James Bond in the eighth film of the official series, 'Live and Let Die', released in 1973.

Moore is the oldest actor to play the role on screen, and he has also recorded the most official Bond appearances. He starred in a further six films, the last of which was *A View to a Kill* (1985). His style as the secret agent was markedly lighter than Sean Connery's, but also proved to be popular with audiences at the box office. Moore was better known from his television work prior to Bond, playing the title role in *Ivanhoe* and Simon Templar in *The Saint*. He teamed up with Tony Curtis for a single TV series of *The Persuaders!* in the early 1970s. Moore's other films include *Gold* (1974), *The Wild Geese* (1978) and *Escape to Athena* (1979). He was awarded a CBE in 1999 and knighted in 2003 for his charity work. Moore became a UNICEF Goodwill Ambassador in 1991.

Peter Carey won the 1988 Booker Prize for 'Oscar and Lucinda'.

The award was the first of two Booker wins for Carey, who was born in Victoria, Australia. After an abortive year as a science undergraduate, Carey began a career in advertising. He wrote fiction in his spare time and, following several rejections, was first published in 1974 (*The Fat Man in History* – a collection of short stories). His debut novel, *Bliss*, appeared in 1981, followed by *Illywhacker* (1985) and then his first Booker-winning title. Carey's other novels include *The Tax Inspector* (1991), *The Unusual Life of Tristan Smith* (1994), *Jack Maggs* (1997) and his second Booker-winning volume *True History of the Kelly Gang* (2000).

James Dyson began UK production of his cyclonic, bagless vacuum cleaner in 1993.

Repeatedly shunned by existing industry players, Dyson brought his vacuum cleaner design to market himself and within two years the DC01 was the UK's best-selling model. Dyson had spent many years developing his bagless product. He filed the first of many patents for the technology in 1979 and made over 5,000 prototypes in order to perfect the design. Dyson's first major success for his cyclonic cleaning method was in the Japanese market where the G-Force vacuum cleaner, launched in 1986, was made under licence. Income from its sales helped him to launch the DC01 under his own brand name seven years later. Dyson's vacuum cleaners have also become successful in many other countries including the US, where they accounted for nearly a quarter of all sales within eight years of entering the market in 2002. His earlier inventions include the Ballbarrow (a wheelbarrow fitted with ball instead of a wheel) and a boat-launcher called the Trolleyball. Dyson was knighted in the 2007 New Year Honours list.

George Foreman won the IBF and WBA heavyweight boxing titles when he defeated Michael Moorer by a tenth-round knockout in 1994.

Foreman had first won the WBA crown in 1973, with a stunning defeat of Joe Frazier in the second round. After two title defences, Foreman faced Muhammad Ali in what was styled the 'rumble in the jungle' in Kinshasa, Zaire. Despite almost constant pressure from Foreman, Ali rebounded to land a knockout blow in round eight. Foreman gave up boxing in 1977, but returned to the ring ten years later. He boxed for the last time at the age of forty-eight in 1997, but lost on points in a non-title fight. Foreman remains the oldest boxer to have won a world title.

46

FORTY-SIX

The 'Sidereus Nuncius' (Sidereal Messenger) by **Galileo Galilei** *was published in 1610.*

Sometimes referred to as the *Starry Messenger*, Galileo's tract contained the astronomical discoveries he had made using his telescope. These included his observations of the mountainous lunar surface and the realisation that the Milky Way was made up of a multitude of stars. It also revealed his discovery of four of the moons of Jupiter (later named Io, Europa, Callisto and Ganymede), that are referred to as the 'Galilean moons' in his honour. In subsequent work he also described the phases of Venus, and observations which supported the sun-centred, as opposed to earth-centred, model of the solar system. Galileo also made contributions to physics such as stating that all bodies fall (without air resistance) at the same rate, and he discovered that the length of a pendulum determines its period. In Galileo's *Dialogue Concerning the Two Chief World Systems*, published in 1632 when he was in his late sixties, he advocated the heliocentric rather than the earth-centred Ptolemaic model for the solar system. This brought him into conflict with the Inquisition, a Roman Catholic tribunal for suppressing heresy. As a result, Galileo had to recant his views and was placed under house arrest for the rest of his life. He died in 1642 at the age of seventy-seven.

Edward Jenner carried out his first vaccination against smallpox, using cowpox, in 1796.

Jenner, a physician and surgeon, was aware of the folklore that people who caught cowpox (a mild infection transmitted from cows) did not get smallpox. When Jenner saw a rash on the hand of dairymaid Sarah Nelmes, he recognised it as cowpox and also saw an opportunity to test the theory that it could provide protection against smallpox. Jenner chose to infect an eight-year-old boy, James Phipps, with cowpox material from Nelmes. He suffered a mild illness but recovered within days. Jenner then tested the efficacy of the vaccine six weeks later by administering Phipps with a dose of smallpox (a practice known as variolation, the intention of which was to produce a mild infection and create future immunity). Despite repeated attempts, he found that Phipps did not develop smallpox. Jenner published his work in 1798. Although there was some resistance to the idea of vaccination, the idea gained ground and in 1853 vaccination by cowpox was made compulsory in Britain (this had occurred earlier in some other countries). Jenner became famous, was welcomed by royalty and Napoleon had a special medal minted in his honour in 1804. He died in 1873 at the age of seventy-three.

William Grenville (Lord Grenville) became prime minister in 1806.

During William Pitt's first period as prime minister, Grenville was made home secretary in 1789 and two years later became foreign secretary, a post that he held until 1801. This was a period that saw the wars of the French Revolution – with France declaring war on Great Britain on 1 February 1793. He was raised to the peerage as Baron Grenville in 1790 and became leader of the House of Lords, a role he continued to play when he became foreign secretary the following year. He left government in 1801 along with Pitt, and others, over the King's refusal to allow Catholic emancipation. Grenville returned as prime minister in 1806 to head a cross-party grouping known as 'The Ministry of all the Talents'. After just over thirteen months it was dissolved, again over the issue of Catholic emancipation, and Grenville was out of office. The ministry's most important achievement was the abolition of the slave trade in 1807. Grenville died in 1834 at the age of seventy-four.

Spencer Perceval succeeded the Duke of Portland as prime minister in 1809.

Perceval was a lawyer by profession and entered Parliament at the age of thirty-three where he proved to be a skilled debater. He became chancellor of the exchequer in 1807 under Portland, and also served as the leader in the Commons. When Portland died in office, Perceval emerged as his successor. During his premiership he had to contend with problems such as the Napoleonic Wars and George III's mental instability. When the King showed no signs of recovering from his illness, Perceval was forced to introduce a bill in 1910 that named the Prince of Wales as Regent, although with some constraints which would remain in place for a year. The regency began in 1811 and continued until the King's death in 1820. Despite expectations that the Regent would replace Perceval as soon as possible, he continued, fatefully as it turned out, in the office of prime minister. In May 1812, at the age of forty-nine, he was assassinated by John Bellingham, a disgruntled merchant who had demanded compensation from the government over his unjust imprisonment in Russia. Bellingham shot Perceval in the lobby of the House of Commons with a single bullet and made no effort to escape after his crime. He was hanged one week later.

Arthur Wellesley, first Duke of Wellington, commanded an Anglo–Allied Army that, along with the Prussian Army under Gebhard von Blücher, defeated Napoleon at the Battle of Waterloo in 1815.

In 1769 Wellington was born Arthur Wesley in Dublin, the fourth son of the first Earl of Mornington. The family later changed its name to Wellesley and Arthur adopted this surname in 1798. Fatherless at the age of twelve, he did not excel at Eton and completed his schooling privately in Brussels and at the Academy of Equitation at Angers. His family's connections secured him a commission as an ensign in the 73rd Regiment of Foot in 1787. Wellesley's military career saw him rise to become the commander of the British Army during the Peninsular War (1807–1814). He was created Duke of Wellington after the successful conclusion of the campaign. Following the victory at Waterloo, Wellington joined Lord Liverpool's government as master-general of the Ordnance in 1819. In 1828, at the age of fifty-eight, he became prime minister for the first time. Six months later, the by-election win of Daniel O'Connell brought the contentious issue of Catholic emancipation to the fore. O'Connell was not permitted by law to take his seat in Parliament because of his religion. Wellington saw the need to push for liberalisation on this issue; feelings ran high, and he ended up fighting a duel with one of his harshest critics, Lord Winchilsea, in Battersea Park. Wellington fired first, intentionally wide, and Winchilsea, who fired into the air, later tendered an apology to his adversary. Catholic emancipation was achieved with the Catholic Relief Act of 1829. Wellington went on to become unpopular with his opposition to parliamentary reform intended to extend and make fairer the franchise. He was out of government in 1830, but voted against the 1832 Reform Act. The Tories returned to power in 1834, but Wellington declined the premiership, although he did act as prime minister in an interim capacity while Robert Peel was out of the country. He then served as foreign secretary. Wellington was made leader of the House of Lords in Peel's second ministry, whose fall in 1846 also marked the end of Wellington's political career. Wellington died in 1852 at the age of eighty-three.

*The building designed by **Joseph Paxton**, dubbed the 'Crystal Palace', was selected in 1850 for the following year's 'Great Exhibition' in Hyde Park.*

Paxton's design for the exhibition used glass, cast iron and wood, which allowed for speedy construction. Its low cost also found favour with the committee in charge of overseeing the exhibition. Paxton did not train as an architect, but was the head gardener at Chatsworth House, a position that he took up in his early twenties. It was at Chatsworth that he gained experience in the creation of large glasshouses. Paxton only entered the contest for the design of the Great Exhibition building weeks before his proposal was chosen. The exhibition opened on 1 May 1851 and ran until the middle of October. Paxton's building was then moved to Sydenham in London where it stood until destroyed by fire in 1936. Paxton was knighted in 1851 and became a Liberal MP in 1854. He died in 1865 at the age of sixty-one.

*In 1867 'Old' **Tom Morris** won golf's Open Championship for the fourth time.*

Morris is the oldest player to have won the Open championship. The annual tournament, which began in 1860, was played exclusively at the Prestwick Golf Club for its first twelve contests (it last featured as the venue in 1925). Morris designed the course and was also the keeper of the greens. Morris was born in St Andrews and returned to the town in 1864 to work for the Royal & Ancient Golf Club as greenkeeper, retiring when he was in his eighties. Morris also ran his own business manufacturing clubs and balls. He died in 1908 at the age of eighty-six. Morris's son, also called Tom, succeeded him as Open champion in 1868 (to become the youngest ever), and also won the next three tournaments to equal his father's tally, but was to die at the early age of twenty-four.

*In 1869 **Ulysses S. Grant** became the eighteenth president of the United States.*

Grant was a former military man. He had fought in the Mexican–American War, and shortly after the start of the American Civil War he was made a brigadier general. He fought on the Union side and, as general-in-chief, he accepted the surrender of his Confederate counterpart Robert E. Lee in 1865. Grant served two terms as president and left office in 1877. He subsequently lost money in a financial fraud, and was diagnosed with terminal cancer. Grant completed his memoirs shortly before his death at the age of sixty-three in order to make provision for his family. They earned a sum of approximately $450,000.

Archibald Philip Primrose *(fifth Earl of Rosebery) became prime minister in 1894.*

In 1886, Primrose became foreign secretary in Gladstone's third administration, but the government fell six months later. Primrose returned to the post in 1892, again under Gladstone who he succeeded as prime minister two years later. Sitting in the House of Lords, his period as prime minister was to be short lived and lacked impact, lasting only fifteen months. Primrose, devoted to horse racing, did however manage to celebrate two of his three Derby wins as an owner while prime minister. Another reputed aim in his life was to marry an heiress, something that he achieved with his marriage to Hannah de Rothschild. Primrose's dying request, in 1929 at the age of eighty-two, was to listen to the Eton boating song.

*In 1901 **King Camp Gillette** filed a patent application for his safety razor with disposable blades.*

The same year, Gillette co-founded the American Safety Razor Company (in 1902 'Gillette' was substituted for 'American' in the company name). The first year of production, 1903, saw sales of only 51 razors and 168 blades, but this increased markedly in 1904 to tens of thousands of each. By the start of the First World War blade sales were counted in the millions. The company's sales were boosted further when all US servicemen were issued with Gillette shaving kits in 1917. Prior to his safety razor, Gillette worked as a travelling salesman, but sought to create a business based on a disposable element in order to generate repeat sales. A utopian socialist, Gillette also wrote several books – including *The Human Drift* (1894) which proposed a future in which all US citizens lived in one giant city called Metropolis, located close to Niagara Falls. Gillette died in 1932 at the age of seventy-seven.

William Durant founded General Motors, which would become the largest car maker in the world, in 1908.

Durant's first commercial success was in the horse-drawn cart and carriage business. In 1904 he joined Buick, then a very small, struggling car-building concern. Soon, he transformed Buick into the major car maker in the US and Durant decided to grow the business further by acquisition. He formed General Motors (GM) in 1908 and quickly added over two dozen firms to the fold including car makers Cadillac and Oakland (later named Pontiac) as well as parts suppliers. Financial trouble lay ahead though; Cadillac had always been profitable, but most units of GM were not and by 1910 the banks took control. Durant then started Chevrolet, along with Louis Chevrolet, the following year and its success meant he was able to take the helm at GM once more in 1916. He added Chevrolet to the roster of marques, but Durant was forced out of GM, for the last time, in 1920. He started another car company the following year – Durant Motors. It achieved modest success, but Durant, a major investor on Wall Street, was to lose heavily as the Depression took hold in the late 1920s. Durant Motors also struggled and was wound up in 1933. Durant was declared bankrupt three years later. He was given a GM pension and was still starting new businesses in his late seventies. He died in 1947 at the age of eighty-five.

*'Waiting for Godot' by **Samuel Beckett** was published in 1952.*

Like many of Beckett's works it was originally written in French (*En Attendant Godot*) and translated into English by Beckett himself. The play is concerned with the musings of its two central characters, the tramps

Estragon and Vladimir, as they await the arrival of someone called Godot who they expect to transform their lives. Completed in 1949, it was Beckett's first play to be published and received its premiere in Paris in 1953. Its London debut came two years later. Beckett was born in Dublin where he later studied at Trinity College. After a short period as a teaching assistant in Paris, he returned to Trinity College in 1930 as a lecturer, but resigned the following year and embarked on some European travels. By his early thirties he had settled in Paris. He remained there during the Second World War, became an active member of the French resistance and was later decorated with the Croix de Guerre. Beckett's first novel *Dream of Fair to Middling Women* was completed in 1932 but failed to find a publisher at the time and eventually appeared in 1992. His first short-story collection *More Pricks than Kicks* was published in 1934 with his debut poetry collection *Echo's Bones and other Precipitates* following a year later. At the age of sixty-three, Beckett was awarded the 1969 Nobel Prize in Literature. He died twenty years later at the age of eighty-three.

Juan Fangio won his fourth consecutive Formula One World Championship in 1957.

Born in Argentina, the son of Italian immigrants, Fangio's title victory in what was his last season before retirement, gave him his fifth championship success only six years after his first in 1951. He is the oldest driver to take the Formula One title. In his other two full seasons, Fangio finished as the runner-up. His Formula One career saw him win nearly half of all the races he entered. Regarded by many as the greatest driver of all time, his championship total was not surpassed until Michael Schumacher claimed the sixth of his seven titles in 2003. Fangio was a mechanic by trade and first tested his racing skills in South America before coming to Europe to compete in 1948. He died in 1995 at the age of eighty-four.

*In 1966 the England football team, managed by **Alf Ramsey**, won the World Cup when they beat West Germany 4–2 after extra time.*

Ramsey began his senior career as a player with Southampton and, as an established full-back, transferred to Tottenham Hotspur in 1949. In his first full season at the club they won the Second Division Championship and the following year became league champions. Ramsey's move also rejuvenated his international career as he amassed most of his thirty-two caps while at Spurs. He captained England on three occasions, played in the 1950 World Cup and gained his last cap in the 6–3 defeat by Hungary in which he scored from the penalty spot. He retired from playing in 1955 and became manager of Third Division South club Ipswich Town. Ramsey's team won promotion and in 1961 they also took the second division title. He then emulated his record as a player with Spurs when newly promoted Ipswich won the first division title in 1962. Later that year Ramsey accepted the job of England manager, but on the condition that he had full responsibility for team selection and tactics. He also stated that he believed that England could win the next World Cup in 1966, when they were also the tournament hosts. After the 1966 victory, there was great expectations of the 1970 tournament, but England could only reach the quarter-finals where they were defeated 3–2 by West Germany (after extra time). England then failed to qualify for the 1974 World Cup and Ramsey was sacked. He had a brief period as the caretaker manager at Birmingham City in the 1977–78 season. Ramsey was knighted in 1967. He died in 1999 at the age of seventy-nine.

John Berger won the 1972 Booker Prize for his novel 'G.'.
Berger was born in London and educated at St Edward's School, Oxford. Following service in the British Army, Berger became a student at the Chelsea School of Art and the Central School of Art. Later, he taught drawing and also became an art critic and writer. His first novel, *A Painter of Our Time*, was published in 1958, and others followed, including *The Foot of Clive* (1962) and *Corker's Freedom* (1964). Berger's book of essays *Ways of Seeing* (1972) arose from the BBC television series in which he offered a new perspective on the appreciation of art. His 2008 novel, *From A to X*, was longlisted for the 2008 Booker Prize.

Larry Hagman starred as J. R. Ewing in the first episode of the mini-series 'Dallas', broadcast in 1978.
Dallas, which recounted the trials and tribulations of a rich Texan oil family, returned for thirteen full series before finally concluding in 1991. The series two finale, when Hagman's character J.R. was shot, led to much speculation as to the identity of the perpetrator. Hagman made his

television debut in 1957 and had his first major hit eight years later with a starring role in the TV comedy *I Dream of Jeannie*, which ran for five series until 1970. His portrayal of J. R. brought him four Golden Globe nominations between 1981 and 1985. Hagman starred alongside other original cast members in a revived producton of *Dallas*, which premiered in 2012. He died later that year, aged eighty-one.

In 1985 **Harold Kroto** *was one of the co-discoverers of a new form of carbon subsequently named buckminsterfullerene.*

Carbon is normally found to exist in two forms or allotropes: graphite and diamond. The properties of each are dictated by the way in which the carbon atoms bond to one another. In graphite they connect together to form sheets or layers, whereas in diamond they bond to create a three dimensional crystalline structure. Kroto and his co-workers (Jim Heath, Sean O'Brien, Yuan Liu, Bob Curl and Rick Smalley) proposed that molecules comprised of sixty carbon atoms (C_{60}) had a spherical structure, similar to a football surface, made up of hexagonal and pentagonal shapes. The name was inspired by architect Buckminster Fuller whose geodesic spheres were evocative of the newly discovered molecule's structure. The finding was actually an unintended consequence of Kroto's desire to investigate red giant carbon stars as a source of long chained carbon molecules such as HC_9N; his experiments at Rice University in Houston, Texas, produced not only the hoped for carbon molecules, but also C_{70} as well as C_{60}. Kroto, Curl and Smalley shared the 1996 Nobel Prize in Chemistry for their discovery. Kroto was also knighted in the same year for his contributions to chemistry.

Jack Nicklaus *won his eighteenth major golf championship when he was victorious at the 1986 US Masters.*

Nicklaus's 1986 US Masters victory was his sixth in a tournament that he first won in 1963. His first professional win was a major: the US Open in 1962 at the age of twenty-two. Nicklaus also claimed victory in this tournament on another three occasions (1967, 1972 and 1980). He has won the Open Championship on three occasions (1966, 1970 and 1978) and the PGA Championship five times. Nicklaus is currently the oldest winner of the US Masters, and holds the record for the most major titles. He joined the Senior PGA tour in 1990 and had further success. In 2005 Nicklaus played his last major, the Open Championship at St Andrews, at the age of sixty-five. He has also run a successful golf course design business for many years, and received the Presidential Medal of Freedom in 2005.

'A Brief History of Time' by **Stephen Hawking** *was published in 1988.*

Hawking's surprise bestseller (it has sold more than nine million copies) was aimed at the layman and discussed topics such as the origin of the universe, the nature of time, black holes and the Big Bang. Hawking has a degree in physics from Oxford University and a PhD from Cambridge University, where he was appointed Lucasian professor of mathematics in 1979. He held this position (once held by Sir Isaac Newton) for thirty years. Hawking is also a sufferer of motor neurone disease which has become progressively worse since his undergraduate days, resulting in almost total paralysis. He is not able to write or speak, but using computer assistance Hawking has been able to carry on his work in theoretical physics. He was awarded a CBE in 1992.

In 1993 **Bill Clinton** *became the forty-second president of the United States of America.*

Clinton's father died in a traffic accident three months before he was born William Jefferson Blythe III in Hope, Arkansas. His mother married Roger Clinton in 1950, and later he officially took the new family name. In the summer of 1963, two memorable events occurred on either side of Clinton's seventeenth birthday. First, while on a visit to the White House as a 'Boys Nation' senator, he met and shook hands with President Kennedy, then, a month later, he listened to Martin Luther King's 'I Have a Dream' speech, which became a lasting source of inspiration. It was around this time of his life that he decided that one day he would like to enter elected public office. He finished his education at Yale Law School in 1973. Five years later, at the age of thirty-two, Clinton was elected as the Governor of Arkansas. Aside from two years in the early eighties when he failed to be re-elected, Clinton served as Governor until 1992, the year of his presidential election victory. Four years later, he became the first Democrat to win a second term in the White House since Franklin Roosevelt in 1936. Clinton is also the third youngest person to take the presidential oath. His time in office was marked by economic prosperity and low unemployment. Scandal surrounding his private life (he was impeached but later acquitted by the Senate) did little to dent his popularity, and he left office with one of the highest approval ratings for a modern-day US president.

47

FORTY-SEVEN

Alexander Fleming made his discovery of penicillin in 1928, which eventually led to its large-scale manufacture in a process developed by Ernst Chain and Howard Florey.

Fleming was investigating the bacterium *Staphylococcus aureus*. By chance, one of his culture plates containing this bacterium had become contaminated by a mould which Fleming noticed was destroying the staphylococci around it. He proceeded to investigate the mould, identified as a member of the genus *penicillium* (it was later more fully defined as *Penicillium notatum* by Charles Thom). Fleming observed that many other types of bacteria were also killed by its action. He named his anti-bacterial agent penicillin and published his findings in 1929. He continued to use it in his bacteriological work, but it was difficult to manufacture and isolate the active ingredient. More than a decade passed before Ernst Chain and Howard Florey saw its medical potential and succeeded in creating a method to isolate and purify the drug for clinical use, which led to its mass manufacture. All three men shared the 1945 Nobel Prize in Physiology or Medicine. Fleming was knighted in 1944. He died eleven years later at the age of seventy-three.

Cecil Powell was awarded the Nobel Prize in Physics in 1950 for his development of photographic emulsions for the study of nuclear interactions and the resulting discovery of the pion.

Silver halide grains are the active component in photographic emulsions, and their interaction with electrically charged particles allows the paths of such entities to be observed following development of the film. Powell championed improvements in this technique by applying better methods and improved emulsion formulations. His work led to the discovery of the pion (or pi-meson) sub-atomic particle in 1946. A scholarship had enabled Powell to attend Sidney Sussex College, Cambridge, where he gained first-class honours in both parts of the natural sciences tripos. He then earned his PhD in physics at the Cavendish Laboratory. His post-doctoral work took him to Bristol University, where he remained for the rest of his academic career, becoming a professor in 1948. Powell died in 1969 at the age of sixty-five.

In 1963 **Gregory Peck** *won the Academy Award for best actor for his portrayal of Atticus Finch in 'To Kill a Mockingbird'.*

Peck, who became one of the major stars of post-war American cinema, made his film debut in *Days of Glory* (1944) and was Academy Award nominated in 1946 for his role in *The Keys of the Kingdom*. He was nominated for best actor in each of the following two years and again in 1950 for *Twelve O'Clock High*. His other films include *Roman Holiday* (1953), *The Million Pound Note* (1954) and *The Omen* (1976). Peck received the highest civilian award in the US, the Presidential Medal of Freedom, in 1969 for his humanitarian work. In 2003, the American Film Institute chose the character of Atticus Finch as the top hero in the past one hundred years of US cinema. Peck died the same year, at the age of eighty-seven.

Ferruccio Lamborghini *founded his sports car company in 1963.*

Lamborghini had already enjoyed considerable success with his tractor manufacturing business, which he formed in 1948. This allowed him to indulge his taste for exotic cars, such as those made by Ferrari and Maserati. A disagreement with his friend Enzo Ferrari, who told him he was better suited to driving tractors than Ferraris, spurred him on to start making his own cars. A prototype of his first car, the 350 GTV, was presented at the Turin Motor Show in October 1963, and was reworked into the 350 GT – the company's first commercial offering. The Miura debuted in 1966 and the Countach in 1974, the year that Lamborghini sold his remaining share of the car company. It has changed hands several times since then and is now owned by Audi AG (a subsidiary of Volkswagen). Lamborghini died in 1993 at the age of seventy-six.

*In 1971 **Alan Shepard** became the fifth man to walk on the moon.*

Shepard, the commander of Apollo 14, was the oldest of the twelve astronauts to land on the moon. His extra-terrestrial career began in 1961 with a fifteen minute sub-orbital flight inside a Mercury capsule, dubbed *Freedom 7*, which made Shepard the first American in space. He reached an altitude of 116 miles during the mission, which took place less than one month after Russian Yuri Gagarin had become the first man to orbit the earth. Shepard was the only one of the original group of seven US astronauts selected for the Mercury flights to participate in a moon landing, and was the first of the Apollo astronauts to hit a golf ball on the lunar surface. He died at the age of seventy-four in 1998.

*'The Godfather', which starred **Marlon Brando** as Don Corleone, was released in 1972.*

Brando's powerful performance won him his second Academy Award for best actor, although he declined it in protest at the portrayal of American Indians by Hollywood and television. His first film, *The Men* (1950), was followed by *A Streetcar Named Desire* (1951) in which he reprised his lauded stage role as Stanley Kowalski. His performance earned him the first of four consecutive Oscar nominations for best actor that culminated in a win for his portrayal of Terry Malloy in *On the Waterfront* (1954). He was nominated again for *Sayonara* (1957) and *Last Tango in Paris* (1972). Following the latter, Brando made only three more films in the 1970s, ending the decade with his role as Colonel Kurtz in *Apocalypse Now* (1979). His last Oscar nomination was for *A Dry White Season* (1989), this time for best supporting actor, after nearly a decade's absence from the big screen. His final film appearance was in *The Score*, released in 2001. Brando died three years later at the age of eighty.

***Thomas Keneally** won the 1982 Booker Prize for 'Schindler's Ark'.*

Schindler's Ark tells the story of Oskar Schindler, the German industrialist who saved approximately 1,200 Jews from certain death in the Nazi extermination camps. The book formed the basis for the acclaimed Steven Spielberg-directed film *Schindler's List* (1993). Keneally, who was born in Sydney, Australia, had previously been Booker-shortlisted for *The Chant of Jimmie Blacksmith* (1972), *Gossip from the Forest* (1975) and *Confederates* (1979). His debut novel, *The Place at Whitton*, was published in 1964 and since then he has written over thirty fictional works as well as volumes of non-fiction. Keneally's more recent novels include *The People's Train* (2009) and *The Daughters of Mars* (2012). He was made an Officer of the Order of Australia in 1983.

John Major *replaced Margaret Thatcher as prime minister in 1990.*

Major had come to public prominence with his appointment in 1989 as foreign secretary and then, only months later, as chancellor under the premiership of Thatcher. Her leadership was challenged in 1990 by Michael Heseltine and her failure to win a big enough margin in the first ballot resulted in her withdrawing from the contest. Major entered it at this point and defeated both Heseltine and Douglas Hurd. He then led the Conservative Party to what was for many a surprising victory at the 1992 general election. Despite party in-fighting (Major resigned the leadership in 1995 in order to reassert his control), he remained as prime minister until defeat by Labour, led by Tony Blair, in the 1997 general election. During his tenure, Major helped to pave the way for progress towards the 1998 peace agreement in Northern Ireland, Britain left the European Exchange Rate Mechanism and the National Lottery was launched. Major left school at sixteen and after a number of jobs entered the banking profession in his early twenties. He had an early interest in politics and was elected to Lambeth Borough Council in 1968, although he would lose his seat three years later. Major first entered Parliament at the 1979 general election and remained in the Commons until 2001. When he came to power, Major was the youngest prime minister for nearly one hundred years. Major was made a Knight of the Garter in 2005.

Clive Woodward *was the coach of the England team that won the Rugby World Cup in 2003.*

The defeat of the hosts and reigning champions Australia brought England the rugby world title for the first time. Woodward gained twenty-one caps playing for England between 1980 and 1984, winning the Grand Slam in his first season. He became the national coach in 1997 and took England to his first World Cup in 1999, where they were defeated by South Africa in the quarter-finals. Woodward was knighted in the 2004 New Year Honours list, the same year that he resigned as England rugby coach.

Barack Obama *was sworn in as the forty-fourth president of the United States of America in 2009.*

Obama was born in Honolulu, Hawaii, to a father from Kenya and a mother from Kansas, who separated two years after his birth. His mother then married Lolo Soetoro, and the family moved to his Indonesian homeland where Obama lived until he was ten. He then returned to Hawaii to live with his grandparents and continued his education at the Punahou Academy. In 1983 he graduated from Columbia University, New York. Obama later enrolled at Harvard Law School and completed his studies there in 1991. He went on to practise civil rights law in Chicago. Obama was elected to the Illinois State Senate in 1996 and served until 2004, when he transferred to the US Senate after his election victory in November of that year. Four years later, he won the presidential election by a comfortable margin, and in 2012 he was re-elected for a second term.

48

FORTY-EIGHT

Henry Pelham *became prime minister in 1743.*

The third prime minister of Great Britain, Pelham spent over ten years in the post and had to contend with the Jacobite Rebellion in 1745 and the War of the Austrian Succession. The rebellion was defeated and the Austrian war ended with a peace treaty in 1748. Pelham's tenure also saw a reform of the calendar with New Year's Day in England being moved from 25 March to 1 January, and the adoption of the Gregorian calendar in place of the Julian calendar throughout Britain in 1752. (In order to achieve alignment, 2 September was followed by 14 September.) Pelham died in office at the age of fifty-nine in 1754. The next prime minister was his brother Thomas, the Duke of Newcastle.

*In 1862 **Alexander Parkes** showed a number of small items made from his invention, Parkesine, the first man-made plastic, at the International Exhibition in London.*

Based on the natural material cellulose, he tried to exploit his invention commercially via the Parkesine Company, formed in 1866. However, the business failed and was wound up two years later. A prolific inventor, Parkes filed over sixty other patents, largely connected to metallurgy. He devised a method to electroplate delicate objects, and on one occasion presented Prince Albert with a silver-coated spider's web. Parkes died in 1890 at the age of seventy-six.

***Grover Cleveland** took office as the president of the United States in 1885.*

Cleveland was voted out after his first term, but returned to the White House four years later, to become the only president in history to regain office. His two separate terms earned him the distinction of being both the twenty-second and twenty-fourth president. Cleveland, the first Democratic president to be elected after the civil war, is also the only president to have married in the White House when he wed the 21-year-old Frances Folsom in 1886. Cleveland actually won more of the popular vote in the 1888 election, but lost out on electoral college votes. He died in 1908 at the age of seventy-one.

***John Boyd Dunlop** applied for a patent for his pneumatic tyre in 1888.*

Inspired by his nine-year-old son John, who complained that the solid rubber tyres fitted to his tricycle made for a rough ride, Dunlop came up with the solution of air-filled tyres which he proved with his own prototypes. Dunlop was born in Dreghorn, Ayrshire, and qualified as a vet at the age of nineteen. He worked in Edinburgh for several years before relocating to Belfast where he established a successful practice. It was there that he developed his pneumatic tyre. Although his first patent was granted in December 1888, it was later ruled invalid since the principle had already been patented in 1845 by fellow Scot Robert William Thomson.

Prior to this, Dunlop had sold his 'patent' to Harvey Du Cros and took shares in the company, Pneumatic Tyre and Booth's Cycle Agency Limited. The setback over the patent was ameliorated by the firm securing other supplementary patents related to the pneumatic tyre. Dunlop resigned his directorship in 1895. In the following year the business was sold and then floated on the stock market as the Dunlop Pneumatic Tyre Company. It would go on to become one of the world's major tyre manufacturers. Dunlop filed many other patents that described improvements to bicycles as well as to the pneumatic tyre. He retired to Dublin where he died, in 1921, at the age of eighty-one.

Howard Carter led the excavations that discovered the tomb of the Egyptian pharaoh Tutankhamen in 1922.

Tutankhamen's tomb was the most intact burial chamber yet discovered in the Valley of the Kings. Carter was employed by George Herbert, fifth Earl of Carnarvon, who had an interest in archaeology and the wealth to fund excavation projects. They first teamed up in 1909 and enjoyed some success in their archaeological quests. In 1914 Carnarvon gained the rights to excavate in the Valley of the Kings, although work would not commence until three years later. By 1922, nothing significant had been found and Carnarvon decided to give up his concession, but Carter persuaded him to finance one more campaign which led to the spectacular discovery later that year. Carnarvon was quickly informed of the find by Carter, who waited on his arrival from England before entering the tomb. Carter spent the next ten years working on the clearance of the tomb; however Carnarvon died months after the discovery. Carter himself died at the age of sixty-four in 1939.

In 1928 mechanically sliced bread first went on commercial sale, in Chillicothe, Missouri, produced using a machine invented by **Otto Rohwedder**.

Rohwedder took out several patents relating to his bread-slicing apparatus which he later sold to the Micro-Westco Company, based in his home state of Iowa. Rohwedder first became interested in creating a bread-slicing machine when he was in his early thirties, but his progress received a setback a few years later, in 1917, when a fire at a factory destroyed his prototype and blueprints. Rohwedder needed to raise funds for a second attempt. Within five years of its arrival in the marketplace, sliced bread was outselling the unsliced version in the US. Rohwedder died in 1960, aged eighty.

In 1956 the Queen laid the foundation stone of Coventry Cathedral, designed by **Basil Spence**.

In 1951 Spence won the competition to design the new Coventry Cathedral, following the destruction of the previous building during World War Two. His proposal left the ruins of the old edifice alongside the new structure which was subsequently consecrated in 1962; the cathedral has since become his most famous work. Born in India to Orcadian parents, Spence completed his schooling in Edinburgh and attended the college of art there, subsequently studying architecture. His career was interrupted by service in the Second World War, but was re-established following his demobilisation. The commission for Coventry Cathedral brought him recognition and Spence found himself in demand for public building projects, many of which were the result of the expansion in higher education in the 1960s. These projects included the new University of Sussex, libraries at Edinburgh and Heriot-Watt universities, Glasgow airport, the British embassy in Rome and also housing developments. The latter did not always prove to be popular. The 'Hutchesontown C' development in the Gorbals area of Glasgow was demolished in 1993, less than thirty years after the first tenants took up residence. Spence, knighted in 1960, died in 1976 at the age of sixty-nine.

Max Perutz *shared the 1962 Nobel Prize in Chemistry for his work on determining the structure of the haemoglobin molecule.*

Born in Vienna, Perutz came to England to undertake his doctoral research at the Cavendish Laboratory in Cambridge in 1936. He began his work on X-ray crystallographic studies of proteins the following year. It took him twenty years of painstaking effort to identify the haemoglobin molecule's structure. Present in red blood cells, the function of this iron-containing protein is to transport oxygen around the body for the process of energy production. His colleague John Kendrew performed similar work on the molecule myoglobin and shared the Nobel Prize award. Perutz died in 2002 at the age of eighty-seven.

*In 1964 **Harold Wilson** became prime minister for the first time when Labour narrowly defeated the Conservatives to take power after a gap of thirteen years.*

Wilson was born in Huddersfield, Yorkshire. A former grammar-school boy, he excelled academically at Oxford, taking a first in politics, philosophy and economics, and became a don in his early twenties. He was placed in the civil service during the Second World War, and in 1945 was first elected to Parliament. Two years later, at the age of thirty-one, Wilson became the youngest Cabinet member of the twentieth century when he was made the president of the Board of Trade. He resigned in 1951 in protest at the budget and months later Labour lost power, which it wouldn't regain until Wilson's victory in 1964. Wilson called another election after eighteen months and in March 1966 his government was returned with its majority boosted from four to ninety-six. Four years later, Labour lost the general election to the Conservatives, led by Edward Heath. Wilson remained as the leader of the opposition and then returned to Downing Street after the first 1974 general election. Labour won more seats than the Conservatives, although they were slightly behind in terms of the percentage of the vote, but a hung Parliament necessitated a second election that year. This gave Labour a slender majority of three and they remained in power until 1979. Wilson announced his resignation as prime minister shortly after his sixtieth birthday in March 1976. Both of Wilson's periods as prime minister were dogged by challenging economic conditions. In foreign policy he had to grapple with the Rhodesian Declaration of Independence, the Vietnam War and Britain's role in Europe. Domestically, he oversaw the abolition of capital punishment and the establishment of the Open University in 1969. He was knighted in 1976 and created Baron Wilson of Rievaulx in 1983 after his departure from the Commons. He died in 1995 at the age of seventy-nine.

*In 1968 **Godfrey Hounsfield** filed a patent application for his computed tomography apparatus (the CT or CAT scan machine).*

Hounsfield's machine worked by detecting X-ray beams fired from various angles which were then combined using a computer to produce images of unparalleled detail of internal body structures. The first clinical trial took place in 1971 and the machine was formally announced in 1972. Initially these machines were used for examining the head, but a full body version was launched three years later. Hounsfield shared the 1979 Nobel Prize in Physiology or Medicine, at the age of sixty, with Allan Cormack who had independently worked on the development of the CAT technique. Hounsfield's background was unconventional for a Nobel science laureate. He joined the RAF as a volunteer reservist at the start of the Second World War and gained experience in radio and radar technology. After the war, Hounsfield attended Faraday House Electrical Engineering College in London where he obtained a diploma. He joined EMI in 1951 and seven years later headed the team that created Britain's first all-transistor computer, the EMIDEC 1100. After transferring to the Central Research Laboratories of EMI, he was given the opportunity to identify new areas that might prove productive, and it was during this period that he conceived the idea of computerised tomography (CT). Among many honours that he received, Hounsfield was elected to the fellowship of the Royal Society in 1975 and was knighted in 1981. He died in 2004 at the age of eighty-four.

'The Godfather' by **Mario Puzo** *was published in 1969.*

Puzo's first novel, *The Dark Arena*, appeared in 1955, followed ten years later by *The Fortunate Pilgrim*. Although well received by the critics, they did not generate high sales and Puzo, in his mid forties with a family to support and in debt, decided to write what he hoped would be a bestseller. He achieved this aim with his fifth novel: *The Godfather*. Puzo also co-wrote the screenplay for the film and its sequel with director Francis Ford Coppola. They shared the Academy Award for 'best adapted screenplay' for both films. They also collaborated on the third part of the trilogy released in 1990. Puzo's screenwriting credits also encompass the first two *Superman* movies. He died in 1999 at the age of seventy-eight.

Ruth Prawer Jhabvala *won the 1975 Booker Prize for 'Heat and Dust'.*

Jhabvala is also an acclaimed screenwriter with two Academy Awards to her credit for her adaptations of *A Room With a View* (1986) and

Howards End (1992). Her long-term collaboration with the film-makers James Ivory and Ismail Merchant began in 1963 when she was commissioned to produce a screenplay of her fourth novel, *The Householder*. To date Jhabvala has worked on over twenty films for their production company, with *The Remains of the Day* (1993) bringing her a further Oscar nomination. Her adaptation of *Heat and Dust* was rewarded with a Bafta in 1984. Jhabvala was awarded a CBE in 1998.

Joan Collins made her first appearance as Alexis Carrington in 'Dynasty' in 1981.

Collins made her debut in the first episode of the second run, and has been credited with transforming the fortunes of the programme, which ran for nine series until 1989. The part brought Collins Golden Globe nominations in six consecutive years (1982 to 1987), and she won once in 1983. Her feature film career began with a minor role in *Lady Godiva Rides Again* (1951). Since then she has appeared in over sixty films and has guest starred in television series such as *Star Trek*, *Tales of the Unexpected* and *Roseanne*. Collins is also a novelist; her first novel, *Prime Time*, was published in 1988. She was awarded an OBE in 1997 for her 'contribution to the arts, culture and charitable causes'.

*'I Dreamed a Dream', the first album by **Susan Boyle**, was released in 2009.*

Boyle's *I Dreamed a Dream* became the biggest-selling album worldwide of 2009 despite only being available for sale from late November. Boyle is also the oldest person to reach number one in the album chart with a debut offering. She shot to fame after her appearance on the ITV programme *Britain's Got Talent*. The Scottish singer's first performance, in which she sang what became the title track for her album, registered millions of hits on the video-sharing website YouTube as Boyle became an instant celebrity on both sides of the Atlantic. Despite this, she came second in the *Britain's Got Talent* final to the dance group Diversity. By the end of the year her first album was number one in several countries. Her second and third albums, *The Gift* and *Someone to Watch Over Me*, released in 2010 and 2011, also went straight to the top of the UK chart.

49
FORTY-NINE

John Stuart, third Earl of Bute, became prime minister in 1762.

Stuart was the first Scottish prime minister following the Act of Union in 1707, and also the first Tory to hold the position. His rise to power was aided by his tutelage of Prince George who ascended to the throne as George III and speedily made Stuart a member of the Privy Council. Following the resignation of Thomas Pelham-Holles, the Duke of Newcastle, Stuart was made prime minister. His closeness to the King made him powerful but unpopular. Although he spent less than a year in office, Stuart was able to negotiate an end to Britain's participation in the Seven Years' War with the Treaty of Paris. However, the settlement did not obtain universal approval; the former prime minister, William Pitt, was one critic and Stuart's opponents attacked him on the issue. His Scottish background was also disliked; it was less than twenty years since the Jacobite rebellion had ended with the Battle of Culloden in 1746. The introduction of a cider tax in 1763 fuelled more discontent and tired of the personal attacks, Stuart resigned. He continued to pursue his interest in botany – along with Princess Augusta he had established the first botanic garden at Kew in 1759. Stuart died in 1792 at the age of seventy-eight and is buried on the Isle of Bute.

*'Monarch of the Glen', by **Edwin Landseer**, was exhibited at the Royal Academy Exhibition in 1851.*

Landseer, known for his paintings of animals, first exhibited his work at the Royal Academy at the age of thirteen with his *Portrait of a Mule* and *Portraits of a Pointer Bitch and Puppy*. He first visited Scotland when he was in his early twenties, and his travels in the Highlands would provide inspiration for many of his major pieces. Although primarily a painter, Landseer also ventured into sculpture and produced the lions at the base of Nelson's Column in Trafalgar Square. The commission took nearly ten years to complete and the lions were unveiled in 1867 when he was sixty-four. Landseer died in 1873 at the age of seventy-one.

*In 1881 **James Garfield** became the twentieth president of the United States.*

A Union Army commander, Garfield was elected to the House of Representatives at the age of thirty, and resigned his military commission at the behest of President Lincoln. He was re-elected for the next eighteen years. Garfield, who narrowly won the popular vote in the 1880 presidential election, asserted the right of the president to make political appointments without undue influence from party factions. However, three months after the eve of his inauguration, he was shot by the disgruntled lawyer, Charles Guiteau, who had sought a diplomatic post. Garfield, with one bullet still lodged near his spine, died eleven weeks later. Guiteau was convicted of murder and hanged the following year.

*The Forth Rail Bridge, designed by **Benjamin Baker** and Sir John Fowler, was officially opened by the Prince of Wales on 4 March 1890.*

The Prince of Wales (the future Edward VII) inserted the last, specially gilded, rivet in the Forth Rail Bridge. Construction of the crossing, which is estimated to have cost up to one hundred men their lives, began in 1883. It held the record for being the longest cantilever bridge span in the world until the building of the Quebec Bridge nearly thirty years later, which has a span approximately twenty-eight metres longer (however, the Forth Bridge is over fifteen hundred metres greater in overall length than the Quebec Bridge). Somerset-born Baker had previously worked with Fowler as an assistant on the engineering of the London Underground. Following the completion of the Forth Rail Bridge, Baker became a consulting engineer for the Aswan Dam project in Egypt – the first dam across the Nile, it was completed in 1902. He was made a KCMG in 1890 and a KCB in 1902. Baker died in 1907 at the age of sixty-seven.

*'Dracula' by **Bram Stoker** was published in 1897.*

Abraham (Bram) Stoker was born in Dublin. His early childhood was marred by a mysterious illness which kept him bedridden and unable to walk until he was seven. Despite this, he later became a champion athlete at Trinity College, Dublin, where he studied science and mathematics. He joined the civil service, but also pursued his literary ambitions by publishing short stories and offering his services for free as a drama critic. The latter brought him into contact with Henry Irving who, in 1878, began to lease London's Lyceum Theatre. He invited Stoker to be the business manager which prompted Stoker's subsequent departure from the civil service. The Lyceum flourished under their auspices and in parallel Stoker was able to work on his writing. Stoker produced his first full-length novel, *The Snake's Pass*, in 1890. He then began researching his novel *Dracula*, originally called *The Un-Dead*. Irving was the role model for the mannerisms and entrancing personality of the Count. Stoker's later works include the novels *The Jewel of Seven Stars* and *The Lair of the White Worm*, as well as the biography *Personal Reminiscences of Henry Irving*. Stoker died in London in 1912, aged sixty-four.

'The Wind in the Willows' by **Kenneth Grahame** *was published in 1908.*

Grahame, denied the funds needed to attend Oxford University, instead took a job at the Bank of England at the age of nineteen. (He notably scored full marks for the essay that was part of the qualifying test.) Grahame's career developed swiftly and he rose to become the secretary of the bank before the turn of the century. In tandem with his duties at the bank, Grahame also began to forge a literary reputation. His first book of collected essays was published in 1893 and was followed by *The Golden Age* (1895), *Dream Days* (1898) and *The Headswoman* (1898). In 1903 he was involved in a bizarre incident at the bank, when he was shot at by a man who had asked him to read some papers. He was uninjured, although the visitor discharged several more shots inside the bank before being apprehended. Grahame retired five years later, shortly before the publication of *Wind in the Willows*. He died in 1932 at the age of seventy-three.

Trygve Lie *was elected as the first secretary-general of the United Nations in 1946.*

A native of Oslo, Lie was elected to the Norwegian Parliament in 1937 and held a number of government posts. He served as foreign minister prior to his UN appointment. Lie's recommendation for UN intervention in the Korean War, and his declaration that North Korea was the aggressor, drew criticism from the Soviet Union who were expected to veto his re-election. Lie's term was extended by a resolution of the General Assembly, but continuing Soviet refusal to recognise his position precipitated his resignation in 1952. He died in 1968 at the age of seventy-two.

The first road-going car to bear the name of **Enzo Ferrari**, *the 125 S, made its debut in 1947.*

The 125 S was the first car to be produced by Ferrari's new company, the aim of which was to use the sale of production models in order to fund Ferrari's motor sport ambitions. Ferrari himself had been a racing driver; ten years into his career in 1929 he formed a racing team, Scuderia Ferrari, initially with the aim of enabling owner-drivers to compete. The team essentially became Alfa Romeo's racing department in 1933 and was later absorbed into a new official Alfa team, which Ferrari left in 1939. A condition of his departure was that he could not use his name for racing cars, or races, for four years. He began the design of the V12-engined 125 S in late 1945 and formed the Ferrari Company in 1947. The Ferrari team secured their debut Formula One Grand Prix win at Monaco in 1950, and took the first of their sixteen constructors' titles – more than any other team – in 1961. Enzo Ferrari died in 1988 at the age of ninety.

The trademark Scrabble, for the word game devised by **Alfred Butts**, *was registered in 1948.*

The origins of Scrabble go back to 1931 when Butts, then an unemployed architect, wanted to create a new game which required a mixture of skill and luck. His first version, which did not use a board, was called Lexiko. In 1938 he added a board, as well as the familiar crossword-style format, and renamed the game Criss Cross Words. There was no interest from the games manufacturers he approached. Finally, ten years later, his creation found a champion in James Brunot who bought the rights, with Butts receiving a royalty payment for every set sold. Some minor adjustments were made and the new name 'Scrabble' was coined. Sales were sluggish in the early years, but the game took off, sales escalated and, in order to keep pace with demand, Brunot licensed its production to one of the manufacturers who had originally turned it down. Butts lived to see the first World Scrabble Championship in 1991. He died two years later at the age of ninety-three.

Wilfrid Brambell *first appeared as Albert Steptoe in a BBC 'Comedy Playhouse' episode called 'The Offer' in 1962.*

'The Offer' spawned the long-running *Steptoe and Son* series, which was broadcast from 1962 until 1974. Brambell, whose television career began in the 1950s, was only thirteen years older than Harry H. Corbett, who played his son Harold in the story of the two rag-and-bone men living in Oil Drum Lane. Brambell also appeared as Paul McCartney's grand-father in the first Beatles' film *A Hard Day's Night*, released in 1964. He died in 1985 at the age of seventy-two.

In 1989 'Foreign Affair' gave **Tina Turner** *her first UK number one album.*

Turner's seventh solo album, *Foreign Affair* entered the UK chart at number one. Several singles were plucked from it, with 'The Best' reaching number five in the UK. Born Anna Mae Bullock in Brownsville, Tennessee, her recording career started as a teenager. Alongside her husband Ike, she enjoyed success in the 1960s with hits including 'River Deep – Mountain High'. Their marriage came to an end in the seventies and she relaunched her career as a solo artist. 'What's Love Got to Do with It', taken from the album *Private Dancer*, gave her a first US number one single in 1984. Approaching seventy, she completed her '50th Anniversary Tour' in 2009.

Michael Ondaatje *was awarded the 1992 Booker Prize for his novel 'The English Patient'.*

The film adaptation of Ondaatje's *The English Patient*, released in 1996, scooped multiple Oscars at the Academy Awards including best picture. Ondaatje was born in Ceylon (now Sri Lanka). He then spent the latter half of his childhood in England before settling in Canada and taking up a teaching position at York University, Ontario. His first novel *Coming Through Slaughter* was published in 1976. Prior to that, Ondaatje completed several volumes of poetry that include *The Dainty Monsters* (1967) and *The Man with Seven Toes* (1969). Ondaatje has published five novels, the latest of which is *The Cat's Table* (2011). He shared the 1992 Booker Prize with Barry Unsworth for his novel *Sacred Hunger*.

Martina Navratilova, *partnered with Bob Bryan, won the mixed doubles title at the 2006 US Open to become the oldest tennis Grand Slam winner in history.*

Navratilova won her first Grand Slam title, aged twenty-one, at Wimbledon in 1978 – the first of a record nine wins at the London venue. She chalked up nine successive appearances in the singles final between 1982 and 1990, only losing in 1988 and 1989. Navratilova's victory in 1990 over Zina Garrison was her final Wimbledon and Grand Slam singles title. A national champion in her native Czechoslovakia aged fifteen, she contested her first Grand Slam final at the Australian Open in 1975. Navratilova has won a career total of eighteen Grand Slam singles tournaments and thirty-one Grand Slam women's doubles tournaments. She stepped back from professional singles competition, at the age of thirty-seven, shortly after her last Wimbledon singles final in 1994 when she lost to Conchita Martinez. Navratilova enjoyed further success in doubles, reaching the final of the women's competition at the 2003 US Open and in the same year winning the mixed doubles at the Australian Open and Wimbledon. In 2004, at the age of forty-seven, she became the oldest winner of a singles match at Wimbledon in the open era, when she triumphed in her first-round tie.

CHAPTER SIX

Quinquagenarians

I never worry about the future. It comes soon enough.

ALBERT EINSTEIN

50
FIFTY

William Harvey published his discovery of the circulation of blood in 1628.

Harvey's account of his medical breakthrough was contained in *Exercitatio Anatomica de Motu Cordis et Sanguinis in Animalibus (Anatomical Exercise on the Motion of the Heart and Blood in Animals)*. His theory, developed over a number of years, challenged the accepted view of blood movement, based on the work of the Greek physician Galen who died in the early third century. Harvey's radical circulatory idea was not immediately accepted, although with time a consensus developed in his favour. Harvey, who was also the court physician to both James I (& VI) and Charles I, died in 1657 at the age of seventy-nine.

George Grenville succeeded the Earl of Bute as prime minister in 1763.

As a prime minister, Grenville was not popular, especially with King George III who dismissed him in 1765 after only two years of service. While in office Grenville's government passed the Stamp Act, which taxed various printed materials in the American colonies. It sowed the seeds of discontent that would subsequently flare up in the American War of Independence. Grenville did not hold high office again after his dismissal, and died five years later at the age of fifty-eight. His son William also became prime minister.

In 1845 James Polk was sworn in as the eleventh president of the United States.

Polk's term as president saw US territory grow significantly. The south west region (including the area of present day California, most of Arizona, Nevada, Utah, and parts of Colorado and New Mexico) was purchased from the Mexicans following the conclusion of the two-year-long Mexican–American War in 1848. Polk also settled the dispute over the Oregon territory with the British. This fixed the boundary with what would later become Canada at the 49th parallel. Today this region largely

353

comprises the states of Oregon, Washington and Idaho. The state of Texas also joined the fold just prior to his inauguration, with the official recognition of its new status confirmed at the end of 1845. Polk's exertions as president damaged his health and he died, at the age of fifty-four, less than four months after leaving office in 1849.

'On the Origin of Species by Means of Natural Selection, or the Preservation of Favoured Races in the Struggle for Life', written by **Charles Darwin**, *was published in 1859.*

A momentous scientific work, Darwin's book elucidated his hypothesis that the diversity of species was due to the process of evolution – gradual changes with time precipitated by the struggle for survival. The idea was particularly controversial for the Victorian era since it ran counter to the belief of a Biblical Creation. Darwin had first conceived his theory some twenty years previously. Its publication in *Origin of Species* was in part spurred on by a similar theory advanced by Alfred Wallace, which was first published in 1856. A joint paper by the two men, with extracts from an 1844 essay by Darwin, was presented to the Linnaean society in 1858. Darwin came from a prosperous family and, expected to follow in his father's footsteps, embarked on the study of medicine at the University of Edinburgh. However, he didn't find the subject to his liking. Darwin was more interested in natural history, which he was able to explore through his extra-curricular activities before leaving Edinburgh without a medical degree. His father guided him instead towards a career in the Church of England. As a first step, Darwin enrolled at Christ's College, Cambridge, for a BA degree, where he became acquainted with the professor of botany, John Henslow. After graduation, it was Henslow who recommended him for the vacancy on the impending voyage of HMS *Beagle* as a collector and companion for the captain, Robert Fitzroy. Its five-year mission gave Darwin a superb opportunity to study the natural environment and equipped him for his work on natural selection. The *Beagle* arrived back in Falmouth, Cornwall, in 1836, and Darwin's findings would occupy him in the coming years, although he did find time to marry his cousin, Emma Wedgwood, in 1839. After the publication of *Origin of Species*, Darwin published further supplementary works on evolution. He died in 1882 at the age of seventy-three and was buried in Westminster Abbey, close to the resting place of Sir Isaac Newton.

Joseph Swan *demonstrated his incandescent light bulb in 1878.*

Swan gave a demonstration of his light bulb, which used a carbon conductor to generate illumination, at a meeting of the Newcastle-upon-Tyne Chemical Society. Swan, whose first experiments in this area dated back to the 1840s, was slow to patent his light bulb technology; he filed his first, for the bulb's evacuation process, in 1880. Others followed, including one for an improved filament. Thomas Edison had patented his light bulb in Britain in 1879, also utilising a carbon filament, and disputes over priority were ended when Swan and Edison joined forces to commercially produce light bulbs in Britain. Swan left school at thirteen to become an apprentice in a firm of druggists and later joined his future brother-in-law in a similar venture. Swan also made many contributions to the development of photography. These included the invention of 'bromide paper', the patent for which was later purchased by George Eastman, the founder of Kodak. Swan was knighted in 1904 by King Edward VII. He died ten years later at the age of eighty-five.

Wilhelm Röntgen *made his first discovery of X-rays in 1895.*

While working at the University of Munich, Röntgen noticed that when he operated his apparatus for studying cathode rays (beams of electrons), nearby crystals of barium platinocyanide glowed. Röntgen proceeded to study this phenomenon, and came to the conclusion that some new type of ray was responsible, which he labelled as X for unknown. The first person to have an X-ray image taken was his wife Anna; the resulting picture of her hand clearly showed the bones of her fingers. Röntgen published his findings at the end of 1895, within weeks of his initial discovery. He refused to take out any patents in connection with X-rays, and was also not keen on the alternative term 'Röntgen rays'. In 1901 he was awarded the first Nobel Prize in Physics for his discovery. Röntgen died in 1923 at the age of seventy-seven.

Robert Baden-Powell *led what was, in effect, the first Boy Scout camp at Brownsea Island, Dorset, in 1907.*

Twenty-two boys had been assembled to test out Baden-Powell's ideas on Scout training, which he published the following year as *Scouting for Boys*. It became one of the biggest-selling books of the twentieth century. The

Scout movement grew rapidly both at home and abroad, with the first World Scout Jamboree being held in 1920 in London. Baden-Powell had had a distinguished career as an army officer, and served in India and Afghanistan. His role during the second Boer War in the siege of Mafeking, where he commanded its defence for over two hundred days until relief arrived in 1900, brought him hero status in Britain. Later in that year he was promoted to major-general. Baden-Powell retired from the army in 1910 to fully devote himself to the Scout movement, and also to the setting up of the Girl Guides in association with his sister Agnes. He met his future wife Olave, who shared his birthday and was thirty-two years younger, in 1912. They married in the same year and she would later take up the running of the Girl Guides. Baden-Powell was proclaimed Chief Scout in 1920, made a baronet in 1922 and a baron in 1929. Four years after his appointment to the Order of Merit in 1937, he died at the age of eighty-three.

In 1918 **Constance Markiewicz** *became the first woman to be elected to the United Kingdom Parliament.*

Markiewicz was elected as the Sinn Féin member for the St. Patrick's division in Dublin, but, as per her party's policy, did not take her seat in the House of Commons. (In 1921 Lady Astor became the first elected woman to sit in Parliament.) Born Constance Gore-Booth in London into an Anglo–Irish family, she spent most of her childhood at the family house in County Sligo, but studied art in London and Paris where she met her future husband, the Polish Count Dunin-Markiewicz. They moved to Dublin in 1908 where she developed an interest in Irish nationalism which led her to participate in the armed 'Easter Rising' in 1916, which aimed to create an independent Irish republic. She later faced the death penalty for her involvement. The sentence was commuted to penal servitude for life and she was released after fourteen months following a general amnesty in June 1917. Markiewicz was re-arrested the following year and it was while she was in prison that she was elected to the House of Commons. Markiewicz was against the Anglo–Irish treaty that set up the Irish Free State and fought for the republican side in the ensuing civil war. She was elected in 1923 to the Free State Parliament, but again did not take her seat, refusing to take the oath of allegiance to the King. Markiewicz died four years later at the age of fifty-nine.

In 1939 'The Big Sleep' was the first novel by **Raymond Chandler** *to be published.*

Chandler was in his forties when his career as a crime-fiction writer began. He started with short stories and had his first, 'Blackmailers Don't Shoot', published in 1933 in the magazine *Black Mask*. His work attracted the attention of a publisher and led him to write his first novel, which introduced the private eye Philip Marlowe. Six further Marlowe books followed in the next twenty years, including *Farewell My Lovely, The High Window* and his last completed novel, *Playback*, published in 1959, the year of his death at the age of seventy. Chandler was also sought out as a Hollywood screenwriter, and was Academy Award nominated along with Billy Wilder for *Double Indemnity* (1944) and on his own account for *The Blue Dahlia* (1946).

Alexander Todd was awarded the 1957 Nobel Prize in Chemistry 'for his work on nucleotides and nucleotide co-enzymes'.

Todd's work was important for the formulation of the DNA double helix model proposed by Crick and Watson in 1953. He also led a group of scientists at Cambridge University who determined the chemical structure of vitamin B12 in 1955, thus enabling its synthetic production. Earlier in his career he was one of the first chemists to investigate the structure of vitamin B1 (thiamine) and he also developed a process for its manufacture. Todd received a knighthood in 1954, a peerage in 1962 to become Lord Todd, Baron of Trumpington, and was appointed to the Order of Merit in 1977. He died twenty years later at the age of eighty-nine.

In 1958 **David Lean** *won the Academy Award for best director for 'Bridge on the River Kwai'.*

Bridge on the River Kwai gave Lean the fourth of his seven best director Oscar nominations, the first coming for *Brief Encounter* in 1947. He also won again with *Lawrence of Arabia* in 1963. Lean's final Academy Award nominations were for his last film, *A Passage to India*, in 1985, when he was up for best director, best adapted screenplay and editing. Lean had established his reputation as an editor early on his career, after rising through the ranks from clapperboard operator. He received the Bafta fellowship in 1974 and was knighted ten years later. Lean never won a competitive Bafta Award (among others he was nominated once for best direction, in 1971, for *Ryan's Daughter*), but after his death in 1991 at the age of eighty-three, Bafta's top directing prize was renamed the David Lean Award in his honour.

In 1965 **Stanley Matthews** *played in the top division of English football for the last time.*

Matthews made his final appearance, at the age of fifty, for Stoke City, in their 3–1 defeat of Fulham. He remains the oldest player to have played in the top division of English football. Weeks before that game, he had been knighted in the New Year Honours list, the first (and so far the only) time that a player has received this honour before retirement from the sport. Matthews began his career with Stoke City and transferred to Blackpool in 1947, where he picked up his only major domestic trophy, the FA Cup, in 1953. In what was dubbed the 'Matthews final', Blackpool came back from 3–1 down, with twenty-five minutes to play, to win 4–3, with Matthews supplying the pass for the winning goal in the dying seconds of normal time. Three years later, he became the first European footballer of the year. In 1957 Matthews was awarded a CBE, and, at the age of forty-two, he played his last game for England in a World Cup qualifier against Denmark. He remains England's oldest football international. Matthews returned to Stoke City for his final seasons in English football and he was able to celebrate the team's promotion back to the first division in 1963. He was never cautioned or sent off as a player. Matthews died in 2000, aged eighty-five.

The inaugural Booker Prize was awarded to **P. H. Newby** *(Percy Howard) in 1969 for 'Something to Answer For'.*

The victory, in which Newby was notified of the outcome by post, won him a trophy and a cheque for £5,000. He made his published debut in 1945 with *Journey to the Interior*, the first of twenty-three novels in a literary career that Newby combined with his work at the BBC. He joined the corporation in 1949 and progressed from radio show production, through appointments such as controller of Radio 3, to reach the position of managing director of BBC Radio in 1975. He published four novels after his retirement from the BBC in 1978, the last of which was *Something About Women* in 1995, two years before his death at the age of seventy-nine. Newby was awarded a CBE in 1972 for his work at the BBC.

The pilot episode of 'Are You Being Served?', co-written by **David Croft** *and Jeremy Lloyd, was first broadcast in 1972.*

The idea for the show was based on Lloyd's short-lived retail experience in the 1950s. Croft and Lloyd were the main writers for the comedy show set in the Grace Brothers department store, which ran for ten series and finally ended in 1985. The show was a huge ratings success. Croft also worked with Jimmy Perry on the hugely popular *Dad's Army*, as well as *It Ain't Half Hot Mum*, *Hi-de-Hi!* and *You Rang, M'Lord*. Croft, who received an OBE in 1978, also scored another hit with Jeremy Lloyd – the series '*Allo 'Allo!*', broadcast between 1982 and 1992. Croft died in 2011 at the age of eighty-nine.

The first book by **Richard Adams** *to be published was 'Watership Down' in 1972.*

An epic adventure novel about a group of rabbits, *Watership Down* grew out of stories that Adams would tell to his two daughters on long car journeys. It became a bestseller and launched his career as a writer, allowing him to leave the civil service where he'd worked for over twenty-five years. He followed up *Watership Down* with *Shardik* in 1974. Adams's other books include *The Plague Dogs* (1977), *The Girl in a Swing* (1980) and *The Outlandish Knight* (1999).

Ian McEwan *won the 1998 Booker Prize for 'Amsterdam'.*

McEwan made his literary debut with a collection of short stories, *First Love, Last Rites*, in 1975. His first novel, *The Cement Garden*, was published three years later. It was followed by *The Comfort of Strangers* (1981), his first to be shortlisted for the Booker Prize, an honour similarly bestowed on *Black Dogs* (1992), *Atonement* (2001) and *On Chesil Beach* (2007). McEwan's other novels include the Whitbread award-winning *The Child in Time* (1987) and *Enduring Love* (1997). Several of his works have been adapted for the cinema, with *Atonement* winning the 2008 Bafta Award for best film. McEwan has also written directly for the screen and made his debut with *The Ploughman's Lunch* in 1983. He was awarded a CBE in 2000.

In 2011 **Colin Firth** *won both the Academy Award and Bafta for best actor for his performance as George VI in 'The King's Speech'.*

Firth had attended the previous Oscar ceremony as a best actor nominee for his role in *A Single Man* (2009), which brought him a first Bafta best actor win. His success at the Academy Awards mirrored his Golden Globe record, with a nomination for *A Single Man* (2009) and a win for *The King's Speech* (2010). Firth's screen career began in the 1980s and before the end of the decade he had received his first Bafta TV best actor nomination for the Falklands War drama *Tumbledown* (1988). His impact as Mr Darcy in the 1995 BBC production of *Pride and Prejudice* provided him with a second Bafta TV nomination. Firth's film career took off in the 1990s with well-received roles in *The English Patient* (1996), *Fever Pitch* (1997) and *Shakespeare in Love* (1998). He played another Mr Darcy in *Bridget Jones's Diary* (2001), picking up a Bafta nomination for best supporting actor. Firth was awarded a CBE in the 2011 Queen's Birthday Honours.

51

FIFTY-ONE

In 1503 it was recorded that **Leonardo da Vinci** *was painting the 'Mona Lisa'.*

Arguably the world's most famous painting, da Vinci's *Mona Lisa* (also known as *La Gioconda*) was created on a poplar wood panel, and now hangs in the Louvre, Paris. It is thought that da Vinci began the work, which featured Lisa del Giocondo (née Gherardini), the wife of a Florentine merchant, in 1503. A towering figure of the Renaissance, da Vinci's talent was wide-ranging and encompassed scientific as well as artistic pursuits. Many of his inventions, for example his flying machines, were ahead of their time. His other artwork includes the celebrated mural, *The Last Supper*, completed in Milan at the close of the fifteenth century, and the drawing referred to as *Vitruvian Man*, which features a human figure within a square and a circle, showing da Vinci's interest in anatomy.

Da Vinci died less than three weeks after his sixty-seventh birthday, in 1519.

The invention of the photographic process developed by **Louis Daguerre** *was announced in 1839.*

Daguerre's technique was the first successful, practicable means of recording an image and could produce spectacular results. However, it also had drawbacks: pictures could not be reproduced, a mirror image was obtained and the surface was extremely fragile. The process was superseded as photography advanced. Daguerre was a scenery painter for the opera, who in the late 1820s began collaborating with Joseph Niépce on a photographic process. (Niépce had been the first person to make a permanent photographic image a few years earlier.) Niépce died in 1833, but Daguerre continued to make progress. He discovered how to develop the image (captured on a copper plate with a light sensitive silver iodide coating) using mercury vapour and how to fix it using a salt solution. Exposure times of twenty minutes in bright light were needed to create a satisfactory image. Daguerreotypes became very popular, particularly as the process was gifted to the world by the French government in 1839, with Daguerre and Niépce's son receiving pensions by way of compensation. (However, in Britain a patent had been taken out on the process shortly before the French government's announcement, which restricted its adoption in Britain and also encouraged the development of alternatives.) Daguerre died in 1851 at the age of sixty-three.

In 1841 **John Tyler** *became the first US vice-president to assume the presidency following the death of an incumbent, namely, William Harrison.*

Tyler entered the highest political office in the US only a month after Harrison's inauguration, to serve as the tenth president. Notable events during his tenure were the bill to allow the annexation of the Republic of Texas (which became the twenty-eighth state in December 1845 after Tyler had left office) and the signing of the Webster–Ashburton treaty which settled a boundary dispute with the British North American colonies (later to become Canada). Tyler was not selected to run for a second term. Prior to the civil war, he supported the view that each state should have the right to determine its status as either 'slave' or 'free'. When the civil war broke out he joined the Confederate side and was elected to their House of Representatives. Tyler died in 1862, at the age of seventy-one, before he could take up his position.

Abraham Lincoln *was sworn in as the sixteenth president of the United States in 1861.*

Lincoln, the first Republican to hold office, did so in a period dominated by the civil war. Born in a Kentucky log cabin, he rose from humble origins (and despite limited formal education) to become a lawyer and politician while still only in his twenties. The potent issue of slavery dominated his attempt to gain election to the Senate in 1858 and his debates with his Democratic rival, Stephen Douglas, brought Lincoln's anti-slavery view to the national stage. (Douglas had argued that individual states should have the right to determine whether slavery was allowed or not.) By the time Lincoln took office, seven southern states had left the Union and declared themselves the Confederate States of America (four more states joined within weeks). The civil war began with a Confederate attack on the Union forces at Fort Sumter just over a month after Lincoln, who was determined to preserve his country's national integrity, was inaugurated. Progress was made on the issue of slavery under Lincoln, with his declaration of freedom for all Confederate slaves coming into effect in 1863. In the same year he made his Gettysburg Address, which redefined the civil war as also a fight for freedom and equality. Lincoln was re-elected in 1864 and the war was won the following year, but he did not live to see the surrender of all the Confederate forces. He became the first US president to be assassinated when John Wilkes Booth, an actor and Confederate sympathiser, shot him while he was watching a play at Ford's Theatre in Washington. Lincoln was fifty-five.

Gottlieb Daimler *and Wilhelm Maybach created the first motorcycle (reitwagen) by fitting an engine into a wooden bicycle frame in 1885.*

The engine was one of Daimler and Maybach's own designs, and was characterised by its lightness and fast running ability. They had both worked at the engine maker Deutz before leaving to develop their own versions. In 1889 they constructed their first car, and the following year the company *Daimler-Motoren-Gesellschaft* (DMG) was formed. The business struggled financially and received investment from several backers, but as a result both Daimler and Maybach were forced out. It was not until 1892, when Daimler was fifty-eight, that DMG sold its first car. He died seven years later. The Mercedes-Benz brand was created after the merger of DMG and Benz & Cie. in 1926.

*The new London department store of **Harry Gordon Selfridge** was opened in Oxford Street in 1909.*

The store, which took Selfridge's name, cost approximately £400,000 to build, and included 130 departments spread over seven levels. It also boasted a library as well as a rooftop garden, offering Londoners a new shopping experience. Selfridge had already had a successful career in American retailing. He worked his way up from the shop floor to become a partner in a major retail outlet in Chicago and amassed a sizeable personal fortune as a result. He left the business in 1904 and moved to London in 1906, where he began planning his new store. Later in life he enjoyed spending his wealth, aided by a passion for gambling. He died in 1947 at the age of eighty-nine.

*In 1948 **Patrick Blackett** was awarded the Nobel Prize in Physics for developing the 'Wilson cloud chamber', and for his discoveries in nuclear physics and cosmic radiation.*

After serving in the Royal Navy during World War One, Blackett read physics and mathematics at Cambridge. He went on to work at the Cavendish Laboratory in Cambridge, where he began to develop the cloud chamber. This apparatus makes visible the tracks created by ionizing radiation, such as alpha particles. In 1924 Blackett used the cloud chamber to obtain, for the first time, pictures of transmutation as one element is transformed into another, in this case nitrogen to oxygen, by its collision with an alpha particle. In 1933 he detected the existence of the positron ('positively charged electron'). He was made a life peer in 1969 and died in 1974, at the age of seventy-six.

***Nadine Gordimer** was awarded the 1974 Booker Prize for 'The Conservationist'.*

The South African author's debut was a short-story collection, *Face to Face*, in 1949. Gordimer's first novel, *The Lying Days*, came four years later and, like later works, was infused with her experience of living in Apartheid-era South Africa. Her opposition to Apartheid led her to join the African National Congress, a then illegal organisation. Gordimer has published numerous short-story collections. Her other novels include *A World of Strangers* (1958), *Burger's Daughter* (1979), *The Pickup* (2001) and her latest, *No Time Like The Present* (2012). Gordimer was awarded the Nobel Prize in Literature in 1991. She shared the 1974 Booker Prize with Stanley Middleton for *Holiday*.

Chris Tarrant *was the quizmaster for the first edition of 'Who Wants to be a Millionaire', broadcast in 1998.*

Tarrant has presented the UK version of the show since its inception. Five contestants have won the top prize of £1,000,000, the first being Judith Keppel in 2000. Tarrant, a former schoolteacher, made his name on television as a co-host on the Saturday morning children's show *Tiswas*, first broadcast in 1974. In addition to *'Millionaire'*, he has also presented *Tarrant on TV*, a programme that takes a look at some of the more unusual TV offerings from around the world. Tarrant was awarded an OBE in 2004.

52
FIFTY-TWO

*'An Inquiry Into The Natures and Causes of The Wealth of Nations', written by **Adam Smith**, was first published in 1776.*

Smith's *The Wealth of Nations* is a key work in the subject of economics. He espoused the benefits of a free-market economy and how it was best suited to deliver a fair outcome for both buyers and sellers. Smith also advocated that a division of labour, breaking up a large task into many smaller ones, would boost productivity. *The Wealth of Nations* was a hugely influential text and still finds resonance today, over two hundred years after its publication. Born in Kirkcaldy, Fife, Smith studied at the University of Glasgow and later at Balliol College, Oxford. He returned to Glasgow in 1751 to become professor of logic and subsequently professor of moral philosophy. Smith's *Theory of Moral Sentiments* appeared in 1759. Later he took up a position as a travelling private tutor, which afforded him the opportunity of a continental tour as well as a pension for life. Smith returned from Europe in 1766 and settled once more in Kirkcaldy where he spent the next few years writing *The Wealth of Nations*. Smith died in 1790 at the age of sixty-seven.

*The steamship 'Britannia', with **Samuel Cunard** on board, made its maiden voyage across the Atlantic from Liverpool to Halifax in 1840.*

The voyage on *Britannia* took fourteen days and eight hours, which was considered swift for the time. In the previous year, Cunard had been granted the first contract to carry mail across the Atlantic by the British government. He subsequently formed with others the British and North American Royal Steam Packet Company, which would later become known as the Cunard Line, to exploit the concession. It was the first company to take passengers on a regularly scheduled transatlantic service, with four steamships in operation on the route. Cunard, a native of Canada, was already a successful merchant and shipowner by the time he won the transatlantic mail contract. He was made a baronet in 1859 and died, at the age of seventy-seven, in 1865.

***Edward Stanley**, fourteenth Earl of Derby, became prime minister for the first time in 1852.*

Stanley entered Parliament in 1820 as a Whig and later served in Lord Grey's government during the 1830s, but resigned after a disagreement with the prime minister over Irish church revenues. He also crossed the floor of the Commons to sit with the Conservatives. Stanley joined Peel's cabinet as colonial secretary in 1841, but again resigned from government, this time over his opposition to the repeal of the Corn Laws. His first premiership lasted less than one year – his second, which began six years later, lasted for nearly sixteen months. (A notable event in this period was the passing of the Government of India Act which transferred the authority for India to the Crown from the British East India Company.) Stanley's third and final stint as prime minister began in 1866 when he was sixty-seven, but again his government was short-lived, lasting only twenty months. However, it did have enough time to pass the Second Reform

Act in 1867, which doubled the size of the electorate. Stanley retired from Parliament the following year due to ill health and was succeeded by Benjamin Disraeli. The Conservatives then lost the general election in 1869, the first after the Reform Act, to the Liberal Party. Stanley had died weeks before, at the age of seventy. He still holds the record as the longest-serving Conservative leader. When he was the colonial secretary in 1845, the capital of the Falkland Islands was named after him.

In 1904 **William Ramsay** *was awarded the Nobel Prize in Chemistry for his work in the discovery of the elements known as the noble or inert gases.*

Born in Glasgow, Ramsay studied at the University of Glasgow and afterwards at Tübingen, Germany, where he received his PhD in chemistry in 1872. Working in tandem with Lord Rayleigh, Ramsay investigated atmospheric nitrogen and in 1894 they made a joint announcement that they had found a new gas which was named argon from the Greek word for 'idle'. In the following year, during experiments with the mineral cleveite, Ramsay isolated the gas helium, previously undiscovered terrestrially, although it had been observed in the sun's spectrum. He postulated that a new eighth group of elements could be added to the periodic table and in 1898, along with his student Morris Travers, proceeded to find the gaseous elements krypton (hidden), neon (new) and xenon (stranger). In later work with Robert Whytlaw-Gray, he showed that the element radon also belonged to the same (eighth) group in the periodic table. He was knighted in 1902, and two years later he became the first British recipient of the Nobel Prize in Chemistry. Ramsay died in 1916 at the age of sixty-three.

In 1955 **Ray Kroc** *opened his first McDonald's restaurant in Des Plaines, Illinois.*

Kroc, a long-established paper cup salesman, changed to selling a new product when he bought the rights to a Multimixer milkshake machine. After many years in this line of work, news reached him of a restaurant in San Bernardino, California, with eight of the Multimixers installed. It was run by Dick and Mac McDonald, and Kroc, then aged fifty-two, decided to investigate. He was impressed with their operation's cleanliness, simple menu, low prices and undoubted popularity, and Kroc saw the opportunity to open more restaurants (which he hoped would generate more Multimixer sales) along the same lines. He struck a deal with the brothers and in 1955

Kroc's first McDonald's restaurant was opened. The hundredth restaurant was opened in 1959 and subsequently Kroc bought out the brothers who gave their name to the chain. The 'Big Mac' first appeared in 1968, created by Jim Delligatti, one of the first McDonald's franchise holders. Ten years later the 5,000th restaurant, located in Japan, opened. Kroc remained as chairman until his death, in 1984, at the age of eighty-one.

Alec Issigonis headed the design team that produced the Mini, which first went on sale in 1959.

The Mini, originally offered by the British Motor Corporation (BMC) as both the Austin Seven and Morris Mini-Minor, used a transversely mounted engine to drive the front wheels. Its design dedicated approximately 80 percent of the car's volume to the passengers and their luggage. The original car sold in its millions, with production finally coming to an end in 2000. Issigonis was born in Smyrna (now Izmir), Turkey, to a father of Greek origin with British citizenship. After his father died, he travelled with his mother to London in 1923 and became an engineering student at Battersea Polytechnic (the forerunner of the University of Surrey). Issigonis left with a diploma and began his engineering career in 1928; he joined Morris Motors in 1936. His first car design, the Morris Minor, was launched in 1948 and continued in production for over twenty years. Issigonis left the merged company of Austin and Morris (BMC) in 1952, but returned three years later to embark on the project that would create the Mini. Issigonis was also responsible for the 1100/1300 range brought out by BMC in the sixties. He was awarded a CBE in 1964 and was knighted in 1969. Issigonis died in 1988 at the age of eighty-one.

Arthur Lowe first appeared as Captain George Mainwaring in the television series 'Dad's Army' in 1968.

Playing the leader of a Home Guard platoon in the fictional Walmington-on-sea, Lowe chalked up nine series of the comedy that concluded in 1977. His first long-running television role was as Leonard Swindley in *Coronation Street* from 1960 to 1965. Lowe's stage work included parts such as Stephano in *The Tempest* and Hudson in John Osborne's *Inadmissible Evidence*. He also appeared in films including *This Sporting Life* (1963) and *O Lucky Man!* (1973). Lowe died in 1982 at the age of sixty-six.

*In 1977 **Jimmy Carter**, representing the Democratic Party, was inaugurated as the thirty-ninth president of the United States.*

Carter, a formal naval officer, peanut farmer and governor of Georgia, defeated the sitting president, Gerald Ford, who had been sworn in after the resignation of Richard Nixon in 1974. Carter's major foreign policy achievements included brokering the Camp David accords that resulted in a peace agreement between Egypt and Israel, the establishment of full diplomatic relations with China and the signing of the Torrijos-Carter treaties that gave control of the Panama Canal to Panama. In the domestic arena he created the Department of Energy and expanded the national park system. Carter also promoted energy conservation and had solar panels installed on the roof of the west wing of the White House (later removed by his successor, Ronald Reagan). His last fourteen months in the presidency were overshadowed by the Iranian hostage crisis, when fifty-two Americans were detained in Tehran. They were released shortly after Reagan was sworn in as president in 1981. Since leaving the White House, Carter has focused on human rights and conflict resolution. He was awarded the Nobel Peace Prize in 2002; the first ex-US president to receive this honour.

__Paul Eddington__ played Jim Hacker in 'Yes, Minister', which was first broadcast in 1980.

Although Eddington had worked as an actor in repertory theatre for thirty years, and played many supporting roles on television, it wasn't until *The Good Life*, the suburban self-sufficiency sitcom first broadcast in 1975, that he caught the public's eye. Eddington won further accolades as Jim Hacker, the Cabinet minister for 'Administrative Affairs' in *Yes, Minister* which ran for three series. Hacker then stepped up to the top job for the sequel, *Yes, Prime Minister*, which aired between 1986 and 1988. Eddington was awarded a CBE in 1987. He died in 1995 at the age of sixty-eight.

*In 1993 **Al Pacino** won the Academy Award for best actor for his portrayal of Lieutenant Colonel Frank Slade in the film 'Scent of a Woman'.*

Pacino was also nominated in the same year for best supporting actor (*Glengarry Glen Ross*) and has had a further five best actor Oscar nominations in his career, the first for the title role in *Serpico* (1973). His performance as Michael Corleone in *The Godfather* (1972), his third film role, brought him international acclaim and his first Academy Award nomination – for best supporting actor. He won the Bafta best actor award in 1976 for his work in *The Godfather: Part II* (1974) and *Dog Day Afternoon* (1975).

*In 1995 **Valery Polyakov** returned to earth after spending over fourteen months in space aboard the 'Mir' space station.*

Polyakov's spaceflight, his second mission, still holds the record for the longest duration (437 days, 18 hours). His first, which ended in 1989, also involved a lengthy time in space – seeing him leave earth for over two hundred and forty days. Construction of the Soviet space station *Mir* began in 1986. Its working life came to an end in 2001 when it was removed from orbit and broke up during re-entry into the earth's atmosphere.

Pat Barker *won the 1995 Booker Prize for 'The Ghost Road'.*

The Ghost Road was the final volume in Barker's First World War trilogy which began with *Regeneration* in 1991 and continued with *The Eye in the Door* two years later. Barker's first published novel was *Union Street* in 1982. It was followed by *Blow Your House Down* (1984), *The Century's Daughter* (1986), later republished as *Liza's England*, and *The Man Who Wasn't There* (1989). Two of her novels have been adapted for the cinema: *Regeneration* (1997) and *Union Street*, which was retitled as *Stanley and Iris* (1989). Barker has received many literary awards, and was also awarded a CBE in 2000. She returned to the First World War for the 2007 novel *Life Class*, and its follow-up, *Toby's Room*, published in 2012.

Cher *reached number one in the UK chart with her single 'Believe' in 1998.*

'Believe', Cher's third solo UK number one, spent seven weeks at the top and was the biggest-selling single of the year. It came over thirty-three years after her first UK chart topper 'I Got You Babe', recorded with her husband at the time, Sonny Bono. Cher is the oldest solo female artist to have a number one single in the UK chart. Born Cherilyn Sarkisian, as a teenager she met Sonny Bono, who was then working for record producer Phil Spector. This marked the start of her music career and also her relationship with Bono that lasted until the mid 1970s. They first recorded together under the names of Caesar and Cleo without success, before changing to Sonny and Cher. Cher has also enjoyed a successful movie career. She picked up a best supporting actress Academy Award for the role of Dolly Pelliker in *Silkwood* (1983) and won an Oscar for best actress for the part of Loretta Castorini in *Moonstruck* (1987).

Paul Nurse was awarded the 2001 Nobel Prize in Physiology or Medicine with Leland Hartwell and Tim Hunt for their discoveries of 'key regulators of the cell cycle'.

In his work, Nurse identified and investigated 'cyclin dependent kinase' (CDK), the gene present in human cells that regulates certain steps in the cell cycle (the process of chromosome duplication and the subsequent division of the cell to create two identical cells). Discoveries in this field have important implications for the development of cancer treatment. Nurse initially studied at the University of Birmingham and completed his doctorate at the University of East Anglia. Following post-doctoral work, he joined the Imperial Cancer Research Fund in the mid 1980s, and was the director-general of the organisation for six years. Nurse was knighted in 1999 and became president of the Royal Society in 2010.

In 2009 **Danny Boyle** *won the Academy Award for best director for 'Slumdog Millionaire'.*

At the age of fourteen Boyle was on course to train for the priesthood, but advice from a priest changed his mind. He instead opted for a career in drama, working initially in the theatre with the Joint Stock Company and then the Royal Court. In the 1980s he began working in television and went on to direct two episodes of *Inspector Morse* and the mini-series *Mr. Wroe's Virgins*. Boyle made his feature-film debut with *Shallow Grave* (1994), for which he picked up several European awards. His next, *Trainspotting* (1996), proved to be even more successful. Boyle's other films include *A Life Less Ordinary* (1997), *The Beach* (2000) and *127 Hours* (2010). Boyle was the artistic director of the much admired opening ceremony for the 2012 London Olympic Games, *Isles of Wonder*.

Andre Geim and Konstantin Novoselov were awarded the 2010 Nobel Prize in Physics for their pioneering work on the material graphene.

Graphene is composed of a layer of carbon atoms, one atom thick, and has several important characteristics. Stronger than an equivalent amount of steel, graphene is also a good conductor of electricity and heat. Geim was in his mid-forties when his paper with Novoselov and their co-workers, which detailed their first investigations of graphene, was published. In earlier work, Geim and his collaborators were able to levitate a frog using a magnetic field, a feat which won Geim and Michael Berry an 'Ig Nobel Prize' in 2000. (Ig Nobels were created to celebrate the more unusual achievements in science, medicine and technology – they were first awarded in 1991. Geim is the first person to have won both a Nobel and an Ig Nobel.) Geim was born in Sochi, USSR, and completed his first degree and doctorate in Russia. He later accepted posts in England, Denmark and Holland before becoming a professor of physics at the University of Manchester in 2001. Geim was knighted in the 2012 New Year Honours.

53
FIFTY-THREE

In 1841 **Robert Peel** *became prime minister for the second time.*

The influence of his MP father, from whom he inherited a baronetcy in 1830, ensured that Peel entered Parliament at the age of twenty-one representing the Irish rotten borough of Cashel. Three years later he accepted the position of Irish chief secretary, and in 1822 he joined the Cabinet as home secretary. Peel oversaw a simplification of the criminal law; ninety-two statutes relating to theft were consolidated into four acts, and the number of offences that carried the death penalty was reduced. When Lord Liverpool stepped down as prime minister due to ill health in 1827, Peel resigned rather than serve under his successor George Canning. However, he subsequently returned to the Home Office under the Duke of Wellington in 1828. The following year he established the Metropolitan Police in London. Nicknames for the officers, such as Bobbies and Peelers, were derived from his own name. Peel's change of stance on the issue of

Catholic emancipation saw him draft and promote the Catholic Relief Bill, which was passed in 1829. Among other measures, it allowed Roman Catholics to sit in Parliament. Peel first held the office of prime minister for only a matter of months at the age of forty-six, but his second ministry lasted for five years. The momentous legislation passed by his government was the repeal of the Corn Laws in 1846. Introduced in 1815 these levied import tariffs on foreign grain when the price rose above a certain level, thus protecting the domestic growers from overseas competition. Peel had initially been a supporter of this measure, but when confronted by a poor harvest and the potato blight in Ireland, he changed his mind and advocated abolition of the Corn Laws, with a gradual lowering of the tariff over a three-year period ending in 1849. (This was to give landowners time for adjustment to the new arrangement.) The bill split the Conservative Party but was passed with the additional votes of the Whigs, and others, in 1846. Peel was then defeated on another bill on the same day and shortly afterwards resigned as prime minister. He died in 1850 at the age of sixty-two, after a fall from a horse.

Samuel Morse *officially opened the first telegraph line between two cities in the US with the message 'What hath God wrought' in 1844.*

The coded words travelled approximately forty miles between Washington and Baltimore, and marked the culmination of years of effort on the part of Morse and his assistants to establish the telegraph. Morse, a gifted artist, had made a living from his paintings and portraits, including one of US president John Adams. He became interested in electricity while studying at Yale, but it was not until he was in his forties that he conceived the idea of a telegraph system. Morse joined the staff of New York University in 1835 and later gained the assistance of a colleague, Leonard Gale, in developing the telegraph apparatus. He also enlisted the support of Alfred Vail, who made further improvements both to the equipment and to Morse's code for transmitting messages. Morse filed his US patent in 1838, which was granted two years later. The US government provided $30,000 to set up the first city-to-city line in 1843 and one year later, with Morse in Washington and Vail in Baltimore, the first message 'What hath God wrought' was sent. Morse died in 1872 at the age of eighty.

Ferdinand de Lesseps struck the first blow in the construction of the Suez Canal in 1859.

De Lesseps was a former French diplomat who promoted the idea of creating a canal between the Mediterranean and the Red Sea. He negotiated the concession to build the canal in 1854, and overcame opposition and doubts about the venture to raise the capital required. The money largely came from French private investors, but Egypt also had a major stake in the canal company. This was later bought out by the British government who overcame their initial objections to the scheme. The canal was officially opened, over ten years after de Lesseps's first strike, in November 1869. De Lesseps then turned his attention to the creation of a Panama Canal. He became the president of the Panama Canal Company and work commenced on the route on New Year's Day 1880 (de Lesseps was seventy-four). Construction problems and disease blighted the project and work came to a halt. The management, including de Lesseps, was charged with financial wrongdoing, and he faced a fine as well as a five-year prison sentence, but the verdict was later overturned. He died at the age of eighty-nine in 1894. The Panama Canal was completed under a modified scheme by the US government and opened in August 1914.

'Harbutt's plastic method and the use of plasticine in the arts of writing, drawing, and modelling in educational work' by **William Harbutt** *was published in 1897.*

Harbutt was an art teacher and his need for a modelling clay which did not dry out inspired him to invent plasticine. He began small-scale manufacture in 1897 and in the same year published his first book to promote its use. Harbutt registered 'plasticine' as a trade mark in 1899 and its success led to the start of commercial production in 1900. He died in 1921 at the age of seventy-seven. Decades later, plasticine, which was used to create the Wallace and Gromit characters, remains popular.

Arthur Balfour succeeded his uncle, Lord Salisbury, as prime minister in 1902.

Balfour remained in power for nearly three and a half years before resigning in December 1905. In the following month his party was heavily defeated at the general election by the Liberals, who won a convincing majority. Balfour also lost his own seat, although he later re-entered Parliament at a by-election. He continued as leader of the opposition until his resignation in 1911, but his political career was not over. During the First World War coalition government he became the first lord of the Admiralty and later foreign secretary, from which office he would issue, in 1917, the 'Balfour Declaration'. This stated the government's preference for a national home for the Jewish people in Palestine, although it added that this should not prejudice the rights of the non-Jewish population. He resigned as foreign secretary in 1919 and was made an earl in 1922. Balfour died in 1930 at the age of eighty-one.

David Lloyd George *became prime minister and leader of the coalition government during World War One, in 1916.*

Lloyd George was born in Manchester to Welsh parents. Following the death of his father when he was one, the family returned to Wales where his uncle would become a major influence on his life. Lloyd George undertook legal training and first entered Parliament at the age of twenty-seven. He became chancellor in 1908, a post that he would occupy until the middle of 1915. In this office, he completed the setting up of the old age pension in 1908, and three years later introduced the national health insurance scheme. His budget of 1909, which among other fiscal measures sought to introduce a tax on land, was rejected by the Lords. This led to the 1911 Parliament Act which removed the right of the upper chamber to veto legislation. His reputation as a war leader was secured with the allied victory in the First World War in 1918, and shortly afterward the coalition government's election win allowed Lloyd George to remain in power for nearly four more years. He led the British side that signed the Anglo–Irish treaty, which established the Irish Free State in 1922. The same year the coalition broke up and Lloyd George resigned from office. He succeeded Asquith as Liberal leader in 1926, but by then they had become the third force in British politics and did not form a government again. Lloyd George remained a member of the Commons until 1945, when he was made an earl. He died the same year at the age of eighty-two.

*Boléro by **Maurice Ravel** premiered at the Paris Opera in 1928.*

By his early thirties, Ravel was an established composer. His early works include 'Pavane pour une infante défunte' (1899), 'Jeux d'eau' (1901), his string quartet in F major (1902–03) and 'Shéhérazade' (1903). Ravel, who saw active service in the First World War, was also a noted orchestrator and performed this task for composers such as Chopin and Mussorgsky. One of his more unusual compositions was his 'Piano Concerto for the Left Hand in D Major', which was commissioned by the Austrian pianist Paul Wittgenstein who had lost his right arm in the First World War. Ravel received a serious head injury in a car accident in 1932 and composed little after this calamity. His health declined and he died after undergoing a brain operation in 1937, aged sixty-two.

In 1951 **Nirad Chaudhuri** made his debut with 'The Autobiography of an Unknown Indian'.

The Autobiography of an Unknown Indian also served to paint a picture of the last decades of British rule in India. Chaudhuri, who worked as a magazine editor and journalist, followed it with his next English language book, *A Passage to England*, published in 1959. He was aged one hundred when his last work, *Three Horsemen of the New Apocalypse*, was published in 1997. He died in 1999 at the age of one hundred and one. Chaudhuri was awarded a CBE in 1992.

Hans Krebs *was awarded the 1953 Nobel Prize in Physiology or Medicine 'for his discovery of the citric acid cycle'.*

The citric acid cycle (also known as the Krebs cycle or tricarboxylic acid cycle) describes the process within a cell whereby food is broken down and a sequence of chemical reactions liberate energy for the cell's functions, as well as carbon dioxide which is breathed out in respiration. Krebs was born in Hildesheim, Germany, and was awarded his doctorate by the University of Hamburg in 1925. Following the rise to power of Hitler, Krebs left for England, where he initially worked at Cambridge University. Krebs, who also identified the urea cycle in 1932, was knighted in 1958. He died in 1981 at the age of eighty-one. Krebs shared the Nobel Prize with Fritz Lipmann for his discovery of 'co-enzyme A' and its importance for cellular metabolism.

In 1970 **Edward Heath** became prime minister following the Conservative victory in the general election.

Heath had become party leader in 1965, and the following year fought unsuccessfully to enter Downing Street at the first attempt in the general election. Although he studied at Balliol College, Oxford, Heath came from a more ordinary background (his father was a builder and carpenter and his mother a maid) than that of previous Tory leaders. He won the organ scholarship at Balliol in his first term and this offered him financial assistance for the remainder of his undergraduate studies. He served in the Second World War in the Royal Artillery and saw at first hand the destruction wrought by the conflict. This experience helped to shape his pro-European stance. First elected to Parliament in 1950, he led the negotiations for Britain's entry into the European Economic Community (EEC) in the early sixties, but UK membership was vetoed by President de Gaulle of France. Heath had the satisfaction of reversing this outcome when he finally secured British entry, as prime minister, in 1973. His time in office was marred by industrial unrest, most notably with the miners, and Heath called an election in 1974 to secure a fresh mandate. The Conservatives won a marginally higher percentage of the overall vote; however, Labour won the most seats and formed a minority government. Labour then gained a slender majority in the second election held that year. Heath remained as Tory leader but was challenged in early 1975 and lost out to Margaret Thatcher. He was made a Knight of the Order of the Garter in 1992 and remained an MP until 2001. He died four years later at the age of eighty-nine.

Telly Savalas *reached number one in the UK singles chart with 'If' in 1975.*
Mainly spoken rather than sung, Savalas's version of 'If' was taken from his album *Telly* which made it to number twelve in the UK chart. Savalas was starring at the time as the eponymous *Kojak* – a detective series based in New York, which made its debut on British television in 1974. Born Aristotelis Savalas in New York to Greek parents, he made his feature-film debut at the age of thirty-nine as Lieutenant Darro in the 1961 production *Mad Dog Coll*. His only Academy Award nomination (for best supporting actor) came two years later for his role as Feto Gomez in *Birdman of Alcatraz* (1962). Savalas was frequently cast as villainous characters and ended the decade with an appearance as Ernst Blofeld in the sixth James Bond film, *On Her Majesty's Secret Service* (1969). The seventies brought fame, as well as Emmy and Golden Globe awards, for his

most recognisable role as Detective Lieutenant Theo Kojak. Savalas died in 1994 at the age of seventy-two.

Margaret Thatcher became Britain's first female prime minister when the Conservatives won the 1979 general election.

Thatcher also won the subsequent general elections in 1983 and 1987, and remained in office until 1990 – the longest continuous prime ministerial term since Lord Liverpool in the nineteenth century. She was born Margaret Roberts in Grantham, Lincolnshire, the daughter of a grocer. She read chemistry at Somerville College, Oxford, and later studied law, being called to the Bar in 1954. Thatcher first entered Parliament at the 1959 general election as the member for Finchley, and following the Conservative victory in 1970, she joined the Cabinet as the secretary for education and science. The Tories lost power in 1974 and the following year Thatcher challenged Edward Heath for the leadership. Victorious, she became the first woman to lead the Conservative Party. Four years later, she made history again when she became prime minister. The beginning of her term in office was to prove difficult with high unemployment, which increased sharply while the government focused on reducing inflation; however, her popularity was boosted by the recapture of the Falkland Islands following the Argentinian invasion in 1982. Divisions within the opposition also contributed to her second electoral success in 1983. The next year saw the beginning of a miners' strike that would endure for twelve months, but due to government readiness and its determination not to capitulate, the strikers were eventually forced back to work. Her term in office is also remembered for policies such as the 'right to buy' for council tenants, various trade union reforms, a major programme of privatisation and the introduction of the community charge, also known as the 'poll tax'. Its unpopularity caused unrest and her position was further weakened by Cabinet resignations that included the chancellor, Nigel Lawson, in 1989 and the foreign secretary, Sir Geoffrey Howe, in 1990. Shortly after Howe's resignation she was challenged for the leadership by Michael Heseltine and, unable to win on the first ballot, she withdrew from the contest. John Major was elected as her successor. Thatcher left the Commons in 1992 and received a life peerage as a baroness.

Malcolm Morley *won the inaugural Turner Prize in 1984.*

Morley was born in London, but left England for New York in 1958. There he developed his style of photorealism, which he termed 'super-realism'. Morley's win, for which he was also awarded a cash sum of £10,000, surprised many since he had not lived in Britain for over twenty-five years. From 1991 onwards the prize has been restricted to artists under the age of fifty, and so Morley is likely to remain not only the first but also the oldest winner of the award.

In 1990 ***Richard Wilson*** *appeared on television for the first time as Victor Meldrew in 'One Foot in The Grave'.*

One Foot in The Grave, written by David Renwick, ran for ten years and brought Wilson two Bafta Awards for best light-entertainment performance (1992 and 1994). Wilson trained as a lab technician after leaving school and later did his National Service in the Royal Army Medical Corps. He was accepted by Rada at the age of twenty-seven and graduated two years later. His other television roles include Gordon Thorpe in four series of *Only When I Laugh* (1979-82), Eddie Clockerty in *Tutti Frutti* (1987) and Dicky Lipton in *Hot Metal* (1988). More recently he has played Gaius in the BBC series *Merlin* which began in 2008. Wilson is also a successful stage actor and director. He was awarded an OBE in 1994.

Blondie, with lead singer ***Deborah Harry****, reached number one in the UK singles chart, in 1999, with 'Maria'.*

Harry is the oldest female singer to have a UK number one single. The group, formed in the 1970s, was recognised as part of the American new wave, but Blondie's first success came in Britain where their breakthrough hit 'Denis' made it to number two in 1978. Their third album *Parallel Lines* made it to number six in the US, and one of its tracks, 'Heart of Glass', gave them their first UK and US number one in 1979. 'Maria', their sixth UK chart topper, would come twenty years later. Harry's first solo album *Koo Koo* was released in 1981. Two years later, she played Nicki Brand in *Videodrome* (1983) in what was her first major film role. Blondie's ninth studio album, *Panic of Girls*, the band's first for eight years, was released in 2011.

Hillary Clinton became the first 'first lady' to be elected to public office in the US when she won a seat in the Senate in 2000, representing New York.

A graduate of Yale Law School, Clinton combined her legal career with support for her husband Bill, who spent twelve years as governor of Arkansas before becoming president in 1992. As First Lady she had a more prominent, political role than her predecessors and chaired the task force on national health care reform. In 2008 she became the first woman to seek the Democratic Party nomination for president, losing out in a closely fought race to Barack Obama. Her eight years representing New York in the Senate came to an end when she was appointed US secretary of state by Obama at the start of his presidency in 2009.

Carol Ann Duffy was appointed as poet laureate in 2009, the first woman to hold the post in its long history.

Duffy is also the first Scot to fill the position, which has been in existence for nearly three hundred and fifty years. Her debut volume of poetry *Standing Female Nude* was published in 1985. Duffy's other collections include the Whitbread award-winning *Mean Time* in 1993 and *The World's Wife* in 1999. Duffy, who was awarded a CBE in 2002, will occupy the post of poet laureate for ten years.

54
FIFTY-FOUR

In 1653 **Oliver Cromwell** *became lord protector of the commonwealth of England, Scotland and Ireland.*

Cromwell made little impact on public life during his first forty years. He was an MP in his late twenties for a year, but made only one speech before Parliament was disbanded by Charles I in 1629. Declining fortunes prompted a sale of almost all of the Cromwell family properties in 1631. He then leased a farmstead at St Ives and worked as a farmer for the next five years. His situation improved with a legacy from his maternal uncle and the Cromwell family moved to Ely. Cromwell also developed a strong puritan faith and in 1640 was chosen to represent Cambridge in Parliament. At the outbreak of the English Civil War in 1642, Cromwell was quick to take action on the side of Parliament and prevented the removal of silver plate from Cambridge that was destined for the King. Cromwell rose through the ranks and became a lieutenant-general of the Parliamentarian forces in 1644. The Parliamentarian 'New Model Army' under Cromwell and Sir Thomas Fairfax secured a decisive victory against the Royalists at Naseby in 1645. War broke out again in 1648 with an attempt by Charles I to regain power, but this was thwarted and would result in his trial and execution in 1649, with Cromwell one of the signatories of his death warrant. Cromwell was appointed as the lord lieutenant of Ireland, where he oversaw brutal massacres at Drogheda and Wexford in 1649. He left Ireland the following year and fought further battles in Scotland and England, finally defeating the supporters of the future Charles II at the Battle of Worcester in 1651. Cromwell's attention turned to political matters. He dissolved the Long Parliament in 1653 and later that year became lord protector. Cromwell was offered the title of king in 1657 and, although the protectorate had developed many of the trappings of royalty, he refused. Cromwell died the following year, at the age of fifty-nine, with his son Richard succeeding him. However, Richard Cromwell could not command the same support and was forced out in 1659, fleeing to France. The monarchy was restored in 1660 under Charles II. Cromwell's body, along with others who had signed the King's death warrant, was disinterred (although there are rumours that a substitute corpse was put in place). It was hung at Tyburn and then decapitated, with the head being placed on a spike outside Westminster Hall, where it remained for over twenty years. The head is then thought to have had a chequered history as an object of curiosity before it was reclaimed by Cromwell's descendants and given to Sidney Sussex, Cromwell's Cambridge college. It was reburied there in an unmarked spot in 1960.

In 1714 **George I** *became King of Great Britain and Ireland following the death of Queen Anne.*

The first monarch of the House of Hanover, George I was born in Osnabruck, now Germany, in 1660. He was granted the throne under the Act of Settlement, which debarred Catholics, who were closer in line, from the succession. George never learned to speak English and, as he was also the Elector of Hanover, spent a proportion of his time out of the country. A Jacobite rebellion in 1715, that sought to place Queen Anne's half-brother James on the throne, was quelled. The Whigs gained the political ascendancy during George's reign, and Sir Robert Walpole, who became recognised as the first de facto prime minister, began his second term as first lord of the Treasury in 1721. George I died in 1727, at the age of sixty-seven and was succeeded by his son, George II.

In 1897 **William McKinley** *became the twenty-fifth president of the United States.*

McKinley fought in the civil war, the last president to have done so, and entered Congress at the age of thirty-four. After fourteen years he was elected as the Governor of Ohio and served for six years until 1896. Major incidents during his presidency included the brief Spanish–American War of 1898, which left the US in control of Puerto Rico, Guam and the Philippines, and the annexation of Hawaii in the same year. McKinley was returned for a second term, but in 1901 he was assassinated by Leon Czolgosz, who shot him twice at close range. Doctors were unable to remove one of the bullets and McKinley died eight days later. Vice-President Theodore Roosevelt was then sworn in to become the youngest president in US history.

Robin Welsh *won an Olympic gold medal as a member of the men's curling team in 1924.*

Welsh, a former rugby player, remains the oldest recipient of a winter Olympic gold medal*, won with his team-mates Willie and Laurence Jackson, and Tom Murray. Curling next appeared, as a demonstration sport, at the 1932 Lake Placid Olympics and did not become an official part of the Games until 1998. Robin Welsh died in 1934 at the age of sixty-five.

---

* The 1924 curling competition was regarded by many historians, although not officially designated at the time, as only a demonstration event. In 2006 the IOC declared that the 1924 event had full Olympic status.

*In 1932 **Franklin Roosevelt** won the first of four consecutive presidential elections to become the thirty-second president of the United States.*

Roosevelt launched the 'New Deal', a series of programmes designed to tackle the economic depression that had followed the stock-market crash in 1929. Early in his presidency he also moved to end prohibition, which had been introduced in 1920 and forbade the sale and manufacture of alcohol. The twenty-first amendment to the US constitution, which repealed it, came into effect in 1933. He worked hard to keep the US out of World War Two, but the attack on Pearl Harbour by Japan in late 1941 brought the country into the conflict. Germany and Italy, shortly afterwards, also declared war on the US. In November 1944, Roosevelt won his fourth term but it was cut short by his death in April 1945, at the age of sixty-three, weeks before the war in Europe ended.

*The rotary internal combustion engine, invented by **Felix Wankel**, was first tested in 1957.*

Known also as the Wankel engine, the engine was developed with the NSU Company, who produced the first car powered by the new rotary unit in 1964. The engine uses a specially shaped triangular rotor, spinning inside a fixed chamber, to perform the four-stroke cycle as generally used in conventional piston engines. It has a better power-to-weight ratio than a piston engine, and also fewer moving parts. The NSU Ro 80 powered by a Wankel engine was named as the European car of the year in 1968. Wankel extensively licensed the technology and the car company Mazda, in particular, has developed the engine further, currently using it to power its RX-8 sports car. Wankel died in 1986 at the age of eighty-six.

*In 1961 **Billy Wilder** won his second Academy Award for best director for 'The Apartment'.*

Wilder worked as a newspaper reporter in Vienna, then as a scriptwriter in Berlin, before he arrived in Hollywood in 1933. He scored his first Academy Award nomination for co-writing the screenplay, with Charles Brackett and Walter Reisch, of *Ninotchka* (1939). He accumulated several other nominations for films such as *Double Indemnity* (1944), *Ace in the Hole* (1951) and *Some Like it Hot* (1959). At the age of thirty-nine, *The Lost Weekend* (1945) won him his first Oscars, for best director and, as co-writer, for best screenplay. More co-writing Academy Awards followed for *Sunset Boulevard* (1950) and *The Apartment* (1960), the latter of which also won the best picture prize. His last film as a director was *Buddy Buddy* (1981). Wilder died in 2002 at the age of ninety-five.

Dorothy Hodgkin was awarded the Nobel Prize in Chemistry in 1964 for her work in determining the structure of important biological molecules by X-rays.

Born Dorothy Crowfoot in Cairo, Egypt, to English parents, she developed an interest in chemistry as a child. She studied the subject at Somerville College, Oxford, where she would later return after her doctorate years at Cambridge. Hodgkin became an expert in X-ray crystallography, and it was using this technique that she determined the structure of penicillin in 1945. After several years of work, Hodgkin and her team also elucidated the structure of vitamin B12 in 1956 and the structure of insulin in 1969. She was the first British woman to be awarded a Nobel Prize, and only the third woman to receive the award in chemistry. In 1965 she became only the second woman to be appointed to the Order of Merit, fifty-eight years after the first, Florence Nightingale. One of her former fourth-year students at Oxford was Margaret Roberts, later to become prime minister as Margaret Thatcher. Hodgkin died in 1994 at the age of eighty-four.

Reg Harris won cycling's British Professional Sprint Championship in 1974.

The achievement capped Harris's return to the sport three years previously at the age of fifty-one. He began to race competitively in his teenage years and won his first national championship in 1944 and his first world title, for the amateur sprint, in 1947. He won two silver medals at the 1948 London Olympics and the following year took the first of three consecutive world professional sprint titles in his debut season at that level. Harris triumphed again in the event in 1954, three years before his original retirement. He received an OBE in 1958. Harris died in 1992 at the age of seventy-two.

In 1979 George Cole made his debut as Arthur Daley in 'Minder' in the episode 'Gunfight at the O.K. Laundrette'.

Minder ran for ten series until March 1994. Cole's film career began in the 1940s and includes the first St. Trinian's film, *The Belles of St. Trinian's* (1954), and its three sequels in which he appeared as 'Flash Harry'. Cole also starred as 'Fingers' in *Too Many Crooks* (1959). His television work after *Minder* includes *Root into Europe* and the sitcom *Dad*. Cole was awarded an OBE in 1992.

Mikhail Gorbachev became general-secretary of the Communist Party of the Soviet Union in 1985.

Gorbachev came from a peasant family in the Stavropol territory of the Russian Republic. He studied law at Moscow State University and graduated in 1955. He rose through the ranks of the Communist Party and in 1980 joined the Politburo, becoming its youngest full member. The death of General-Secretary Konstantin Chernenko in 1985 (the third leader to die in as many years) led to Gorbachev's appointment to the highest political office in the USSR. His reformist agenda was soon apparent. The policies of *perestroika* (restructuring) and *glasnost* (openness) sought to transform the Soviet Union's economic and social fabric by making the former more market-orientated and the latter more liberal. Gorbachev also transformed international relations and played a key role in the ending of the Cold War. He sanctioned Soviet disengagement from the Eastern Bloc countries (which resulted in the fall of the Berlin Wall in 1989), the replacement of communist regimes throughout the region and the reunification of Germany. Gorbachev was elected president of the USSR in 1990 and was awarded the Nobel Peace Prize in the same year. As increased freedom allowed the expression of pent-up nationalist sentiment in the Soviet republics, hard-liners sought to re-establish central control and staged a coup against Gorbachev in 1991. Gorbachev was detained, liberated after three days and resumed office, but the rapid disintegration of the Soviet Union led to his resignation on Christmas Day 1991. He formed the Gorbachev Foundation in 1992, the Social Democratic Party of Russia in 2001 and the Union of Social Democrats in 2007.

*In 1987 **Michael Caine** won the Academy Award for best supporting actor for his role as Elliot in 'Hannah and Her Sisters'.*

Caine's career as an actor began after his National Service in the British Army in the early 1950s. He made little headway in his first decade, although he did settle on his final stage name, inspired by the Humphrey Bogart film *The Caine Mutiny* (1954). Finally his breakthrough role came, in his early thirties, with the film *Zulu* (1964) in which he played the aristocratic Lieutenant Gonville Bromhead. He then had his first outing as Len Deighton's spy Harry Palmer in *The Ipcress File* (1965). Caine's role as the eponymous philanderer in *Alfie* (1966) brought him his first Academy Award nomination for best actor. Two Harry Palmer sequels, his first US-made film *Gambit* (1966) and the robbery escapade *The Italian Job* (1969) added to his reputation. In the next decade, he gave memorable performances in films such as *Get Carter* (1971); *Sleuth* (1972), which gave him his second Academy nomination for best actor; and *The Man Who Would be King* (1975). His role as Frank Bryant in *Educating Rita* (1983) secured a Bafta best actor award and another Oscar best actor nomination. His performance in *The Quiet American* (2002) brought him his sixth overall Academy nomination. Caine won a second Oscar, again for best supporting actor, for *The Cider House Rules* (1999). Awarded a CBE in 1992, Caine received the Bafta Fellowship and was knighted in 2000.

In 1990 **A. S. Byatt** *(Antonia Susan) won the Booker Prize for 'Possession'.*
Byatt made her publishing debut in 1964 with the novel *The Shadow of the Sun*. It was followed by the first of her two books on Iris Murdoch: *Degrees of Freedom: The Early Novels of Iris Murdoch* (1965) and *Iris Murdoch: A Critical Study* (1976). Her third novel, *The Virgin in the Garden* (1978), was the first in a quartet that includes *Still Life* (1985), *Babel Tower* (1996) and *A Whistling Woman* (2002). In 1983 Byatt left her job as a senior lecturer in English at University College London, in order to write full-time. Her recent novel, *The Children's Book*, was shortlisted for the 2009 Booker Prize. Byatt was awarded a CBE in 1990 and a DBE in 1999.

In 1992 **Anthony Hopkins** *won both the Academy Award and Bafta for best actor for his portrayal of Hannibal Lecter in 'The Silence of the Lambs'.*
The Silence of the Lambs also gave Hopkins his first Academy Award nomination and he received three more in the 1990s for *Remains of the Day* (1993), *Nixon* (1995) and *Amistad* (1997). He made his film debut in *The White Bus* (1967) and became an established stage and television performer, winning a Bafta TV award in 1973, for best actor, for his

portrayal of Pierre Bezukhov in *War and Peace*. His other notable films include *The Elephant Man* (1980), *84 Charing Cross Road* (1987) and *Shadowlands* (1993), the latter giving him a second Bafta best actor award. Hopkins was knighted in 1993 and awarded the Bafta Fellowship in 2008.

In 2001 **George W. Bush** *became the forty-third president of the United States.*

Bush is the eldest son of the former president, George Bush, and the second US leader, after John Quincy Adams, to have been the son of a previous president. Bush, who prior to the presidency spent six years as the governor of Texas, narrowly achieved victory in the 2000 election over the sitting vice-president, Al Gore. The result hinged on the vote in the state of Florida which, after recounts, declared Bush the winner by 537 votes. A Supreme Court ruling on the vote counting, over one month after the election, was also in Bush's favour. Bush was finally accorded 271 electoral votes to Gore's 266 – Gore though had won the popular vote by over half a million votes. Bush's presidential priorities were significantly altered by the destruction of the World Trade Center in New York and the strike on the Pentagon by hijacked passenger planes on 11 September 2001, which killed nearly three thousand people. A fourth hijacked jet was brought down by its passengers before it reached its target. Bush declared a 'war on terror' and responded to the attacks with US-led military action in Afghanistan in October 2001. In 2003 the US, concerned about the threat posed by possible weapons of mass destruction, led a controversial invasion of Iraq which removed Saddam Hussein from power, although evidence of the weapons' existence was not found. Bush was re-elected in 2004, and on that occasion did win the popular vote as well as the majority in the electoral college.

Nick Skelton, *riding Big Star, won a gold medal at the 2012 London Olympics as a member of Great Britain's showjumping team.*

Skelton was appearing in his sixth Olympic Games and the team's victory, following a jump-off against the Netherlands, brought him his first Olympic medal and made him the oldest competitor to win gold at the London Games. It was also Britain's first showjumping gold medal since 1952. Skelton's success was all the more remarkable given the fact that he broke his neck after falling from his horse during preparations for the Sydney Olympics in 2000. The accident forced him to retire from the sport until he made a comeback in 2002. Over a career of nearly forty years, Skelton's achievements include three team bronzes, a team silver and an individual bronze at the World Championships; seven team medals, including three gold, at the European Championships; four King George V Gold Cup victories and three consecutive Hickstead Derby wins. He also holds the British record for clearing the highest fence (7 feet 7 inches and 5/16th inch), which he set in 1978 with Lastic. Skelton, who was awarded an OBE in the 2012 Queen's Birthday Honours, shared the 2012 Olympic team gold medal with Scott Brash, Peter Charles and Ben Maher.

55
FIFTY-FIVE

Alessandro Volta presented his invention of the 'voltaic pile', essentially the first electric battery, to the Royal Society of London in 1800.

Volta's creation consisted of alternate plates of silver and zinc separated by cardboard soaked in salt water. He had been inspired by the findings of Luis Galvani, whose experiments with frogs led him to theorise that the electric current he observed was a constituent of the animal itself. However, Volta disagreed and proved with his invention that he was indeed correct. Volta, a professor of physics, was also responsible for other inventions, as well as the discovery of the gas methane. He was awarded the title of 'Count' by Napoleon in 1810, and, in the 1880s, his name was given to the unit of electrical potential difference – the volt. Volta died in 1827 at the age of eighty-two.

William Lamb, second Viscount Melbourne, became prime minister in 1834.

Lamb first entered Parliament at the age of twenty-six as the Whig MP for Leominster. He had recently married Lady Caroline Ponsonby and their union was to bring him some unwelcome attention as a result of her liaisons with the poet, Lord Byron, who she famously labelled as 'mad, bad and dangerous to know'. The Lambs separated in 1825 and Lady

Caroline died three years later with William at her bedside. Lamb inherited the title of Viscount Melbourne in 1828 and as a result transferred to the House of Lords. He served as home secretary between 1830 and 1834 before replacing Earl Grey as prime minister after his resignation. Melbourne's ministry was dismissed by King William IV after only four months, but he returned to power in 1835 after Sir Robert Peel was unable to command an outright majority following the election earlier in the year. The young Queen Victoria ascended to the throne in 1837 with Melbourne as her first prime minister and he became a trusted advisor and mentor. He resigned from office in 1841 and died seven years later, at the age of sixty-nine. The Australian city of Melbourne was named after him in 1837.

Coca-Cola, invented by **John Pemberton**, *first went on sale in Jacob's Pharmacy in Atlanta, Georgia, in 1886.*

Pemberton, a successful pharmacist, also served on the Confederate side in the civil war and was wounded in the Battle of Columbus. Coca-Cola evolved from a popular drink that he had created called Pemberton's French Wine Coca, itself inspired by Vin Mariani, a successful tonic drink containing cocoa. Temperance legislation prompted Pemberton to produce a non-alcoholic version of his drink, which was given its name, Coca-Cola, by Frank Robinson, a bookkeeper for the Pemberton Chemical Company. Robinson also wrote the name in the flowing Spencerian script that would become widely recognised as its trademark. Pemberton also claimed his drink had health benefits and could alleviate many ailments, but he did not live long enough to see how phenomenally popular his drink would become. Pemberton sold shares in Coca-Cola to raise funds and only months before his death he sold all his remaining rights to Asa Candler. Candler successfully marketed and expanded the business, and formed the Coca-Cola Company in 1892. Pemberton died in 1888 at the age of fifty-seven.

Ivan Pavlov *was awarded the 1904 Nobel Prize in Physiology or Medicine for his research relating to the physiology of digestion.*

Pavlov's most famous work, his description of the 'conditioned reflex', was first published in 1903. In his examination of the digestive process in dogs, Pavlov found that the canines, which normally only salivated when presented with food, could be conditioned to salivate using an external stimulus such as ringing a bell. He did this by giving food and ringing the bell at the same time. Eventually the dogs would salivate if the bell was rung, even if no food was offered. Pavlov was held in high esteem in post-revolutionary Russia and the Soviet government ensured that he had the means to continue his research, which he was able to do until his death in 1936 at the age of eighty-six.

Herbert Asquith became prime minister in 1908, taking over after the resignation of Henry Campbell-Bannerman due to ill health.

Unusually, Asquith had to travel to Biarritz in south west France, where King Edward VII was holidaying, in order to 'kiss hands' as prime minister. Asquith, a graduate of Balliol College, Oxford, was called to the Bar in 1876. He entered Parliament at the age of thirty-three as the Liberal member for East Fife, became home secretary in 1892 and chancellor in 1905. Asquith's last budget, which he delivered a month after becoming prime minister, included the plan to introduce pensions for everyone over the age of seventy – legislation that would be completed by his successor as chancellor, David Lloyd George. Asquith, via the Parliament Bill which became law in 1911, was also instrumental in neutering the power of the Lords to veto legislation. He also had to grapple with the campaign for women's suffrage, the Irish Home Rule issue and Britain's entry into World War One. In 1915 Asquith formed a coalition government, but was forced to resign the following year. He continued to lead the Liberals, even after losing his seat in 1918, but the party never recovered electorally from the split between its Asquith and Lloyd George factions. Asquith was made an earl in 1925 and died three years later, at the age of seventy-five.

Ferdinand Porsche set up his own engineering and design consultancy in 1931.

Porsche was born in Bohemia, now in the Czech Republic, in 1875. He displayed an aptitude for mechanics at an early age and, although he received scant formal training in engineering, Porsche made his mark early with his work for the System Lohner-Porsche electric carriage, exhibited at the Paris World Fair in 1900 when he was twenty-five. Its wheel hub electric motors were his creation and he also developed what was the first hybrid vehicle when he added a petrol engine to create the Lohner-Porsche Mixte. At the age of thirty-one, he became the technical director at Austro-Daimler. He received an honorary doctorate from the Vienna University of Technology in 1917 and six years later left Austro-Daimler, subsequently becoming the technical director at DMG which soon merged with Benz & Cie. to form Daimler-Benz. Porsche's desire to create a small, light car was not supported by the board and he resigned in 1929. A brief spell at the Steyr Company ended when it collapsed and Porsche found himself out of work; he decided to form his own consultancy business. Its most famous and enduring design was the 'People's Car', later popularly known as the Volkswagen Beetle, which was commissioned in the 1930s by the German dictator Adolf Hitler who required a cheap and reliable form of transport for the masses. After the Second World War, it would become the world's best-selling car. Production ended in 2003 after over 21 million Beetles had been manufactured. The first vehicle to bear the Porsche name, the 356, began production in 1948 and was created by Ferdinand's son, Ferry. It bore many similarities in design to the Beetle. Ferdinand Porsche died in 1951 at the age of seventy-five.

Pablo Picasso *completed the first sketch for his painting 'Guernica' in 1937.*

The large mural-sized canvas was painted by Picasso as a reaction to the bombing of Guernica during the Spanish Civil War, and depicts the horror of conflict and its effect upon individuals. *Guernica* was first exhibited at the 1937 World Fair in Paris and, following showings in many countries, it was placed in the care of the Museum of Modern Art in New York. Picasso did not allow the painting to revisit Spain under General Franco, but it was returned in 1981, six years after Franco's death. Picasso was born in Málaga, Andalusia, in 1881, and as a young boy displayed a precocious talent for art. His father, also a painter, was his early teacher. As a teenager, Picasso trained in Barcelona where his father had obtained a professorship at the School of Fine Arts. Picasso also studied briefly in Madrid before moving to Paris as a young man. His life's work encapsulated many styles: from his early blue and rose periods to cubism, classicism and surrealism. As well as painting, Picasso's oeuvre includes etching, sculpture, ceramics and lithography. He was also a highly prolific artist, producing tens of thousands of works during his lifetime. Picasso died in 1973 at the age of ninety-one.

Edward Appleton was awarded the 1947 Nobel Prize in Physics for his research into the ionosphere and his discovery of the Appleton layer.

The ionosphere forms the uppermost part of the earth's atmosphere. It consists of charged particles and ions, created by the action of the sun's radiation. In 1902, Oliver Heaviside and Arthur Kennelly had each postulated the existence of a reflecting layer of ionized gas, which could explain Marconi's successful radio transmission across the Atlantic Ocean in the previous year. Appleton's work confirmed its existence in 1924 and he went on to identify an upper layer, beginning at approximately 230km above the surface, which is now known by his name. It is responsible for reflecting short-wave radio signals around the earth. As well as radio communication, his methods and findings were also important for the development of radar. Appleton was knighted in 1941. He died in 1965 at the age of seventy-two.

Lyndon Johnson became US president following the assassination of John F. Kennedy in 1963.

Johnson entered Congress as a representative from Texas, his home state, in 1937. He joined the navy after the attack on Pearl Harbour and was awarded the silver star for gallantry. In 1949 he moved to the Senate to represent Texas. Four years later, at the age of forty-four, he became the Democrat's youngest leader in the Senate. In 1954 he became the majority leader. Johnson left the Senate in 1961 to become vice-president. Shortly after Kennedy's assassination, Johnson was sworn in as president on board Air Force One when it was on the ground at Love Field Airport, Dallas. He completed the passage of Kennedy's Civil Rights Act (which outlawed racial segregation) in 1964, and later that year won a landslide victory in the presidential election. The Voting Rights Act, which was introduced in 1965, made discriminatory voting practices illegal. However, the escalating conflict in Vietnam proved increasingly unpopular and Johnson declined to run for another term in office. He died in 1973 at the age of sixty-four.

In 1963 **William Hartnell** *became the first actor to play Doctor Who.*

Hartnell's first adventure as the Doctor was called 'An Unearthly Child' and he went on to play the role for nearly three years before leaving during the fourth series in 1966. Hartnell's film career began in the 1930s and included roles in *Brighton Rock* (1947), *Carry on Sergeant* (1959) and *This Sporting Life* (1963). He returned to the part of Doctor Who in the 'The Three Doctors', a four-part special first broadcast at the end of 1972. Hartnell died three years later at the age of sixty-seven.

Rodney Porter *was awarded the 1972 Nobel Prize in Physiology or Medicine for his discoveries in relation to the 'chemical structure of antibodies'.*

Porter was a graduate of Liverpool University and, after service in the Second World War, undertook his doctoral work at Cambridge under the supervision of the future double Nobel Prize winner Frederick Sanger. Porter developed an interest in the immune system which was to last throughout his scientific career. During his investigation into immuno-globulins (also called antibodies, these are protein molecules that are created to fight infections), Porter was able to break the molecules apart, using the protein-splitting enzyme papain, to make them easier to study. In 1962 he became the first person to put forward the four-chain structure of immunoglobulin. Porter was killed in a road accident in 1985; he was sixty-seven and still involved in his research. The 1972 Nobel Prize was shared with Gerald Edelman.

Stanley Middleton *was awarded the 1974 Booker Prize for 'Holiday'.*

Holiday was Middleton's fourteenth novel in a prolific literary career which explored the mores of provincial life. His first novel, *A Short Answer* (1958), was published when he was in his late thirties. He combined his writing with his career as an English teacher in his native Nottinghamshire, completing, on average, one book per year. Middleton's other novels include *Harris's Requiem* (1960), *The Daysman* (1984) and *Married Past Redemption* (1993). His forty-fifth, *A Cautious Approach*, was completed shortly before his death in 2009 at the age of eighty-nine, and was published the following year. Middleton shared the 1974 Booker Prize with Nadine Gordimer for *The Conservationist*.

Robin Day *chaired the first edition of the BBC television programme 'Question Time' in 1979.*

Day presented *Question Time* for the next ten years as it established itself as one of the most popular political programmes on television. He read law at Oxford and was called to the Bar in 1952, but opted instead for a career in journalism and broadcasting. In 1955, at the age of thirty-two, he became one of the first newsreaders on the newly constituted ITV. Day also carved out a reputation as an interviewer, with his inquisitorial approach replacing the previous air of deference shown to politicians. He stood for Parliament as a Liberal candidate in 1959, but lost to the sitting Tory MP and returned to television to work as a freelancer at the BBC. Day, who was knighted in 1981, also presented *Panorama* and, on radio, *The World at One*. He died in 2000 at the age of seventy-six.

In late 1980, the company founded by **John DeLorean** *produced its first car: the DMC-12.*

Intended for the American market, the V6-engined DeLorean, with its gull-wing doors, was manufactured in a purpose-built factory in Northern Ireland. It had a suggested retail price of $25,000 and every car had unpainted stainless-steel body panels. The company received substantial investment from the British government (approximately £80 million); however, only around nine thousand cars were made before the closure of the factory in 1982. There had been problems with quality, and the car was relatively expensive at a time of recession in the US. The lack of sufficient sales soon gave the DeLorean Motor Company (DMC) financial problems and, unable to raise more investment, it was declared bankrupt. For DeLorean, who had left his job as a vice-president at General Motors (GM) in 1973 to create his own car company, it was the end of a dream. A graduate in mechanical and automotive engineering, DeLorean joined GM in 1956 after jobs at Chrysler and Packard. He rose rapidly at GM and at the age of forty became the youngest general manager of a division in the company when he took over Pontiac. As well as his business troubles in 1982, DeLorean also found himself charged with drug offences. He was implicated in an attempt to obtain and supply millions of pounds worth of cocaine in a desperate bid to raise funds for his company. However, despite incriminating video evidence, he was acquitted in 1984, with the jury unanimously clearing him on eight separate charges after he had claimed that he had been a victim of an entrapment operation by the FBI. DeLorean was declared bankrupt in 1999. He died in 2005 at the age of eighty, but his car continues to be held in affection, helped in part by its role in the *Back to the Future* films as a time machine.

***John Vane** was awarded the 1982 Nobel Prize in Physiology or Medicine for his 'discoveries concerning prostaglandins and related biologically active substances'.*

Prostaglandins, discovered in the 1930s by the Swede Ulf von Euler, can exist and be created in virtually every cell of the body. They have a variety of effects which include activation of the inflammatory response, such as fever, and the production of pain. Prostaglandins also play a role in the mechanism of blood clotting and the induction of labour. Vane was the first to discover that the drug aspirin, manufactured since the start of the twentieth century, worked by preventing the generation of prostaglandins, thus solving a decades old mystery. Vane's team also discovered prostacyclin, a prostaglandin which performs as a blood clot inhibitor. A graduate of the universities of Birmingham and Oxford, Vane was knighted in 1984. He died in 2004 at the age of seventy-seven. Vane shared the Nobel Prize with Sune Bergström and Bengt Samuelsson.

***Trevor Baylis** filed his patent application for a generator to power a wind-up radio in 1992.*

Baylis was inspired to create a wind-up radio after seeing a television programme about the spread of Aids in Africa. Public education programmes about the disease could be broadcast by radio, but receivers that relied on battery power were costly, inconvenient and limited the potential audience. His first prototype was featured on the television programme *Tomorrow's World* in 1994, and the interest it generated led to the backing that enabled its commercialisation in 1997, the same year that he was also awarded the OBE, one of many accolades that he has received for his invention.

***David Dimbleby** became the chairman of the BBC television programme 'Question Time' in 1994.*

Dimbleby has presided over the programme for more than eighteen years, making him the longest-serving chairman. The son of the late Richard, and brother of Jonathan (also both broadcasters), Dimbleby joined the BBC in the 1960s. He became a presenter on *Panorama* in the following decade and in 1979 anchored his first general election results programme; a duty that he has performed for the BBC ever since. He has also presented other series for the corporation on subjects such as art and architecture. In 2010, Dimbleby hosted the final live party leaders' debate prior to the UK general election.

*The television quiz show 'The Weakest Link', presented by **Anne Robinson**, first aired in 2000.*

Prior to becoming a broadcaster, Robinson worked as a journalist for newspapers that included the *Daily Mail, The Sunday Times* and the *Daily Mirror* (she also worked as an assistant editor for the latter). Her first regular television slot was as the presenter of the viewers' comments show *Points of View*, which she remained with until 1999. She also fronted the consumer complaints show *Watchdog* for several years, which she rejoined in 2009. However, she is probably best known for presenting *The Weakest Link*, which ended in 2012 after thirteen series.

56
FIFTY-SIX

*In 1889 the Eiffel Tower, designed by **Gustave Eiffel**, was opened in Paris.*

The tower had been constructed for the Exposition Universelle, a world fair held during the year of the 100th anniversary of the French Revolution. Originally conceived as a temporary construction to last only twenty years, the Eiffel Tower has become one of the world's top tourist attractions, and, until 1930, was the tallest structure on the planet. Eiffel's other creations include bridges, viaducts and the internal framework that supports the Statue of Liberty in New York, a gift from France to the United States in 1876. Eiffel was also recruited to build the locks for the Panama Canal project led by Ferdinand de Lesseps. However, the failure of the canal company in 1889 due to bankruptcy resulted in charges of fraud, which also extended to Eiffel who received a sentence of two years in prison (plus a fine) on his conviction. The decision was later overturned on appeal and Eiffel was cleared of any wrongdoing. He spent the remaining thirty years of his life pursuing scientific interests, living and working in his eponymous tower. He died in 1923 at the age of ninety-one.

Woodrow Wilson *took the oath of office as the twenty-eighth president of the United States in 1913.*

Wilson's election victory was aided by a split in the Republican vote, with both President Taft and his predecessor Theodore Roosevelt appearing on the ballot paper. Wilson was born in the state of Virginia and graduated from the College of New Jersey (now Princeton University) in 1879. He then studied law at the University of Virginia and began his legal practice in 1882. Wilson gave it up and returned to academia, receiving a doctorate from John Hopkins University in 1886 (Wilson is the only president to have earned a PhD). He accepted various academic positions before being made president of Princeton University in 1902. Wilson was elected to the governorship of New Jersey in 1910 and two years later gained the Democratic nomination for the presidency. Legislation passed in his first term included the Federal Reserve Act, which established the central banking system of the US, and the Clayton Antitrust Act, which outlawed anti-competitive business behaviour. Wilson strove to keep the US out of the First World War and, partly due to this achievement, won re-election in 1916. He attempted to broker an end to the conflict, however the resumption of unrestricted German U-boat warfare forced Wilson's hand and made him decide that there was no alternative to a US declaration of war against Germany. The US entered World War One in April 1917. In a speech at the beginning of 1918, he enunciated his 'Fourteen Points' for peace. It was on the basis of these that Austro-Hungary and Germany surrendered in 1918. The last of the fourteen points called for the establishment of an 'association of nations' which became the 'League of Nations' founded by the post-war Versailles treaty. Despite Wilson's best efforts the United States did not join the League, with the Republican-controlled Senate voting against membership. His transcontinental campaign to win support for the League took its toll on his health and Wilson suffered a stroke in 1919 which left him seriously weakened and partially paralysed. He continued as president and died three years after leaving office in 1924, aged sixty-seven. Amendments to the US constitution enacted during his presidency included the prohibition of alcohol in 1919 (repealed in 1933) and the right to vote for women in 1920.

*In 1929 **Margaret Bondfield** became the first woman to become a Cabinet minister in Britain.*

Prior to winning her seat as a Labour MP in 1923, Bondfield was a notable trade unionist who had first become active in the National Union of Shop Assistants, Warehousemen and Clerks in the latter years of the previous century. She held the post of the union's assistant secretary for several years and later became the secretary of the Women's Labour League. Bondfield also, for a time, held the chair of the TUC General Council; the first woman to do so. In 1924 she became the first woman minister when she served as a parliamentary secretary in the inaugural Labour government, led by Ramsay MacDonald, in 1924. Bondfield was defeated in the general election of that year, but returned to Parliament two years later. Labour was once again in government in 1929 and MacDonald appointed her to the Cabinet as the minister of labour. Bondfield's political career in the Commons ended with defeat in the 1931 general election. She died in 1953 at the age of eighty.

***Jules Rimet** presented the football World Cup trophy to its inaugural winners, Uruguay, in 1930.*

Rimet, who was born in France and trained as a lawyer, was not a footballer himself, but the football World Cup was his brainchild. He became the third president of FIFA in 1921 and advocated the creation of a world football tournament, which was finally agreed to by the organisation in 1928. Prior to the World Cup, the Olympic Games had been the premier international football competition, and Uruguay, the winners in 1924 and 1928, were selected as hosts for the first World Cup. This decision was helped by the Uruguayan government's offer to pay all travelling and accommodation expenses. Nevertheless, only four European teams (many had been deterred by the long sea journey) travelled to Uruguay to compete: France, Belgium, Romania and Yugoslavia. Three second-half goals gave victory to the host nation as they defeated Argentina 4–2 in the final. The solid gold trophy they were presented with was renamed after Jules Rimet in 1946. Brazil were allowed to keep it after their third win in 1970, but thirteen years later the trophy was stolen and never recovered. Rimet served as FIFA president until 1954, during which time there was a four-fold increase in membership. He died in 1956 at the age of eighty-three.

Richard Nixon *took office as the thirty-seventh president of the United States in 1969.*

A lawyer by profession, Nixon was elected to the House of Representatives aged thirty-three, the Senate aged thirty-seven and as Dwight Eisenhower's vice-president two years later. In the latter post he served two terms and was the natural choice to run against John F. Kennedy in the 1960 presidential election. However, Nixon was narrowly defeated and two years later he also lost the election to become the governor of California. At the time, Nixon viewed this latest setback as the end of his political career, but he returned in 1968 to win the Republican nomination and the presidency. Nixon went on to win a second term in 1972 and became the first person to have won twice as a vice-president and as a president. The ongoing Vietnam War provided the backdrop to his period in the White House; a ceasefire was agreed in 1973, but the war finally ended in 1975 after Nixon had left office. Nixon became the first US president to visit the People's Republic of China in 1972, and talks with the Soviet leadership produced the first nuclear weapons limitation agreement. The scandal that emerged from a break-in at the offices of the Democratic National Committee, at the Watergate building in Washington during the 1972 campaign, led to Nixon's resignation in 1974, the first ever by a US president. Nixon denied any personal involvement, but tape recordings indicated that he had been involved in attempts to cover up the incident. Facing the threat of impeachment and removal from office, Nixon resigned. He died in 1994 at the age of eighty-one.

Anita Brookner *won the Booker Prize in 1984 for 'Hotel du Lac'.*

Brookner, an art historian and the first woman to become the Slade professor of art at Cambridge University, made her debut as a novelist at the age of fifty-two with *A Start in Life* (1981). It was followed by *Providence* (1982), *Look at Me* (1983) and then her Booker-winning title. Since then,

Brookner has typically written one novel per year. Her other titles include *A Friend from England* (1987), *Incidents in the Rue Laugier* (1995) and more recently, *Strangers* (2009). Her first published works were on the subject of art history and include *Watteau* (1968) and *The Genius of the Future* (1971). She was awarded a CBE in 1990.

Seamus Heaney *was awarded the Nobel Prize in Literature in 1995.*
Heaney, born and raised in Northern Ireland, studied English language and literature at Queen's University Belfast, and returned there as a lecturer in 1966. In the same year his first, widely acclaimed volume of poetry, *Death of a Naturalist*, was also published. Heaney's other collections include *Door into the Dark* (1969), *Wintering Out* (1972) and *North* (1975). Heaney was elected in 1989 to a five-year term as the professor of poetry at the University of Oxford.

John Walker *was awarded the 1997 Nobel Prize in Chemistry for his investigations into the mechanism of adenosine triphosphate (ATP) synthesis.*
The ATP molecule is the universal carrier of energy within the cell. It acts both as a store of energy and the means to transfer energy in all living things. The enzyme ATP synthase creates ATP from adenosine diphosphate (ADP) and phosphate building blocks. Walker and his co-workers determined the structure of ATP synthase, and confirmed the mechanism for its interaction with ATP, put forward by Paul Boyer, with whom he shared half of the 1997 Nobel Prize (the other half was awarded to Jens Skou for the 'discovery of an ion-transporting enzyme'). Walker graduated with a degree in chemistry from St Catherine's College, Oxford, in 1964, and was awarded a DPhil degree five years later. He held various research positions abroad and then returned to England in 1974 to work at the Medical Research Council's Laboratory of Molecular Biology in Cambridge. Walker remained there for the next twenty-four years, before becoming the director of the MRC Mitochondrial Biology Unit in Cambridge. He received a knighthood in 1999.

Gordon Brown *became prime minister in 2007.*
Brown participated in a 'fast track' programme that saw him enter high school two years earlier than normal and subsequently enrol at the

University of Edinburgh when he was sixteen to study history. Brown subsequently graduated with first-class honours in history and completed a PhD. Unusually, he was also elected as rector while still a student. Prior to entering the Commons at the 1983 general election, at the age of thirty-two, he worked as a lecturer and as a television journalist. Following the Labour general election victory in 1997, Brown's first Cabinet post was as chancellor of the exchequer and upon entering office Brown announced a significant shift when he transferred interest rate setting policy to the Bank of England. His ten years as chancellor made him the longest serving since Sir Robert Walpole in the eighteenth century. Unopposed in the Labour leadership election following Tony Blair's resignation, he became prime minister in 2007. His time as premier was largely dominated by the financial crisis that unfolded both at home and abroad. Brown failed to secure a majority at the 2010 general election and was replaced as prime minister by David Cameron at the head of a Conservative/Liberal Democrat coalition. Subsequently, Brown also stepped down as leader of the Labour Party.

57

FIFTY-SEVEN

William Pitt, first Earl of Chatham, became prime minister in 1766.

Pitt entered Parliament at the age of twenty-six, representing the five electors of the pocket borough of Old Sarum. His superb oratorical skills were deployed in opposition to the prime minister, Sir Robert Walpole. In 1746, four years after Walpole had left office, Pitt joined the government, becoming paymaster-general in the administration led by Henry Pelham. The financial integrity he displayed, scrupulously ensuring that he profited by no more than his salary from the post, found favour with the public. Pelham died in 1754 and was replaced by his brother, the Duke of Newcastle. In the following year, Pitt was dismissed as paymaster due to his criticism of Newcastle's ministry. In 1756, Pitt returned to government, under the premiership of the Duke of Devonshire, as the secretary of state of the southern department, a post with responsibilities for foreign policy; an area in which Pitt would make his most significant contributions. Newcastle returned as prime minister in 1757, but Pitt maintained his office, continuing to direct foreign policy and the prosecution of the Seven Years' War. Pitt's strategy ensured significant territorial gains for the British Empire, although he resigned in 1761 when unable to win support for a pre-emptive strike against Spain. Pitt was back five years later, this time as prime minister and now sitting in the Lords as the Earl of Chatham. Ill health prompted his resignation in 1768 and he died ten years later at the age of sixty-nine. His second son, also William, became the youngest British prime minister in 1783, at the age of twenty-four.

George Washington took office as the first president of the United States in *1789.*

Washington was born of English planter stock in Virginia, in 1732. He gained his early military experience when he joined the Virginia militia in 1752. Two years later he was commissioned as a lieutenant colonel in the Virginia regiment, and was involved in confrontations with the French over territorial claims – the first hostilities of what would become the Seven Years' War (also known as the French and Indian War). Washington saw further action, accepted a command with the rank of colonel, but resigned in 1758, the same year that he made his first entry into elected politics as a member of the Virginia House of Burgesses. Washington also applied for a commission in the British Army, but was rejected. He was against the Stamp Act of 1765, which introduced taxation of the American colonies by Britain and was repealed the following year. However, other contentious legislation followed and matters escalated between the colonies and the Crown. In 1775 war finally broke out and Washington became the commander-in-chief of the continental army. The French joined the conflict on the side of the Americans in 1778, and three years later the Battle of Yorktown resulted in a decisive victory against the British. A peace treaty was signed in 1783, the same year that Washington resigned his army post. He presided over the convention in 1787 that produced the US constitution, and two years later Washington was unanimously elected under its auspices as the first president of the United States. He served two terms before retiring and returning to his estate, but died in 1799 at the age of sixty-seven, less than three years after leaving office.

*In 1801 **Thomas Jefferson** became the third president of the United States.*

Jefferson was born in Shadwell, Virginia, to a prosperous and well-connected family. A graduate of the College of William and Mary, he then read law and was admitted to the Bar in Virginia in 1767. In 1774, aged thirty-one, his pamphlet *A Summary View of the Rights of British America* was published. This advocated that the American colonies should be free from British authority and taxation. Two years later, Jefferson was the primary author of the Declaration of Independence, which was approved by Congress on 4 July 1776. Jefferson became the first secretary of state in 1790 under the presidency of George Washington, but resigned in 1793 after a dispute with the treasury secretary, Alexander Hamilton. He narrowly lost the presidential contest in 1796 and subsequently served as vice-president until 1801 when he took office as president. Jefferson's major success in his first term was the purchase of the Louisiana territory from Napoleon for $15 million in 1803 which doubled the area of the country. Jefferson was re-elected in 1804. He sought to maintain a neutral line in the war between Britain and France, but his policy of preventing American ships sailing to European ports was not a success and harmed the US economically. It was repealed just before Jefferson left office in 1809. He retired to his home state where he established the University of Virginia. Jefferson died on 4 July 1826 at the age of eighty-three.

***George IV** ascended to the throne in 1820.*

The eldest son of fifteen children, George had acted as regent since 1811 as a result of the ill health of his father George III. His secret marriage to Mrs Maria Fitzherbert in 1785, twice widowed and a Roman Catholic, was declared legally void since the Royal Marriages Act of 1772 required the King's consent for any royal weddings. An official royal union between George and a cousin, Caroline of Brunswick, took place in 1795. George only agreed to the marriage in order to improve his finances since his prodigal lifestyle had seen him accumulate considerable debt. However, it proved to be a failure and the couple separated, although they did have one daughter, Charlotte, who later died in childbirth. Echoing his youthful extravagance, the coronation of George IV in 1821 was a grand affair. He was reluctantly pressed into accepting Catholic emancipation in 1829 and died the following year at the age of sixty-seven. Although his personal conduct made him unpopular, George was an enthusiastic patron of the arts. He purchased and commissioned many paintings, oversaw the restoration of Windsor castle and instigated the development of Buckingham House into Buckingham Palace.

George Canning *became prime minister in 1827.*

Canning had entered Parliament at the age of twenty-three and became foreign secretary in 1807, at the age of thirty-six. As foreign secretary, he oversaw the seizure of the Danish fleet to prevent it falling into the hands of Napoleon. A quarrel with Lord Castlereagh, the war minister, led to the two men fighting a duel in 1809. Canning, who had never fired a shot before, missed Castlereagh, but he himself was wounded. Canning went on to hold the office of chancellor and became prime minister in 1827. However, he died suddenly after only one hundred and nineteen days in office, making him the shortest-serving prime minister in British history.

In 1924 **Ramsay MacDonald** *became Britain's first Labour prime minister.*

For MacDonald, who also took on the role of foreign secretary in the minority administration, it was a dramatic turnaround in events. Only six years earlier he had failed to win re-election, only being returned to Parliament in 1922 following the general election, which also made Labour the second largest party in the Commons, and MacDonald the leader of the opposition. They remained the second largest party after the 1923 election, but the lack of a sufficient electoral mandate for the Conservatives to continue in office resulted in MacDonald's appointment as prime minister. However, the government fell months later. The ensuing election was bitterly fought and it returned the Conservatives to power with a clear majority. Labour lost forty seats but the Liberal Party lost nearly three times that amount as the election pushed them into a poor third place: a new two-party system was being formed. The election of 1929 produced another hung Parliament and MacDonald formed his second Labour minority government. Economic turbulence caused by the stock market crash and rising unemployment plunged the government into crisis. In 1931, the Labour Cabinet split over plans that would result in cuts to government spending, including unemployment benefit. The resulting cabinet resignations precipitated the end of the Labour administration. MacDonald also resigned, but was persuaded to remain as prime minister at the head of a coalition National Government. The new Cabinet consisted of Labour, Conservative and Liberal members, but many in MacDonald's own party felt betrayed. These feelings were intensified when in the general election held later that year the Labour Party was reduced to fifty-two seats with the National Government winning 554 (most of these Conservative). MacDonald remained as prime minister until the summer of 1935 when, with his health and vigour in decline, he resigned. He died two years later at the age of seventy-one. A public funeral was held in Westminster Abbey and his ashes were interred in his home town of Lossiemouth in Scotland.

In 1948 **Ronald Colman** *won the Academy Award for best actor for his part as Anthony John in 'A Double Life'.*

Colman, born in Richmond, Surrey, was seriously injured during the First World War and invalided from the army. He then pursued his interest in acting and appeared in various stage productions as well as in a few short silent films. In his late twenties he performed on the American stage, which led to the start of his US film career with a leading role opposite Lillian Gish in *The White Sister* (1923). His other silent films include the classic *Beau Geste* (1926). His smooth, agreeable voice ensured an easy and successful transition into the era of the 'talkies', and he was first nominated for the best actor Oscar at the third Academy Awards ceremony, held in 1930, for his roles in *Bulldog Drummond* (1929) and *Condemned* (1929). His film output in the 1930s included *Raffles* (1930), *A Tale of Two Cities* (1935), *Lost Horizon* (1937) and *The Prisoner of Zenda* (1937). In the next decade he made fewer films, but was still Academy Award nominated for his role in *Random Harvest* (1942) and won the best actor award for *A Double Life* (1947). Television and radio were his mainstay in the 1950s with his last film, *The Story of Mankind* (1957), released in the year of his death at the age of sixty-seven.

Anthony Eden *succeeded Winston Churchill as prime minister in 1955.*

Eden was educated at Eton and Christ Church, Oxford, where he graduated with a first in oriental languages in 1922. In-between Eton and Oxford, he saw active service in the First World War during which he was awarded the Military Cross. Eden also lost two of his brothers during the war. He was first elected to Parliament at the 1923 general election at the age of twenty-six as the Conservative member for Warwick and Leamington. Twelve years later Eden entered the Cabinet as foreign secretary. He was the youngest person to hold the post in the twentieth century and was also one of the longest serving. His first spell ended with his resignation after just over two years, following a disagreement with Chamberlain over the direction of foreign policy. Eden rejoined the government under Churchill during World War Two, and returned to the post of foreign secretary five years to the day since his first appointment. Following Labour's election victory in 1945, Eden was out of government. He became foreign secretary again in 1951, and held the position until he replaced Churchill as prime minister in 1955. Nine days after taking office in April 1955, Eden called a general election which returned the Conservatives to power with an increased majority. Less than two years later, Eden resigned due to ill health following the Suez crisis. The military operation (conducted with France and Israel) to retake the Suez Canal after its nationalisation by Egypt initially went well, but diplomatic pressure, particularly from the United States, forced the declaration of a ceasefire after less than ten days. British and French forces withdrew from Egypt in December 1956 and the Israelis followed suit three months later. The whole operation had aroused controversy, British public opinion was divided and its ignominious conclusion for Britain damaged Eden's reputation. He resigned as an MP in 1957. Already a Knight of the Order of the Garter since 1954, he entered the House of Lords as the Earl of Avon in 1961. Eden took seriously ill during a US trip in 1977 and was flown home by the RAF. He arrived back in Britain twenty years to the day after his resignation as prime minister. He died five days later at the age of seventy-nine.

Maria Goeppert-Mayer was awarded the 1963 Nobel Prize in Physics for her work on nuclear shell structure.

Goeppert-Mayer is one of only two women to have been awarded the Nobel Prize in Physics (Marie Curie was the first). Born Maria Goeppert in Kattowitz within the German Empire (now Katowice, Poland), the family moved to Göttingen where she later entered the university and received her doctorate in 1930. In the same year, Goeppert married physical chemist

Joseph Mayer and they left Europe for his home country of the United States. She continued to work in science, but usually on an unpaid basis (she was fifty-three years old before she attained a full university professorship). In 1948, Goeppert-Mayer started to work on a theory to explain why certain atomic nuclei with a number of protons or neutrons equal to one of the 'magic numbers' (now recognised as 2, 8, 20, 28, 50, 82 and 126) were more stable. She proposed the nuclear shell model of atomic nuclei. Her fellow Nobel laureate, Hans Jensen, also worked independently on the same problem and came to similar conclusions. He and Goeppert-Mayer then collaborated to produce the book *Elementary Theory of Nuclear Shell Structure*, published in 1955. Goeppert-Mayer moved to the University of California at San Diego in 1960. She died in 1972 at the age of sixty-five.

Paul Scott *won the 1977 Booker Prize for 'Staying On'.*

Scott became profoundly interested in India, which provided his major literary inspiration, when he was posted to the country as an officer cadet in 1943. He returned to England after the end of the Second World War and took a job as an accountant before becoming a literary agent with clients that included Muriel Spark and John Braine. Scott's first novel, *Johnny Sahib*, was published in 1952; others followed, and eight years later Scott decided to become a full-time writer. He visited India again to reacquaint himself with the country that would be the focus for his *Raj Quartet*. The first volume, *The Jewel in the Crown*, was published in 1966 when Scott was forty-six. *The Day of the Scorpion* (1968), *The Towers of Silence* (1971) and *A Division of the Spoils* (1974) completed what became his major literary achievement. The quartet was later adapted to become the television series *The Jewel in the Crown*, first broadcast in 1984. *Staying On*, his Booker Prize-winning novel and a sequel to his *Raj Quartet*, was to be his last. Scott was too ill to make the prize-giving ceremony and died only months later, in 1978, at the age of fifty-seven.

Hilary Mantel *won the 2009 Man Booker Prize for 'Wolf Hall'.*

Set in Tudor England during the reign of Henry VIII, *Wolf Hall* depicts the rise to power of Thomas Cromwell, who became the King's main advisor. Mantel's first published novel was *Every Day is Mother's Day* (1985). Seven others followed, including *Fludd* (1989), *A Place of Greater*

Safety (1992) and *An Experiment in Love* (1995), before *Beyond Black* (2005) became her first to be shortlisted for the Man Booker Prize. Mantel's sequel to *Wolf Hall*, *Bring up the Bodies*, won the 2012 Man Booker Prize, making her the first woman and the first British author to win the award a second time. She was awarded a CBE in 2006.

58

FIFTY-EIGHT

'Travels into Several Remote Nations of the World' by **Jonathan Swift** *was published in 1726.*

Swift's book is better known as *Gulliver's Travels* and was published under the pseudonym of Lemuel Gulliver. His most famous work, it satirises human nature while also parodying 'voyage literature'. During four different voyages, Gulliver visits places including Lilliput, Brobdingnag and Laputa, and meets creatures such as the Houyhnhnms and Yahoos. The book was an immediate success and its first edition sold out within a week. Swift was born in Dublin in 1667. A graduate of Trinity College, he was ordained as a priest in the Church of Ireland aged twenty-seven. His early works of satire include *The Battle of the Books* and *A Tale of a Tub*, both published in England in 1704. Swift also wrote political pamphlets – originally supporting the Whigs and later the Tories. He became the editor of a Tory newspaper, *The Examiner*, in 1710. However, the Tories did not gift him an English church position as he'd hoped, although he was made the Dean of St. Patrick's Cathedral in Dublin in 1713. In the following year, the death of Queen Anne and the ascendancy of the Whigs dashed any remaining hopes of advancing his clerical career in England. From then on, he largely remained in Ireland and after a break of several years returned to writing. He died in 1745 at the age of seventy-seven.

In 1809 **James Madison** *was inaugurated as the fourth president of the United States.*

Madison, born in Virginia, was a graduate of the College of New Jersey (now Princeton University). He was the principal architect of the

Virginia Plan which became, in essence, the basis of the United States Constitution (Madison is often referred to as the 'Father of the Constitution'). A member of the House of Representatives between 1789 and 1797, Madison was the author of the first ten amendments to the constitution, known as the 'Bill of Rights', ratified in 1791. He was President Thomas Jefferson's secretary of state, during which time the Louisiana purchase was completed which doubled the area of the United States. The Napoleonic Wars affected the Americans as well, with seizures of their ships and the disruption of trade by the British creating tension between Britain and America. Madison, who succeeded Thomas Jefferson as president, decided in favour of war with Britain in 1812, a decision which was backed by Congress. Although the British did manage to occupy Washington D.C. in 1814, and set fire to many public buildings including the White House, the conflict ended in stalemate and was formally concluded in 1814. Madison left office in 1817 and died in 1836, at the age of eighty-five.

In 1817 **James Monroe** *became the fifth president of the United States.*

A former secretary of state under James Madison, Monroe also served for a time as the secretary of war. Notable events during his two terms as president included the cessation of Florida from Spain, the espousal of what later became known as the 'Monroe doctrine' and the 'Missouri compromise'. The Monroe doctrine was contained in a message to Congress in 1823 in which the president stated that there should be no further colonisation of the Americas by European powers (although existing colonies were unaffected), and that the United States would not become involved in any European conflicts. The 'Missouri compromise' was the agreement reached in the dispute over whether or not Missouri would be a 'slave state' or a 'free state' when it was admitted to the Union. It stated that slavery would not be allowed north of the 36 degree 30 minute parallel except in the proposed state of Missouri (its southern border was located on this parallel). Missouri was the fifth and last state to be admitted to the Union during Monroe's presidency (following Mississippi, Illinois, Alabama and Maine). He left office in 1825 and was replaced by John Quincy Adams. Monroe died in 1831 at the age of seventy-three.

James Spangler filed his patent application for a 'Carpet Sweeper and Cleaner' in 1907.

Although not the first vacuum cleaner, Spangler's was the first portable 'upright' model, and sported a rotating brush at the front to agitate the carpet dust and allow it to be drawn into the machine. Spangler invented the machine while working as a janitor in a department store where the task of floor sweeping aggravated his asthma. He built his first machine out of a collection of everyday items that included a broom handle, pillow case and soapbox. He tried to exploit his invention via his Electric Suction Sweeper Company, but a turning point came when William Hoover bought Spangler's patent because he saw its potential to create products to replace his declining leather goods business. Spangler remained with the company and continued to receive royalties, as sales of the vacuum cleaners began to multiply. He died in 1915 at the age of sixty-six. The Electric Suction Sweeper Company was renamed Hoover in 1922.

William D'Arcy received news in 1908 that his exploration team had struck oil in Persia.

D'Arcy, a lawyer by profession, was already a successful and wealthy businessman with a fortune amassed from his mining interests in Australia, the country his family had immigrated to when he was a teenager. He returned to England in 1889, although he maintained links with his Australian enterprise. In 1901, acting through a representative, he obtained exclusive exploration rights in south west Persia to look for oil. However, the team, headed up by George Reynolds and funded by D'Arcy, had no success in this quest. An agreement with the Burmah Oil Company provided further investment, but it took another three years until they struck oil: the first major find in the Middle East. They had been close to the point of giving up, but now the fortune that D'Arcy had staked on the venture was safe. In the following year the Anglo-Persian Oil Company, the forerunner of British Petroleum (BP), was formed. D'Arcy died in 1917, aged sixty-seven.

William Butler Yeats was awarded the 1923 Nobel Prize in Literature.

Born in Dublin in 1865, Yeats spent time, as a child, in London and Sligo, which was the home of his maternal grandparents. The time he spent in Sligo nurtured his interest in celtic myth and legend that would permeate his early work, in particular. His first publications appeared when he was in his twenties and included *The Wanderings of Oisin and Other Poems* (1889) and his lyric poem *The Lake Isle of Innisfree* (1890). Although from an Anglo–Irish background, Yeats was a fervent supporter of Irish nationalism and was a key figure in the Irish Literary Revival at the cusp of the twentieth century. He co-founded the Irish Literary Theatre, later to become the Abbey Theatre, which opened with Yeats's *The Countess Cathleen* in 1899. The middle period of Yeats's poetry signalled a shift away from Celtic mysticism towards contemporary subjects as seen in his 1910 collection *The Green Helmet and Other Poems*. Yeats became a senator in the newly formed Irish Free State in 1922, one year before his Nobel award – the first for an Irish national. His later writing, which includes the volumes *The Tower* (1928) and *The Winding Stair* (1929), is considered by many to be his finest. He died in France, at the age of seventy-three, in 1939. Yeats's body was re-interred in County Sligo in 1948.

Peter Mitchell was awarded the 1978 Nobel Prize in Chemistry for his work on biological energy transfer and he was cited in particular for his 'formulation of the chemiosmotic theory'.

Mitchell first published a paper on the chemiosmotic theory when working at the University of Edinburgh zoology department in 1961. Its aim was to explain the mechanism by which adenosine triphosphate (ATP), a biological compound which stores and transports energy, is formed. The photosynthesis of plants, and respiration in animals, results in energy being amassed in ATP. This compound is then split into adenosine diphosphate (ADP) and inorganic phosphate, which releases energy and fuels various biological processes. Mitchell's theory covers the conversion of ADP back into ATP. He proposed that in addition to a transfer of electrons, hydrogen ions (protons) also undergo movement, with the resultant potential difference providing energy for the creation of ATP. His theory was initially received with scepticism by the scientific community, but further work in this area by others vindicated his proposal. Mitchell left the University of Edinburgh in 1963, and in 1965 established the Glynn Research Institute, a small charitable organisation based in Cornwall. He died in 1992 at the age of seventy-one.

*In 1982 **Clarence 'Gatemouth' Brown** won the Grammy Award for best traditional blues album for 'Alright Again!'*

Brown was born in Louisiana but raised in Orange, Texas. His father, a railroad worker, was also a musician, and as a child Brown learned to play guitar, violin and the drums. His music teacher described him as having a 'voice like a gate' and the name stuck. Brown first performed as a drummer aged sixteen, but his guitar playing was showcased when he gave an impromptu turn in 1947, taking the stage after T-Bone Walker had left mid-show due to illness. His performance attracted the attention of the club's owner, Don Robey, who became his manager and signed him to his Peacock record label. Brown's early hits included 'Okie Dokie Stomp' and 'Boogie Rambler'. His career hit a lull in the sixties before its resurgence in the following decade. Brown's music developed into a fusion of blues, country, jazz and other influences, and he continued to record and perform up to his death in 2005 at the age of eighty-one. His last studio album, *Timeless*, was released in 2004.

* **Tim Hunt** was awarded the 2001 Nobel Prize in Physiology or Medicine for his discovery of cyclins.*

The cell cycle is the sequence of steps involved in cell division, in which a single cell splits and duplicates itself. Cyclins are proteins that play an important part in the regulation of this process and their level varies throughout the cell cycle. Hunt made his discovery in 1982 while working with sea urchin eggs. A graduate of Clare College, Cambridge, he shared the 2001 Nobel Prize with Leland Hartwell and Sir Paul Nurse, who also made discoveries that contributed to improved understanding of the cell cycle. Tim Hunt was knighted in 2006.

* **Steve Fossett** completed the first solo round-the-world balloon flight in 2002.*

Setting off from Australia, Fossett took approximately two weeks to complete his circumnavigation of the Southern Hemisphere aboard his balloon *Bud Light Spirit of Freedom*. Fossett graduated in economics from Stanford and earned an MBA from Washington University. He was involved with computer systems for the first few years of his career, but then became a financial trader and set up his own companies, Lakota Trading and Marathon Securities. Their success made his fortune and provided him with the means to fund his record attempts. Fossett has set over one hundred world records using various forms of transport: balloons, boats, gliders, airships and aircraft, and the majority of these still stand. He had also swum the English Channel and competed in dog sled races in Alaska. Fossett's other records include one for the longest distance aircraft flight when he flew nearly 26,000 miles in 2006. Tragedy struck in the following year when his light aircraft went missing on a routine flight near the Nevada and California border. The initial search and rescue missions drew a blank, but one year later identification cards belonging to Fossett were found in the vicinity by a hiker. Plane wreckage and remains, later confirmed as belonging to Fossett by DNA analysis, were then recovered. He was sixty-three.

In 2010 **Kathryn Bigelow** *won both the Academy Award and Bafta for best director for 'The Hurt Locker'.*

Bigelow is the first woman to win either the Academy Award or Bafta for best director. She also shared the Oscar for best picture with Mark Boal, Nicolas Chartier and Greg Shapiro. A graduate of Columbia University's film school, her first feature (co-directed with Monty Montgomery) was *The Loveless* (1982). Her other films include *Blue Steel* (1989), *Point Break* (1991) and *Strange Days* (1995). Her former husband, James Cameron, was a fellow nominee for best director in 2010 for the film *Avatar (2009)*.

59
FIFTY-NINE

Edward VII, *of the House of Saxe-Coburg and Gotha, succeeded to the British throne in 1901.*

Born in Buckingham Palace, he was the eldest son of Queen Victoria and Prince Albert. His coronation took place in August 1902, weeks after an operation for appendicitis carried out by Sir Frederick Treves (the British surgeon who had befriended Joseph Merrick, better known by the epithet 'the elephant man'). Edward VII founded the Order of Merit in the same year; admission into the order is the gift of the sovereign and restricted to twenty-four living members in addition to foreign recipients. It recognises 'great achievement in the fields of the arts, learning, literature and science'. Edward was connected to most of the other European monarchies: for example, the German Emperor Wilhelm II was his nephew. Fluent in French (and German), his visit to Paris in 1903 helped to pave the way for the agreements between Britain and France known as the Entente Cordiale, which were concluded the following year. Edward died in 1910, at the age of sixty-eight, only nine years after his coronation. He was succeeded by his eldest living son, who ruled as George V.

Jack Warner starred as the title character in the television series 'Dixon of Dock Green', first broadcast in 1955.

Warner first played police constable George Dixon in *The Blue Lamp* (1950), in which his character is fatally shot in the course of duty. Dixon was resurrected for the small screen, allowing Warner to become famous playing a policeman at an age when real-life police officers would be retiring. The series ran for nearly twenty-one years, with Warner making his final bow at the age of eighty. His career as an entertainer began with variety-show appearances, before he moved on to radio and film. Warner made his film debut in *The Dummy Talks* (1943) and four years later made his first appearance as Joe Huggett in *Holiday Camp* (1947), a character he returned to in three more films. Warner, who was awarded an OBE in 1965, died in 1981 at the age of eighty-five.

*In 1968 Manchester United, managed by **Matt Busby**, became the first English side to win the European Cup.*

Manchester United defeated Benfica 4–1 at Wembley after extra time to claim their first European trophy. Lanarkshire-born and raised, Busby began his senior playing career in 1928, at United's local rivals Manchester City, when he was eighteen. He played in two FA Cup finals, losing the first to Everton in 1933 by three goals to nil (it was the first final in which players wore numbered shirts), but gave an inspirational performance the following year when they defeated Portsmouth by two goals to one, despite Portsmouth leading the match with only seventeen minutes to play. Busby transferred to Liverpool in 1936, but the outbreak of war ended his senior playing career. He joined Manchester United as manager in 1945, and his team's first success was winning the FA cup in 1948. They finished as championship runners-up four times, before winning the first of five league titles with Busby at the helm in 1952. The young team he assembled in the 1950s became known as the 'Busby babes', and they won the League Championship in 1956 and in 1957, when they also reached the semi-final of the European Cup and the FA Cup final. The following season was overshadowed by the Munich air disaster which claimed the lives of twenty-three people, eight of them United players, when their plane crashed on take-off following a refuelling stop on the way back from a European tie. Busby himself was seriously injured and close to death. After his recovery, he rebuilt the side, won the FA Cup in 1963 and two more League Championships, and then, ten years after the Munich disaster, the European Cup. Busby retired from management in the following season, although he returned for the end of the 1970–71 campaign following the dismissal of his successor Wilf McGuinness. Busby was knighted in 1968. He died in 1994 at the age of eighty-four. Manchester United next won European football's top prize in 1999 on what would have been Busby's ninetieth birthday.

*In 1968 **Alec Rose** arrived in Portsmouth at the end of his solo round-the-world sailing voyage.*

Rose's trip was self-funded and included a short stay in Australia to visit his son and daughter-in-law as well as an enforced stop in New Zealand to repair damage sustained to his boat, a ketch named *Lively Lady*. Rose rounded both the Cape of Good Hope and Cape Horn during his 28,500 mile voyage, which took 354 days. The Portsmouth greengrocer received a knighthood the day after his arrival back in England. He died in 1991 at the age of eighty-two.

***Bernard Katz** was awarded the 1970 Nobel Prize in Physiology or Medicine for his work on the transmission of nerve impulses.*

Katz was born and brought up in Germany, but left for England in 1935 where he completed his doctorate at University College London. Katz moved to Australia in 1939. He served in the Royal Australian Air Force as a radar officer during the war before returning to England. His research into the way that a nerve impulse creates muscle activity showed that the transmitter chemical between the two (acetylcholine) was released in discrete quantities, always a multiple of a fundamental packet, or quantum, of the substance. Katz was knighted in 1969. He died in 2003 at the age of ninety-two. The 1970 Nobel Prize in Physiology or Medicine was shared with Ulf von Euler and Julius Axelrod.

Iris Murdoch won the 1978 Booker Prize for 'The Sea, The Sea'.

The central character of *The Sea, The Sea* is Charles Arrowby, whose chance meeting with his first love kindles an obsession that disrupts the solitude he sought by moving to live beside the sea. Murdoch was born in Dublin to Anglo-Irish parents and moved at an early age with her family to London. She won a scholarship to Somerville College, Oxford, to read Greats (classics, philosophy and ancient history) in which she obtained a first-class degree. She became a fellow and tutor in philosophy at St Anne's College, Oxford, in 1948. Murdoch's first novel, *Under the Net* (1954), was published at the age of thirty-four and followed her first book, the philosophical tract, *Sartre: Romantic Rationalist*, published in the previous year. She completed a further twenty-five novels over the next forty-one years that included *The Bell* (1958), *A Severed Head* (1961) and her last, *Jackson's Dilemma* (1995). A further five of Murdoch's books were shortlisted for the Booker Prize: *The Nice and the Good* (1968), *Bruno's Dream* (1969), *The Black Prince* (1973), *The Good Apprentice* (1985) and *The Book and the Brotherhood* (1987). She was awarded a CBE in 1976 and was made a DBE in 1987. Murdoch died in 1999 at the age of seventy-nine.

CHAPTER SEVEN

Sexagenarians

What's a man's age? He must hurry more, that's all;
Cram in a day, what his youth took a year to hold.

ROBERT BROWNING

60

SIXTY

Thomas Pelham-Holles, Duke of Newcastle upon Tyne (and first Duke of Newcastle under Lyme), became prime minister in 1754.

Pelham-Holles took over as prime minister from his brother, Henry Pelham, following his death in office (he added Holles to his name as a condition of inheriting the estate of his uncle John Holles). Pelham-Holles's first term was to last for two and a half years and saw clashes with France in North America in 1754, and then the outbreak of the Seven Years' War which called into question Pelham-Holles's foreign policy strategy. Poor progress in the war forced his resignation in 1756. He returned to office as prime minister the following year, with William Pitt leading the government in the Commons. Their coalition proved successful, but the death of George II in 1760, whose patronage Pelham-Holles had enjoyed, marked the beginning of the end of his premiership. He resigned in 1762 and was replaced by George III's favourite, the Earl of Bute. Pelham-Holles died six years later, at the age of seventy-five.

In 1810 Nicolas Appert won the prize offered by Napoleon for a food preservation technique that would be of use in helping to feed the military.

Appert had worked for many years on his food preservation method, which involved placing items into glass jars, sealing them and then placing them in boiling water. The 12,000 franc prize was awarded to Appert by Napoleon himself. Shortly afterwards, Appert published *L'Art de Conserver Pendant Plusieurs Années, Toutes les Substances Animales et Végétales* (The Art of Preserving Animal and Vegetable Substances for Many Years), the first cookbook if its kind. Appert died in 1841 at the age of ninety-one.

William Robertson was promoted to field marshal in 1920, becoming the first soldier to have advanced from the lowest to the highest rank in the British Army.

Robertson enlisted as a private in the 16th Lancers at the age of seventeen. He made steady progress through the ranks and joined the 3rd Dragoon Guards, who were then serving in India, as a second lieutenant in 1888. Robertson's advancement was aided by his aptitude for languages; he spoke French and German, as well as a number of Indian languages. He returned from India in 1896 to attend the military staff college at Camberley, the first former private to gain admission. During the First World War, Robertson became the quartermaster-general and subsequently chief of the Imperial General Staff. Following the armistice of 1918, he commanded the British Army of the Rhine. Robertson became a baronet in 1919 and was promoted to field marshal, the highest army rank, in 1920. He died in 1933 at the age of seventy-three.

Harry Truman became the thirty-third president of the United States in 1945, when he assumed office after the death of President Franklin Roosevelt.

Harry Truman was born and raised in Missouri where he joined the National Guard in 1905. He saw active service in Europe in the First World War as an artillery officer. After his return to the US he opened a haberdashery in Kansas City; however, the business failed and left Truman with debts he paid off in the coming years. Truman was elected to the Senate in 1934, where he remained until he took office as Franklin Roosevelt's vice-president in January 1945. Less than three months later, Roosevelt's death resulted in Truman becoming president. The war in Europe soon ended with the fall of Berlin. Weeks later, Truman's decision to drop the atomic bomb on the Japanese cities of Hiroshima and Nagasaki led to the surrender of Japan. However, a new conflict was about to begin: the 'Cold War' with the Soviet Union. Truman responded to the 1948 blockade of the western sectors of Berlin with an airlift of supplies, which led to a climb-down by the Soviets. Truman was re-elected in the same year for a second term. War was again on the agenda, with Truman committing the US military, under the auspices of the UN, to the defence of South Korea following its invasion by North Korea (the captured territory was recovered and a ceasefire signed in 1953). Other significant events during Truman's presidency included the US recognition of Israel, the Marshall Plan to provide economic aid to rebuild post-war Europe and the founding of NATO. Truman decided not to stand for re-election in 1952. He died at the age of eighty-eight in 1972.

T. S. Eliot (Thomas Stearns) was awarded the 1948 Nobel Prize in Literature.

Eliot was born in St. Louis, Missouri, in 1888, and graduated with a degree in philosophy from Harvard. After periods of postgraduate study at the Sorbonne and back again at Harvard, Eliot won a scholarship to Merton College, Oxford, in 1914. The following year, he married Vivienne Haigh-Wood, whom he'd known for only a few weeks. Eliot settled in England and took up teaching before accepting a position at a London bank in 1917. His first major poetical work, 'The Love Song of J. Alfred Prufrock' was published in 1915 and Eliot's complex, pioneering verse, 'The Waste Land' followed in 1922. It first appeared in *The Criterion*, a literary magazine established by Eliot, and for which he served as editor from its inception in 1922 until its closure in 1939. He left his position at the bank in 1925 to join Faber and Gwyer (later Faber and Faber) as literary editor, and also to serve on the board of directors. His other major works include the poems 'The Hollow Men' (1925) and 'Four Quartets' (1943), and the plays *Murder in the Cathedral* (1935) and *The Cocktail Party* (1949). The musical *Cats* was based on his *Old Possum's Book of Practical Cats*, published in 1939. As well as receiving the Nobel Prize in 1948, Eliot was also admitted to the Order of Merit. He died in 1965 at the age of seventy-six.

Alec Douglas-Home, fourteenth Earl of Home, became prime minister in 1963 following the resignation of Harold Macmillan.

The foreign secretary since 1960 in Macmillan's Conservative government, Douglas-Home sat in the House of Lords but chose to renounce his peerage and fight the Kinross and West Perthshire by-election, caused by the death of its sitting MP. He is the last prime minister to have been a member of the upper House, albeit for only a short time. (After leaving the Lords, and prior to his by-election victory, he was prime minister, although not actually an MP.) Douglas-Home (who was appointed as a Knight of the Order of the Thistle in 1962) was in office for one year before losing narrowly to Labour under Harold Wilson at the 1964 general election. He returned to government as foreign secretary in Edward Heath's Cabinet, between 1970 and 1974. Home left the Commons at the second general election in 1974 and returned to the House of Lords as a life peer. He died in 1995 at the age of ninety-two.

Margaret Atwood won the Booker Prize in 2000 for 'The Blind Assassin'.

In addition to her work as a novelist, the Canadian-born author has also produced nearly twenty poetry collections, children's books and non-fiction works. Atwood's first publication was the volume of poetry *Double Persephone* (1961) and her debut novel, *The Edible Woman*, was published eight years later. Atwood has won many awards and accolades for her writing; in addition to her Booker Prize win in 2000, she has been short-listed on four other occasions for: *The Handmaid's Tale* (1986), *Cat's Eye* (1989), *Alias Grace* (1996) and *Oryx and Crake* (2003). *The Year of the Flood*, a companion to *Oryx and Crake*, was published in 2009.

John Sulston was awarded the 2002 Nobel Prize in Physiology or Medicine for his work in studying the cell divisions in the nematode from fertilised egg to complete organism.

Sulston tracked and identified all the cell divisions that are necessary to create the complete organism *Caenorhabditis elegans* (*C. elegans*), an approximately one millimetre long nematode comprised of 959 cells. He found that the process was identical in different individuals and that certain cells are programmed to die during the organism's formation (a total of 131). He also discovered the first gene linked to this phenomenon, *nuc-1*. Corresponding genes also exist in higher species, including man. Sulston shared the 2002 award with Sydney Brenner, who identified *C. elegans* as a suitable experimental vehicle, and Robert Horvitz who discovered and characterised further genes controlling cell death in *C. elegans*. Sulston, a graduate of Pembroke College, Cambridge, joined the MRC Laboratory of Molecular Biology in 1969. In 1992 he began an eight-year period as the first director of the Sanger Centre for genome research in Cambridge. He was knighted in 2001.

61

SIXTY-ONE

*In 1797 **John Adams** became the second president of the United States.*

Immediately before his appointment, Adams had served for eight years as the first vice-president of the US. Educated at Harvard, Adams was a successful lawyer. He played a prominent role in the independence movement and was a delegate to the first and second Continental Congresses. Relations with post-revolutionary France, then at war with Britain, figured greatly during his single term; the French seizure of US merchant ships amounted to an undeclared or 'quasi war', prompting the US to build up their navy to counter this threat. In 1800 a peace agreement was concluded between the US and France. Adams left office the following year to be replaced by Thomas Jefferson, his former vice-president. In 1812 the two men, both now ex-presidents, set aside their rivalry and began a remarkable correspondence that would last until their deaths, on the same day: 4 July 1826, the fiftieth anniversary of the Declaration of Independence. Adams was ninety.

Frederick Abel and James Dewar patented their invention of cordite in 1889.

Cordite is a smokeless propellant, formed primarily of nitroglycerine and guncotton, used in firearms and larger guns. Abel was appointed to the presidency of a 'special committee on explosives', formed by the British government in 1888. The committee, which also included Dewar, was tasked with investigating which of the smokeless powders was most suitable for the British military. None of these were ideal, and so Abel and Dewar devised their own compound. The committee was given access to information on modern explosives, including ballistite, a smokeless propellant patented by Alfred Nobel. Abel and Dewar patented their invention the following year, prompting legal action from Nobel who claimed that his ballistite patent had been infringed. However, after three years the case was decided in the House of Lords in favour of Abel and Dewar, where it was decided that the wording of Nobel's patent did not cover the composition of cordite. It became the main propellant used by the British Army. Cordite's formulation was modified in the early twentieth century; however, it has now been superseded. Abel became a Knight of the Order of the Bath in 1891 and was made a baronet two years later. Abel died in 1902 at the age of seventy-five.

The maiden flight of Ferdinand von Zeppelin's first airship, the LZ1, took place in 1900.

Although the first flight by an airship had taken place almost fifty years earlier when Henri Giffard piloted his dirigible over Paris, Zeppelin pioneered the development of the rigid airship. The maiden flight of the LZ1 lasted for approximately seventeen minutes, during which time it covered nearly four miles. Despite setbacks, Zeppelin persevered with airship development and, in 1910, the first commercial airline passenger service was started by Deutsche Luftschiffahrts-Aktiengesellschaft (Delag) using Zeppelin airships. Prior to his ventures in the field of aviation, Zeppelin had had a career in the Prussian Army and had also worked as a military observer for the Union side in the American Civil War. It was during his time in the US that he made his first balloon flight. Zeppelin retired from the Prussian Army when he was in his early fifties and devoted himself to airship development. He died in 1917 at the age of seventy-eight.

Joshua Millner *won a gold medal at the 1908 London Olympic Games for the 1,000 yards men's free rifle.*

Millner, who was born in Dublin and represented Great Britain and Ireland, scored ninety-eight out of a possible one hundred to take first place. He is the oldest winner of an individual Olympic event in the modern Games (Oscar Swahn became the oldest overall gold medallist as part of the Swedish running deer shooting team in 1912). Millner served in the Territorial Army where he reached the rank of colonel. As well as shooting, he was interested in the breeding of Irish Setters; his book on the breed was published in 1924 when he was seventy-six. Millner died in 1931 at the age of eighty-four.

Robert Robinson *was awarded the 1947 Nobel Prize in Chemistry for 'his investigations on plant products of biological importance, especially the alkaloids'.*

Alkaloids are a group of naturally occurring chemicals typically found in plants. They are renowned for both their medicinal and poisonous properties, and examples include nicotine, morphine and caffeine. Robinson's work did much to further our understanding of the alkaloids, both in terms of their structure and the processes that could be used to create them in the laboratory. He demonstrated that larger 'chemical building blocks' could be used to assemble them. Robinson's other contributions to chemistry included his synthesis of the blue and red pigments of flowers and his work on penicillin. He first studied chemistry at Victoria

University, Manchester, and in his mid-twenties he became the first professor of pure and applied chemistry at the University of Sydney. Robinson returned to England three years later and, after several academic appointments, as well as a spell working for the British Dyestuffs Corporation, he joined the University of Oxford as the Waynflete professor of chemistry in 1929. He was knighted in 1939 and admitted to the Order of Merit a decade later. Robinson died in 1975 at the age of eighty-eight.

Franchised from **Harland Sanders**, *the first Kentucky Fried Chicken restaurant opened in 1952.*

Located in Salt Lake City, Utah, Leon 'Pete' Harman renamed his restaurant 'Kentucky Fried Chicken' after striking an agreement with Sanders to sell his fried chicken recipe. Sanders combined the use of a pressure cooker to speed up the preparation with a coating that included eleven herbs and spices to produce his distinctive fried chicken (the exact recipe remains a closely guarded secret). Before opening his first restaurant, attached to a filling station, in Corbin, Kentucky, Sanders had worked as a farm hand and insurance salesman, among other jobs. The restaurant was named Sanders Court & Café and it was there that Sanders developed his 'secret recipe' in the late 1930s. His venture was successful, but the arrival of the interstate in the 1950s dramatically reduced passing trade and Sanders, then in his sixties, sold up and began franchising his chicken business instead. By 1965 there were over six hundred Kentucky Fried Chicken outlets across the United States, at which point Sanders sold the business for $2 million, with his image remaining as the official face of the brand. The first UK restaurant, which was also the first US-based 'fast food' outlet in Britain, was opened in 1965 in Preston. Sanders received the honorary title of 'Kentucky Colonel' from the state governor in the mid-1930s. He died in 1980 at the age of ninety.

Patrick White *was awarded the 1973 Nobel Prize in Literature.*

White was born in London to Australian parents and spent the early period of his life both in their homeland and in England, where he read modern languages at King's College, Cambridge, graduating in 1935. He became interested in writing at a young age and his first novel, *Happy Valley* (1939), was published when he was twenty-six. During the war he was posted to the Middle East as an air force intelligence officer, but he was still able to produce a second novel, *The Living and the Dead*, in 1941. Post-war, he settled in Australia where he wrote the novels *The Aunt's Story* (1948) and *The Tree of Man* (1955). His other books include *Voss* (1957); *The Vivisector* (1970), which was nominated for the 'lost' Man Booker Prize in 2010; and his last, *Memoirs of Many in One* (1986). His autobiography, *Flaws in the Glass*, was published in 1981. White died in 1990 at the age of seventy-eight. He used the money from his Nobel Prize to found the Patrick White Award.

*In 1974 **Gerald Ford** took the oath of office as president of the United States when he succeeded Richard Nixon.*

As a result of the Watergate scandal, Nixon was the first US president to resign from office. Ford granted him an unconditional pardon within weeks of assuming power, a measure that attracted controversy at the time. A graduate of Yale Law School, Ford practised law both before and after the Second World War, during which he served in the US Navy. He was elected to the House of Representatives in 1948, where he became the Republican leader in 1965. Ford continued in this role until assuming the vice-presidency in 1973 following Spiro Agnew's resignation. Ford won his party's nomination for the 1976 presidential election, but was defeated by Jimmy Carter. He died in 2006 at the age of ninety-three, after enjoying the longest lifespan of any US president.

*In 2007 **Helen Mirren** won the both the Academy Award and Bafta for best actress for her portrayal of Elizabeth II in 'The Queen'.*

Acting was an early ambition for London-born Mirren and her performance as Cleopatra in the National Youth Theatre Production of *Antony and Cleopatra* at the Old Vic brought her to prominence at the age of twenty. She subsequently joined the Royal Shakespeare Company where her roles included Ophelia in *Hamlet* and Lady Macbeth. Mirren made her film debut in *Herostratus* (1967) and went on to appear in *O Lucky Man!* (1973) and *The Long Good Friday* (1980). Her first Bafta best film actress nomination was for *Cal* (1984). Her portrayal of Detective Chief Inspector Jane Tennison in the TV drama *Prime Suspect*, first broadcast in 1991, brought Mirren Bafta TV wins for best actress for three consecutive years. In addition to her win for *The Queen*, Mirren has also received three further Academy Award nominations. Two of these were for the best supporting actress category for *The Madness of King George* (1994) and *Gosford Park* (2001). Her role as Tolstoy's wife Sophia in *The Last Station* (2009) earned Mirren a second best actress nomination. She was awarded a DBE in 2003.

62

SIXTY-TWO

*In 1829 **Andrew Jackson** was sworn in as the seventh president of the United States.*

As a major general in the war against the British that started in 1812, Jackson became a hero when he led his troops to victory at the Battle of New Orleans in 1815, despite being outnumbered by the British forces. Jackson had also fought in the Revolutionary War and at one point was held as a prisoner by the British. He pursued a legal and political career and became the first representative for Tennessee after it was granted statehood in 1796. He won the popular vote in the 1824 presidential election, but lost on the electoral college vote. However, Jackson was successful four years later and went on to be re-elected for a second term. In 1830 Jackson signed into law the 'Indian Removal Act', which he strongly supported. This act gave the president the power to offer unsettled land in the west to Native Americans east of the Mississippi, the intent being to move them outside the existing state boundaries. Tens of thousands of Native Americans were displaced during Jackson's presidency, with many of them forced to accept the terms of resettlement. Two states were admitted to the Union during Jackson's presidency: Arkansas in 1836 and Michigan in 1837. Jackson died at the age of seventy-eight in 1845.

***Louis Pasteur** carried out the first successful treatment for rabies in 1885.*

Although the vaccine had previously only been tried on dogs, Pasteur decided – after consulting with colleagues – to use it on a nine-year-old boy, Joseph Meister, who had been badly bitten by a rabid dog. He carried out a sequence of injections over a period of eleven days to try to save Meister from a highly probable death. Pasteur's treatment plan and vaccine proved to be a success. Meister was protected from the disease and his life saved. Pasteur also conducted experiments which vindicated the germ theory of disease, and devised the process called pasteurisation which heat-treats foodstuffs, such as milk, to destroy harmful bacteria. Pasteur died in 1895 at the age of seventy-two. He is interred beneath the research institute in Paris, inaugurated in 1888, which bears his name.

In 1930 **George Arliss** *won the Academy Award for best actor, for the title role in 'Disraeli'.*

In what was the third Academy Awards ceremony, Arliss became the first British actor to win an Oscar. Born in London in 1868, his acting career took him to America at the start of the twentieth century where he would live for the next twenty-two years. In 1911, he first played Benjamin Disraeli on stage in a production that was adapted for a 1921 silent film. He then played Disraeli again, this time with sound, for his Oscar-winning film role; his spouse, Florence, played his screen wife. Arliss also portrayed historical figures in many of his other later films; he played the title characters in *Voltaire* (1933) and *Cardinal Richelieu* (1935) and the Duke of Wellington in *The Iron Duke* (1934). He made his last film appearance in 1937 as the eponymous *Doctor Syn*. Arliss died in 1946 at the age of seventy-seven.

The steam engine 'Mallard', designed by **Nigel Gresley**, *set the official world speed record for a steam locomotive in 1938.*

Running between Grantham and Peterborough, *Mallard* recorded a speed of 126mph while pulling seven coaches. *Mallard* was one of a number of streamlined class A4 pacific locomotives built by the London and North Eastern Railway (LNER) works at Doncaster for the East Coast mainline between London King's Cross and Edinburgh. The first went into service in 1935 and all were withdrawn from operation by the mid-1960s. Gresley was born in Edinburgh in 1876, and was brought up back in the family home in Derbyshire. He was educated at Marlborough College and then joined the London and North Western Railway as an engineering apprentice in 1893. By his mid-thirties, he had become the chief mechanical engineer for the Great Northern Railway (GNR). When the LNER was formed in 1923 from the merger of several smaller companies (including the GNR), Gresley maintained his position as chief mechanical engineer. The class A3 locomotive *Flying Scotsman*, designed by Gresley, was built in 1923 and eleven years later it became the first steam locomotive to officially reach 100mph. Gresley was knighted in 1936. He died at the age of sixty-four in 1941.

In 1945 **Clement Attlee** *became prime minister of the first majority Labour government following a landslide victory in the first post-war election.*

Attlee also became the first Labour leader to serve a full term as prime minister, in an administration which was one of the most radical of the twentieth century. It oversaw the establishment of the National Health Service and nationalisation of the railways, the steel industry, the coal mines and the Bank of England. In foreign affairs, both India and Burma were granted independence in the first major events of decolonisation. His government authorised the creation of Britain's independent nuclear deterrent and the UK became a member of NATO on its formation in 1949. Attlee was born the seventh of eight children in Putney, London, and enjoyed a comfortable middle-class upbringing. He graduated from Oxford with a degree in history, then studied law and was called to the Bar in 1906. Attlee also worked as a volunteer at a Stepney Boys' Club that was supported by his old school, Haileybury. He later became the club's manager and his experience of poverty at such close quarters shifted his political views to the left. In 1908 he joined the Independent Labour Party and became active in local politics. Attlee served in the First World War as an officer and was wounded in the Gallipoli campaign. He ended the war with the rank of major and resumed his involvement in East End politics, becoming the mayor of Stepney in 1919; he was elected three years later to Parliament. Attlee played a junior role in the Ramsay MacDonald administrations of the 1920s, but did not join his cross-party National Government in 1931. Four years later he became Labour leader. In the wartime coalition under Churchill, Attlee became a member of the War Cabinet and for the last three years held the title of deputy prime minister. After Churchill was defeated in the general election of 1945, Attlee became prime minister. A much reduced majority in the 1950 general election resulted in Attlee calling another election the following year, but this time the Conservatives were returned to power. He remained as leader of the opposition and fought the 1955 general election but lost out again, this time to Anthony Eden. He relinquished his twenty-year leadership of the Labour Party, left the Commons and joined the Lords as the first Earl Attlee. He died in 1967 at the age of eighty-four.

In 1953 **Dwight Eisenhower** *became the thirty-fourth president of the United States.*

Nicknamed 'Ike', Eisenhower first had a career in the US military before going into politics. In the latter stages of World War Two he served as the supreme commander of the allied expeditionary force in Europe and was in charge of the 'D-Day' Normandy landings in 1944. Just under one year later, General Eisenhower accepted the German surrender. His army career began in 1911 at the age of twenty with admission to the US military academy at West Point. Eisenhower advanced through the ranks, but did not experience active service in the First World War. It was not until 1942 that, as a lieutenant general and commander-in-chief of the allied landings in North Africa, he first commanded troops in combat. The first post-war Republican president, he spent two terms in the White House, the maximum allowed as a result of the twenty-second amendment to the constitution ratified by his predecessor, Harry Truman. He signed a peace deal in 1953 which brought the fighting in the Korean War to an end. Three years later Eisenhower came out against Britain and France in the Suez crisis, forcing a ceasefire and the subsequent withdrawal of their troops from the canal zone. At home he expanded the social security system and signed legislation to create the interstate highway system. His presidency also saw the admission of the forty-ninth (Alaska) and fiftieth (Hawaii) states to the Union. Eisenhower left office at the age of seventy, handing over to John F. Kennedy, who was nearly thirty years his junior. He died in 1969 at the age of seventy-eight.

'The Fellowship of the Ring', the first part of the Lord of the Rings trilogy, by **J. R. R. Tolkien** *(John Ronald Reuel), was published in 1954.*

The second volume of Tolkien's trilogy, *The Two Towers*, appeared later in 1954 and the final instalment, *The Return of the King* was published the next year. The epic novel, set in a fantasy world in which Frodo Baggins takes possession of an all-powerful ring which he must try and destroy in the fire of Mount Doom, was a sequel to Tolkien's 1937 work *The Hobbit, or There and Back Again*, published when he was forty-five. Tolkien was born to English parents in Bloemfontain (now in present-day South Africa) in 1892, and moved to England aged three. Tolkien lost both his parents in childhood – his father at the age of four and his mother eight years later. Despite these calamities, he did well at school where he displayed an aptitude for languages. He graduated from Exeter College, Oxford, in 1915, taking a first in his English language and literature finals. He served in the First World War, including at the Battle of the Somme, but was invalided back to England suffering from trench fever. In 1920, he began his academic career at the University of Leeds where he became a professor of English language in 1924 at the age of thirty-two. He shortly returned to Oxford to take up a post as a professor of Anglo-Saxon, a position he held for twenty years. He then became a professor of English language and literature in 1945, retiring fourteen years later. Tolkien was awarded a CBE in 1972 and died the following year, at the age of eighty-one.

Harold Macmillan succeeded Anthony Eden as prime minister in 1957.
The son of a publisher and his American wife, Macmillan was educated at Eton and Balliol College, Oxford. He saw action with the Grenadier Guards in the First World War and was wounded on three occasions – the last incident, during the Battle of the Somme in 1916, was serious enough to prevent him taking any further part in the war. Macmillan entered Parliament in 1924 as the MP for Stockton-on-Tees, lost his seat in 1929, but recaptured it two years later. He served in the wartime coalition government of Winston Churchill, but found himself out of the Commons again in 1945, as the Labour Party won a landslide victory. He returned months later and the Conservative general election win in 1951 resulted in his appointment as minister for housing and local government. Macmillan then had a quick succession of Cabinet jobs: minister of defence, foreign secretary and chancellor, before succeeding Sir Anthony Eden who had resigned for health reasons in the aftermath of the Suez crisis. Macmillan was re-elected in 1959 at the age of sixty-five with an

increased majority, largely thanks to a favourable economic climate. During the next four years, National Service was abolished, Britain's application to join the EEC was rejected and a nuclear test ban treaty with the US and the USSR was agreed. Macmillan resigned in October 1963 and left the Commons the following year. He then focused on his publishing interests, his memoirs and also his chancellorship of Oxford University. He was appointed to the Order of Merit in 1976. Twenty years after leaving Parliament he returned, at the age of ninety, to make his maiden speech in the Lords as the newly created first Earl of Stockton. He died two years later.

In 1969 **Carol Reed** *won the Academy Award for best director for 'Oliver!'*

Reed's first solo directorial effort was *Midshipman Easy* (1935). Several other features followed, including the well received coal-mining drama *The Stars Look Down* (1940). His first post-war film, *Odd Man Out* (1947), won the 1948 Bafta Award for best British film; his next, *The Fallen Idol* (1948), with a screenplay by Graham Greene, brought him his first Academy Award nomination for best director. He collaborated with Greene again on *The Third Man* (1949), which tells the story of Harry Lime in post-war Vienna. The film won a Bafta for best British film and earned Reed another Oscar nomination. His later films, including *The Man Between* (1953) and a third Greene-scripted feature, *Our Man in Havana* (1959), were less successful. However, Reed's first musical, *Oliver!* (1968), provided a major upturn and won him his only Oscar – he was also nominated for both a Bafta and a Golden Globe. Reed was knighted in 1953. He died in 1976 at the age of sixty-nine.

In 1970 **John Wayne** *won the Academy Award for best actor for his portrayal of Rooster Cogburn in 'True Grit'.*

True Grit was Wayne's second and final acting nomination at the Oscars, the first coming for his role as Sergeant John Striker in *Sands of Iwo Jima* (1949). He was born Marion Morrison in Iowa, but the family later moved to California where he gained his nickname 'Duke'. He won a scholarship to the University of Southern California in Los Angeles and also began to work in the local film industry as a prop mover and extra. It was at this time that he first met John Ford, who would later direct Wayne when he played the Ringo Kid in his breakthrough film *Stagecoach* (1939). Wayne went on to become one of American cinema's top box-office stars, taking the leading role in films such as *Flying Leathernecks* (1951), *The Quiet Man* (1952) and *The Searchers* (1956). He directed, produced and starred as Davy Crockett in *The Alamo* (1960), which was nominated for a best picture Oscar. Mostly famed for westerns and war films, Wayne made his last screen appearance as the gunfighter J. B. Books in *The Shootist* (1976). He died three years later at the age of seventy-two. Wayne was posthumously awarded the Presidential Medal of Freedom in 1980.

Penelope Fitzgerald *won the 1979 Booker Prize for 'Offshore'.*
Fitzgerald's first book to be published, at the age of fifty-eight in 1975, was a biography of the Victorian artist Edward Burne-Jones. She earned a first in English from Somerville College, Oxford, in 1938 and took a job at the BBC. Fitzgerald came from a literary family. Her father, Edmund Knox, had been the editor of *Punch* magazine, and her uncle, Ronald Knox, was a crime writer (and priest). They featured in Fitzgerald's second book, the biographical *The Knox Brothers*, which also included their other male siblings – Dillwyn, a Bletchley Park cryptographer; and Wilfred, a clergyman and theologian. Fitzgerald's first novel, *The Golden Child*, was published in 1977, and her second, *The Bookshop*, was shortlisted for the 1978 Booker Prize. Her last three novels were: *The Beginning of Spring* (1988), *The Gate of Angels* (1990) – both of which were Booker shortlisted – and *The Blue Flower* (1995). Fitzgerald died in 2000 at the age of eighty-three.

Frederick Sanger *was awarded the 1980 Nobel Prize in Chemistry for his work in developing a technique to determine the sequence of base pairs in DNA.*
Deoxyribonucleic acid (DNA) consists of a double helix structure made up of a sequence of four 'bases'. The order of these bases, which can be shown by Sanger's technique, form the genetic code of an organism. Sanger shared one half of the Nobel Prize with Walter Gilbert, who independently developed a different method to achieve the same aim (each was awarded one quarter of the prize fund. The third recipient was Paul Berg, who received the remainder of the award for his studies of nucleic acids). It was Sanger's second Nobel Prize in Chemistry; his first was awarded in

1958 for his determination of the amino acid sequence in the protein insulin. Sanger is the only person to have received two Nobel awards in chemistry, and only one of three people to have won more than one award in a scientific discipline (along with John Bardeen and Marie Curie). Sanger had originally intended to study medicine at university, but switched to science and graduated from St John's College, Cambridge, in 1939. He obtained his doctorate four years later and remained in Cambridge where he joined the staff of the Medical Research Council in 1951, moving to their newly created Laboratory of Molecular Biology in 1962. Sanger retired in 1983 and was appointed to the Order of Merit in 1986. The Sanger Institute, for genome research, is named in his honour.

*In 1987 **Paul Newman** won the Academy Award for best actor for his portrayal of Fast Eddie Felson in 'The Color of Money'.*

Newman originally played the character of Felson in *The Hustler* (1961), which gained him his second Academy Award nomination for best actor. Newman amassed a total of nine nominations in this category, with films that included *Hud* (1963), *Cool Hand Luke* (1967), *Absence of Malice* (1981) and *The Verdict* (1982), before his final nomination, at the age of seventy-eight, for *Road to Perdition* (2002). This was also Newman's last film appearance as an actor, although he later voiced the character of Doc Hudson in the animated feature *Cars* (2006). His successful screen partnership with Robert Redford only encompassed two films: *Butch Cassidy and the Sundance Kid* (1969) and *The Sting* (1973). Newman made his film debut in his late twenties in *The Silver Chalice* (1954). However, he was displeased by his performance and thought it might spell the end of his film career. Newman recovered from the setback and four years later he received his first best actor Oscar nomination for *Cat on a Hot Tin Roof* (1958). Newman was also passionate about motor sport and was involved both as a competitor and as a racing team owner. He first raced professionally in 1972 and seven years later, at the age of fifty-four, came second in the Le Mans 24-Hour race. He was still competing at the age of seventy, achieving a class win at the '24 Hours of Daytona' event in 1995. Newman launched his own brand of food products in 1982, beginning with salad dressing, and stipulated that all profits would go to charity – a figure that has reached over $300 million. Newman died in 2008 at the age of eighty-three.

Betty Boothroyd *was elected as the first female Speaker of the House of Commons in 1992.*

Boothroyd was elected to Parliament in 1973, at the age of forty-three, when she won the West Bromwich by-election. It was her fifth attempt to enter Parliament in over fifteen years, during which time she worked as a political assistant and secretary, and also had a spell as a local councillor. In her younger days, she was a member of the Tiller Girls dance troupe. Boothroyd became the Deputy Speaker of the Commons in 1987, then Speaker five years later. She resigned both as Speaker and as an MP in 2000, and subsequently entered the House of Lords as Baroness Boothroyd. She was appointed to the Order of Merit in 2005.

63
SIXTY-THREE

Jacob Roggeveen *was the leader of the expedition that, in 1722, made the first recorded European sighting of Easter Island.*

The island was first spotted on Easter Sunday, thus giving rise to its name, although it is more usually known as Rapa Nui by its native population. Roggeveen's party landed on the island the next day. Roggeveen had set out from Amsterdam in 1721 with three ships to explore the southern hemisphere. The expedition eventually reached Batavia (present-day Jakarta) in the autumn of 1722. Easter Island was visited by the Spanish nearly fifty years later and by Captain James Cook in 1774. Situated in the Pacific Ocean and annexed by Chile in 1888, it is home to approximately 5,000 inhabitants and is one of the world's most isolated human populations. Easter Island is famous for its hundreds of stone statues known as 'moai'.

In 1868 ***Benjamin Disraeli*** *became prime minister for the first time following the resignation of the Earl of Derby.*

'I have climbed to the top of the greasy pole' was Disraeli's remark after taking office, although his position as prime minister was to last less than a year, after defeat in the general election by the Liberals led by William Gladstone, with whom Disraeli enjoyed a fierce rivalry. His first term as prime minister came over thirty years after Disraeli had entered Parliament as an MP at the fifth attempt. Overlooked by Sir Robert Peel for a place in the Cabinet in 1841, he attained high office at the age of forty-seven as chancellor under Lord Derby in 1852. He occupied this post for less than a year before the government fell, but Disraeli enjoyed two more spells as chancellor. During the latter one he was a leading advocate of the 1867 Reform Bill, which, when enacted nearly doubled size of the electorate. (Ironically it was the Liberals and not the Conservatives who were to win the first general election under the new rules and thus remove Disraeli from office in 1868.) Disraeli was sixty-nine when he replaced Gladstone to become prime minister for the second time in 1874. His ministry was to endure for over six years and this time the Conservatives enjoyed a parliamentary majority. Their main achievement in domestic affairs was social measures that included a public health act, a new factory act and an education act. It was also under Disraeli that Britain secured a large share in the Suez Canal Company in 1875. He was elevated to the House of Lords in 1876, from where he continued to lead the government, when Queen Victoria conferred upon him the title of Earl of Beaconsfield. Gladstone returned to power in 1880, which was also the year that Disraeli published his final complete novel *Endymion*; he had published his first novel, *Vivian Grey*, in his early twenties. Disraeli's last novel, *Falconet*, was unfinished at the time of his death in 1881, at the age of seventy-six.

Antonio Meucci filed a caveat for his telephone device, the teletrofono, in 1871.

A caveat was a way to protect an invention prior to the submission of a full patent application. They were also cheaper to register, but Meucci, out of work and living on welfare assistance, failed to renew it in 1874 due to his financial circumstances. Alexander Graham Bell's patent for the telephone was filed in 1876 and Meucci (and others) challenged his right to primacy in the matter. However, Meucci died in 1889, while legal proceedings were still ongoing. He was eighty-one. The Bell patent expired over three years later and Meucci's challenge to it was subsequently dropped, thus the right of precedence was never established in court. (In 2002, the US House of Representatives recognised Meucci's telephone work with a special resolution.)

Cecil Day-Lewis *was appointed as poet laureate in 1968.*

Day-Lewis was born in Queen's County (present-day County Laois), Ireland, in 1904. He was raised in London by his father with the assistance of an aunt, after the death of his mother when he was four. He graduated from Wadham College, Oxford, in 1927, where he met W. H. Auden who influenced his early writings. Day-Lewis helped to finance the publication of his first volume of poetry, *Beechen Vigil*, in 1925, but it was with the collection *Transitional Poem*, published four years later, that Day-Lewis began to forge his reputation. He worked as a schoolmaster for several years after leaving Oxford, but by the mid-1930s he had embarked on a career as a full-time writer, with his earnings augmented by his twenty crime novels, written under the pen name of Nicholas Blake. The first was *A Question of Proof*, published in 1935. During the Second World War he was the commander of a Home Guard platoon in Devon before joining the Ministry of Information in London. After the war, he became the Oxford professor of poetry in 1951 for a five-year term. Day-Lewis died in 1972 at the age of sixty-eight and is buried close to the grave of Thomas Hardy in Dorset. His son by his second marriage is the actor Daniel Day-Lewis.

In 2006 ***Margaret Beckett*** *became Britain's first female foreign secretary.*

Beckett served for just over a year in the role of foreign secretary in what was Tony Blair's last Cabinet. Her parliamentary career began with her election as the MP for Lincoln, at the second attempt, in 1974. She held junior positions in the Labour government of the 1970s, before losing her seat at the 1979 general election. She returned to the Commons in 1983 and became a prominent opposition politician. Beckett was elected to the post of deputy leader in 1992 and, following the death of Labour leader John Smith in 1994, she took on his parliamentary and party duties until the completion of the leadership election, won by Tony Blair, in which she also stood as a candidate. When Labour entered government in 1997 she became the president of the Board of Trade. Her subsequent Cabinet positions were leader of the House of Commons and secretary of state for environment, food and rural affairs prior to becoming foreign secretary in 2006. She was made a Dame in the 2013 New Year Honours.

64

SIXTY-FOUR

Oscar Swahn won a gold medal in the running deer single shot event at the 1912 Olympic Games, held in Stockholm.

Swahn was representing Sweden in the team event and remains the oldest sporting gold medallist in the history of the modern Olympics. He first won gold at the Olympics four years earlier in London for both the individual and team running deer single shot events. (This involved firing at a moving deer-shaped target marked with concentric circles. A hit in the centre scored four points giving a maximum possible of forty points from the ten attempts. Swahn scored twenty-five, to claim the 1908 individual gold medal by one point.) At his last Olympics in 1920, Swahn took home, at the age of seventy-two, a silver medal as part of the Swedish team in the 'running deer, double shots' to become the oldest sporting medallist in Olympic history. He died in 1927 at the age of seventy-nine.

Andrew Bonar Law became prime minister in 1922.

The withdrawal of Conservative support for the ruling coalition precipitated the resignation of David Lloyd George as prime minister and the invitation to Bonar Law from the King to form a government. In the general election held later in the same year, the Conservatives, led by Bonar Law, won a majority, with the Labour Party emerging, for the first time, as the main opposition after the Liberals (the combined Lloyd George and Asquith factions) were pushed into third place. Forced to resign due to ill health, Bonar Law's premiership was to last one day short of seven months. He died two months later, at the age of sixty-five, after the shortest premiership of the twentieth century.

James Callaghan became prime minister in 1976 following the resignation of Harold Wilson.

Upon taking office as prime minister, Callaghan became the only person to have held the four major offices of state. He was appointed as chancellor by Harold Wilson when he was fifty-two, following Labour's election victory in 1964. Following the decision to devalue the pound in 1967 he resigned, but remained in the Cabinet and swapped places with Roy Jenkins to become home secretary. Defeated in 1970, Labour returned to power in 1974 and Callaghan became foreign secretary for a two year period before taking office as prime minister. During his premiership he had to contend with a small, then non-existent majority, which forced him to make deals with the minority parties, notably the Liberals, in order to remain in power. He declined to call an election in 1978, which many believed Labour would have won. Later in the year the country's long-term economic woes flared up in what became known as the 'Winter of Discontent': a series of strikes over pay rises that dented public support for the government. In 1979 Callaghan's administration was defeated in a no-confidence motion by one vote, and lost the subsequent election to the Conservatives led by Margaret Thatcher. Callaghan remained as leader until the following year. He left the Commons at the 1987 general election after nearly forty-two years as an MP, and was made Baron Callaghan of Cardiff. The longest-lived British prime minister, he died eleven days after his wife Audrey in 2005, on the eve of his ninety-third birthday.

Kingsley Amis won the 1986 Booker Prize for 'The Old Devils'.
Amis was thirty-one when, in 1954, *Lucky Jim* became his first published novel. It won the Somerset Maugham award in 1955 and went on to sell over a million copies in the United States alone. His output was prodigious over the remaining forty years of his life and included a further twenty-three novels. *Ending Up* and *Jake's Thing* were shortlisted for the Booker Prize in 1974 and 1978 respectively, before he won with *The Old Devils* in 1986. Amis was knighted in 1990. His last novel, *The Biographer's Moustache*, was published in 1995, the year of his death at the age of seventy-three.

James Black was awarded the 1988 Nobel Prize in Physiology or Medicine for his discovery of propranolol, the first beta blocking drug, and cimetidine, which is used for the treatment of stomach ulcers.
Black won a scholarship to St Andrews University to study medicine and afterwards pursued an academic career before joining ICI in the late

1950s. Early in the next decade he led the team that discovered and developed propranolol, the first clinically useful 'beta blocker'. These drugs reduce the workload of the heart by blocking the beta-receptor sites thereby preventing the binding of hormones such as adrenalin, which increase the heart rate. Propranolol has been widely used for the treatment of cardiac-related illnesses. Black left ICI, joined Smith Kline French and went on to develop with his colleagues the drug cimetidine (brand name Tagamet). It restricts the production of acid in the stomach and therefore plays an important role in the treatment of peptic ulcers and heartburn. Both propranolol and Tagamet (launched in the UK in 1976) have sold in huge quantities, with the latter achieving annual sales of approximately $1 billion. Black was knighted in 1981 and appointed to the Order of Merit in 2000. He died ten years later at the age of eighty-five. The 1988 Nobel Prize in Physiology or Medicine was shared with Gertrude Elion and George Hitchings for their work on drug development.

George Bush was inaugurated as the forty-first president of the United States in 1989.

Bush succeeded fellow Republican Ronald Reagan, whom he had served as vice-president for eight years. Born in Massachusetts in 1924, Bush flew in nearly sixty combat missions during World War Two and was decorated with the Distinguished Flying Cross. Following the war, he graduated with a degree in economics from Yale and then moved into the Texan oil industry where his efforts made him a millionaire. Bush turned to politics in the 1960s. Although, unsuccessful in his attempt to win a seat in the US Senate in 1964, he was elected to the House of Representatives two years later. He failed to get elected in another bid for the Senate in 1970, but served the Republican administrations of the 1970s in roles that included ambassador to the UN and director of the CIA. He was president during a time of dramatic change in Europe with the fall of the Berlin Wall and the collapse of the Soviet Union. Closer to home, he sent US troops into Panama to depose General Noriega. Bush was instrumental in assembling the multinational coalition that liberated Kuwait following its invasion by Iraq in 1990. He was defeated by Bill Clinton in the 1992 presidential election, but his son George W. became president eight years later, only the second occasion that a son has followed his father into the highest political office in the United States.

*In 1999 **Judi Dench** won both the Academy Award and Bafta for best supporting actress for her portrayal of Queen Elizabeth in 'Shakespeare in Love'.*

Dench recorded one of the shortest Oscar-winning performances in history, with less than eight minutes of screen time. She made her first film appearance at the age of twenty-nine in *The Third Secret* (1964), but her early career was focused on the theatre with the Royal Shakespeare Company and the Old Vic Company. Dench won her first Laurence Olivier award in 1977 for *Macbeth*. She picked up two Baftas for playing Laura Dalton, opposite her husband Michael Williams, in the TV comedy series *A Fine Romance*, which aired between 1981 and 1984. She began to take on more film roles and won best supporting actress Bafta Awards for *A Room with a View* (1985) and *A Handful of Dust* (1988). Dench has also played the secret service boss 'M' in recent James Bond films, beginning with *Goldeneye* in 1995. She garnered a Bafta win and an Oscar nomination (her first) for best actress for *Mrs Brown* (1997). Since then, Dench has been a regular nominee at the Oscars; she was cited for best actress for *Iris* (2002), *Mrs Henderson Presents* (2006) and *Notes on a Scandal* (2007), and for best supporting actress for *Chocolat* (2000). *Iris* (2002) gave her a second Bafta film best actress award, the year after she received the Bafta Fellowship. Dench received an OBE in 1970 and was made a DBE in 1988. She has won a record six best actress Olivier awards and received a special Olivier award that recognised her contribution to British Theatre in 2004.

*****Menzies Campbell** became the leader of the Liberal Democrats in 2006.*

Campbell was first elected to Parliament in 1987, at the age of forty-six. He became the Liberal Democrats' foreign affairs spokesman ten years later, and kept this role until his leadership victory in 2006. Campbell resigned nineteen months later following party dissatisfaction with his impact as leader, and questions over his suitability to advance the Liberal Democrats' fortunes at the age of sixty-five. He was replaced by the 40-year-old Nick Clegg. Campbell studied law at the University of Glasgow and was called to the Scottish Bar in 1968. He was also a sprinter in his youth, and represented Great Britain at the 1964 Tokyo Olympics in both the 200m and the 4x100m relay. Between 1967 and 1974 he held the British 100m record. Campbell was knighted in the 2004 New Year Honours.

*In 2007 **Martin Scorsese** won the Academy Award for best director for 'The Departed'.*

Scorsese's sixth nomination for the category of best director at the Oscars came over a quarter of a century after his first, for *Raging Bull* (1980). He had considered becoming a priest as a teenager, but instead opted to pursue his interest in cinema; after studying for a first degree in English, he graduated from New York University's film school in 1966. He made his full-length directorial debut with *I Call First* (1967), which was later retitled as *Who's That Knocking At My Door*. Scorsese's breakthrough came with *Mean Streets* (1973) starring Harvey Keitel and regular future collaborator Robert De Niro. He had further success with *Taxi Driver* (1976), which went on to win the Palme d'Or at Cannes and notched up four Academy Award nominations including best picture. His religious-themed film, *The Last Temptation of Christ* (1988), aroused controversy, but also secured him a second directorial Academy Award nomination. Scorsese was similarly nominated for *Goodfellas* (1990), *Gangs of New York* (2002) and *The Aviator* (2004).

65
SIXTY-FIVE

*In 1857 **James Buchanan** was sworn in as the fifteenth president of the United States.*

Buchanan's single term as president was profoundly affected by the issue of slavery, as the southern and northern states disagreed violently about whether to support or abolish it. The last months of his time in office saw the Union break apart as the southern states opted to form their own confederacy following the election of Buchanan's successor, the Republican northerner, Abraham Lincoln, in 1860. Buchanan's response to the crisis was seen by many as ineffectual as no action was taken under his watch against the rebel states. The civil war began shortly after he had left office. Buchanan is the only president who remained unmarried, and his niece Harriet Lane served as his 'First Lady'. He lived to see the conclusion of the civil war in 1865 and died three years later, at the age of seventy-seven.

*In 1895 **Robert Cecil**, third Marquess of Salisbury, became prime minister for the third and last time.*

Cecil first entered Parliament at the age of twenty-three in 1853, and moved to the Lords in 1868 after the death of his father. Two years prior to this he had become the secretary of state for India, but resigned within eight months over his opposition to plans for electoral reform that would extend the franchise. He became foreign secretary in 1878 under Disraeli and, following Disraeli's death in 1881, succeeded him as the leader of the Conservatives. Five years later, Cecil became prime minister for the first time, although his minority administration only lasted seven months. However, following the disarray of the Liberal Party over Irish home rule, he was swiftly returned to office where he remained for thirteen of the next sixteen years, a spell only interrupted by Gladstone's fourth and last premiership, which began in 1892. For most of Cecil's tenure, he also occupied the office of foreign secretary. Notable legislation during his second administration included the Local Government Act which established elected county councils in England and Wales in 1889. The second Boer War began in 1899, during his third term, and Cecil resigned in 1902 shortly after its conclusion. He was replaced as prime minister by his nephew, Arthur Balfour. Cecil died the following year, at the age of seventy-three. Aside from a few days in the 1960s before the Earl of Home renounced his title, Cecil was the last member of the House of Lords to lead the government.

*'Little House in the Big Woods', by **Laura Ingalls Wilder**, was published in 1932.*

Wilder's debut volume in what became the Little House series, was also her first book to be published. It recounts tales of her early childhood on the western frontier of the United States during the latter half of the nineteenth century. The book was rewritten with material from her unpublished (and rejected) autobiography, *Pioneer Girl*, with assistance from her daughter Rose. She followed her successful debut with *Farmer Boy* in 1933, which was based on a year in the boyhood of her husband, Almanzo Wilder. *Little House on the Prairie* was published in 1935, and five more books were added to the series during Wilder's lifetime (a ninth was published posthumously in 1971). She died in 1957 at the age of ninety.

In 1940 **Winston Churchill** *became prime minister for the first time.*

Churchill succeeded Neville Chamberlain to lead the wartime coalition government. Although he lost the first post-war general election to Clement Attlee's Labour Party, Churchill remained as leader of the opposition and returned to power, at the age of seventy-six, in 1951. He stepped down four years later to be succeeded by Sir Anthony Eden. He continued as an MP until the 1964 general election, when he retired from the Commons at the age of eighty-nine. Churchill was born at Blenheim Palace in 1874, the son of Conservative politician Lord Randolph Churchill and his American wife (née Jennie Jerome). He attended Harrow and then the military college at Sandhurst, before receiving a commission as an officer and seeing action in India and the Sudan. He also took the opportunity to work as a wartime correspondent, and after leaving the army in 1899, and failing to enter Parliament at the Oldham by-election of that year, he returned to this role in the South African War. He was captured by the Boers but made a daring escape. Churchill then became an officer in the South African Light Horse regiment and also continued to work as a war correspondent. He returned to England in 1900 and, at the age of twenty-five, was elected to Parliament as a Conservative member for Oldham. His advocacy of free trade caused him to cross the House and join the Liberals in 1904. He became president of the Board of Trade in 1908, home secretary in 1910 and first lord of the Admiralty in 1911. His reputation was tarnished four years later by the failed Dardanelles campaign during the First World War, and he resigned. He returned to the army and saw active service on the western front, but when his battalion was merged with another and he relinquished his command, Churchill took the opportunity to return home and resume his political career. Lloyd George appointed him as the minister of munitions in 1917 and, after the end of the First World War, he became secretary for war and air. Churchill found himself out of Parliament in 1922. He tried to regain a seat in 1923 (his last campaign as a Liberal), but was thwarted in this attempt and a subsequent one in 1924, when he stood as an 'independent anti-socialist' in a by-election. His political fortunes turned later in the year when he was adopted by the Conservatives as a candidate in the forthcoming general election. They were returned with a majority and Churchill, rejoining his old party, became chancellor for four and a half years. Out of government in 1929, Churchill's next decade saw his influence wane – his pronouncements on insufficient rearmament and the growing Nazi threat were disregarded. Following the declaration of war in September 1939, Churchill returned to his post as first lord of the Admiralty in the War Cabinet, and within months had replaced Chamberlain as prime minister at the head of a coalition government. His influential speeches and broadcasts rallied the nation and with the Allied victory in 1945, his reputation as a national hero was secured. He was given a state funeral following his death twenty years later, at the age of ninety. Churchill had lived twice as long as his father, who had died on the same day seventy years previously. In addition to being a politician and soldier, Churchill also wrote prolifically and was awarded the 1953 Nobel Prize in Literature. He also enjoyed painting and is best known for his impressionist land-scapes. In 2002 he was voted as the 'Greatest Briton' in a poll of the British public. Churchill received numerous public honours including the Order of Merit in 1946 and became a Knight of the Order of the Garter in 1953. Ten years later, he was made an honorary citizen of the United States – a US Navy destroyer was named after him in 2001.

In 1967 **Francis Chichester** *completed his solo round-the-world voyage in his yacht, Gypsy Moth IV.*

After nine months and one day, during which time Chichester had made one stop in Sydney and rounded both capes, he returned to his starting point of Plymouth Sound. Chichester was appointed as a knight shortly before leaving Sydney to embark on the return leg, and was formally invested by the Queen at Greenwich a few weeks after his successful return to Britain. She used the same sword that Elizabeth I had used to dub Francis Drake. The voyage had not been Chichester's first adventurous exploit. In his late twenties, he became the first person to fly solo across the Tasman Sea from New Zealand to Australia. His navigation skills allowed him to locate two tiny islands en route and thus make the necessary refuelling stops for his Gypsy Moth plane. At the age of fifty-eight aboard Gipsy Moth III, Chichester was victorious in the first single-handed transatlantic yacht race. He also set a record time of under forty-one days for the crossing. Chichester, aged seventy, had to retire from his fourth transatlantic yacht race due to ill health in 1972. He died in the month after his return to Plymouth.

Jacob Bronowski wrote and presented the television series 'The Ascent of Man', first broadcast in 1973.

In the thirteen-part series, Bronowski put forward his account of the development and impact of science. The series won many plaudits both for its intellectual scope and production quality, and he was awarded the Royal Television Society's silver medal for outstanding creative achievement. Bronowski was born in what is now Poland, in 1908. The family moved to Germany during World War One before settling in England in 1920. He read mathematics at Cambridge, and after completing his doctorate became a lecturer at the University College of Hull. After wartime work in operational research for the British government, he was appointed as the director of the coal research establishment of the National Coal Board, during which time he oversaw the development of smokeless fuel. As well as his scientific interests, Bronowski also had a love of literature; he wrote several books and won an Italia Prize for one of his radio plays. He died in 1974 at the age of sixty-six.

*The technique of in vitro fertilisation (IVF) developed by **Patrick Steptoe** and Robert Edwards resulted in the birth of the first 'test tube' baby in 1978.*

Louise Brown was born at Oldham and District General Hospital as a result of IVF. The procedure involved the extraction of eggs from her mother, and their fertilisation externally, before re-implantation. Steptoe qualified as a doctor before the Second World War and then served in the Royal Navy. He spent two years as a prisoner of war following the sinking of his ship in the Mediterranean. In 1951 he was recruited to the post of consultant obstetrician and gynaecologist in Oldham. Steptoe was concerned with female infertility and pioneered gynaecological laparoscopy in Britain. He first met Robert Edwards in 1968 with whom he began a collaboration that produced their infertility treatment breakthrough a decade later. Steptoe was awarded a CBE in 1988 – shortly before his death, in the same year, at the age of seventy-four.

Anthony Leggett was awarded the 2003 Nobel Prize in Physics for his theoretical work on the helium-3 isotope in its superfluid state.

Unusually for a Nobel laureate in physics, Leggett did not study the subject at school, nor was it his first choice for a university degree. Instead, he focused on the classics (Greek and Latin) and he graduated with a first in Greats from Balliol College, Oxford. Leggett then undertook a second degree, this time in physics, at Merton College. He was awarded a first and went on to gain his doctorate in 1964. Leggett became a lecturer at the University of Sussex in 1967, where in the following decade he produced his theory to explain the properties of superfluid helium-3 (helium with only one neutron). Leggett, who was knighted in 2004, shared the Nobel Prize with Alexei Abrikosov and Vitaly Ginzburg.

*In 2009 **Ranulph Fiennes** reached the summit of Mount Everest to become the oldest Briton to have successfully climbed the peak.*

The successful 2009 ascent by Fiennes was his third attempt to scale the world's highest mountain, and came four years after his first assault on the peak in 2005 (two years before this he had undergone a triple heart bypass following a heart attack). Fiennes's reputation for undertaking physical challenges was forged over many decades. He completed the first longitudinal circumnavigation of the world, along with Charles Burton, in 1982. In their nearly three-year-long global odyssey they travelled from Greenwich to the South Pole, and then returned via the North Pole. At birth, Fiennes inherited the baronetcy awarded to his grandfather in 1916.

Julian Barnes won the 2011 Man Booker Prize for 'The Sense of an Ending'.

Barnes's first Man Booker triumph in 2011 came after three previous shortlistings for *Flaubert's Parrot* (1984), *England, England* (1998) and *Arthur and George* (2005). *The Sense of an Ending* (2011), his eleventh novel, examines the themes of memory and time through the experience of the middle-aged Tony Webster. Barnes, who was born in Leicester and grew up in Middlesex, read modern languages at Magdalen College, Oxford, and then worked for three years as a lexicographer for the *Oxford English Dictionary* before moving into journalism. He published his debut novel, *Metroland* (1980), at the age of thirty-four, which won him the Somerset Maugham Award, the first of many literary prizes. Barnes's other novels include *Staring at the Sun* (1986) and *A History of the World in 10½ Chapters* (1989).

66

SIXTY-SIX

Charles Grey, *second Earl Grey, became prime minister in 1830.*

Grey first entered Parliament in 1786 at the age of twenty-two and quickly made his mark with a maiden speech attacking the prime minister, William Pitt (the younger), and government policies. Grey became a member of the Whig opposition and was out of power until 1806 when, following Pitt's death, he joined the 'Ministry of all the Talents', under William Grenville, as first lord of the Admiralty. Grey became foreign secretary and leader of the Whigs after the death of Charles Fox, but the government fell in 1807 over the issue of Catholic emancipation, which was supported by Grey and Grenville, but opposed by the King. Grey's father had been granted an earldom during the 'Talents' administration, and he inherited the title in 1807. Moving to the Lords, Grey remained in opposition until the Whigs returned to power in 1830. As prime minister, he oversaw the passing of the 1832 Reform Act, which reformed the House of Commons by increasing the size of the electorate and abolishing 'pocket' and 'rotten' boroughs. It had been Grey's third attempt to get a reform bill through the Lords. Another key legislative measure enacted by his government was the abolition of slavery within the British Empire in 1833. Grey retired from politics the following year, after over three and a half years as leader. He died in 1845 at the age of eighty-one. His name is also associated with a blend of tea (flavoured with bergamot) called Earl Grey.

In 1968 **Louis Armstrong** *spent four weeks at number one in the UK singles chart with 'What a Wonderful World'.*

Armstrong's vocal performance gave him his only British number one in a UK chart career that began in 1952 with 'Takes Two to Tango'. Music offered Armstrong an escape from a life of poverty and poor prospects in Louisiana. Following his arrest for firing a pistol in the street to mark the New Year celebrations of 1914, Armstrong ended up in a waifs' home – which provided him with his first opportunity to receive some musical training. His virtuoso trumpet and cornet playing made him a highly influential figure in the development of jazz. In 1964 Armstrong's cover of 'Hello Dolly' gave him, at the age of sixty-two, his only other UK top-five hit, and a US number one. He died in 1971 at the age of sixty-nine.

John Betjeman *was appointed as poet laureate in 1972.*

Betjeman was born in 1906 in London, the only child of a furniture manufacturer. He attended Magdalen College, Oxford, where he regularly contributed poetry and architectural pieces to the student press. However, he left Oxford after three years without completing his degree, in 1928. He eschewed a career in the family business and instead worked as a preparatory schoolmaster, then as the assistant editor of the *Architectural Review* and later as the London *Evening Standard* film critic. Betjeman's first collection of poems, *Mount Zion*, was published in 1931. A second, *Continual Dew, A Little Book of Bourgeois Verse*, appeared in 1937. *Ghastly Good Taste: Or, a Depressing Story of the Rise and Fall of English Architecture*, his first prose work, was published in 1933. Betjeman continued to produce further volumes of poetry and his *Collected Poems* (1958) sold over 100,000 copies. In addition, he produced more architectural tomes as well as guidebooks. Betjeman also emerged as a popular broadcaster. He received the Queen's Medal for Poetry and a CBE in 1960, and was knighted nine years later. Betjeman died in 1984 at the age of seventy-seven. A statue of Betjeman was unveiled in London's redeveloped St Pancras station in 2007 – a building that he had campaigned to save from demolition in the 1960s.

'Angela's Ashes', the first book by **Frank McCourt**, *was published in 1996.*

The memoir recounted his bleak childhood growing up in Brooklyn, New York, and Limerick, Ireland, and went on to win the Pulitzer Prize for 'biography or autobiography' in 1997. The book became a bestseller and also was made into a film in 1999. McCourt's next book was another memoir, *'Tis*, its narrative following on from his debut. He died in 2009 at the age of seventy-eight.

Martin Evans was awarded the 2007 Nobel Prize in Physiology or Medicine for his discovery of embryonic stem cells and their application in producing 'specific gene modifications in mice'.

In a letter to the journal *Nature* in 1981, co-written with his collaborator Matt Kaufman, Evans reported that he had discovered embryonic stem cells in mouse embryos, and was able to propagate these in the laboratory. Such stem cells are capable of developing into any specialised cell within the organism, for example skin cells, liver cells etc. Evans then demonstrated that the genetic code of stem cells could be changed in a specific way. Embryos with these modified stem cells would develop into mice that contained the modification and were able to transmit it to the next generation. This opened the door to further research on the effect of a single gene and – due to the similarities in the genetic makeup of people and mice – shed light on many human ailments. For example, Evans was the first to cure cystic fibrosis in mice using gene therapy. He shared his prize with Mario Capecchi and Oliver Smithies, who had developed a technique to alter DNA at the molecular level. Evans studied at Christ's College, Cambridge, and then took up a research assistant position at University College London, where he completed his PhD in 1969. He was knighted in 2004.

67
SIXTY-SEVEN

*In 1841 **William Harrison** took the oath of office as the ninth president of the United States.*

Harrison delivered the longest address in US presidential history which took approximately two hours to read and ran to nearly 8,500 words. He did not wear a coat or hat at his inauguration, despite it being a cold and rainy March day, and subsequently caught a cold. The cold developed into pneumonia, and Harrison died exactly one month after taking office. The succession of Vice-President John Tyler to the presidency established the convention that would govern similar occurrences in the future. Harrison remains the shortest-serving US president. His grandson Benjamin became the twenty-third president in 1889.

*In 1935 **Stanley Baldwin** became prime minister for the third time.*

Baldwin had become prime minister for the first time twelve years previously when he took over from Andrew Bonar Law, who had resigned due to ill health after only 211 days. Baldwin's premiership did not last much longer as the Conservatives lost their majority in the election that he called in late 1923. The first ever Labour government was then formed with Ramsay MacDonald as prime minister, but it was a minority administration and was defeated in the Commons in October 1924. The subsequent general election returned the Conservatives and Baldwin to power with a large majority. He had to face the general strike of 1926, but preparations made for such an eventuality by the government helped to defuse the situation and the strike ended after nine days. Baldwin's government equalised the voting age for men and women to twenty-one in 1928. The Conservatives lost the election the following year, the first under the new franchise, but in 1931 Baldwin became part of the coalition National Government and, in 1935, its prime minister at the age of sixty-seven. During his third and last period in office he had to deal with the abdication crisis of King Edward VIII; his discreet handling of the situation drew praise from all quarters and boosted his political standing. Baldwin resigned as prime minister in 1937 and shortly afterwards was made Earl Baldwin of Bewdley. He died ten years later at the age of eighty.

Michael Foot was elected as the leader of the Labour Party in 1980.

Foot took over from James Callaghan following a leadership election. A major figure on the left of the party, Foot was unable to stem the dissatisfaction of the Labour right with the direction of policy and this led some prominent ex-Cabinet ministers to break away and form the Social Democratic Party in 1981. Foot led the Labour Party into the 1983 general election at the age of sixty-nine, but the party suffered a heavy defeat. Shortly afterwards, Foot stood down as leader and was succeeded by Neil Kinnock. He remained in Parliament, was re-elected in the 1987 general election at the age of seventy-one and finally retired from the Commons in 1992. Foot declined elevation to the House of Lords. It was the end of his parliamentary career, which began when he was elected as the member for Plymouth Devonport in 1945, when he had just turned thirty-two. By that time Foot had started to forge a career as a journalist, following his time at Wadham College, Oxford, where he converted to socialism and moved away from his family's attachment to Liberalism (his father had been a Liberal MP) to join the Labour Party. He found himself out of Parliament in 1955, but returned five years later as the member for Ebbw Vale. Sometimes at odds with Labour Party policy, Foot declined a post in government during Labour's period in office that began in 1964, but ten years later he finally joined the Cabinet as employment secretary. (He stood for election as leader when Harold Wilson resigned in 1976, but lost out to James Callaghan.) Foot wrote many books, including biographies of H. G. Wells and Aneurin Bevan. He was a lifelong fan of his hometown football club, Plymouth Argyle, and for his ninetieth birthday he was registered as an honorary player and given shirt number ninety. Foot was listed in the club's programmes and became the oldest registered professional player in football history. He joined the Argyle board in 2001 and served for four years. Foot died in 2010 at the age of ninety-six.

In 2005 **Morgan Freeman** *won the Academy Award for best supporting actor for his role as Eddie Dupris in 'Million Dollar Baby'.*

Million Dollar Baby (2004) brought Freeman his second nomination for best supporting actor, with the first coming for *Street Smart* (1987). Freeman, who was born in Memphis, Tennessee, worked for a spell as a United States Air Force mechanic, but gave it up and took various jobs as he pursued his acting ambitions. His first screen appearance was as an extra in *The Pawnbroker* (1964). Freeman also continued with stage work, but it was his role in the 1970s kids' series *The Electric Company* that first brought him to the attention of the media. The next decade saw him make further television and film appearances before he picked up his first Oscar nomination, for best supporting actor, for playing Fast Black in

Street Smart (1987). Two years later he notched up his first Academy Award nomination for best actor with *Driving Miss Daisy* (1989). The nineties brought memorable performances in, among others, *Unforgiven* (1992), *The Shawshank Redemption* (which secured his second best actor nomination in 1995), *Se7en* (1995) and as the US president in *Deep Impact* (1998). The next decade saw him take on the role of God in first *Bruce Almighty* (2003) and then its sequel *Evan Almighty* (2007). His third best actor nomination at the Academy Awards was for his role as Nelson Mandela in *Invictus* (2009).

*In 2009 **Barbra Streisand** reached number one in both the UK and US album charts with 'Love is The Answer'.*

Love is The Answer is the sixty-third album by the multi-award-winning Brooklyn-born singer and actress. Streisand released her first, *The Barbra Streisand Album*, which won three Grammy Awards, at the age of twenty in 1963. The following year she starred in the Broadway musical *Funny Girl* as Fanny Brice and, in what was her first feature film, won a best actress Oscar for the role when it was transferred to the big screen. Her other early films include *Hello, Dolly!* (1969), *What's Up, Doc?* (1972), and *The Way We Were* (1973), which earned her an Academy Award nomination for best actress. Streisand starred as Esther Hoffman in *A Star is Born* (1976) and shared the film's only Oscar for the best original song, 'Evergreen' (music by Streisand, lyrics by Paul Williams). She made her directorial debut with *Yentl* (1983), which she also co-wrote, co-produced and starred in as the title character. Streisand has also appeared more recently on screen in *Meet the Fockers* (2004) and in its sequel, *Little Fockers* (2010).

68

SIXTY-EIGHT

*The timepiece H4, designed by **John Harrison**, began its first long-distance sea trial with a journey to the West Indies, in 1761, aboard the ship 'Deptford'.*

In 1714 the British government offered a reward of £20,000 for a sufficiently accurate means to determine the longitude position at sea, a major problem for sailors at the time. Accurate timekeeping was one approach to the issue since the difference between the local time and that of Greenwich could readily be translated into a measure of longitude. John Harrison, a carpenter and joiner in his thirties, took up the challenge of creating a marine timekeeper good enough to win the prize. He had already made clocks; his early pieces being constructed entirely of wood. Harrison's first sea clock, H1, was demonstrated in 1735 and two more versions were to follow before his pièce de résistance, H4, a large watch design, was completed in 1760, the year before its sea trial on the journey to the West Indies. It proved, over an eighty-one-day voyage, to be accurate to within almost five seconds after an allowable adjustment based on its performance on land. However, the longitude board was not fully satisfied that the requirements had been met and a further trial was ordered. This took place in 1764 and again the Harrison timepiece performed superbly and was accurate enough to win the £20,000 award, but again the board stalled on paying out and made further demands. Harrison had to disclose the workings of H4 (for which he was granted half of the prize) and also provide two more watches in order to receive the remainder of the award. Eventually, and by now in his late seventies, Harrison appealed to King George III for assistance in the matter. The King was sympathetic to his position and encouraged an appeal to the prime minister, Lord North, which finally resulted in the issue being settled with a payment of £8,750 that brought Harrison's total remuneration (which included money to assist in the development of his chronometers) to more than the original £20,000 on offer. Harrison died three years later at the age of eighty-three.

*The Menai Suspension Bridge, designed by **Thomas Telford**, was opened to the public in 1826.*

Construction of the Menai Suspension Bridge, which connects the island of Anglesey to the Welsh mainland across the Menai Strait, began in 1819. Telford was born in Dumfriesshire, the son of a shepherd who died four months after his birth. Brought up by his mother, he was apprenticed to a stonemason after leaving school and later worked in Edinburgh and then London, when he was in his mid-twenties. It was there, in 1783, that he met William Pulteney, MP for Shrewsbury, whose patronage did much to advance Telford's career through commissions and recommendations. In 1787 Telford became the county surveyor of public works in Shropshire. The startling design of the Pontcysyllte Aqueduct, opened in 1805, was one of Telford's first major civil engineering achievements. Created in partnership with the more experienced canal builder William Jessop, and originally part of the Ellesmere Canal, the aqueduct was named as a UNESCO world heritage site in 2009. His other works encompassed roads, canals (for example, the Caledonian, initially in partnership with Jessop), numerous bridges and docks. Telford died in 1834 at the age of seventy-seven.

George Hamilton Gordon, *fourth Earl of Aberdeen, became prime minister in 1852.*

Gordon had already held high office on two occasions, as foreign secretary, first under Wellington at the age of forty-four, and then under Sir Robert Peel thirteen years later. The collapse of the government led by the Earl of Derby resulted in Gordon becoming prime minister as the head of a coalition of Whigs and Peelites. However, his premiership foundered on the matter of the Crimean War. Britain and France had declared war on Russia in March 1854, but blame for the poor prosecution of the conflict fell on Gordon. A large parliamentary majority voted to hold an enquiry into the conduct of the war in January 1855. Taking this as a vote of no confidence, Gordon resigned the following day. He held no further political office and died nearly six years later, at the age of seventy-six.

Frederick Hopkins *was awarded the 1929 Nobel Prize in Physiology or Medicine for his discovery of vitamins.*

Hopkins was born in Eastbourne, Sussex, in 1861. After leaving school at seventeen, he spent six months as an insurance clerk before being articled to a consulting chemist for three years. He then took up a post as an analytical assistant at Guy's Hospital and studied for an external degree in chemistry at University College London. Prior to graduating, Hopkins also became a medical student at Guy's Hospital, London, and qualified in 1894. Hopkins was invited to become a lecturer in chemical physiology at Cambridge in 1898, where he would remain for the rest of his career.

Experiments that he began in the first decade of the twentieth century using rats clearly showed that 'accessory factors' (later called vitamins), in addition to basic constituents such as carbohydrates, proteins etc. in the diet, were essential for proper nutrition. He published a full account of his work in 1912, when he was in his early fifties. Hopkins, who shared the Nobel Prize with Christiaan Eijkman for his discovery of the 'antineuritic vitamin', was knighted in 1925 and appointed to the Order of Merit ten years later. Hopkins died in 1947 at the age of eighty-five.

Neville Chamberlain *became prime minister in 1937.*

Chamberlain's prime ministership was the culmination of a Westminster political career which began at the relatively late age of forty-nine. (No one older has entered Parliament for the first time and risen to the highest office.) Chamberlain's father, Joseph, had been a Liberal Cabinet minister under Gladstone and his older half-brother, Austen, served as chancellor and later as foreign secretary during the first two decades of the twentieth century. Unlike Austen, Neville was earmarked for a career in business rather than politics. He attended Mason College in Birmingham and was later apprenticed to a chartered accountancy. He left to supervise a business venture of his father's in the Caribbean (a sisal plantation) while still in his twenties, but despite his best efforts the enterprise failed. He returned to Birmingham, where he was more successful in the manufacturing business. Chamberlain became active in local politics with his election to the Birmingham city council as a Liberal Unionist candidate. In 1915 he became lord mayor and proved adept at leading the city during wartime. He resigned to take up the newly created position of director-general of National Service at the end of 1916, but he resigned after less than nine months and began his parliamentary career the following year. In 1923 he became minister of health and, five months later, was advanced to the chancellorship following Baldwin's succession as prime minister due to Bonar Law's ill health. Out of power briefly, Baldwin's Conservative government returned in 1924 and Chamberlain returned to the Ministry of Health, where he was able to concentrate on social reform with measures that included reform of the Poor Law. In 1929 the Conservatives began two years in opposition, after which Chamberlain joined the coalition National Government, initially as minister of health again, but in 1931 he switched to the post of chancellor – where he would remain until taking the reigns as prime minister in 1937. Europe was heading for war, but Chamberlain was determined to avert it and, for the first time in autumn 1938, flew to meet Hitler in Germany to discuss his territorial demands concerning Czechoslovakia. Two further meetings followed and, with an agreement reached, Chamberlain declared that 'peace for our time' had been achieved. However, within months the Nazis had occupied Prague and on 1 September 1939, they invaded Poland. Two days later, Chamberlain made a radio broadcast to the nation announcing that Britain was 'now at war with Germany'. Chamberlain remained as prime minister until May 1940 but lacking the necessary support from the Labour Party to form a coalition government, and also facing criticism over his conduct of the war, he resigned. He served in Churchill's government but was diagnosed with terminal cancer and died before the end of 1940, at the age of seventy-one.

John Hicks *and Kenneth Arrow were awarded the 1972 Nobel Prize in Economics.*

The prize was awarded for 'pioneering contributions to general economic equilibrium theory and welfare theory'. Hicks became the first British recipient of the award, which was inaugurated in 1969. Hicks, who was born in Warwick, graduated with a degree in philosophy, politics and economics from Balliol College, Oxford, and secured a lectureship at the London School of Economics. He later held professorships at the University of Manchester and the University of Oxford. Hicks was knighted in 1964. His most famous tract on economics is *Value and Capital*, published in 1939. Hicks died in 1989 at the age of eighty-five.

The debut Wallace and Gromit animation, 'A Grand Day Out', featuring the voice of **Peter Sallis***, received its first broadcast on Christmas Day in 1989.*

Although Sallis is a Londoner, he brings Wallace to life with a northern accent. The story of Wallace and Gromit's trip to the moon was the basis of a student project by Nick Park and had been several years in the making. Sallis has also been acclaimed for his role as Norman Clegg in the long-running BBC series *Last of the Summer Wine*, which made its first appearance as part of the Comedy Playhouse strand in 1973, when Sallis was fifty-one. Sallis and actress Jane Freeman were the only members of the original cast still with the programme when it completed its thirty-first, and final, series in 2010. Sallis, who delivered the closing line, was the only one of the pair to appear in the concluding episode. He was awarded an OBE in 2007.

Howard Jacobson *won the 2010 Man Booker Prize for his novel 'The Finkler Question'.*

Jacobson's winning book explores the nature of Jewishness through the characters of Julian Treslove, Treslove's old school friend Sam Finkler and their former teacher Libor Sevcik. Jacobson's success made him the second oldest recipient in the award's history, behind Sir William Golding. Jacobson, a graduate of Downing College, Cambridge, made his debut with *Coming From Behind* in 1983. His later novels include *No More Mister Nice Guy* (1998), as well as the Booker-longlisted titles *Who's Sorry Now?* (2002) and *Kalooki Nights* (2006).

69
SIXTY-NINE

Henry Campbell-Bannerman became prime minister in 1905.

Days after taking his position at the head of the government, Campbell-Bannerman became the first incumbent to be officially recognised with the title prime minister. Previously, the office holder had been known as the 'first lord of the Treasury', a title that still resides with the prime minister. He was born in Glasgow in 1836. He studied at the University of Glasgow, and then at Trinity College, Cambridge. Aged thirty-two, he entered Parliament and a few years later he added the suffix Bannerman to his name to fulfil an inheritance requirement regarding his maternal uncle's estate. In 1886, during Gladstone's brief third ministry, he became secretary of state for war at the age of forty-nine. He returned to the post in 1892 and held it until the Liberals lost power three years later. He was knighted shortly after. Campbell-Bannerman became Liberal leader in 1899 and, after becoming prime minister at the end of 1905, he called a general election which returned his party to power with a large majority. He was the oldest prime ministerial debutant in twentieth-century British politics, but had little time to make a significant impact as ill health forced his resignation in 1908, two years after his decisive election victory. He died in Number 10 Downing Street less than three weeks later at the age of seventy-one. Herbert Asquith succeeded him as prime minister.

John Boyd Orr *was awarded the 1949 Nobel Peace Prize.*

A qualified doctor, Orr abandoned his medical career to study nutrition and became the director of a new Aberdeen-based nutrition institute. The First World War intervened and Orr served in both the army (in which he was decorated for bravery) and navy, before returning to Aberdeen. Orr pushed for better facilities and, with a combination of government money and donations (principally from John Rowett), a new institute (named after Rowett) was opened in 1922. The institute was concerned with both animal and human nutrition. One outcome based on its findings was the provision of free milk in schools, pioneered in Scotland and subsequently extended to England. Orr became the first director of the Food and Agriculture Association in 1945. He attempted to establish a world food board which would act to stabilise prices and alleviate shortages, but lack of support from the major powers saw the idea founder. The Nobel Prize recognised his efforts in the field of nutrition and his belief that eliminating hunger in the world would remove one of the causes of war. Orr was knighted in 1935 and made a baron in 1949. He died in 1971 at the age of ninety.

In 1980 **William Golding** *won the Booker Prize for 'Rites of Passage'.*

Golding's first published novel, at the age of forty-two, was *Lord of the Flies* in 1954. Rejected numerous times, the manuscript had originally been submitted under the title *Strangers from Within*, but was later changed by its eventual publishers, Faber & Faber, to its now familiar form. The success of the book, with its tale of marooned schoolboys and their descent into violence, brought Golding financial security and he was able give up his teaching career to write full-time. His next novel, *The Inheritors* (1955), was followed by others including *The Pyramid* (1964), *The Scorpion God* (1971) and the first part of his To the Ends of the Earth trilogy, *Rites of*

Passage, which won him the 1980 Booker Prize at the age of sixty-nine (Golding is the oldest recipient of this literary award). The final volume in the triumvirate, *Fire Down Below* (1989), was the last of his novels to be published before his death in 1993 at the age of eighty-one. *The Double Tongue* was published posthumously in 1995. Golding was awarded the 1983 Nobel Prize in Literature, and became the first Booker winner to be made a laureate. Knighted in 1988, Golding died five years later at the age of eighty-one.

Ronald Reagan *was sworn in as the fortieth president of the United States in 1981.*

An ex-actor and former governor of California, Reagan became the oldest person ever elected to the presidency when he defeated the incumbent Jimmy Carter. Reagan's movie career began with *Love is On the Air* (1937), the first of over fifty films he appeared in, and concluded with *The Killers* (1964). Originally a Democrat, Reagan became a Republican and made a stirring nationally televised speech in support of Barry Goldwater, the Republican's candidate for the presidency in 1964, which raised large sums for the campaign. Although Goldwater lost the subsequent contest, it effectively launched Reagan's political career. He was elected as the governor of California in 1966 at the age of fifty-five and served eight years following re-election in 1970. He was unsuccessful in obtaining the Republican nomination against President Gerald Ford in 1976, but led his party's ticket four years later. Weeks after taking the oath of office, Reagan survived an assassination attempt in which he was shot; the bullet narrowly missed his heart. The domestic economic situation was a prime focus in his first term and Reagan embarked on cuts to both taxes and government spending as a strategy to stimulate recovery. An economic upturn aided his re-election, secured with a record number of electoral college votes in 1984. The US relationship with the Soviet Union figured large in Reagan's second term; he was a vociferous critic of Communism. The coming to power of Mikhail Gorbachev in 1985 shifted relations to a more diplomatic arena, which resulted in the signing of a treaty to remove intermediate nuclear missiles in 1987. At home, his presidency was engulfed in the Iran-Contra scandal which involved the covert sale of arms to Iran with the profits being diverted to rebel contra forces in Nicaragua. Reagan was not directly implicated in the dealings although questions were asked about his conduct. Despite the scandal, he remains one of the most popular presidents in public opinion polls. He died in 2004 at the age of ninety-three.

V. S. Naipaul *(Vidiadhar Surajprasad) was awarded the 2001 Nobel Prize in Literature.*

Born in Trinidad, Naipaul came to England in 1950 after winning a scholarship to Oxford where he read English. His first novel, *The Mystic Masseur*, was published in 1957. Four years later his fourth book, *A House for Mr Biswas*, established his literary reputation. Naipaul, who won the 1971 Booker Prize for *In a Free State*, is one of only four writers to have won both the Booker Prize and the Nobel Prize in Literature. He was knighted in the 1990 New Year Honours.

CHAPTER EIGHT

Septuagenarians

Age is opportunity no less
Than youth itself, though in another dress,
And as the evening twilight fades away
The sky is filled with stars, invisible by day.

HENRY WADSWORTH
LONGFELLOW

70

SEVENTY

*'De revolutionibus orbium coelestium' (On the revolutions of the heavenly spheres), by **Nicolaus Copernicus**, was published in 1543.*

Copernicus's book, which detailed his model for a heliocentric universe, appeared in print shortly before his death at the age of seventy. The result of many years of work, it placed the sun as the fixed point – a radical alternative to the accepted earth-centred, or geocentric, system that had been proposed by Ptolemy fourteen hundred years earlier. Copernicus is reputed to have received the first printed copy of his work on his deathbed.

*
Henry Temple, third Viscount Palmerston, became prime minister in 1855.*

Palmerston is the oldest prime ministerial debutant in British political history. Although he succeeded his father as viscount at the age of seventeen, the title belonged to the Irish peerage and therefore did not confer the right to sit in the House of Lords. Instead, Palmerston was able to enter the Commons, which he did in 1807 at the age of twenty-two. Palmerston spent nearly two decades as the secretary at war until his resignation in 1828. It was to be his last position as a Tory; Palmerston joined the Whigs soon after. His speeches on foreign policy caught the attention of Lord Grey, who offered him the post of foreign secretary when he came to power in 1830; Palmerston was then forty-six. He retained this position for a total of nearly sixteen years, split over three periods in office. Palmerston's reputation as foreign secretary was formed by his stout defence of British interests coupled with his use of 'gunboat diplomacy'. During his time in office, Palmerston played an important role in the creation of Belgium. The Opium War with China also saw Britain gain control of Hong Kong in 1842. Palmerston's approval of the coup d'état of Louis Napoleon in France, offered without consultation with his colleagues or the monarch, forced his resignation in 1851. Palmerston exacted political revenge, weeks later, by bringing down the Earl Russell government he was forced to leave. The following Conservative administration was short lived and Palmerston returned as home secretary for a period of just over two years in the Whig/Peelite coalition that replaced them. In 1855 he succeeded the Earl of Aberdeen, who had been criticised for the lack of progress in the Crimean War, as prime minister. The conflict was successfully ended the following year, and Palmerston's first term in office continued until 1858 when his government was defeated. He returned as premier sixteen months later, to begin his second term at the age of seventy-four. He won the general election of 1865 with an increased majority but died three months later, at the age of eighty. The last prime minister to die while in office, Palmerston was accorded a state funeral and buried at Westminster Abbey.

In 1926 **George Bernard Shaw** *received the 1925* Nobel Prize in Literature.*

Shaw was born in Dublin in 1856. He moved to London as a young man, where he could often be found in libraries or the British Museum reading room as he pursued a career as a novelist. Although he was unsuccessful, Shaw did begin to make an impact as a critic and essayist, but it would be as a playwright that he would have his greatest success. Shaw was thirty-six when his first play to be staged, *Widowers' Houses*, opened in 1892; a harsh criticism of slum landlords that reflected his socialist beliefs. He wrote over five dozen plays that include *Arms and the Man* (1894), *Candida* (1894), *The Devil's Disciple* (1897) and *Pygmalion* (1912). A 1938 cinema production of the latter won Shaw an Oscar for 'best writing, screenplay', shared with three others (he is the only person to have won a Nobel Prize and an Oscar). *Pygmalion* was also adapted as a stage musical, *My Fair Lady*, which when transferred to the big screen won eight Oscars, including best picture, in 1965. Shaw, who wrote his plays mostly in shorthand, was an advocate of spelling reform and left a sum in his will to develop a new alphabet based on phonetics. He died in 1950 at the age of ninety-four.

Philip Noel-Baker *was awarded the Nobel Peace Prize in 1959.*

Noel-Baker had been a lifelong campaigner for disarmament and peace. A graduate of King's College, Cambridge, he was involved in the drafting

---

* Shaw was aged seventy when the prize, withheld from the previous year, was announced in November 1926. It was presented in the following month.

of the charters of both the League of Nations and its successor the United Nations. He served as a Labour MP, held several ministerial posts and retired from the Commons in 1970. Noel-Baker also represented Britain at the Olympics on two occasions, winning a silver medal for the 1500m at the Antwerp Games in 1920. Noel-Baker was made a life peer in 1977 and died five years later, at the age of ninety-two.

Lorna Johnstone was an equestrian competitor for Great Britain at the 1972 Munich Olympic Games.

Johnstone secured Britain's highest finish in the individual dressage event in Munich, when she took twelfth place out of thirty-three competitors in her third and final Games. It was her best individual Olympic result. She had made her Olympic debut in 1956 at the age of fifty-three in the individual dressage event (curiously, the equestrian events were held in Stockholm, Sweden, and not in the host country of Australia due to quarantine restrictions). Johnstone remains the oldest female competitor at the Olympics. She died in 1990 at the age of eighty-seven.

In 1983 'Jumping the Queue' became the first novel by **Mary Wesley** *to be published.*

Jumping the Queue marked the start of Wesley's adult literary career, which flourished well into her eighties. She produced another nine novels including *The Camomile Lawn* (1984), later adapted for television; *A Sensible Life* (1990); and her last, *Part of the Furniture* (1997). Born Mary Farmar in Egham, Surrey, to a well-to-do family, her education largely consisted of a series of governesses. Her first published books were for children: *Speaking Terms* and *The Sixth Seal*. Both were published in 1969, the year before her second husband's death. *Jumping the Queue*, written when Wesley was facing an uncertain financial future, was rejected by several publishers before being accepted by Macmillan. It was the start of a late-blooming but prolific literary career that restored her fortunes and made her a household name. Wesley was awarded a CBE in 1995. She died in 2002 at the age of ninety.

In 1999 **James Coburn** *won the Academy Award for best supporting actor for his portrayal of Glen Whitehouse in 'Affliction'.*

Coburn had never received an Academy nomination before his

Oscar-winning year. His career spanned more than four decades and began with his appearance in *Ride Lonesome* (1959). His performance in John Sturges's western *The Magnificent Seven* (1960) led to his casting in another Sturges's hit of the early sixties: *The Great Escape* (1963). Coburn remained busy throughout the decade, notably playing Derek Flint in the spy spoof *Our Man Flint* (1966). The 1970s saw him team up with director Sam Peckinpah for *Pat Garrett & Billy the Kid* (1973) and *Cross of Iron* (1977). Coburn died in 2002, aged seventy-four.

Peter Mansfield *was awarded the 2003 Nobel Prize in Physiology or Medicine for his work in the development of magnetic resonance imaging.*

Mansfield did not do well enough in the 11-plus exam to get a place at the local grammar school, and subsequently left school at fifteen to work as a printer's assistant. He then became interested in rocketry and took a job at the Ministry of Supply's Rocket Propulsion Department. After completing his National Service, he returned to the ministry and decided to also study part-time for A-levels. He subsequently secured a place to study physics at Queen Mary College at the University of London. It was there that he first worked on the topic of nuclear magnetic resonance (NMR) as part of his undergraduate project. (NMR is an investigative technique which makes use of the fact that certain atoms when placed in a magnetic field can absorb and re-emit radio waves.) Mansfield graduated with first-class honours and, following his PhD and postdoctoral research, joined the University of Nottingham as a lecturer in 1964. Mansfield began his work on the imaging applications of NMR in the 1970s, and his contribution to the mathematical analysis of the detected signals helped to develop it as a clinical technique. Mansfield's efforts also resulted in the introduction of the 'echo-planar scanning' method, which accelerated the image-gathering process. He shared the Nobel award with Paul Lauterbur, who discovered that a two-dimensional image could be created by using gradients in the magnetic field. Mansfield was knighted in 1993.

Shirley Bassey *entered the UK singles chart in 2007 with 'The Living Tree' to become the oldest solo female artist to reach the top forty.*

Bassey had her first UK hit single five decades earlier with a number eight placing for 'The Banana Boat Song'. She has also notched up two British number one singles, 'As I Love You' and 'Reach For The Stars/ Climb Ev'ry Mountain', and sold an estimated 135 million records worldwide. Bassey scored her first US hit single with the first of her Bond theme tunes, 'Goldfinger', in 1964. 'Diamonds are Forever' (1971) and 'Moonraker' (1979) complete her trio of 007 songs. She was awarded a damehood in 2000.

71
SEVENTY-ONE

Alben Barkley took office as the thirty-fifth vice-president of the United States in 1949.

Barkley won office in the 1948 election on the Democratic ticket along with Harry Truman, the incumbent president, to become the oldest United States vice-president in history. Despite an impoverished background, Barkley studied law and was called to the Kentucky Bar in 1901. He became a representative in the US Congress at the age of thirty-five in 1913. Barkley joined the Senate fourteen years later, a position he held until becoming vice-president in 1949. He was a popular occupant of the office and became known by the nickname coined by his grandson: 'the Veep'. Barkley, a widower, also made history by becoming the first vice-president to marry while in office when he wed Jane Hadley (who was nearly half his age). He made an attempt to win the presidential nomination for the 1952 campaign, but his age counted against him. He returned to the Senate after the vice-presidency and served there until he collapsed and died while making a speech at a Democratic meeting in 1956. Barkley was seventy-eight.

Max Born was awarded the 1954 Nobel Prize in Physics for his contribution to quantum mechanics.

Born was cited in particular for his 'statistical interpretation of the wave function', a mathematical entity which describes the wave characteristics of a particle. Born put forward the idea that the wave function relates to the probability of the particle being found at a future place and time, thus opening up a clear dividing line between the world of classical physics, in which a particle's future position can be known with certainty based on its current status, and quantum mechanics. Born was born in the city of Breslau within the German Empire (now Wrocław in Poland). He studied in Breslau, Heidelberg and Göttingen where he became a professor of theoretical physics in 1921. It was there that he reviewed Werner Heisenberg's seminal paper on quantum mechanics and was swift to see the potential to use mathematical matrices as a means to express Heisenberg's theory. Born was relieved of his post at Göttingen due to the anti-Jewish laws put in place by the Nazis and travelled to Britain where he became a professor at the University of Edinburgh. Born, who is the grandfather of Olivia Newton-John, shared the Nobel Prize with Walther Bothe. Born died in 1970 at the age of eighty-seven.

*Dennis **Gabor** was awarded the 1971 Nobel Prize in Physics for his invention of holography.*

Gabor was born in Budapest, Hungary, where he studied at the technical university. He continued his education in Berlin where he received his doctorate in electrical engineering in 1927. Following Hitler's rise to power, Gabor moved to England in 1934. Two years later he carried out his first basic experiments in holography. Gabor gave the technique its name (from the Greek *holos*, meaning whole), and he initially developed it as a means to improve the resolution of the electron microscope. The hologram creates an interference pattern by capturing the interaction of light from an object with a reference beam of light. When this pattern is then illuminated with the reference beam alone, a three dimensional image of the original object is reconstructed. However, it wasn't until the 1960s, when lasers became available, that high-quality optical holograms could be created. Holography was not his only invention – Gabor filed over 100 patents in his lifetime. He died in 1979 at the age of seventy-eight.

*In 1974 **John Houseman** won the Academy Award for best supporting actor for his portrayal of Charles Kingsfield in 'The Paper Chase'.*

Born in Romania in 1902 to a British mother and a father from Alsace, and educated in England, Houseman moved to the US where he pursued his interest in drama. In 1937 he co-founded the Mercury Theatre with

Orson Welles; the company's first production was Shakespeare's *Julius Caesar*. Their radio version of *The War of the Worlds* reportedly panicked many listeners who believed they were hearing an account of an actual alien invasion. Houseman and Welles fell out in 1939, although they did work together again on *Citizen Kane* (1941). Houseman continued his career with production and directing roles – *Julius Caesar* (1953), produced by Houseman, was nominated for a best picture Academy Award. In later life he became the director of the acting division of the Juilliard School for the Arts in New York, which he had helped to establish in 1968. His first major film role was as Charles Kingsfield in *The Paper Chase* (1973), and it was one that he returned to in the subsequent television series that aired between 1978 and 1986. He died in 1988 at the age of eighty-six.

In 1979 **Laurence Olivier** *received a second honorary Academy Award.*

Olivier, one of the foremost actors of his generation, was also nominated for best actor for his portrayal of Ezra Lieberman in *The Boys from Brazil* (1978). Olivier's first honorary prize from the Academy was presented in 1947 for his work on *Henry V* (1944) as an actor, producer and director. The title role also brought him, at the age of thirty-nine, his only best actor Oscar, a category he was nominated for a total of nine times. He was first nominated for his performance as Heathcliff in *Wuthering Heights* (1939); his other nominations include *Richard III* (1955), *Othello* (1965) and *Marathon Man* (1976). Olivier was knighted in 1947, made a life peer in 1970 (becoming Baron Olivier) and admitted to the Order of Merit in 1981. London's theatrical awards were renamed in his honour in 1984. Olivier died five years later at the age of eighty-two.

72
SEVENTY-TWO

The Forth Rail Bridge, designed by **John Fowler** *and Benjamin Baker, was officially opened in 1890.*

A native of Sheffield, Fowler worked as an engineer on many railway projects in the nineteenth century. He played a prominent role in the creation of the metropolitan line in London, the world's first underground railway. Benjamin Baker was also a collaborator on this project, the first section of which was opened in 1863. Sixteen years later the Tay Railway Bridge, designed by Sir Thomas Bouch, collapsed during a storm and took with it the train that was crossing at the time causing seventy-five deaths. As a result, Bouch's suspension-bridge design for the Forth crossing was cancelled and Fowler and Baker took on the task instead. Construction of their cantilever design began in 1883. Fowler, who had been knighted in 1885, also received a baronetcy shortly after the official opening of the bridge by the Prince of Wales in 1890. Fowler consulted widely on railway projects in many countries including India, Germany and the United States. He died in 1898 at the age of eighty-one.

In 1948 **Edmund Gwenn** *won the Academy Award for best supporting actor for his part as Kris Kringle in 'Miracle on 34th Street'.*

Gwenn's recognition by the Academy, in what was his first nomination, came towards the end of an acting career that had begun on stage in the 1890s. London-born Gwenn worked steadily throughout the early years of the twentieth century, building a reputation as a character actor. Army service in World War One intervened, although during the war he did manage to make his screen debut in the short film *The Real Thing at Last* (1916). Post-war he supplemented his theatrical work with further film parts, including an early starring role as Hornblower in *The Skin Game* (1921). In the mid 1930s, he also began appearing in Hollywood productions. Gwenn garnered a second Academy Award nomination for best supporting actor at the age of seventy-five for his part in *Mister 880* (1950). He continued to notch up appearances in films such as the sci-fi flick *Them!* (1954) and Hitchcock's *The Trouble with Harry* (1955), as well as taking roles on television. Gwenn died in 1959 at the age of eighty-one.

Niels Jerne *was awarded the 1984 Nobel Prize in Physiology or Medicine for his work on the immune system.*

Jerne proposed three major theories on the immune system. The first to be published, in 1955, when he was forty-four, was his 'natural selection theory' of antibody formation. This stated that the body's capacity to recognise and confront foreign agents was in-built from an early stage of foetal development, with the antibodies required to fight off infection being selectively promoted when the body was exposed to attack. Jerne's second theory, published in 1971, concerned the maturation and development of the immune system and his third discussed the interactive processes at work in the immune response. Jerne was born in London to Danish parents. He initially studied physics for two years at university, before switching to medicine. Jerne died in 1994 at the age of eighty-two. He shared the Nobel Prize with Georges Köhler and César Milstein.

*In 2007 **Alan Arkin** won the Academy Award for best supporting actor for his part as Edwin Hoover in 'Little Miss Sunshine'.*

Arkin's first Oscar triumph came forty years after his initial nomination, for his role as Lieutenant Rozanov in *The Russians Are Coming The Russians Are Coming* (1966), which was also Arkin's major feature-film debut. He missed out on the Oscar to Paul Schofield that year, but did pick up a Golden Globe award. Arkin also took on the role of Inspector Clouseau in the 1968 film, after Peter Sellers had declined to return as the French detective for a third time. The following year Arkin earned a second Academy Award nomination for best actor; this time for *The Heart is a Lonely Hunter* (1968). Two years later, he starred as Captain Yossarian in the film adaptation of Joseph Heller's *Catch-22* (1970).

73
SEVENTY-THREE

*Robert Cecil **was awarded the 1937 Nobel Peace Prize.***

Cecil was recognised for his work in the establishment and promotion of the League of Nations which came into existence after the First World War, and endured for nearly thirty years before being replaced by the United Nations. He helped to draft the League's covenant and the affairs of the organisation were to dominate his later political life. Cecil was the son of the third Marquess of Salisbury, the long-serving Conservative prime minister. Qualified in law, he also pursued a parliamentary career, and was first elected to the Commons in 1906. He moved to the Lords in 1923 as Viscount Cecil of Chelwood. Cecil died in 1958 at the age of ninety-four.

*In 1992 **Jack Palance** won the Academy Award for best supporting actor for his portrayal of Curly Washburn in 'City Slickers'.*

Palance surprised the audience at the Oscar ceremony by performing a sequence of one-handed press-ups after accepting the award. A former professional heavyweight boxer, he also scored back-to-back best supporting actor Oscar nominations in the 1950s for *Sudden Fear* (1952) and *Shane* (1953). Palance's acting break came when he was selected as the understudy to Marlon Brando in a 1947 Broadway production of *A Streetcar Named Desire*. It was directed by Elia Kazan who would later cast him in *Panic in the Street*s (1950), his big-screen debut. He died in 2006 at the age of eighty-seven.

***Bob Dole** was selected as the Republican candidate for the 1996 US presidential election.*

Dole became the oldest debutant as a presidential candidate, but failed to defeat the incumbent Bill Clinton in the November 1996 election. He gained just over 40% of the popular vote but lost heavily in the electoral college. Twenty years earlier Dole had been Gerald Ford's vice-presidential running mate, but they lost out to Democrats Jimmy Carter and Walter Mondale in the election. Dole, a native of Kansas, saw active service in World War Two and was seriously injured fighting in Italy. Decorated for bravery, he spent over three years in hospital recovering. Dole later trained as a lawyer and was elected to the House of Representatives in 1960, at the age of thirty-seven. Eight years later he was elected to the senate where he remained until 1996, the year of his presidential campaign.

***John Pople** was awarded the 1998 Nobel Prize in Chemistry for his 'development of computational methods in quantum chemistry'.*

Pople won a scholarship to Trinity College, Cambridge, and completed part two of the mathematical tripos in 1945. Awarded his PhD in 1951, he directed his mathematical skills to the field of theoretical chemistry.

Pople created the Gaussian computer program which used quantum mechanical laws to model the properties of molecules and their interactions. The first version of the program appeared in 1970 and was made publicly available. It has since evolved further and has been widely used in the study of chemistry and biochemistry, including in the development of new drugs. Pople was knighted in 2003. He died the following year, at the age of seventy-eight.

74

SEVENTY-FOUR

*In 1982 **Katharine Hepburn** won the Academy Award for best actress for her role as Ethel Thayer in 'On Golden Pond'.*

Hepburn's win gave her a record fourth best actress Oscar. She first won for her part as Eva Lovelace in *Morning Glory* (1933), and then triumphed in successive years with *Guess Who's Coming to Dinner* (1967) and *The Lion in Winter* (1968). Hepburn was nominated on a further eight occasions for the best actress Oscar, and her total of twelve nominations overall is only second to Meryl Streep for this category. She formed an on-screen (and a clandestine off-screen) partnership with Spencer Tracy that spanned nine films, beginning with *Woman of the Year* (1942) and concluding with her Oscar-winning role in *Guess Who's Coming to Dinner* (1967). Hepburn died in 2003 at the age of ninety-six.

*In 1984 **Harriet Doerr** won a national book award in the US, for first fiction, for her novel 'Stones for Ibarra'.*

Published in 1983, *Stones for Ibarra* was later adapted for television. Doerr's second novel, *Consider This, Señora*, was published in 1993, and she also completed two short-story collections. Doerr enrolled as a student at Stanford in the late 1920s, but left after two years to marry and raise a family. She returned to Stanford after her husband's death in 1972 and graduated in 1977 with a degree in history at the age of sixty-seven. Doerr then joined a creative-writing programme, which set her on course to publish her first book. Doerr died in 2002 at the age of ninety-two.

*In 2005 **Clint Eastwood** won his second Academy Award as a director for 'Million Dollar Baby'.*

Million Dollar Baby (2004) also brought Eastwood a share of the best picture award and a nomination for best actor. Eastwood's film career had begun fifty years earlier with an uncredited appearance in *Revenge of the Creature* (1955), one of his many minor roles in the 1950s. However, he achieved his big break on television when he played Rowdy Yates in the long-running series *Rawhide* (1959 to 1965). Eastwood's big-screen ambitions were then boosted by his appearance in a trio of 'spaghetti westerns' – concluding with *The Good, The Bad and the Ugly* (1966) – as the enigmatic 'man with no name'. Starring roles in films such as *Coogan's Bluff* (1968) and *Kelly's Heroes* (1970) followed, but it was at the age of forty-one that Eastwood first played one of his most famous characters, police inspector Harry Callaghan, in *Dirty Harry* (1971). He made his directorial debut with *Play Misty for Me* (1971), in which he also starred as a disc jockey pursued by a female stalker. The familiar terrain of the western gave Eastwood, at the age of sixty-one, his first Academy Award nominations for *Unforgiven* (1992). The film was listed in three categories: best actor, best picture and best director, and picked up wins in the latter two. His other Oscar nominations for best director are for *Mystic River* (2003) and *Letters from Iwo Jima* (2006), both of which were contenders for best picture.

*In 2007 **Peter O'Toole** was nominated for best actor at the Academy Awards for his portrayal of Maurice in 'Venus'.*

This was O'Toole's eighth Oscar nomination for best actor, but, as on the previous seven occasions, he was to be unsuccessful – leaving him with the dubious record of being the most nominated actor or actress without a win (although he did receive an honorary award in 2003). Born to an Irish father and Scottish mother, he made his film debut in *Kidnapped* (1960). He then shot to stardom with his acclaimed performance as T. E. Lawrence in David Lean's *Lawrence of Arabia* (1962), a role which gave him his first Academy Award nomination and a Bafta Award for best British actor. He has enjoyed greater success at the Golden Globes with wins for *Becket* (1964), *The Lion in Winter* (1968) and *Goodbye, Mr. Chips*

(1969). Equally accomplished on stage, O'Toole has performed at the Bristol Old Vic and with the Royal Shakespeare Company. He announced his retirement from acting in July 2012.

75
SEVENTY-FIVE

Charles Sherrington was awarded the 1932 Nobel Prize in Physiology or Medicine for his work on the function of neurons.

Sherrington made many important findings in his study of the nervous system. For instance, he explained the reciprocal innervation of muscles, in which there is a co-ordination between excited and inhibited muscles to control, for example, movement of a limb. His 1906 book *The Integrative Action of the Nervous System* is a seminal text in neurophysiology. It was also Sherrington who proposed the word 'synapse' for the gap between nerve cells. He was knighted in 1922 and appointed to the Order of Merit two years later. Sherrington died in 1952 at the age of ninety-four. He shared the Nobel Prize with Edgar Adrian.

Friedrich Hayek was awarded the 1974 Nobel Prize in Economics.

Hayek was born in Vienna, where he studied at the university and graduated with a degree in law. At the age of thirty-two, he became a professor of economic science and statistics at the London School of Economics where he remained until 1950. The books he published in this period include *Prices and Production* (1931), *Profits, Interest and Investment* (1939), *The Pure Theory of Capital* (1941) and *The Road to Serfdom* (1944). The latter, his most famous book, argued that liberty itself was at stake from unwarranted central economic planning by governments. An abridged Reader's Digest version, published in 1945, ensured that *The Road to Serfdom* reached a wide audience. Hayek concluded his career with positions at the universities of Chicago and Freiburg. He died in 1992 at the age of ninety-two. The Nobel Prize was shared with Gunnar Myrdal of Sweden.

*In 1992 **John Lee Hooker** scored his highest UK singles chart position with 'Boom Boom' which reached number sixteen.*

The Mississippi bluesman also saw the album of the same name achieve one place better in the UK. Both entries marked the start of a brief flurry of chart activity for Hooker who was to last enter the UK singles chart in 1996, at the age of seventy-eight, with 'Baby Lee', performed with Robert Cray. Prior to the 1990s, Hooker had only recorded one other UK chart entry, a number twenty-three placing for 'Dimples' in 1964. However, he was an influential figure in popular music whose stateside recording career began in 1948, at the age of thirty-one, with 'Boogie Chillen'. Hooker died in 2001 at the age of eighty-three.

*In 1994 **Nelson Mandela** became the first democratically elected president of South Africa.*

Mandela was released from prison in 1990 after serving twenty-seven years of a life sentence for treason and sabotage against the apartheid regime in South Africa. The ban on the African National Congress had also been lifted shortly before his release and Mandela resumed his leadership of the organisation. He received the 1993 Nobel Peace Prize, together with F.W. De Klerk, the South African president who sanctioned Mandela's release and supported the move to full democracy. Mandela served a five-year term as president, before retiring in 1999.

***Michael Atiyah** and Isadore Singer were awarded the 2004 Abel Prize.*

The annual award, which was first given in 2003, is named after the Norwegian mathematician Niels Abel (1802–1829) and honours outstanding work in the field of mathematics. It is bestowed by the Norwegian Academy of Science and Letters, and presented by the King of Norway. Atiyah is the first, and so far only, British mathematician to receive the prize, which recognised the Atiyah-Singer theorem developed with his fellow Abel laureate. First published in 1963, the theorem is concerned with differential equations. Atiyah was also a recipient of the Fields Medal at the age of thirty-seven in 1966 (this is an award made every four years to up to four mathematicians under the age of forty). Atiyah was knighted in 1983 and admitted to the Order of Merit in 1992.

Harold Pinter was awarded the Nobel Prize in Literature in 2005.

In addition to his work as a playwright, Pinter also acted, wrote screenplays and directed in the theatre. He made his playwriting debut with *The Room*, which was first performed in 1957. It was followed by his first full-length work, *The Birthday Party*, which received generally poor reviews and closed quickly after its London debut, although it is now regarded as a modern masterpiece. Pinter completed twenty-nine plays in his career, including *The Caretaker* and *The Homecoming*. Screenwriting brought him two Oscar nominations in the 1980s for the films *The French Lieutenant's Woman* (1981) and *Betrayal* (1983). He was awarded a CBE in 1966 and made a Companion of Honour in 2002. Pinter died in 2008 at the age of seventy-eight.

Yuichiro Miura successfully climbed Mount Everest in 2008.

The ascent was Miura's second climb to the top of Everest as a septuagenarian, having first reached the summit at the age of seventy-one. Decades earlier Miura, at the age of thirty-seven, became the first person to ski on Mount Everest. His descent began just below 26,000 feet, but ended shortly after with a fall; one that probably saved his life, since he avoided descending into a crevasse.

76
SEVENTY-SIX

In 1708 the last stone was placed on the lantern of St Paul's Cathedral, designed by **Christopher Wren**.

The first service had already taken place in the partially finished St Paul's in 1697 and the cathedral was officially declared complete by Parliament in 1710. Wren was in his mid-thirties when he was asked to design a new St Paul's, following the damage sustained by the old cathedral as a result of the Great Fire of London. Wren was also responsible for the construction of over fifty churches in the capital, similarly destroyed by the fire, although his plans for a more wide-ranging redevelopment of the area around St Paul's were never implemented. Although now most famous as an architect, Wren was also a prominent figure in the world of science. At the age of twenty-four he became the professor of astronomy at Gresham College, London, and four years later accepted the same position at the University of Oxford. Wren was also instrumental in the founding of the Royal Society, inaugurated in November 1660. Nine years later, his appointment as the Surveyor of the King's Works gave Wren the status and resources to further his architectural ambitions. He was knighted in 1673 at the age of forty-one. Wren's other buildings include the Royal Observatory at Greenwich, the Chelsea Hospital and Trinity College Library in Cambridge. He died in 1723 at the age of ninety and is buried in St Paul's where the Latin inscription on his gravestone reads *Si monumentum requiris, circumspice* (If you seek a monument, look around you).

*'Wide Sargasso Sea' by **Jean Rhys** was published in 1966.*

A prequel to Charlotte Brontë's *Jane Eyre*, *Wide Sargasso Sea* was Rhys's first novel to be published in twenty-seven years and became her most successful work. It won her the W.H. Smith annual literary award the following year and revived interest in her early catalogue. Rhys began her writing career with the short-story collection *The Left Bank and Other Stories* in 1927 and went on to publish four more early novels, the last of which was *Good Morning, Midnight* (1939). A BBC dramatisation of this work in 1957 marked her emergence from obscurity and provided the impetus for Rhys to write again. She was born Ella Gwendolen Rees Williams in Dominica (then a British colony) in the West Indies and moved to England at the age of sixteen. She attended Rada and then worked as a chorus girl. After the First World War she travelled through continental Europe with her husband and met the author Ford Madox Ford in Paris, who encouraged her literary ambitions. Rhys followed up *Wide Sargasso Sea* with several collections of short stories and an unfinished autobiography. She died in 1979 at the age of eighty-eight.

*In 1982 **Henry Fonda** won the Academy Award for best actor for his portrayal of Norman Thayer in 'On Golden Pond'.*

Fonda's only Oscar capped a career that had begun more than half a century earlier on the amateur stage. He made his debut screen appearance, at the age of thirty, in *The Farmer Takes a Wife* (1935). The first of his two best actor nominations came six years later for his part as Tom Joad in *The Grapes of Wrath* (1940). Fonda starred in, and co-produced, the jury-room drama *12 Angry Men* (1957), for which he shared an Academy Award nomination with Reginald Rose for best picture. Fonda is the oldest recipient of the best actor prize from the Academy. He died less than five months after the award, at the age of seventy-seven.

In 2002 **Robert Altman** *was nominated for best director at the Academy Awards for 'Gosford Park'.*

Altman's nomination for *Gosford Park* (2001) was the fifth time that he had been in the running for the best director Oscar having previously been cited for *MASH* (1970), *Nashville* (1975), *The Player* (1992) and *Short Cuts* (1993). Although unsuccessful in the competitive categories, he did however receive an honorary award from the Academy in 2006. After some initial post-war forays into acting, songwriting and writing for the screen, Altman's film career got underway with a job in his hometown, Kansas City, making various educational and industrial short films. He also produced television commercials and went on to direct a large raft of television shows in the 1960s, including episodes of *Bonanza* and *Bus Stop*. At the start of the next decade, aged forty-four, he directed his breakthrough feature film, *MASH* (1970) – a project that had been turned down by several other directors, but became a commercial and critical success. Altman died in 2006 at the age of eighty-one.

The BBC television show 'Strictly Come Dancing' first aired in 2004, co-hosted by **Bruce Forsyth** *and Tess Daly.*

Given a Saturday evening slot, *Strictly Come Dancing* quickly became a ratings success. Forsyth has continued to co-host the show, completing the tenth series in 2012 at the age of eighty-four. Forsyth had started out in the entertainment business over sixty years before as 'Boy Bruce, The Mighty Atom'. He then trod the boards in variety and cabaret shows for many years before his big break came at the age of thirty, as a compère of the hit ITV variety show *Sunday Night at the London Palladium*. In the seventies Forsyth hosted *The Generation Game* on BBC1, which was another major success (he later rejoined the series for a period in the nineties). He returned to ITV for game shows such as *Play Your Cards Right* and

The Price is Right. Forsyth was knighted in the 2011 Queen's Birthday Honours.

Charles Kao *was awarded the 2009 Nobel Prize in Physics for his work on fibre optic communications.*

Kao's efforts in this field date back to the 1960s when he showed that the losses sustained in the optical fibres available at the time were due to impurities in the glass, rather than a fundamental limitation of the technology. Kao and his colleague, George Hockham, published their findings in 1966. This paved the way for the development of high purity glass fibres and their ubiquitous presence in modern communication systems. They confer a host of advantages over conventional copper-wire technology, including higher carrying capacity, thinner dimensions and less signal degradation. Kao was born in Shanghai, China, in 1933. He graduated from Woolwich Polytechnic (now the University of Greenwich), and then worked as an engineer for telecommunications company STC, before joining their research laboratory (STL) in Harlow, Essex. While working there he completed his doctorate in electrical engineering in 1965. Kao shared the Nobel Prize with Willard Boyle and George Smith for their invention of the charge-coupled device (CCD) sensor.

77
SEVENTY-SEVEN

The cause for which **Mohandas Gandhi** *had long campaigned, the independence of India, was achieved in 1947.*

Later popularly known as Mahatma (great soul), Gandhi was born in 1869 in Porbandar, western India, the youngest child of four. Growing up, he absorbed the values of tolerance and peaceful co-existence that drove his later political vision. At the age of eighteen Gandhi arrived in England to study law and three years later he was called to the Bar. This period exposed him to Western customs, but also marked the beginning of his study of Hinduism and Christianity, and his move towards a more ascetic lifestyle. He returned to India, but his legal career foundered. In 1893 he accepted a one-year contract to work for an Indian law firm in South Africa; this was to be a transformative experience for Gandhi. Ultimately he would spend more than twenty years in South Africa, and it was there that his campaigning zeal, focused on anti-Indian discrimination, came to the fore. He became a noted public figure who embraced non-violent protest as the way to right injustice. Despite this, he was imprisoned on several occasions. In his mid-forties, during the First World War, Gandhi returned to India. Gradually, he pushed for Indian independence, with the movement gaining a new momentum after the massacre at Amritsar in 1919 by British troops. He led a policy of non-cooperation with the British Raj and this earned him a two-year spell in prison. Gandhi would be incarcerated again as a result of campaigns that included the 1930 'March to the Sea' protest against the tax on salt and the intensified demand for independence during World War Two. Post-war, negotiations began on Indian independence and these culminated in the Mountbatten Plan of 1947. This divided the Indian subcontinent along religious lines, creating a separate Pakistan alongside an independent India. Gandhi had wished to preserve national unity, and he tried to quell the internal strife between the different religious groupings both before and after independence. However, he was assassinated in Delhi by a Hindu nationalist, Nathuram Godse, in January 1948. Gandhi was seventy-eight.

In 1982 **John Gielgud** *was awarded the Academy Award for best supporting actor for his portrayal of Hobson in 'Arthur'.*

Gielgud made his professional stage debut at the Old Vic aged seventeen, playing a herald in a production of Shakespeare's *Henry V*. He went on to attain a considerable reputation as a Shakespearean actor, particularly for his performances as Richard II and Hamlet. Gielgud was also an accomplished director; his productions included plays by Chekhov, Wilde and Shakespeare. He won a 1961 Tony Award for best director for *Big Fish, Little Fish*. Gielgud's acclaimed one-man play *Ages of Man*, which was constructed from Shakespearean excerpts, won a special Tony Award in 1958. He made his film debut in *Who is the Man?* (1924), but it was only in later life that he really embraced the medium with appearances in films such as *Julius Caesar* (1953), which gave him a Bafta Award for best British actor, and *Becket* (1964), which brought him his first Academy

Award nomination. He also won a Bafta for his role in *Murder on the Orient Express* (1974) and starred in *The Elephant Man* (1980) and *Prospero's Books* (1991). Gielgud's performance in *Shine* (1996), released when he was ninety-two, gained him his final Bafta nomination, for best supporting actor. He was knighted in 1953 and appointed to the Order of Merit in 1996. Gielgud died at the age of ninety-six in 2000.

In 1985 **Peggy Ashcroft** *won the Academy Award for best supporting actress for her role as Mrs Moore in 'A Passage to India'.*

Ashcroft is the oldest winner of the best supporting actress category at the Oscars. Although she made her film debut in the early 1930s, her main focus was the theatre and she recorded many acclaimed Shakespearean performances in her career, including as Juliet in *Romeo and Juliet* and as Rosalind in *As You like It*. Ashcroft also played Margaret of Anjou in *The Wars of the Roses*, which was an adaptation of Shakespeare's *Henry VI* trilogy and *Richard III*. She was awarded a CBE in 1951 and a DBE five years later. Ashcroft's film and television appearances became more frequent from the late 1950s onwards. Her first Bafta nomination was for best British actress in *The Nun's Story* (1959). She enjoyed a trio of Bafta best actress wins in the 1980s, including the television award for *The Jewel in the Crown* (1984) and a Bafta for her Oscar-winning performance in *A Passage to India* (1984). Ashcroft continued to work into her eighties and was twice Bafta nominated in 1990, both in film and television. She died in 1991 at the age of eighty-three.

In 1986 **Don Ameche** *won the Academy Award for best supporting actor for his part as Art Selwyn in 'Cocoon'.*

This was Ameche's only Oscar nomination in a career spanning more than fifty years. He landed his first starring role in *Sins of Man* (1936), played Charlie Dwyer in the best picture nominated *Alexander's Ragtime Band* (1938) and memorably portrayed the title character in *The Story of Alexander Graham Bell* (1939). Ameche also enjoyed a successful radio career, notably playing one half of an argumentative couple in *The Bickersons*, which first aired in 1946. His film roles started to dry up in the 1950s, but he remained a popular television actor. His turn as Mortimer Duke in the comedy *Trading Places* (1983) reinvigorated his movie career and two years later he won an Oscar for his role as Art Selwyn in *Cocoon*. He returned to the role in the sequel, *Cocoon: The Return* (1988), and completed his last film, *Corrina, Corrina* (1994), shortly before his death, in 1993, at the age of eighty-five.

In 1998 **John Glenn** *became the oldest person to go into space.*

Glenn's nearly nine-day experience on board the space shuttle *Discovery* was considerably longer than his previous spaceflight of just under five hours, in 1962, during which he piloted his Mercury capsule, *Friendship 7*, to become the first American to orbit Earth. In the period between his brace of space missions, Glenn left NASA to pursue a career in politics. He was elected to the US Senate in 1974 as a Democrat for the state of Ohio, a position he held until his retirement in 1999.

Jack Kilby *was awarded the 2000 Nobel Prize in Physics 'for his part in the invention of the integrated circuit'.*

Kilby's Nobel award (shared with Zhores Alferov and Herbert Kroemer for their work in developing semiconductor heterostructures) came over forty years after he had filed his patent for 'miniaturized electronic circuits'. Kilby demonstrated that it was possible to fabricate more than one electronic component in a small area of semiconductor material, therefore creating what is known as the integrated circuit. The drive for greater miniaturisation gathered pace over the next decades, allowing electronic-based devices to become increasingly practical and popular. Robert Noyce (who died in 1990) worked independently on a similar invention to Kilby and both are generally credited with the invention of the technology. The gap between the reason for Kilby's citation and his award is one of the longest in Nobel history. Kilby died in 2005 at the age of eighty-one.

78
SEVENTY-EIGHT

Douglas Hyde *was inaugurated as the first president of Ireland in 1938.*

Despite suffering a stroke in 1940, Hyde served a full seven-year term as president (the Irish Free State established in 1922, which had dominion status under the British Crown, was replaced by the Irish Republic in 1937). Hyde had been expected to follow his father into the clergy of the Church of Ireland, but instead, after graduating with a degree in modern literature and divinity, he studied law, although he opted to not pursue a legal career either. Hyde became passionately involved in the promotion of the Irish language and culture, and was instrumental in the founding of the Gaelic League, serving as its first president. Hyde also became the first professor of modern Irish at University College Dublin. He died in 1949, just over four years after leaving the office of president, at the age of eighty-nine.

Bertrand Russell *received the Nobel Prize in Literature in 1950.*

Russell's Nobel citation noted 'his varied and significant writings in which he champions humanitarian ideals and freedom of thought'. The grandson of a former prime minister, Lord John Russell, he was orphaned at the age of three and raised by his grandmother. He excelled in mathematics and philosophy at Trinity College, Cambridge, subsequently becoming a fellow soon after graduation. The first volume of his landmark work *Principia Mathematica* (co-written with Alfred Whitehead) was published in 1910. Its overriding thrust was to show that mathematical truths could be derived from logic. A further two volumes, published in 1912 and 1913, completed the work. His pacifist stance resulted in his dismissal from his position at Trinity College during the First World War and a six-month prison sentence, during which he wrote *Introduction to Mathematical Philosophy*. After the war he applied his intellect to a wider range of issues and produced volumes on Bolshevism, China and education among other topics. He inherited an Earldom in 1931 following the death of his older brother. *A History of Western Philosophy*, published when in his early seventies, became a best-seller. Russell rejoined Trinity College in 1944 and five years later was appointed to the Order of Merit. At the age of eighty-five he became, in 1958, the first president of the Campaign for Nuclear Disarmament (CND); Russell's strong support for its aims would bring him another prison sentence, albeit for only one week, in 1961. He died nine years later at the age of ninety-seven.

*In 1989 **Charles Crichton** was nominated for best director at the Academy Awards for 'A Fish Called Wanda'.*

Crichton also shared a nomination with John Cleese for best original screenplay for *A Fish Called Wanda*. He started work in the British film industry in the 1930s, mainly as an editor. Crichton made his directorial debut with *For Those in Peril* (1944), but he is most remembered for his work on the 'Ealing comedies', the first of which (directed by Crichton) was *Hue and Cry* (1947). Others include *The Lavender Hill Mob* (1951), which was voted best film of the year by the British Academy, and *The Titfield Thunderbolt* (1953). From the sixties onwards the bulk of Crichton's work was for television, with *A Fish Called Wanda* (1988) becoming his first feature film for over twenty years. It was also to be his last. Crichton died in 1999 at the age of eighty-nine.

79
SEVENTY-NINE

*In 1939 three paintings by **Grandma Moses** were displayed in an exhibition entitled 'Contemporary Unknown Painters' at the Museum of Modern Art in New York.*

Born Anna Robertson in New York State in 1860, Moses only began painting when she was in her late seventies. Her artwork was spotted, in a drugstore window, by an art collector from New York City who bought the paintings, and others by Moses. Her paintings appealed both to the critics and the public, and her first solo exhibition, *What a Farm Wife Painted*, was staged in 1940. She conjured up the scenes in her pictures from memory, and during the remainder of a long life completed over one thousand paintings. Moses's work was exhibited widely in the United States and Europe, and also appeared on Hallmark Christmas cards. She continued to paint until weeks before her death, at the age of one hundred and one, in 1961. Moses's painting *Sugaring Off* (1943) sold for $1.2 million in 2006.

*In 1980 **Melvyn Douglas** won the Academy Award for best supporting actor for his part as Benjamin Rand in 'Being There'.*

Douglas's performance in *Being There* gave him a second best supporting actor win; his first had been for *Hud* (1963). Seven years after *Hud*, he also picked up his only Oscar nomination for best actor for his portrayal of Tom Garrison in *I Never Sang for My Father* (1970). Following work on the stage, his film career began in the 1930s with *Tonight or Never* (1931) starring Gloria Swanson and also featuring a pre-Frankenstein Boris Karloff. At the end of the decade he played opposite Greta Garbo in *Ninotchka* (1939), which had the tagline 'Garbo laughs!' (courtesy of Douglas's character in the film). However, it was his later career which brought recognition by the Academy, as well as a Tony Award in 1960 (for *The Best Man*), and an Emmy in 1968 for the television drama *Do Not Go Gentle Into That Good Night*. He continued working up until his death in 1981, at the age of eighty.

*In 1984 **Asa Long** became the oldest person to win the US Draughts Championship.*

Long already held the record as the youngest winner of the title, which he took at the age of eighteen. He also was victorious in the British Open Championship in 1984, and challenged for the world title (which he won in 1934 and 1936) the following year, but lost out to Marion Tinsley. Long died in 1999 at the age of ninety-five.

*In 1986 **John Huston** was nominated for best director at the Academy Awards for 'Prizzi's Honor'.*

Huston's nomination for *Prizzi's Honor* (1985) was his fifteenth and final one in a directing career that had begun with *The Maltese Falcon* (1941). *The Treasure of the Sierra Madre* (1948) provided his only Oscar triumphs, with Huston winning for best director and 'best writing, screenplay' (incidentally, his father Walter also took home the best supporting actor award for the same film). John Huston also gained Academy recognition for his work in front of the camera with a nomination for best supporting actor for his role in *The Cardinal* (1963). His portrayal of Noah Cross in Roman Polanski's *Chinatown* (1974) also brought acclaim. Huston's other directorial credits include *The Asphalt Jungle* (1950), *The Man Who*

Would Be King (1975), *Escape to Victory* (1981) and *Under the Volcano* (1984). He also directed *The Misfits* (1961), the last completed film of both Clark Gable and Marilyn Monroe. Although the Academy did not reward him with an Oscar for *Prizzi's Honor* (1985), his daughter Angelica won the best supporting actress award for the same film. Houston died in 1987 at the age of eighty-one.

In 2000 **Richard Farnsworth** *was nominated for the Academy Award for best actor for his role as Alvin in 'The Straight Story'.*

Farnsworth spent nearly forty years working as a stunt man before turning to acting in the 1970s. At the age of fifty-nine he received his first Academy Award nomination, for best supporting actor, for *Comes a Horseman* (1978). His other film appearances include *The Grey Fox* (1982), *The Natural* (1984) and *Misery* (1990). *The Straight Story* (1999) was his last film; just over six months after the Oscar ceremony Farnsworth, who had been diagnosed with terminal cancer, was found dead from a self-inflicted gunshot wound. He remains the oldest male to be nominated for the top acting award at the Oscars.

CHAPTER NINE

Octogenarians

Let us cherish and love old age; for it is full of pleasure if one knows how to use it.

SENECA

80

EIGHTY

In 1968 **Edith Evans** *won the Bafta Award for best British actress for her role as Mrs Ross in 'The Whisperers'.*

Evans made her stage debut at the age of twenty-two in 1910 and two years later started her professional stage acting career, where she built a reputation playing Restoration and Shakespearean roles. Although Evans made three silent movies in her twenties, there was a lengthy gap before she resumed her screen output in the late 1940s, beginning with *The Queen of Spades* (1949). She reprised one of her most famous stage roles, as Lady Bracknell, in a 1952 film production of *The Importance of Being Earnest* and continued to work in cinema and television until her death in 1976, at the age of eighty-eight. Evans's work in film brought her three Oscar nominations: best supporting actress for *Tom Jones* (1963) and *The Chalk Garden* (1964), and best actress for *The Whisperers* (1967). Evans was awarded a damehood in 1946.

In 1976 **George Burns** *won the Academy Award for best supporting actor for his part as Al Lewis in 'The Sunshine Boys'.*

Rather than becoming a swansong, the success of *The Sunshine Boys* (1975) revitalised Burns's acting career. He went on to act in several more films with his last, *Radioland Murders* (1994), released when he was ninety-eight. Born Nathan Birnbaum, one of twelve children, in New York City, Burns cut his teeth as an entertainer in Vaudeville, but enjoyed scant success until he teamed up with his future wife, Gracie Allen, in his mid-twenties. Originally Burns was the comic half of the duo, but switched places to become the straight man when he realised that Allen was getting more laughs. Their double act proved to be popular and transferred success-fully to both radio and television. He was grief-stricken by her death in 1964 at the age of fifty-nine. Burns died over thirty years later in 1996, less than a month after his hundredth birthday.

*In 1990 **Jessica Tandy** won the Academy Award for best actress for her portrayal of Daisy Werthan in 'Driving Miss Daisy'.*

Tandy was born in London, where she made her stage debut at the age of eighteen and her Broadway debut two years later. Her first film role was a walk-on appearance in the British production *The Indiscretions of Eve* (1932), but by the end of the decade she was playing more substantial parts. Tandy moved to the US and made her Hollywood debut in *The Seventh Cross* (1944). Her performance as Blanche DuBois in Tennessee Williams's *A Streetcar Named Desire*, which opened on Broadway in late 1947, won her plaudits and a Tony Award for best actress. Tandy is the oldest winner of the Academy Award for best actress to date. She appeared infrequently in films over the next two decades, although she continued to work in the theatre, receiving a second Tony Award for *The Gin Game* in 1977. A third, for *Foxfire*, followed in 1983. Her film career blossomed as a septuagenarian, with appearances in *The Bostonians* (1984) and *Cocoon* (1985). At the age of eighty-two her role as Ninny Threadgoode in *Fried Green Tomatoes at the Whistle Stop Café* (1991) brought her a second and final Oscar nomination, this time for best supporting actress. Tandy's last film, *Nobody's Fool* (1994), was released shortly after her death at the age of eighty-five in 1994.

*In 1994 **Larry Adler**, in a duet with Kate Bush, reached number twenty-seven in the UK singles chart with 'The Man I Love'.*

This was to be Adler's only appearance in the British top thirty, but the virtuoso harmonica player went on to score a number two position in the album chart in the same year with *The Glory of Gershwin*, which contained his Kate Bush collaboration and many others. A native of Baltimore, Maryland, Adler's skill with the mouth organ enhanced its status as an instrument; composers including Malcolm Arnold and Ralph Vaughan Williams created pieces especially for Adler and the harmonica. He also wrote music himself and received an Oscar nomination for the soundtrack of *Genevieve* (1953). Adler died in 2001 at the age of eighty-seven.

*In 2007 **Andy Williams** reached number twenty-one in the UK singles chart with 'It's the Most Wonderful Time of the Year'.*

A reissue of his original 1963 recording, 'It's the Most Wonderful Time of the Year' made Williams the oldest solo artist to feature in the UK chart. Williams also reached number nine in 1999 with 'Music to Watch Girls By' and number twenty-three with 'Can't Take My Eyes Off You' – a duet with Denise Van Outen – in 2002. Williams's first UK hit, 'Butterfly', in 1957, was also his first and only number one in Britain. He was a regular entrant of the UK charts in the sixties and seventies, and also fronted his own award-winning TV variety show between 1959 and 1971. Williams died in 2012 at the age of eighty-four.

81

EIGHTY-ONE

*In 1831 **Johann Wolfgang von Goethe** completed the manuscript of part two of 'Faust'.*

Part one of *Faust*, in which the title character gains earthly pleasures by making a pact with the devil, was published in 1808 when Goethe was in his late fifties; more than thirty years after he had begun writing what would become his greatest work. Part two of *Faust* was published posthumously in 1832, the year of his death at the age of eighty-two. Goethe was born into a prosperous family in Frankfurt am Main, then an Imperial Free City of the Holy Roman Empire. He studied law at university, but his interests were wide-ranging and included philosophy, science, drama, poetry and literature. His novel *The Sorrows of Young Werther*, published in his mid-twenties, brought him early success as a writer. Shortly afterwards, Goethe became a privy councillor to the young Duke of Weimar. He would reside in the Duchy for the rest of his life and became involved in the administration of the territory. Goethe's scientific investigations included research in the fields of optics and anatomy. His book, *Theory of Colours*, was published in 1810. Goethe's other literary works include the epic poem *Hermann and Dorothea* (1798), the novel *Wilhelm Meister's Apprenticeship* (1796) and the poem *Marienbad Elegy* (1823).

Barbara McClintock was awarded the 1983 Nobel Prize in Physiology or Medicine 'for her discovery of mobile genetic elements'.

McClintock's pioneering, independent work in the 1940s and 1950s, which for the first time revealed the movement of pieces of genetic code within or between chromosomes, was largely ignored at the time by her contemporaries, who doubted the possibility of such a phenomenon. Her breakthrough research focused on maize and was first published in the early fifties, before the discovery of the structure of DNA in 1953. It would be around two decades before her work was vindicated by similar findings in bacteria. Further evidence of mobile genetic elements, also called transposons, has been found in various other species, for example the fruit fly *Drosophila*, as well as man. McClintock, who completed her doctorate at Cornell University at the age of twenty-four, remains the only woman to have been awarded an unshared Nobel prize in the category of physiology or medicine. It was one of a number of awards she received later in life which finally recognised the importance of her work. McClintock died in 1992 at the age of ninety.

82

EIGHTY-TWO

*In 1892 **William Gladstone** became prime minister for the fourth time.*

Gladstone was born in Liverpool into a prosperous family and attended Eton and Christ Church College, Oxford, where he took a double first in classics and mathematics. Aged twenty-three, he entered Parliament as a Tory at the first general election held after the Reform Act of 1832. He joined the Cabinet as the president of the Board of Trade in 1843 in the administration of Robert Peel which, split over the repeal of the Corn Laws, fell three years later. He was elected as an MP for Oxford University in 1847 and five years later joined the coalition of Whigs, Peelites and Liberals under Lord Aberdeen as chancellor of the exchequer. His first budget speech in 1853, delivered with bravura, was close to five hours in duration, with tariff simplification its main thrust. It also included a measure to lower the income tax threshold. Gladstone was back in opposition in

1855 but returned to the chancellorship in 1859 when he joined Lord Palmerston's Liberal Government. The Conservatives regained power in 1866 and the following year Gladstone became the leader of the Liberal Party. He became prime minister after their general election victory in 1868. His first five years in office included measures to introduce a national schooling system for children between five and twelve in England and Wales, as well as the introduction of the secret ballot for elections. The Liberals were soundly defeated at the 1874 general election, Disraeli became the Conservative prime minister and Gladstone resigned the leadership of his party. Six years later the Liberals were victorious, and he returned as prime minister at the age of seventy for another five-year term (his tree-felling hobby helped to keep him physically fit). He also acted as chancellor for the latter part of his first term and for nearly the first three years of his second term. His Liberal Government enacted further electoral reform, but the defeat of their budget brought about Gladstone's resignation. He returned as prime minister for the third time the following year but, after barely six months and despite Gladstone's efforts, the government's Irish Home Rule bill was defeated in the Commons leading him to dissolve Parliament and fight an election. The Liberal Party, split over Irish Home Rule, lost to the Conservatives. At the age of eighty-two Gladstone returned for his fourth and last time as prime minister in 1892. This time, he managed to pilot another Irish Home Rule bill through the Commons, but it was rejected by the Lords. Gladstone resigned in 1894 as the support of his Cabinet drained away. He died four years later at the age of eighty-eight. He is the oldest person ever to occupy the office of British prime minister.

Oliver Smithies was awarded the 2007 Nobel Prize in Physiology or Medicine for his work in developing the process of 'gene targeting'.

The technique of 'gene targeting' has made it possible to add genes to mice from another species (including humans), or create mice with certain genes inactivated or 'knocked out'. It is therefore an important tool in the investigation of inherited diseases such as cystic fibrosis. Smithies was born in Halifax, Yorkshire, and studied at Balliol College, Oxford, for his undergraduate and doctoral degrees, but since 1960 has lived and worked in the US. His Nobel Prize-winning work was largely completed in the 1980s. He shared the award with Mario Capecchi (who independently developed a similar technique), and Sir Martin Evans for his work with embryonic stem cells.

In 2012 **Christopher Plummer** *won both the Academy Award and Bafta for best supporting actor for his part as Hal Fields in 'Beginners'.*

In addition to the Oscar, the role also brought Plummer his first success at the Baftas and Golden Globes, making him the oldest person to have won an acting award at each event. Plummer's first Academy nomination also came late in life, at the age of eighty, for playing Leo Tolstoy in *The Last Station* (2009). He was born in Toronto in 1929, the same year as the inaugural Academy Awards were held in Los Angeles. Plummer made his Broadway debut at the age of twenty-four as George Philips in *The Starcross Story*, but the play closed after only one night. Later in 1954, his next Broadway production, *Home is the Hero*, enjoyed a longer run and five years later *J.B.* brought Plummer the first of his six Tony nominations. Since then he has won twice: for *Cyrano* in 1974 and *Barrymore* in 1997. He made his feature-film debut in *Stage Struck* (1958), but for many his most memorable screen role remains that of Captain Von Trapp in what was his fourth film, the hugely successful *The Sound of Music* (1965). His other films include *The Man Who Would Be King* (1975), *The Amateur* (1981), *The Insider* (1999) and *A Beautiful Mind* (2001).

83

EIGHTY-THREE

The meridian at Greenwich, established by **George Airy**, *was declared to be the official prime meridian for the world at a special conference in 1884.*

Airy, the astronomer royal, had built the 'transit circle' telescope in the Greenwich Observatory at the start of the 1850s; zero degrees longitude was defined by the cross-hairs in the eyepiece. It was the fourth meridian to be defined in Greenwich, following those established by previous astronomer royals John Flamsteed, Edmond Halley and James Bradley. The global need for an agreed location for the meridian resulted in delegates from twenty-five nations meeting in Washington in 1884 to decide the issue. The location of Greenwich, as defined by Airy, was approved by a resounding majority: only San Domingo voted against, with France and Brazil abstaining. Airy was born in Alnwick, Northumberland, and was educated at Trinity College, Cambridge, where he became the Lucasian professor of mathematics at the age of twenty-five. Not much more than a year later, he vacated this chair to become the Plumian professor of astronomy at the university. At the age of thirty-three he was appointed as the seventh astronomer royal, a post which he held until his resignation in 1881. Airy was knighted in 1872 and died twenty years later, at the age of ninety.

84

EIGHTY-FOUR

*In 2003 the Danish architect **Jørn Utzon** was announced as the winner of the Pritzker Architecture Prize.*

In the award citation, particular mention was made of Utzon's design for the iconic Sydney National Opera House. Utzon had won the contest to design the Opera House in 1957 at the age of thirty-eight. A dispute over fees, and disagreement with the New South Wales government over the escalating cost of the Opera House's construction, resulted in his resignation from the project in 1966. The building was officially opened by the Queen in 1973. Utzon never returned to Australia after his resignation and so never paid a visit to his most famous creation. In 1999 Utzon was recommissioned as the building's architect. The reception hall with an interior designed by Utzon was renamed in his honour. He died in 2008 at the age of ninety.

*In 2008 **Frank Lautenberg** won re-election to the US Senate to represent New Jersey for a fifth term.*

Lautenberg, a native of New Jersey, did not begin his career as a senator until the age of fifty-eight when he was elected on the Democratic ticket, in 1982. He was re-elected twice and served until January 2001, but declined the opportunity to stand in the elections of the previous year. However, Lautenberg became a candidate again in 2002, and subsequently won his fourth term in the Senate. Currently the oldest member of the US Senate, his latest six-year term will expire when he is ninety.

85
EIGHTY-FIVE

*The first solo exhibition of artwork by **Bill Traylor** took place in Montgomery, Alabama, in 1940.*

Born into slavery, Traylor was eventually able to farm his own land. He had only started drawing in his eighties after he had moved to nearby Montgomery, Alabama, where he began working in a shoe factory. After rheumatism prevented him working, he lived on welfare in the back room of a funeral parlour. He initially drew with pencil on cardboard, and was championed by a local artist, 25-year-old Charles Shannon, who organised his first solo exhibition; another was staged in New York in 1942. Shannon supplied encouragement and materials and Traylor completed hundreds of drawings, but it wasn't until the late 1970s that his work found a receptive audience. His drawings can now be found in several galleries including the Metropolitan Museum of Art in New York. Traylor died in 1949 at the age of ninety-five.

***John Fenn** was awarded the 2002 Nobel Prize in Chemistry for developing the technique of electrospray ionisation (ESI) which is used to facilitate the analysis of large molecules using mass spectrometry.*

Mass spectrometry is a key method used to determine the substances present in a sample. The basis of the technique is to ionise the material under investigation and then accelerate it in an electromagnetic field. From this procedure, the components can be identified by their charge-to-mass ratio. Although it had become well established in the twentieth century, difficulties remained with the analysis of large molecules (macromolecules) such as proteins. Fenn's solution to this problem, electrospray ionisation, enabled these to be successfully ionised and therefore be capable of analysis using mass spectrometry. Fenn, a graduate of Berea College and Yale University, did not begin his work on ESI until later life, and was seventy when he first presented the successful identification of macromolecules using the technique in 1988. He shared the Nobel Prize with Koichi Tanaka (who in contrast to Fenn used a laser pulse in his work to perform the task of ionisation) and Kurt Wüthrich for his application of nuclear magnetic resonance (NMR) to macromolecules. Fenn died in 2010 at the age of ninety-three.

In 2008 the painting 'Benefits Supervisor Sleeping' by **Lucian Freud** *set a new auction record for a work by a living artist.*

The 1995 Freud painting, posed for by Sue Tilley, sold in New York for nearly $34 million. The grandson of Sigmund Freud, Lucian was born in Berlin, but moved with his family to England in 1933. He studied art in London and served in the merchant navy during World War Two. His first solo exhibition, which included his work *The Painter's Room*, took place at the Lefevre Gallery, London, in 1944. Freud's realistic style, particularly demonstrated in his nudes, made him one of the most distinguished British artists of recent times. Appointed to the Order of Merit in 1993, Freud died in 2011, aged eighty-eight.

Robert Edwards *was awarded the 2010 Nobel Prize in Physiology or Medicine for his work in developing in vitro fertilisation (IVF).*

Edwards, who studied at the University of Wales, Bangor, and the University of Edinburgh, began researching the biology of fertilisation in the 1950s. Approximately a decade later he was joined in his work to create a treatment for human infertility by the gynaecologist Patrick Steptoe. Their collaboration culminated in the birth of the world's first 'test-tube' baby, Louise Brown, at Oldham and District General Hospital in 1978. The technique of IVF has resulted in approximately four million births worldwide. Edwards received a knighthood in 2011.

86

EIGHTY-SIX

In 1996 double Academy Award winner **Luise Rainer** *returned to screen acting after a break of more than fifty years.*

Rainer appeared in *The Gambler* (1997), adapted from the novel by

Fyodor Dostoevsky. Born in Germany in 1910, Rainer gained experience in stage acting and film work before moving to the US for her first Hollywood production: *Escapade* (1935). Her next, *The Great Ziegfeld* (1936), brought her a first Oscar win for best actress, at the age of twenty-seven. She repeated this success with *The Good Earth* (1937) to become the first person to win twice, and to win consecutively, a top acting category at the Academy Awards. Unhappy with the roles she was offered, she would make only six more features prior to *The Gambler* (1997), the last of which was *Hostages* (1943). Rainer continued to act on stage and also took on occasional television roles. She celebrated her one hundred and third birthday in 2013.

In 2013 **Emmanuelle Riva** *attended the Academy Awards ceremony as the oldest ever nominee for best actress for her role as Anne in 'Amour'.*

Riva, enjoying her first Oscar nomination, also celebrated her eighty-sixth birthday on the day of the Awards ceremony. Earlier in 2013, she became the oldest winner of the best actress category at the Bafta Awards for her performance in *Amour*. Her only previous Bafta nomination was in 1961, for best foreign actress, for her first major film, *Hiroshima, Mon Amour* (1959). The French actress's other films include *Thérèse Desqueyroux* (1962), *Three Colours: Blue* (1993) and *C'est la Vie* (2001).

87

EIGHTY-SEVEN

Peyton Rous *was awarded the Nobel Prize in Physiology or Medicine in 1966 'for his discovery of tumour-inducing viruses'.*

Rous had first reported his findings that viruses could play a role in the transmission of certain forms of cancer over half a century before his Nobel recognition. His initial work focused on a sarcoma present on a chicken, which Rous showed could be transferred to healthy birds by viral infection (known today as the Rous sarcoma virus No. 1). He went on to identify further avian tumours precipitated in this way, but the full significance of Rous's discovery was not recognised for decades. However, from the 1950s onwards renewed interest in cancer-causing viruses led to a vindication of Rous's work. He died in 1970 at the age of ninety. The 1966 Nobel Prize was shared with Charles Huggins 'for his discoveries concerning hormonal treatment of prostrate cancer'.

Joseph Rotblat was awarded the 1995 Nobel Peace Prize.

Rotblat, the oldest Nobel Peace laureate, shared the award with the Pugwash Conferences on Science and World Affairs, which he helped to establish in the 1950s. He became the first secretary-general of Pugwash (named after the town in Nova Scotia which hosted the initial event) and subsequently became chairman of the British group. Rotblat also became the president of the overall organisation, which sought to assemble scientists and other notables to discuss the social impact of science as well as the threat from nuclear weapons and ways to reduce it. Rotblat was born in present-day Poland, where he abandoned an apprenticeship to study physics, the subject of his doctorate in 1938. Before the outbreak of war in 1939, he joined James Chadwick's group at the University of Liverpool, and subsequently became involved in the British atomic weapon programme. In 1944, Rotblat joined the US Manhattan Project at Los Alamos, but continued to have misgivings about the development of atomic weapons. The news that Germany was not on course to develop their own version meant he could no longer justify his involvement and he returned to Britain, where he became involved in the field of medical physics. He pursued his desire for nuclear disarmament with great energy through Pugwash, and donated his share of the Nobel Prize money to the organisation. Rotblat was knighted in 1998 and died in 2005, at the age of ninety-six.

*In 1998 **Gloria Stuart** was nominated for an Academy Award for best supporting actress for her portrayal of the older Rose in 'Titanic'.*

Directed by James Cameron, *Titanic* scooped a record-equalling eleven Oscars, but Stuart, for whom it was her first Academy nomination, lost out to Kim Basinger. Stuart's film career began with *Street of Woman* (1932), and during the next fourteen years she appeared in more than forty movies, but major stardom proved elusive. She took a break from acting in the 1940s, but returned thirty years later, initially doing television work. Her first film in later life was *My Favourite Year* (1982), and she made further film appearances in the remainder of the decade. There was then a lull until her success in *Titanic* (1997) led to more film roles; the last, *Land of Plenty* (2004), was released when she was ninety-four. She remains the oldest person to have been nominated for an acting award at the Oscars. Stuart died in 2010 at the age of one hundred.

88

EIGHTY-EIGHT

Raymond Davis Jr. *was awarded the 2002 Nobel Prize in Physics for his work in detecting solar neutrinos.*

Neutrinos are elementary particles which are generated by nuclear reactions, or by specific kinds of radioactive decay. Electrically neutral, they have very little mass and can easily travel through ordinary matter. These factors make them exceedingly difficult to detect. The sun, which is powered by the fusion of hydrogen atoms to create helium, produces vast quantities of neutrinos as a result of this reaction. Davis was the first to detect these solar neutrinos and thus confirm experimentally the source of the sun's energy. The apparatus he used consisted of a 100,000 gallon tank of tetrachloroethylene (a source of chlorine) which was placed nearly 5,000 feet underground to shield it from other sources of radiation. Although the process has a low probability, a neutrino can transform a chlorine atom into a radioactive isotope of argon. The detection of any argon present in the tank therefore gave a measure of the number of neutrinos that had been captured. The experiment was conducted over a period of more than twenty years, but the final results, published in 1998, yielded only one third of the neutrinos expected. (This was later shown to be due to the fact that the detector employed by Davis was only sensitive to one of the three types of neutrino.) Davis, a native of Washington, D.C., graduated from the University of Maryland with a degree in chemistry. Following the completion of his master's degree, he moved to Yale university to undertake his PhD in physical chemistry. After periods in the military and industry, he joined Brookhaven National Laboratory in 1948 and shortly afterwards began researching neutrinos. He shared the Nobel Prize with Masatoshi Koshiba and Riccardo Giacconi. Davis, the second oldest laureate in Nobel history and the oldest in a scientific discipline, died in 2006 at the age of ninety-one.

Doris Lessing *was awarded the 2007 Nobel Prize in Literature.*

Lessing was born in Persia (modern-day Iran) to British parents, but moved at an early age with her family to Southern Rhodesia (present-day Zimbabwe). Self-educated after the age of fourteen, Lessing arrived in England in 1949. Her debut novel, *The Grass is Singing*, which was set in colonial southern Africa, was published the following year when she was thirty. Although successful, it was her third novel, *The Golden Notebook* (1962), which really established her reputation. She has been nominated for the Booker Prize on three occasions: for *Briefing for a Descent into Hell* in 1971, *The Sirian Experiments* in 1981 and for *The Good Terrorist* in 1985. Her latest novel, *Alfred and Emily*, was published in 2008.

89
EIGHTY-NINE

In 1956 work commenced on the construction of the new Guggenheim Museum in New York, designed by **Frank Lloyd Wright***.*

Wright was commissioned to design the New York Guggenheim Museum in 1943. The building, in which he created a novel spiral-ramp exhibition space, is one of his most recognised designs. Wright left university without graduating to pursue a career in architecture and at the age of twenty-six he set up his own practice in Chicago. Wright, whose output was prolific, became an exponent of what was later dubbed the 'prairie style', characterised by low-pitched roofs and horizontal lines that echoed the prairie landscape. He became America's most celebrated architect and enjoyed a global reputation. One of Wright's most famous buildings is Fallingwater, a house located in Pennsylvania that was completed in the late 1930s. Wright imaginatively integrated the building's design into the surrounding landscape by constructing it over a waterfall. The house has been open to the public since the mid-1960s and has become a major attraction. He died in 1959, aged ninety-one, six months before the official opening of the New York Guggenheim Museum. The first European building from a Wright design was constructed in 2007, in County Wicklow, Ireland, using plans from an unused commission for a house. Wright's only other work outside the United States was the Imperial Hotel in Japan, which was one of the few buildings in Tokyo to survive a major earthquake in 1923.

CHAPTER TEN

Nonagenarians

The longer I live, the more beautiful life becomes.

FRANK LLOYD WRIGHT

90
NINETY

Leonid Hurwicz was awarded the 2007 Nobel Prize in Economics for his contribution to 'mechanism design theory'.

Mechanism design theory was first put forward by Hurwicz in 1960. In what is a complex area, it aims to understand the optimal framework (and incentives) that can achieve the best resolution for the participants in a given situation. (One simple example is the best way to involve two children in the division of a cake that they will share. One mechanism is to let one child cut the cake and offer the other the choice of pieces, thus creating an incentive for the first child to cut the cake fairly.) Hurwicz was born to Polish parents in Moscow and graduated from Warsaw University in 1938 with a degree in law. He had also studied economics as part of his degree course and this subject caught his interest. He spent a few months studying at the London School of Economics, but his visa expired and he travelled to Geneva to continue his studies. He was living in Switzerland when the Second World War broke out. From there, Hurwicz managed to obtain passage to Chicago, sailing from Estoril, Portugal. One of his early posts in the US was as a research assistant to the economist Paul Samuelson (the winner of the 1970 Nobel Prize in Economics). Although he never took an economics degree himself, in 1951 Hurwicz became a professor in the subject at the University of Minnesota, where he would later develop his idea of mechanism design theory. Hurwicz shared the award with Eric Maskin and Roger Myerson, who also made significant contributions in this area. Hurwicz is the oldest person to become a Nobel laureate. He died in 2008 at the age of ninety.

91

NINETY-ONE

Hulda Crooks climbed Mount Whitney, the highest peak in the forty-eight adjoining states of the US, in 1987.

Crooks also became the oldest woman to successfully reach the summit of Mount Fuji (12,388ft) in Japan that same year. Her Mount Whitney climb was the last of her twenty-three ascents of the 14,494-foot mountain in Southern California, which she'd first climbed at the age of sixty-six. Crooks was honoured by the US Congress in 1990 when Day Needle, a peak close to Mount Whitney, was renamed Crooks Peak. She died in 1997 at the age of one hundred and one.

92

NINETY-TWO

In 2009 Vera Lynn became the oldest person to top the UK album chart, with 'We'll Meet Again: The Very Best of Vera Lynn'.

Lynn was born Vera Welch in East Ham, London, and at the age of seven was already singing in local clubs. Aged eleven, she joined a singing troupe and also opted for her grandmother's maiden name as her professional name. She left school at fourteen and the following year her vocal talent was spotted by a local bandleader, Howard Baker, who took her on as a singer. In 1935 her recording career began and she also made her first radio broadcast, with the Joe Loss Orchestra. Lynn's debut solo record, 'Up the Wooden Hill to Bedfordshire', followed in 1936 when she was still eighteen. The Second World War broke out three years later during which she made her most famous recordings. The sentiment of songs such as 'We'll Meet Again' and 'The White Cliffs of Dover' resonated with many in wartime Britain. Lynn, who also performed for troops stationed abroad, became known as the 'Forces' Sweetheart'. Her popularity continued after the war and in 1952 Lynn, singing 'Auf Wiederseh'n Sweetheart', became the first British artist to top the US singles chart. The first ever UK singles chart was published in November of that year and three of her records occupied places in its top ten. Two years later she made it to number one with 'My Son, My Son'. She received an OBE in 1959 and was made a Dame in 1975. A life-size Vera Lynn cut-out has been included in the millennium vault, which will not be opened until the year 3000, after she topped a nationwide poll which asked the public who best represented the spirit of the twentieth century. Her autobiography and song recordings are also included in the vault at Guildford Castle in Surrey.

Acknowledgements

First, I must convey my thanks to my wife Carol. Her encouragement, enthusiasm and unflagging support have kept me on track as many more months of researching and scribbling ticked by than I had originally envisaged. My thanks also go to Hannah Adcock for expertly editing the text; and to literary consultant Claire Wingfield, who provided some much needed encouragement at the half-way point and skilfully proofread the manuscript. They have both suggested many improvements and have been a delight to work with. My gratitude is also extended to the staff at the superb resource that is the National Library of Scotland in Edinburgh. Without exception they have proved themselves to be courteous, efficient and incredibly helpful. Finally, I would like to also express my appreciation to the writers and researchers of the various sources which helped to furnish the factual content of the book. The further reading section lists the main sources consulted both online and in print.

Abbreviations

ATP	Association of Tennis Professionals
BA	Bachelor of Arts
Bafta	British Academy of Film and Television Arts
BASIC	Beginners All Purpose Symbolic Instruction Code
BBC	British Broadcasting Corporation
BSc	Bachelor of Science
CAT	Computerised Axial Tomography
CBE	Commander of the Order of the British Empire
CEO	Chief Executive Officer
CIA	Central Intelligence Agency
DBE	Dame Commander of the Order of the British Empire
DNA	deoxyribonucleic acid
DPhil	Doctor of Philosophy
EMI	Electric and Musical Industries Ltd
FA	Football Association
FIDE	World Chess Federation [*Fédération Internationale des Échecs*]
FIFA	International Federation of Association Football [*Fédération Internationale de Football Association*]
GM	General Motors
IAAF	International Association of Athletic Federations
IBF	International Boxing Federation
IBM	International Business Machines
IBO	International Boxing Organisation
IOC	International Olympic Committee
ITV	Independent Television
KBE	Knight Commander of the Order of the British Empire
KCB	Knight Commander of the Order of the Bath

KCMG	Knight Commander of the Order of St Michael and St George
MBE	Member of the Order of the British Empire
MP	Member of Parliament
MRC	Medical Research Council
NASA	National Aeronautics and Space Administration
NATO	North Atlantic Treaty Organisation
NBC	National Broadcasting Company
OBE	Officer of the Order of the British Empire
PGA	Professional Golfers' Association
PhD	Doctor of Philosophy
Rada	Royal Academy of Dramatic Arts
RAF	Royal Air Force
RCA	Radio Corporation of America
SI	International System of Units (*Système International*)
TT	Tourist Trophy
UEFA	Union of European Football Associations
UK	United Kingdom
UN	United Nations
UNESCO	United Nations Educational, Scientific and Cultural Organisation
UNICEF	United Nations International Children's Emergency Fund
US/USA	United States of America
USSR	Union of Soviet Socialist Republics
WBA	World Boxing Association
WBC	World Boxing Council
WBO	World Boxing Organisation

Note on Awards

Academy Award

Also known as the Oscars, these annual film awards were first presented in 1929. The Academy of Motion Picture Arts and Sciences has a membership of approximately six thousand professionals (e.g. actors, directors, producers, editors) involved in the creation of films. For most awards the nominations are determined by the votes of each particular Academy grouping, i.e. directors select directors, although all voting members may nominate for the best picture category. The winners are then decided by a ballot of all Academy members. For feature films to be eligible for an award they must be commercially exhibited for at least seven consecutive days in Los Angeles county during the calendar year prior to the award ceremony. There is no restriction on the country of origin, but foreign language films must contain English subtitles (note that for the award of best foreign language film, the Los Angeles screening requirement is waived, but must be met if the film is to be considered for other awards). Feature films must also receive their first screening in a cinema.

Bafta

These awards are governed by the British Academy of Film and Television Arts, which has a membership of approximately 6,500 industry professionals. Most of these are eligible to vote and decide the winners of the annual awards, which also recognise work in television (presented in a separate ceremony to the cinema awards). Membership is open to those involved for at least five years in the production of feature films shown in the UK, television in the UK, or video games in the UK. Previous nominees and winners are also eligible. Additionally, those located outside the UK must either show a connection to the British industry, be born in the UK or Ireland, or be a British citizen. The main criterion for a feature film to be considered is that it has had at least a one-week-long commercial screening in the UK in the calendar year prior to the awards ceremony.

Emmy

Emmys were first awarded in 1949 to recognise achievements in the field of television. Three organisations administer their own Emmy Awards. The Academy of Television Arts & Sciences presents the primetime Emmy Awards which recognise primetime transmissions within the US. The National Academy of Television Arts & Sciences confers Emmy Awards in the fields of daytime, sports, news and documentary, while the International Academy of Television Arts & Sciences, founded in 1969, recognises programmes created outwith the US.

Golden Globe

The Hollywood Foreign Press Association (HFPA), which comprises approximately ninety international journalists based in southern California, decides the winners of the Golden Globes, first awarded in 1944. They were extended to cover achievements in television as well as cinema in the mid 1950s.

Grammy

These awards are voted for by eligible members of the National Academy of Recording Arts and Sciences in the US and were first presented in 1958. Their aim is to honour 'artistic achievement, technical proficiency and overall excellence in the recording industry'.

Man Booker Prize

This was first constituted as the Booker-McConnell Prize in 1968, after its initial sponsors. In 2002, the title was updated to reflect its new sponsors: Man Group plc. The prize is open to any full-length novel, which has not been self-published, and is written in the English language by a citizen of the Commonwealth, the Republic of Ireland or Zimbabwe. A judging panel, freshly assembled each year, bestows the award.

Nobel Prize

Established by the will of Alfred Nobel, prizes for outstanding achievement in the fields of physics, chemistry, literature, physiology or medicine, and peace were first awarded in 1901, five years after Nobel's death. A prize in economics was created in 1968, as a result of a donation from Sveriges Riksbank, and it was first awarded in 1969 (its official name is the Sveriges Riksbank Prize in Economic Sciences in Memory of Alfred Nobel). For the prizes in physics, chemistry and economic sciences, approximately three thousand invitations to nominate are issued to selected academics and former Nobel laureates, among others, in each particular field. Once received, the nominations are reviewed and scrutinised, in a process that takes several months, to produce a list of final candidates. This is put before the Royal Swedish Academy of Sciences which then decides, through a majority vote, the Nobel laureates. The award for the prize in physiology or medicine follows a similar process, except that the final decision is taken by the Nobel Assembly at Karolinska Institutet. For the literature prize, approximately seven hundred nominations are invited from distinguished academics and others, with the Swedish Academy taking the final vote to decide the winner. The Norwegian Nobel committee is responsible for administering the peace prize, which is, uniquely, presented in Oslo, Norway. Nominations for this prize, which can also be awarded to associations and institutions, are requested from academics, politicians, former winners and others. All prize categories can be divided between, at most, two separate pieces of work, and the total number of laureates per discipline cannot exceed three. Posthumous nominations are not allowed, but the prize may still be awarded if the prize winner dies before the presentation ceremony. The recipient of the prize in each discipline receives a diploma, gold medal and a cash award – shared when there is more than one winner – which for 2012 was 8 million Swedish Kroner (approximately £750,000).

Olivier

Considered to be the British equivalent of the Tonys, they were first constituted as The Society of West End Theatre Awards in 1976 and were renamed as the Laurence Olivier Awards eight years later. The Society of London Theatre (SOLT) administers the Oliviers through four panels for theatre, opera, dance and affiliates. The panellists include professionals and members of the public who decide on the winners in each area. For the theatre awards only, the membership of SOLT is also consulted prior to the final shortlist, from which the respective panellists select the winners.

Order of the British Empire

Founded in 1917 by George V, this award, which recognises achievement in a range of fields, consists of five ranks: Knight/Dame Grand Cross (GBE), Knight/Dame Commander (KBE/DBE), Commander (CBE), Officer (OBE) and Member (MBE). People can be nominated by individuals, organisations or government departments, after which they enter a review process which decides on the recipients who receive final formal approval from the monarch. The list of honours to be bestowed is published twice a year: in mid-June (on the Queen's official birthday) and at New Year. The Order, which has civil and military divisions, has as its motto 'For God and the Empire'.

Order of Merit

The Order of Merit (post-nominally OM) was founded by Edward VII in 1902, and is bestowed as a personal gift of the monarch to recognise 'great achievement in the fields of the arts, learning, literature and science' by a citizen of one of the sixteen Commonwealth realms. The order is limited to a total of twenty-four members, but there can be additional foreign recipients.

Tony

Formally called the Antoinette Perry Award, these were established in 1947 to honour achievement in the theatre. Productions that are staged in eligible Broadway theatres, as defined by the award rules, can be considered for recognition in the main categories. The awards, administered by the American Theatre Wing and The Broadway League, are ultimately decided by the votes of approximately seven hundred theatrical professionals.

Turner Prize

The Turner Prize was first awarded in 1984 and was initially open to anyone who had made the 'greatest contribution to art in Britain in the previous twelve months'. It is now restricted to artists and, since 1991, potential winners must be under the age of fifty. The prize now recognises 'an outstanding exhibition or other presentation in the previous twelve months' by a British artist. An independent jury is appointed each year to decide the winner.

Further Reading

American National Biography
This contains biographies of over 17,400 lives that have had an impact on the US. Available online at www.anb.org by subscription.

Chambers Biographical Dictionary
The ninth edition, published in 2011, contains over 18,000 wide-ranging biographies condensed into a single volume. Also available online at corp. credoreference.com from Credo Reference.

Encyclopaedia Britannica
First published in the latter half of the eighteenth century, this regularly-updated reference work has also been available online at www.britannica. com since the 1990s.

www.imdb.com
Arguably the web's premier resource for information on everyone involved in the film and television industries. The website includes career histories, awards, biographies and much more.

The Oxford Dictionary of National Biography
A repository of over 57,000 biographies of deceased men and women connected to the history of the British Isles. The online edition (www. oxforddnb.com) is normally accessible at home via membership of a local British library.

www.nobelprize.org
This is the official website of the Nobel Prize and contains biographies of Nobel laureates as well as information on their award-winning work.

It also includes the presentation speeches, laureate lectures, press releases, and other material.

The Times Digital Archive

The archive contains every edition of the newspaper from 1785 to 1985. It is available by subscription or may be accessible via a British library membership.

The Times Literary Supplement Historical Archive

This includes every edition from its beginning in 1902 to 2007. More information is available at www.tlsarchive.com/tlsp/ and the archive can be accessed by subscription and some library memberships.

Additional websites

www.bafta.org – British Academy of Film and Television Arts
www.boxofficemojo.com – feature-film box-office statistics
www.boxrec.com – boxing records
www.espncricinfo.com – cricket data and statistics
www.espnscrum.com – rugby union data and statistics
www.guardian.co.uk – *The Guardian* newspaper online
www.ibdb.com – Broadway theatre information and statistics
www.independent.co.uk – *The Independent* newspaper online
www.nasa.gov – the National Aeronautic and Space Administration
www.number10.gov.uk – includes brief histories of British prime ministers
www.officialcharts.com – UK album and singles chart information
www.olympic.org – the official Olympic website
www.oscars.org – the Academy of Motion Picture Arts and Sciences
www.royal.gov.uk – the official website of the British monarchy
www.screenonline.org.uk – British Film Institute's film & TV history
www.telegraph.co.uk – the *Daily Telegraph* newspaper online
www.themanbookerprize.com – official site for the literary award
www.thetimes.co.uk – *The Times* newspaper online
www.whitehouse.gov – includes biographical sketches of US presidents
www.wikipedia.org – popular, free online encyclopaedia

Selected books

Attenborough, David, *Life On Air*, (London: BBC Books, 2002).

Baren, Maurice, *How It All Began, The Stories Behind Those Famous Names* (Otley: Smith Settle, 1992).

Bostridge, Mark, *Florence Nightingale: The Woman and Her Legend*, (London: Viking, 2008).

Birks, John L., *John Flamsteed: The First Astronomer Royal at Greenwich*, (London: Avon Books, 1999).

Bragg, Melvyn, *Rich: The Life of Richard Burton* (London: Hodder and Stoughton, 1988).

Branson, Richard, *Losing My Virginity* (London: Virgin Books, 2002).

Brayer, Elizabeth, *George Eastman: A Biography*, (Baltimore; London: John Hopkins University Press, 1996).

Button, Virginia, *The Turner Prize*, (London: Tate Publishing, 2005).

Campbell-Smith, Duncan, *Masters of the Post: The Authorized History of the Royal Mail*, (London: Allen Lane, 2011).

Carpenter, Humphrey, *That Was Satire That Was*, (London: Phoenix, 2002).

Clegg, Barbara, *The Man Who Made Littlewoods: The Story of John Moores*, (Sevenoaks: Hodder & Stoughton, 1993).

Cooper, Jackie, *Please Don't Shoot My Dog*, (New York: Berkley, 1982).

Cooper, John Milton, *Woodrow Wilson: A Biography*, (New York: Alfred A. Knopf, 2009).

Corina, Maurice, *Pile It High, Sell It Cheap: The Authorised Biography of Sir John Cohen, founder of Tesco*, (London: Weidenfeld and Nicolson, 1971).

Cowell, Simon, *I Don't Mean To Be Rude, But . . .*, (London: Ebury Press, 2004).

Crombac, Gérard, *Colin Chapman: The Man and His Cars*, (Wellingborough: Patrick Stephens, 1986).

Dale, Rodney, *The Sinclair story*, (London: Duckworth, 1985).

Davies, Hunter, *The Beatles*, (London: Ebury Press, 2009).

De Havilland, Geoffrey Raoul, *Sky Fever: The Autobiography of Sir Geoffrey de Havilland*, (Shrewsbury: Airlife Publications, 1979).

Dimbleby, Jonathan, *Richard Dimbleby*, (Sevenoaks: Coronet, 1977).

Dyson, James, *Against the Odds: An Autobiography*, (London: Orion, 1997).

Ferguson, Alex, *Managing my life: My Autobiography*, (London: Hodder & Stoughton, 1999).

Fraser, Antonia, *Cromwell: Our Chief of Men*, (London: Phoenix, 2002).

Garland, Ken, *Mr. Beck's Underground Map*, (Harrow Weald: Capital Transport Publishing, 1994).

Hague, William, *William Pitt the Younger*, (London: HarperCollins, 2004).

Hamilton, James, *Faraday: The Life*, (London: HarperCollins, 2002).

Harris, Kenneth, *Attlee*, (London: Weidenfeld and Nicolson, 1982).

Hughes, Kathryn, *The Short Life & Long Times of Mrs Beeton*, (London: Harper Perennial, 2006).

Kallir, Otto, *Grandma Moses*, (New York: Abrams, 1973).

Lamarr, Hedy, *Ecstasy and me: My Life as a Woman*, (London: W.H.Allen, 1967).

Lawson, Twiggy, *Twiggy in Black and White*, (London: Simon & Schuster, 1997).

Martin, Peter, *Samuel Johnson: A Biography*, (London: Weidenfeld & Nicolson, 2008).

McCormick, Neil, *U2 by U2*, (London: HarperCollins Entertainment, 2008).

McKibben, Gordon, *Cutting Edge: Gillette's Journey to Global Leadership*, (Boston: Harvard Business School Press, 1998).

Meyers, Jeffrey, *Hemingway: A Biography*, (London: Macmillan, 1986).

Moore, Patrick, *Eighty Not Out*, (London: Contender, 2003).

Nasaw, David, *The Chief: The Life of William Randolph Hearst*, (London: Gibson Square, 2002).

Palm, Carl Magnus, *Bright Lights, Dark Shadows: The Real Story of Abba*, (London: Omnibus Press, 2002).

Perry, Fred, *Fred Perry: An Autobiography*, (London: Hutchinson, 1984).

Phoenix, Helia, *Lady Gaga: Just Dance, The Biography*, (London: Orion, 2010).

Pressnell, Jon, *Haynes Publishing: The First Fifty Years 1960-2010*, (Sparkford: Haynes Publishing, 2010).

Robertson, W.R., *From Private to Field-Marshal*, (London: Constable & Co. 1921).

Rogan, Johnny, *Starmakers and Svengalis*, (London: Queen Anne Press, 1988).

Sadie, Stanley, *Mozart*, (London: Macmillan, 1982).

Shapiro, Helen, *Walking Back to Happiness: My Story*, (London: HarperCollins, 1993).

Tomalin, Claire, *Charles Dickens: A Life*, (London: Viking, 2011).

Torekull, Bertil, *Leading by Design: The IKEA Story*, (New York: HarperBusiness, 1999).

Torvalds, Linus, *Just For Fun: The Story of an Accidental Revolutionary*, (New York, London: Texere, 2001).

Walton, Sam, *Sam Walton: Made in America*, (New York: Bantam, 1993).

Westfall, Richard S., *Never at Rest: A Biography of Isaac Newton*, (Cambridge: Cambridge University Press, 1980).

Wogan, Terry, *Is it me?*, (London: BBC, 2000).

Wood, Jonathan, *Bugatti: The Man and the Marque*, (Marlborough: Crowood, 1992).

Wootton, David, *Galileo: Watcher of the Skies*, (New Haven; London: Yale University Press, 2010).

Copyright Acknowledgements

Index

Page numbers in bold type indicate a main entry for a person.

Oscars *see* Academy Awards
Osmond, Jimmy **8**
O'Sullivan, Ronnie **36**
Otis, Elisha **284**
O'Toole, Peter **476**
Ottey, Merlene **272**
Otto, Nikolaus **295**
Owen, David **249**
Owen, Mark 59
Owens, Jesse **74**
oxygen, elemental nature of 274

Pacino, Al **368**
package tour **186**
Packard, David 113
Page, Jimmy 57
Page, Larry **121**
Pakistan, founding of 483
Palance, Jack **474**
Palin, Michael **130**
Panama Canal 286, 368, 373, 395
Pankhurst, Emmeline **317**
Paralympics 19, 49, 203, 211, 221
Park, Nick **183**, 457
Parkes, Alexander **338**
Parkesine 338
Parkinson, Michael **227**
Parliament Act 374
particle accelerator 206
Pasteur, Louis **427**
Pavarotti, Luciano **118**
Pavlov, Ivan **388**
Paxman, Jeremy **260**
Paxton, Joseph **326**
Peacock, Jonnie **49**
Peck, Gregory **334**
Peel, John **152**
Peel, Robert **371**, 436, 455, 496
Pelham, Henry **337**
Pelham-Holles, Thomas (Duke of Newcastle) 344, **419**
Pemberton, John **388**
Pendleton, Victoria **144**
penicillin 256, 333, 383
penny post 307
Pepys, Samuel **123**
Perceval, Spencer **324**
periodic table 214, 237, 366
Perkin, William **37**

Perry, Fred **113**
Perry, Grayson **303**
Perry, Jimmy **312**
Perry, Matthew **120**
Pertwee, Jon 271
Perutz, Max 320, **340**
Petit, Philippe **104**
Petty-Fitzmaurice, Henry **110**
Phelps, Michael **145**
phlogiston theory 274
phonograph 61
photocopier 187
photography
    calotype process 265
    daguerreotype 361
    for nuclear interactions 333
    instant 40
    invention of roll film 111
Picasso, Pablo **390**
Pierre, DBC **292**
Piggott, Lester **15**
pillar box, UK introduction 178
Pink Floyd 65, 162
Pinsent, Matthew **202**
Pinter, Harold **479**
pion (pi-meson) 334
Piper, Billie **25**
Pitman, Jenny **229**
Pitt, William, (Earl of Chatham – 'Pitt the elder') 344, **400**, 419
Pitt, William ('Pitt the younger') **92**, 284, 294, 324, 448
Planck, Max **286**
planetary motion, laws of 232
Plant, Robert **57**
plasticine 373
Plath, Sylvia 129
Playboy 140
Plomley, Roy **149**
Plummer, Christopher **498**
Plunkett, Roy **138**
Pluto 204
poet laureate 129, 437, 449
    first female 379
Polaroid Corporation 40
Polgár, Judit **24**
Police, the (band) 142
polio 270
Polk, James **353**